ISLAM IN TRANSITION

ISLAM IN TRANSITION
MUSLIM PERSPECTIVES

Second Edition

Edited by

John J. Donohue
St. Joseph's University, Beirut, Lebanon

John L. Esposito
Georgetown University, Washington, D.C.

New York   Oxford
OXFORD UNIVERSITY PRESS
2007

Oxford University Press, Inc., publishes works that further Oxford University's
objective of excellence in research, scholarship, and education.

Oxford New York
Auckland   Cape Town   Dar es Salaam   Hong Kong   Karachi
Kuala Lumpur   Madrid   Melbourne   Mexico City   Nairobi
New Delhi   Shanghai   Taipei   Toronto

With offices in
Argentina   Austria   Brazil   Chile   Czech Republic   France   Greece
Guatemala   Hungary   Italy   Japan   Poland   Portugal   Singapore
South Korea   Switzerland   Thailand   Turkey   Ukraine   Vietnam

Published by Oxford University Press, Inc.
198 Madison Avenue, New York, New York 10016
http://www.oup.com

Oxford is a registered trademark of Oxford University Press

Library of Congress Cataloging-in-Publication Data

Islam in transition: Muslim perspectives / [edited by] by John J. Donohue and John L.
    Esposito.—2nd ed.
      p.   cm.
    Includes bibliographical references.
    ISBN-13: 978-0-19-517430-4—ISBN-13: 978-0-19-517431-1 (pbk.)
    ISBN 0-19-517430-5—ISBN 0-19-517431-3 (pbk.)
    1. Islam—20th century.   2. Religious awakening—Islam.   I. Donohue, John J.
II. Esposito, John L.

BP163.I674 2006
97.2'7—dc22
                                                                    2005049855

9   8   7   6   5   4   3   2   1

Printed in the United States of America
on acid-free paper

For
Elizabeth (Donohue) Scavone
and
Jeanette P. Esposito

CONTENTS

vii

III Islam and Social Change   143

IV Islam and Contemporary Issues 261

PREFACE

Much has happened since the publication of the first edition of *Islam in Transition: Muslim Perspectives*. Nothing symbolizes this more than 9/11 and the threat of global terrorism to both Muslim and non-Muslim societies. Islam and Muslims have experienced many transformations, challenges, and threats in recent decades. These include the emergence of new Islamic republics and governments, the fall of the Taliban, democratization movements from North Africa to Southeast Asia, and the global impact and ongoing threat from Muslim extremists, epitomized by Osama Bin Laden and al-Qaeda. These resulted in the decision to bring out a second, thoroughly revised edition. We have retained those texts that remain relevant to understanding the development and trajectory of Muslim thought and have added many new selections that reflect the changing dynamics of Muslim discourse and politics.

Fortunately, since the publication of *Islam in Transition*, many books have been published on Islam and Muslim politics and societies. Collections of Muslim writings have appeared, focusing on what their editors often call Islamic fundamentalism or liberal Islam. However, the continued relevance (and value) of *Islam in Transition* remains its scope, which encompasses the nineteenth to the twenty-first centuries and documents the diversity of Muslim voices on topics ranging from responses to European colonialism and the rise of Islamic modernist and fundamentalist movements to issues of legal reform, gender, bioethics, violence and terrorism, globalization, and democratization. There are, of course, many Muslim voices and possible selections. We have tried to provide a selection of representative topics, issues, and authors reflecting conservative, fundamentalist, and modernist or liberal reformers. Our emphasis, therefore, was not on the historical significance of the authors, though certainly many are important and prominent figures, but on the positions they articulated. Thus, as in the first edition, we provide very brief biographies and introductions.

Please note that we have retained spelling, transliteration, and diacritics as they appear in the original selections. In some selections, footnotes have been edited or deleted.

Finally, we would like to thank Natana DeLong-Bas and Abdullah al-Arian for their assistance in this project.

ISLAM IN TRANSITION

ISLAM IN TRANSITION: MUSLIM PERSPECTIVES

The history of humankind has seen the rise and decline of vast empires and civilizations. Perhaps no rise has been more astonishing than that of Islamic civilization, both for the speed and breadth of its geographic expansion as well as for the development of its rich cultural heritage.

Islamic civilization provided a remarkably coherent system, a world-view and a way of life that gave meaning and direction to the lives of Muslims for some twelve centuries. However, in the modern period (late nineteenth and twentieth centuries) the Islamic tradition has encountered its greatest challenges, both political and ideological. The central question has been: "Can Islam meet the political, social, and economic demands of modernity?"

This volume is designed to enable the reader to better appreciate and understand the varied ways in which Muslims have grappled with the problems of change during the modern period—from the late nineteenth century to the present. This will be accomplished by exploring the view-points of Muslims—those for whom the question of tradition and change is not simply an academic inquiry but an important existential concern. Although modern Muslim authors have addressed themselves to these problems, their writings are often inaccessible owing to lack of adequate translation and/or ready availability of their writings.

In response to this lacuna, this volume seeks 1) to provide direct access to modern Muslim thinkers as they grapple with the question of Islam and socio-political change; and 2) to do this in a way that reflects the diversity of Muslim thought and so avoids the all-too-common tendency to present Islam as a monolithic structure.

Because the Islamic tradition has been central to Muslim identity and self-understanding, some knowledge of this tradition is necessary to appreciate both the crisis of modernity and the heritage that influences Muslim responses to this crisis.[1]

Seventh-century Arabia saw the advent of a movement that in time would sweep across the Middle East, Europe, Asia, and Africa and which today includes over 1.3 billion adherents. The central fact and inspiration of this movement is the one, true God (Allah) and his revelations to the Prophet Muhammad, which were recorded in the Quran, the final, complete and perfect revelation of God's will for all of humanity. Islam means "submission" to this divine will. A Muslim, then, is one who submits to the will of God as revealed in the Quran. However, this submission is not understood in a passive sense, since the Quran declares that the Muslim's vocation is to strive (jihad) to realize God's will in history. This universal mission to spread the realm of Islam (dār al-islām) throughout the world was the driving force behind Muhammad and the early Muslims who established a religio-political community (umma) in Medina. After a protracted struggle, Mecca, the commercial and religious center of Arabia, was conquered and the tribes of the Arabian Peninsula were consolidated within an Islamic state. Within a hundred years of the prophet Muhammad's death, successive conquests, including the Byzantine and Persian (Sasanid) Empires, produced an empire, stretching from North Africa to South Asia, that was greater than any the world had known.

Muslim self-understanding is based upon the Quran and this early glorious history. For succeeding generations of Muslims, the time of the Prophet and his immediate successors has constituted the ideal period—the embodiment and epitome of the Islamic way of life. As a result, basic to Muslim identity was the belief that the divinely mandated vocation to realize God's will in history was communal as well as individual. There was an organic holistic approach toward life in which religion was intimately intertwined with politics, law, and society. The traditional Islamic structure of state and society that had developed provided the paradigm or ideal to be emulated for centuries to come. The Islamic state was to be a community of believers whose common religious bond replaced individual tribal allegiance, which had been based on blood kinship. Allah was the sovereign of the state; Muhammad, his messenger on earth, served as prophet and leader of the community. Upon Muhammad's death, his successors (caliphs), as leaders of the community, were to ensure the faithful following of the divine will as expressed in the sacred revealed law (Sharia) of Islam.[2] Thus, both ruler and ruled, according to Islamic political theory,

---

1. For a better appreciation of the history of Islamic civilization in primary sources see William H. McNeill and Marilyn R. Waldman, eds., *The Islamic World* (Oxford University Press, 1977).
2. *Sharia*: road or path, the divinely ordained law (straight path) which is to govern all aspects of Muslim life and society.

were subject to the *Sharia*. Law, then, provided the blueprint for Islamic society. Based upon the Quran and the example (Sunna) of the prophet,[3] a comprehensive law was formulated which served as a guide for every aspect of life—duties to God (worship, fast, pilgrimage, etc.) as well as duties to one's fellow Muslims. The latter category included prescriptions that fall within the domains of commercial, penal, and family law. Questions of contract, banking, marriage, and divorce were all part of the *Sharia*. But who was to interpret and apply the *Sharia*? This was the province of a class of scholars (*ulama*, "learned ones") of the *Sharia* whose task it was to interpret the law and to advise the ruler. These scholars, where necessary, might also act as a curb on the government when and if a ruler's policies were un-Islamic. While this relationship between the ruler and the *ulama* might be mutually supportive, it has often been tension-filled. Given the comprehensive scope of the *Sharia*, the *ulama*, who serve as legitimizers of political rulers and their policies (political, social and economic), have the power to declare a government's policies, or even the government itself, to be un-Islamic as demonstrated by the role of the *ulama* in toppling the ruling governments in Pakistan and Iran.

For Muslims, then, the traditional Islamic socio-political system was rooted in revelation; its truth was validated by Islamic history, which attested to Allah's divine guidance of the community. Indeed, Muslims could look back to the glorious past—the vast expansion of the first Islamic centuries and the flourishing of a rich culture whose springs fed the Christian West. Despite the gradual breakdown of the Islamic Empire (*c.* 1000) and its destruction with the fall of the 'Abbāsid Empire (1258) to the Mongols, Muslims could nevertheless witness Allah's continued guidance in the subsequent conversion of their conquerors and the eventual reemergence and rule of three Muslim empires: the Ottoman (Middle East), Safavid (Persia), and Mughal (Indian subcontinent) which extended down to the modern period (late nineteenth and early twentieth centuries).

However, from the seventeenth century onwards a long process of Western intervention and presence began which was to result in the most serious challenge ever encountered by the Islamic world. Gradual colonial economic control gave way to political and military dominance in the nineteenth century. Thus, for the first time in Islamic history, Muslims found themselves subjugated and ruled by the Christian West—foreign unbelievers who were their colonial masters and whose missionaries often claimed that their success was due to the superiority of Western Christian civilization. This challenge raised profound questions of identity for

---

3. *Sunna*: the exemplary behavior of the Prophet Muhammad (what he said, did, or permitted), became normative for the Muslim community. Therefore narrative traditions (*hadīth*) regarding his activities were preserved and written down and eventually brought together in vast collections.

Muslims. What had gone wrong in Islam? Where was the divine guidance that had assured past success? How could Muslims realize the divine imperative to spread the realm of Islam (*dār al-islām*)? Could one be a good Muslim in a non-Muslim state which was ruled by unbelievers and whose laws were not *Sharia* laws? Was there any contradiction between revelation and reason, science and technology? Was the Islamic way of life capable of meeting the demands of modernity? The beginnings of Muslim modernist thought resulted from this soul-searching inquiry and from the attempts of the "Fathers of Muslim Modernism," Jamāl al-Dīn al-Afghānī, Muhammad 'Abduh (Egypt), and Sir Sayyid Ahmād Khān (India), to provide a response and thus revive and renew their people.

Gradually in the twentieth century, Muslim political fortunes began to change with the rise of independence movements, the shedding of colonialist rule, and the founding of separate independent nation states throughout the Muslim world. Islam (Islamic religious leaders, parties, and symbols) often played an important role in liberation movements. With the establishment of modern Muslim nations, questions of Islamic identity, viz. the role of religion in the state (its constitution, laws and institutions), reemerged. While varying accommodations occurred, Islam seemed to recede from the public sphere as most states followed a more Western, secular path of modernization. Deep-seated questions regarding Islamic identity remained unresolved. This state of affairs has been reflected in con-stitutional debates regarding the status of Islam as the state religion, its role in national ideologies (Arab nationalism and Islamic socialism), the place of the *Sharia* in the state's legal system, the question of separate (secular and religious) judicial and educational systems, and especially the change in the status of women and the family through the reform of Muslim family law. Recently, these unresolved tensions regarding Islamic identity have been reflected in the political upheavals in Iran and Pakistan, and, more generally, in the calls for a more Islamic state and way of life which have been heard throughout the Muslim world. Such movements are often characterized popularly by such terms as the "Islamic resurgence," "Islamic renaissance" and "Islamic fundamentalism."

The Iranian revolution of 1978–1979 focused attention on what is termed "Islamic fundamentalism," and with it the spread of political Islam in other parts of the Muslim world. This contemporary revival had its origins and roots in the late 1960s and early 1970s from such disparate areas as Egypt, Sudan, and Libya as well as Pakistan, Malaysia, and Indonesia. The ongoing failures of many governments and their economies, growing disparities between rich and poor, and corruption, as well as the impact and disruption of modernity, spawned disillusionment and a sense of failure within modern Muslim states. American political-military policies toward Islam and the Muslim world were often seen by many Muslims as due to a militant "Christian Crusader" mentality, influenced by Orientalism and Zionism.

In the 1990s Islamic revivalism emerged in many small radical groups or organizations on the periphery of society. This "quiet revolution" produced a new generation and class of modern educated, but Islamically oriented elites and organizations coexisting alongside their secular counterparts. They became part and parcel of mainstream religion and society and were found among the middle and lower classes, educated and uneducated, professionals and workers, young and old, men, women, and children.

With the end of the Cold War, Islam, or Islamic fundamentalism, came to be seen by some as a new global political and demographic threat. The record of Islamic experiments in Iran, Sudan, and Pakistan and the Taliban's Afghanistan reinforced fears of the export of religious extremism, violence, and terrorism. At the same time, Islam and Muslims had become the second- and third-largest religion in Europe and America, respectively. Policymakers and experts engaged in heated debates, often using the phrase "clash of civilizations," a clash between Islam/the Muslim world and the modern secular or Judeo-Christian democratic values and culture of the West.

The 9/11 attacks, subsequent acts of terrorism by Muslim extremists from Madrid to Bali, and Osama Bin Laden and al-Qaeda's commitment to a global jihad reinforced fears of a global terrorism that threatened Muslim countries and the West. Within Islam and the global Muslim community, mainstream Muslims and extremists seemed locked in a struggle for the soul of Islam as reformers sought to marginalize extremists and engage in a process of widespread reinterpretation and reform. Critical questions were raised about the relationship of Islam to religious extremism, violence and terrorism, global jihad and suicide bombing, modernization, democracy, gender equality, human rights, and globalization.

As we have seen in this brief introduction, for almost thirteen centuries Islam provided a divinely sanctioned political and social order, a coherent worldview, which gave direction and meaning to Muslims both as individuals and as a community. Through changing political fortunes, this ideal framework of state, society, and law assured a general stability and sense of identity. With the breakup of Muslim empires, the intervention of the West, and the establishment of modern Muslim nation states, these traditional societies have been subjected to all the pressures (intellectual, political, and social) associated with the process of modernization or development.

As we survey Muslim responses to the challenge of modernity, a number of considerations should be kept in mind. Muslim nations that have emerged from centuries of colonial rule have had but several decades as independent states to make a transition that in the West took several centuries. Out of this period, new Islamic responses and perhaps fresh syntheses are emerging. The formative period of Islam can serve as an inspiration, as Muslims look to their early history and the sources of Islam. For once again the Islamic community faces the challenge of a creative interpretation (*ijtihād*) and reapplication of Islamic values to meet the needs of changing Muslim societies.

We hope that the selections included in this sourcebook will provide our readers with some insight into the complexity of the problems that characterize this period of transition and the broad spectrum of responses that have issued from the Muslim world.

I

EARLY RESPONSES: CRISIS AND THE SEARCH FOR IDENTITY

The selection of texts presented here takes us through a century of Muslim contact with the West and Muslims' reflections on their own plight. Rifā'a Badawī Rāfi' al-Tahtāwī first went to Paris in 1826 and began to recount what he saw and what Egyptians should do to be "civilized." He was concerned mainly with explaining the new world to the old and removing hesitations born of isolation. Political and economic organization, patriotism and civic concern, and science appeared to be the keys to European power and progress—and they were there for the borrowing. It all seemed so easy.

By the end of the nineteenth century, the climate had changed. Jamāl al-Dīn al-Afghānī marked the turning point, as he roamed from India to Egypt arousing Muslims to resist the incursions of imperialism by galvanizing their forces as individual nations or as the Muslim "nation" (depending on his audience) to regain lost power and glory. He was an occasional critic of religion, an unhesitating advocate of science and philosophy, and also a proponent of a return to Islam, which touched traditional sensibilities.

Afghānī was the catalyst; Muhammed 'Abduh was the synthesizer. With considerable erudition and dedication, he reread Islamic history to discover, hidden under the silt of ages, that very rationality that the West was vaunting. In fact, the admirable traits of the West derived from its contact with Islam. Thus, there was no problem being modern and Muslim.

A disciple of 'Abduh's, 'Ali 'Abd al-Rāziq, pushed this rereading of Muslim history a bit further in 1926, trying to disprove the Muslim axiom that "Islam is both religion and state." He went beyond the tolerated limits and was retired to obscurity. Islam may be all that Europe was, potentially, at least, but for the guardians of Islamic tradition Islam was much more, and that more was different from the West. This sense of being different is always present in some form or other in the texts, but rarely is it defined clearly. This, of course, is the problem of identity.

7

The search for identity among the Muslims of South Asia was characterized by a somewhat different process. A Muslim minority had ruled the
Hindu majority of the Indian subcontinent for centuries. From the eighteenth
century onwards, British colonial presence had meant increased military,
economic, and political controls. As a result of the so-called Sepoy Mutiny
of 1857 (which many South Asian historians prefer to call the First War of
Independence) de facto British control gave way to British rule with British
removal of the Mughal emperor.

Surveying the heavy price of Muslim political and cultural resistance to
British rule and the inner weakness of the community, Sir Sayyid Ahmad
Khān determined that the revival (indeed, survival) of the Muslim community was dependent upon Muslim acceptance of and accommodation
with British rule and, most importantly, an inner renewal through religious,
social, and educational reforms. Ahmad Khān maintained that Islam was
the religion of reason and nature and, like Afghānī and 'Abduh, argued that
there was no inherent conflict between Islam and modern thought.

He studied at al-Azhar University and was appointed imām of
the first large student mission sent by Muhammad ʿAlī to Paris.
His five years in France left a lasting impression, and his account
of his impressions circulated widely. He learned French, read
avidly, and translated some twenty books into Arabic. He headed
the new school of languages and was editor of the first official
gazette.

Fatherland and Patriotism

The wisdom of the Almighty King has seen it fit that the sons of the
fatherland[1] be united always by their language, by their allegiance to one
king and by their obedience to one divine law and political administration.
These are some of the indications that God disposed men to work together
for the improvement of their fatherland and willed that they relate to one
another as members of one family. God willed that the fatherland would,
so to speak, take the place of father and mother and tutor and would be
the locus of the happiness shared by men. Thus, it is not fitting that one
nation be divided into numerous parties on the basis of different opinions,
because partisanship begets contradictory pressures, envy, and rancour with
consequent lack of security in the fatherland. This is especially so because
the holy law and the political administration which put all men on an equal
footing require that they be of one heart and consider no one their enemy
save him who sows discord among them by his treachery. They must
beware of such people, lest their sovereignty be flawed and order disrupted.
The obvious enemy is he who does not want the people to be faithful to
their fatherland or to enjoy fully their freedom.

The son of the fatherland—whether he be native born or a refugee who
has been naturalized—has a relation to the fatherland, which is expressed
in various ways. Sometimes he is referred to in terms of the fatherland itself,
for example he may be called "Egyptian," or in terms of his people, then
he is called by an adjective derived from their name, or he may be described
in terms of the idea of fatherland and be called a "patriot." This means

---

1. The concepts of fatherland (*watan*) and patriotism (*wataniyyah*) were new to Muslim
thought. Tahtāwī appears to have been the first to introduce them into Arabic. See
M. ʾAmārah, ed., vol. I, p. 123. [Ed.]

From *Kitāb al-Murshid al-amīn lil-banāt wa-al-banīn* [The faithful guide for girls and boys],
(Beirut: Arab Foundation, 1973), pp. 433–35, 469–71, 480–81.

that he enjoys the rights of his country, the greatest of which is complete freedom in that human society. The patriot, though, can be described in terms of freedom only if he is obedient to the law of the fatherland and aids its execution so that his subservience to the principles of his country necessarily entails that the fatherland will guarantee him the enjoyment of civil rights and municipal privileges. In this sense he is a patriot and a native, signifying that he is counted a member of the city and ranks as a member of its body. This is considered the greatest privilege in civilized nations. The people of the majority of nations had been deprived of this privilege, which is one of the greatest characteristics (of civilization.) This was so in those times when governors commanded according to their whims and acted as they wished. The people at that time had no channel by which they could oppose their rulers and no protection provided by the rules of the holy law. They were not able to inform their king that they considered certain things inappropriate nor could they write about his policies or administration. They could not express their opinion on any matter. Consequently, they were like foreigners with regard to the affairs of government, and they were not appointed to any functions or posts other than those which were below their merits. Now ideas have changed, and these dangers have been removed from the sons of the fatherland. Now the heart of a true patriot can be filled with love for his fatherland because he has become one of its members. . . .

The quality of patroitism demands not only that a man seek his due rights from the fatherland, but also that he fulfill his obligations to it. If one of the sons of the fatherland does not fulfill his obligations to it, then he loses the civil rights to which he had title.

The Romans in olden times demanded that a patriot who reached twenty years of age swear an oath that he would defend his fatherland and his government, and they bound him by covenant to this. The formula of the oath was: I take God as my witness that I will freely and willingly bear the weapon of honor for my fatherland and its people whenever there is occasion for me to aid them. And I call God to witness that I will fight, alone or with the army, to protect fatherland and religion. . . .

From this it can be understood how tenaciously the nation of the Romans loved their fatherland and why they came to rule over all the countries of the world. When this quality of patriotism declined, failure took hold of the members of this nation, and their situation deteriorated. Their organization was unravelled by the countless differences among princes and by the multiplicity of governors. After having been ruled by one Caesar, they split into East and West with two Caesars: Caesar of Rome and Caesar of Constantinople. From one great power they became two weak powers. They met defeat in all their wars and finally, after having reached the pinnacle, they dissolved into nothingness. Such is the case of a nation with divided government and a nation without organization.

CIVILIZATION, ISLAM, AND REASON

The civilization of the fatherland consists in the acquisition by the people of the inhabited area of the instruments necessary to better their conditions sensibly and spiritually. It is an expression of their superiority in ameliorating their morals and customs and education, and an indication of their capacity to acquire praiseworthy qualities, attain the perfections of civilization, and make progress in refined living. This is what civilization is with respect to the nation which resides in the fatherland, but the individuals of this civilized nation differ one from another in the degree of progress and betterment each attains. Thus civilization is applied both to nations and to individuals in an equivocal sense. . . .

The opposite of civilization is crudity; it is a lack of refinement in the level of life. There is no doubt that the mission of God's messengers bringing holy laws is at the root of the true civilization, which is the norm and pole of attraction for all civilizations. The civilization which Islam brought with its principles and rules civilized the countries of the world without exception and diffused the light of guidance to all horizons. The Messenger of God said: "I have brought you the pure holy law which no prophet before me has brought, not even my brother Moses, and the other prophets in my time try only to follow my holy law."

Anyone who has devoted himself to the science of the principles of jurisprudence and has an understanding of the restraints and rules it contains, will judge that all the rational deductions arrived at by the intellects of the other civilized nations, which they have made the basis for drawing up the laws and rules of their civilization, rarely go beyond these principles on which the branches of jurisprudence are built and around which human relations turn. Consequently, what we call the science of the principles of jurisprudence, they call natural laws or the laws of instinct. These consist in rational rules, good and bad, and on them they base their civil laws. What we call the branches of jurisprudence, they call civil laws or regulations. What we call justice and good works, they call freedom and equality. The love of religion and the passion to protect it, which the people of Islam hold so tenaciously and which give them an advantage over other nations in power and force, they call love of fatherland. However, among us, the people of Islam, love of the fatherland is just one branch of the faith, and the defense of religion is its capstone. Every Islamic kingdom is a fatherland for all those in it who belong to Islam; it combines religion and patriotism. Its defense is a duty on its sons by reason of these two aspects. However, it was customary to confine oneself to religion because it is so important a force, along with the will of the fatherland. The zeal for a specific fatherland may be incited by mere nationality and family, one can talk of sentiment, which is Qaysi, Yamani, Misri and Shami. However, in the fatherland all humans are put on the same level, so you will find two parties who differ from one another but unite against a foreigner in defense of their fatherland or their religion or their species.

The benefits of civilization are many and around them pivot all the sciences of harmonious living and of mutual enmity. For this reason some have said: whenever the orbit of civilization of the kingdoms of the earth widens, wars lessen, attacks decrease, conquests become more humane, reversals and triumphs more rare, until they finally cease altogether. Lawless tyranny and enslavement are wiped out, and poverty and wretchedness are removed. . . .

THE NATURAL LAW AND THE *SHARĪ'A*[2]

Man's actions must be in accord with these causes mentioned above; he must observe them, otherwise he will receive divine punishment for going contrary to the creator of these causes. For example, if a man wants to see in the pitch darkness of night and makes every effort to do so, or if he goes contrary to what the temporal seasons require, thinking that it is simple to obtain what only the seasons can produce, or if he contradicts the intrinsic nature of the elements, for instance, wishing to live permanently in water or to touch fire without being burned or to drink poison without dying, then he will be punished for his actions in this life to the degree that he contravenes the customary causes. He will drown or be burned, will choke or die. On the contrary, if he observed these causes and their intrinsic nature as much as possible, then he will protect himself to the same degree, since they are drawn up by the divine wisdom to guard and protect, to aid and help.

The regulations of the *Sharī'a* do not go contrary to most of these natural laws. They represent the innate character which God created along with man and made obligatory for him in existence. They are like a mold formed according to his likeness and fashioned to fit him. It is as if they were written on the tablet of his heart by divine inspiration without any intermediary. Then, later, there came the holy laws of the prophets through intermediaries and books which did not render these laws void in any way, for they preceded the legislation of holy laws among the peoples and nations. In former times the laws of the first sages and leaders of nations were based on these natural laws. From them they garnered guidance for mapping out the way of life in time past. On the basis of these laws, the ancients of Egypt, Iraq, Persia, and Greece arrived at a type of organization for human society. This can be attributed to God's kindness toward mankind, guiding them in their manner of living through the appearance of sages in their midst who legislated civil laws, especially those which are necessary like the protection of property, life and offspring, etc. . . .

2. *Sharī'a*: The *Sharī'a* or path is the general term given to the corpus of rules and precepts governing all aspects of a Muslim's personal and social life. The rules are derived from the Qur'ān, the Sunna (practice) of the Prophet, from analogical reasoning, and consensus. The *Sharī'a* is considered to be divinely revealed. Also, the Qur'ān indicates that each people was given its *Sharī'a* by God. [Ed.]

SAYYID JAMĀL AL-DĪN AL-AFGHĀNĪ
1838–1897

Philosopher, writer, orator, journalist, and political activist, he traveled widely from India and Afghanistan to Istanbul, Cairo, Paris, and London, stirring in Muslims the consciousness of their potential strength in the face of colonialism. He is the father of modern Muslim nationalism, proponent of pan-Islam, and the main inspiration for the reform movement in Islam. He expresses almost all the attitudes and themes that are commonplace in Muslim apologetics from 1900 to the present.

An Islamic Response to Imperialism

In the human world the bonds that have been extensive . . . have been two. One is this same unity of language of which nationality and national unity consist, and the other is religion. There is no doubt that the unity of language is more durable for survival and permanence in this world than unity of religion since it does not change in a short time in contrast to the latter. We see that a single people with one language in the course of a thousand years changes its religion two or three times without its nationality, which consists of unity of language, being destroyed. One may say that the ties and the unity that arise from the unity of language have more influence than religious ties in most affairs of the world. . . .

RELIGION AND PROGRESS

All religions are intolerant, each one in its way. The Christian religion, I mean the society that follows its inspirations and its teachings and is formed in its image, has emerged from the first period to which I have just alluded; thenceforth free and independent, it seems to advance rapidly on the road of progress and science, whereas Muslim society has not yet freed itself from the tutelage of religion. Realizing, however, that the Christian religion preceded the Muslim religion in the world by many centuries, I cannot keep from hoping that Muhammadan society will succeed someday in breaking its bonds and marching resolutely in the path of civilization after the manner of Western society. . . . In truth, the Muslim religion has tried to stifle science and stop its progress. . . .

From *An Islamic Response to Imperialism: Political and Religious Writings of Sayyid Jamāl al-Dīn al-Afghānī*, trans. and ed. Nikki R. Keddie (Berkeley: University of California Press, 1968), pp. 56, 87, 102–7.

SCIENCE AND PROGRESS

The Europeans have now put their hands on every part of the world. The English have reached Afghanistan; the French have seized Tunisia. In reality this usurpation, aggression, and conquest have not come from the French or the English. Rather it is science that everywhere manifests its greatness and power. Ignorance had no alternative to prostrating itself humbly before science and acknowledging its submission.

In reality, sovereignty has never left the abode of science. However, this true ruler, which is science, is continually changing capitals. Sometimes it has moved from East to West, and other times from West to East. More than this, if we study the riches of the world we learn that wealth is the result of commerce, industry, and agriculture. Agriculture is achieved only with agricultural science, botannical chemistry, and geometry. Industry is produced only with physics, chemistry, mechanics, geometry, and mathematics; and commerce is based on agriculture and industry.

Thus it is evident that all wealth and riches are the result of science. There are no riches in the world without science, and there is no wealth in the world other than science. In sum, the whole world of humanity is an industrial world, meaning that the world is a world of science. If science were removed from the human sphere, no man would continue to remain in the world. . . .

The science that has the position of a comprehensive soul and the rank of a preserving force is the science of *falsafa* or philosophy, because its subject is universal. It is philosophy that shows man human prerequisites. It shows the sciences what is necessary. It employs each of the sciences in its proper place.

If a community did not have philosophy, and all the individuals of that community were learned in the sciences with particular subjects, those sciences could not last in that community for a century, that is, a hundred years. That community without the spirit of philosophy could not deduce conclusions from these sciences.

The Ottoman Government and the Khedivate of Egypt have been opening schools for the teaching of the new sciences for a period of sixty years, and until now they have not received any benefit from those sciences. The reason is that teaching the philosophical sciences was impossible in those schools, and because of the nonexistence of philosophy, no fruit was obtained from those sciences that are like limbs. Undoubtedly, if the spirit of philosophy had been in those schools, during this period of sixty years they themselves, independent of the European countries, would have striven to reform their kingdoms in accord with science. Also, they would not send their sons each year to European countries for education, and they would not invite teachers from there to their schools. I may say that if the spirit of philosophy were found in a community, even if that community did not have one of those sciences whose subject is particular, undoubtedly their philosophic spirit would call for the acquisition of all the sciences.

The first Muslims had no science, but, thanks to the Islamic religion, a philosophic spirit arose among them, and owing to that philosophic spirit they began to discuss the general affairs of the world and human necessities. This was why they acquired in a short time all the sciences with particular subjects that they translated from the Syriac, Persian, and Greek into the Arabic language. . . .

Jurisprudence among the Muslims includes all domestic, municipal, and state laws. Thus a person who has studied jurisprudence profoundly is worthy of being prime minister of the realm or chief ambassador of the state, whereas we see our jurisconsults after studying this science unable to manage their own households, although they are proud of their own foolishness.

The science of principles consists of the philosophy of the *Shari'a*, or *philosophy of law*. In it are explained the truth regarding right and wrong, benefit and loss, and the causes for the promulgation of laws. Certainly, a person who studies this science should be capable of establishing laws and enforcing civilization. However, we see that those who study this science among the Muslims are deprived of understanding of the benefits of laws, the rules of civilization, and the reform of the world.

Since the state of the *'ulamā'* has been demonstrated, we can say that our *'ulamā'* at this time are like a very narrow wick on top of which is a very small flame that neither lights its surroundings nor gives light to others. A scholar is a true light if he is a scholar. Thus, if a scholar is a scholar he must shed light on the whole world, and if his light does not reach the whole world, at least it should light up his region, his city, his village, or his home. What kind of scholar is it who does not enlighten even his own home?

The strangest thing of all is that our *'ulamā'* these days have divided science into two parts. One they call Muslim science, and one European science. Because of this they forbid others to teach some of the useful sciences. They have not understood that science is that noble thing that has no connection with any nation, and is not distinguished by anything but itself. Rather, everything that is known is known by science, and every nation that becomes renowned becomes renowned through science. Men must be related to science, not science to men.

How very strange it is that the Muslims study those sciences that are ascribed to Aristotle with the greatest delight, as if Aristotle were one of the pillars of the Muslims. However, if the discussion relates to Galileo, Newton, and Kepler, they consider them infidels. The father and mother of science is proof, and proof is neither Aristotle nor Galileo. The truth is where there is proof, and those who forbid science and knowledge in the belief that they are safeguarding the Islamic religion are really the enemies of that religion. The Islamic religion is the closest of religions to science and knowledge, and there is no incompatibility between science and knowledge and the foundation of the Islamic faith. . . .

SAYYID JAMĀL AL-DĪN AL-AFGHĀNĪ
Islamic Solidarity

A study of the particular identity which characterizes some nations and an examination of their beliefs prove to anyone blessed with a clear and accurate sense of observation that in most nations there is a spirit of ethnic solidarity which in turn produces a sense of pride. Those whom this spirit animates are proud of the glorious deeds of their ethnic brothers. They become angry with any misfortune which touches them to the point where, in order to combat it, they kill without thinking about the reasons or the causes of the sentiment which pushes them to act. This is why many who are seeking for truth have come to the conclusion that a strong feeling of ethnic identity must be counted as integral to human nature. Yet their opinion is not correct, as we can ascertain by the behavior of a child who, born in one country subsequently is taken before he reaches the age of conscious thinking into the territories of another nation; if he grows up and reaches the age of reason in that place, he will not mention his birthplace or display any natural partiality for it. He will have no idea about his birthplace. Indeed, perhaps he will be more attached to the place where he grew up. Yet, that which is truly natural does not change.

Therefore, we do not think that such a feeling is natural to man, but rather that is is composed of a number of accidental attributes which necessity stamps upon the feelings. Actually, wherever he is, the human being has many wants. Individuals have a tendency to set themselves apart and to seek profit for themselves when they have not been properly taught. Also, they have a tendency to have numerous selfish desires which, when united with power, gives them an aggressive character. That is why some men find themselves struggling against the aggression of others. After fighting troubles for long years they were constrained to band together according to their parentage and in various ways until they formed ethnic units. That is how they became divided into nations such as the Indians, the Russians, the Turkomans, etc. Each of these groups, thanks to the combined strength of its members, was able to preserve its interests and to safeguard its rights from any encroachment by another group. Moreover, they have gone even farther than necessary as is common in the evolution of man: they have reached the point where each group is bitter if it falls under the rule of another. It believes that domination will be oppressive even if it is just. . . .

However, if necessity has created this sort of individualistic racial solidarity, there is no doubt that such solidarity can disappear just as it can arise. Such can take place when an arbiter is accepted and the contending forces are brought together. . . . This arbiter is the Prince of all things, the

From *The Emergence of the Modern Middle East: Selected Readings*, trans. and ed. Robert G. Landen (New York: Van Nostrand Reinhold Company, 1970), pp. 105–10.

Conqueror of heaven and earth. . . . When men recognize the existence of the Supreme Judge . . . they will leave it entirely to the possessor of sacred power to safeguard good and repel evil. No longer will they have any need for an ethnic sentiment which has lost its purpose and whose memory has been erased from their souls; judgment belongs to Allah, the Sublime, the Magnificent.

That is the secret of the aversion which Muslims have for manifestations of ethnic origin in every country where they live. That is why they reject all clan loyalty with the exception of Islamic sentiment and religious solidarity. The believers in Islam are preoccupied neither with their ethnic origins nor with the people of which they are a part because they are loyal to their faith; they have given up a narrow bond in favor of a universal bond: the bond of faith.

Actually, the principles of the Islamic religion are not restricted to calling man to the truth or to considering the soul only in a spiritual context which is concerned with the relationship between this world and the one to come. . . . There is more besides: Islamic principles are concerned with relationships among the believers, they explain the law in general and in detail, they define the executive power which administers the law, they determine sentences and limit their conditions; also, they are concerned with the unique goal that the holder of power ought to be the most submissive of men to the rules regulating that power which he gains neither by heritage, nor inheritance, nor by virtue of his race, tribe, material strength, or wealth. On the contrary, he acquires it only if he submits to the stipulations of the sacred law, if he has the strength to apply it, and if he judges with the concurrence of the community. Thus, in truth, the ruler of the Muslims will be their religious, holy, and divine law which makes no distinction among peoples. This will also be the summary of the ideas of the nation. A Muslim ruler has no other privilege than that of being the most ardent of all in safeguarding the sacred law and defending it.

In safeguarding the rights and the protection of people, of property, and of reputations, the lawgiver has not taken any account of lineage, nor of ancestral privilege. Moreover, any bond, with the exception of the bond of Islamic law, was disapproved by Him. Whoever relies upon such bonds is subject to blame and whoever advocates them deserves criticism. The Prophet said, in this matter: "Tribal solidarity should not exist among us; it does not exist among those of us who are bound by religion; it does not exist among those of us who die believers." The *hadīths* (tradition) of the Prophet all agree upon this point. In summary, whoever surpasses all men in piety, that is to say, in the practice of Islamic law, will be distinguished by the respect and veneration accorded to him: "The noblest among you in the eyes of God, is the most pious" (Qur'ān 49: 13). It has followed, down through many ages, and in spite of the differences in generations, that power has been wielded by men who are not noble in their race, nor especially privileged in their tribe; who do not hold sovereignty because of hereditary royalty, or do not claim it by virtue of their noble descent or highborn antecedents; they are raised to power only because of their obedience to the law and to the intense zeal they display in observing it.

The amount of power given to Muslim rulers is a product of their observance of divine regulations, of the way in which they follow the good directions which these prescribe, and of the absence of all personal ambition in them. Each time a ruler tries to distinguish himself by surpassing all others in luxury or the magnificence of his mode of life, or each time that he tries to assume a greater dignity than his people, then the people return to their tribal loyalties, differences arise, and the ruler's power declines.

Such is the lesson which one can learn from the history of the Muslims from the day their religion was revealed up to our own time. They set little value on either ethnic ties or racial sentiment but take only religious ties into consideration. That is why one can say that an Arab has no aversion to domination by Turks, why the Persian accepts the sovereignty of the Arab, and why the Indian obeys the laws of the Afghan without any bitterness or hesitancy among them. That is why one also can assert that the Muslim does not revolt or protest against either the regimes which impose themselves over him or against the transfer of power from one tribe to another so long as the possessor of authority maintains religious law and follows it precepts. But if these regimes stray in their conduct and unjustly deviate from the laws' teachings and attempt to execute that which is not right, then the hearts of the Muslims are detached from them and they become the object of disaffection, and even if they are a Muslim people's own blood brothers, they will appear more odious than foreigners in the people's eyes.

One can also say that Muslims are different from the adherents to other religions because of the emotion and regret they feel if one piece of Muslim territory is cut off from an Islamic government, whatever may be the ethnic origin of the inhabitants of this territory or the group which has taken it over.

If among the Muslims one found a minor ruler of whatever racial origin, who followed the divine commandments, was zealous in applying them, compelled the people to apply the punishments which they ordain, obeyed the law himself like his subjects, and gave up trying to distinguish himself through vain pomp, it would be possible for this ruler to enjoy widespread power and great influence. He could assume great authority in Muslim-inhabited countries. He would not encounter great difficulty in doing this, for he would not have to spend money, or build up his army, or conclude alliances with the great powers, or seek the assistance of partisans of civilization and freedom. . . . He could accomplish all this by following the example of the orthodox caliphs [the early caliphs of Islam in the seventh century A.D., Ed.] and by returning to the original sources of Islamic religious law. His conduct would bring a revival of strength and a renewal of the prerequisites of power.

Let me repeat for you, reader, one more time, that unlike other religions, Islam is concerned not only with the life to come. Islam is more: it is concerned with its believers' interests in the world here below and with allowing them to realize success in this life as well as peace in the next life. It seeks "good fortune in two worlds." In its teachings it decrees equality among different peoples and nations.

The times have been so cruel and life so hard and confusing that some Muslims—they are rare—have lost patience and assert with difficulty that Islamic principles are their oppressors and they give up using religious principles of justice in their actions. They resort, even, to the protection of a foreign power but are filled with regret at the things that result from that course of action. . . . Actually, the schisms and divisions which have occurred in Muslim states originate only from the failure of rulers who deviate from the solid principles upon which the Islamic faith is built and stray from the road followed by their early ancestors. Certainly, opposition to solidly based precepts and wandering away from customary ways are the very actions that are most damaging to power. When those who rule Islam return to the rules of their law and model their conduct upon that practiced by early generations of Muslims, it will not be long before God gives them extensive power and bestows strength upon them comparable to that wielded by the orthodox caliphs, who were leaders of the faith. God give us the will to act with justice and lead us upon the road to integrity.

SHAYKH MUHAMMAD 'ABDUH
1849–1905

He received a traditional religious education but was transformed by his contact with Jamāl al-Dīn al-Afghānī. Exiled by the British, he spent time in Beirut and Tripoli, then in Paris where he edited a review with Afghānī for a brief time. He returned to hold high religious posts, including that of Mufti of Egypt. His desire to reform Islam and put it in harmony with modern times by a return to primitive purity pushed him to theological reflection and writing, which make him the founder of the modernist school in Islam.

Islam, Reason, and Civilization

At all events, religion must not be made into a barrier, separating men's spirits from God-given abilities in the knowledge of the truths of the contingent world as far as in them lies. Rather, religion must promote this very search, demanding respect for evidence and enjoining the utmost possible devotion and endeavour through all the worlds of knowledge—and all within the true proportions of the goal, holding fast the while to sound itself. Any who assert the contrary do not know what religion is and do despite to it which the Lord of the worlds will not forgive. . . .

How then can reason be denied its right, being, as it is, the scrutineer of evidences so as to reach the truth within them and know that it is Divinely given? Having, however, once recognised the mission of a prophet, reason is obliged to acknowledge all that he brings, even though unable to attain the essential meaning within it or penetrate its full truth. Yet this obligation does not involve reason in accepting rational impossibilities such as two incompatibles or opposites together at the same time and point. For prophecies are immune from bringing such follies. But if there comes something which appears contradictory, reason must believe that the apparent is not the intended sense. It is then free to seek the true sense by reference to the rest of the prophet's message in whom the ambiguity occurred, or to fall back upon God and His omniscience. There have been those among our forebears who have chosen to do either one or the other. . . .

When religions first began, men understood their well-being, whether general or particular, only in a most rudimentary way, rather like infants lately born, who know only what comes within their senses and distinguish

From *The Theology of Unity*, trans. Ishaq Musa'ad and Kenneth Cragg (London: George Allen & Unwin, 1966), pp. 103–4, 107–8, 133–35, 145–46, 148–50.

only with difficulty between the present and the past. . . . The religions took men and gave them straight commands and firm restraints, to which they required obedience to the utmost possible degree. Though the meaning and purpose were there to be known, obedience was irrespective of actual comprehension and intelligent knowledge. Religions came with astonishing and impressive miracles and laid upon men the forms of worship consonant with their condition.

At length, human society reached a point at which man came to his full stature, helped by the moral of the earlier vicissitudes. Islam supervened, to present its case to reason, to call on mind and intelligence for action, to take emotion and feeling into partnership for man's guidance to both earthly and heavenly blessedness. It clarified the things that provoked human discords and demonstrated that religion with God was one in all generations, that there was a single Divine purpose for their reform without and their cleansing within. Islam taught that the sole aim of outward forms of worship was to renew the inward recollection of God and that God looks not on the form but on the heart. It required the devotee to care as well for his body as for the soul, enjoining outward as well as inward integrity, both of which it made mandatory. Sincerity was made the very heart of worship and rites were only laid down in so far as they conduced to the hallowing of moral character. "Verily prayer preserves men from foul and evil things." (Qur'ān 29:45.) "Man is created restless. When evil befalls him he despairs, but touched with good fortune he becomes niggardly— though not those who pray." (Qur'ān 79:19–22.) The rich man who remembers to be grateful is raised by Islam to the same level as the poor man who endures patiently. Perhaps Islam even esteems him higher. Islam deals with man in its exhortations as a wise and sober counsellor would deal with a mature person summoning him to the full harnessing of his powers, both outward and inward, and affirmed this quite unequivocally to be the way of pleasing God and showing thankfulness for His grace. This world is the seedplot of the world to come. Men will not come by ultimate good save as they endeavour a present well-doing.

Islam removed all racial distinctions within humanity, in the common dignity of relationship with God, of participation in human-kind, in race group and particular setting, as well as the dignity of being in the way of the highest attainments prepared by God for men. This universal dignity contrasts sharply with the exclusive claims of those who pretend to privileged status denied to others and consign allegedly inferior mortals to permanent subjection, thus strangling the very spirit of the peoples, or most of them, and reducing them to walking shadows. . . .

Now the nations had what they were looking for—a religion with a mind to think. Now they had a faith which gave justice its due place. The main factor which deterred a massive and spontaneous accession to Islam to enjoy these things long-desired lay in the system of class privilege under which the nations laboured. By this some classes lorded it over others, without right. Rulers wrecked nothing of the interests of the common people if the desires of the higher classes conflicted with them. Here was a religion which regulated human rights and gave equal respect to persons of all classes, their beliefs, their dignity and their property. It gave, for example, to a poor non-Muslim woman the perfect right to refuse to sell her small dwelling, at any price, to some great amīr, ruling absolutely over a large territory, who wanted it, not for private purposes, but in order to enlarge a mosque. When, in this particular case, he doubled the price and took forcible steps to acquire it and she raised a complaint to the Caliph, he issued an order to ensure her possession and reproached the amīr for his action. Islamic justice permitted a Jew to take up a case before the judge against no less a person than 'Alī ibn Abī Tālib, who was made to stand with the plaintiff in the court-process until judgement was given.

The foregoing makes clear how the message and relationships Islam brought endeared even its enemies to it, and so revolutionized their outlook as to make them its allies and protégés. . . .

ISLAM CIVILIZES ITS CONQUERORS

The light of Islam shone in the lands where its devotees went, and the only factor at work in their relation with the local people was the Word of God heard and apprehended. At times the Muslims were pre-occupied with their own affairs and fell away from the right path. Then Islam halted like a commander whose allies have disappointed him and is about to give ground. "God brings about what He intends." (Qur'ān 65:3.) The Islamic lands were invaded by the Tartar peoples, led by Jenghiz Khan, pagans who despoiled the Muslims and were bent on total conquest, plunder and rapine. But it was not long before their successors adopted Islam as their religion and propagated it among their kin with the same consequences as elsewhere. They came to conquer the Muslims and they stayed to do them good.

The West made a sustained attack against the East, involving all the kings and peoples, and continuing more than two hundred years, during which time the West engendered a quite unprecedented zeal and fervour for religion. With military forces and preparations to the utmost of their capacity, they advanced towards the Muslim heart-lands, fired by religious devotion. They overran many countries of Islamic allegiance. Yet in the end these violent wars closed with their evacuation.

Why did they come and why did they return? The religious leaders of the West successfully aroused their peoples to make havoc of the eastern world and to seize the sovereignty over those nations on what they believed to be their prescriptive right to tyrannize over masses of men. They came in great numbers of all sorts of men, estimated in millions, many settling in Muslim territory as residents. There were periods of truce in which the angry fires abated and quieter tempers prevailed, when there was even time to take a look at the surrounding culture, pick up something from the medley of ideas and react to what was to be seen and heard. It became clear that the exaggerations of their idle dreams which had shaped into such grievous efforts had no vestige of truth. And, furthermore, they found freedom in a religion where knowledge, law and art could be possessed with entire certitude. They discovered that liberty of thought and breadth of knowledge were means to faith and not its foes. By God's will they acquired some experience of refined culture and went off to their own territories thrilled with what they had gained from their wars—not to mention the great gains the travellers gathered in the lands of Andalusia by intercourse with its learned and polished society, whence they returned to their own peoples to taste the sweet fruits they had reaped. From that time on, there began to be much more traffic in ideas. In the West the desire for knowledge intensified and concern grew to break the entail of obscurantism. A strong resolve was generated to curb the authority of religious leaders and keep them from exceeding the proper precepts of religion and corrupting its valid meanings. It was not long after that a party made its appearance in the west calling for reform and a return to the simplicities of the faith—a reformation which included elements by no means unlike Islam. Indeed, some of the reforming groups brought their doctrines to a point closely in line with the dogma of Islam, with the exception of belief in the prophetic mission of Muhammad. Their religion was in all but name the religion of Muhammad; it differed only in the shape of worship, not in meaning or anything else.

Then it was that the nations of Europe began to throw off their bondage and reform their condition, re-ordering the affairs of their life in a manner akin to the message of Islam, though oblivious of who their real guide and leader was. So were enunciated the fundamental principles of modern civilization in which subsequent generations as compared with the peoples of earlier days have found their pride and glory.

All this was like a copious dew falling on the welcoming earth, which stirs and brings forth a glad growth of every kind. Those who had come for strife, stayed to benefit and returned to benefit others in turn. Their rulers thought that in stirring up their peoples they would find an outlet for their rancour and secure their own power. Instead they were shown up for what they were and their authority foundered. What we have shown about the nature of Islam, well enough known to every thoughtful student, is acknowledged by many scholars in western countries and they know its validity and confess that Islam has been the greatest of their mentors in attaining their present position. "God's is the final issue of all things." (Qur'ān 22:41.)

'ALĪ 'ABD AL-RĀZIQ
1888–1966

A disciple of 'Abduh, he studied at al-Azhar and later at Oxford University. In the debate that followed the abolition of the caliphate in 1924, he offered a contribution entitled *Islam and the Bases of Power*, which led to his condemnation by a council of *ulama* of al-Azhar University. He was forbidden from holding any public office, so he devoted his efforts to the Academy of Arabic Language in Cairo.

The Caliphate and the Bases of Power

APOSTLESHIP AND GOVERNANCE

We hope that the reader will not be alarmed by this study, which aims at discovering whether or not the Prophet was a king. One should not think that research like this is dangerous for religion or harmful to faith for those who undertake it. Reflection reveals that the matter is not so serious as to push a believer beyond the bounds of faith or to upset anyone's piety.

What makes the question seem grave is its connection with the dignity and rank of the Prophet. Nonetheless, it does not in any way touch the essence of religion or the foundations of Islam.

This research is probably new in Islam. Muslims have never faced the question frankly, and their *'ulamā'* have no clear and well-formed doctrine on the matter. Consequently, if, after study, one concludes either that the Prophet was a king as well as an apostle or that he was an apostle only, it can hardly be branded heresy or heterodoxy with regard to the opinions professed by Muslims. The study falls outside the area of those beliefs which the *'ulamā'* have treated and on which they profess well-established opinions. It belongs more to the area of scientific research than to that of religion. Let the reader follow us without fear and with a tranquil soul.

It is well known that prophecy is something other than royalty: there is no intrinsic connection between the two notions. Prophecy is one sort of dignity, royalty another. How many kings there are who were neither prophets nor apostles. How many prophets God raised up without making them kings. In fact, the majority of known prophets were prophets only.

Jesus, son of Mary, was the apostle of Christianity and head of the Christians, and yet he preached submission to Caesar and accepted his

From "L'Islam et Les Bases Du Pouvoir" [Islam and the bases of power], trans. from Arabic by L. Bercher in *Revue Des Etudes Islamiques*, VIII (1934), pp. 171–73, 185–87, 190–91, 200–208, 211–13, 218–22.

authority. It was Jesus who addressed those profound words to his followers: "Render unto Caesar the things that are Caesar's and unto God those that are God's." . . .

In the history of the prophets we find only rare examples of persons whom God permitted to accumulate the dignity of prophet along with that of king. Was Muhammad one of these, or was he prophet only and not king?

To our knowledge, not one of the 'ulamā' has expressed a clear opinion on this question: in fact, none has spoken about it. But by way of induction we can affirm this: Muslims in general tend to believe that the Prophet was both prophet and king and that he established with Islam a political government of which he was king and head. This is the opinion that best corresponds to the dominant taste of Muslims and the position to which they most easily relate. No doubt this is also the opinion of the majority of the 'ulamā' in Islam. When it comes to treating certain points which touch on the question, these people are inclined to consider Islam as a political unity and as a government founded by the Prophet. . . .

PROPHETIC PRIMACY

Thus we have seen the almost insurmountable difficulties facing those who wish to side with the opinion that the Prophet was both apostle of God, political sovereign and founder of a political government. . . .

There remains only one opinion for the reader to adopt. . . . This opinion holds that Muhammad was solely an apostle. He dedicated himself to purely religious propaganda without any tendency whatsoever towards temporal sovereignty, since he made no appeal in favor of a government. This same opinion maintains that the Prophet had neither temporal sovereignty nor government, that he established no kingdom in the political sense of the word nor anything synonomous with it, that he was a prophet only, like his brother prophets who preceded him, and that he was neither a king nor the founder of a state, nor did he make any appeal for a temporal empire.

This is not a very common opinion. In fact, it is so singular that it may clash with Muslim understanding. However, it is perfectly worthy of consideration and rests on solid reasons.

Before setting forth these reasons, we should put the reader on his guard against an error which anyone lacking sufficient wisdom and caution could easily commit. Actually, the prophetic mission itself demands that the Prophet have a sort of primacy in his nation, a form of authority over his people. But this has nothing in common with the primacy of temporal sovereigns, nor with their authority over their subjects. Therefore, we should not confuse prophetic primacy with that of temporal sovereignty. We must remember that major differences set them apart one from the other. . . .

An effective religious appeal implies that the one making it have a certain perfection which is first of all physical—he should not bear any physical defect, and his senses should be perfectly sound. There should be nothing about his physical person which would alienate and since he is chief, he should inspire in all a reverential fear and manifest a sympathy which attracts men and women. For the same reasons and because of his constant relations with the other world, he should also possess spiritual perfection.

The prophetic state demands that the prophet have a clearly privileged social rank in his nation. There is a *hadīth* which says: God never raises up a prophet who is not honored by his people and who is not powerful in his family.

The prophetic state demands, moreover, that the prophet possess a power which permits him to see that his injunctions are executed and his preaching followed, for God does not consider the prophetic mission a vain thing. He does not raise up a prophet as carrier of the truth without having decided that his preaching will be effective, that its fundamentals will be engraved on the tables of eternity and that it will be incorporated intimately into the truths of this life. "We sent no messenger save that he should be obeyed by God's leave." (Qur'ān 4:64) . . .

The prophet may have a role similar to that of monarchs in the political direction of the nation. But he has a role which is proper to him and which he shares with no one, namely it is his role to touch the soul which inhabits the body and to pull back the veils covering hearts in order to know them. He has the right or rather the duty to open the hearts of his followers and touch the sources of love and hate, of good and evil, and to know the intimate thoughts, the folds wherein temptation hides, the sources of man's designs and the matrix within which their character is formed. He has an obvious role in governing the masses, but he also accomplishes a hidden work which regulates the relations among associates and allies, masters and slaves, parents and children. . . . He has the right to scrutinize the internal as well as the external aspects of life. It is his business to direct the affairs of the body and of the soul, our temporal and our spiritual relations: his is the governance of this world and all that is concerned with the next world. . . .

MUHAMMAD'S AUTHORITY

We wish also to draw the reader's attention to another point, for we come across words which are sometimes used as synonyms and at other times are given different meanings. Often this is a cause for debate, divergence and incoherent judgements. These words include "king," "sultan," "chief," "prince," "caliph," "state," "kingdom," "government," "caliphate," etc.

By asking ourselves if the Prophet was or was not a king, we are trying to discover if he had a quality other than that of apostle which would lead us to believe that he effectively founded or at least initiated the foundation of a political unit. . . .

We do not doubt that Islam forms a religious unit; that Muslims as such form a unique community; that the Prophet preached unity and that he realized it before his death; that he was at the head of this religious unit as the unique guide, unrivaled director, and master whose orders were never contested and whose instructions were never transgressed. We know that to make Islamic unity triumph, the Prophet fought with word and sword, that he obtained divine aid and victory, that the angels and the power of God aided him so effectively that he brought his apostolate to term, accomplished the task confided to him and exercised an authority over his nation such as no king before or since has ever wielded. . . .

If we want to call this religious unit a "state," give that unlimited power which was the Prophet's the name of kingdom or the dignity of caliphate, and give the Prophet himself the title of king, caliph, sultan, etc., we are free to do so. These are only words, and we should not stop at words. The important thing, as we have said, is the meaning, and we have defined that meaning for the reader.

What is important for us to know is whether the preeminence of the Prophet in his nation was that of an apostle or that of a king: if the manifestations of authority which we notice at times in the life of the Prophet were the manifestations of a political government or those of religious primacy, and whether this unit of which the Prophet was head was a unity of government and a state or a purely religious unity which was not political. In sum, we want to know if the Prophet was prophet only, or both king and prophet.

The Qur'ān clearly confirms the opinion that the Prophet had no connection with political royalty. The verses of the Holy Book reinforce one another in affirming that the heavenly work of the Prophet did not surpass the limits of the message which was completely foreign to the notion of temporal power. "He who obeys the Prophet obeys God. As for those who turn away, we have not sent you to be their guardian." (Qur'ān 4:80) "Your people have denied it, though it is the truth. Say, 'I am not in charge of you.' For every announcement there is a term, and you will come to know." (Qur'ān 6:66–7). . . .

Thus it is seen that it is not the Qur'ān alone that forbids us to believe that the Prophet, besides his religious preaching, engaged in propaganda with a view to constituting a political government. Nor is it the Sunna alone which prohibits a similar belief. It is reason and the true signifance and nature of the prophetic mission which join with the Qur'ān and the Sunna to reject this opinion.

The authority of Muhammad over the believers was the authority of apostleship; it had nothing in common with temporal power.

No, there was neither government, nor state, nor any type of political aspiration, nor any of these ambitions proper to kings and princes.

Perhaps the reader has now succeeded in finding the answer to the question he posed touching the absence of every manifestation of temporal authority and of established government in the time of the Prophet. No doubt he will have understood why there was no governmental organization, no governors, no judges, no ministers. . . .

A UNIVERSAL RELIGIOUS MESSAGE, NOT AN ARAB STATE

Islam, as we have seen, is a sublime appeal enunciated by God for the good of the entire world, East and West, Arab and non-Arab, man and woman, rich and poor, learned and ignorant. It is a religious unity by which God wished to unite humanity and which he willed to extend to all the countries of the earth. . . .

Arabia, as is known, contained Arab groupings belonging to different tribes and peoples, speaking different dialects, living in different regions and tied to various political groupings. . . .

These nations, divided though they were, all rallied to the call of Islam in the time of the Prophet and gathered under his standard. These peoples, by God's grace, became brothers, joined together by the sole bond of religious feeling, held in check by one factor only: the primacy of the Prophet and his goodness and mercy. They became one nation with but one chief: the Prophet.

This unity which existed from the time of the Prophet was in no respect a political unity. It had none of the aspects of a state or a government. It was never anything other than a religious unity free from any admixture of politics. It was based on a unity of faith and religious dogma, not on a unity of state or a system of temporal authority.

What proves this is the conduct of the Prophet. We have no knowledge indicating that he sought to interfere in the political direction of the various nations, or that he changed anything in their mode of government or in the administrative or judicial regime of their tribes. Nor did he try to change the social and economic relations existing among the peoples or between them and other nations. We never hear that he deprived a governor of office, named a judge, organized a police force for these peoples, or regulated their commerce, agriculture or industry. On the contrary, the Prophet left to them concern for all these interests, saying: "You know better than anyone." Thus, all these nations with the civil and political unity which they respectively enjoyed, with the anarchy or the order found among them were joined together only by the tie to which we referred, namely, the unity of Islam, its precepts and its morals.

The following objection, however, could be raised: these fundamental precepts, these moral rules, these laws which the Prophet brought to both Arab and non-Arab nations were very numerous and had considerable effect on most aspects of life in these nations. . . .

However, if we reflect attentively, we note that all the rules prescribed by Islam, all the obligations imposed by the Prophet on Muslims, all these rules, precepts and moral injunctions had nothing in common with the methods of political government or the civil organization of the state. All these taken together do not form even a feeble part of the political principles and legislation indispensible for a civil government. All that Islam brought in the areas of dogma, juridical relations, customs, and penal law belongs to the religious domain; its intention is God alone and the service of the religious interests of humanity, nothing more. . . .

The Arabs, though reunited by the law of Islam, remained divided both politically and in their civil, social, and economic life. That is to say, the Arabs were formed into many different states, if we may be allowed to call the manner of life of the Arabs at that time by terms such as "state" or "government."

Such was the situation of the Arabs at the death of the Prophet. They formed a general religious unity embracing, with rare exceptions, completely different states. This is an indisputable truth. . . .

The Prophet went to his celestial repose without having named anyone to succeed him and without having indicated who might take his place in the nation.

There is no doubt about this. During all his life the Prophet made no allusion to anything which could be called an "Islamic State" or an "Arab state." It would be blasphemy to think otherwise. The Prophet did not leave this earth until he had entirely accomplished the mission given him by God and had explained to his nation the precepts of religion in their entirety without leaving anything vague or equivocal. How, then, if his work comprised the creation of a state, could he have left the Muslims without any precise directions concerning that state, especially since it was fated that after his death they would slip back into their old contentions and start killing one another? How could he have failed to concern himself with the question of succession to power when this has always been the primary concern of those who have founded governments? How could he have left the Muslims with nothing to guide them in this domain, abandoning them to incertitude? How could he leave them to grope in the darkness and to massacre one another while the body of the Prophet was still in their midst and his funeral had scarcely been held? . . .

The Prophet went to his celestial repose only after the religion had been completed, when grace had reached its fullness and the preaching of Islam had become a solid reality. On that day only did he die. His mission was accomplished, and that sublime union which in his august person joined heaven and earth came to an end.

THE CONFUSION BETWEEN PROPHETIC
PRIMACY AND CALIPHAL RULE

The primacy of the Prophet was, as we have said, a religious primacy attributable solely to his prophetic mission. The prophetic mission finished with the death of the Prophet and, at the same time, the primacy ceased. It was not given to any person to succeed him in that primacy nor in his prophetic mission.

If it was absolutely necessary that one of the followers of the Prophet take a position of preeminence after his death, then that preeminence would have to be entirely new and different from that which we recognized in the Prophet. . . .

The Muslims knew then that they were instituting a civil or temporal government and nothing more. This is why they allowed themselves the liberty to revolt against this government and oppose it. They knew full well that their lack of accord centered on a question of the temporal order only and that their disagreement touched a question of political interest which did not affect their religion nor upset their faith. . . .

We do not hesitate for an instant to affirm categorically that the major part of what is called the "war of apostasy" in the first days of the caliphate of Abū-Bakr was not a war of religion but a purely political war. The masses believed it was a religious struggle, but, in fact, its goals were not entirely religious. . . .

There were circumstances particular to Abū-Bakr which aided the masses to fall into the error of attributing a religious character to the leadership of Abū-Bakr. For instance, there was the fact that Abū-Bakr enjoyed an elevated and privileged rank alongside the Prophet. He had a reputation for religious proselytism and was highly esteemed by the Muslims. . . .

Thanks to these explanations, the reader can understand that this title of "Caliph of the Prophet of God" given to Abū-Bakr was one of the sources of the error which spread among the mass of Muslims, leading them to believe that the institution of the caliphate was a religious dignity and that he who was charged with the direction of Muslims' affairs held the place occupied by the Prophet.

Thus it is that since the first days of Islam the opinion has been propagated that the institution of the caliphate is a religious office occupied by a successor to the Prophet, author of the law.

It was in the interest of monarchs to give credence to this error in public so that they could use religion as a shield protecting their thrones against the attacks of rebels. They maintained this policy in diverse ways, and anyone who looks into the matter will find how numerous were the means they employed. They let it be understood publicly that obedience to the imāms was part of obedience to God and a revolt against them was rebellion against God. That was not all. The caliphs were not the sort of men who would rest content with that nor would they be satisfied with what satisfied Abū-Bakr. That appellation which provoked his anger would not upset them; they went further and made the sovereign "the successor of God on earth and his shadow over his servants." But the "glory of God is too high to be affected by that which they wanted to associate with Him." (Qur'ān 9:31). . . .

And so the question of the office of caliph was added to religious studies and came to be integrated into the dogmas of theology. Muslims studied it along with the attributes of God and the prophets; the theory of the caliphate became as much a part of dogma as the profession of Muslim faith: "There is no God but God and Muhammad is the Prophet of God."

Such was the crime that kings in their tyranny committed against Muslims. They concealed aspects of the truth from them and made them swerve from the right path. In the name of religion they barred their way from the paths of light, treated them arbitrarily, humiliated them and prohibited them from studying political science. Also, in the name of religion they betrayed them and snuffed out their intelligence in such a way that they could find no recourse other than religion even in questions of simple administration and pure politics. . . .

The final result of all this was the death of the spirit of scientific research and intellectual activity among Muslims. They were stricken with paralysis in the area of political thought, incapable of examining anything connected with the institution of the caliphate or the caliphs.

The truth is that the Muslim religion is innocent of this institution of the caliphate such as it is commonly understood by Muslims. It is innocent of all the apparel of seduction and intimidation, and the pomp of force and power with which they surrounded the institution of the caliphate. This institution has nothing in common with religious functions, no more than the judiciary and the other essential functions and machinery of power and state. All these functions are purely political; they have nothing to do with religion. Religion neither admits nor denies them. It neither orders nor forbids them. It simply leaves them to our free choice so that we will have recourse to rational judgement in their regard and base our judgement on the experience of the nations and the rules of politics. . . .

There is nothing in religion which prohibits Muslims from rivaling other nations in all the political and social sciences. Muslims are free to demolish this worn-out system (of the caliphate) before which they have debased and humiliated themselves. They are free to establish the bases of their kingdom and the organization of their state according to more recent conceptions of the human spirit and according to the principles of government whose excellence and firmness have been consecrated by the experience of the nations. . . .

SIR SAYYID AHMAD KHĀN
1817–1898

He was for several decades a member of India's civil service and during the Mutiny of 1857 remained loyal to the British. In addition to his own prolific reformist writings, he founded a translation society for the introduction of modern Western texts (1864) and the Anglo-Muhammadan Oriental College at 'Aligarh (1874), modeled on the British university system. In 1886 he established the Muhammadan Anglo-Oriental Educational Conference, which promoted Western education, the translation of Western scientific works, and women's education.

India and English Government

A great calamity over India, the Mutiny of 1857, had passed. We attributed it to want of education in India, and to the fact that the Indians did not understand what right the Government, whose subjects we are, had upon us, and what was our duty towards it. Combined with these was the want of intercourse between the rulers and the ruled for want of education. By this time universities were established in India with the object of imparting high education. Most of the statesmen approved of high education and considered it the duty of Government, while a few of them were against it. No one, however, thought for a moment that simultaneously with education a proper training was essential, inasmuch as a man could not become a man (civilised) through mere education, nor could his moral character be improved, but would rather become like a restive horse which does not remain within its rider's control. . . .

In our opinion, if the children of respectable Muhammadan families received, alongwith high education, a proper training and were at the same time given moral discipline, formed into a good society which is most essential for moral development, then, of course, they would, on attaining high education, be not a burden but a boon to the community. At all events the education imparted at this time to the Hindu Bengalis, the Parsis of Bombay, and the Brahmins and Mahrattas of Bombay and Poona, and which is termed high education, has not borne good fruit for India. First of all they considered themselves as highly educated and as eminent statesmen. Then they argued that the English Goverment should govern India in the same way as it governs in Europe, and make no distinction between the

From Shan Muhammad, ed., *The Aligarh Movement: Basic Documents 1864–1898* (New Delhi: Prakashan, 1978), Vol. III, pp. 1069–72.

conquerors and the conquered. Again, they learnt the word "liberty" and understood it to mean that they might say what came on their tongue or what passed in their mind; whether it was right or wrong, suited to the occasion or otherwise, whether there were sufficient reasons in support of it or not; they have fully to speak and print and publish throughout India. Then they came across the word "agitation" and said, "Look at the people of Ireland, how much agitation they make on the Government measures, establish clubs and societies for fomenting agitation, and say what they please on the platform and in the press." Then it came into their head that the English Government is a Government that is afraid of general agitation, and that nothing could be obtained from the Government without spreading agitation. And again it occurred to them that unless an agitation is widespread and the general public or all the people of a country agree on agitating, there could be no agitation, proper and advantageous. So they tried to make agitation widespread.

So long as the acts of a Government, right or wrong, proper or improper, are not spread widely among the masses, no agitation can be got up against Government, and on this theory the National Congress came into existence. The Congress did all it could to have the sins of the Government made generally known throughout India. . . .

We do not believe for a moment that this party of agitators mean to rebel, or to incite the people to rebel, against the Government; but what they have done, and are still doing is enculated [*sic*] to spread general discontent against the Government, and what is to be regretted the more is that discontent is mostly or rather generally improper and unjustified, and is in itself calculated to create rebellious thoughts among the people. The advocates of this movement, no doubt, call themselves well-wishers of the Government. It may probably be true. But what they do creates general discontent and antagonism against the Government. . . .

Musalmans, with a few exceptions, have not up to this time joined the National Congress and its agitation, and those that have thrown in their lot do not understand what harm is thereby being, and will in future be, done both to their community and the country. Those who are against the agitation are styled by the agitators flatterers of the Government. They may say what they please, but the oppositionists believe with certainty that if the Government accedes to the wishes of the agitators (which is, however, quite impossible) there would be a great danger to the administration and peace of India. This belief, and not flattery of the Government, has impelled them to oppose the movement.

Although the Musalmans do not take any part in the agitation of the National Congress, still their newspapers which are in the hands of Muslim editors have with a few exceptions, imitated other papers and gone out of their way, and in writing articles have not restrained their pens, a fact which is much to be regretted. But they must understand that supposing all the Hindus and Muhammadans of India join the National Congress in its agitation, and all papers, Hindu and Muhammadan, agree on publishing articles distorting the facts and opposed to the Government, still no harm can be done to the Government. The Government will of course be compelled to curtail the sphere of liberty which is now allowed, and to frame a law for taking away the liberty of the press. The Government will not have to be blamed for this course; whatever it will do will be a punishment for actions of the Indians themselves.

Who can say that the Government is to be blamed for having, after the Mutiny of 1857, taken away arms from the people of India and prohibited their possession without a license? It was a punishment to the Indians for the misdeeds they committed during the Mutiny of 1857. Every fair-minded person will admit the Indians had in their evil deeds gone so far that the Government was compelled to pass the Arms Act. . . .

The well-being of the people of India, and especially of the Musalmans, lies in leading a quiet life under the benign rule of the English Government. They must understand that the religion of Islam enjoins us to remain faithful to those under who we live as their subjects and enjoy peace, and to dispel from our minds any idea of disloyalty, and to keep aloof from such persons as entertain such notions, and to consider them our worthy king, and our Creator as the king of kings and our real Lord. . . .

SIR SAYYID AHMAD KHĀN

Islam: The Religion of Reason and Nature

You know well that in our time a new wisdom and philosophy have spread. Their tenets are entirely different from those of the former wisdom and philosophy [of the Greeks]. They are as much in disagreement with the tenets of ordinary present-day Islam as the tenets of Greek wisdom and philosophy were with the tenets of customary Islam during their time. . . . Yet the Muslim scholars of that time accepted them like religious tenets, . . . and this has made things even more difficult.

[Former science and modern science.] My friends! Another problem is the big difference between critical research today [and its results] and the tenets of Greek wisdom of old, because the tenets of former wisdom were based on rational and analogical arguments and not upon experience and observation. It was very easy for our forbears whilst sitting in the rooms of mosques and *khānqahs*,[1] to disprove teachings arrived at by analogous reasoning and to refute rational teachings by rational demonstrations, and not to accept them. But today a new situation has arisen which is quite different from that [brought about] by the investigations of former philosophy and wisdom. Today doctrines are established by natural experiments [i.e. experiments in natural science] and they are demonstrated before our eyes. These are not problems of the kind that could be solved by analogical arguments or which can be contested by assertions and principles which the *'ulamā'* of former times have established. . . . One highly necessary subject has been neglected by the *'ulamā'*. They did much to confront Greek wisdom and philosophy, but nothing or very little to satisfy the heart of the denier or doubter of Islam, by the way they would present to them the religion of Islam. It is neither sufficient for the firm believer, nor does it satisfy the mind of the doubter, to say simply that in Islam this has been taught in this way and has to be accepted.

[Need for a new theology] In the same way there are many other reasons for which in our time Muslims need to adopt new methods in controversy. The person who considers Islam to be true and believes firmly in it, his heart will testify that Islam alone is true—whatever changes may occur in logic, philosophy and natural science, and however much the doctrines of Islam seem to be in contradiction with them. This attitude is sufficient for those who believe with a true and uncomplicated mind in Islam, but not for those who reject or doubt it. Furthermore, it is by no

---

1. *khānqah*: a monastery of the Sūfī orders.

From "Lecture on Islam," *Sir Sayyid Ahmad Khān: A Reinterpretation of Muslim Theology*, trans. Christian W. Troll (Atlantic Highlands, N.J.: Humanities Press, Inc., 1978), pp. 311–19.

means a work of proper protection to confess just by the tongue that Islam is true, and to do nothing to strengthen it in its confrontation with the modern propositions of wisdom and philosophy. Today we need, as in former days, a modern theology ['ilm al-kalām] by which we either render futile the tenets of modern sciences or [show them to be] doubtful, or bring them into harmony with the doctrines of Islam. . . .

I happen to believe that there is nobody who is well acquainted with modern philosophy and modern and natural science as they exist in the English language, and who at the same time believes in all the doctrines which are considered doctrines of Islam in present-day under-standing. . . . I am certain that as these sciences spread—and their spread-ing is inevitable and I myself after all, too, help and contribute towards spreading them—there will arise in the hearts of people an uneasiness and carelessness and even a positive disaffection towards Islam as it has been shaped in our time. At the same time, I believe firmly that this is not because of a defect in the original religion but rather because of those errors which have been made, willfully or not, to stain the face of Islam. . . . The person that states Islam to be true must also state how he can prove the truth of Islam. . . . in order to arrive at the truth it is necessary that we discover a criterion and establish a touchstone which is related to all religions in the same manner and by which we can prove our religion or belief to be true. . . .

By this criterion I shall justify without any wavering what I acknowl-edge to be the original religion of Islam which God and the Messenger have disclosed, not that religion which the 'ulamā' and preachers have fashioned. I shall prove this religion to be true and this will be the decisive difference between us and the followers of other religions. . . . the only criterion for the truth of the religions which are present before us is whether the religion [in question] is in correspondence with the natural disposition of man, or with nature. If yes, then it is true, and such correspondence is a clear sign that this religion has been sent by that person which has created man. But if this religion is against the nature of man and his natural constitution and against his forces and faculties, and if it hinders man from employing these profitably, then there can be no doubt that this religion is not sent by the person that created man, because everyone will agree that religion was made for man. You can turn this and state to the same effect that man was created for religion.

So I have determined the following principle for discerning the truth of the religion, and also for testing the truth of Islam, i.e. is the religion in question in correspondence with human nature or not, with the human nature that has been created into man or exists in man. And I have become certain that Islam is in correspondence with that nature. . . .

I hold for certain that God has created us and sent us his guidance. This guidance corresponds fully to our natural constitution, to our nature and this constitutes the proof for its truth. . . .

After determining this criterion I clarified that Islam is in full accordance with nature. So I formulated that "Islam is nature and nature is Islam." God is the Creator of all things, as He is the Creator of heaven and earth and what is in them, and of all creatures; so is He also the Creator of nature. What a tremendous slander is it, therefore, when my opponents state that I call nature Creator or—God forbid—nature God. What I declare to be created, they accuse me of calling Creator.

[This path is not entirely new in the history of Islam.] Can anybody say that the path I have outlined above is not apt to strengthen Islam? . . . No doubt it is a new path, and yet in it I have followed the ancient *'ulamā.'* As they developed a theology [*'ilm-al-kalām*] in a new fashion, so I, like them, have developed a new method to prove the same truth. We cannot exclude the possibility of a mistake. Yet future *'ulamā'* will render it fully correct and will help Islam. In my view Islam can be reaffirmed against doubters in this way and not in any other.

II

ISLAM AND THE MODERN STATE

ISLAM AND NATIONALISM

The concern of the first modern reformers in the Middle East was directed toward adopting European political systems and toward restating Islam as a religion in perfect harmony with modernity. But the solutions which appeared so facile engendered much more serious questions about the basis of political organization and the function of religion in society. In the section which follows, the writings of Rashīd Ridā and Shakīb Arslān slip easily from national identity to Muslim nationalism, as if they were conditioned by their allegiance to the Ottoman Empire, the last of the Muslim Empires. Sāti' al-Husrī addresses the problem clearly: any new union raises the question of political organization and for the Arabs, common language, history and geography, not religion, are the only solid bases for political union. The Arabism advocated by al-Husrī found less of a response in Egypt than in other Arab countries, as the selection from Tāhā Husayn demonstrates. He dismisses the problem of East/West as inapplicable to Egypt, but his countryman Hasan al-Bannā shows that Tāhā Husayn's judgments had not filtered down to the masses. It was impossible to dismiss Islam, and so we find 'Abd al-Rahmān al-Bazzāz adroitly showing how Arabism and Islam are completely in harmony. This marks the attempt at a new synthesis of Islam and Arab nationalism. But note that the references to Islam in al-Bazzāz are basically historical. Islam, as such, is not seen as the basis of political organization.

Questions of independence and national identity went through two important phases in South Asia during the first half of the twentieth century. Initially, Hindus and Muslims of the Indian National Congress and the Muslim League had worked together in the independence movement. Yet, progressively, many Muslims came to fear for the rights of a Muslim minority in a Hindu-dominated secular state. Thus, for example, Muhammad 'Alī, once president of the Indian National Congress and a founder of the

Muslim League, quit the Congress in 1930. Muhammad Iqbāl, regarded by many as the spiritual father of Pakistan, articulated this Muslim communal concern in his presidential address before the All-India Muslim League (December 19, 1930) in which he called for a separate state for Muslims within India.

However, there were those in India who argued that any form of nationalism (whether Indian nationalism or Muslim nationalism) was antithetical to Islam, since the Islamic community or state (*umma*) is one that transcends all ethnic, tribal, regional, and racial divisions. We see this line of argument in the writings of Mawlānā Abū-l-'Alā' Mawdūdī. Mawdūdī sharply contrasts the ideals and values of Islam vis-à-vis nationalism—the one sustained by a divinely revealed law and the other by force.

RASHĪD RIDĀ
1865–1935

He studied at the Ottoman government school and at Shaykh Husayn Jisr's school, both in Tripoli, Lebanon. Here he made his first contact with Muhammad 'Abduh, and later, in 1897, when he took refuge in Egypt, he became 'Abduh's faithful disciple and guardian of his ideas. In 1898, Ridā founded the periodical *al-Manār*, which was the most important voice of Islamic reform in the Arab world. The following selection is a *fatwā* (legal opinion) given by Ridā in response to an inquiry from an Indonesian Muslim.

Patriotism, Nationalism, and Group Spirit in Islam

To the Excellent and Learned Shaykh Rashīd Ridā, may God give you long life.

Greetings and peace. In my country, Indonesia, at present there is a strong movement for independence involving a continual struggle against the colonialists. Unfortunately, in the midst of this holy war a group of *'ulamā*'[1] have risen up forbidding patriotism and making war on patriots in the name of the Islamic religion and its doctrines. They claim the patriots have deviated and are inciting enmity among the masses and their leaders. As a result the patriots are caught between two fires, that of the colonialists and that of the *'ulamā*'.

I am aware of the development of the national movement in Egypt and I know that religious men were in the avant garde of the combatants carrying the banner of nationalism. . . . Yes, I refer to the men, the students, and the *'ulamā*' of al-Azhar[2] who led demonstration after demonstration and fell in the squares and in the streets. Because of this I turn to you to ask for clarification on these matters, especially the following questions. An answer will help Indonesia and point out the way of truth and guidance.

1. Is it correct that there are *hadīths* forbidding the notion of patriotism and nationalism?

---

1. *'ulamā*': religious scholars. [Ed.]
2. al-Azhar University: Center of Islamic learning in Cairo. [Ed.]

From *Fatwās*, trans. from *al-Manār*, vol. 33 (1933), pp. 191–92.

2. Are his (Muhammad) sayings "There is no group feeling in Islam" and "There is no one among us who invokes the invocation of the *jāhiliyya*"[3] two clear *hadīths* forbidding patriotism?

3. Is there a distinction between group feeling and patriotism? Is patriotism included in the notion of group feeling? What was group feeling among the Arabs?

4. What is the view of Islam concerning the idea of patriotism and does this idea run counter to Islamic unity? What is intended by Islamic unity?

5. It is known that Shaykh Muhammad 'Abduh, the great philosopher, was the father of patriotism and of patriots. In his house in Halwan, Sa'd (Zaghlul) grew up and there the men of Egypt met. What do you, his disciple and biographer, judge in this matter?

6. What kind of patriotism should Muslim youth have?

   Answer of *al-Manār*:
These questions on the subject can be reduced to one problem with subdivisions. . . . Consequently, we will answer them with a single comprehensive yet brief answer. . . . "Group feeling" among the Arabs is related to "the group," i.e. a man's people who take sides with him; that is, they protect and defend him and aid him whenever he needs help or is wronged. The word "group" originally signifies the relatives of a man who are his heirs; then it becomes used in a wider sense. The word derives from *'isb*, an ivy plant which winds itself around a tree or the like.

It is well known that one of the imperatives of Islam is its prohibition of partisanship in wrong for the sake of relatives, people, or fatherland. It prohibits enmity and divisions among Muslims arising from the partisanship of any group, country, or region against their brothers in religion and against others except those against whom war should be waged.

The Prophet made this clear in his words: "Group spirit is a man's supporting his people in wrong." The Imām Ahmad[4] related this.

It is also well known that another imperative of Islam obliges its people to attack and combat the foreigners who attack them. All the jurisprudents have declared that holy war is a duty incumbent on all individuals when an enemy commits aggression against Muslims or occupies any of their lands. This is warding off wrong, so it is shameful ignorance to prohibit it and to deduce the prohibition from the group feeling of the Jāhiliyya, such as that which existed between the 'Aws and the Khazraj[5] among the Ansār,[6] which was prohibited by some *hadīths*.[7]

3. Jāhiliyya: the period of "ignorance" before Islam. [Ed.]
4. Ahmad ibn Hanbal: founder of one of the four main Sunni legal schools. [Ed.]
5. 'Aws and Khazraj: tribal groupings at Medina. [Ed.]
6. the Ansār: "helpers" of Muhammad at Medina. [Ed.]
7. *Hadīths*: traditions of the Prophet Muhammad; narratives of what the Prophet said, did, or permitted. [Ed.]

This is the summary answer to the first three questions.

The contemporary notion of patriotism expresses the unity of the people of different religions in their homeland, and their cooperation in defending the homeland they share. They cooperate to preserve its independence, to win it back if it was lost, and to develop it. In the islands of Indonesia this does not appear as it does in Egypt.

Islam's view of this is that Muslims are obligated to defend the non-Muslim who enters under their rule and to treat him as an equal according to the just rules of the *Sharī'a*.[8] Consequently, how could it not be allowed to join with them in defending the country, preserving its independence and developing it? The Companions of the Prophet exempted the *dhimmī*[9] who joined them in war from the head tax during the Caliphate of 'Umar, as we have demonstrated from evidence in the tenth volume of the *Manār Commentary*.[10]

The type of patriotism that should adorn a Muslim youth is that he be a good example for the people of the homeland, no matter what their religious affiliation, cooperating with them in every legitimate action for independence, for developing science, virtue, force, and resources on the basis of the Islamic law of preferring the closest relations in rights and duties. In his service of his homeland and his people he must not, however, neglect Islam which has honored him and raised him up by making him a brother to hundreds of millions of Muslims in the world. He is a member of a body greater than his people, and his personal homeland is part of the homeland of his religious community. He must be intent on making the progress of the part a means for the progress of the whole.

8. *Sharī'a*: Islamic law. [Ed.]
9. *dhimmī*: the protected people in a Muslim country, i.e. the Jews and Christians. They paid a head tax for this protection. [Ed.]
10. *Manār Commentary*: a commentary on the Qur'ān begun by Muhammad 'Abduh and continued by Ridā, published in the periodical *al-Manār*. [Ed.]

AMĪR SHAKĪB ARSLĀN
1869–1946

A member of a leading Lebanese Druze family, he studied at the American school in Shwayfat, then at al-Hikmah school in Beirut. In 1889 a trip to Egypt brought him into contact with 'Abduh and his circle. He was elected to the Ottoman parliament in 1913, but after the First World War he spent much of his time in Europe. He was a link between Middle Eastern and North African Islam, and a proponent of Arab causes at the League of Nations. He published a periodical *La Nation Arabe*. His writings emphasize the Islamic nature of Arab Nationalism.

Our Decline and Its Causes

It may be said without exaggeration about the Muslims that their condition, spiritual as well as material, is deplorably unsatisfactory. With very few exceptions, in all countries where Muslims and non-Muslims live side by side, the Muslims lag far behind in almost everything. . . .

It cannot, however, be gainsaid that throughout the Islamic world, there has been a great stir, a powerful convulsion and an awakening in matters spiritual and temporal which is indeed phenomenal. The Europeans are carefully observing these revolutionary manifestations and are studying their directions and tendencies. That some of them are indeed apprehensive and suspicious of this awakening and stir is vouched for by the articles and books they have published. But it can easily be seen that this forward movement of the Muslims has not advanced so far as to enable them to come anywhere near the nations of Europe, America, or Japan.

This, then, is the general condition of the modern Muslims. What are the causes that led to the general degradation of Muslims? Was it not the Muslims who were credited with leadership in the East as well as in the West, for about eight or nine centuries, and acquired name and fame all over the world? Let us, therefore, first of all examine the factors that contributed to their greatness and advancement, before investigating the causes that led to their decline and fall.

The causes of the advancement of the Muslims were, briefly, those originating in Islam, which made its advent in the Arabian Peninsula. Its birth gathered together and consolidated the scattered races and tribes of

From *Our Decline and Its Causes: A Diagnosis of the Symptoms of the Downfall of Muslims*, trans. M.A. Shakoor (Lahore, 1944; reprint ed., 1968), pp. 1–4, 6–8, 10–13, 15, 29, 39–40, 44–45, 48, 68–71, 73–75, 83–86, 96–97, 99, 132, 134.

Arabia, brought them out of barbarism into civilization, replaced their hardheadedness with mutual love and sympathy, eradicated idolatry and restored the worship of the one God. . . . Renovated and inspired by this dynamic force they made themselves masters of half the world in the short span of half a century. But for the internecine strife which lifted its head once again among them, towards the close of 'Uthmān's Caliphate and during the Caliphate of 'Alī,[1] no power on earth could have prevented them from conquering the whole world. . . .

As we scrutinize the matter minutely, it will be found that the greater part of the inspiring force that accounted for their victories and achievements has disappeared, although vestiges of it are visible here and there like the fading lines on a tattooed hand. Were it only for the bearing of the designation of "Muslims" without ever performing the duties of a Muslim, that God had promised the reward of greatness, glory and honor for the Believers, we could have, with justice, asked, "Where is the honor for the Muslims?" as according to the Qur'ānic verse, "Honor belongs to God and to His Apostle and to the Believers."

> And it was due from Us
> To aid those who believed (Qur'ān 30:47)

Do these words of God mean that they are only to proclaim themselves Muslims but never need encounter the tribulations of life in the field of action? If it be so, one cannot but wonder at the decline and degradation of the Muslims. But the Qur'ānic verses do not mean this; nor does God break His promises; and the Qur'ān has remained the same as it then was. Not a syllable has been changed in its text. The change has occurred in the Muslims themselves:

> Verily, never will God change the condition of a people until they
> change it themselves (Qur'ān 13:11)

How can you expect that God will help a nation that shuns the field of action, and that He will shower upon them the magnificent rewards once bestowed on their glorious and heroic ancestors, although they have none of the valour, vitality and stout-heartedness of the latter? . . . How absurd it would be for the present-day Muslims to desire that they should get for the five per cent work they do, the same reward as their illustrious forbears who performed their one hundred per cent work. . . .

Today that zeal of our ancestors, their fervor and their ennobling devotion to their faith, has disappeared from among the Muslims. This spirit is found transfused in the enemies of Islam, though they received no such inspiration from the scriptures of their religions. . . .

---

1. 'Uthmān and 'Alī: the third and fourth Caliphs or leaders of the Muslim community after the death of Muhammad. [Ed.]

Can anyone point out a single Muslim nation of modern times which has sacrificed men and money as unstintingly and unhesitatingly for their country and their nation as these Christian nations of Europe have done for theirs (during World War I). . . .

If, therefore, the Islamic nations, following in the footsteps of their illustrious ancestors, act as they have been commanded, or at least, like the Europeans, sacrifice their persons and properties for defending their honor and heritage and for resisting aggressors, they will certainly be entitled to the same blessings as others have enjoyed by dint of their sufferings and sacrifices, and will find themselves in safety and security by the grace of God.

But without sufferings and sacrifices, without the spirit of self-abnegation and readiness to court death, without spending their wealth and properties, without the burning zeal for pursuing the right path prescribed by God, the Muslims instead hope to defend their dignity, honor and independence, by merely praying to God for help! . . .

But Islam is, on the contrary, not confined to prayer, fasting, meditation or supplication. Is God to accept the prayers of those who, while they are capable of positive work and sacrifices in person and material, choose to live a negative life of idleness and apathy to action? . . .

If the foreign intruders in Muslim countries are enraged at those Muslims who refuse to betray their own brethren in pursuance of foreign behests, it is because most Muslims offer help to these foreigners betraying their own brethren and enthusiastically assist them with advice against their own nation and faithfully cooperate with these foreigners from greed and perfidy. But for the assistance obtained by the foreigners through the treachery of one section of the Muslims and the zeal with which the latter rendered them help against their own countrymen and brethren, these foreigners would have neither usurped their sovereignty and established their rule over them nor acted in such a manner as to contravene and supercede their religious laws and undermine the foundations of those social codes and conventions which are the offsprings of those laws, nor would they have dragged down the Muslims into the valley of the shadow of death and laid them to a disgraceful death. . . .

These Muslims would hardly deserve any recompense from God even if they had not engaged in conspiracies against their own religion, or placed themselves at the beck and call of the covetous foreigners for undermining their own nation, or lent their shoulders to be used as a ladder for the foreigner to climb on to power and wealth. They believe they have performed their religious duty when they have said their prayers, uttered the formulas, chanted a few verses, sung their hymns and spent their time in supplications. This is all Islam means to them. If this were all that was needed to be a Muslim and to be victorious in this world as well as in the next, then the Qur'ān would never have been so full of counsels, commands, and inspiring words calling upon the Muslims to serve Islam with their minds, bodies, and material wealth, to make the greatest sacrifices, to be steadfast in honesty and patience, to work for the benefit of their fellow believers, to maintain justice and equity and to acquire all noble qualities. . . .

There are people who ask why degradation has overtaken the Muslims and why they are not able to keep pace with others. Anyone who realizes how they differ from others in the degree of awakening, devotion, and sense of duty and self-respect, will easily find the answer to these questions. . . .

Another important cause of the decline of Muslims is the blind obstinacy with which they insist upon the maintenance of hackneyed conventions. Serious are the dangers to a nation from men who condemn everything old as absurd and worthless, without giving thought to their intrinsic value, simply because they are "old"; no less serious are the dangers that arise from the conservative school, which insists that no change can be permissible in anything. . . . Thus these sophisticated "ultra-moderns" and the conservative conventionalists are ruining Islam between themselves. . . .

The best examples in this matter are the Europeans. Study them as closely as we may; we shall not find even a single nation among them that desires to lose its identity in another. The English would remain but English. The French want to remain French, etc. . . . To the extent the European civilization is sufficient for the Europeans, to the same extent is Japanese civilization sufficient for the Japanese. In other words, the civilizations of both are confined within the bounds of their nationalities, languages, customs, religions, their conceptions of freedom, ethical peculiarities, modes of thought, etc. . . .

Every nation adheres rigorously to its religion and clings steadfastly to its religious heritage, traditions, and national characteristics and peculiarities. They never speak of these things with contempt or ridicule. The Muslims alone seem not to understand their value. If anyone tells them that they should hold fast to the Qur'ān, their faith, their religious traditions, and their natural characteristics, or that they should not abandon the Arabic language, or that they should preserve their oriental mode of life and conduct and etiquette, they would yell like lunatics: "Down with your traditionalism . . . in these civilized days how can you progress like others with your outworn traditions and customs of the Middle Ages?" . . .

As for the conservative Muslims . . . they have made the Muslims helpless victims of poverty and indigence by reducing Islam to a religion of mere other-worldly preoccupations. . . . It is these conservatives who declared war on natural science, mathematics, and all creative arts, condemned them as the practices of infidels and thereby deprived Muslims of the fruits of science. . . .

The quintessence of Islamic teaching is that man should make proper use of his intellect which God has given him as a guiding light to help him think for himself, and that having done everything in his power, he should resign himself to the Will of God, for the happy fructification of his labor. . . .

Islam is by its very nature and genius a revolt against all degenerate tradition. It dug the grave for the abominable and debased traditions and usages of old and cut off all relationship with what was false and untrue. How can it then be called a religion of static inaction and conservatism. . . .

In order that Muslims may awake, arise and ascend the highest pinnacle of advancement and progress, like any other modern nation, it is their sacred duty to embark on a *jihād*[2] by sacrificing their life and wealth in consonance with the oft repeated commandments of the Qur'ān. It is this kind of *jihād* that is known in modern parlance as "sacrifice." No nation has achieved victory but by sacrifice. . . .

If Muslims will resolve and strive, taking their inspiration from the Qur'ān, they can attain the rank of the Europeans, the Americans and the Japanese in learning and science and making progress. Yet withal they can preserve their own faith, just as others have done. Nay more, if we derive our inspiration from the Qur'ān, we would be better qualified for progress than others.

---

2. *jihād*: "to strive, struggle" to realize God's Will. The term applies to moral (spiritual perfection), intellectual (the reasoning or interpretation of *ijtihād*), and military (holy war) efforts or struggles. [Ed.]

SĀTIʿ AL-HUSRĪ
1880–1964

Born in North Yemen of Syrian parents, he was educated as
an official in the Ottoman Empire. After the Arab Revolt, he
was Minister of Education for Faysal's brief reign in Syria. The
leading proponent of Arab unity and Arabism between the two
world wars, he became Director General of Cultural Affairs for
the Arab League and then Dean of the Institute of Higher Arab
Studies in Cairo.

Muslim Unity and Arab Unity

I have read and heard many opinions and observations concerning Muslim
unity and Arab unity, and which is to be preferred. I have been receiving
for some time now various questions concerning this matter: Why, it is
asked, are you interested in Arab unity, and why do you neglect Muslim
unity? Do you not see that the goal of Muslim unity is higher than the goal
of Arab unity, and that the power generated by Muslim union would be
greater than that generated by Arab union? Do you not agree that religious
feeling in the East is much stronger than national feeling? Why, then, do
you want us to neglect the exploitation of this powerful feeling and to spend
our energies in order to strengthen a weak feeling? Do you believe that the
variety of languages will prevent the union of the Muslims? Do you not
notice that the principles of communism, socialism, Freemasonry, and other
systems unite people of different languages, races, countries, and climates;
that none of these differences have prevented them from coming to understanding, from drawing nearer to another, and from agreeing on one plan
and one creed? Do you not know that every Muslim in Syria, Egypt, or Iraq
believes that the Indian Muslim, the Japanese Muslim, or the European
Muslim is as much his brother as the Muslim with whom he lives side by
side? Whence, then, the impossibility of realizing Muslim union? Some say
that Muslim unity is more powerful than any other and that its realization
is easier than the realization of any other. What do you say to this? Some
pretend, mistakenly, that the idea of Arab union is a plot the aim of which
is to prevent the spread of the idea of Muslim union, in order to isolate
some of the countries of the Muslim world and facilitate their continued
subjugation. What is your opinion of this allegation? . . .

From Sylvia G. Haim, ed., *Arab Nationalism* (Berkeley: University of California Press, 1962),
pp. 147–53.

I think that the essential point which has to be studied and solved when deciding which to prefer, Muslim unity or Arab unity, may be summarized as follows: Is Muslim unity a reasonable hope capable of realization? Or is it a utopian dream incapable of realization? And assuming the first alternative, is its realization easier or more difficult than the realization of Arab unity? Does one of these two schemes exclude the other? And is there a way of realizing Muslim unity without realizing Arab unity? When we think about such questions and analyze them, we have, in the first place, to define clearly what we mean by Muslim unity and by Arab unity and to delimit without any ambiguity the use of the two expressions.

It goes without saying that Arab unity requires the creation of a political union of the different Arab countries the inhabitants of which speak Arabic. As for Muslim unity, that naturally requires the creation of a political union of the different Muslim countries, the inhabitants of which profess the Muslim religion, regardless of the variety of their languages and races. It is also well known that the Muslim world includes the Arab countries, Turkey, Iran, Afghanistan, Turkestan, parts of India, the East Indies, the Caucasus, North Africa, as well as parts of Central Africa, without considering a few scattered units in Europe and Asia, as in Albania, Yugoslavia, Poland, China, and Japan. Further, there is no need to show that the Arab countries occupy the central portion of this far-flung world.

Whoever will examine these evident facts and picture the map of the Muslim world, noticing the position of the Arab world within it, will have to concede that Arab unity is much easier to bring about than Muslim unity, and that this latter is not capable of realization, assuming that it can be realized, except through Arab unity. It is not possible for any sane person to imagine union among Cairo, Baghdad, Tehran, Kabul, Haiderabad, and Bukhara, or Kashgar, Persia, and Timbuctoo, without there being a union among Cairo, Baghdad, Damascus, Mecca, and Tunis. It is not possible for any sane person to conceive the possibility of union among Turks, Arabs, Persians, Malayans, and Negroes, while denying unity to the Arabs themselves. If, contrary to fact, the Arab world were more extensive and wider than the Muslim world, it would have been possible to imagine a Muslim union without Arab union, and it would have been permissible to say that Muslim union is easier to realize than Arab union. But as the position is the exact opposite, there is no logical scope whatever for such statements and speculations. We must not forget this truth when we think and speak concerning Muslim unity and Arab unity. The idea of Muslim unity is, it is true, wider and more inclusive than the concept of Arab unity, but it is not possible to advocate Muslim unity without advocating Arab unity. We have, therefore, the right to assert that whoever opposes Arab unity also opposes Muslim unity. As for him who opposes Arab unity, in the name of Muslim unity or for the sake of Muslim unity, he contradicts the simplest necessities of reason and logic.

Having established this truth, to disagree with which is not logically possible, we ought to notice another truth which is no less important. We must not forget that the expression "unity," in this context, means political unity; and we must constantly remember that the concept of Islamic unity greatly differs from that of Muslim brotherhood. Unity is one thing and affection another, political unity is one thing and agreement on a certain principle another. To advocate Muslim unity, therefore, is different from advocating the improvement of conditions in Islam and different also from advocating an increase in understanding, in affection, and in cooperation among Muslims. We can therefore say that he who talks about the principle of Muslim brotherhood, and discusses the benefits of understanding among the Muslims, does not prove that Muslim unity is possible. Contrariwise, he who denies the possibility of realizing Muslim unity does not deny the principle of Muslim brotherhood or oppose the efforts toward the awakening of the Muslims and understanding among them. What may be said concerning the ideal of brotherhood is not sufficient proof of the possibility of realizing Muslim unity. Further, it is not intelligent or logical to prove the possibility of realizing Muslim unity by quoting the example of Freemasonry or socialism or communism, because the Freemasons do not constitute a political unity and the socialist parties in the different European countries have not combined to form a new state. Even communism itself has not formed a new state, but has taken the place of the Czarist Russian state. We have, therefore, to distinguish quite clearly between the question of Muslim brotherhood and that of Muslim unity, and we must consider directly whether or not it is possible to realize Muslim unity in the political sense.

If we cast a general glance at history and review the influence of religions over the formation of political units, we find that the world religions have not been able to unify peoples speaking different languages, except in the Middle Ages, and that only in limited areas and for a short time. The political unity which the Christian Church sought to bring about did not at any time merge the Orthodox world with the Catholic. Neither did the political unity which the papacy tried to bring about in the Catholic world last for any length of time. So it was also in the Muslim world; the political unity which existed at the beginning of its life was not able to withstand the changes of circumstance for any length of time. Even the 'Abbāsid caliphate, at the height of its power and glory, could not unite all the Muslims under its political banner. Similarly, the lands ruled by this caliphate did not effectively preserve their political unity for very long. Nor was it long after the founding of the caliphate that its control over some of the provinces became symbolic rather than real; it could not prevent the secession of these provinces and their transformation into independent political units. It deserves to be mentioned in this connection that the spread of the Muslim religion in some areas took place after the Muslim caliphate lost effective unity and real power, so much so that in some countries Islam spread in a manner independent of the political authority, at the hands of missionary tradesmen, holy men, and dervishes. In short, the Muslim world, within its present extensive limits, never at any time formed a political unity. If, then, political unity could not be realized in past centuries, when social life was simple and political relations were primitive, when religious customs controlled every aspect of behavior and thought, it will not be possible to realize it in this century, when social life has become complicated, political problems have become intractable, and science and technology have liberated themselves from the control of tradition and religious beliefs.

I know that what I have stated here will displease many doctors of Islam; I know that the indications of history which I have set out above will have no influence over the beliefs of a great many of the men of religion, because they have been accustomed to discuss these matters without paying heed to historical facts or to the geographical picture; nor are they used to distinguishing between the meaning of religious brotherhood and the meaning of political ties. They have been accustomed to confuse the principles of Islamic brotherhood, in its moral sense, and the idea of Islamic unity, in its political sense. I think it useless to try to persuade these people of the falsity of their beliefs, but I think it necessary to ask them to remember what reason and logic require in this respect. Let them maintain their belief in the possibility of realizing Islamic unity, but let them at the same time agree to the necessity of furthering Arab unity, at least as one stage toward the realization of the Islamic unity in which they believe. In any event, let them not oppose the efforts which are being made to bring about Arab unity, on the pretext of serving the Islamic unity which they desire. I repeat here what I have written above: whoever opposes Arab unity, on the pretext of Muslim unity, contradicts the simplest requirements of reason and logic, and I unhesitatingly say that to contradict logic to this extent can be the result only of deceit or of deception. The deceit is that of some separatists who dislike the awakening of the Arab nation and try to arouse religious feeling against the idea of Arab unity, and the deception is that of the simple-minded, who incline to believe whatever is said to them in the name of religion, without realizing what hidden purposes might lurk behind the speeches. I therefore regard it as my duty to draw the attention of all the Muslim Arabs to this important matter and I ask them not to be deceived by the myths of the separatists on this chapter.

Perhaps the strangest and most misleading views that have been expressed regarding Arab unity and Islamic unity are the views of those who say that the idea of Arab unity was created to combat Islamic unity in order to isolate some Islamic countries, the better to exercise continuous power over them. I cannot imagine a view further removed from the realities of history and politics or more contradictory to the laws of reason and logic. The details I have mentioned above concerning the relation of Muslim unity to Arab unity are sufficient, basically, to refute such allegations. Yet I think it advisable to add to these details some observations for further proof and clarity. It cannot be denied that the British, more than any other state, have humored and indulged the Arab movement. This is only because they are more practiced in politics and quicker to understand the psychology of nations and the realities of social life. Before anybody else they realized the hidden powers lying in the Arab idea, and thought it wise, therefore, to humor it somewhat, instead of directly opposing it. This was in order to preserve themselves against the harm they might sustain through it and to make it more advantageous to their interests.

We must understand that British policy is a practical policy, changing with circumstances and always making use of opportunities. We must not forget that it was Great Britain who, many times, saved the Ottoman state, then the depository of the Islamic caliphate, from Russian domination. She it was who halted Egyptian armies in the heart of Anatolia to save the seat of the Muslim caliphate from these victorious troops, and she it was who opposed the union of Egypt with Syria at the time of Muhammad 'Alī. Whoever, then, charges that the idea of Arab unity is a foreign plot utters a greater falsehood than any that has ever been uttered, and he is the victim of the greatest of deceptions. We must know full well that the idea of Arab unity is a natural idea. It has not been artificially started. It is a natural consequence of the existence of the Arab nation itself. It is a social force drawing its vitality from the life of the Arabic language, from the history of the Arab nation, and from the connectedness of the Arab countries. No one can logically pretend that it is the British who created the idea of Arab unity, unless he can prove that it is the British who have created the Arabic language, originating the history of the Arab nation and putting together the geography of the Arab countries. The idea of Arab unity is a natural concept springing from the depths of social nature and not from the artificial views which can be invented by individuals or by states. It remained latent, like many natural and social forces, for many centuries, as a result of many historical factors which cannot be analyzed here. But everything indicates that this period is now at an end, that the movement has come into the open and will manifest itself with ever-increasing power. It will, without any doubt, spread all over the Arab countries, to whom it will bring back their ancient glory and primeval youth; it will indeed bring back what is most fertile, most powerful, and highest in these countries. This ought to be the faith of the enlightened among the speakers of the *dad* [Arabic].

TĀHĀ HUSAYN
1889–1973

A childhood accident rendered him totally blind, but he persisted in studies, going on to al-Azhar and attending lectures at the new Egyptian University in Cairo. He became a member of the circle that formed around Lutfī al-Sayyid and the newspaper *al-Jarīdah*. In 1915 he went to France for studies for four years and returned to front stage in the literary and academic life in Egypt. He was a university administrator and later Minister of Education. His ideas were precocious for Egypt of the early twentieth century: in 1926 his book rejecting pre-Islamic poetry as forgery caused a scandal and was taken off the book stands, and in 1938 his *Future of Culture in Egypt* was equally provocative.

The Future of Culture in Egypt

I do not like illusions. I am persuaded that it is only God who can create something from nothing. I therefore believe that the new Egypt will not come into being except from the ancient, eternal Egypt. I believe further that the new Egypt will have to be built on the great old one, and that the future of culture in Egypt will be an extension, a superior version, of the humble, exhausted, and feeble present. For this reason we should think of the future of culture in Egypt in the light of its remote past and near present. We do not wish, nor are we able, to break the link between ourselves and our forefathers. To the degree that we establish our future life upon our past and present we shall avoid most of the dangers caused by excesses and miscalculations deriving from illusions and dreams.

At the outset we must answer this fundamental question: is Egypt of the East or of the West? Naturally, I mean East or West in the cultural, not the geographical sense. It seems to me that there are two distinctly different and bitterly antagonistic cultures on the earth. Both have existed since time immemorial, the one in Europe, the other in the Far East.

We may paraphrase the question as follows: Is the Egyptian mind Eastern or Western in its imagination, perception, comprehension and judgment? . . .

The meaning of all this is very clear: the Egyptian mind had no serious contact with the Far Eastern mind; nor did it live harmoniously with the Persian mind. The Egyptian mind has had regular, peaceful, and mutually beneficial relations only with the Near East and Greece. In short, it has been

From *The Future of Culture in Egypt*, trans. S. Glazer (Washington, D.C.: American Council of Learned Societies, 1954), sections 2–5, 7, 10.

influenced from earliest times by the Mediterranean Sea and the various peoples living around it. . . . I clearly, indeed intuitively, understand our consciousness of the positive relationships existing between us and the Near East not only because of identity of language and religion, but also because of geographical propinquity as well as similarity of origin and historical evolution. When we go beyond the Near East, however, these factors no longer obtain, except for religion and temporary considerations of a political or economic nature.

History shows that religious and linguistic unity do not necessarily go hand in hand with political unity, nor are they the props on which states rely. The Muslims realized this a long time ago. They established their states on the basis of practical interests, abandoning religion, language, and race as exclusively determining factors before the end of the second century A.H. (eighth century of the Christian Era). . . .

Egypt was one of the earliest among the Islamic states to recover her ancient, unforgotten personality. History tells us that she violently opposed the Persians and Macedonians, the latter being eventually absorbed into the local population. Egypt yielded to the Western and Eastern Roman rulers only under duress and had to be kept under continuous martial law. History further relates that she acquiesced most reluctantly even to Arab domination. The spirit of resistance and rebelliousness that followed the conquest did not subside until she regained her independent personality under Ibn Tūlūn and the dynasties that followed him.

From earliest times Muslims have been well aware of the now universally acknowledged principle that a political system and a religion are different things, that a constitution and a state rest, above everything else, on practical foundations. . . . Islam arose and spread over the world. Egypt was receptive and hastened at top speed to adopt it as her religion and to make the Arabic of Islam her language. Did that obliterate her original mentality? Did that make her an Eastern nation in the present meaning of the term? Not at all! Europe did not become Eastern nor did the nature of the European mind change because Christianity, which originated in the East, flooded Europe and absorbed the other religions. If modern European philosophers and thinkers deem Christianity to be an element of the European mind, they must explain what distinguishes Christianity from Islam; for both were born in the geographical East, both issued from one noble source and were inspired by the one God in whom Easterners and Westerners alike believe. . . .

The essence and source of Islam are the essence and source of Christianity. The connection of Islam with Greek philosophy is identical to that of Christianity. Whence, then, comes the difference in the effect of these two faiths on the creation of the mind that mankind inherited from the people of the Near East and Greece? . . .

No, there are no intellectual or cultural differences to be found among the peoples who grew up around the Mediterranean and were influenced by it. Purely political and economic circumstances made the inhabitants of one shore prevail against those of the other. The same factors led them to treat each other now with friendliness, now with enmity.

The development of modern communications has served to link Egypt closely to Europe, as indeed they linked all parts of the world. Although the renaissance of Egypt, which began early in the nineteenth century, is still unclear in some respects, its modern orientation is unmistakable. As far as the materialistic side of life, particularly among the upper classes, is concerned, it is purely European. The other classes more or less resemble their European counterparts, depending only on the capabilities and wealth of the various individuals and groups. We adopted and still retain the European attitude toward the external manifestations and embellishments of existence. Whether we did so consciously and deliberately or not, I do not know, but the fact remains that there is no power on earth capable of preventing us from enjoying life the way they do.

Like the Europeans, we have built railroads, telegraph lines, and telephones. We learned from Europe to sit at the table and eat with a knife and fork. We wear the same kind of clothes. All this we did without discrimination, without examination to know what is actually bad and what is unsuitable for us. So far has the European ideal become our ideal that we now measure the material progress of all individuals and groups by the amount of borrowing from Europe. Moreover, even the intangible aspects of life, surface differences notwithstanding, show the same influence. We did not hesitate, for example, to adopt the European system of government; and if we criticize ourselves for something, this is simply that we have been slow in following European administrative and political practices. Our political life in recent times has been in a state of confusion between absolute government and limited government, for which we have no precedent in our Middle Ages. I mean that our modern absolute government was affected by the European absolutism prevalent before the rise of democracy; in similar fashion our form of limited government was shaped by the systems of limited government also existing in Europe.

Those who sought to impose arbitrary rule on modern Egypt patterned themselves upon Louis XIV rather than 'Abd al-Hamīd. Proponents of a form of limited government based on justice but without the people's participation accepted curbs to their power that were European not Eastern. They set up national courts and enacted civil laws in conformity with European rather than Islamic codes. Their administrative, fiscal, and economic statutes were almost wholly Western. They sought no guidance from the procedures of the medieval Muslim kings and caliphs. The cabinet, governmental ministries, and the several administrative agencies connected with them are European in origin, spirit, and form. Until the modern era the Muslims had never heard of them.

Certain old Islamic institutions, to be sure, have survived because of their more or less close association with religion, but even these have changed greatly, at least in form, under the strong influence of their European counterparts. Take the *Sharī'a* courts, for example; there is no doubt that if a Muslim judge were to be resurrected today he would find many of the legal procedures unfamiliar. Although we have kept the institution of the *waqf* (endowed foundation), we set up without delay a special ministry to administer it in a way that I believe the ancients would neither recognize nor approve if they were returned to life. Most of us, however, feel that this ministry is still too backward for the times. Some would like to abolish or change the institution of *waqf* itself in conformity with modern economic requirements.

We have also retained al-Azhar University, which has been in a serious condition since before the time of Ismā'īl. The crisis, in my opinion, will not end soon, but will continue until the struggle between the old and the new reaches a state of balance. The available evidence indicates, however, that the institution is proceeding very rapidly in the direction of the new. Indeed, if God were to resurrect the Azhar scholars who lived at the beginning of the modern era, they would beg Him in all sincerity to return them to their graves so that they would not have to look upon the great innovations that have already been introduced into the university.

The dominant and undeniable fact of our times is that day by day we are drawing closer to Europe and becoming an integral part of her, literally and figuratively. This process would be much more difficult than it is if the Egyptian mind were basically different from the European.

This is not all. Since the world war we have taken such decisive steps forward that any attempt to retrace them or abrogate the rights won would, I am certain, be violently resisted by many Egyptians. Which one of us is willing to see Egypt retreat from the progress she had made toward democracy, or who would go back to a system that did not center about a constitutional representative government? This form of government, although adopted from Europe, became almost immediately a vital and inseparable part of our being. Anyone urging Egyptians to return to the way of life characteristic of Pharaonic, Greco-Roman, or early Islamic times would be ridiculed by the people, including the arch-conservatives and those who loathe any tampering whatsoever with our ancient heritage. We must also realize, too, that our signatures on the treaties by which we gained our independence and rid ourselves of the capitulations have clearly obliged us to follow the Europeans in government, administration, and legislation.

Our educational system is also based on exclusively European methods, which are applied through our primary, secondary, and higher schools. If for the sake of argument we suppose that the mentality of our fathers and grandfathers may have been Eastern and essentially antithetic to the Europeans, we must see that our children are quite different. We have been putting into their heads modes of thought and ideas that are almost completely European. I cannot conceive of anyone seriously advocating abandonment of the European system in our schools and revival of

techniques used by our ancestors. As a matter of fact, the Europeans borrowed the methods that prevailed in the Islamic world during the Middle
Ages. They did then just what we are doing now. It is essentially a matter
of time. They began their new life in the fifteenth century, while we were
delayed by the Ottoman Turks until the nineteenth century. If God had
preserved us from the Ottoman conquest, we should have remained in
unbroken touch with Europe and shared in her renaissance. This would
certainly have fashioned a different kind of civilization from the one in
which we are now living.

However, God has bestowed on us a boon to compensate for our
misfortune and calamities. The world has struggled for hundreds of years
to attain the present stage of progress. It is within our power to reach it in
a short time. Woe to us if we do not seize the opportunity! . . . Obviously
then I am pleading for a selective approach to European culture, not wholesale and indiscriminate borrowing. . . .

HASAN AL-BANNĀ
1906–1949

After studies at a teachers' training college, he went to Dār al-ʿUlūm in Cairo. He was fired with religious zeal as a student, and once he began his career as a teacher, he was not long in founding the Muslim Brotherhood (1928), which soon became one of the best organized and largest of the political groups in Egypt. He preached a return to the sources of Islam and a rejection of currents from abroad. The military arm of the Muslim Brothers was implicated in some political assassinations; this led to Hasan al-Bannā's assassination in 1949. The Muslim Brothers are still a strong influence throughout the Arab world.

The New Renaissance

When we observe the evolution in the political, social, and moral spheres of the lives of nations and peoples, we note that the Islamic world—and, naturally, in the forefront, the Arab world—gives to its rebirth an Islamic flavor. This trend is ever-increasing. Until recently, writers, intellectuals, scholars, and governments glorified the principles of European civilization, gave themselves a Western tint, and adopted a European style and manner; today, on the contrary, the wind has changed, and reserve and distrust have taken their place. Voices are raised proclaiming the necessity for a return to the principles, teachings, and ways of Islam, and, taking into account the situation, for initiating the reconciliation of modern life with these principles, as a prelude to a final "Islamization."

CAUSES

This development worries a good number of governments and Arab powers, which, having lived during the past generations in a state of mind that had retained from Islam only lessons of fanaticism and inertia, regarded the Muslims only as weak drudges or as nations easily exploitable by colonialism. In trying to understand the new movement [the Brotherhood], these governments have produced all sorts of possible interpretations: "It is the result," said some, "of the growth of extremist organizations and fanatical groups." Others explained that it was a reaction to present-day political and economic pressures, of which the Islamic nations had become

From Kemal H. Karpat, ed., *Political and Social Thought in the Contemporary Middle East* (New York: Praeger, 1968), pp. 118–22.

aware. Finally, others said, "It is only a means whereby those seeking govern-ment or other honors may achieve renown and position."

Now all these reasons are, in our opinion, as far as possible from the truth; for this new movement can only be the result of the following three factors, which we will now examine.

THE FAILURE OF THE WEST

The first of the three is the failure of the social principles on which the civilization of the Western nations has been built. The Western way of life—bounded in effect on practical and technical knowledge, discovery, invention, and the flooding of world markets with mechanical products—has remained incapable of offering to men's minds a flicker of light, a ray of hope, a grain of faith, or of providing anxious persons the smallest path toward rest and tranquillity. Man is not simply an instrument among others. Naturally, he has become tired of purely materialistic conditions and desires some spiritual comfort. But the materialistic life of the West could only offer him as reassurance a new materialism of sin, passion, drink, women, noisy gatherings, and showy attractions which he had come to enjoy. Man's hunger grows from day to day: he wants to free his spirit, to destroy this materialistic prison and find space to breathe the air of faith and consolation.

PERFECTION OF ISLAM

The second factor—the decisive factor in the circumstances—is the discovery by Islamic thinkers of the noble, honorable, moral, and perfect content of the principles and rules of this religion, which is infinitely more ac-complished, more pure, more glorious, more complete, and more beautiful than all that has been discovered up till now by social theorists and reformers. For a long time, Muslims neglected all this, but once God had enlightened their thinkers and they had compared the social rules of their religion with what they had been told by the greatest sociologists and the cleverest leading theorists, they noted the wide gap and the great distance between a heritage of immense value on one side and the conditions experienced on the other. Then, Muslims could not but do justice to the spirit and the history of their people, proclaiming the value of this heritage and inviting all peoples—nonpracticing Muslims or non-Muslims—to follow the sacred path that God had traced for them and to hold to a straight course.

TYPE OF DEVELOPMENT

The third factor is the development of social conditions between the two murderous world wars (which involved all the world powers and monop-olized the minds of regimes, nations, and individuals) which resulted in a set of principles of reform and social organization that certain powers, in deciding to put them into practice, have taken as an instructional basis. These principles have become the prey of change and transformation, in fact subject to disappearance and ruin. Muslim thinkers looked on, observed, and returned to what they already possessed in their own right— the great Book of God, the brilliant manifest example of their Prophet and their glorious history. There was nothing of value they could accredit to any existing regime that could not be already found inspiring their thought and conduct and already inscribed in Islamic social organization. There was no blemish against which the social organization of a watchful Islam could not guard [its people] by showing them its fearful consequences.

The world has long been ruled by democratic systems, and man has everywhere glorified and honored the conquests of democracy: freedom of the individual, freedom of nations, justice and freedom of thought, justice for the human soul with freedom of action and will, justice for the peoples who became the source of power. Victory at the end of World War I re-inforced these thoughts, but men were not slow to realize that their collective liberty had not come intact out of the chaos, that their individual liberty was not safe from anarchy, and that the government of the people had not in many cases freed society from camouflaged dictatorship that destroyed responsibility without limiting jurisdiction. Quite the contrary, vice and violence led to the breaking loose of nations and peoples, to the overthrow of collective organization and family structure, and to the setting up of dictatorial regimes.

Thus, German Nazism and Italian Fascism rose to the fore; Mussolini and Hitler led their two peoples to unity, order, recovery, power, and glory. In record time, they ensured internal order at home and, through force, made themselves feared abroad. Their regimes gave real hope, and also gave rise to thoughts of steadfastness and perseverance and the reuniting of different, divided men around the words "chief" and "order." In their resolutions and speeches, the Führer and the Duce began to frighten the world and to upset their epoch.

What happened then? It became evident that in a powerful and well-knit regime, where the wishes of the individual were based on those of their chiefs, the mistakes of the chiefs became those of the regime, which shared also in their acts of violence, their decline, and their fall; then, everything was at an end, all had been cut down as in a single day, but not until the world had lost in a second war thousands of men, the flower of her youth, and masses of wealth and material.

The star of socialism and Communism, symbol of success and victory, shone with an increasing brilliance; Soviet Russia was at the head of the collectivist camp. She launched her message and, in the eyes of the world, demonstrated a system which had been modified several times in thirty years. The democratic powers—or, to use a more precise expression, the colonialist powers, the old ones worn out, the new ones full of greed—took up a position to stem the current. The struggle intensified, in some places openly, in others under cover, and nations and peoples, perplexed, hesitated at the crossroads, not knowing which way was best; among them were the nations of Islam and the peoples of the Qur'ān; the future, whatever the circumstances, is in the hands of God, the decision with history, and immortality with the most worthy.

This social evolution and violent, hard struggle stirred the minds of Muslim thinkers; the parallels and the prescribed comparisons led to a healthy conclusion: to free themselves from the existing state of affairs, to allow the necessary return of the nations and peoples to Islam.

THE THREE REGIMES AND PRAYER

In a whimsical moment, I happened to say to my audience at a meeting—which, thanks to God, was a complete success—that this Islamic prayer which we perform five times a day is nothing but a daily training in practical social organization uniting the features of the Communist regime with those of the dictatorial and democratic regimes. Astonished, my questioners demanded an explanation. "The greatest value of the Communist regime," I said, "is the reinforcement of the notion of equality, the condemnation of class distinction, and the struggle against the claim to property, source of these differences." Now this lesson is present in the mind of the Muslim; he is perfectly conscious of it and his spririt is filled with it the moment he enters the mosque; yes, the moment he enters, he realizes that the mosque belongs to God and not to any one of his creatures; he knows himself to be the equal of all those who are there, whoever they may be; here there are no great, no small, no high, no low, no more groups or classes. And when the muezzin calls, "Now is the hour of prayer," they form an equal mass, a compact block, behind the *imām*.[1] None bows unless the *imām* bows, none prostrates himself unless the *imām* prostrates himself; none moves or remains motionless unless following the *imām's* example. That is the principal merit of the dictatorial regime: unity and order in the will under the appearance of equality. The *imām* himself is in any case limited by the teachings and rules of the prayer, and if he stumbles or makes a mistake in his reading or in his actions, all those behind him—young boys, old men, or women at prayer—have the imperative duty to tell him of his error in order to put him back on the right road during the prayer, and the *imām* himself is bound absolutely to accept this good advice and, forsaking his error, return to reason and truth. That is what is most appealing in democracy.

How, therefore, can these regimes be superior to Islam, which astonishingly unites all their merits and avoids all their sins? "If this message came from some other than God, many contradictions would be found in it" (Qur'ān).

---

1. The *imām* referred to here is a leader of prayer, and should not be confused with the Shī'īte *Imām*, who is the supreme head of the community.

NO INCENTIVE FOR TROUBLE

As I have said, [the people of] the West—and with them those who are blind—are worried by this development, which they consider serious, since they see themselves forced to combat it by every means, being less accustomed to finding themselves facing such a situation than to seeing the success of their reactionary principles on the less developed nations, in contempt of all the rules of civilization followed by cultivated and orderly peoples; judgment steeped in error and the flagrant suppression of rights can be seen as clearly as daylight. Here, our intention is to demonstrate to the West two points:

1. Demonstration of the excellence of Islamic principles of collective organization, and their superiority over everything known to man until now, these principles being:

   a. Brotherly love: condemnation of hatred and fanaticism.
   b. Peace: Error is committed by the misguided thinking on the legitimacy of the Holy War.
   c. Liberty: Error is committed by those who suspect Islam of tolerating slavery and interfering with liberty.
   d. Social justice: obvious character of the Islamic theory of power and class structure.
   e. Happiness: manifest error in the appreciation of the reality of abstinence.
   f. Family: matters concerning the rights of women, number of wives, and repudiation.
   g. Work and profit: matters concerning the different kinds of profit, and error in the appreciation of the fact of relying on God.
   h. Knowledge: Error is committed by those who accuse Islam of encouraging ignorance and apathy.
   i. Organization and determination of duties: Error is committed by those who see in the nature of Islam a source of imperfection and indolence.
   j. Piety: the reality of faith, and the merit and reward attached to it.

2. Demonstration of the following facts:

   a. For the good of man in general, Muslims must move toward a return to their religion.
   b. Islam will find in this return her principal strength on earth.
   c. Far from receiving impetus from a blind fanaticism, this movement will be inspired by a strong regard for the values of Islam which correspond fully to what modern thought has discovered as most noble, sound, and tested in society. It is God who says what is true and who shows the way.

Lawyer, historian, and man of politics, he was Dean of the
Law School at Baghdad in 1955, and in 1965 he became Prime
Minister. After the Ba'th coup in 1968, he fell out of favor, spent
a few years in prison, and died in exile. His speeches and writings emphasize the accord between Arabism and Islam.

Islam and Arab Nationalism

Before I begin, I had better explain the significance of the title of this
talk and limit its scope somewhat. . . . All I aim at this evening is to define
the relation of Arab nationalism, insofar as it is a "belief and a movement,"
to the Islamic *Sharī'a*,[1] insofar as it is "a religion, a civilization, and a
philosophy of life". . . . The question is: Is it possible for one of us to be a
loyal nationalist and a sincere Muslim, at one and the same time? Is there
a fundamental contradiction between Arab nationalism, in its precise
scientific sense, and true Muslim feeling? And does the acceptance of the
one entail the rejection of the other?

I think the apparent contradiction between Islam and Arab nationalism
which is still present in the minds of many people is, in the first place, due
to misunderstanding, misrepresentation, and misinterpretation, involving
both Islam and Arab nationalism.

The misunderstanding of Islam is due to the wrong significance
attributed to the word "religion." We are influenced here—as a result of the
intellectual imperialism under which a group of us still labor—by the Western
concepts which restrict religion within narrow limits not extending beyond
worship, ritual, and the spiritual beliefs, which govern a man in his behavior,
in relation to his God and to his brother man, in his capacity of an individual
independent of society. Islam does not admit this narrow view of religion,
but opposes it and the purpose it serves to the utmost. Many people still
believe that Islam is similar to Christianity or Buddhism, and consists in
devotional beliefs and exercises, ethical rules and no more. But, in fact, Islam,
in its precise sense, is a social order, a philosophy of life, a system of economic principles, a rule of government, in addition to its being a religious
creed in the narrow Western sense. Some of the Western thinkers have come

1. *Sharī'a*: Islamic law. [Ed.]

From Sylvia G. Haim, ed., *Arab Nationalism* (Berkeley: University of California Press, 1962),
pp. 172–76, 178–88.

to realize the wide difference between the comprehensive nature of Islam and the limited nature of Christianity; Christianity pays more attention to the individual, as such, and to his spiritual purity, than to the individual as part of a whole and to his relation to this whole. This was inevitable because of the difference in the nature of the two religions, their circumstances, and the periods in which they were revealed. Christ was a member of the Israelite society which, under the authority of the Roman state, was devoid of any active share in the existing political organization. But the Prophet—Peace be on Him—was a leader and a statesman, as much as he was a social reformer and a religious teacher. . . . Because Islam is a political religion . . . it does not therefore necessarily contradict Arab nationalism, unless their political aims differ. But this is unthinkable, as we shall see later.

Just as Islam has been misunderstood, so has Arab nationalism. The reason for this may be that some think that nationalism can be built only upon racial appeal or racial chauvinism, and that it would therefore be contrary to the universal nature of Islam. The exaggeration of some nationalists has undoubtedly been one of the important reasons for this misunderstanding; and no doubt what some Umayyad governors, princes, and walis have done in their enthusiastic tribal chauvinism and their racial propaganda was contrary to the nature of Islam. But the Arab nationalism in which we believe, and for which we call, is based, as our national pact stipulates, not on racial appeal but on linguistic, historical, cultural, and spiritual ties, and on fundamental vital interests. In this respect, too, there is no contradiction between Arab nationalism and Islam. Many young people have greatly misunderstood Arab nationalism. They know something of the history of the West, of its national revivals, and have found there obvious signs of contradiction between Christianity and these national movements; this is, of course, natural in Western societies. The Church, which used to claim great spiritual power over all the Christians, looked askance on all political movements which aimed at shaking off ecclesiastical authority. In other words, European society gave allegiance to two fundamental authorities, the spiritual authority of the Pope and the temporal authority of the Emperor.

This dualism, although it has come to us in some stages of our slow social evolution, is not known in true Islam, where it is not admitted. On the contrary, the unity of creed has led to the unity of life, and the unity of life has made the caliph of the Muslims the leader in prayer, the leader of the army, and the political head at the same time. The opposition of German or Italian nationalism to Christianity, for instance, does not therefore necessarily mean that Arab nationalism should be opposed to Islam. It befits us to remember here the great difference between the relation of Christianity to the West, and the relation of Islam to the Arabs. Christianity is a religion introduced to the West. It arose out of the spirituality of the East, and is in complete opposition to the nature of the Teutonic tribes in Germany and the Celtic in France; that is why the German or the French nationalist finds great difficulty in reconciling it with the elements of the nationality which he cherishes, and realizes that Christianity has not found it possible to penetrate to the roots of Germanic and Celtic life. The opposite is true of Islam and its influence over Arab society and the Arab nation, as we shall explain in some measure. . . .

The correct scientific explanation of the emergence of the Arabs in the first period of Islam is that it was one of the waves out of the Arabian Peninsula, although it was the most venerable of these waves and the most illustrious in the history of the Arabs themselves and in the history of the whole of mankind. There is no contradiction at all between our sincere Muslim feeling and our holding precious the ancient Arab civilizations. . . . Islam abandoned only what was bad in our customs and what was false in our laws and traditions. Islam holds, as the noble *hadīth* has it, that men are metals like gold and silver, those among them who were the best in the *jāhiliyya* remain the best in Islam. It would not have been possible for the Arabs to achieve such a revival and accomplish such tremendous actions, in war, politics, legislation, literature, art, sociology, and the other aspects of life, in such a short time, if their metal had not been pure and their abilities latent in them from long ago, their nature creative and their spirit strong and true. There could not shine among the Arabs, in one or two generations, men like Abū-Bakr, 'Umar, 'Alī, Ibn Ubayda, Sa'd, Khālid, Ibn 'Abbās, Abū-Dharr, and Ibn Mas'ūd, or women like Khadīja, Fātima, 'Ā'isha, Asma', al-Khansa, and many other men and women of genius of that age, had the Arabs not inherited an ancient and continuous civilization and had they not been prepared by their instinct to create and build and renovate. The fact that the Prophet Muhammad was Arab was not a matter of chance; a genius, he belonged to a nation of great abilities and qualities. . . .

It is clear from all this that the Arabs are the backbone of Islam. They were the first to be addressed in the verses of Revelation; they were the *Muhājirīn* and the *Ansār*; their swords conquered countries and lands, and on the whole they are as 'Umar has described them in a saying of his: "Do not attack the Arabs and humiliate them for they are the essence of Islam."

After this clear exposition of the intellectual problems and the factors that contribute to the mistaken belief that there is a contradiction between the principles of Islam and Arab nationalism, it befits us to define the meaning of nationalism, more particularly of Arab nationalism and of its assumptions, and to look into these assumptions in order to see which are accepted by Islam and which, if any, are rejected.

Nationalism is a political and social idea which aims, in the first place, to unify each group of mankind and to make it obey one political order. The factors and the assumptions of nationalism are varied, and we do not intend to analyze them in this lecture. But we can assert that modern nationalism is based on language, history, literature, customs, and qualities. On the whole, the ties that bind individuals together and make them into a nation are both intellectual and material. If we examine these assumptions carefully and inquire into the position of Islam toward each of them, we find a great similarity, and sometimes complete agreement, between what Arab nationalism teaches and what is affirmed by Islam. Language, then, is the primary tenet of our national creed; it is the soul of our Arab nation and the primary aspect of its life. The nation that loses its language is destined to disappear and perish. It is the good fortune of the Arabs that their language is not only a national duty but also a religous one, and the influence of Islam on its propagation and preservation is very great. . . . Moreover, as we have explained above, the Arabs had a glorious history before Islam, and their history is even more glorious and of greater moment after Islam; the Muslim Arab, when he exalts his heroes, partakes of two emotions, that of the pious Muslim and that of the proud nationalist.

In fact, the most glorious pages of Muslim history are the pages of Arab Muslim history, as the Western historians themselves admit. . . .

As for Arabic literature which is the result of Arab feeling and emotion all through the ages, its greatest and most venerable parts came from Islam, and indeed, the Qur'ān itself, in addition to being a book of direction, is the most awesome example of the elevated prose which the Arab, irrespective of his religion, exalts. How I wish the youth especially would read a small original book, *Descriptive Technique in the Qur'ān*, by Sayyid Qutb to see the artistic beauty of the style of the Qur'ān. Who can belittle the influence of the Qur'ān on Arabic literature? As for pre-Islamic poetry, and especially descriptive and wisdom verse, there is in most of it nothing which contradicts the spirit of Islam.

The fourth element in Arab nationalism consists of "the good Arab customs and qualities." Here, undoubtedly, there is similarity, not to say complete identity, between the ethical ideal of Arab nationalism and that prescribed by Islam. . . . We do not pretend to say that all the pre-Islamic customs of the Arabs were good, but we maintain that Islam has confirmed all that was best in Arab character. In our national call for exalting the Arab character, we mean those polished virtues which elevate man and make of him a being worthy of the description "polite."

Let us leave the Arab factors aside and examine nationalism as a political movement working to unite the Arabs and to give them self-government. The national movement is "democratic," "socialist," "popular," and "coöperative." Islam, although it did not lay down in detail the organization of government, requires consultation, and does, without any doubt, accept completely democratic organization. Its financial legislation and juristic principles are, in essence, socialist; Sayyid Qutb has succeeded in explaining this in his book *Social Justice in Islam*. It is enough to remember something of the life of the Prophet and of the caliphs, to realize the extent of the coöperative and the popular spirit of Islam. The position being such, the government for which we call does not in any way contradict Islam.

But to say this is not to imply a call for Pan-Islamism. To say that Islam does not contradict the Arab national spirit is one thing, and to make propaganda for Pan-Islamism is another. Pan-Islamism, in its precise and true meaning, aims to form a comprehensive political organization which all the Muslims must obey. This organization, although it may be desired by all the pious Muslims, is not possible in practice, for many reasons—geographical, political, social—or, at least, it is not possible under the present conditions, even if we agreed to limit this union to the parts of the Muslim homeland which are contiguous. And even if we assumed that these parts could be united, then the unification of the parts which speak the same language, inherit the same literature, and have the same history, is more urgently needed and more worthy of consideration; it is not natural to expect the union of Iraq with Iran or Afghanistan, for instance, before Syria and Jordan are united. A view contrary to this is nonsense and deserves no answer. It follows, therefore, that the call to unite the Arabs—and this is the clearest and most important objective of Arab nationalism—is the practical step which must precede the call for Pan-Islamism. It is strange, however, to find that some of those who call themselves supporters of Pan-Islamism in the Arab countries are the most violent opponents of Pan-Arabism. If they would understand things as they are and would appreciate matters properly, if they did not follow mere emotion, they would admit that their call is misplaced, until the first aim of the Arab nationalists is fulfilled, namely the erection of a collective organization for the Arabs in Asia and Africa.

The conclusion is that no fundamental contradiction or clear opposition exists between Arab nationalism and Islam. The nearest analogy for the relation between them is that of the general to the particular. If we wanted to represent that relationship geometrically, we can imagine Islam and Arabism as two circles overlapping in the greater part of their surface, and in what remains outside the area that is common to the two circles the two are not in fundamental opposition to each other. This is a truth which we must realize, and it befits the Arabs to rejoice in this great good fortune, that their nationalism does not contradict their religion; the Muslim Turk, for instance, who wants to glory in his nationalism, finds an insoluble difficulty in reconciling this sentiment with his sincere religious feeling. His national feeling requires him to be proud of his language and to purify it of other foreign languages; this may drive him to belittle Arabic, which is the flowing source from which Turkish language and literature drew from the earliest days. And if he wants to exalt the glorious actions and the heroes of the past, this will drive him, in most cases, to feel that the Muslim Arabs were strangers to him and that they were, in spite of external appearances, his real colonizers, mentally, spiritually, and culturally; the nationalist Muslim Arab will not often encounter this kind of difficulty.

I do not know whether it is necessary for me to say that our call for Arab nationalism and for a comprehensive Arab being does not, under any circumstances, make us antagonistic to the non-Arab Muslims; for, as our national pact defines it, we consider the group of the Islamic peoples the nearest of all other groups to us; we see in this group a great force which we cherish, and we work to strengthen the ties with it and to coöperate with it. Our relation to the non-Arab Muslims who inhabit the Arab homeland is a brotherly one, for they are the brothers of the Arabs and have all the rights and all the duties of the Arabs. There is not in our nationalism a call to persecute any of the human races; on the contrary, there is no empty national arrogance nor blind racial chauvinism in it. When we take pride in our great actions and cherish our nationality, we want to inspire our nation to reach the place which it deserves among the peoples and the nations of the earth. This is a natural right, accepted by all religions, and recognized by the principles of justice. There is in it no feeling of superiority over others and no desire to oppress other races.

It also befits us to make it clear that there is nothing in this national call of ours which need exercise the non-Muslims among the Arabs or diminish their rights as good compatriots. Chauvinism, in all its aspects and forms, is incompatible with the nature of the Arabs; the non-Muslim Arabs used to enjoy all their rights under the shadow of the Arab state, from the earliest times, and the scope open to them was wide. The loyal nationalists among the Arab Christians realize this and know that Islam and the civilization which accompanied it are an indivisible part of our national heritage, and they must, as nationalists, cherish it as their brother Muslims cherish it.

I realize indeed that this talk of mine and tens of other better ones on this subject will not be enough to dispel all the common myths and mistakes about the meaning of Arab nationalism and Islam, and will not succeed in removing all the illusions which assume the existence of contradictions between the two. What those harmful pictures and wrong explanations, what past centuries have left, cannot be erased or effaced if we do not realize the three following matters:

First. We must free ourselves from the intellectual power of the West and its imported concepts, and we must think independently and with originality about our problems, affairs, and history. We must abandon false standards in intellectual and social matters, because the difference of the borrowed concepts and the variation in the factors and conditions will lead us to mistaken results and false judgments. We must become intellectually independent and consider things objectively; we must not borrow from the West, or when we do we must borrow and reject after a careful examination and a full and complete comparison.

Second. We must work earnestly and sincerely to present anew our nation's past and to write our history in a correct scientific manner, in order to eradicate these distorted pictures and to put a stop to these iniquitous judgments, to tear out those black pages which the pens of prejudiced intriguers have drawn. . . .

Third. Last but not least, we must look to Islam, which we cherish so much and which we believe to be the reflection of the Arab soul and its spiritual source which does not exhaust itself. We must look at it as a whole, devoid of its communal and sectarian character, the Book of God and his Sunna flowing out of its clear and original sources, as our ancient ancestors used to understand it before some backward Muslims burdened it with what there remained in their subconsious of the influence of Zoroastrianism, of Buddhism, of the Israelite traditions, of Roman and Greek sophistry. We must receive it straight from its clear Arab environment, not mixed in an imaginary international environment, and not weighed down by the chains of symbolic Sufism or burdened by the dead hand of a petrified clergy.

MUHAMMAD IQBĀL
1875–1938

No other single person has captured the minds and imaginations of Muslims in India-Pakistan as has Iqbāl. After an early classical Islamic education, he studied at Cambridge and Munich, earning a doctorate in philosophy as well as a law degree. Conversant with Western philosophical and scientific thought, Iqbāl advocated a fundamental rethinking of Islamic thought as reflected in his *The Reconstruction of Religious Thought in Islam*. A prolific author, his poetry and prose touched every area of Muslim life—religion, politics, and society.

A Separate Muslim State in the Subcontinent

What, then, is the problem and its implications? Is religion a private affair? Would you like to see Islam, as a moral and political idea, meeting the same fate in the world of Islam as Christianity has already met in Europe? Is it possible to retain Islam as an ethical ideal and to reject it as a polity in favour of national polities in which religious attitude is not permitted to play any part? This question becomes of special importance in India where the Muslims happen to be in minority. The proposition that religion is a private individual experience is not surprising on the lips of a European. In Europe the conception of Christianity as a monastic order, renouncing the world of matter and fixing its gaze entirely on the world of spirit, led by a logical process of thought to the view embodied in this proposition. The nature of the Prophet's religious experience, as disclosed in the Qur'ān, however, is wholly different. It is not mere experience in the sense of a purely biological event, happening inside the experient and necessitating no reactions on its social environment. It is individual experience creative of a social order. Its immediate outcome is the fundamentals of a polity with implicit legal concepts whose civic significance cannot be belittled merely because their origin is revelational. The religious ideal of Islam, therefore, is organically related to the social order which it has created. The rejection of the one will eventually involve the rejection of the other. Therefore, the construction of a polity on national lines, if it means a displacement of the Islamic principle of solidarity, is simply unthinkable to a Muslim. This is a matter which at the present moment directly concerns the Muslims of India.

From *Struggle for Independence: 1857–1947* (Karachi, 1958), App. IV, pp. 14–18.

. . . It is, however, painful to observe that our attempts to discover such a principle of internal harmony have so far failed. Why have they failed? Perhaps we suspect each other's intentions, and inwardly aim at dominating each other. Perhaps in the higher interests of mutual co-operation, we cannot afford to part with the monopolies which circumstances have placed in our hands, and conceal our egoism under the cloak of a nationalism, outwardly simulating a large-hearted patriotism, but inwardly as narrow-minded as a caste or a tribe. Perhaps we are unwilling to recognise that each group has a right to free development according to its own cultural traditions. But whatever may be the causes of our failure, I still feel hopeful. Events seem to be tending in the direction of some sort of internal harmony. And as far as I have been able to read the Muslim mind, I have no hesitation in declaring that if the principle that the Indian Muslim is entitled to full and free development on the lines of his own culture and tradition in his own Indian homelands is recognized as the basis of a permanent communal settlement, he will be ready to stake his all for the freedom of India. The principle that each group is entitled to free development on its own lines is not inspired by any feeling of narrow communalism. There are communalisms and communalisms. A community which is inspired by feeling of ill-will towards other communities is low and ignoble. I entertain the highest respect for the customs, laws, religious and social institutions of other communities. Nay, it is my duty, according to the teaching of the Qur'ān, even to defend their places of worship if need be. Yet I love the communal group which is the source of my life and behaviour; and which has formed me what I am by giving me its religion, its literature, its thought, its culture, and thereby recreating its whole past, as a living operative factor, in my present consciousness.

Communalism, in its higher aspect, then, is indispensable to the formation of a harmonious whole in a country like India. The units of Indian society are not territorial as in European countries. India is a continent of human groups belonging to different races, speaking different languages and professing different religions. Their behaviour is not at all determined by a common race-consciousness. Even the Hindus do not form a homogeneous group. The principle of European democracy cannot be applied to India without recognising the fact of communal groups. The Muslim demand for the creation of a Muslim India within India is, therefore, perfectly justified. The resolution of the All-Parties Muslim Conference at Delhi is, to my mind, wholly inspired by this noble ideal of a harmonious whole which, instead of stifling the respective individualites of its component wholes, affords them chances of fully working out the possibilities that may be latent in them. And I have no doubt that this house will emphatically endorse the Muslim demands embodied in this resolution. Personally I would go further than the demands embodied in it. I would like to see the Punjab, North-West Frontier, Sind and Baluchistan amalgamated into a single state. Self-government within the British Empire, or without the

British Empire, and the formation of a consolidated North-West Indian Muslim state appears to me to be the final destiny of the Muslims, at least of North-West India.

The idea need not alarm the Hindus or the British. India is the greatest Muslim country in the world. The life of Islam as a cultural force in this country very largely depends on its centralisation in a specified territory. This centralisation of the most living portion of the Muslims of India whose military and police service has, notwithstanding unfair treatment from the British, made the British rule possible in this country, will eventually solve the problem of India as well as of Asia. It will intensify their sense of responsibility and deepen their patriotic feeling. Thus, possessing full opportunity of development within the body-politic of India, the North-West Indian Muslims will prove the best defenders of India against a foreign invasion, be that invasion one of ideas or of bayonets. . . .

. . . the Muslim demand . . . is actuated by a genuine desire for free development which is practically impossible under the type of unitary government contemplated by the nationalist Hindu politicians with a view to secure permanent communal dominance in the whole of India.

Nor should the Hindus fear that the creation of autonomous Muslim states will mean the introduction of a kind of religious rule in such states. I have already indicated to you the meaning of the word 'religion,' as applied to Islam. The truth is that Islam is not a church. It is a state, conceived as a contractual organism long before Rousseau ever thought of such a thing, and animated by an ethical ideal which regards man not as an earth-rooted creature, defined by this or that portion of the earth, but as a spiritual being understood in terms of a social mechanism, and possessing rights and duties as a living factor in that mechanism. . . . I, therefore, demand the formation of a consolidated Muslim state in the best interests of India and Islam. For India it means security and peace resulting from an internal balance of power; for Islam an opportunity to rid itself of the stamp that Arabian Imperialism was forced to give it, to mobilize its law, its education, its culture, and to bring them into closer contact with its own original spirit and with the spirit of modern times.

Mawlānā Mawdūdī received an early traditional religious
education, which was supplemented by his self-taught knowledge
of Western thought. He pursued a career in journalism and in
1933 assumed editorship of *Tarjuman al-Qur'ān* [Exegesis of
the Quran], which throughout the years served as a vehicle of
his thought. He has been perhaps the most systematic modern
Muslim writer, and his many writings have been translated into
English and Arabic and circulated throughout the Muslim world.
In 1941 Mawdūdī established the Jamā'at-i-Islāmī [the Islamic
Association], an extremely well organized association committed
to the reestablishment of an Islamic world order or society (politically, legally, and socially). Although originally against any form
of nationalism and thus opposed to the establishment of Pakistan,
Mawdūdī nevertheless migrated to Pakistan, after the partitioning, where the Jamā'at-i-Islāmī has been very active in politics.

Nationalism and Islam

Even a cursory glance at the meaning and essence of nationalism would
convince a person that in their spirit and in their aims Islam and nationalism are diametrically opposed to each other. Islam deals with man as man.
It presents to all mankind a social system of justice and piety based on creed
and morality and invites all towards it. And then it admits him in its circle,
with equal rights, whosoever accepts this system. Be it in the sphere of
economics or politics or civics or legal rights and duties or anything else,
those who accept the principles of Islam are not divided by any distinction
of nationality or race or class or country. The ultimate goal of Islam is a
world-state in which the chains of racial and national prejudices would be
dismantled and all mankind incorporated in a cultural and political system,
with equal rights and equal opportunities for all, and in which hostile competition would give way to friendly co-operation between peoples so that
they might mutually assist and contribute to the material and moral good
of one another. Whatever the principle of human good Islam defines, and
whatever the scheme of life it prescribes, it would appeal to mankind in
general only when they would free themselves of all ignorant prejudices and
dissociate themselves altogether from their national traditions, with their
sentiments of racial pride, and with their love of sanguinary and material

From *Nationalism and India* (Lahore: Maktaba-e-Jama'at-e-Islami; new edition, 1947),
10–12, 24–28, 30–34.

affinities, and be prepared, as mere human beings, to enquire what is truth, where lies righteousness, justice and honesty, and what is the path that leads to the well-being of, not a class or a nation or a country, but of humanity as a whole. . . .

As opposed to this, nationalism divides man from man on the basis of nationality. Nationalism simply means that the nationalist should give preference to his nationality over all other nationalities. Even if he were not an aggressive nationalist, nationalism, at least, demands that culturally, economically, politically and legally he should differentiate between national and non-national; secure the maximum of advantages for his nation; build up barriers of economic preferences for national profit; protect with tenacity the historical traditions and the traditional prejudices which have come down to wake his nationality, and breed in him the sentiments of national pride. He would not admit with him members of other nationalities in any walk of life on an equal basis. Whenever there is a chance of his nation obtaining more advantages, as against the other, his heart would be sealed against all sentiments of justice and propriety. His ultimate goal would be a nation-state *rather* than a world-state, nevertheless if he upholds any world ideology, that ideology would necessarily take the form of imperialism or world domination, because members of other nationalities cannot participate in his state as equals, they may do so only as "slaves" or subjects. . . .

THE FUNDAMENTAL DIFFERENCE BETWEEN NATIONALISM AND ISLAM

. . . The law of God (the *Sharī'a*) has always aimed at bringing together mankind into one moral and spiritual framework and make them mutually assistant to one another on a universal scale. But nationalism at once demolishes this frame-work with the noxious instruments of racial and national distinction, and by creating bitterness and hatred between nations makes them fight and exterminate rather than help one another.

The *Sharī'as* of God provide the highest opportunities of free contact between man and man because on this very contact depends the progress of human civilisation and culture. But nationalism comes in the way of these contacts with a thousand hindrances; it makes the mere existence of foreign nationals in a country impossible.

The *Sharī'as* of God want that every individual, every nation, every race should obtain full opportunities of developing its natural characteristics and its inherent potentialities so that it may be able to subscribe its due share to the collective progress of mankind. But nationalism urges upon every race, every nation, that it should secure power and degrade and disgrace and belittle other races and nations and bring them under servility, and deny them any chance of developing their natural talents and resources, and deprive them even of the primary right of mere existence.

The fundamental principle of the *Sharī'as* of God is that the rights of man are based on moral code and not on force. That is, if the moral law sanctions a right to a weak individual or weak people, the powerful individual or the powerful people must honour this right. But in contrast to this nationalism establishes the principle that "might is right" and that the weak has no right because he has no might. . . .

Again an essential feature of this nationalism is that it makes man opportunist. The *Sharī'as* of God are given to man to make him live by principles and relate his behaviour to permanent laws which would not alter with individual or national interests. But, unlike it, nationalism makes man unprincipled. A nationalist has no principles in the world except that he wishes the good of his nation. If the laws of ethics, injunctions of religion, and principles of culture serve his purpose he would put his faith in them gladly, but if they interfered with his interest he would set them aside and invent and adopt some other principles and theories.

But a more direct conflict between nationalism and the *Sharī'as* of God occurs in yet another way. It is obvious that whatever messenger is sent by God, he must take birth in some nation and in some country. Again, the Book of Laws which he would be given must necessarily be in the language of the country to which he has been deputed. Moreover, the sacred and holy places associated with the mission of that Rasūl [messenger, prophet] must be situated mostly in that particular country. But in spite of these limitations the truth and that divine teaching which a Rasūl brings from God, is not confined to one nation or country, it is intended for humanity at large. The entire human race is called upon to believe in that Rasūl and his teachings, and whether that Rasūl has a limited mission, as Noah and Moses and many other Rasūls had, or a universal mission, as Abraham and Muhammad had, in either case all mankind are ordered to respect and believe in every Rasūl and when the mission of a Rasūl is universal, it is natural that the Book of Laws given to him by God must acquire an international status; the cultural influence of the language he speaks must be international; the sacred places associated with his mission, in spite of their being situated in one country must become centres of international importance. And not only that Rasūl but also his companions and the prominent persons taking part in his movement at its inception, in spite of their being connected with one nation would become the heroes of all nations. All this falls contrary to the taste, temperament, sentiments and thoughts of a nationalist. The national self-consciousness of a nationalist can never brook it that he should take as his heroes persons who do not belong to his nationality; accept the central importance and sanctity of such places as are not situated within his country; admit the cultural influence of a language which may not be his own; secure inspiration from traditions which may have been imported from outside. He would regard all these things not only as foreign but would look upon them with that displeasure and hatred with which everything of foreign invader is received, and would endeavour his best to eliminate and cast out all these external influences from the life of his nation. It is the natural demand of his nationalistic sentiment that he should associate his sentiments of sacredness and sanctity with his own homeland, that he should sing hymns to rivers and mountains of his own country, that he should revive his ancient national historical traditions (traditions which this foreign religion describes as the relics of the age of ignorance) and pride in them, that he should relate his present with his own past and link his national culture with that of his ancestors in a chronicle sequence, that he should take as his heroes, historical or legendary, persons from his own nation and take inspiration only from their deeds, imaginary or real. In short, it is in the nature and constitution of nationalism that it should condemn everything that comes from outside and praise all those things which are the products of its own home. The ultimate goal to which this path leads is that even the religion which has been imported must be completely abandoned, and those religious traditions which may have come down to a nationalist from the "age of ignorance" of his own national history be praised and glorified. Many nationalists might not have reached this ultimate goal and might be lingering somewhere midway, but the path they are traversing only leads to this goal.

ISLAM AND SOCIALISM

In the wake of World War II, attitudes in the Muslim world began to change radically. The West's creation of Israel in 1948 spelled the demise of the liberal nationalist current of political thought in most of the Arab world. A series of military coups d'état brought to power regimes that were disillusioned with the liberal West and attracted by the progress of socialism in Russia and Eastern Europe. For the new generation of leaders, independence meant positive neutrality and a concern for authentic Arab identity. Arab socialism became the shibboleth that separated the "progressives" from the "reactionaries." Nāsirism and the ideology of the Ba'th Party became the two major forces in the area. Egypt's Jamāl 'Abd al-Nāsir espoused socialism, and Shaykh Mahmūd Shaltūt, the leading religious figure in Egypt (Shaykh al-Azhar), gives assurance that Arab socialism fits perfectly with Islam. After Nāsir's death in 1970 it has not been easy to say exactly what Nāsirism is, but one version is given in the selection from Libyan leader Mu'ammar al-Qadhdhāfī, a fervent disciple of Nāsir.

Arab specificity is also the preoccupation of the Ba'th Party and selections from one of the founding fathers Michel Aflāq, a Christian, present a rather original attempt at weaving Islam into the pattern of Arab revolutionary thought.

Both Nāsirism and Ba'thism represent new forms of nationalist thought. But they did not have the political stage entirely to themselves; there were also universalist currents present trying to establish a popular base. At one pole was Marxism, never too popular, represented here by Sadiq al-'Azm, and at the opposite pole was Islamic socialism, represented here by Mustafā al-Sibā'ī and Sayyid Qutb, spokesman for the Muslim Brotherhood. South Asia has witnessed similar concerns to relate Islam to socioeconomic reform and to do so in the name of Islamic socialism.

Finally, A. K. Brohi reflects the position of many Muslims who believe that Islam provides its own blueprint for a socially just society and who object to the association of Islam with the term "socialism."

SHAYKH MAHMŪD SHALTŪT
1892–1963

Born in Minya, Mahmud Shaltut studied and then taught in
Alexandria. In 1927 he joined the faculty of al-Azhar University
and was among those who proposed the reform of al-Azhar. He
was dismissed from his post in the 1930s because of his reformist
views. However, he later returned and in 1958 became the Rector
of al-Azhar (Shaykh al-Azhar).

Socialism and Islam

ISLAM AND SOCIETY

Islam is not only a spiritual religion, as some wrongly imagine, thinking
that it limits itself to establishing relations between the servant and his Lord,
without being concerned with organizing the affairs of the community and
establishing its rules of conduct. On the contrary, Islam is universal in
character. Not only does it determine the relations between man and his
Lord, but it also lays down the rules that regulate human relations and
public affairs, with the aim of ensuring the welfare of society. . . .

MUTUAL SOCIAL AID AMONG MUSLIMS

Members of human society cannot be considered independent of one
another. On the contrary, as a result of their existence in this world and
the very conditions of their lives, they render each other mutual service and
cooperate to satisfy their needs. . . .

This bond is, in Islam, the "religious brotherhood" among Muslims.
It is in the "brotherhood" that rights and social duties are expressed in the
most sincere fashion. It is this that constitutes the most powerful factor
leading toward clemency, sympathy, and cooperation; and giving a sense
of the idea, it leads society toward good and banishes evil.

Islam has established this "brotherhood" among Muslims. "The
believers are a band of brothers" (Qur'ān 49:10), and the Prophet said,
"Muslim is brother to Muslim." Moreover, Islam has raised the religious
brotherhood over and above the blood relationship.

Muslims have attained social solidarity to a unique degree in their
Islamic society, which God has immortalized in His Book, which says,
"Prize them above themselves, though they are in want" (59:9). . . .

From Kemal H. Karpat, ed. *Political and Social Thought in the Contemporary Middle East*
(New York: Praeger, 1968), pp. 126–32.

SOCIAL SOLIDARITY AMONG MUSLIMS

Social solidarity among Muslims is of two kinds—the moral and the material. Moral solidarity derives from two factors. The first is recognizing good and virtue and inviting one's neighbor to conform to it with sincerity and fidelity. "You are the noblest nation that has ever been raised up for mankind. You enjoin justice and forbid evil. You believe in Allah" (Qur'ān 3:106).

The second allows one to hear the Word of God and receive it with gratitude and acknowledgment. "Give good news to My servants, who listen to My precepts and follow what is best in them, These are they whom Allah has guided. These are they who are endued with understanding" (Qur'ān 39:19–20).

The interaction of these two forces makes cooperation between members of a Muslim society more sound.

Material solidarity consists of meeting the needs of society, of consoling the unfortunate, of helping to achieve what is in the general interest, i.e., whatever increases the standard of living and serves all individuals in a beneficial manner.

It is not to be doubted that all those foundations on which life rests, such as perfection, happiness, and grandeur, matters of science, health, greatness, dignity, civilization, power, and strength, cannot be attained without wealth.

In its attitude toward allowing man to assure his needs. Islam considers wealth realistically. Islam has made wealth an "ornament" of this life (Qur'ān 18:44). It also qualified it as the "support of man." Wealth is not an end in itself. It is only one of the means of rendering mutual service and procuring what one needs. Used thus, it is a good thing, both for the one who possesses it and for society. Considered as an end in itself, and with the sole aim of being enjoyed, wealth becomes for its owner the cause of great harm, and at the same time sows corruption among men. . . .

That is why the Qur'ān regards wealth as a good thing, on condition that it is acquired legally and spent for the good of others, and that it remains not an end in itself but simply a means.

Agriculture, industry, and commerce, on which the material life of society depends, are the sources of wealth. Society needs agriculture for the foodstuffs that are produced by the soil. It also needs the various industries that are necessary to man. Clothing, housing, agriculture, machinery, roads, waterways, and railways are also necessary for the protection and defense of the state. All these can be acquired only through industry.

Agriculture, industry, and commerce must therefore be developed as much as possible. That is why the men of Islamic religious learning ['ulamā'] teach that it is a collective obligation to learn to make all that one cannot do without, and that if this obligation is not fulfilled the sin that falls back on the whole nation can be effaced only if a part of the nation discharges the obligation.

There is no doubt that this obligation consists in working for the achievement of the principle that Islam imposes on its followers, i.e., the autarky [or establishment of self-sufficiency] that allows the Muslim community itself to meet all its needs. . . .

Muslim jurists are unanimous in recognizing the right of authorities to expropriate [land] in order to enlarge the place of prayer [i.e., the jurisdiction of Islam] until the whole world becomes a mosque. They also have the right to act likewise to enlarge a street or any other public service, in the interests of both individuals and the community. . . .

Worldly possessions are the possessions of God, given by Him to His servants for the benefit of the universe. God sometimes claims possession of these goods: "Allah gives without measure to whom he wills" (Qur'ān 24:38). At other times, He attributes them to their previous owners: "Do not give to the feeble-minded the property with which Allah has entrusted you for their support" (Qur'ān 4:4).

God has clearly established that the possessors of goods, who are the holders after Him, must preserve, increase, and spend them in a manner laid down by Him: "Give in alms of that which He has made your inheritance" (Qur'ān 57:7). God also has put his wealth at the disposal of all men equally: "Allah created the heavens and the earth to reveal the truth and to reward each soul according to its deeds. None shall be wronged" (Qur'ān 45:12).

If worldly possessions are the possessions of God, if all men are the servants of God, and if the life in which they toil and do honor to the possessions of God belongs to God, then wealth, although it may be attributed to a private person, should also belong to all the servants of God, should be placed in the safekeeping of all, and all should profit from it. "Men, serve your Lord, who has created you and those who have gone before you, so that you may guard yourselves against evil; who has made the earth a bed for you and the sky a dome, and has sent down water from heaven to bring forth fruits for your sustenance" (Qur'ān 2:19–21).

Thus, to be rich is a social function whose aim is to ensure the happiness of society and satisfy its needs and interests.

So that all men may profit from worldly goods and their souls be free from all greed in this regard, Islam has opposed all who hoard and jealously watch over their wealth. . . . "Proclaim a woeful punishment to those who hoard up gold and silver and do not spend it in Allah's cause. The day will surely come when their treasures shall be heated in the fire of Hell, and their foreheads, sides, and backs branded with them. Their tormentors will say to them: 'These are the riches which you hoarded. Taste then the punishment which is your due'" (Qur'ān 9:36).

Similarly, Islam has fought the stupidity that leads to the squandering of goods uselessly: "The wasteful are Satan's brothers" (Qur'ān 17:29).

Islam has fought luxury, which has created hatred among the social classes, which menaces a peaceful and stable life, not to mention corruption and anarchy. . . .

Islam has traced the straight path of the ideal society; it is a path of solidarity by which the nation lives and which ensures the strength of society. With this end in view, Islam has abolished from the minds of owners [of property] and capitalists such vices as meanness, the taste for squandering the luxury. It has employed all means to encourage men to give generously and to be afraid of appearing miserly and of neglecting the right of the people and of society, to such a point that it has raised liberality to the rank of faith. . . .

"The true servants of the Merciful are those who walk humbly on the earth and say 'Peace!' to the ignorant who accost them; . . . who are neither extravagant nor niggardly but keep the golden mean; who invoke no other God besides Allah . . ." (Qur'ān 25:64–66).

For Islam, avarice similarly is one of the traits that condemn the infidel: "'What has brought you into Hell?' They will reply: 'We never prayed or fed the hungry . . .'" (Qur'ān 74:43–44).

Islam has maintained this view for so long that it considers it a denial of the Judgment not to encourage giving to the needy: "Have you thought of him that denies the Last Judgement? It is he who turns away the orphan and does not urge others to feed the poor" (Qur'ān 107).

Briefly summarized, such is the doctrine of Islam regarding the relations among men from the point of view of the solidarity of members of society. It contains in detail all the solid foundations necessary to make our nation a magnificent stronghold, a haven of happiness for those who shelter there.

The doctrine also contains a clear statement of what the socialism of Islam is, for adoption by those who wish to adopt it. Can man find a more perfect, more complete, more useful, and more profound socialism than that decreed by Islam? It is founded on the basis of faith and belief, and all that is decreed on that basis participates in the perpetuation of life and doctrine.

MU 'AMMAR AL-QADHDHĀFĪ
1942–

He studied history at Benghazi University while training at the
Military Academy. In 1969 he was one of the leaders of the
Libyan revolution and emerged as Chairman of the Revolutionary
Council and President of the country. A devoted admirer of Jamāl
'Abd al-Nāsir, he has developed his own Islamic ideology, which
he labels the "Third Way."

The Third Way

We will fasten our tie to the past and reconsider our present in order to
cut our way through to the future, generation after generation. This is no
simple task. The advance began in the East and went West. Now . . . here
we are speaking in the Libyan Arab Republic, on the subject of the third
theory which, as we said, is not new. It exists, and it was the first and
will be the last . . . in our theory we focus on the Qur'ān, since the Qur'ān
is the perfect book which contains nothing false whatever, is from God
Almighty, may He be praised, who created man and created the rules
(*sunan*) which govern the universe.

We must take the Qur'ān as the focal point of our journey in life
because the Qur'ān is perfect; it is light, and in it are solutions to the
problems of man . . . from personal status . . . to international problems.

Both the East and the West want to corrupt us from within, obliterate
every distinguishing mark of our personality and snuff out the light which
guides us. Both have focused their sights on the Qur'ān in a menacing way
and have zeroed in on religion . . . in order to tie religion to reactionism
and to associate it with superstitions. As a result we began returning to
the pagan society which existed at the time Islam first appeared. When the
heavenly messages were revealed, the pagans used to charge that the
revealed books were fables, or poetry, or the saying of some seer or crazy
man. Have we returned to that pagan society in which one speaks those
same words the pagans spoke when the heavenly messages appeared . . . an
appeal to morality is called reactionism . . . religion is labeled fables. . . .
Any personal action on our part springing from our personality or from
our values is cast into doubt, and we ourselves have begun to doubt. That
precisely is how colonialism has affected us. And this is what I want to
repeat: I say that we must be awake and alert. We must reconsider so that

From *Fīl-Nazariyyah al-Thālithah* [The third way], (n.p.:n.d.), pp. 65–71.

we will know . . . what word we will speak? What are the needs in which we believe? . . . We want to reconsider our situation because we were in darkness. We were prey, but now . . . the prey is standing on its own two feet and desires to resist its predators and wants to live on an equal footing with them. . . . The prey must re-examine itself . . . treat its wounds and regain strength of movement.

With our theory or our creed we have no need of communism nor capitalism; we did not need East or West in our creation, nor do we need them in our resurrection. This does not mean that we have no need of East or West in our human and international relations. No, we interact with the world; we affect it and are affected by it in turn. We are part of mankind, whether men be communist or capitalist. What we want to say is that we have no need for anyone to reconstruct us brick by brick, to restructure our personality and dictate the positions we should take. We must have the possibility to profit from the experience of mankind, but we too have an experience which others should respect and profit from. In this way we interact with the world that it may benefit from us as we benefit from it. But if someone thinks he can come and rebuild us from zero and mold us into new forms according to his lights, we will resist stubbornly. We will not allow ourselves to be molded into slaves of some new creator. We are slaves to no one but God, God it is who created us.

The details of the theory, its component parts and its elucidation, are not my specialization. They are the specialization of every cultured and learned person, every thinker, every *mujtahid* [one capable of interpretation], every researcher. This is their task . . . to refute the calumnies leveled against us; to expose the economic, military, legal, social and political aspects of the Qur'ān; to demonstrate how the foundations of present civilization were established by the Arabs. The Arabs, deformed by colonialism, were beginning to doubt themselves. It was becoming impossible for them to believe that the foundations of contemporary civilization were laid by Arabs and Muslims because a comparison of the present flourishing civilization with the backward state of the Arabs was embarrassing. It meant that this backwardness was the artisan of this progress and anyone lacking literary courage would be embarrassed to say that the Arabs and Muslims were the architects of the present civilization.

In fact, there is a certain justification for this embarrassment because the backwardness in which we live makes us too embarrassed to attribute anything progressive to ourselves. Courage is needed to speak these words. Anyone who looks at the books of astronomy we have today will find all the names of the stars are Arabic . . . this means that the Arabs or the Muslims created the science of astronomy. The sciences of chemistry, accounting, algebra, medicine, all have authors who are known by name. . . .

The time has come to manifest the truth of Islam as a force to move mankind, to make progress, and to change the course of history as we changed it formerly.

We must establish the fact that religion is the effective motive in the life of man and that the world in its long history was moved by religion which, along with nationalism, played the basic role. That is, nationalism and religion are the two forces that have moved history and have set the tempo for the march of all humanity. A disavowal of the role of religion and nationalism in the movement of history is obstructionism born of disbelieving despair; it has no pretext except the desire to dominate by force.

As for capitalism, we must oppose it forcefully in order to demonstrate the corruption of wealth, the corruption of exploiting capital. If capital is amassed, it is transformed into evil; we must demonstrate this from the Qur'ān. The Qur'ān is replete with sayings about those living in luxury, those who squander, and those who are prodigal. There are verses from the Qur'ān which we can take as titles for the volumes we will compose by our practice because the Qur'ān does not give details for everything. The Qur'ān is verses which explain a very large part of life. When the Qur'ān says "Nay, but verily man is rebellious, that he thinketh himself independent" (96:6–7), this verse is an encyclopedia in itself, it says clearly that if a man sees he is rich and has wealth and power, it is inevitable that he will be conceited and tyrannical; and tyranny begets corruption and absolutism, it enslaves people and debases life. Sowing corruption on earth . . . the meaning of "that he thinketh himself independent" is that if he sees himself rich he will be tyrannical. So the problem is that riches or wealth, power or possessions by themselves push man to tyranny. Thus, wealth is a problem which must be treated and solved. Restraints must be part of it. And as long as wealth is sometimes an evil, we must search out other things and other states in which wealth will not be evil. We must search for justice in this subject. . . .

We must search out the causes of corruption to discover what it is that makes man sow corruption on earth in order to eliminate these causes so that man may be just and society may be just. We will establish the ideal society.

The world, East and West, is incapable of arriving at a true solution, and attempts to solve the problem by extremist solutions have failed. . . . One sets wealth at liberty and allows all things to follow their inclinations arbitrarily until they arrive at some result which society must adapt to in a spontaneous way . . . the other maintains: there is no way except for us to interfere violently, uproot everything and then reshape it all even though it be contrary to the nature of man such as is done in communism. . . . Thus, the world is not led to the true path. We have the true path . . . it was present before communism and before capitalism. America is only a century old, whereas these words have been present with us for more than a thousand years. The rights of man existed among us before the American society was formed. When we articulated the rights of man, the American continent was devoid of human life. Now they have been present for 100 years and have started bragging that they are the ones who have fashioned the rights of man . . . also the communist revolution of 1917 is of very recent vintage.

We are a people with authentic roots set deep in history, and the truths about which we speak were present before the formation of American society which leads capitalism, and present before Marxist philosophy, the philosophy of the communists who lead communist society. These truths were present before they were, and we call these truths the first theory and the last theory. Because of this, we call it "the third theory" in the sense that we have here a third thing which may be the first, in fact, is the first, and also the last.

But in the vast struggle between the other two systems, this authentic system marking out the middle way was lost sight of. We see that all civilizations have ended in doubt. The offspring of non-Islamic civilizations brought man to the world of doubt; all of them ended in doubt. Islamic civilization is the only one that brought man to certainty and faith. This subject is extremely important, if only the perplexed generations in the East and West today would come to recognize this. . . . Here is a civilization that leads to faith and to certainty, quite the contrary of the civilizations which led man to doubt. Decidedly man by nature does not want to live in doubt; it is inevitable that he search for the path that will lead him to faith and certainty. Islamic civilization is the one which leads to this result. All other civilizations lead to doubt.

MICHEL AFLĀQ
1910–1989

After obtaining a licentiate in history at the Sorbonne, he taught
in Damascus. In 1940 he joined with Salāh al-Dīn Bitār to form
the Ba'th (Resurrection) Party. He was Minister of Education
in 1949 and in 1956 fused his party with the Socialist party of
Akram Hourani to form the Arab Ba'th Socialist party, which
ruled in Syria and Iraq. He was expelled from the party in Syria
in 1966 but remained in favor with the Iraqi branch.

The Arab Personality
Between Past and Present

We are faced with the fact that our glorious past has been cut off from or
rather is in contradiction to our shameful present. The Arab personality was
a unified whole. There was no difference between its spirit and thought, its
words and action, its specific and general morality. . . .

Now is the time for us to remove this contradiction and to restore unity
to our Arab personality and wholeness to our Arab life. . . .

Our affiliation with our heroic forebears has been mere formalism,
nothing more, and our modern history has had no organic relation with our
glorious past but has fed on it like a parasite. Today we must resurrect
our specific characteristics and act in a manner which will justify our official
lineage and demonstrate our legitimacy. In as far as we are able we must
root out stagnation and decline so that our glorious, authentic blood will
flow back into our veins. . . .

The movement of Islam represented in the life of the Prophet was no
mere historical event for the Arab. True, it can be described by time and
place, cause and effect; but because of its profundity, its ardor and its
breadth, it was directly tied to the life of the Arabs. It gives a true picture
and stands as complete eternal symbol of the nature of the Arab soul with
all its rich possibilities and its authentic bent. Accordingly, we are correct
in considering that it is continually capable of renewal in spirit, not in form
or letter. Islam is the vibrant convulsion which shook the forces latent in
the Arab *umma* and mobilized them in a surge of life which rocked the barriers of tradition and the bonds of convention to reestablish its connection
with the profound sense of being. The *umma* was gripped by fervor and a

From *Dhikrā-l-Rasūl al-'Arabī* [In remembrance of the Arab prophet] (Beirut: Arab
Foundation 1972), pp. 5–24.

sense of wonder which it expressed in new syllables and in magnificent works. It was no longer capable of keeping within its bounds; its thoughts and actions flowed out to other nations, and thus it became all-enveloping. The Arabs, then, by means of this crucial moral experience know how to rebel against their own reality and to divide in order to go beyond themselves to a stage in which a higher unity is achieved. In it they tested their souls in order to uncover their potential and strengthen their virtues. Whatever fruit Islam later bore in conquests and civilization was already present seminally in the first twenty years of its mission (ba'tha). Before the Arabs conquered the earth, they conquered themselves; they sounded their depths and tested their inner self. Before they ruled nations, they ruled themselves; they dominated their passions and mastered their will. The sciences they developed, the arts they created, the civilization ('umrān) they raised up were nothing, but the partial, material, limited realization of the powerful, all-embracing dream they lived in those years with all its strength—nothing but a faint echo of that heavenly voice they heard, a pale shadow of that enchanting vision they saw the day that the angels fought in their ranks and paradise flashed off their swords.

This experience is not an historical event remembered with pride for the moral it holds, rather it is a permanent predisposition of the Arab *umma*—if Islam is correctly understood. This *umma* arises every time matter dominates spirit and outward forms weight on its essence. Then it divides within itself to reach a higher unity and a sound harmony. . . .

The life of the prophet mirrors the Arab soul in its absolute reality, but this reality cannot be grasped by the mind; it is known only by living experience. . . .

Until now we have been looking at the life of the Prophet from the outside, as a marvelous picture held up for our admiration and reverence. We must begin to look at it from within in order to give it life. Every Arab at the present time can enliven the life of the Arab Prophet . . . as long as he is affiliated with the *umma* which mobilized all its forces to give birth to Muhammad, or more exactly, as long as this man is an individual of this *umma* which Muhammad mobilized all his forces to bring forth. In a past time the life of a whole *umma* was epitomized in one man; today the life of this *umma* in its new renaissance must become a detailed exposition of the life of its greatest man. Muhammad was all the Arabs, so let all the Arabs today be Muhammad.

The dazzling truth, which only the stubborn would deny, is that the Arabs were chosen to bring the message of Islam because of their basic characteristics and virtues, and the choice of the era for the appearance of Islam was due to the fact that the Arabs had matured and were in a perfect state for receiving a message like this and carrying it to mankind. The triumph of Islam was postponed for all those years so that the Arabs could arrive at the truth by their own proper effort. This truth would be the result of their experience of themselves and the world, tempered by hardship and sorrow, despair and hope, failure and victory. In other words, in order that faith would spring from the depths of their souls, thus true faith would be blended with experience and be rooted in the marrow of life. Islam, then, was an Arab movement. Its meaning was the renewal and perfection of Arabism. The language in which it was revealed was Arabic, its comprehension of things was filtered through the Arab intellect. The virtues it strengthened were Arab virtues, explicit or latent. The faults it fought against were Arab faults already on the way to extinction. The Muslim at that time was nothing but an Arab, but he was a new Arab, evolved and perfected. Today we label many individuals of the *umma* "patriot" or "nationalist"—though all the *umma* should be "nationalist." We use this term to characterize the group who believe in their country because they possess the qualities and virtues necessary to make them conscious of their deep affiliation to their *umma* and ready to bear the consequent responsibilty. The Muslim was the Arab who believed in the new religion because he had the qualities and virtues necessary to understand that this religion represented the leap of Arabism to unity, power, and progress.

But does this mean that Islam should be limited to the Arabs? To say this would be to stray from the truth and contradict reality. Every great nation, with profound ties to the eternal sense of being, is oriented from its inception to all-embracing immortal values. Islam is the most eloquent expression of the orientation of the Arab *umma* to immortality and comprehensiveness. In its reality it is Arabic and in its ideal goals it is human. The message of Islam is the creation of Arab humanity.

The Arabs are singled out from other nations by this characteristic: their national consciousness is joined to a religious message; or more precisely this message is an eloquent expression of that national consciousness. They did not expand for the purpose of expansion nor did they conquer countries and rule for merely economic motives, for reasons of race or for the desire of dominating and subjugating . . . but to fulfill a religious duty which was truth, guidance, mercy, justice, and sacrifice. They shed their blood for this and counted their sacrifice trivial as they went forward rejoicing in the face of God. As long as the tie between Arabism and Islam remains strong and as long as we see in Arabism a body whose soul is Islam, there is no reason to fear that the Arabs will go to extremes in their nationalism. It will never attain the fanaticism of injustice and colonialism. . . .

Naturally, the Arabs cannot fulfill this duty unless they are a strong, active nation because Islam can be personified only in an Arab nation with its authentic virtues, morals and talents. Accordingly the first duty imposed by the humanism of Islam is that the Arabs be strong and sovereign in their lands.

Islam is universal and immortal, but its universality does not mean that it expands once for all to embrace various concepts and currents. Rather, in every critical period of history and at every decisive stage of development, it expresses one of the infinite concepts concealed within it since the beginning. Its immortality does not mean that it is frozen so that no change or transformation overtakes it or that life passes over it leaving it untouched. Rather, it means that despite its continuous changing—it discards garments which wear thin and sloughs off old skins—its roots remain one and the same, and its ability to grow, generate, and create is one and the same. It is never deficient; it is never ephemeral. It relates to specific times and places with absolute meaning and action, within the limits of this time and this place.

Do these zealots who want to make Islam a knapsack which includes everything, a factory producing various vehicles and medicines, do they understand that instead of proving its force and guarding its basic charism from every extraneous change, they annihilate its spirit and its personality and make it lose its vital, independent characteristics? And from another angle, they smooth the way for propagandists of injustice and masters of despotic rule. In their attempt to arm themselves with Islam, they discredit the very matter of Islam, that is, the Arab nation.

Therefore, the meaning that Islam expresses in this critical period of history and at this decisive stage of development is that all efforts should be directed to strengthening and resuscitating the Arabs and that these efforts should be confined to the frame of Arab nationalism.

The Arabs' connection with the West is commonly traced back to Bonaparte's campaign against Egypt and symbolized by his act of hanging up verses from the Qur'ān beside a text of the "rights of man." Since that time, the Arabs (or the leaders spuriously converted to Arabism) have been pushing their new renaissance in this distorted direction. They contort themselves and warp the texts of their history and the Qur'ān to show that not only is there no difference between the principles of their civilization and creed and those of Western civilization, but they, in fact, preceded the Westerners in their declaration and application of the same. This means only one thing: they stand as accused before the West, affirming the soundness and superiority of Western values. . . . Before long they pushed this logic to its conclusion by admitting that with European civilization they had no need of their own. The ruse of European colonialism was not that it led the Arab mind to acknowledge immortal principles and concepts; it had acknowledged them and adopted them as its base from the beginning. The ruse was in seizing on the inertia and creative incapacity of the Arabs to force them to adopt the peculiar European content of these concepts. We have no argument with the Europeans about the principle of freedom, but we contest their assumption that they alone are the purveyors of true freedom.

Europe today, as in the past, fears Islam, but it knows now that the force of Islam (which formerly expressed the force of the Arabs) has revived and appears in a new form which is Arab nationalism. For this reason Europe turns all its weapons against this new force while it befriends and aids the old form of Islam. International Islam, which is limited to superficial worship and pale general themes, is about to be Europeanized.

The day will come when the nationalists will find themselves the sole defenders of Islam, and they will be forced to breathe into its proper meaning if they want the Arab nation to remain the sound basis for survival.

The modern Arab mind has been infiltrated by two European notions of nationalism and humanism which are false and present a grave danger. The notion of abstract nationalism in the West is logical; Westerners decided to separate nationalism from religion, since religion having entered Europe from without was foreign to its nature and its history. Religion was a distillation of the creed and morals of the hereafter; it was not revealed in their national languages, it did not express the needs of their milieu, nor was it woven into their history. Whereas Islam, in relation to the Arabs, is not merely a creed of the hereafter nor is it mere morals, it is of this world, expressing their universal feelings and their view of life; it is the strongest expression of the unity of their personality. . . . Over and above that, it is the image of their language and literature and the most weighty part of their national history. We cannot sing of any one of our immortal heroes merely as Arab while neglecting or avoiding his quality as a Muslim. The relation of Islam to Arabism is not like the relation of a religion to any nationalism. The Christian Arabs will know, once their nationalism has fully awakened within them and their authentic nature has returned, that Islam is their national culture. They must fill themselves with it until they understand it and love it. Then they will guard Islam as they guard the most precious thing in their Arabism. Since reality remains far from this aspiration, the new generation of Arab Christians has the task of realizing it with daring and freedom, sacrificing its pride and advantages, since nothing is equal to Arabism and the honor of being affiliated to it.

The second danger is the European notion of abstract humanity; it leads in the last analysis to considering peoples as blocs of static, homogeneous humanity with no roots in the earth, unaffected by time. Consequently, it is possible to apply to any one of these groups the reforms and alternatives which developed to meet the needs and dispositions of another. . . .

It is not enough that theories and reforms be intelligible in themselves; they must spring in a vital way from the general spirit which was their source and origin. Today some think that bringing various reforms into the Arab milieu will suffice to revivify the nation. We think this attitude is another indication of our decline because it is content to mirror others and puts the branch in place of the root and the effect in place of the cause. The fact is that these reforms are branches which must spring from a root as blossoms flower on trees, and this root is above all psychological. It is the nation's faith in its mission and the faith of its sons in it.

From the preceding, it is clear why we attach all our concern to profound and alert national feelings. They are the root because they alone guarantee that social reforms will be vibrant, effective and courageous and in harmony with the spirit and the needs of the people, who will accomplish them because they want them.

We celebrate the memory of the hero of Arabism and Islam. What is Islam if not the offspring of pains, the pains of Arabism. These pains have returned to the land of the Arabs to a degree more excruciating and deeper than the Arabs of the *jāhiliyya* (pre-Islamic period) ever knew. How appropriate it would be if there welled up in us today a purifying formative revolution like that whose banner was borne by Islam. It is only the new Arab generation that can assume the revolution; they appreciate its necessity because the pains of the present have prepared them to carry its standard. Their love of their land and their history have led them to know the spirit of revolution and the direction it must take.

We, the new Arab generation, have a mission not a policy; we have faith and creed not theories and words. That band of Shuʿūbīyya[1] supported by foreign weapons, moved by racial envy against Arabism, do not frighten us because God and the nature of history are with us. . . . No one understands us except those who believe in God. We may not be seen praying with those who pray or fasting with those who fast, but we believe in God because we have a pressing need for him. Our burden is heavy, our road is rough and our goal is distant. We arrived at this faith, we did not begin with it. . . . I do not reckon that an Arab youth who is conscious of the corruption deeply embeded in his nation and who appreciates the dangers surrounding the future of Arabism . . . can dispense with faith in God. That is, faith in the right, the inevitable victory of right and the necessity of striving so that right may be victorious.

---

1. *Shuʿūbīyya*: the *Shuʿūbīyya* were the anti-Arab Muslims, or Persianizers, of the eighth and ninth centuries who vaunted Persian values and belittled Arab culture.

SADIQ AL-'AZM
1936–

The descendent of a prominent Syrian political family and graduate of American University of Beirut, he holds a Ph.D. in philosophy from Yale University. His Marxist criticism of religious thought published in 1970 caused a scandal. He was brought to trial in Beirut in the same year on charges of provoking religious troubles but was acquitted.

A Criticism of Religious Thought

Even before the defeat of 1967, the Arab liberation movement knew that Arab reactionaries and their international allies were using religious thought as an ideological weapon, and yet no great importance was attached to this fact. Apparently no one saw the necessity of disarming the reactionaries by exposing their thought to a critical, scientific analysis to reveal the forgeries they employ to exploit the Arab man. In fact, the political and intellectual leaders of the Arab liberation movement espoused a negative attitude which abetted the conservative position inasmuch as they refrained from any criticism of the Arab intellectual and social heritage and refused to seek out ways of effecting change at the higher levels corresponding to the changes which had occurred in the composition of the society's infrastructure. The Arab liberation movement considered the cultural superstructure worthy of respect and veneration. It surrounded retarded mental habits, bedouin and feudal values, backward human relations, and obscurantist, quietistic world views with an aura of sacredness which put them outside the pale of scientific criticism and historical analysis. . . .

The fact is that the Arab liberation movement changed some of the economic and social conditions of the Arab man but, at the same time, placed all sorts of obstacles on the path leading to parallel changes in the intellect and conscience of the Arab man, which would aid his "view of himself, of life and the world to evolve". . . . To put it another way, the Arab liberation movement stood "on its head rather than on its feet". . . in the sense that it wanted to put the revolutionary economic and social changes it introduced and its use of modern science and technology at the service of existing social relations and class divisions. . . . This posture found expression in the cultural policies of the Arab liberation movement such as its superficial but conservative preoccupation with the religious heritage,

From *Naqd al-Fikr al-Dīnī* [A criticism of religious thought] (Beirut: Dār al-Talī'ah, 1970), pp. 10–13, 20–25, 26–31, 40–43, 45–51, 57–58, 60–62, 64–69, 76–78.

traditions, values, and thought, which, of course, impeded the hoped for changes in the Arab man. . . . Under the cover of protecting the people's traditions, values, art, religion, and morals, the cultural effort of the Arab liberation movement was used to protect the backward institutions and the medieval culture and thought of obscurantist ideology. . . .

In our view, the old religious position, full of serenity and optimism, is collapsing completely. We are passing through a stage of real renaissance marked by a complete scientific and cultural upheaval and a radical industrial and socialist transformation. We have been affected by the two most important books of the last two centuries: *Capitalism* and *The Origin of the Species*. The corpse of traditional feudal society has been shredded by the machine, and its bones have crumbled under the weight of modern economic and social organization, and with it has passed the fateful, positive attitude toward religion and its problems.

In this frantic atmosphere two problems loom large, the first is of a general cultural and ideological nature—the problem of the struggle between science and religion (Islam, for us). The second is a special problem, which is the concern of everyone radically affected by the scientific culture, which has begun to flood his society and milieu and forces him to face up to a basic question: "Can I accept in all honesty and sincerity the religious tenets my father and grandfathers accepted without betraying the principle of intellectual integrity?" . . .

There is a widely accepted opinion claiming that the struggle between science and religion is only apparent and that the difference between scientific knowledge of religious creeds is merely superficial. The propagandists of this opinion also claim that the spirit of Islam, for example, cannot conflict with science and that apparent conflicts are between science and the extraneous silt of the ages which has buried the true spirit. I would like to expand a bit to clarify this opinion, criticize it and explain the opposite viewpoint, to show that religion as it enters the core of our life and affects our intellectual and psychological makeup is in opposition to science and scientific knowledge—heart and soul, literally and figuratively.

First, we should not forget that more than two-and-a-half centuries passed in Europe before science was decisively victorious in its long war against the religious mentality which was dominant on that continent and before it established itself definitively in its cultural heritage. Science is still fighting a similar war in developing countries, including the Arab homeland, even though the battle is hidden and its lineaments are only occasionally apparent to all.

Second, the Islamic religion comprises opinions and tenets on the growth, composition, and nature of the universe, on the origin, history, and life of man through the ages which form an inseparable part of the religion. It is not necessary to emphasize that these opinions and tenets are clearly in opposition to our scientific information on these subjects. But contradictions between religion and science concerning their convictions on a limited subject is not very important. The conflict and struggle go much deeper than that when they touch the problem of the methodology which must be adopted to arrive at our convictions and knowledge in the subjects mentioned. It is a question of the way we must follow to be certain of the truth or falsehood of these convictions. Islam and science in this matter are on contradictory paths. For the Islamic religion (as for other religions) the correct methodology for arriving at knowledge and conviction is to return to specified texts considered as sacred or revealed, or to go back to the writings of the sages and the learned who studied and explained these texts. That is, the justification of the whole operation is reduced to faith and blind trust in the wisdom at the source of these texts and their freedom from error. It goes without saying that the scientific path to arrive at knowledge and conviction concerning the growth and nature of the universe and man and his history is completely incompatible with this subservient methodology which dominates religion because scientific methodology rests on observation and deduction and because the unique justification for the soundness of the results arrived at by this methodology is the degree of its internal logical harmony and its conformity with reality.

Third, among the essential things that the Islamic religion insists on is that all basic truths that touch the core of man's life and all knowledge connected with his destiny in this life and the next were uncovered at one specific and decisive moment in history (the revelation of the Qur'ān and perhaps the other books before it). For this reason we find the gaze of believers always directed backwards to that time in which they believe these truths and this knowledge were uncovered by God through angels and messengers. The result is that the function of the believer, sage, philosopher, and learned man is not to discover new essential truths or gain important knowledge not known previously but only to work for a more profound view and more comprehensive grasp of the revealed texts. The scientific spirit is far removed from the logic of this religious view because science does not acknowledge the existence of texts which are impervious to objective criticism and serious study and because the most outstanding characteristic of scientific thought is discovery. . . . But religion from the nature of its firm, stable, and limited beliefs lives in eternal verities and looks backwards seeking inspiration from its infancy. For this reason religion has always formed a metaphysical obscurantist justification for the social, economic, and political status quo. It has always been and is still a strong fortress against those who exert effort for a revolutionary change of these conditions. . . .

There is a resemblance between religion and science in that both attempt to explain events and define causes. Religion is an imaginative substitute for science. But the problem arises when religion claims for itself and its beliefs a type of veracity which no imaginative substitute is capable of claiming. The attempt to efface the features of the struggle between religion and science is nothing but a hopeless effort to defend religion. It is resorted to every time religion is forced to concede a traditional position and every time it is forced to withdraw from a center it formerly held. . . .

Now we turn to what we called our particular problem. The question around which our study will center can be summarized as follows: what should be the position of a man who has been exposed to scientific culture and has been radically affected by it vis-à-vis traditional religious beliefs and the institutions in which they are embodied? Can this man continue to believe in Adam and Eve, hell and heaven, that Moses divided the Red Sea and turned his rod into a serpent? What can be the position of a man who had a religious upbringing and accepted it lock, stock, and barrel vis-à-vis the natural scientific view of life, the universe, and man? It is difficult to find among us a person enjoying a bit of sensitivity and even a modest share of intelligence and scientific education who does not feel at some stage of his life and development the anxiety which surrounds this question and the worry it provokes. The intellectual and psychological state which this question expresses has become a basic part of our makeup; sometimes it floats on the surface of consciousness and we feel its existence strongly; at other times it is buried deep within us where it affects our conduct and thought in hidden ways. In any case it is always active. . . .

VARIOUS EXPLANATIONS CONCERNING
SCIENCE AND RELIGION

The First Solution: Concordism. Among the sayings repeated by "concordist" speakers to confirm their claim that there is no conflict between religion and science is the Prophetic Tradition saying, "Seek science even if it is in China," and numerous well-known Qur'ānic verses which encourage man to think and meditate on things and to seek science and knowledge, etc. They attempt to demonstrate that Islam's concern for science and intellect extends back to its beginning. Naturally these thinkers attribute an absolute sense to these Islamic phrases. They speak as if these phrases belong to no time or place and can be separated from the historical context and the circumstances which gave them meaning and import at the time. It is clear to us that the science which Islam encourages one to seek is essentially religious and legal science and what is associated with it, and not physics and chemistry, for example. The intellect which Islam encourages man to use seeks knowledge of God by meditating on what he has created as did Hayy ibn Yaqzān in the story of Ibn Tufayl. The aim is not the formation of the dialectical theory of matter or the theory of Durkheim on religious customs and worship, or a theory of a convex universe. Islam is not at fault for that. At that time religious sciences were regarded as the most lofty and weighty, the extreme limit sought by anyone seeking science.

In this regard it should be remarked that the vast majority of these "concordists" know only very little about modern science, its methods of research, and what we may call the "scientific soul" or the "scientific spirit." However, they stand perplexed and breathless before the achievements of science and its practical applications. They are forced to respond to its effects in their everyday life and for this reason find that they can do nothing but announce perfect harmony and complete concord between their Islam and this great force. Therefore, Islam and modern science are harmonious and concordant in everything! No wonder then that they fall into strange contradictions. . . .

This type of thought declaring concord between Islam and contemporary life is concerned with justifying the social and political conditions which exist, no matter what they may be, on the basis of their complete harmony with the pure religion, its doctrines and law. The religious men of Islam supervise this operation defending the *status quo* and its personalities and policies. They put all their effort into laying a veneer of Islamic law over the political and social order, no matter what it may be, with which they are associated.

We find that every Arab system of government, no matter what its color, is not lacking esteemed Islamic institutions ready to issue *fatwās*[1] declaring that its policy is in complete harmony with Islam and contradicts it in nothing. There is no need to point out that the Islamic institutions in each state amass Qur'ānic verses, prophetic traditions, and legal opinions to demonstrate that the position of the given state is truth itself. . . .

Also, this methodology of concord between Islam and modern science is epitomized in the derivation of all modern sciences, theories and methodologies from verses of the Qur'ān. It is an arbitrary and ridiculous exercise of cramming every bit of modern science, great and small, into verses of the Qur'ān, then claiming that the Qur'ān contained all science from the beginning. In other words, the proponents of this current lie in wait for every new scientific theory and every scientific discovery, then exert themselves to find a verse in the Qur'ān claiming that it contained the theory and the discovery for fourteen centuries if not forever. . . .

The Second Solution: The complete rejection of scientific theory and all the ideas and opinions it contains, and complete enclosure within the religious view to defend it unto death. In fact it is very difficult to take this view either individually or as a group because in its most extreme form it is a kind of intellectual suicide, and in its moderate form it leads to a progressive cleavage between man and the world around him. It is a type of escape that saves man from the effort of facing up to truths that do not harmonize with his own emotional, intellectual, and religious makeup. If he cannot bear this contradiction between his inner world and the world which surrounds him, then he will manifest the symptoms of the disease: complete nervous collapse or a type of general paralysis preventing any

---

1. *fatwā*: a formal legal opinion given by a jurist (*muftī*) on a legal problem submitted to him either by an individual or a judge.

productive or frutiful work. He is hypersensitive to the burden which the religious heritage and the culture of the past place on him, and he is unable to adapt to the new conditions surrounding him. . . .

The Third Solution: Distinguishing between the temporal and the eternal or spiritual dimensions of religion by saying that all that we find in religion concerning nature and history, etc., is included under the temporal dimension, which can be ceded completely to science. The spiritual dimension, however, has absolutely no connection with science; it is the area of eternal truths, hidden things, faith, and mystical experience. The proponents of this current say that scientific method and knowledge do not go beyond the scope of nature and for that reason it is not easy for them to investigate religious beliefs which are supported by pure faith not by intellectual argument nor by science and its proofs. In other words the propagandists for this opinion say that religious knowledge differs specifically from scientific and intellectual knowledge. For this reason we always fail when we try to apply logic to religious knowledge. It always appears to contradict logic and to be incompatible with the scientific mentality because this special kind of knowledge is the result of mystical experience or of the leap of pure faith or something similar.

The question which confronts me is this: Is it possible for me, a son of this century and a stepson of its civilization and science, to believe with the faith of miracles what appears to me with certainty to be in clear contradiction with science, knowing that my faith, or lack of it, will never change the pitch of this contradiction or diminish it? If I accept this clear contradiction, what prevents me from accepting all other contradictions which I find in all religions and fables and stories? This claim for naive acceptance of matters which appear contradictory to the intellect opens wide the door to things that modern science has struggled for long years to eradicate from the intellect of man. Every attempt to reinstate them ruins scientific values and confounds objective methodology and its application for the solution of the great and difficult problems of man. . . .

The Fourth and Final Solution. Now we will proceed to the solution which William James presented in the article . . . "The Will to Believe." In that article James establishes a general principle for verifying the opinions and judgments presented to us. It is this: we cannot accept or reject any opinion as long as sufficient indications and testimonies to its truth or falsehood are not present. As long as these conditions are not met, we must suspend judgment. Likewise, the force with which we defend any given opinion we hold should be proportionate to the strength of the arguments supporting it and the number of signs indicating its correctness. There is no doubt that this principle enunciates a noble ideal which man can realize only to a certain degree, no matter how intelligent or how free he may be from fanaticism and passion in forming his studied opinions on the various subjects of life. . . . James asks if there are various cases in which a man is right in affirming a matter despite the clear lack of indications and confirmation of its truth or falsehood. He answers that religious belief or faith in the existence of God is one of these cases. According to James the person who faces the difficult choice between belief in the existence of God or lack of belief will never find any intellectual confirmation or scientific demonstration proving God's existence or non-existence. Here James confirms the right of this man to believe in the existence of God relying on what his emotional nature indicates about this subject. . . . But the question which comes to our mind is, why do we give the question of religion this preference and privilege to the point of excepting it from the comprehensive moral principle which governs the operation and content of certainty? . . . Harmonizing our opinions with our emotional nature cannot form acceptable justification for our belief in these opinions, not if we wish to have studied opinions rather than merely inherited views. . . .

This does not mean that I want to invalidate religious feelings in man's experience of existence, but I think it is necessary to distinguish religion from religious feeling. Those feelings ground down by the burden of petrified traditional religious beliefs and the weight of frozen rites and rituals must be freed from their prison so that they may flower and express themselves by ways and means appropriate to our conditions of life in twentieth century civilization. For this reason we must renounce the traditional notion stating that existence is a special religious truth, and we must direct our concern towards religious feelings liberated from these weights and burdens. Likewise it seems to me that it is not necessary to attach religious feelings to hidden beings, concealed existences and strange forces as was always done. These feelings constitute a property which can shape all our other feelings, thoughts and goals. We can look to these feelings to bring order, harmony and assurance to our view towards the changing events of life. In this sense, religious feelings may be represented in the artist's view of beauty, or in the scientist's search for truth, or in the militant's conception of the goals he works to achieve, or in the view of the common man towards fulfilling the daily duties of life.

MUSTAFĀ SIBĀʿĪ
1915–1964

He was head of the Syrian branch of the Muslim Brothers and editor of their publications, *al-Manār* (Damascus) and *al-Muslimīn*. He studied at al-Azhar University and later taught at Damascus University where he became Dean of the Sharia College. In 1949 he was elected to the Syrian parliament.

Islamic Socialism

Islamic socialism rests on five fundamental rights that must be guaranteed to all its citizens:

1. The right to live and, as its corollary, the safeguarding and protection of health and illness.
2. The right to liberty in all its forms, and particularly to political liberty.
3. The right to knowledge: This right extends to all the knowledge the nation needs, both spiritual and material.
4. The right to dignity, in all its aspects.
5. The right to property, subject to certain conditions.

I have also mentioned in my book the most important principles on which property is based in Islam:

1. Work—the most important way of acquiring property. All work leads to possession; it is legal if it involves neither fraud nor injustice.
2. Private property is an indefeasible right. The state guarantees it and punishes those who interfere with it.
3. Property is a social function; the state forbids its utilization as a means of oppression and exploitation.
4. Wealth involves social duties: legitimate charity, pensions for relatives, mutual social aid.
5. Inheritance is a legitimate right protected by the state.

Nationalization can be applied to goods and articles necessary to society only if their possession by one or several individuals involves the

From Kemal H. Karpat, ed. *Political and Social Thought in the Contemporary Middle East* (New York: Praeger, 1968), pp. 123–26.

exploitation of society, on condition also that economic experts agree that it is in the obvious interest of the nation.

Henceforth, when the state has recourse to nationalization in cases of social or economic necessity, it is obliged to afford adequate compensation to the dispossessed proprietors.

The principles of Islam, our social situation, and the obligation placed upon us by our religion to wipe out oppression and give human dignity to the peasants—all this renders the limitation of landed property legal in the eyes of the law and makes it one of the duties of the state. Nevertheless, it must be applied in all fairness and in conformity to the general interest, and not merely to satisfy rancor and vengeance.

Moreover, the seizure of private goods should be carried out only under certain conditions, especially in cases of extreme danger, invasion, public disaster, famine, flood, or earthquake. Only if the state treasury and the funds held by the authorities are inadequate to guard against any danger is it lawful to deduct from people's wealth what is strictly necessary to meet such necessity, as proclaimed by the 'ulamā' of Islam, such as al-Nawāwī, al-Ghazzālī, etc.

I have then cited the rules of mutual social aid. Numbering twenty-nine, they guarantee the fulfillment by the state of this obligation vis-à-vis its subjects, thus assuring them as well as their children a decent life in case of incapacity, illness, or unemployment.

Briefly summarized, such is the conception of Islamic socialism that I have set out in my book. I have then compared it with the socialism of the extreme left.

1. In recognizing the lawful character of private property, Islamic socialism allows those with talent to participate in constructive competition, an essential condition for the expansion of civilization and the development of production.

2. This socialism encourages and leads to cooperation and friendship, not to class struggle.

3. It is a moral socialism based on sound morals, of which it makes a foundation in its doctrine.

4. All that concerns man comes under the care of this socialism: religion, morals, education, clothing, food, and not only the material aspects of life.

5. It is an integral part of the credo of the Muslim, who can but apply it. It constitutes a more rapid and more effectual method than any other socialism for the reform of our society.

As for the socialism of extreme left, this is what I wrote: "Its roots are not in the depths of the human soul; it is not based upon religion or human nature or conviction. It cannot therefore be applied except by force and in an atmosphere of terror."

Such are the aspects and characteristics of socialism in Islam. Without doubt, it is totally different from the type of socialism that attaches no importance to religious values, relies on the class struggle in society, seizes private property without good reason, nationalizes industry and economic concerns that contribute to the national economic prosperity, paralyzes initiative and competition in the individual as well as the community, impoverishes the rich without enriching the poor, originates from hate and not from love, claims to work for the people while it terrorizes them, impoverishes them, and humiliates them. A socialism of this kind is as far removed as possible from Islam and has nothing in common with it. Moreover, Islam foresees in it the inevitable ruin of any society where it reigns and exercises influence.

Finally, since our revolutionary order [the Syrian revolution] and our government have agreed on socialism as a social regime, and since they have published a detailed program which is in no way contrary to Islam, it is good—and I say this in all sincerity and frankness—that the cause of Islamic socialism should be encouraged, because of its profound influence on the minds of the masses and its facility for building a worthwhile society, unique and advanced in its economy and its social relations. It is also desirable that this socialism should be embraced by every zealous defender of our nation who is anxious to avert the danger of extreme left-wing socialism.

In fact, Islamic socialism conforms to human nature. It satisfies the dignity of all citizens as well as their interests. To the workers, it grants a decent standard of living and an assured future; to the holder of capital, it opens up wide horizons as regards production under state control. Finally, it applies to all citizens without discrimination, and is not the prerogative of the followers of one religion to the exclusion of those of another.

SAYYID QUTB
1906–1966

Son of a landowner, he completed secondary and college studies
in Cairo, obtaining a licentiate in Arabic language and literature
from Dār al-ʿUlūm. After a brief tenure as an inspector in the
Ministry of Education, he left to devote himself to writing. In
1939 he turned to more religious writing. In 1948 he published
Social Justice in Islam and then spent two years in the United
States studying educational organization. On his return to Egypt
he joined the Muslim Brothers. He spent ten years in prison under
Nāsir; he was freed in 1964, only to be imprisoned again and
executed in 1966 on suspicion of plotting against the government.

Social Justice in Islam

Islam grew up in an independent country owing allegiance to no empire and
to no king, in a form of society never again achieved. It had to embody this
society in itself, had to order, encourage, and promote it. It had to order
and regulate this society, adopting from the beginning its principles and its
spirit along with its methods of life and work. It had to join together the
world and the faith by its exhortations and laws. So Islam chose to unite
earth and Heaven in one spiritual organization, and one that recognized no
difference between worldly zeal and religious coercion. Essentially Islam
never infringes that unity even when its outward forms and customs change.
. . . One of the characteristic marks of this faith is the fact that it is essentially a unity. It is at once worship and work, religious law and exhortation. Its theological beliefs are not divorced in nature or in objective from
secular life and customs. . . . However we approach the question, there can
be no shadow of doubt that the theory of society is obviously reflected in
the beliefs and the customs of this religion, and that these latter represent
the basic, powerful, and universal theory of all social life. So if in any age
we find a desire to over-emphasize the pietistic aspect of this faith and to
divorce it from the social aspect, or to divorce the social aspect from it, it
will be the fault of that age rather than that of Islam. . . .

We have, then, not a single reason to make any separation between
Islam and society, either from the point of view of the essential nature of
Islam, or from that of its historical course; such reasons as there are attach
only to European Christianity. And yet the world has grown away from

From *Social Justice in Islam*, trans. John B. Hardie (Washington, D.C.: American Council of
Learned Societies, 1953/Octagon Books reprint, 1970), pp. 7–9, 13–16, 24–28.

religion; to it the world has left only the education of the conscience and the perfecting of piety, while to the temporal and secular laws has been committed the ordering of society and the organizing of human life.

Similarly we have no good grounds for any hostility between Islam and the thought of social justice, such as the hostility that persists between Christianity and Communism. For Islam prescribes the basic principles of social justice, and establishes the claim of the poor to the wealth of the rich; it lays down a just principle for power and for money, and therefore has no need to drug the minds of men, and summon them to neglect their earthly rights in favor of their expectations in Heaven. On the contrary, it warns those who abdicate their natural rights that they will be severely punished in the next world, and it calls them "self-oppressors." "Surely the angels said to those who died when they were oppressing themselves, 'In what circumstances were you?' They answered, 'We were poor in the earth.' The angels said, 'Was not Allah's earth wide enough for you to migrate?' 'The abode of such is Hell—an evil place to go.'" Thus Islam urges men to fight for their rights; "and he who fights without injustice, the same is a martyr." So while Europe is compelled to put religion apart from the common life, we are not compelled to tread the same path; and while communism is compelled to oppose religion in order to safeguard the rights of the workers, we have no need of any such hostility to religion.

But can we be certain that this "two-in-one" social order which was established by Islam in one specific period of history will continue to have the potential for growth and renewal? Can we be sure that it is suitable for application to other periods of history whose circumstances differ to a greater or lesser degree from those which obtained in the age which gave birth to Islam?

This is a fundamental question. It is not possible to give an exhaustive answer to it here, as it will be answered in detail in what is to follow; first, we must examine this social order itself, define its sources and roots, and scrutinize its applications in everyday life. Suffice it here—for we are still in the stage of general discussion—to say that Islam has already experienced such an historical process, and the social, economic, and intellectual developments connected with it.

This process Islam has survived by laying down the general, universal rules and principles, and leaving their application in detail to be determined by the processes of time and by the emergence of individual problems. But Islam itself does not deal with the incidental related issues of the principle, except insofar as such are expressions of an unchanging principle whose impact is felt universally. This is the limit of the authority which can be claimed by a religion, in order that it may guarantee its flexibility and ensure the possibility of its own growth and expansion over a period of time. . . .

The conclusion from this is that we should not put away the social aspect of our faith on the shelf; we should not go to French legislation to derive our laws, or to communist ideals to derive our social order, without first examining what can be supplied from our Islamic legislation which was the foundation of our first form of society. But there is a wide ignorance of the nature of our faith; there is a spiritual and intellectual laziness which is opposed to a return to our former resources; there is a ridiculous servility to the European fashion of divorcing religion from life—a separation necessitated by the nature of their religion, but not by the nature of Islam. For with them there still exists that gulf between religion on the one hand and learning and the State on the other, the product of historical reasons which have no parallel in the history of Islam.

This does not mean that our summons is to an intellectual, spiritual, and social avoidance of the ways of the rest of the world; the spirit of Islam rejects such an avoidance, for Islam reckons itself to be a gospel for the whole world. Rather our summons is to return to our own stored-up resources, to become familiar with their ideas, and to proclaim their value and permanent worth, before we have recourse to an untimely servility which will deprive us of the historical background of our life, and through which our individuality will be lost to the point that we will become merely the hangers-on to the progress of mankind. Whereas our religion demands that we should be ever in the forefront: "You are the best nation which I have produced among men; you encourage what is approved of God, and you forbid what is disapproved." . . .

While we are examining this universal theory which takes its rise from the nature of Islamic thought about the world and life and humanity, we may study also the fundamental outlines of social justice in Islam. Above all other things it is a comprehensive human justice, and not merely an economic justice; that is to say, it embraces all sides of life and all aspects of freedom. It is concerned alike with the mind and the body, with the heart and the conscience. The values with which this justice deals are not only economic values, nor are they merely material values in general; rather they are a mixture of moral and spiritual values together. Christianity looks at man only from the stand-point of his spiritual desires and seeks to crush down the human instincts in order to encourage those desires. On the other hand Communism looks at man only from the standpoint of his material needs; it looks not only at human nature, but also at the world and at life from a purely material point of view. But Islam looks at man as forming a unity whose spiritual desires cannot be separated from his bodily appetites, and whose moral needs cannot be divorced from his material needs. It looks at the world and at life with this all-embracing view which permits of no separation or division. In this fact lies the main divergence between Communism, Christianity, and Islam.

Thus, in the Islamic view, life consists of mercy, love, help, and a mutual responsibility between Muslims in particular, and between all human beings in general. Whereas in the Communist view, life is a continual strife and struggle between the classes, a struggle which must end in one

class overcoming the other; at which point the Communist dream is realized. Hence it is patent that Islam is the undying goodness of humanity,
embodied in a living faith, working in the world; while communism is the
evil of human nature, limited to a single nation.

There are, then, these two great facts: the absolute, just, and coherent
unity of existence, and the general, mutual responsibility of individuals
and societies. On these two facts Islam bases its definition of social justice,
having regard to the basic elements of the nature of man, yet not unmindful of human abilities. . . .

Accordingly, when Islam comes to lay down its rules and laws, its
counsels and controls, that natural "love of gain" is not overlooked, nor
is that deep natural avarice forgotten; selfishness is rebuked, avarice is dealt
with by regulations and laws, and the duty laid on man is that of liberality. At the same time, Islam does not overlook the needs and the welfare of
society, nor does it forget the great achievements of individuals in life and
society in every age and among different nations, which is inconsistent with
justice, when the greed and cupidity of the individual prey upon society; or
that same oppression may also take the form of society preying upon the
nature and ability of the individual. Such oppression is a sin, not against
one individual alone, but against the whole principle of the community. It
is an encroachment upon the freedom of the individual whose natural rights
are infringed; but its evil effects do not touch merely the welfare and rights
of that one individual; they go beyond him to touch the welfare of the whole
community, because it cannot profit to the full from his abilities. So the
regulations lay down the rights of the community over the powers and
abilities of the individual; they also establish limiting boundaries to the freedom, the desires, and the wants of the individual, but they must also be ever
mindful of the rights of the individual, to give him freedom in his desires
and inclinations; and over all there must be the limits which the community must not overstep, and which the individual on his side must not
transgress. Nor must there be interference with great individual achievements; for life is a matter of mutual help and mutual responsibility according to Islam, and not a constant warfare, to be lived in a spirit of struggle
and hostility. Thus there must be freedom for individual and general
abilities, rather than repression and a restrictive constraint. Everything that
is not legally forbidden is perfectly permissible; and everything that is not
useless is of value. So the individual is to be encouraged by having every
freedom in a life which reflects the Divine nature and which gives promise
of the highest achievement.

This breadth of vision in the Islamic view of life, together with the fact
that it goes beyond merely economic values to those other values on which
life depends—these things make the Islamic faith the more powerful to
provide equity and justice in society, and to establish justice in the whole
of the human sphere. It also frees Islam from the narrow interpretation
of justice as understood by Communism. For justice to the Communist is

an equality of wages, in order to prevent economic discrimination; but within recent days when theory has come into opposition with practice, Communism has found itself unable to achieve this equality. Justice in Islam is a human equality, envisaging the adjustment of all values, of which the economic is but one.

In the Islamic view values are so very composite that justice must include all of them; therefore Islam does not demand a compulsory economic equality in the narrow literal sense of the term. This is against nature, and conflicts with the essential fact, which is that of the differing native endowments of individuals. It arrests the development of outstanding ability, and makes it equal to lesser ability; it prevents those who have great gifts from using their gifts to their own advantage and to that of the community, and it discourages the community and the individual from producing such gifts. . . .

Islam does, of course, acknowledge a fundamental equality of all men, and a fundamental justice among all, but over and above that it leaves the door open for achievement of preeminence through hard work, just as it lays in the balance values other than the economic. "Verily the noblest among you in Allah's eyes is the most pious." "Allah will raise up in degrees of honor those of you who believe, and to whom knowledge has been brought." "Wealth and children are an ornament to life in the world, but the things which endure, the works of righteousness are better in thy Lord's eyes—better for reward and better for hope." From this it is apparent that there are values other than the merely economic; with these values Islam reckons, and these it brings into relation with the idea of justice in society, since different individuals have different methods of gaining their livelihood. Islam admits the reasonable causes of these differences, as being differences in strength and in endowment. It does not admit differences that depend on rank and station; such it absolutely denies. . . .

Islam, then, does not demand a literal equality of wealth, because the distribution of wealth depends on men's endowments, which are not uniform. Hence absolute justice demands that men's rewards be similarly different, and that some have more than others—so long as human justice is upheld by the provision of equal opportunity for all. Thus rank or upbringing, origin or class should not stand in the way of any individual, nor should anyone be fettered by the chains that shackle enterprise. Justice must be upheld also by the inclusion of all kinds of values in the reckoning, and by the freeing of the human mind completely from the tyranny of the purely economic values, and by the relegation of these to their true and reasonable place. Economic values must not be given an intrinsically high standing, such as they enjoy in those human societies which lack a certainty of true values, or which give to them too slight an importance; in such conditions money alone becomes the supreme and fundamental value.

In Islam money is not given this value; Islam refuses to admit that life can be reckoned in terms of a mouthful of bread, the appetites of the body, or a handful of money. Yet at the same time it demands a competence for every individual, and at times more than a competence, in order to remove the fear of destitution. On the other side it forbids that unbridled luxury in possessions and desires, which produces social divisions and classes. It prescribes the claims of the poor upon the wealth of the rich, according to their needs, and according to the best interests of society, so that social life may be full, just, and productive. Thus it is not unmindful of any one of the various aspects of life, material, intellectual, religious and worldly; but it organizes them all, that they may be related together and thus furnish an all-embracing unity in which it will be difficult to neglect any one of their various integral parts. So these departments of life become an organized unity, similar to the great oneness of the universe, and to that of life, of the nation, and of all mankind.

THE NATIONAL CHARTER OF THE ALGERIAN
POPULAR DEMOCRATIC REPUBLIC
1976

The Algerian Charter, published July 5, 1976, as the highest source for national policy and state law, was drawn up by the Front for National Liberation, the sole political party in the country.

Islam and the Socialist Revolution

The Algerian people is a Muslim people.

Islam is the state religion.

As an integral part of our historic personality, Islam is one of our strongest defenses against all attempts at depersonalization. In the worst hours of colonial domination, the Algerian people, driven by a sense of justice and equality, entrenched themselves in a militant, austere Islam and drew from it that moral energy and that spiritual sense that preserved them from despair and allowed them to overcome.

The decline of the Muslim world cannot be explained by moral causes alone. Other factors of a material, economic, and social nature such as foreign invasions, internal struggles, the rise of despotism, the spread of feudal oppression and the disappearance of certain world trade routes played a determining role in this. Also, the rise of superstitions and the general preoccupation with the past should not be considered as causes but as effects. To concentrate attacks on aberrant practices while neglecting social conditioning is to fall into inefficacious moralism. As a matter of fact, the Muslim world has only one way out of its predicament to regeneration: it must go beyond reformism and commit itself to the path of social revolution.

Revolution fits easily into the historical perspective of Islam. Islam, if its spirit is correctly understood, is not tied to any particular interests, to no specific clergy, to no temporal power. Neither feudalism nor capitalism can claim it as their own. Islam brought to the world a lofty notion of human dignity which condemns racism, chauvinism, and the exploitation of man by man. Its fundamental egalitarianism can find an expression adapted to every epoch.

It behooves the Muslim people, whose destiny today is mingled with that of the Third World, to become aware of the positive aspects of their spiritual and cultural patrimony and to reassimilate them in the light of

From *Charte Nationale* (République Algérienne, 1976), pp. 21–22.

contemporary values and mutations. That is to say that every undertaking which aims at a reconstruction of Muslim thought today if it wishes to be credible, must necessarily refer to a much vaster undertaking: the total refashioning of society.

In our period of decisive social transformation, the Muslim peoples are called to shake off the anachronistic yoke of feudalism, despotism, and every form of obscurantism.

The Muslim peoples are coming to realize more fully that it is in re-inforcing their struggle against imperialism and in adopting resolutely the path of socialism that they respond best to the imperatives of their faith and make their action accord with its principles.

A. K. BROHI
1915–1987

A leading lawyer and statesman, A. K. Brohi held numerous posts in Pakistan's government, among them Minister of Law and Religious Affairs. He oversaw the establishment of the Sharī'a College in Islamabad.

The Concept of Islamic Socialism

One of the terms which nowdays so frequently appears in the daily Press, or is heard *ad nauseam* within the so-called intellectual circles, is that of *Islamic Socialism*. It is claimed that "Islamic Socialism" if we could only realise it as a practical possibility is a panacea for all our ills. Speaking for myself, I find much difficulty in understanding precisely what is meant by the concept of Islamic Socialism. The term "socialism" one can understand; and, to some extent, I suppose I understand what "Islam" is. But it is, if I am permitted to so put it, the spurious concoction of these two concepts which creates complications for the rational mind. The dilemma posed to normal human intelligence by this hybrid expression "Islamic Socialism" can be presented as follows: If "Socialism" is precisely what Islam enjoins us to accept, then Socialism by itself should be acceptable to us as our national ideology. If, however, it is not the conventional type of Socialism that Islam enjoins upon us to accept, then in what essential particulars, one may ask, has Islam modified this concept so that it must be designated as *Islamic Socialism* to distinguish it from its non-Islamic varieties. Why is the word "Islam," which is substantive, being degraded into becoming an adjective of "socialism" is a question that no one that I know of in this country can, consistently with logic, honestly answer. On the one hand we say (do we not?) that Islam provides a comprehensive code of life bearing upon questions related to the economic, political and social organisations of mankind; yet, on the other hand, we are called upon to say that there is an ideology called "Socialism" which is what we need provided we could somewhat modify it: thus it is said, not Islam simply, but Islamic Socialism will redeem us and will help us to organise our lives much more meaningfully than we are able to do so at present.

If Islam is a universal religion, that is to say, a way of life which is valid for all time, for all people, and for all geographical habitats, then why does it not also have an adequate answer to those specific economico-political

From *Islam in the Modern World* (Lahore: Publishers United Ltd.), pp. 93–98.

problems with which we are confronted in Pakistan—so that we are forced to borrow our "model" from an alien culture and civilization? If Socialism may be defined as a theory or a policy of social organisation which advocates the ownership and control of the means of production, capital, land, property etc., by the community as a whole and their administration or distribution in the interests of all, it is clear that Islam cannot have much to say in the matter. If you think that is the only way to secure justice, you may subscribe to the theory or the policy of Socialism; but on the other hand, if you think that it will not advance the cause of justice but frustrate it, you may not subscribe to its doctrine. But what has that got to do with Islam, anyway! This strategy of Socialism may be of some importance today to realise the ideal of justice but tomorrow it may not—it is no use, therefore, implicating Islam in this manoeuvre.

By "Socialism" one ordinarily understands an economic philosophy which enjoins upon its votaries the necessity of regarding the instruments of production and the questions relating to the distribution of wealth to be matters exclusively for state's ownership and concern. In the context of the Marxian philosophy, which necessarily is a part and parcel of the materialistic interpretation of history, we are asked to believe in the primacy of economic categories. Contrary to this view, within the framework of a Muslim view of life, this avowedly materialistic approach must be rejected, since it is in conflict with the contention of the Qur'ān, that it is the moral and spiritual categories which are primary and fundamental.

There is, accordingly, no place in Islam for the materialistic interpretation of history so that you might, with some justification, be able to argue for the primacy of the economic factor. Therefore socialism, as an offspring of materialistic interpretation of history, cannot be acceptable to a Muslim. Hence, no wonder, efforts are afoot to suggest that "socialism" can be spiritualised—and this is sought to be achieved by the simple device of labelling it as "Islamic."

I suspect that the word "Islam" is in Pakistan constantly being utilised as a cloak for importing alien stuff—be these ideologies or institutions. By this device, ideologies and cognate principles of social organisation which have been sanctioned by the growth of atheistic, nihilistic, and materialistic philosophies of the West in our time are given an air of plausibility, an appearance of respectability. I have often heard it said: if you add God to Communism the product becomes equal to Islam. Although I am a philosopher by training, I confess, I do not know much about this "dialectical arithmetic" and I will not therefore venture to say anything about it. But what I can say with some authority is this: that God is too all-comprehensive to be added to anything, and Communism which is assuredly based on the cult of Godlessness cannot survive for you to accept it, if you are to be a believer in God. You cannot have both together: you have to make up your mind as to what you want and then you have some choice in the matter. "Theistic Communism" is absurd—as is "Islamic Socialism" or "Islamic Capitalism."

To the age-old question: "What is the state to do for the individual where the individual is not able to provide for himself those bare necessities of life which he is to have if he is to survive?" Islam has its own answer to return. It is the responsibility of the State to provide conditions upon which not only the mind and character of its citizens must develop but also the conditions upon which its citizens are to win by their own efforts all that is necessary to full civic efficiency. It is not for the State to feed, house or clothe them. It is for the State to take care that the economic conditions are such that the normal man, who is not defective in mind or body or will can, by useful labour, feed, house, and clothe himself and his family. The "right to work" and "the right to a living wage" are just as valid as the rights of persons or property—that is to say, they are integral conditions of a good social order. This was the concept of social order upon which "liberalism" of the nineteenth-century European politics was based. Man's pre-occupation with the task of founding a just society is as old as the hills. This was long before Socialism—or, as a matter of fact, long before any "ism" was born. What could you say of the economic and political system of Abū-Bakr, or 'Umar or 'Uthmān or of 'Alī? Were they socialists? The instruments of production were not owned by the state of their day nor had they the type of control which a socialist state claims to have on the means of distribution of wealth. And yet they were, I suppose, consistently with conditions that obtained in their times, practising the Gospel of Islam by founding society on justice.

ISLAM IN THE CONTEMPORARY SECULAR STATE

This section presents a more contemporary treatment of the problem of Islam and the modern state. A new generation building on the efforts of their predecessors feels more free to criticize as well as to explicate what was implicit in much of the preceding argumentation. We have included the section from 'Abdallāh Laroui's *Contemporary Arab Ideology* because it brings out so well the three basic mentalities (cleric, politician, and technocrat)—caricatures perhaps, but nonetheless instructive, indicating how the basic confrontation has not been skirted. Hichem Djait, however, does not skirt the issue; he attacks it head-on and calls for a radical change in mentality. But lest the reader take away the impression that these selections represent the dominant thought of today, we have included a selection from the very popular Egyptian writer Mustafā Mahmūd. The other authors wrestle with the roots of the problem and address intellectuals; Mustafā Mahmūd focuses on showing how one can be modern and still be a tradition-oriented Muslim. He treats the problem at a popular level for a much broader audience. Note that in practically all the selections there is a desire to maintain a specific identity free of the West in its capitalist and Marxist forms.

The Muslims of India, the fourth-largest Muslim population in the world, have faced a unique situation. As a result of the partitioning in 1947, those who did not migrate to Pakistan became a minority in India, a land they had once ruled. Moreover, whereas historically the Islamic community had always been understood to be a religio-political state or empire, Indian Muslims were now living in a secular state, a community in which religion and the state were separate, a situation which many saw as antithetical to the Islamic way of life.

Mushīr-ul-Haq, writing several decades after India's independence, distinguishes between Indian Muslims' acceptance of a secular state and the majority's rejection of secularism, which they saw as a threat to their distinctive identity and traditions. Yet the importance of change ("fashioning a new social order") and the *ulama*'s role in legitimating it, continue to be the major challenges facing the Muslim community in a secular India.

At the turn of the twenty-first century, the Islamic reformer Asghar Ali Engineer again addressed the issue of Islam and secularism. He argues that Islam is not a static religion; it has been and is today capable of multiple interpretations, conservative and liberal. Just as early Muslim interpretations of the Quran were in response to socio-historical contexts, so today Islam, reinterpreted in light of Quranic teachings, can support a liberal pluralism that is compatible with a liberal secularism.

'ABDALLĀH LAROUI
1933–

He is a historian and political theoretician, active in the Moroccan national movement. He studied in Paris and is now professor of history at Muhammad V University, Rabat.

Contemporary Arab Ideology

For three quarters of a century the Arabs have been asking themselves one and the same question: "who is the other and who am I?"

In February 1952 Salama Mūsa entitled one of his articles, "Why Are They powerful?" The "they" have no need to be defined; "they," "them" are the others who are always present beside us, in us. To think is, first of all, to think of the other. This proposition, whether true or false for the individual, is true at every instant for our life as a collectivity. This, then, is where we should begin.

Who is the other for the Arabs? For a long time the other was called Christianity and Europe; today it bears a name vague and precise at the same time, that of the West.

THREE MEN, THREE DEFINITIONS

In contemporary Arab ideology it is possible to distinguish three principle ways of grasping the essential problem of Arab society: the first situates itself in religious faith, the second in political organization, and the last in scientific and technical activity.

1. The Cleric

The man of religion keeps the East-West opposition in the frame of an opposition between Christianity and Islam. He carries on a twelve-century-old tradition of the East and West of the Mediterranean basin. For a long time, victories and defeats alternated. This time, however, the war was rapid and the defeat durable: the enemy takes up his position and organizes himself according to his own norms. Nonetheless, the cleric can maintain the illusion that it is the old confrontation that continues. Besides, for this type of accident, he has a justification which is always ready: "When we want to make a city perish, we order the rich and they give themselves

From *L'idéologie arabe contemporaine* [Contemporary Arab ideology] (Paris: Maspero, 1967), pp. 15, 19–28.

over to their villainry. The word against that city fulfills itself and we destroy it entirely," says the Qur'ān (17: 16). There is no need then to study the enemy; he is nothing but the instrument of evil. Everything finally resolves itself in the relations of society with its God. This position has an unlimited advantage because, in theory, it settles the problem definitively.

Whether the years of misery are numbered by tens or by hundreds, they are explained and justified once for all.

Why is it, then, that at a given moment this satisfaction wears off? Because of the dialogue which the other imposes.

A response, then, is called for, so the cleric, having guarded an inspired silence, begins a study which is condemned in advance: reducing everything to the letter of dogma, he tries to find there the secrets of strength and weakness, and naturally he finds nothing but words.

He hears it said: "the weakness of Islam derives from fanaticism and superstition." He takes up his texts, reads and re-reads them, and finds there nothing but tolerance and reasoned faith. Islam, he replies, is recognition of God according to the paths of reason; absolute monotheism, it abrogates all false divinities, human and inhuman, and thus guarantees the most absolute liberty to the individual; a religion clear and without mystery, it has more chance than any other religion to unite reasonable men around the one God.

He also hears it said: "the strength of the West is based on reason and liberty." While trying to get an idea of that liberty in history, he comes across anti-clerical writers, not by chance, and is horrified to hear that Galileo was imprisoned, Descartes was calumniated, Rousseau persecuted, and Giordano Bruno perished at the stake because he dared to defend the rights of reason against the state. His thoughts turn to Abraham in the Qur'ān, hero of personal investigation, and he asks himself: How can Christians dare to speak of tolerance after so many crimes? Of course, he does not think for a moment about the persecution of the Muʿtazilites by the Caliph Mutawakkil[1], nor about the auto-da-fés of the Almoravids.[2] In the history of Islam he sees nothing but the translators of Ma'mūn[3] hunched over their Greek and Syriac books, and the rare manuscripts of Hakam[4] which the Spanish barbarians, it is said, grabbed up after the fall of Cordova[5] to use for making cheap bridges.

However, it is not long before a complication arises which risks putting the whole system of polemic in jeopardy. If reason is truly on the side of Islam and fanaticism on the side of Christianity, how explain the

1. Caliph Mutawakkil in the ninth century stamped out the somewhat nationalist theological school of the Mu'tazilites. [Ed.]
2. Almoravids: Muslim dynasty controlling North Africa and Spain (1049–1145). [Ed.]
3. Ma'mūn: Caliph in the ninth century, predecessor of Mutawakkil who encouraged the Mu'tazilites and also the translation of Greek science and philosophy. [Ed.]
4. Hakam II: most famous of Umayyad Caliphs of Spain. Under him in the tenth century Cordova became an intellectual capital. [Ed.]
5. Fall of Cordova from Muslim control in second quarter of thirteenth century. [Ed.]

blossoming of the one and the decadence of the other? Muhammad 'Abduh wrote: If we can validly judge a religion according to the actual state of those who practice it, we can affirm that there is no tie between Christianity and modern civilization.

Then the cleric recalls certain facts: the solitude of the philosophers Fārābi (d. 950) and Rāzi (d. 1209), the duplicity of Averroes (d. 1198), the anonymity of the "Brothers of Purity"[6] who, in the fourth century A.H. wanted to amalgamate Islamic faith and Greek philosophy. Henceforth he wants to recall all the ruses which reason had to use to defend its right to life, and he answers: "The cause of our weakness? It is our infidelity to the divine message." The cleric then separates dogma from life. The first is kept pure and spotless while actual history is seen as nothing but a series of avatars of a revelation betrayed.

Previously, God, tired of being humiliated by his chosen people, took refuge among the Arabs, but later reason, hemmed-in by despotism and obscurantism, withdrew, in spite, to the Christians and gave them glory, power, and riches despite their religion. Andalusia[7] is no longer a land like others, conquered then lost. It becomes the symbol of reason which unloved and too often abandoned, abandoned us in turn. Fortunately, it is not vindictive; it can be tamed again if we decide to return to ourselves. Such are the thoughts of the modern cleric.

By that slight nudge everything is pushed back into order, and the promise God made to "his good servants" can be realized once more. This vision, still put forth by the man of religion, is not ephemeral. All through modern history it is found repeated by the pens of Arab publicists. It begins first by creating unanimity, then little by little loses its adepts, but remains in groups generally considered as backward. However, is it necessary to scratch very deeply to rediscover it, barely changed, among men who pretend to be open to objective truth?

2. The Politician

Little by little the West is better known. Western history is studied for itself and not in small pieces for polemic. In the end, one is persuaded that if reason is perhaps absent from Christianity, it is certainly not absent from Europe and, in any case, whether it came from Andalusia or elsewhere, it has found propitious soil in the West.

To the extent that the cleric searches for polemical arguments against the Church everywhere and finds them especially in the writers of the century of enlightenment, to the same extent he opens the way for the domination that this century is going to exercise, little by little, over the Arab intelligence.

6. Brothers of Purity: anonymous authors of some fifty letters, mid-tenth century, representing Ismāʿīlī doctrine. [Ed.]
7. Andalusia: for Muslims, includes practically all the Iberian peninsula, which was held by the Muslims for seven centuries. [Ed.]

The eighteenth century still fascinates the Arabs. This century will always be loved for good and bad reasons because it supplies most of the arguments against the Church and its depravity and because it gives credibility to certain myths. What language is sweeter than that of Rousseau when he criticizes the duality of power in the Christian world and writes: "Muhammad had sound views; he tied his political system together in good fashion and as long as his form of government existed under his successors, the Caliphs, the government was one and good." A single law ruling over this world and the next, guaranteed by the infallible instinct which God put in the heart of every man, isn't this the very essence of the Muslim city described by Rousseau which he justifies without knowing its ultimate goal?

However, can one read Rousseau continually without drawing close to Montesquieu, can one use indefinitely the philosophy of light uniquely against the Church? The moment comes when the unity of the system appears, and the Arab reader no longer sees Europe as the domain of the Pope and bishops alone. He begins to notice the Emperor also and the feudal noble, especially if he comes from Egypt or Syria where he suffered from Turkish tyranny and hears it said that those ancient lands of civilization fell precisely because of the Turkish occupation. When Montesquieu dissects oriental despotism, the Middle Eastern reader feels hatred for the Turkish usurper rise in himself. Still, he recognizes willingly that the Caliph, even in the brilliant periods of Muslim empire, governed according to his own good pleasure; conquered people were persecuted; the state had no end other than the exploitation of subject populations. He recognizes that property was precarious, commerce was discouraged, taxes were unequal, administration was venal, and justice was subjective. Yes, he finishes by admitting it was a reign of violence, fear, the unlimited power of one, and the slavery of all. The Caliph, shadow of God on earth, respected neither the life nor property of his subjects, and his violence, punctuated by brief and bloody revolts, resembled that of all who ruled over the ancient land of Asia.

The new man, the politician who has taken the place of the cleric on front stage, thinks: our decadence certainly had secular slavery as its ultimate cause. All of a sudden, all the classical judgments, which he read formerly but did not assimilate, are going to regain force: that the slave could neither work well or fight, that agriculture, commerce, science, and philosophy can never flower in servitude. Like many others he reflects on the misadventures of Athens and Rome and lets himself be convinced that the fall of empires is always the victory of liberty over slavery.

Then Islam will be disassociated from decline, and the Turk will become the symbol of misery and failure. It will be said: as long as Islam was Arab it was free, tolerant, and victorious. Once it became Turkish it changed its nature and declined. Turkish Islam was victor as long as Europe was subservient and fatalistic, but as soon as it liberated itself at the time of the reformation, it conquered everywhere.

The new man, jurist and politician, is going to amalgamate Rousseau and Montesquieu and understand ideal democracy after the fashion of the English watchmaker.

Since the evil has been diagnosed, the remedy has been found. The Turkish regime was the power of a sole ruler; therefore, we should elect an assembly. The Turkish regime regulated all activities, therefore we should give free reins to private enterprise. The Turkish regime accommodated itself to ignorance, then we must sacrifice everything to spread instruction.

This jurist-politician is going to put himself to the task with quibbles and subtleties. The Prophet was wrong once concerning the technique of pollinating date palms and frankly admitted his error. From that the conclusion is abusively drawn that Islamic dogma does not impose a strict organization of public powers and that it can, consequently, accommodate itself to any regime whatever that Muslims choose.

Ijmā' (juridical consensus) becomes a veritable democratic charter, corroborated by the procedure which the Caliph 'Umar chose to designate his successor. Ignorant or forgetful of the lessons of ethnology, he claims that the Arab is by nature free and that he cannot independently found a regime which is not democratic—an argument which at base takes up the racist determinism of E. F. Gautier.

Thus dogma is saved a second time because every classical despotic organization is declared non-Muslim and with the same stroke the future is uncovered: let us organize a representative democracy and power will return to us again. Everyday floods of eloquence are going to be poured out at the feet of creative liberty, and this great hope, now visible after so many years, takes on the melancholy aspect of a youth betrayed by destiny. Tāhā Husayn after twenty-five years reflected on his dreams, contradicted by reality, and lamented: "Believe me, the good, all the good for a man of culture and courage is to escape with his heart, his spirit and his conscience far from these times. If he cannot go elsewhere, let him at least exile himself in one of the epochs of past history."

This liberal vision which carries in itself both diagnosis and therapy, is still found in all Arab countries. In certain countries like Egypt, discredited by its failures, it scarcely dares to make itself heard from time to time in the university or the parliament; in others like Morocco, it still has sufficient self-confidence to present itself openly.

3. The Technocrat

Political liberty and parliaments do not give power; daily experience was not long in demonstrating this. No one yet doubted the real representation of the deputy, but knew very well that his speeches were forgotten as soon as they were delivered in the temple of the nation. This deputy: lawyer, doctor, journalist, or professor, fought to occupy high positions, but when he arrived there he sensed correctly that everything, politics and administration, escaped him and that his presence was necessary only during official feasts. He consoled himself knowing that his chief had no more power than he. Sometimes the latter explained to him that the big boss himself is only the shadow of a shadow. For a long time he used an image: the people, an invincible force; now he mouths it with bitterness. Even the people, guided by their elected representatives, keep an obstinate silence. The politician asks: liberty we have, but power? Since he believes that power is his due, he turns against the people. For the first time, with necessary distance, he sees the people as they are: ignorant, squalid, drowsy. Then the residences of the great families are fortified, the clubs close, and the cars streak along the streets with shades drawn to protect oneself against sights which are too violent. The peasant becomes the expression of another world, another humanity, and the politican-jurist no longer rejects with indignation the insinuation of foreigners about the influence of climate, race, and sun. Exasperated and disillusioned, betrayed by events, the man of quibbles keeps silence.

A newcomer then takes the floor. He is neither lawyer, magistrate, nor doctor. Son of a shop-keeper, perhaps a peasant, occasionally from a minority, in short the one who up till now was marginal. During this period of silence, he has acquired a new image of the West shaped by various pressures, and this image will serve as the norm by which he judges the society and the work of his elders.

The West, he will say, is not defined either by a religion without superstitions nor by a state without despotism, but simply by a material force acquired by work and applied science. Henceforth he will laugh at the ideas of the West the cleric and the politician shaped for themselves. In the great amphitheatre of Cairo University, Salama Mūsa in 1930 will pose the following question to Egyptian youth: "Do the Westerners have the same religion? the same racial origin? the same institutions?" And he answered: "During the past quarter of a century a single truth has become clear to me, and it is this: the difference which separates us from civilized Europeans is industry and industry alone." The technocrat will cite often the example of Japan: does a religion more foreign to reasoned monotheism exist, is there a history more bloody, a people more subservient than those we find in Japan of the Samurai? Nonetheless, in little time Japan conquered whites and yellows simply because it went straight to the secret of the West. Let us do likewise; let us not waste our time any longer in theological discussions and in lamentations over an unfinished destiny. Science is certainly very beautiful, but it must be subordinated to technique; culture is a noble goal, but it comes after a specialized trade. Salama Mūsa affirms: "Today civilization is industry; its culture is science. Whereas the culture of agrarian societies is literature, religion and philosophy."

The criticism of Islamic history which the liberal politician had timidly begun is now totally put aside. The technocrat feels no need to interpret dogma or to warp it from its traditional sense. He simply ignores it, since it does not determine the strength or weakness.

In excluding tradition from the discussion, he helps save it for the last time. The technocrat answers the argument of the preceding generation with: "Was it not under Cromwell that England laid the bases of its maritime hegemony? Was it not under the two Napoleons that France became an industrial power? Despotism hinders nothing; perhaps it is even a condition for the advancement of a people."

This man, worshiper of technology, is often sad and quiet, but intellectually he is a terrorist; he refuses to put himself in question, and he scorns disinterested science. For him, the West is no longer opaque as it was for the cleric. He feels at home there, speaks its language, follows its logic and slowly, the past and its problems grow dim in his mind. He no longer asks: "What was our greatness?", nor "Why, our decadence?" Insipid questions, he thinks, and goes off crying out: truth is for tomorrow, truth is technology. He believes he has gone beyond the cleric and the liberal politician; actually he has appropriated the West for himself by a short, effortless leap, having jettisoned his past a bit too easily. For all that, the West has not really become clearer to him; it is his history which has become more opaque.

While the liberal politician, betrayed by events, discredited himself more each day, the technocrat was preparing intellectually for the installation of the new state. When this day arrives, the technocrat will cry victory and will say as did Salama Mūsa in July 1952: "It is the most beautiful day of my life." But the new state will not be long in recognizing that this technocrat is most often not a technician; it will listen to him for a while, then turn away quickly.

The question will be asked:

What do these three men represent in reality? Were they picked at hazard? Are they the expurgated editions of actual writers? If so, why were they not presented under their true names?

These three men, in fact, represent three moments of the Arab conscience which has been trying since the end of the last century to understand itself and to understand the West. They were described abstractly because they are found in diverse forms of literature (essays, newspaper articles, plays), and they are not incarnated in the same man for all the Arab countries.

No doubt there is already a presentiment that to judge these forms of conscience several questions must be answered: Do they form an historical sequence? Who has given them their general problematic? What relation is there between each of them and the social forces active in Arab society or in the West? However, it can be affirmed presently that the worst methodological error would be to deny the interdependence, already so evident, between Arab ideology and Western ideology.

HICHEM DJAIT
1935–

He studied at Tunisia's Sadiqi College and went to Paris to
continue studies, first at the Ecole normale supérieure and then
at the Sorbonne. He is *agrégé* in history and now teaches at the
University of Tunis.

Islam, Reform, and the New Arab Man

How can we follow the wake of our glorious historical tradition, holding
to a course stable enough to avoid lurches into alienation and flexible
enough to adjust to the dynamics of change? Reformism and modernism
asked themselves this question and gave answers which were fragmentary
and biased, each in its own way. For the fundamentalism of 'Abduh, for
example, Islamic society and the modern world confront each other in the
context of our reality. The fundamentals of the first must be maintained,
the second must be absorbed as a foreign body. Moreover, it is the material manifestations (the signs of power) of the second that are sought
more than the spirit which gives them life. Imperialism and the plasticity of
eternal Islam! A *ruse de guerre* and a defensive tactic at one and the same
time despite appearances; the cart has been put before the horse. We do not
start with evidence of the perennial nature of Islamic society—such as it has
been defined up to now—in order to adapt the benefits of the modern world
to it; rather we set out from the necessity of implanting modernity in our
society without severing society from its Arab-Islamic tradition. Or rather,
we start by abandoning ourselves to the dynamism of history, a history
we will shape to fit our aspirations once we have defined our hopes. In
our view, Islam cannot be the unique positive foundation of present-day
society as the reformism of *al-Manār* would have it.[1] Nor, on the contrary,
can Islam be merely a condiment, an historic decoration: playing a minor
role in the great theatre of Arabism, as the diverse tendencies of Arab
neo-modernism would have it. One cannot deny to the individual Arab, if
and when he wishes, the possibility of interiorizing Islam as a religion, a
source of moral inspiration and a metaphysic, without falling into a narrow

---

1. *al-Manār*—periodical published from 1897 to 1935 which served as principal vehicle for
reformist thought of Muhammad 'Abduh and continued as such even after his death in
1905 under his disciple Rashīd Ridā.

From *La personnalité et le devenir arabo-islamiques* [The future of the Arab-Islamic
personality] in *Collections Esprit—La Condition Humaine* (Paris: Editions du Seuil, 1974),
pp. 126–35.

materialism devoid of any consideration for the validity of religious action. No systematic de-Islamizing of conscience, then, but a de-Islamizing of the central and operative core of the society.

However, it is clear that an interiorized Islam and a society in the process of being rationalized will interpenetrate, or, to be more precise, religion will have to adapt itself to a different humanity. Up to the present, religion has been closely coupled to a certain form of society which it helped to shape and which in turn affected it; tomorrow it will be able to correlate differently.

Contemporary reflection has become mired in an impossible problem because it has not been able to separate Islam and society correctly—the confusion derives from the West's medieval apprehension of Islam as an antagonistic, monolithic religious form. But an Islam rethought, reformulated, and revitalized can respond to the modern, rationalized conscience to the extent that it associates itself with new dimensions of affectivity and reason. But how can we do this without disfiguring Islam, without depriving it of its historic asset of authority, the sacred part of its scriptural bases, and finally, that which is its major contribution, the perspective of going beyond the human which it contains within itself to the transcendence which it offers to every anxious soul? Have no doubts, this will be an intellectual and moral struggle cut to the measure of those who are inspired both by religious faith and faith in the future of modern man, and who live out that double affiliation in conflict. It is for them to redefine the essence of the Islamic design and to redirect the very structure of Islamic religious sensibility towards other paths. In any case, this may be a rearguard action, because humanity is well on the way to abandoning all religious structures of the classical type.

To contract Islam to its pure and positive religious content and to plumb its depths will mean, in a sense, to separate religion from society. The latter must be freed from the closely knit structures of "Islam-society" which still weigh heavily upon it from the very distant past. The state can act as the catalyst for this liberation, but action from above will not suffice if it is not accompanied by an interior movement which is both broad and deep, that is to say, by a resounding affirmation of new ideas and new ways of acting.

To tell the truth, the principal obstacle to such changes lies in the close solidarity of the elements under discussion, and this solidarity has not been explained clearly. Islam cannot abandon the positions it holds in the social fabric by title of ancient conquest unless it ceases to be on the defensive, and it will not lower its guard unless new spiritual perspectives are opened up for it. Furthermore, the collective mentality of society will not accommodate itself to new plans of action unless they are coherent and carry in themselves the germ of a better life, and to make this accommodation, the collective mentality must be rationalized, that is to say, secularized. This poses the problem in its full dialectical breadth.

The solution will come from the dynamism and creativity of the future which will jar the weight of the past. History must be set in motion once again to press out new strata and new traditions. *The Arab problem is one of a totality which seeks a vital, inner motive force.*

Once the voyage is begun, our authentic values must be reaffirmed as the guides of our human action; the reel of history must roll smoothly.

The motive force of which we spoke is a determination springing from the depths of our Arab being; it is the unleashing of latent potentiality and a reorientation of the spirit that animates society.

In this present phase of our history, because of human resources and a thousand and one other reasons . . . it is impossible to imagine Arab society becoming completely neutral vis-à-vis ideology, whether religious or secular. An Arab society sterilized and remade such that its actvity will be directed to the pure co-existence of all men who are motivated by material well-being—a well-being which is still hypothetical—is impossible today. What is more, the voice of Arab conscience rejects it.

But in a contrary sense, an Arab society dominated by a "lay ideology of progress" in the form of a specific Marxism is fully possible. History is contingent; it may or may not follow this direction. All we know for certain is that at the present time Arab Marxism is a minority current. In any case, we do not desire this solution. The reason is not that it would entail a loss of our historic personality: Soviet Marxism was adept in wedding itself to Russian nationalism and Chinese Marxism. Despite the universal horizons it projects for itself, it is, in fact, the new destiny of eternal China. No, our reason is that at the heart of the Arab dialectic the question is not merely one of finding a recipe for socio-economic development; nor is it one of making ourselves presentable to the outside world; rather it is much more a question of living in a society made of better human stuff and of participating in a civilization of quality.

Judging from models which exist, we fear that an Arab-Marxism would mean the modern perpetration and legitimation of the oriental totalitarianism which is still present in society's bias towards a medieval type of ethno-religious constraint and present also in the structure and function of Arab states. Man, society, and power must be liberated. Above all, we refuse to let this violent world lose its soul and shut itself up again in a drab, suffocating structure. We do not deny that Marxism represents a hope for humanity as a whole, but, in any case, some non-Arab countries have assumed responsibility for its continued existence and survival.

In short we want neither an ideologically neutral society like that of the post-industrial West, nor a society propelled by Marxist ideology—true Marxism can be grasped but not its pale substitutes which we think are stripped of value—nor, finally, and *a fortiori*, a society obsessed with static souvenirs which go back to the sources of medieval unanimity and is closed in on itself. Arab society should find the way for its own fulfillment and start searching for its own ideology.

This ideology should synthesize contradictory aspirations and exigencies: tradition and modernity, profound interior appeal (past and present) and necessary rapport with the outside world. If we reformulate the problems in another manner, we can move beyond certain false problems and allow the real, absorbing, and urgent questions to come into the full light of conscience. This is how the alternatives Islam-Marxism, Islam-westernization should be surmounted, and, *a fortiori*, that of tradition-modernism. For us the problem lies in reconciling an Arab personality, which, for the most part, we only tolerate even though we love it, with a future to be chosen. Tensions like this are common in periods of mutation —recall the inner divisions which rent France, or those which were the lot of the Church, in the process of incorporating the values of the modern world, even though these values issued from Western soil and matured slowly.

In the Arab and Islamic case, modernization has always been a deformed superimposition; it has appeared as an attack or the repercussion of a previous attack. Modernity has to be nationalized; it must be acclimatized and wedded to our deep personality. If we make modernity identical with either westernization or Marxization, we will falsify our personality in exchange for a borrowed future; this may be progress, but the price paid is alienation. The truth is that this modernity has sprung free from its country of origin and is now in universal orbit. To grasp it in its universal dimensions, to integrate it and make it ours, to add to it and express it in the language of our own particularity, this is our primary goal: it is the dialectic of perpetuity in renovation.

What is demanded of Arab humanity today is not to promote a model for universal revolution which will make the Arabs the avant garde of their time as they once were with Islam. This type of historical miracle does not repeat itself. Nor will the European renaissance, the French revolution, or the Russian revolution be repeated. Arab humanity is asked to totalize its experience and that of humanity, to remain itself while taking on a new body, and to make its identity a source of energy which penetrates the whole effort and enlivens it part by part.

Though open to criticism, the Arab renaissance of the nineteenth century did prepare the way for the present epoch. Like every renaissance it advocated a return to sources, straddling between a recent and burdensome tradition and a more ancient tradition seen as disfigured or betrayed. But, apart from the fact that this renaissance limited itself to its own cultural horizons, there is also the danger that such a movement if prolonged in the same sense risks focusing us on the past and its grandeur. As we already suggested, we have to break with the past in a certain sense. A second renaissance will not have the sense of progress unless its anxious search for the authentic and its intention to restore are put in proper perspective so that the essential thing stands out, namely, the unspoken things must come to full maturity and we must be ready to fecundate our reality and our being. In this way, the renaissance will rediscover its true function, that of giving new birth by means of the ancient. From this pro-classical illusion will arise the promise of a culture, not renewed, but new, expressing the universal in an original way. The radically new, the *jamais vu*, by projecting itself onto the nostalgia for the ancient, will mature—but the new will be formless and consequently ineffable.

A true renaissance is both a revival of certain privileged sectors of the past and a leap into the unknown. It is an affirmation of creative liberty and presupposes peeling away the scales of certain parts of our being. The Arab renaissance, if understood in a sense other than pure nostalgia or mere repetition, must recover its breadth culturally so that it can show us that we are as able as the ancients and as capable as our contemporaries. Then it will become a cultural birth, not merely a resur-rection. But given the ambiguity of the term "renaissance," we prefer to speak in terms of an Arab future which will be a total, complex, and powerful dialectic. It will not be possible to stop at a cultural and religious superstructure and from there to preach renaissance and reform, allowing the political concept of revolution to fade out of focus. No, our aim must be a general, long-term action in which the confrontation with oneself will be completed by a confrontation with the other. The spark once struck penetrates and sets fire to the deepest social, political, and mental strata. The rhythm of the movement will be one of accompaniment, simultaneity, and solidarity; it will group all the elements present. This totalizing action, based on clear objectives, is our only way out of the vicious circle which hems us in. It is clear, for example, that our mentality will not evolve towards rationality unless there is an anterior material development. But one can also claim that the latter presupposes the former. In the same vein, the overthrow of present structures will yield only ephemeral and fictive results unless it is supported by the allegiance of vital social forces. Inversely, an action from on high will never be effective unless mature aims and ideals are developed. Adopting techniques and inventions will have no meaning if this adoption is separated from the tendencies and historic roots of popular identity.

There is more: The principal stake, to wit, the quality of civilization and the framework of life within which man can expand to the maximum. For this and for the rest, a fundamental revision of the values by which we live is necessary. We need a radical redefinition of our image of man, and we should start with the complex network of Arab humanity. Here the role of thought comes into play; it lays the foundations for action. Nothing of value will be accomplished among the Arabs unless three capital elements of their existence are revised: religion and its place in society; man himself and his personality; and the relations between state and society, or, if you wish, the model of development. Reform in the religious order, rational-ization of the individual, mutation in society—this triptych is the *sine qua non* condition of this renewal, which we wish to be a leap forward and a pledge for the future. Coupled with the affirmation of the Arab personality, under its ideologies—cultural form or as political destiny—it constitutes, in our eyes, the praxis for the Arab universe, the surest preface to its emancipation.

MUSTAFĀ MAHMŪD
1921–

After primary and secondary education at Tanta, he entered the medical college of Cairo University and on graduation practiced medicine in Cairo from 1952 to 1966. In the mid-fifties he began writing on religion and modern problems and now has become a full-time writer and spiritual counselor.

Islam vs. Marxism and Capitalism

As developing nations we normally look at two pioneering experiences only: communism in the East and capitalism in the West. We can hardly imagine that there may be another solution, so if we discover that both the two experiences are not advantageous to us we begin to search for a solution midway between the two schools and we start to manufacture an appropriate composite.

If we were to look to Islam we would find a source of thought and truth which surpasses both systems in its progressiveness and contemporaneity. We would find that everything we reckon new in scientific socialism was old hat thirteen centuries ago in Islam. Islam came establishing, from the very beginning, the principle of equal opportunity, guaranteeing minimal needs to the individual and achieving a balance between the liberty of the individual to profit and the rights of society, the principle of private and public property (private and public sectors), the principle of state interference in the economy—this is what we call today a directed economy—the principle of confiscating the wealth of exploiters for the benefit of the poor and the oppressed.

Islam does not allow classes and forbids that wealth circulate among a limited group of rich.

"That it become not a commodity between the rich among you" (Qur'ān 59:7).

Rank in Islam is based on piety not riches.

"The noblest of you in the sight of God is the best in conduct" (Qur'ān 49:13).

"God does not look at your form or your wealth but only at your hearts and your actions" (Prophetic Tradition).

"People are equal like the teeth of a comb; there is no preference for the Arab over the non-Arab except in piety" (Prophetic Tradition). . . .

From *al-Marksiyyah wal-Islām* [Marxism and Islam] (Cairo: Dār al-Ma'arif, 1975), pp. 66–79.

128

Islam is against excessive disparity in resources. There is more than one verse against luxury and the luxurious. "The wrongdoers followed that by which they became opulent, and were guilty" (Qur'ān 11:116). "Till when we grasp their luxurious ones with the punishment, behold they supplicate" (Qur'ān 23:64). . . .

Despite this, Islam is not against the rich man if he is restrained.

"There is no objection against the rich man who is pious" (Prophetic Tradition). "Yes, just wealth for the just servant" (Prophetic Tradition). "In their wealth the beggar and the outcast had due share" (Qur'ān 51:19).

The minimum for life must be guaranteed to all. "People share in three things: water, pasture and fire" (Prophetic Tradition).

The wealth of the rich is illegal if there is one poor person in the society who cannot find food. "There is no one of us who goes to sleep full when his neighbor is hungry" (Prophetic Tradition). "Let him who has surplus give to him who has not" (Prophetic Tradition).

We have seen examples of state interference in the economy under 'Umar ibn al-Khattāb.[1] . . .

'Umar refused to let Muslims take possession of land conquered in raids, considering it the property of the community, just as he refused to allow possession of beneficient trusts, mines, and underground resources, considering them under the rule of the public sector.

'Umar forbade the buying and consumption of meat two days in succession when meat was scarce, and anyone violating the prohibition he struck with an udder, saying: "Now your stomach will close up for two days."

'Umar bought monopolized products forcibly from the monopolists for a symbolic price and used to fix the price for certain items to prevent arbitrary pricing which might harm people. . . .

Abū-Dharr al-Ghiffārī[2] considered the wealth of the wealthy fair game for others as long as there was one poor man in the society who could not find sufficiency.

Private property is inviolable in Islam as is public property. "The blood, honor and wealth of every Muslim is inviolable" (Prophetic Tradition).

The one who violates private property has his hand cut off like the one who violates public property.

In Islam, formal logic is joined with dialectical logic. (Formal logic is Aristotelian and talks of the permanence of existing things, so what is a tree today will be a tree tomorrow. Dialectical logic is Hegelian dialectical logic and talks of the continual change of existing things, so every existing thing carries the seed of its own destruction.) These two are the logics of permanence and evolution. Islam joins adherence to permanent dogmatic principles with personal interpretation (*ijtihād*) in derived branches, details,

1. 'Umar b. al-Khattāb: second Caliph after death of Muhammad.
2. Abū-Dharr al-Ghiffārī: companion of the Prophet, known for his humility and asceticism. Because of his criticism of abuses of wealth he has been adopted recently as the first socialist.

and applications (this is what we call development). It says that derived
rules change with changes in time and place. This is what jurisprudents call
"difference of time and place," not difference in argument and proof. Hence
the Prophetic Tradition: "differences among Imāms is a blessing," because
they are differences in details necessitated by changing circumstances.

For this reason we say that economic policy in Islam is divine policy in
what concerns principles but positive policy in what concerns application
and detail.

The divine principles in the Islamic program are based on the notion of
accommodation of the interests of the individual with those of the group.
It does not crush the individual for the good of the group (as in communism)
nor does it crush the group for the good of the individual (as in capitalism).

But if accommodation is impossible as in time of war or famine or
plague, the Islamic application chooses the group interest and decrees that
people divide food equally, though all may be only half full. . . .

However, in a normal situation the Islamic program is bound by divine
principles which aim at a delicate balance between individual and community interest. . . .

For this reason anyone who thinks Islam is capitalistic is mistaken.
Likewise anyone who thinks Islam is communistic is mistaken. And so too,
the one who thinks Islam is a mathematical mean between the two systems
or a concoction from both is mistaken. The truth is that Islam has a distinctive economic program which proceeds from basically different points
of departure, although some point or other may be in accord with this or
that system.

It proceeds from the notions of accomodation, interest, cooperation,
and complementarity, not from the notion of class struggle and contradiction. It seeks a balance between the individual and the group, not the
melting of individuals into the group (as in scientific socialism) nor the sacrifice of the group for the good of a minority of individual capitalists (as in
capitalist throught). Accomodation and interest are always the starting point.

In capitalist economics we find that the freedom of the individual
for gain is the principle and the interference of the state is the exception. In
scientific socialism we find that the interference of the state and its isolated
role in economic activity is the principle and the granting of some freedom
to the individual is the exception. It is clear, then, that in Islam we are in
the presence of something very different.

Individual freedom to profit is a principle in the Islamic system along
with individual property, so too are state interference in the economy and
public property principles. And when Islam established the *zakāt*[3] it legalized state interference and set up the first institution of social security. Islam
makes interference a duty so that wealth will not remain among the rich as
the monopoly of one class to the exclusion of the rest of the citizens. . . .

---

3. *zakāt*: obligatory tax on capital holdings enjoined by Muhammad.

The freedom of the individual to gain is a principle, but Islam does not allow it to become an absolute. It puts fetters on it, so production of wine, usurious transactions, monopoly, amassing wealth and spending it foolishly or gathering it by graft, and infringement on the rights of others and over-pricing are not allowed.

The Islamic economic program is characterized by another thing not found in capitalism or in scientific socialism, namely its satisfaction of spiritual as well as material needs. Relations with God and acting to please him in expenditure and performance of good deeds is a principle. Our prophet says: "Alms fall into God's hand before they reach the hand of the deprived."

This gives the economic program a lofty goal and enables economic activity. The believer feels he is dealing directly with God.

Also, it provides the governor with a two-fold supervision over his actions in addition to the supervision of the commissioner of taxes, namely, the supervision of God and the supervision of his conscience.

This spiritual satisfaction protects the society from the psychological emptiness and malaise which occur in opulent European societies like Sweden or in socialist atheistic societies in the East where we find the high-est proportion of insanity and suicide despite the abundant guarantees of life for all.

The reason is that the system does not satisfy spiritual needs and does not quench that holy thirst within man, the thirst for the true God, even though it satisfies his stomach and natural dispositions. They do not under-stand that man is not merely stomach and instincts. . . .

There is no separation in Islam between the spiritual and the material. . . . Sincere, upright action before God is both material and spiritual.

Wealth is not sought for itself in Islam but is sought as a means to piety and a way to upright, merciful, and loving action. This marks it as very different from the meaning of wealth in materialist capitalist economy and materialist socialist economy. These latter look at wealth as economic power and as a means for domination and conquest. Activity without a spiritual sense is dry and lifeless.

We, however, say, "Seek, in what God gives you, this life and the next." This makes our use of wealth in construction and development something similar to prayer or obligatory devotions by which we seek the next life in pleasing the Creator. . . .

Were we to execute our economic plan with this religious, devotional spirit we would accomplish miracles in a few years and overtake the cav-alcade of progress with the speed of a rocket. The Arab states complement one another economically and form a nation which could become richer and stronger than the American nation—a geographical area with petroleum, iron, coal, copper, magnesium, gold, and uranium in addition to abundant agricultural produce, unlimited animal and marine resources and a numer-ous work force. Imagine the possibilities were we to join the potential of

Saudi Arabia, Kuwait, and the Gulf States with that of Egypt, Sudan, and
North America; if only we did the necessary planning, brought them
together and exploited our possibilities. . . .

Only by searching into the depths of Islam, the Qur'ān and the Sunna[4]
for this Islamic economic plan and by searching for its limits and its
specifications will we all be saved from stumbling around between capitalism and scientific socialism (which is not scientific as we saw). By this too
we will be saved from patching up our great civilization with civilizations
which are in fact either in old age and decline (like capitalism) or in a stage
of trial and experiment (like scientific socialism). Both these civilizations are
materialistic standing on hypothetical philosophies oriented to dry material
interest without any trace of spirit or divine knowledge and lacking that
certainty which is supported by heaven and sustained by God.

Islamic economics, as we saw, gives us the advantages which are found
in scientific socialism plus spiritual satisfaction and dogmatic enthusiasm
along with more progressive and contemporary points of view and more
humanistic procedures. Moreover, it will help us to avoid the pitfalls,
errors, and presumptions of materialistic thought and that strangeness
which it has for us as imported thought which remains at the door of our
hearts and does not enter no matter what propaganda or tyranny the ruler
may use. We are a believing people. Faith for us is our pillar, our heart, and
our backbone. In this valley [Nile] we came to know God and worshipped
him during seven thousand years when these "civilizers" were barbarians
who did not know how to talk. . . .

4. Sunna: the practice of the Prophet.

MUSHĪR UL-HAQ
1933–

After graduation ('Ālim) from Nadwat al-Ulema, Lucknow, Mushīr ul-Haq earned his B.A. (Jamia Millia Islamia, Delhi) and M.A. (Muslim University, Aligarh) in Islamic and Arabic studies. In 1967, he received a Ph.D. in Islamic studies from McGill University. He has been a member of the Institute of Advanced Studies in Simla and is presently Chairman of the Department of Arabic Studies, Jamia Millia University.

Islam in Secular India

The Constitution of India designates the country a "Sovereign Democratic Republic" but makes no mention of "secularism." For the last two decades Indians have been talking of secularism, yet the term remains vague and ambiguous. One may, therefore, be justified in asking: what does secularism really mean—especially in the Indian context? . . .

It should be remembered that when India became independent the makers of the Indian Constitution had hardly any alternative to taking secularism as their guideline. The leaders of the Independence Movement were so committed to a noncommunal and non-religious policy that even after the partition of the country they could not retreat from their stand. The Muslim community of India also welcomed the idea of a secular state because they feared the alternative would be a "Hindu state." . . .

All through the freedom struggle hardly any national leader dared to question the importance of religion. The leaders of both the Hindu and the Muslim communities most of the times used a religous vocabulary in their speeches and writings to achieve political ends. In the case of the Hindu community one may say that religion did not mean a codified and systematized set of principles, rather it was understood in term of higher moral values. But this cannot be said about the Muslims. Religion to them was not just moral values: it was the *Sharī'a*, a system, an institution: Muslims were told this time and again. . . .

The *Sharī'a* (which means a "way") and is usually translated as "Islamic law") is believed by generality of the Muslims to be "the Islamic way of life, comprehending beliefs, ritual, practices, public and personal law, and being stretched even to include dress, personal appearance and rules of behaviour in social intercourse. . . ."

From *Islam in Secular India* (Simla: Indian Institute of Advanced Study, 1972), pp. 6, 8–9, 14–16, 19–21, 85–86.

The Indian Muslims generally hold "Islam" as "faith" and "*Sharī'a*" or "the practical exhibition of the faith" to be inseparable. Faith must show in action. And action has to be strictly in line with the rules and regulations formulated by the *fuqahā'* ("jurists") in the golden days of Islam, chiefly on the basis of the Qur'ān and the Prophetic traditions. Therefore no part of life is regarded to be outside of the purview of the *Sharī'a*, and its violation is considered "crime" as well as "sin."

Thus secularism and secular state are to be accepted or rejected on the basis of the *Sharī'a*. The secular state, as we have seen, has a precedent in Islamic history and is, therefore, acceptable, but secularism as a doctrine is believed to be incompatible with Islam. Since no serious effort has so far been made to explain to the Indian Muslims—as it has been done in the case of Turkey—that "secularism" is a foreign word, and in Islamic society it can be interpreted quite differently from what it is understood in a Christian society, naturally we find the Indian Muslims still groping after the meaning of secularism. . . .

On the question of secularism, however, Indian Muslims appear broadly divided into two sections. The first group, in a minority and rather contemptuously called "secularist" includes mostly modern educated Muslims who hold that religion, as a faith, can co-exist with secularism. The second group, led by the *'ulamā'*, stands by the view that religion is not only faith but *Sharī'a* also. Faith may co-exist with secularism, but *Sharī'a* cannot. . . .

There are then two groups of Indian Muslims—the "secularists" and the "nationalist" *'ulamā'*—who are suspect in the eyes of many Muslims, but there is little hope of their joining hands. These two are quite different from each other. They have practically nothing in common in their education, or mental make-up, or in their approach to this world and the next, in short, in anything. The only point common to them is that both are frowned upon by the generality of the Muslims, of course, for different reasons altogether.

In short it can be said that the Indian Muslims are in a dilemma: so far as the secular state is concerned, it is acceptable, for one thing, no alternative is available and, for the other, a secular state guarantees religious freedom. But the philosophy of secularism is considered to be a poison for religious life. . . .

CONCLUSION

The key to understanding the Muslims' lack of response to the demand for secularization appears to lie in two words: innovation and tradition. If secularism places worldly life outside the control of religion, this is an innovation without precedent in Islamic history: hence, to the faithful, unacceptable. But if secularism denotes only that the state does not favour any particular community in matters of religion, it is believed to be in accord with Islamic tradition which gives religious freedom to every citizen. This concept of secularism is not alien to a Muslim and therefore he sees no conflict between his religion, Islam, and secularism.

However, secularism becomes anti-religion when it demands a share in what belongs to God. At this point a devout Muslim hesitates to accept secularism as a way of life because it is not the life of this world which he lives for; it is the "next" for which he is supposed to live and work. It is true that in the past Muslims have quite often allowed Caesar to take what he wished and to leave for God what he pleased: British rule in India is a recent example of the fact. Thus, one may say, it would not have been very difficult for the Muslims to let the tradition continue. But it is often forgotten that the Muslims' participation in the struggle for freedom was mostly inspired by the promises from their religious leadership, the *'ulamā'*, that after the departure of the British from India they would have an opportunity to live a life according to their religion. The partition blighted the Muslim hope of religious revival in India: yet the prospect of living in a secular state which is supposed to guarantee freedom of religious belief and practice to all its citizens without any distinction restored their confidence in their religious future.

Had religion meant to the Muslims only a personal relation between man and God, they might have surrendered unconditionally to the forces of secularization. But they are constantly told by their religious leaders, the *'ulamā'*, that Islam is not just a philosophy; it is man's total and unconditional submission to God: its demands from the adherents are much more than those of a state. This makes the Muslims hesitate to cooperate in building up a completely secular society.

Some people may not like to be told that the Muslim community, by and large, is still religious in the sense that it invariably seeks a religious sanction for every innovation, but we have seen how strongly they believe in the institutionalized procedures for seeking this sanction. To be fully accepted an innovation has to transform itself into a tradition. It appears, therefore, that until secularism is "blessed" by the *'ulamā'*, it will not make much headway in the Muslim community. . . .

ASGHAR ALI ENGINEER
1939–

Born and raised in Salumbar, India, Asghar Ali Engineer received an Islamic and secular education, graduating in civil engineering. A longtime rights activist and scholar of Islam, he has been especially concerned with communal violence. He is head of the Institute of Islamic Studies and the Centre for the Study of Society and Secularism; his many books include *The Rights of Women in Islam, Islam and Revolution*, and *A Rational Approach to Islam*.

Islam and Secularism

Many people feel that Islam is quite incompatible with secularism. Some even maintain that as long as one is Muslim he cannot be a secularist. This is further reinforced by the propaganda by some Muslim countries like Saudi Arabia that secularism is *haram* [forbidden] and that all secular nations are enemies of Islam. Maulana Maududi, the founder chief of Jamat-e-Islami also said while leaving for Pakistan in 1948 that secularism is *haram* and all those who participate in secular politics in India will be rebels against Islam and enemies of the messenger of Allah.

How far is it true? Are Islam and secularism really incompatible? Is Saudi propaganda against secularism justified? Was Maulana Maududi right? These are important questions and we must search for answers. We must bear in mind that in every religion there are different intellectual trends—both liberal as well as conservative. Both quote scriptures in support of their respective positions. Since a scripture or religious tradition for that matter has to deal with complex social situations, one finds differing or even contradictory statements responding to the differing or contradictory situations.

In scriptural hermeneutics one has to take the situation in totality and develop certain keys to deal with the evolving situation. The commentators often deal with the situation as if it is static. Social situations can never be static. It continually evolves and changes. The way scriptural statements were understood by early commentators conformed to their own socio-cultural situation. Their hermeneutics should not be binding on the subsequent generations as it will not conform to the changed situation. For every age there are some keys which help us understand the scripture in our own age. Also, a commentator should have a vision of society and this vision

From *Rational Approach to Islam* (New Delhi: Gyan Publishing House, 2001), pp. 43–52.

evolves from one's own social situation. Allah's creative power cannot be treated as static anyway. The Qur'an also refers to His dynamism when it states "every day He manifests Himself in yet another (wondrous) way. Which, then, of your Sustainer's powers can you disavow?" (29:55). This Allah manifests Himself every day in a new state (*sha'n*). And the word *yaum* literally means day, but figuratively it can also mean a whole epoch, a period. Taking the word *yaum* in this sense, the verse will mean Allah manifests His Glories in new ways from period to period, from epoch to epoch.

The early commentators of the Qur'an, on which depends the conservative view of the *'ulama*, were a product of their own socio-religious and socio-cultural situation. In the early days of Islam, particularly in the period of four caliphs succeeding the Holy Prophet, state was very closely identified with religion of Islam. In the Arabia of those days there did not exist even a state before advent of Islam, let alone any laws associated with the state. But a state came into existence when Islam united people of Arabia, transcending tribal bonds.

The state needed laws to deal with the fast evolving situation. First they took help of the Qur'an and then Sunnah of the Prophet. Even then if they could not solve the problem, they held the assembly of the companions of the prophet and tried to solve the problem in consultation with them. Their collective wisdom was often of great help. But it is quite obvious that they heavily drew from their own experiences in the social milieu they lived in. This social milieu also heavily influenced their understanding of the Qur'anic verses. And some Qur'anic verses were integrally related to the situation obtaining there.

The problem really arose when the subsequent generations treated the understanding of the Qur'anic verses by the companions of the Prophet or the early commentators who drew their own understanding heavily from the pronouncements of these companions and their followers (*tabi'in*). The companions were thought to be—and rightly so—as great authorities as the Qur'an was revealed during their life time and in their presence and who could understand it better than these companions. Most of the subsequent commentators simply referred to these companions, and their followers' pronouncements became the only source of understanding the Qur'anic verses. Until today the commentators of the Qur'an are repeating those very ideas and these ideas have become sacred and any deviation is considered heresy by most of the orthodox commentators of the Qur'an.

The Islamic state which came into existence after the death of the Prophet, as pointed out above, also became a model for the subsequent generation though this model was hardly followed even in the early period of Islamic history. The Umayyad and the Abbasid empires which came into existence after what is called khilafat-e-rashidah (i.e., the rightly guided period of khilafat, Islamic state) never followed this religious model. Both the empires were based on personal and authoritarian rule and were Islamic only in name. The Umayyad and the Abbasid Caliphs followed their own personal desires rather than the Qur'anic injunctions or the Shari'ah rules. They just symbolically made their obeisance to religion and followed what was in their personal interest. Thus theirs were what we can call "semi-secular" states.

And the states which came into existence after the Abbasid state were even more secularised except the Fatimid state which was more or less based on the Isma'ili theology. Even the Fatimid Imams had to face serious problems as their Isma'ili followers were very few in their domain and the vast majority belonged to the Sunni faith. Thus they often separated affairs of the state from Isma'ili theological considerations. A separate department of Isma'ili theology (Fatimi Da'wah) had to be established.

Though the Khilafat model was never repeated in the history of Islam, in theory it remained the objective of all the Islamic theologians to establish the state on the model of early Khilafat, and any state which did not follow that model came to be condemned as un-Islamic and it was even more strongly condemned if the state claimed to be secular. Maulana Maududi opposed Jinnah [Ali Jinnah, the founder and first leader of modern Pakistan] vehemently because his vision of Pakistani state was based on the secular concept giving all citizens equal rights irrespective of their religious faith. The Maulana refused to support the Pakistan movement as Jinnah would not agree to set up an Islamic state.

Now the question is whether Islam as a religion is compatible with secularism? Does it aim at setting up an Islamic state and nothing less? Can there be a Muslim country with a secular state? These are some of the crucial questions one has to answer in order to deal with the subject of Islam and secularism. Of course, we should remember that there cannot be uncontested answers. Every answer that we attempt would be, and could be, contested by those with differing viewpoints. Ours is a liberal and inclusive approach and we will, of course, attempt to answer from this viewpoint. . . .

Now the important question is can Islam and secularism go together? We have already said above that religion and secularism can go together or not, depending on the interpretation of both religion as well as secularism. If religion is interpreted in keeping with very conservative traditions, it may be difficult for it to go along with secularism which demands more liberal disposition and not only tolerance but also promotion of pluralism. On the other hand, if secularism is interpreted too rigidly (i.e., if it is equated with atheism), as many rationalists do, then also the two (i.e., religion and secularism) will find it difficult to go together.

Islam too, as pointed out above, can be interpreted rigidly, or liberally. If both Islam and secularism are interpreted liberally, there should not be any problem with Islam in a secular setup. In fact if one studies the Qur'an holistically one can find strong support for "liberal or non-atheistic secularism." No religion will support atheistic secularism for that matter. If we talk of liberal secularism, what do we mean by it? We must clearly define it. Liberal secularism does not insist on belief in atheism. Secondly, it promotes pluralism and respect for all faiths, and thirdly it guarantees full freedom of religion for all citizens. Also, secularism guarantees equal rights for all citizens irrespective of one's caste, creed, race, language or faith.

Islam can hardly clash with this liberal secularism. The Qur'an, in fact, directly encourages pluralism (its verse 5:48). This verse clearly states that every people have their own law and a way (i.e., every nation is unique in its way of life, its rules, etc.). It also says that if Allah had pleased He would have created all human beings a single people, but He did not do so in order to test them (whether they can live in harmony with each other despite their differences in laws and way of life). Thus it is a clear assertion of pluralism. One must respect the other's faith and live in harmony with him/her.

The Qur'an also asserts that every people have their own way of worshiping God (see 2:148). One should not quarrel about this. Instead one should try to excel each other in good deeds. In the verses 60:7–8 we find that Allah will bring about friendship between Muslims and those whom you hold as enemies. And Allah does not forbid you from respecting those who fight you not for religion, nor drive you forth from your homes and deal with them justly. Allah loves doers of justice.

The above verse is a good example of secular ethos. If others do not fight you in matters of your faith and allow you to profess, practice and propagate your faith, you should respect them and deal with them justly. This is precisely what our own secular constitution says and this is what secular constitutions world over emphasise. Also, in 6:109 the Qur'an prohibits Muslims from abusing people of other faiths or their gods as in turn they will abuse Allah. This verse also makes a much more significant statement that Allah has made for every people their deeds fair-seeming (i.e., every community thinks its beliefs and deeds are fair and good and social harmony lies in accepting this situation rather than quarreling about each other's beliefs and practices).

The Qur'an also states in 22:40 that no religious place should be demolished as in all religious places, be it synagogue, or church or monastery, name of Allah is remembered and hence all these places should be protected. This is another tenet of liberal secularism which is upheld by the Qur'an.

The Islamic tenets, it will be seen, do not disapprove of a composite or pluralistic way of life. Even the Covenant of Madina (called Mithaq-i-Madina) clearly approves of pluralistic setup. When the Prophet migrated from Mecca to Madina owing to persecution in Mecca at the hands of Meccan tribal leaders, he found Madinese society a pluralistic society. There were Jews, pagans and Muslims and also Jews and pagans were divided into several tribes, each tribe having its own customs and traditions. The Prophet drew up a covenant with these tribes guaranteeing them full freedom of their faith and also creating a common community in the city of Medina with an obligation to defend it, if attacked from outside.

This was in a way a precursor of a modern secular nation, every citizen free to follow his/her own faith and tribal customs and their own personal laws but having an obligation towards the city to maintain peace within and defend it from without. The Prophet clearly set an example that people of different faiths and traditions can live together in peace and harmony, creating a common bond and respecting a common obligation towards the city/country.

Yet another question which remains to be answered is about equal rights to all citizens in a country with Muslim majority. It is often argued that Muslims are reluctant to accord equal citizenship rights to religious minorities. No doubt there is some truth in this assertion but not the whole truth. Some Muslim majority countries certainly do not allow non-Muslims equal rights, but many other countries do. We have already given examples of countries like Indonesia and Malaysia. Both countries, though Muslim majorities, do allow all their citizens, including the non-Muslims, equal political rights. Pakistan too, until Zia-ul-Haq's time, enjoyed equal citizenship rights and joint electorate. It was Zia who created a separate electorate for non-Muslims.

In the Qur'an, as pointed out elsewhere, there is no concept of state, nor of territorial nationalism. In fact religious scriptures are hardly supposed to deal with such questions. It nowhere states that it is obligatory for Muslims to set up a religious or a theocratic state. The Qur'an does not refer, not even indirectly, to any concept of state. Its whole emphasis is on truth, justice, benevolence, compassion, tolerance and wisdom as far as life in this world is concerned. As long as people conform to these values, it does not matter what religious faith they belong to. They can coexist in peace and harmony. Thus the concept of a purely Islamic state is a historical construct attempted by Muslim jurists over a period of time. It is these jurists who laid down detailed rules of Shari'ah and also drew up a configuration of an Islamic state defining the rights of non-Muslims in such a state. Moreover it was a very different historical situation and the Qur'anic verses were interpreted under the influence of their own social and religious ethos.

The rights of non-Muslims, in other words, will have to be rethought and reformulated. The Qur'an nowhere states that religion can be the basis of political rights of the people. This was the opinion of Muslim jurists of the medieval period when religion of the ruler determined the status of the ruled. Such a formulation cannot be considered a necessary part of the political theory of Islam. The only model for this purpose can be the Mithaq-i-Madina and this Covenant, as pointed out above, did not make any distinction between people of one religion and the other in matters of political rights. This Covenant, at least in spirit, if not in form, provides a valuable guidance for according political rights to citizens of a modern state irrespective of one's religion. It is unfortunate that the later political theorists of Islam almost wholly neglected this significant political document drawn up by the Prophet of Islam. In fact he was far ahead of his time in according non-Muslims equal religious and political rights. The theory of political rights in the modern Islamic state should be based on this document.

There is a great deal of emphasis on freedom of conscience and human rights in the modern civil society. It is highly regrettable that most of the Muslim countries do not have a good record in this field. Freedom of conscience, human rights and democracy are quite integral to each other. In most of the Muslim majority countries today which have declared themselves as "Islamic countries," even the democratic discourse is banished, let alone human rights discourse. It is not right to maintain that an Islamic society cannot admit of human rights. The lack of democracy and human rights is not because of Islam or Islamic teachings but due to authoritarian and corrupt regimes which totally lack transparency in governance. Again, if we go by the sunnah of the Prophet and record of governance of the rightly guided caliphs, we see that the principle of accountability and transparency in governance was quite fundamental. The people who had experienced the conduct of the Prophet were so sensitive to the doctrine of accountability that there was a great uprising when the regime of the third Caliph deviated from this doctrine for various reasons not to be discussed here. The Prophet of Islam and his companions had sensitised the Muslims to such an extent in respect of accountability and transparency in governance that any deviation from it was strongly protested. But when authoritarian regimes came into existence and khilafat turned into monarchy beginning with the first Umayyad monarch Yazid, this doctrine vanished into thin air. . . .

From all this will be seen that Islamic teachings as embodied in the Qur'an and Sunnah of the Prophet (and not opinions of the jurists) are not against the concept of human rights and individual freedom (freedom of conscience). It is authoritarian rulers of some Muslim countries who denounce the concept of human rights as alien to Islam. Islam, in fact, is the first religion which legally recognised other religions and gave them dignified status and also accepted the concept of dignity of all children of Adam (17:70) irrespective of their faith, race, tribe, nationality or language (49:13).

The verse 2:213 is also quite significant on the unity of all human beings which is what is the intention of Allah. All differences are human and not divine and these differences should be resolved in a democratic and goodly manner (29:46). These are the norms laid down by the Qur'an, but the rulers of Muslim countries deviate from these norms to protect their hold on power and blame it on Islam.

Islam upholds pluralism, freedom of conscience and human and democratic rights and thus does not clash with the concept of secularism. It is also interesting to note that in a secular setup like India's the *ulama* accepted secular principles of governance and never objected to it. In fact, the *ulama* in India stress secularism and urge upon Muslim masses to vote for secular parties. . . . Of late the Jama'at-e-Islami-i-Hind has also accepted secular democracy and has even set up a secular democratic front of its own, particularly after demolition of Babri Masjid and the riots that followed it. Thus it will be seen that the Indian *ulama* have shown a way in this respect by accepting secularism. Islam and secularism can and should go together in the modern world.

III

ISLAM AND SOCIAL CHANGE

MODERNIZATION OF ISLAMIC LAW

Under the impact of the West, modern change in Islamic law first occurred in the nineteenth century in the Ottoman Middle East and in the Indian subcontinent. This was accomplished through the enactment of commercial and penal codes, which, both in form and substance, were derived from European models. In addition, secular (*nizamiyya*) courts were established to handle civil and criminal cases, and thus the religious (Sharia) courts' jurisdiction was limited to the area of family law. At the same time, the first attempts at codification of civil law took place, resulting in, for example, the Ottoman *Mejelle* of 1877. Thus, from the latter part of the nineteenth century, Islamic law in much of the Muslim world was restricted to the domain of family law.

The twentieth century saw the continuation of the trend toward modernization through the adoption of Western secular codes. In some Muslim countries the functions of the Sharia courts were absorbed by the civil court system, thus ending the dual court system (religious and secular) which had been created during the nineteenth century. In addition, as will be discussed, for the first time changes were introduced in Muslim family law; however, the methodology employed was one of reinterpretation and reform of the Sharia rather than its displacement by secular codes.

Although Turkey decided to follow a path of complete secularization and adopted the Swiss Civil Code (1928) even in the area of family law, she was a unique exception. Most Muslim countries have continued to acknowledge the Sharia as "a source" (if not "the source") of their nations' law. In effect, these Muslim nations have developed modern legal systems in which the Sharia has been primarily restricted to family law.

In the contemporary Islamic world there have been renewed demands for a return to a more Islamic way of life. This reemergence of Islam in the political sphere has been accompanied by demands for a more Islamic legal system by those who maintain that it is the Sharia that determines the Islamic character of a state and its people.

The first two selections exemplify two quite divergent approaches to the problem of Islamic legal reform. Subhī Mahmasānī advocates the need to reinterpret and adapt Islamic law to the modern world; however, Āsaf A. A. Fyzee espouses a secular path and thus argues the need for modern Islam to separate religion from politics and law.

The contemporary resurgence of Islam has resurrected the issue of Islamic legal reform as many Muslims have responded to calls for the reintroduction of Islamic law. Central to any discussion is the role of women in the Quran. Amina Wadud looks at the rights and roles of women, rereading the text from a woman's perspective. Ahmad Zaki Yamani analyzes and comments on the political competence of women in classical Islamic law. Muhammad Sa'id al-'Ashmawi assesses the positions of conservatives, militants, and reformers and offers his methodology for Islamic legal reform. Heba Raouf Ezzat examines the future of women and politics, specifically with regard to their political participation and the need for a major paradigm shift. Sisters in Islam, a Malaysian NGO, provides an example of how a women's organization has responded to the state and its legal system on issues of Islamic law.

The major and most contested area of Islamic legal reform has occurred in Muslim family law (laws governing marriage, divorce, and inheritance). Family law is the heart of the Sharia, reflecting the importance of the family in Islam. Although modern legal reform began in the nineteenth century, reform in family law did not occur until the twentieth century. The process of legal adaptation employed differed from that which had previously occurred in other areas of Islamic law. With few exceptions Muslim family law reform was characterized not by the replacement of Islamic law with Western-based codes but by the incorporation of selective changes based on reform through a process of reinterpretation that drew on the Islamic legal tradition for its rationale and its new provisions.

Family law reform, however, did not occur without a great deal of debate between conservatives and modernists on both methodological and substantive legal questions. The conflict over family law reform was graphically portrayed in the debate that surrounded Pakistan's *Muslim Family Laws Ordinance* of 1961. The Commission on Marriage and Family Laws was established in 1955. The majority (laypersons) and minority (the sole member of the ulama) reports reflected the deep-seated questions all reform encounters: Who shall do it? How shall it be accomplished? What may or may not be changed?

In addition to legal reform, another way in which law has been relevant to the process of modernization is the use of fatwas (fatwa; pl. fatwas)—formal legal opinions or interpretations given by a mufti (a legal specialist). Fatwas have been used to legitimate social changes from the veil (*hijab*) to bioethics (organ donation, genetic engineering, birth control, surrogate motherhood, and abortion).

SUBHĪ MAHMASĀNĪ
1911–1986

An LL.B. and *Docteur en Droit* (University of Lyons), he has
served as magistrate, president of the Appeals Court (1944–46),
member of Parliament, and minister of Economy (1966). He has
taught at a number of universities, including the American
University of Beirut and the Lebanese University.

Adaptation of Islamic Jurisprudence to Modern Social Needs

CLOSING THE DOOR OF IJTIHĀD AND NEGLECT OF EDUCATION

Islamic Jurisprudence dealt with questions of religion and acts of worship,
and with legal transactions, along with all provisions, rules, and particulars derived from them. That is why jurists in Islam were at once men of
religion and jurisprudence. They were called "scholars" (*'ulamā'*) because
their field of study included all departments of ancient knowledge. As a
result, Islamic jurisprudence played such a significant role in the history of
Islamic thought as well as in all aspects of Muslim life.

It is known that Islamic jurisprudence is based on various sources;
some religious, the Qur'ān and the Sunna, and some secondary accepted by
the majority of the jurists: *ijmā'* (consensus of opinion) and *qiyās* (analogy).
There are other sources acknowledged by some schools but refuted by
others. These are based on necessity, custom and equity; such as *istihsān*
(appropriateness) in the Hanafī school, *al-masālih al-mursalat* (excepted
interests) in the Mālikī school, and the like.

The jurists took up all these sources, known as evidence (*adillat*) of
law, in a special branch of knowledge called *'ilm al-usūl* (science of basic
sources). They began to work at discovering legal solutions from such
sources and evidences. This sort of activity was referred to as *ijtihād*
(endeavor or interpretation). It was a cause for expanding legal provisions
to comprise new cases, as well as a strong factor in the development of
Islamic law according to the needs of different countries and the conditions
of changing times. Thus, *ijtihād* had led to the flourishing of Islamic
jurisprudence, especially at the early stage of the 'Abbāsid period.

From "Muslims: Decadence and Renaissance" *in Muslim World* 44 (1954), pp. 186–91,
196–97, 199–201.

When Baghdad fell in the middle of the seventh century A.H., intellectual activities diminished, and Arab civilization began to decline. This took place after the Sunni jurists unanimously agreed to close the door of *ijtihād* and to be contented with the four known Sunnite schools: the Hanafite, the Mālikite, the Shāfi'ite, and the Hanbalite. The result was that Islamic thought met a dead end, and imitation and stagnation in jurisprudence and other Arabic and Islamic learning became predominant.

In fact, the closure of *ijtihād* violates the provisions and concepts of Islamic jurisprudence and condemns all Muslims to permanent stagnation and exclusion from the application of the laws of evolution. It imposes upon them to maintain the same conditions prevailing at the time of ancient jurists, and to follow the pattern they had set for themselves and for the Muslims of their days and the days that will follow until eternity.

No doubt, the remedy lies in opening what the ancients had closed or attempted to close. The door of *ijtihād* should be thrown wide open for anyone juristically qualified. The error, all the error, lies in blind imitation and restraint of thought. What is right is to allow freedom of interpretation of Islamic jurisprudence, and to liberate thought and make it capable of true scientific creativeness. . . .

ADHERENCE TO DOUBTFUL TEXTS

What brought about disagreement in law is the fact that the Prophet did not order the writing of the *Sunna* as he did regarding the Qur'ān. On the contrary, he prohibited such an action by saying: "Don't write down from me, and whoever wrote down from me other than the Qur'ān should have it destroyed. There is no harm in relating from me." (*Sahīb Muslim*, Vol. 8, pp. 229). This made 'Umar ibn al-Khattāb refuse to compile the traditions. He was afraid lest the people would take them up and leave the Qur'ān.

However, despite such discouragement, traditions were forged in great number during certain periods of Islamic history. This was done to serve and support certain policies or factions, or to popularize storytelling or to achieve other purposes. Consequently, the traditions became impossibly numerous. Many unreliable and absurd traditions could not possibly stand in logic and reason.

Faced with this situation, Muslim jurists began to study and examine them. They laid down a set of scientific rules by which to judge and determine their authenticity. These rules came to constitute a special science called the Science of Traditional Method (*Mustalah al-Hadīth*). In addition, many were prompted to write, warning their readers of false traditions. As a result, there was agreement among jurists regarding some traditions and disagreement regarding others. As an example of fabricated traditions, one may cite the following: "The sea is of hell." "The mouse is Jewish." "Eggplant is the cure of all sickness."

Modernist jurists, such as Ibn Taimiyyat and Muhammad 'Abduh, also revolted against this deplorable situation. They began to examine traditions in the light of the principles of jurisprudence and reason. . . .

The remedy of this evil is obvious and within reach. All forged traditions without exception should be discarded. Nothing should remain except those authentic traditions on which agreement by jurists of the known schools had been unanimous.

In compliance with this warning, Muslim reformists should liberate themselves from the remnants of error, forgery, falsehood and fabrication. They must discard made-up traditions which are incompatible with legal texts and principles, or with the rules laid down by the Science of the Sources of Law (*Usūl al-Fiqh*), or by logic and reason, on which all provisions of Islamic jurisprudence are based.

ADHERENCE TO FORMALISM AND PARTICULARS

The provisions of Islamic jurisprudence are based less on the texts than on interpretations of the jurists. The texts form the bases of the principles and universal rules; whereas most details and particulars are based on the interpretation of jurists by way of unanimity, (*ijmā'*) analogy (*qiyās*), or other legal sources. These details and particulars fill huge volumes of legal work, so that research regarding them requires a long time and considerable effort.

Furthermore, this great body of particulars often dominated the general principles, and, with repeated imitation, took a rigid and formalistic taint alien to the original substance. Some jurists of late adhered to them and through blind imitation transmitted them as basic obligatory provisions, without any discrimination or examination in the light of the original principles and texts and without the criterion of reason and thought. Thus, details dominated the basis and the form overshadowed the substance. Such a state of things was one of the causes which led to the decline and stagnation of Islamic culture. . . .

SECTARIAN DIFFERENCES

. . . In general, disagreements among schools were not on the whole disagreements on basic principles and doctrines, but rather on details as a result of diversity of interpretations and differences of views in applying principles to practical cases.

The existence of diversity of opinions was a reason for flexibility in Islamic jurisprudence, as well as a cause of relief to the people. Thus it was said: "Disagreement among jurists is the nation's bliss." This is supported by the fact that the Ottoman Empire which adopted the Hanafite School in law and religion borrowed from other schools many legal provisions, particularly in its Family Code. . . .

However, alongside those advantages of diversity of schools there were disadvantages too, most important of which was sectarianism, with all its outcome of discord, animosity and hatred. Followers of each school were often so by inheritance and tradition rather than by reason and conviction. They displayed strong fanaticism towards their own school and its leaders and attacked other schools and leaders with flagrant bitterness. There were days when strife became intense between the Shī'ites and the Sunnites as well as among the different schools and sects within these two groups. Such a strife was one of the causes leading to disunity and backwardness among Muslims.

THE SOURCES OF LAW AND MODERN LEGAL REFORM

To cure this evil, struggle must be waged against sectarian partisanship, Efforts must be made to reconcile all hearts and unite the various schools. This, in my opinion, can be achieved by a return to the same and only original sources of law. Such a return should take into consideration the following bases:

I. To adopt the provisions of the Qur'ān as the first basis for Islamic teachings and jurisprudence; to distinguish in this respect between compulsory and voluntary or directive provisions on the lines already attempted by interpreters of the Qur'ān and scholars of the Science of Legal Sources; and then to apply these provisions in accordance with their respective significance.

II. To adopt the Sunna in all obligatory religious provisions, provided that this Sunna is authentic and acceptable in the various Muslim schools and that it is not inconsistent with the text of the Qur'ān.

III. To adopt the rest of the Sunna, that is to say the traditional teachings and precepts whose authenticity had been disputed by reliable leaders of the schools, provided they are consistent with reason and acceptable to jurists and scholars of the Science of Legal Sources ('Ilm al-Usūl) on the basis of the principle mentioned above, namely that the truly traditional is always consistent with the truly rational.

IV. To choose from the legal rules based on interpretations of jurists those which are most suitable to the needs of modern society, public interest and principles of justice and equity.

Such are the practical fundamental lines which will lead to the unification of Muslim schools—a unification that has become at the present time an urgent necessity. . . .

Moreover, the idea of unifying the various schools is consistent with the spirit of Islamic jurisprudence and its teachings.

"Those who are discordant in their religion and separated into parties, do not belong to you." (Qur'ān 4:159).

If Islam prohibits religious fanaticism and demands brotherhood and tolerance between Muslims and the rest of the world, for better reason it does not allow sectarianism among Muslims themselves. . . .

Muslim jurists, as we have already mentioned, studied Islam as being a religion, a law and a social system. This is why Islamic jurisprudence contained provisions pertaining to acts of worship as well as to legal transactions.

As a consequence, there has been an inter-action between the teachings of religion and ethics on the one hand, and the provisions of law on the other hand. Thus we find justice and charity, coupled by the Qur'ān in one single verse: "God enjoins justice and charity," so that it has become a rule of justice not to do harm to one another, and a duty in legal transactions to abide by the principles of honesty and tolerance. All of this, no doubt, has been a source of benefit for the Muslims. It has made Islamic jurisprudence human and just.

Accordingly, earlier Muslim jurists made a differentiation in certain cases between the legal and the religious rulings, a differentiation similar to that made today between civil and natural obligations. They were, for instance, of the opinion that if a man had the right to repudiate his wife in law, his repudiation in order to be valid in religion must be based on justifiable grounds. Otherwise it would be proof of rashness and ingratitude towards the blessings of marriage which is based on love and mercy.

However, some jurists were influenced by dominant pre-Islamic customs and therefore did not go beyond this imperfect step. They declined to apply in such cases the ruling imposed by the teachings of religion. If they had done so, giving religious and ethical principles more consideration, along with as much implementation in law as had been possible, their attitude would have been closer to the spirit of Islamic jurisprudence and teachings.

In addition, we find that some jurists, especially during the period of imitation and decline, had, despite their differentiation between legal and religious rulings, discarded such differentiation with regard to other matters. They mixed religion with the daily ways of life and studied Islam as comprising both categories in similar degree. They were, thus, unmindful of the fact that the basis in Islam is the religion and its teachings and that the world and its affairs are only the accessories. Indeed, their excess in this respect was such that incidental worldly matters were placed on the same level with the original, essential and immortal provisions of religion.

As a result, stagnation in Islamic thought and culture was bound to take place. Muslims of earlier days adhered to trivialities, so much so that they condemned as a prohibited innovation anything unknown during the time of the Prophet or their time. Thus, for instance, they advocated the prohibition of the study of foreign languages, eating with the fork, wearing the hat, and other worldly trivial matters.

But if we refer to the essence of Islamic jurisprudence, we find that the teachings of the Prophet do not bind the Muslims except in cases pertaining to religion and ethics, along with their accessories. Traditions which refer to secondary matters of daily living and which the Prophet had mentioned as a matter of opinion, are not mandatory. In support of this statement, we may cite the tradition included by Muslim in his collection of traditions (Vol. 7, p. 95), namely that the Prophet once passed by some people who were fecundating-palm trees and he asked: "What are these people doing?" The answer was that they were fecundating palm trees. To this the Prophet said: "If they would not do that (the trees) would be prolific." When they were told of his words they stopped that pollination. But the fruits did not ripen. Upon learning about this, the Prophet said: "I am only a human being; If I order you to do something regarding your religion you must comply. But if I order you to do something on the basis of my opinion, well I am just a human being. You know better in matters concerning your worldly affairs."

Therefore, no relation whatever exists between Islam and matters of daily living, unless these are concerned with a principle of religion. By religion, here, is meant the provisions of the faith, the unity of God, acts of worship, along with the principles of ethics and the fundamental rules of legal transactions. Outside these, the above-mentioned tradition leaves to the Muslims freedom in secondary matters relating to their daily life. It is because they know more about such matters, and because such matters are subject to changes in accordance with their needs and interests.

Muslims must comprehend this rule, and thereby separate provisions of religion from matters of daily life in the manner explained. They ought to adhere to their religion and ethical code, and manage their ways of life according to the spirit of Islam and requirements of science and civilization. It is by so doing that they will be able to put an end to their backwardness in this respect and to rise towards happiness and prosperity.

To sum up, the most important factor in the decline of Muslims is their neglect of the duties of Islam. Improvement of their condition can be brought about by their return to the true principles of Islam, their understanding of the effective causes of legal rules, and their giving what belongs to religion to religion and what belongs to the world to the world, along with their determination to destroy the walls of ignorance and imitation, to reject unauthentic texts, formalistic technicalities, particulars, and details, together with sectarian partisanship—all of which have distorted the real essence of Islam.

Muslims have to choose between two courses: the course of ignorant imitators, thereby accepting darkness and ignorance and oblivion; or the course of the pious predecessors which leads to light and knowledge and life. . . .

ĀSAF A. A. FYZEE
1899–1981

He was a distinguished jurist, professor of law, and former Vice-Chancellor of the University of Jammu and Kashmir as well as a former visiting professor at Cambridge University and U.C.L.A. Among his more important works are *Outlines of Muhammadan Law* and *A Modern Approach to Islam*.

The Reinterpretation of Islam

In Islam law is not distinct from religion. The two streams flow in a single channel and are indistinguishable. They are known as *Sharīʿa* (Pers., Tur., Urdu,—*Sharīʿa*) and *fiqh*, the two aspects of the religious law of Islam. *Sharīʿa* is the wider circle, it embraces in its orbit all human actions; *fiqh* is the narrower one, and deals with what are commonly understood as legal acts. *Sharīʿa* always reminds us of revelation, that *ʿilm* (knowledge) which we could never have possessed by for the Qurʾān or *hadīth*; in *fiqh*, the power of reasoning is stressed, and deductions based upon *ʿilm* are continuously cited with approval. The path of *Sharīʿa* is laid down by God and His Prophet; the edifice of *fiqh* is erected by human endeavour.

It must, however, be candidly confessed that the line of distinction is by no means clearly drawn, and very often the Muslim doctors themselves use the terms synonymously: for, the criterion of all human action, whether in the *Sharīʿa* or in the *fiqh*, is the same—seeking the approval of Allah by conforming to an ideally perfect code. . . . The faith of Islam teaches the belief in one God and His Messengers; but it cannot and ought not to lay down how it can enforce such obedience. By "enforce" is meant (*a*) order the doing of a thing and (*b*) punish its disobedience. How can a matter of faith be a matter of enforcement by an outside agency? A teacher may teach me; he can inspire me by his example; he can fire my enthusiasm. But how can he make me believe? Thus there is a clear difference between a rule of law which can be enforced by the state, and a rule of conscience which is entirely a man's own affair.

Today in Islam this is the greatest difficulty. *Sharīʿa* embraces both law and religion. Religion is based upon spiritual experience; law is based upon the will of the community as expressed by its legislature, or any other law-making authority. Religion is unchangeable in its innermost kernel—the love of God for His own sake is sung by *sūfīs* and mystics throughout

From *A Modern Approach to Islam* (Bombay: Asia Publ. House, 1962), pp. 85–96, 98–108.

the world. If *sharī'a* is the name given to this duality, then one of the forces constantly pulls in the other direction. The cognition of God is a mystery, and man is forever pursuing it. In this pursuit, all men of faith regardless of their particular religion are equal. But laws differ from country to country, from time to time. They must ever seek to conform to the changing pattern of society. The laws of the Arabs cannot be applied to the Eskimos; and the laws of the bushmen of Australia are unsuitable for the fertile basin of Uttar Pradesh. Laws are like metals in the crucible of time and circumstance; they melt, they gradually solidify into different shapes; they re-melt and assume diverse forms. This process of evolution is coterminous with human society. Nothing is static except that which is dead and lifeless. Laws can never be static. India is changing with the rest of the world before our own eyes. These changes are the result of our powers over nature, our views on life, and our desire to improve the social conditions of men. Our legislature pours out a stream of statutory law, and this legislative activity attempts to regulate our dealings in society.

But the mind and conscience of man is free. He must be permitted to believe what he will in respect of the ultimate things in the universe, and he cannot be fettered in his faith and imagination. There is thus an internal strife in Islam. First, the ageless concepts of the religious law come into conflict with modern civil law, e.g. insurance or the loans which Government raises. Insurance and the giving or taking of interest is forbidden by the *Sharī'a*; while it is not only permitted but encouraged by the modern state.

Secondly, in order to do away with the rigours of the older law, principles of a newer system are engrafted upon the ancient law of Islam; or a new set of laws replaced the *Sharī'a*. An illustration of the former is the Muhammadan law of Gifts in India, where the principles of English equity are grafted upon the *fiqh* (Islamic law, proper). An illustration of the latter is the Evidence Act in India, which completely replaces the Islamic law of Evidence. Everywhere in Islamic countries this dual process is at work—*qānūn*, the secular law, is eating into and replacing the laws of the *Sharī'a*. In North Africa, French jurisprudence; in Central Asia, the Soviet laws; in India, the English common law; in Indonesia, the Dutch law and above all, International law, are profoundly influencing not only the body of law but the meaning of justice as it affects the Muslims.

We have seen that the *Sharī'a* is both law and religion. Law is by its very nature subject to change. The heart of religion, on the other hand, is unchangeable, or at any rate, the belief in God is an unalterable ideal, a perennial quest. If two such divergent forces are made to live together, there will be a clash. . . . My solution is (*a*) to define religion and law in terms of twentieth century thought, (*b*) to distinguish between religion and law in Islam, and (*c*) to interpret Islam on this basis and give a fresh meaning to the faith of Islam. If by this analysis some elements that we have regarded as part of the essence of Islam have to be modified, or given up altogether, then we have to face the consequences. If, on the other hand, belief in the innermost core can be preserved and strengthened, the operation although painful will produce health and vigour in an anaemic body which is languishing without a fresh ideal to guide it. . . .

GENERAL PRINCIPLES OF REINTERPRETATION

Historical Approach

The message of Islam was sent to the world fourteen centuries ago. Does it need reinterpretation? Is it not meant for the whole world and for all time? The answer to both questions is in the affirmative. Even if a message is true, and, in a sense eternal, it is by the very premises essential to understand it in accordance with the science, philosophy, psychology, metaphysics and theology of the modern world; nay, the sum-total of the world's thinking and its blazing light should be brought to bear upon it. . . . No language remains static. The evocative power of words and phrases increases and decreases; it is not a constant factor, it is one of the known variables. . . . I wish to *understand* the Qur'ān as it was understood by the Arabs of the time of the Prophet only to *reinterpret* it and apply it to my conditions of life and to believe in it, so far as it appeals to me as a twentieth-century man. I cannot be called upon to live in the desert, to traverse it on camel back, to eat locusts, to indulge in vendetta, to wear a beard and a cloak, and to cultivate a pseudo-Arab mentality. I must distinguish between poetic truth and factual truth. I must distinguish between the husk and the kernel of religion, between law and legend. I am bound to understand and accept the message of Islam as a modern man, and not as one who lived centuries ago. I respect authority, but cannot accept it "without how" (*bilā kayfa*) in the matter of conscience.

Islam is based upon the Qur'ān, and the Qur'ān is to be interpreted in its historical setting and on chronological principles. We must first study the main principles of Judaism and Christianity before approaching Islam. . . .

SPECIFIC RULES OF INTERPRETATION

Fundamental Principles

The six principles which are proposed for a modern reinterpretation of Islam are as follows:

  i. Study of History of Religions.
 ii. Comparative Religion of the Semitic Races.
iii. Study of Semitic languages and philology.
 iv. Separation of Law and Religion.
  v. Re-examination of *Sharī'a* and *kalām*.
 vi. Reinterpretation of cosmology and scientific facts. . . .

Separation of Law from Religion

The separation of *civil* law from the *moral* or *religious* law can now no longer be delayed in Islam. We must in the first instance distinguish between the universal moral rule, such as, truthfulness, marital purity, honesty, etc., and the particular moral rules, such as the prohibition of ham and of wine. The former are enjoined by all religions; the latter are not. A difference of emphasis is clearly indicated in such cases.

And then we must deal with the law. The first task is to separate logically the dogmas and doctrines of religion from the principles and rules of law. The essential faith of man is something different from the outward observance of rules; moral rules apply to the conscience, but legal rules can be enforced only by the state. Ethical norms are subjective, legal rules are objective. The inner life of the spirit, the "Idea of the Holy," must be separated to some extent from the outward forms of social behaviour. The separation is not simple; it will even be considered un-Islamic. But the attempt at a rethinking of the *Sharī'a* can only begin with the acceptance of this principle. . . .

Such a liberal interpretation would affect the constitution of an Islamic country. According to Islam, God is the owner of everything; He is the true sovereign in a state. Such a theory would be impractical in the modern world, and the only workable principle is as laid down by numerous modern democratic constitutions, namely, that the people of a country are sovereign within their own domain. If religion is gradually freed from the shackles of civil law, and law (*qānūn*) is allowed to grow and develop freely, Muslim society is bound to progress rapidly. . . .

Re-examination of Sharī'a and Kalām (Theology)

The theology of Islam must be re-examined in all its aspects, and modern philosophy, metaphysics, ethics, psychology and logic should be applied to formulate and restate its essential dogmas. The scholastic theology of Islam (*'ilm al-kalām*) in its various aspects has not been substantially reformed since the days of Ghazālī. The current stream of European thought; the great advances made by Protestant thinkers from Luther downwards, and by the scholastics from St. Thomas Aquinas and Suarez down to Maritain and Berdyaev; and the speculations of Jewish and other thinkers of the modern world must be used with discrimination to fortify and re-shape Islamic theological principles. . . .

Subsidiary Principles. When a rule is laid down in the Qur'ān or *Sharī'a* it is necessary to determine whether it is a rule of law or a rule of ethics. If it is a rule of law, the state should enforce it; if it is a rule of ethics, the state cannot enforce it. Once it is determined in accordance with the foregoing principles that there is a *clear rule of law laid down in the Qur'ān*, the question assumes importance. The law of God, it is said, cannot be disobeyed. This statement, it is respectfully submitted, requires careful re-examination.

The Qur'ān may lay down a *fundamental* rule governing the actions of man; or it may speak of a *particular* by-law, restricted by time and circumstance, not laying down an eternal verity, or it may speak in the language of poetry, metaphor, myth or legend: *He it is Who hath revealed unto thee (Muhammad) the Scripture wherein are clear revelations* (muhkamāt)— *They are the substance of the Book—and others (which are) allegorical* (mutashābihāt), Qur'ān 3:7.

In such a case, we may come to the conclusion that it is a question of interpretation and that law can be changed, but religion is more permanent and need not be altered.

In order to examine a clear dictate of the Qur'ān . . . we must follow a certain procedure. The procedure submitted is as follows:

1. *What was the rule or custom before Islam?* . . .

2. *How did the Prophet try to reform it?* . . .

3. *What were the results of such reform?* The case of *women* may be taken as an illustration. The law of marriage in Islam, with certain important reservations, is beneficial to women; and so is the law of inheritance. Why is it that almost everywhere in Islamic countries women have been denied rights by custom over immovable property? That is so in India, Indonesia, Egypt, Persia, and North Africa. And what is more disturbing is that not only is woman denied her Qur'ānic rights but she is considered *inferior* to man and not fit for certain political rights. Travel in Muslim countries demonstrates the painful fact that woman is considered the plaything of man and seldom a life-companion, co-worker, or helpmate. It is not enough to brush this aside by saying that a particular practice is un-Islamic or contrary to the spirit of Islam. It is necessary to face facts, to go to the root of the matter, to give up inequitable interpretations, and to re-educate the people. The Qur'ānic verse: *Men are in charge of women, because God hath made one of them to excel the other* (Qur'ān 4:34) should be reinterpreted as purely local and applicable only for the time being. Its wider application should be reconsidered; and it may be possible to construe it as a rule of social conduct which was restricted to conditions existing in Arabia at the time of the Prophet, and as being no longer applicable in modern life.

4. *How were the rules applied and interpreted in the various schools of law in the succeeding centuries?* The two rules mentioned above are closely connected. Contemporary sources, particularly independent and critical accounts, will have to be scrutinized to discover what the immediate results were, and the historical evolution of the doctrines will have to be examined. Were the commands obeyed in the latter and the spirit in the succeeding centuries? Were they misunderstood or changed or distorted? Were they used for political or personal ends? These are some of the questions that arise.

5. *What is the present state of the personal law? How far does it fall short of the highest norms fixed by modern juristic thinking? In what way*

can the rules be sustained, amended, or repealed, so as to conform to mod-
ern concepts of social justice and to promote the social well-being of the
Muslim community as an integral part of society in general? This method
of interpretation deals with the personal law in India; a similar process can
be applied to theological and moral rules.

If the complete fabric of the *Sharī'a* is examined in this critical manner, it is obvious that in addition to the orthodox and stable pattern of religion, a newer "protestant" Islam will be born in conformity with conditions
of life in the twentieth century, cutting away the dead wood of the past and
looking hopefully at the future. We need not bother about nomenclature,
but if some name has to be given to it, let us call it *"Liberal Islam."*

RESULTS

The greatest gift of the modern world to man is freedom—freedom to think,
freedom to speak, freedom to act. . . .

And what does Islam do, so far as religious doctrine is concerned? It
closes the Gate of Interpretation. It lays down that legists and jurisconsults
are to be divided into certain categories, and no freedom of thought is
allowed. Iqbāl and 'Abdur Rahīm amongst recent Indian writers have
rebelled against this doctrine, and yet none ventures to face the wrath of
the *'ulamā'*. Some ten years ago, there were disturbances in Pakistan and
an inquiry was instituted. The Chief Justice of Pakistan questioned several
'ulamā' regarding Islam and its essential tenets; and, according to his
analysis, some of the *'ulamā'* were, in the opinion of their fellow-*'ulamā'*,
unbelievers. Such is the degree to which *fossilization* of thought has taken
place in our faith. Islam, in its orthodox interpretation, has lost the
resilience needed for adaptation to modern thought and modern life.

It must be realized that religious practices have become soulless
ritual; that large numbers of decent Muslims have ceased to find solace or
consolation in the traditional forms of prayer and fasting; that good books
on religion are not being written for modern times; that women are treated
badly, economically and morally, and that political rights are denied to
them even in fairly advanced countries by the *fatwās* of reactionary *'ulamā'*;
that Muslims, even where they constitute the majority in a country, are
often economically poor, educationally backward, spiritually bankrupt and
insist on "safeguards"; that the beneficial laws of early Islam have in many
instances fallen behind the times; and that the futile attempt to plant an
Islamic theocracy in any modern state or fashion life after the pattern of
early Islam is doomed to failure.

And finally, that the time for heart-searching has come. Islam must be
reinterpreted, or else its traditional form may be lost beyond retrieve. . . .

AMINA WADUD
1952–

An expert on the Quran and Islam, Amina Wadud was trained
at the University of Michigan, taught at the International Islamic
University in Kuala Lumpur, and is currently a professor of
Islamic studies in the Department of Philosophy and Religious
Studies at Virginia Commonwealth University.

Rights and Roles of Woman

It would be impossible to have a discussion on any topic in the Qur'an
which would exhaust the material covered in the text itself. Nor would
it be possible to conclude in definitive terms the significance of all the
material in the Qur'an concerning humankind on earth. The text was
revealed to the inhabitants of the earth, while they inhabited the earth, and
we are all on the earth as we read and discuss the text. As such, our earthly
existence transforms our perceptions of the text and is equally potentially
transformed by the text. More importantly, because of the Qur'an's
intention to guide the affairs of humans, a certain emphasis is placed on
understanding and applying the text while we are here on earth.

In my consideration of woman on earth from the Qur'anic perspective,
there are certain problems inherent in our understanding of what the
Qur'an depicts. Our operations on the earth are shaped by our world-view
(and vice versa). We have not yet attained the Qur'anic utopia. Whenever
Qur'anic support is given for conflicting opinions on how to operate in this
world, controversies arise. Many popular or dominant ideas about the role
of woman do not have sanction from the Qur'an. Pointing these out causes
problems, not so much with logical analysis of the text, but with application of the new analysis in the context in which Muslim societies operate.

Hermeneutics of any text must confront three different aspects in order
to support its conclusions: 1. the context in which the text was written
(in the case of the Qur'an, in which it was revealed); 2. the grammatical
composition of the text (how it says what it says); and 3. the whole text,
its *Weltanschauung* or world-view. Often, differences of opinion can be
traced to variations in emphasis between these three aspects.

I will discuss selected concepts, terms or verses from these perspectives:
1. There is no inherent value placed on man or woman. In fact, there is no
arbitrary, pre-ordained and eternal system of hierarchy. 2. The Qur'an does

From Amina Wadud, *Qur'an and Woman: Rereading the Sacred Text from a Woman's
Perspective* (New York: Oxford University Press, 1999), pp. 62–91.

not strictly delineate the roles of woman and the roles of man to such an extent as to propose only a single possibility for each gender (that is, women must fulfil this role, and *only* this one, while men must fulfil that role and only men *can* fulfil it).

To demonstrate these points, I will make a detailed analysis of Qur'anic passages which have been interpreted to imply the superiority of males over females. In doing this, I will demonstrate a more integrated communal perspective on the rights and responsibilities of the individual in society using certain Qur'anic concepts.

Overall, my analysis tends to restrict the meaning of many passages to a particular subject, event, or context. These restrictions are based on the context of the verses or on application of general Qur'anic concepts of justice towards humankind, human dignity, equal rights before the law and before Allah, mutual responsibility, and equitable relations between humans. . . .

FUNCTIONAL DISTINCTIONS ON EARTH

The Qur'an treats woman as an individual in the same manner as it treats man as an individual. Their only distinction is on the basis of *taqwa* (God-conscious piety). *Taqwa* is not determined by gender. The Qur'an also focuses on how we function in society. It acknowledges that we operate in social systems with certain functional distinctions. The relationship that the Qur'an shows between these worldly distinctions and *taqwa* is important in my consideration of equity among people. More importantly, functional distinctions included in the Qur'an have been used to support the idea of inherent superiority of men over women.

Functional distinctions are indicators of roles and role expectations. To what extent does the Qur'an delineate functions for each gender? Are there certain exceptions and exclusions for males or females? Does the Qur'an value certain functions above others?

WOMAN IS NOT JUST BIOLOGY

Because woman's primary distinction is on the basis of her child-bearing ability, it is seen as her primary function. The use of 'primary' has had negative connotations in that it has been held to imply that women can only be mothers. Therefore, women's entire upbringing must be to cultivate devoted wives and ideal mothers in preparation for this function.

There is no term in the Qur'an which indicates that child-bearing is 'primary' to a woman. No indication is given that mothering is her exclusive role. It demonstrates the fact a woman (though certainly not all women) is the exclusive human capable of bearing children. This capacity is essential to the continuation of human existence. This function becomes primary only with regard to the continuity of the human race. In other words, since only the woman can bear children, it is of primary importance that she does.

Although it does not restrict the female to functioning as a mother, the Qur'an is emphatic about the reverence, sympathy, and responsibility due to the female procreator. 'O humankind . . . have *taqwa* towards Allah in Whom you claim your rights of one another, and (have *taqwa*) towards the wombs (that bore you)' (4:1). This verse is often interpreted as indicating respect for women in general. I specify this verse as indicating respect for the needed procreative capacity of women. I do not diminish respect from women as a class, but I do specify, from the Qur'anic perspective, the significance of the function of child-bearing, which is exclusively performed by women. The reverence given to the fulfilment of this function helps to explain how the Qur'an explicitly delineates a function for males which creates a balance in human relations.

No other function is similarly exclusive to one gender or the other. This brings to mind the popular misconception that since only males have had the responsibility of *risalah*, it indicates something special about that class. Both men and women have been included in divine communication as the recipients of *wahy*, but there is no Qur'anic example of a woman with the responsibility of *risalah*. However, all those chosen for this responsibility were exceptional.

This is not a biological association with males representing their primary function and expressing a universal norm for all men. In fact, given the difficulty they have faced in getting others to accept the message when these exceptional men have come from poor classes, the likelihood of failure for the message might have been greater if women, who are given so little regard in most societies, were selected to deliver the message. It is a strategy for effectiveness, not a statement of divine preference.

Besides the two functions discussed above, every other function has real or potential participation by both males and females. However, there is still a wide range of functional distinctions between individuals considered in the Qur'an. The questions that must be asked then are: What is the value of the functional distinctions between individuals? Do these functional distinctions and the values placed on them delineate specific values for males and females in society? Are these values intra-Qur'anic or extra-Qur'anic?

In particular, several verses from the Qur'an have frequently been used to support the claims of the inherent superiority of males over females. These verses contain two terms which have been used to indicate value in the functional distinctions between individuals and groups on earth. I will review these terms, how they have been used in the Qur'an, and in the overall context of Qur'anic justice.

The first term is *darajah* (pl. *darajat*), 'step, degree or level'. A *darajah* exists not only here on earth between people but also between the Hereafter and earth, between levels in Heaven and in Hell. The other term, *faddala* is often used in conjunction with *darajat*. I have translated *faddala* 'to prefer', with a verbal noun (*tafdil*) meaning 'preference'. Often the preference given is spoken of in terms of *fadl*, which I translate as (Allah's) 'benevolence'.

DARAJAH

An individual or group can earn or be granted a *darajah* over another. The Qur'an specifies, for example, that by striving in the way of Allah with one's wealth and one's person (4:95) or by immigrating for Allah (9:20), one can obtain a *darajah*. However, most often the *darajah* is obtained through an unspecified category of doing 'good' deeds (20:75, 6:132, 46:19).

Distinguishing between individuals or groups on the basis of 'deeds' involves problems with regard to the value of women in society and as individuals. Although the Qur'an distinguishes on the basis of deeds, it does not set values for particular deeds. This leaves each social system to determine the value of different kinds of deeds at will. They have always done this and 'every society has distinguished men's work from women's work'. The problem is that 'Men's work is usually regarded as more valuable than women's work, no matter how arbitrary the division of labor'.

On the one hand, the Qur'an supports distinctions on the basis of deeds, but on the other hand, it does not determine the actual value of specific deeds. This leads to the interpretation that the Qur'an supports values of deeds as determined by individual societies. Actually, the Qur'an's neutrality allows for the natural variations that exist.

With regard to the *darajah* obtained through deeds, however, the Qur'an has stipulated several points which should affect evaluation in society. First, all deeds performed with *taqwa* are more valuable. Second, 'Unto men a fortune from that which they have earned and unto women a fortune from that which they have earned' (4:32). The deeds may be different, but recompense is given based on what one does. It does not matter how the deeds are divided between the males and the females in a particular social context.

Another implication of a 'fortune from what one earns' is that whenever anyone performs tasks normally attributed to the other gender in addition to his or her own normal tasks, he or she will earn an additional reward. For example, Moses meets two women from Madyan, where ordinarily the males tended the animals. However, because there was no able-bodied male in the family to perform this task according to the norm (the father being an old man), the women were required to be *extraordinarily* useful.

There is no indication that these women were immoral in their performance of this task, because fulfiling the tasks needed for survival takes precedence over socially determined roles. Similarly, in post-slavery America, the Black female was given employment instead of the Black male. In many families, she became the sole supporter. This necessity, in addition to her fulfilment of the ordinary tasks of bearing and rearing children, should have given her more. A flexible perspective on the fulfilment of necessity would have benefited her. Instead, she was subject to a double burden and, often, violence at home from a husband who felt displaced.

Each social context divides the labour between the male and the female in such a way as to allow for the optimal function of that society. The Qur'an does not divide the labour and establish a monolithic order for every social system which completely disregards the natural variations in society. On the contrary, it acknowledges the need for variations when it states that the human race is divided 'into nations and tribes that you might know one another' (49:13). Then it gives each group, and each member of the group—the males and the females—recompense in accordance to deeds performed.

This is an important social universal in the Qur'an. It allows and encourages each individual social context to determine its functional distinctions between members, but applies a single system of equitable recompense which can be adopted in every social context. This is also one reason why certain social systems have remained stagnant in their consideration of the potential roles of women. The Qur'an does not specifically determine the roles, and the individual nations have not considered all the possibilities.

As for the *darajah* which is 'given' by Allah, it is even more illusive than the *darajah* for unspecified deeds. There is a distinction on the basis of knowledge: 'Allah will exalt those who believe among you, and those who have knowledge, to high ranks [*darajat*]' (58:11). 'We raised by grades [*darajat*] (of mercy) whom We will, and over all endued with knowledge there is one more knowing' (12:76).

There are also social and economic distinctions: 'We have apportioned among them their livelihood in the life of the world, and raised some of them above others in ranks [*darajat*] that some of them may take labour from others; and the mercy of Allah is better than (the wealth) that they amass' (43:32). It is also clear, however, that wealth is not a 'real' distinguishing characteristic, but a functional distinction apparent to humankind and valued within society.

The *darajah* given by Allah serves another significant function—to test the inhabitants of the earth: 'He it is Who has placed you as viceroys of the earth and has exalted some of you in ranks [*darajat*] above others, that He may try you by (the test of) that which He has given you' (6:165).

Finally, it is necessary to discuss the one verse which distinguishes a *darajah* between men and women:

Women who are divorced shall wait, keeping themselves apart, three (monthly) courses. And it is not lawful for them that they conceal that which Allah has created in their wombs if they believe in Allah and the Last Day. And their husbands would do better to take them back in that case if they desire a reconciliation. And [(the rights) due to the women are similar to (the rights) against them, (or responsibilities they owe) with regard to] the *ma'ruf*, and men have a degree [*darajah*] above them (feminine plural). Allah is Mighty. Wise (2:228).

This verse has been taken to mean that a *darajah* exists between all men and all women, in every context. However, the context of the discussion is clearly with regard to divorce: men have an advantage over women. In the Qur'an the advantage men have is that of being individually able to pronounce divorce against their wives without arbitration or assistance. Divorce is granted to a woman, on the other hand, only after intervention of an authority (for example, a judge).

Considering the details given, *darajah* in this verse must be restricted to the subject at hand. To attribute an unrestricted value to one gender over another contradicts the equity established throughout the Qur'an with regard to the individual: each *nafs* shall have in accordance to what it earns. Yet, the verse is presumed to state what men have believed and wanted others to believe: that society operates hierarchically with the male on top.

Finally, this verse states: '[(the rights) due to the women are similar to (the rights) against them, (or responsibilities they owe) with regard to] the *ma'ruf*.' The term *ma'ruf* occurs in other instances with regard to the treatment of women in society. Pickthall translates it as 'kindness', but its implications are much wider than that. It is a passive participle of the verbal root 'to know', and as such indicates something 'obvious', 'well known' or 'conventionally accepted'. However, with regard to treatment, it also has dimensions of equitable, courteous and beneficial.

In this verse (2:228), it precedes the *darajah* statement to indicate its precedence. In other words, the basis for equitable treatment is conventionally agreed upon in society. With regard to this, the rights and the responsibilities of the woman and the man are the same. Again, the expression places a limitation rather than a universal perspective on this issue because convention is relative to time and place.

FADDALA

As with *darajah*, the Qur'an states explicitly that Allah has preferred [*faddala*] some of creation over others. Like *darajah*, this preference is also discussed in specific terms. First, humankind is preferred over the rest of creation (17:70). Then, occasionally, one group of people have been preferred over another. Finally, some of the prophets are preferred over others (2:253, 6:86, 17:55). It is interesting to note, however, that 'preference' is not absolute. Although the Qur'an states that some prophets are preferred over others, it also states that *no distinction* is made between them (2:285). This indicates that, in the Qur'anic usage, preference is relative.

Like *darajah*, *faddala* is also given to test the one to whom it is given. Unlike *darajah*, however, *faddala* cannot be earned by performing certain deeds. It can only be given by Allah, Who has it and grants it to whom He wishes and in the form He wishes. Others do not have it and cannot give it. They can only be recipients of His *fadl*.

With regard to *faddala*, men and women, the following verse is central:

Men are [*qawwamuna 'ala*] women, [on the basis] of what Allah has
[preferred] (*faddala*) some of them over others, and [on the basis] of what
they spend of their property (for the support of women). So good women
are [*qanitat*], guarding in secret that which Allah has guarded. As for those
from whom you fear [*nushuz*], admonish them, banish them to beds apart,
and scourge them. Then, if they obey you, seek not a way against them
(4:34).

Needless to say, this verse covers a great deal more than just preference. This is classically viewed as the single most important verse with
regard to the relationship between men and women: 'men are *qawwamuna
'ala* women'. Before discussing this, however, I want to point out that this
correlation is determined on the basis of two things: 1. what 'preference'
has been given, and 2. 'what they spend of their property (for support of
women),' i.e. a socioeconomic norm and ideal.

The translation I have inserted, 'on the basis of,' comes from the *bi* used
in this verse. In a sentence, it implies that the characteristics or contents
before *bi* are determined 'on the basis' of what comes after *bi*. In this verse
it means that men are *qawwamuna 'ala* women only if the following two
conditions exist. The first condition is 'preference', and the other is that they
support the women from their means. 'If either condition fails, then the man
is not '*qawwam*' over that woman'.

My first concern then is *faddala*. The verse says the position between
men and women is based on 'what' Allah has preferred. With regard to
material preference, there is only one Qur'anic reference which specifies
that Allah has determined for men a portion greater than for women:
inheritance. The share for a male is twice that for the female (4:7) within a
single family. The absolute inheritance for all men will not always be more
than that for all women. The exact amount left depends on the family's
wealth in the first place.

In addition, if verse 4:34 refers to a preference demonstrated in
inheritance, then such a materialistic preference is also not absolute. This
connection is often favoured because the other condition for *qiwamah* is
that 'they spend of their property (for the support of women)'. Thus, there
is a reciprocity between privileges and responsibilities. Men have the
responsibility of paying out of their wealth for the support of women, and
they are consequently granted a double share of inheritance.

However, it cannot be overlooked that 'Many men interpret the above
passage' as an unconditional indication of the preference of men over
women. They assert that 'men were created by God superior to women (in
strength and reason)'.

However, this interpretation, . . . is (i) unwarranted and (ii) inconsistent with
other Islamic teachings . . . the interpretation is unwarranted because there
is no reference in the passage to male physical or intellectual superiority.

Faddala cannot be unconditional because verse 4:34 does not read 'they (masculine plural) are preferred over them (feminine plural)'. It reads '*ba'd* (some) of them over *ba'd* (others)'. The use of *ba'd* relates to what obviously has been observed in the human context. All men do not excel over all women in all manners. Some men excel over some women in some manners. Likewise, some women excel over some men in some manners. So, whatever Allah has preferred, it is still not absolute.

If 'what' Allah has preferred is restricted to the material (and specifically inheritance), then the extent and nature of the preference is explained by the Qur'an. Even if 'what' Allah has preferred is more than just the preference given in inheritance, it is, nevertheless, still restricted to 'some of them' over 'some others' by the wording in this context:

> 'men are '*qawwamun*' over women in matters where God gave *some* of the men more than *some* of the women, *and* in what the men spend of their money, then clearly men as a class are not '*qawwamun*' over women *as a class*.

However, further understanding of this distinction requires further explanation of *qawwamuna 'ala*. What does it mean, and what are the parameters of its application?

As for the meaning, Pickthall translates this as 'in charge of'. Al-Zamakhshari says it means that 'men are in charge of the affairs of women'. Maududi says 'Men are the managers of the affairs of women because Allah has made the one superior to the other. . . .' Azizah al-Hibri objects to any translation which implies that men are protectors or maintainers because 'The basic notion here is one of moral guidance and caring' and also because:

> only under extreme condition, (for example, insanity) does the Muslim woman lose her right to self-determination. . . . Yet men have used this passage to exercise absolute authority over women. They also use it to argue for the male's divinely ordained and inherent superiority.

Some questions beg asking concerning the parameters of application: Are all men *qawwamuna 'ala* all women? Is it restricted to the family, such that the men of a family are *qawwumuna 'ala* the women of that family? Or, is it even more restricted, to the marital tie, such that only husbands are *qawwumuna 'ala* wives? All of these possibilities have been given.

Generally, an individual scholar who considers *faddala* an unconditional preference of males over females does not restrict *qiwamah* to the family relationship but applies it to society at large. Men, the superior beings, are *qawwamuna 'ala* women, the dependent, inferior beings.

Sayyid Qutb, whose discussion I will consider at length, considers *qiwamah* an issue of concern for the family within society. He restricts verse

4:34, in some ways, then, to the relationship between the husband and the wife. He believes that providing for the females gives the male the privilege of being *qawwamuna 'ala* the female.

He gives *qiwamah* a decided dimension of material maintenance. The rationale behind restricting this verse to the context of husband and wife is partly due to the fact that the remainder of the verse discusses other details of concern to the marital relationship. In addition, the following verse uses the dual, indicating that it is concerned with the context between the two: the husband and wife. However, preceding verses discuss terms of relations between male members of society and female members of society.

I apply this verse to society at large—but not on the basis of inherent superiority of men over women, or of Allah's preference of men over women. Rather, I extend the functional relationship, which Sayyid Qutb proposes between the husband and the wife, towards the collective good concerning the relationship between men and women in society at large. My main consideration is the responsibility and right of women to bear children.

Sayyid Qutb says. 'The man and the woman are both from Allah's creation and Allah . . . never intends to oppress anyone from His creation. Both the man and the woman are members of the most significant institution of society, the family. The family is initiated by marriage between one man and one woman. Within the family, each member has certain responsibilities. For obvious biological reasons, a primary responsibility for the woman is child-bearing.

The child-bearing responsibility is of grave importance: human existence depends upon it. This responsibility requires a great deal of physical strength, stamina, intelligence, and deep personal commitment. Yet, while this responsibility is so obvious and important, what is the responsibility of the male in this family and society at large? For simple balance and justice in creation, and to avoid oppression, his responsibility must be equally significant to the continuation of the human race. The Qur'an establishes his responsibility as *qiwamah*: seeing to it that the woman is not burdened with additional responsibilities which jeopardize that primary demanding responsibility that only she can fulfil.

Ideally, *everything* she needs to fulfil her primary responsibility comfortably should be supplied in society, by the male: this means physical protection as well as material sustenance. Otherwise, 'it would be a serious oppression against the woman'.

This ideal scenario establishes an equitable and mutually dependent relationship. However, it does not allow for many of today's realities. What happens in societies experiencing a population overload, such as China and India? What happens in capitalistic societies like America, where a single income is no longer sufficient to maintain a reasonably comfortable life-style? What happens when a woman is barren? Does she still deserve *qiwamah* like other women? What happens to the balance of responsibility when the man cannot provide materially, as was often the case during slavery and post-slavery US?

All of these issues cannot be resolved if we look narrowly at verse 4:34. Therefore, the Qur'an must eternally be reviewed with regard to human exchange and mutual responsibility between males and females. This verse establishes an ideal obligation for men with regard to women to create a balanced and shared society. This responsibility is neither biological nor inherent, but it is valuable. An attitude inclined towards responsibility must be cultivated. It is easy enough to see the cases in which it has not been acquired.

However, such an attitude should not be restricted to mere material *qiwamah*. In broader terms, it should apply to the spiritual, moral, intellectual, and psychological dimensions as well. Such a perspective on *qiwamah* will allow men to truly fulfil their *khilafah* (trusteeship) on the earth, as ordained by Allah upon human creation. Such an attitude will overcome the competitive and hierarchical thinking which destroys rather than nurtures.

Men are encouraged to fulfil their trusteeship of the earth—especially in relationships with women, the child-bearers and traditional caretakers. What women have learned through bearing and caring for children, men can begin to experience, starting with their attitudes to and treatment of women.

NUSHUZ: DISRUPTION OF MARITAL HARMONY

Finally, with regard to this verse, I will discuss whether this portion,

> So good women are *qanitat*, guarding in secret that which Allah has guarded. As for those from whom you fear (*nushuz*), admonish them, banish them to beds apart, and scourge them. Then, if they obey you, seek not a way against them.

means that a woman *must* obey her husband, and if she does not, he can beat her (here translated 'scourge'). I believe the passage intends to provide a means for resolving disharmony between husband and wife.

First, the word *qanitat*, used here to describe 'good' women, is too often falsely translated to mean 'obedient', and then assumed to mean 'obedient to the husband'. In the context of the whole Qur'an, this word is used with regard to both males (2:238, 3:17, 33:35) and females (4:34, 33:34, 66:5, 66:12). It describes a characteristic or personality trait of believers towards Allah. They are inclined towards being co-operative with one another and subservient before Allah. This is clearly distinguished from mere obedience between created beings which the word *ta'a* indicates.

Sayyid Qutb points out that this choice of words indicates that the Qur'an intends there to be a personal emotional response rather than the external 'following of orders' which the *ta'a* (obey) would suggest. As for the use of that word *ta'a* and the remainder of the verse, 'As for those (feminine plural) from whom you fear *nushuz* . . .', it should first be noted that the word *nushuz* likewise is used with both males (4:128) and females (4:34), although it has been defined differently for each. When applied to the wife, the term is usually defined as 'disobedience to the husband'. With the use of *ta'a* that follows. Others have said this verse indicates that the wife must obey the husband.

However, since the Qur'an uses *nushuz* for both the male and the female, it cannot mean 'disobedience to the husband'. Sayyid Qutb explains it as a state of disorder between the married couple. In case of disorder, what suggestions does the Qur'an give as possible solutions? There is 1. A verbal solution: whether between the husband and wife (as here in verse 4:34) or between the husband and wife with the help of arbiters (as in 4:35, 128). If open discussion fails, then a more drastic solution: 2. separation is indicated. Only in extreme cases a final measure: 3. the 'scourge' is permitted.

With regard to regaining marital harmony, the following points need to be raised. First, the Qur'an gives precedence to the state of order and emphasizes the importance of regaining it. In other words, it is not a disciplinary measure to be used for disagreement between spouses. Second, if the steps are followed in the sequential manner suggested by the Qur'an, it would seem possible to regain order before the final step. Third, even if the third solution is reached, the nature of the 'scourge' cannot be such as to create conjugal violence or a struggle between the couple because that is 'un-Islamic'.

It appears that the first measure is the best solution offered and the one preferred by the Qur'an, because it is discussed in both instances of the word *nushuz*. It is also in line with the general Qur'anic principle of mutual consultation, or *shura*, being the best method for resolving matters between two parties. It is obvious that the Qur'an intends a resolution of the difficulties and a return to peace and harmony between the couple when it states: '. . . it is no sin for the two of them if they make terms of peace between themselves. *Peace is better*' (4:128). It is peace and 'making amends' (4:128) that are the goals, not violence and forced obedience.

The second solution is, literally, to 'banish them to beds apart'. First, the significance of 'beds apart' is possible only when the couple continually shares a bed (unlike polygamy when husband and one wife do not), otherwise, this would not be a meaningful measure. In addition, 'beds apart' indicates that at least one night should pass in such a state. Therefore, it is a cooling-off period which would allow both the man and the woman, separately, to reflect on the problem at hand. As such, this measure also has equally mutual implications.

As one night apart can lead to many nights apart before any resolution is made, this separation could go on indefinitely. This does not indicate that a man should then begin to physically abuse his wife. Rather, it allows for a mutually found peaceable solution, or a continued separation—divorce. Divorce also requires a waiting period, and beds apart is characteristic of that waiting. Thus, this measure can be taken as part of the overall context of irreconcilable differences between the married couple.

It cannot be overlooked, however, that verse 4:34 does state the third suggestion using the word *daraba*, 'to strike'. According to *Lisan al-'Arab* and *Lanes's Lexicon, daraba* does not necessarily indicate force or violence. It is used in the Qur'an, for example, in the phrase '*daraba Allah mathalan* . . .' ('Allah *gives* or *sets* as an example . . .'). It is also used when someone leaves, or 'strikes out' on a journey.

It is, however, strongly contrasted to the second form, the intensive, of this verb—*darraba*: to strike repeatedly or intensely. In the light of the excessive violence towards women indicated in the biographies of the Companions and by practices condemned in the Qur'an (like female infanticide), this verse should be taken as prohibiting unchecked violence against females. Thus, this is not permission, but a severe restriction of existing practices.

Finally, the problem of domestic violence among Muslims today is not rooted in this Qur'anic passage. A few men strike their wives after completely following the Qur'anic suggestions for regaining marital harmony. The goal of such men is harm, not harmony. As such, after the fact, they cannot refer to verse 4:34 to justify their action.

Finally, the word *ta'a* in this verse needs a contextual consideration. It says 'if they obey (*ta'a*) you do not seek a way against them.' For the women, it is a conditional sentence, not a command. In the case of marriages of subjugation—the norm for Muslims and non-Muslims at the time of the revelation—wives were obedient to husbands. The husbands are commanded 'not so seek a way against' wives who are obedient. The emphasis is on the male's treatment of the female.

The Qur'an never orders a woman to obey her husband. It never states that obedience to their husbands is a characteristic of the 'better women' (66:5), nor is it a prerequisite for women to enter the community of Islam (in the Bay'ah of the women: 60:12). However, in marriages of subjugation, wives did obey their husbands, usually because they believed that a husband who materially maintains his family, including the wife, deserves to be obeyed. Even in such cases, the norm at the time of the revelation, no correlation is made that a husband should beat his wife into obedience. Such an interpretation has no universal potential, and contradicts the essence of the Qur'an and the established practices of the Prophet. It involves a severe misreading of the Qur'an to support the lack of self-constraint in some men.

With regard to the relationship between maintenance and obedience, it can be observed that even husbands who are unable or unwilling to provide for their wives believe they should be obeyed. In fact, this widespread characteristic of Muslim marriage is only one example of the association of men as natural leaders deserving obedience.

- This belief in the need to obey the husband is remnant of marriages of subjugation and is not exclusive to Muslim history. It has not progressed, although today couples seek partners for mutual emotional, intellectual, economic, and spiritual enhancement. Their compatibility is based on mutual respect and honour, not on the subservience of the female to the male. The family is seen as a unit of mutual support and social propriety, not an institution to enslave a woman to the man who buys her at the highest price and then sustains her material and physical needs only, with no concern for the higher aspects of human development.

If the Qur'an was only relevant to this single marriage type, it would fail to present a compatible model to the changing needs and requirements of developing civilizations worldwide. Instead, the Qur'anic text focuses on the marital norm at the time of revelation, and applies constraints on the actions of the husbands with regard to wives. In the broader context, it develops a mechanism for resolving difficulties through mutual or extended consultation and arbitration.

In conclusion, the Qur'an prefers that men and women marry (4:25). Within marriage, there should be harmony (4:128) mutually built with love and mercy (30:21). The marriage tie is considered a protection for both the male and the female: 'They (feminine plural) are raiment for you (masculine plural) and you are raiment for them' (2:187). However, the Qur'an does not rule out the possibility of difficulty, which it suggests can be resolved. If all else fails, it also permits equitable divorce.

AHMED ZAKI YAMANI
1930–

Born in Mecca, Saudi Arabia, he was educated at Cairo
University and at New York University Law School; he received
his LL.M. from Harvard University School of Law. He serves as
Minister of State and was Saudi Arabia's Minister of Petroleum
from 1962 to 1986 and subsequently OPEC's first Secretary
General. A specialist in law and Islamic law, he is regarded as the
founder of many of the kingdom's modern laws and regulations.

The Political Competence
of Women in Islamic Law

One of the most controversial topics in our Arab and Islamic societies is
the question of women participating in public life and, particularly, working in the political arena. The opinions pro and con are generally based
upon texts that are interpreted in different ways according to local custom,
the social environment and the particular jurist's willingness to respond to
changing circumstances.

There are people who look at the question of women's political activity with a western eye and who attempt to force Islamic texts into a sem-
blance of agreement with the western point of view; but while the political
emancipation of women in the West was due to secular development the
Muslim position on reform and progress actually stems from the sacred
texts of both the Qur'an and the Sunnah, illuminated by the *maqasid* [pur-
poses and objectives] of Shari'ah, prevailing circumstances, and customs
which do not clash with the texts but rather move companionably alongside them.

Perhaps one of the most important distinctions between the Islamic
point of view and the western point of view, whether it be secular or religious, is that Islam is based on the concept of *tawhid* [oneness] in belief
and in life. God is one and unique, humanity is one.

The idea of oneness for Muslims derives basically from their belief in
one God, one universe and one humanity. Muslims therefore do not conceive of duality or trinitarianism in their religious belief, their pattern of life
or their view of the universe.

Another important concept in Islamic philosophy is the *khalifah* vested
by God in man. For when God created Adam and before He breathed His

Reprinted by permission of the author.

spirit into him He said to the angels: "I am putting on earth a khalifah." The khalifah here was not for Adam alone but for Adam and Eve and their offspring male and female.

The Qur'an is repeatedly inclusive as in "And their Lord responded I do not allow your deeds—be you male or female—to go to waste. You are of each other." "Whosoever, male or female, does good deeds and is a believer We will give unto them a good life and their reward shall be yet better than their deeds." "O people we have created you of male and female and made you into nations and tribes that you may get to know one another. The most honored amongst you in the eyes of God is the one who heeds Him most, for God is knowing of all things."

The concept of the khalifah rests on the oneness of women and men within a relationship expressed in the Qur'an as ". . . and the believers, men and women, guardians over each other. . . ." This is a common and mutual guardianship, governed by a bond of faith within the framework of one nation. So it is proved that equality between men and women is the original condition, an equality between partners in God, and so it is that the Prophet said "Women are an equal part of men."

Men and women are equal in their human value, their social rights, their responsibilities and their subjection to reward and punishment. This equality, in turn, is built upon the oneness of their origin and their destiny: their accountability on the Day of Judgment.

Some may put forward the rules specific to woman such as her liberation from some economic burdens or her different portion of inheritance. But these are exceptions to be seen against the backdrop of the general rule of equality. They have obvious financial reasons and cannot in any way affect the general principle of equality.

Al-Imam Ibn Hazm says "As the messenger of God was sent equally to men and to women, and as the speech of both God and His Prophet was addressed to men and women, it is not permissible to exclude women from any part of this except on the evidence of a clear text or unanimous opinion as this would be *takhsis al-zahir* [qualifying the obvious] which is not permissible."

This position is not weakened by the attempts of some jurists in the past to exclude women from Qur'anic discourse except where there is clear evidence to the contrary, for other jurists insisted that women cannot in fact be excluded from Qur'anic discourse except where the evidence for such exclusion is clear. It is to the latter school that the opinion of Ibn Hazm quoted above belongs.

Work or action ['amal] is an essential component of Islamic belief and Shari'ah as proclaimed by the Qur'an. [In the classification of actions], political action falls into the category of wajib [duty] . . . a duty which—although obligatory—does not have to be performed by every individual as long as enough individuals perform it, the rest are relieved of it. . . .

There is a clear difference here between political rights as a western concept, and the Islamic view which sees political action as a duty stemming naturally from the concepts of oneness and stewardship working for the good of the nation as defined by Shari'ah.

This duty, known in the West as political rights, falls upon every Muslim individual whether male or female in accordance with their ability, competence and resources. It is both an individual political duty and a communal co-operative duty; individuals are required to assist those who perform the communal duty and to assist the State in carrying out its obligations.

The difference between seeing political action as a right and seeing it as a duty is, of course, that a duty *has* to be performed while a right may or may not be used.

The Islamic concept is flexible, vital, dynamic. The imposition of a duty is in harmony with its own freedom of movement, with the legitimate interests of the individual and her/his ability to perform the action, for no-one may be commissioned to perform an action which they are unable to perform and God requires of each person only what that person is capable of.

When we study the question of woman's right to the offices of State, therefore, we ask: Which woman? What are her abilities? What is her degree of competence? We do not speak of "woman" in general and thus exclude her from the legal discourse describing a Muslim's duties.

WOMEN'S POLITICAL COMPETENCE

Although many Muslim writers love to hold forth on the rights gained by women under Islam, many of them have also adopted the concept of the social division of work: a woman's work is in the home looking after the family, while a man's work is out in the public realm earning money for the family. These writers admit that equality between men and women in both rights and duties is the base line in Islam, and yet some of them see that women should not push themselves into political affairs and that the political participation of women at the time of the Prophet and the four khalifahs following him was a matter of individual cases.

No Muslim man or woman is required to perform legal duties or obligations—including political duties—unless they are competent to perform them. Jurists divide competence into a "competence of duty" and a "competence of performance." The first describes a person's suitability for a legal requirement (or right) to fall upon her/him. The second is a person's suitability to act in a manner that is recognized legally.

Books of jurisdiction and civil law are full of explanations and detailing of competence in various areas—but not the political. The political competence of a woman is her suitability to participate in every activity in an Islamic society. Muslim jurists have affirmed women's competence in all civil matters—although their opinions vary on some details—but many of them have reservations regarding her political competence and have considered it deficient. They have employed evidence such as the hadith "deficient in mind and in religion" and considered deficiency a corollary of femaleness. This led to the removal of some duties from Muslim women such as jihad and attending public meetings, and from non-Muslim women such as payment of the *jizyah* [the tax payable by non-Muslims in lieu of the zakah tax paid by Muslims]. In this the jurists took no account of the different levels of political competence which fall into:

a. The "general competence" of all Muslims to take part in, for example, the bay'ah and the shurah

b. The "general competence in a specific area" such as the communal duties which may become—in certain circumstances—individual duties, e.g. jihad, where preparation and training are needed.

c. The competence specific to duties that can only be communal such as the holding of office: this is the competence that requires innate or natural abilities but which may also benefit from acquired skills.

So much for the political competence of woman, it remains to be said that her actual practice of her duties in this field has to be related to her degree of political awareness and know-how; she should have attained a level of education, knowledge and experience which enables her to exercise her political competence. In this she is no different from man.

There is no doubt that the social conditions prevailing in Muslim society have a crucial role to play in enabling women to play their part in political life—or in rendering them unfit to perform this duty. I will come to this later.

In the early days of Islam God lightened women's load and did not oblige them to attend public meetings. But they were obliged to attend communal prayers for the two major festivals: 'Id al-Fitr [the festival marking the end of Ramadan], and 'Id al-Adha [the festival, during the pilgrimage, celebrating Abraham's sacrifice of a sheep instead of his son].

The attendance of women at the 'Id prayers is not simply permissible; it is obligatory, as is their attendance at communal prayers called to discuss important matters or make known important news.

Participating in communal prayers where important public matters are discussed is one of the duties of women.

But the weakness which afflicted Islamic progress after the age of the Prophet gradually had a negative effect on the status of women. And it was helped by the pressure of custom; legislating texts started to be used in a manner that reflected custom and ignored the overall vision of those texts and the purposes of Shari'ah.

We have seen the importance of the level of a woman's awareness in her performing her political duties. We should now examine the influence of the social conditions that encourage or deter this political participation.

Social conditions were changing from the start, and the change was to the advantage of the society of Madinah rather than that of Makkah. The female Companions, particularly from the Ansar, took part in various activities. They attended prayers at the mosque and listened to the sermon. Some of them opened their houses to guests and hosted the immigrant Companions.

This development in the social conditions of Madinah took place under the aegis of Islamic Shari'ah and not in conflict with it. It is an example of social change that can now be broadened and extended. But it needs an effort from women to raise themselves to the task, and it needs juristic endeavor to support them in this—all within the framework of the definite texts of the Qur'an and the Sunnah and taking into account their purposes and their occasions.

In the West, woman's participation in politics is built on the bond of citizenship. It is a right that woman demands, a goal she works towards, a social status she desires. In the Islamic view this participation is a legal duty and a responsibility a woman has to prepare herself to fulfill. A major juristic interpretative effort should support her with the aim of effecting change in the social climate so that it accepts this participation and approves it.

The political participation of women in the West generally begins with the vote. This participation is then channeled through institutions and is aimed at influencing the decision-makers and promoting political stability. The Islamic view of the political participation of women starts with the idea of the religious-legal good, maslahah. The ummah, the nation, is the prime mover; institutions are merely instruments to bring about this maslahah. Women's political action therefore is in harmony with the rules and purposes of Shari'ah and with maslahah, the public interest. Bay'ah, wilayah and shurah are the means by which the main purpose—al-maslahah—is attained.

In Islam bay'ah is the most prominent political act. It is bay'ah that legitimizes a government, it is the contract of loyalty to that government and it is the right of every Muslim male or female.

The bay'ah has more or less disappeared from the political life of most Islamic states (except for some who cling to its form) but it is important for understanding the Islamic basis of our research on the public wilayah of women, or women and the offices of state.

It is difficult to find in the books or religious-legal politics or the works of jurisprudence generally a specific definition for public wilayah. In books that appeared in the later ages there are definitions—but they vary. We can say that wilayah is a legal authority that derives its power from religious law, Shari'ah. In this it differs from a post or an office which derives its power from the State and conforms to its rules and laws.

Public wilayah includes the Supreme Wilayah which is the khilafah, the leadership itself, followed by the judiciary, the hisbah and the shurah. These are all communal wilayahs, they are not posts but responsibilities.

Jurists are unanimous in that woman is not eligible for the khilafah because it includes religious duties which she cannot perform—even though she might be competent to perform its worldly or temporal duties. This opinion therefore does not affect her right to be Head of State or Prime Minister if that falls within her competence in a democratic state based on shurah.

With regard to the judiciary some jurists have seen that a woman may be a judge of matters in which she can bear witness, others have said simply that she may be a judge. Among those is Ibn Jarir al-Tabari who allowed that a woman may be an absolute judge of anything. He was followed by many jurists, among them Ibn Rushd (Averroes), Ibn Qudamah, Ibn Hazm and al-Shukani. We note here that women have become judges in the Islamic Republic of Iran.

As for hisbah, Ibn al-Khattab, appointed al-Shaffa'—a woman—for the judicial hisbah of the markets in Madinah.

We know also that women performed the duty of shurah and gave their opinion on many occasions in the time of the Prophet and the khilafah immediately following. Women perform their consultative duties in various ways: for example, to interpret the texts and give an opinion is a communal duty, jurists are unanimous therefore in allowing women's participation in discussions in jurisprudence of a legislative nature. Women also take part in consultation on specialized or technical matters where the criterion is professional competence. This too is a communal duty. They participate too in the general shurah as members of the ummah. This is an individual and binding duty.

It is true that women's actual practice of public wilayah only appeared intermittently during the Madinah years, but the fact that it appeared at all indicates its obligatory nature under different social conditions. The original condition for this wilayah is that it is obligatory but it was not possible to impose it on a society that was not yet ready to accept it in its fullest form. It was necessary to implement the idea gradually taking into account customs and the social environment, for we have seen how custom affected the position of women in Makkah, then in Madinah and so on.

The gradual introduction of rules is a known and accepted process in Islam; if the complete prohibition of alcohol had been suddenly announced Muslims might not have obeyed it.

I have restricted this paper on the public wilayah of woman to the opinions that have allowed it and their evidence for it on the basis of the Qur'an, the Sunnah, al-ijma', al-qiyas and al-maslahah.

Today, all Muslims should look at the activities in which woman takes part on the basis of her political competence in the Islamic system, we should look at them from an *usuli* perspective; that is the perspective of what was practiced originally (in the time of the Prophet). I have presented this as an example that can be followed and applied to our political life today in standing for parliament, the right to vote, the right to hold political office such as ministerial posts, or to hold posts in the judiciary. These should all be determined by the ability of a woman and her knowledge, adapted to social conditions and within the framework of the texts and purposes of Shari'ah.

I should point out that the Muslim woman has practiced her political competence with distinction. Biographies speak of the many women who spoke publicly against Mu'awiyah and supported the Imam 'Ali ibn Abi Talib. And even after Mu' awiyah took power the books speak of the women's debates and disputations with him. We mention Sawdah bint 'Imarah ibn al-Ashtar, Bakkarah al-Hilaliyyah, al-Zarqa' bint 'Udayy ibn Ghalib ibn Qais al-Hamadhaniyyah, 'Akrashah bint al-Atrash, Darmiyyah al-Hajuniyyah and Arwa bint al-Harith ibn 'Abd al-Muttalib. Looking through the history books one wonders at their eloquence, their rhetoric and their personalities. One admires their political astuteness. Note Hind bint Yazid al-Ansariyyah who opened her house in Iraq to become a political club for those opposed to Mu'awiyah. Men went there to consult with each other and Hind herself was eloquent, logical and persuasive. Ibn Jarir has written of her work and her rhetorical skill.

In the vanguard of women who distinguished themselves through effective and powerful political action is Umm Kulthum bint 'Ali ibn Abi Talib. It was she who accompanied (her nephew) 'Ali ibn al-Husayn ibn 'Ali to Kufah in the year 61 of the hijra where her speeches moved people to such an extent that al-Imam Khaddam al-Asadi wrote of her: "I have never seen a more eloquent woman . . . as though she spoke with the tongue of the Prince of the faithful, 'Ali. She gestured to the people to stop and their very breathing ceased, then she spoke and their tears ran into their beards."

In the fields of religious studies and hadith narrative (riwayah) women distinguished themselves over men in that there is not one known case of a woman accused of inaccuracy in her riwayah. But this is a topic which is far too large to go into here.

It is also important to remember that the history of Islam is full of Muslim women rulers and administrators. We mention Lubna who was appointed by the khalifah, al-Hakam ibn 'Abd al-Rahman al-Nasir, to head his office. She wrote his letters to the governors and those in authority, she administered his affairs and kept his secrets. We mention also Queen Arwa bint Ahmad, the wife of King al-Akram. She reigned in Yemen for 40 years at the end of the 5th century hijrah (the 11th century AD) and many books have been written documenting and analyzing her scientific, political and administrative achievements. Then there is Safiyyah Khatun (the niece of the Sultan Salah al-Din al-Ayyubi) who took the throne in Aleppo in the year 643 of the hijrah after the death of her father, Kung al-'Aziz, and ruled for six years. And Fatimah bint al-Hasan ibn Muhammad 'Ali, the Queen of San'a' in the Yemen, who annexed Sa'da and Najran. And Safwat al-Din Banishah bint Qutb al-Din (daughter of the sixth king of the Qatghali dynasty), Queen of Karman. Two queens ruled in India in Islamic times:

Skandar Begum and Shah Jihan, besides the Empress Nur Jihan who ruled Northern India in 1620 AD and had Indian coinage struck in her name. She was famous for her resolution, her wisdom and her good management of her country's political and military affairs. In Indonesia several women ruled between the years 1641 and 1688 AD, among them Safiyyat al-Din Taj al-'Alam, Naqiyyah Shah, 'Inayet Shah and Kemalet Shah.

These shining examples in the chronicles of Muslim women fulfilling their political duties fill us with pride. They also fill us with sorrow at the condition of women in some of our Islamic societies, at the way they are treated and at their being deprived of their God-given rights.

I end this paper by saying that Islam does not minimize the political competence of woman or deny it. That a woman's execution of her communal duties in this field is contingent on her abilities—and these are clearly developing and maturing—and on the social conditions of her society. The view that Islam prohibits men and women from mixing and holds that women should therefore refrain from taking part in any political activity (since that necessitates mixing) is a view to be rejected. The society of Madinah at the time of the Prophet saw men and women mixing in the markets and the mosque. What is prohibited in Islam is for a man and a woman to be alone illegitimately. The example we can give of this is a man visiting a woman in the absence of her husband [mughibah]. In this case the Prophet's instructions were that one man could not visit her alone but with one or two other to prevent suspicion. So is the visit of two or three men to the wife of a friend not mixing?

Then there is the case of Fatimah bin Shurayk whom the Prophet described as a women of many guests—to the extent that he forbade Fatimah bin Qays from spending her 'iddah in her home as it was a house full of men.

It is the duty of Muslim jurists, whose minds God has illuminated so that they have understood Islam,—its Shari'ah and the purposes of this Shari'ah, and who have at heart the religious-legal interest of the nation —it is their duty to use their interpretative abilities to the full and to declare their opinions frankly and clearly, so that the status of women in our Islamic societies is not made to develop outside the framework of Islam.

It is the duty of Muslim rulers in societies controlled by the rigid, fossilized, narrow-minded rules which are ascribed to Islam to carry the banner of a true and developed Muslim campaign.

I am not a jurist and I do not carry the responsibility of declaring juristic opinions, but the rapid plunge towards a terrible abyss has alarmed me. I have offered this contribution as an appeal to be heard by specialists who understand the Shari'ah and its purposes, and who are as concerned as I about our current circumstances and what our future seems to be. Perhaps others will step forward to research and write and give their contributions, but God alone is our support and it is He who will guide us to the righteous path.

MUHAMMAD SA'ID AL-'ASHMAWI
1932–

Former Chief Justice of the High Court of Cairo, Egypt, he is widely recognized for the forcefulness of his writings in the struggle to redefine Islam in the modern world. His refutation and condemnation of Islamic fundamentalists and extremists earned him praise from many liberals as well as criticism from conservative Muslims, and death threats from extremists in Egypt.

Reforming Islam and Islamic Law

REFORMING ISLAM AND LAW

Despite the fact that Islam dawned in a desert environment, it carried the potential to create a vast civilization. When the Arabs conquered Persia, Syria and Egypt in the first century of Islam, they were faced with well-established civilizations and superpowers of the day. The Arabs lost no time in selecting the most pertinent endowments of each civilization for the new civilization they intended to establish. In time, Islam itself became a well-established civilization, spreading across most of the Middle East. This civilization respected ethics and humanity.

Over the centuries a variety of schools were founded propounding various legal rules, theologies and philosophies. Unfortunately, their debates often raged over minor matters that were difficult to prove. The *mū'atazīla*, or withdrawers, thought rationally but stressed that the Qur'ān is created and not eternal. Opposing the mū'atazīla were the traditionalists, who deemed the Qur'ān eternal and uncreated. Had the debate centered on the historical context of the Qur'ān, the debate would have been profitable and effective. Instead, the debate moved from the philosophical sphere into the political sphere. Under Caliph Ma'amun (813–833 C.E./198–218 A.H.), the mū'atazīla came to power. Despite their advocacy of rationalism, they sought to impose their doctrine with the backing of state force.

A few years later, the mū'atazīla were ousted from power and were replaced by the traditionalists. Wary of the mū'atazīla, the traditionalists judged reason and the mind dangerous, liable to arouse strange ideas to be applied with force. Led by theologians Ashaari (873–941 C.E.) and Al-Ghazzali (1059–1111 C.E./606 A.H.) the traditionalists argued that since God is omnipotent and ruler over all, the mind, reason and causality could

From *Against Islamic Extremism*, ed. Carolyn Fluehr-Lobban (Gainesville, FL: University of Florida Press, 2001), pp. 119–26.

effect nothing and man's actions are acts of God not of the individual. Al-Ghazzali added that there was only one causality—that of God. Fire is not caused by striking a match, nor wetness by throwing water. Both fire and water are the products of the will of God. Thus, everything is owned by God, and man, reason and causality are active agents; they are mere illusions to delude mankind.

Al-Ghazzali set down his ideas in his book *The Revival of Religious Sciences*, in which he classified all human activities in chapters replete with citations from fabricated prophetic traditions. Al-Ghazzali's book was deemed the core of Islam and not a book written by man, despite its reliance on fabrication. With the loss of causality and free will, the Islamic mind closed, and Islam lost its vitality and potential for development. Thereafter, Islam, as a philosophical system, slipped into degeneration.

Two hundred years ago Muslims were rudely awakened by European enlightenment. With the French invasion of Egypt in 1798–1800 C.E., Egypt, and later the rest of the Middle East, felt the shock of Western civilization. Egypt led in the renewal of spirit and mind. Egyptian youth were dispatched to the universities of Europe. Egyptian confidence and know-how returned, and soon Egypt felt competent to rule in place of the Western powers that occupied its land. In Egypt's battle for liberation, Western colonization was viewed by some people as a second round of the Crusades, sparking enmity against the West.

For the past three decades the West has been transformed into a global civilization, while the Islamic world has produced little or nothing at all. Paradoxically, many Muslims curse international civilization as a neo-Western invasion, yet surround themselves with Western technology (products, gadgets). Muslims, particularly those in the Gulf, indulged in Western technology in a way that could have been a boon to Islamic power and mind but instead became its bane. The passive acquisition of technology or gadgets, dislocated from the science of production, monopolized Islamic activities without refining the mind. Even today, this lack of refinement besets the Islamic world. Electronic means of communication—from airplanes to faxes—have reduced the meaning of time and space, leaving only the unfilled vacuum of leisure.

Many Muslims have called for the reform of Islam, but differ about how to set about it. One proposal calls for a return to the Golden Age in which contact with international civilization is severed. This reform, however, provides no solution as to how to make do without lasers, airplanes and telephones. This proposal advocates blind faith, giving rise to a false feeling of peace.

A second proposal calls for the wholesale adoption of modern technology so that the Islamic world can be absorbed into international civilization. While the first proposal seeks to return the Islamic world to the ideas of Ashaari and Al-Ghazzali, the second proposal struggles to embrace the new reality of contemporary civilization.

A third proposal for reform, which I advocate, fails between the two extremes. This proposal calls for a revival of Islamic mind, ethics and human rights and an integration of these with contemporary civilization so that we can share effectively in developing civilization instead of merely consuming it. This reform calls for the abandonment of the Ashaari and Al-Ghazzali doctrine. Instead Muslims should respect causality and the potential of man, without which thinking, invention and science are void. Man, not God, must be made responsible for his works. This understanding places man in history. Religious ideas evolve, moving in time and space, through history and place.

In addition, this proposal cares deeply for human rights, even if the term was not coined by Islamic civilization. Human rights ensure that every Muslim may speak according to what he believes. Human rights ensure that every Muslim respect the human brotherhood and recognize that God is for all human beings—good and evil, believers and unbelievers. This proposal advocates employing the technology of civilization while integrating it with *true* Islamic values. The notion of participating in humanity's technological evolution and respecting human rights is slowly but surely taking root in the Islamic world. However, at the same time, its advocates have become a target for militants. Militants have created movements of terror across the Islamic world and have disseminated their practices abroad. By their misdeeds they have distorted the image of Islam, and isolated Muslims from history. Those who seek to adapt the Islamic world, to accommodate contemporary civilization, are attacked and intimidated into silence. Those, such as myself, who seek to grasp the technology of contemporary civilization and blend it with Islamic identity are also attacked and intimidated into silence.

The Islamic world has been torn between the liberals and the militants. Unfortunately, few Muslims have put forward strategies to heal the divisions. Meanwhile the world continues evolving apace, augmenting its capacities by the minute, leaving the vast morass of Muslims to detach themselves from time and space by their behavior, moving nowhere but backward. Muslims opt not for sharing, but for resisting civilization, opposing its forces and consuming its products, then reacting to this consumption by violence against themselves, their society and the world. In addition, Islamic religious institutions operate de facto and religious officials defend their wealth and align themselves with militants and reactionaries against progress.

Moreover, in Egypt, the moderates and enlightened are subject to punishment by the nation's legislation. Under Article 98(f) of the penal code, it states, "Whosoever writes against the deity or vilifies it or any of its sects, should be imprisoned for no less than six months and no more than five years, or be fined E£500." Militant Muslims, who include religious authorities, have implored the government to bring the moderates and enlightened to trial charged with infringement of Article 98. Since religious officials hold that they are the sole legitimate representatives of Islam, they consider any vilification of themselves to be a vilification of Islam. Thus, they call on the government to apply the article on all who preach or write against their closed and narrow-minded instructions. . . .

Similarly Article 161 of the penal code punishes with imprisonment for three years and a fine ranging from E£100 to E£500 all who publish anything judged against any faith accepted in Egypt. Islam, Christianity and Judaism are all faiths accepted in Egypt but only militant Muslims turn to Article 161 to punish their opponents. Militant Muslims see the moderates and enlightened as assaulting Islam itself rather than seeking its reform, In most of the Islamic world, the situation has become critical. Without an Islamic reformation—renewal of the Islamic mind, ethical code and respect for human rights—Muslims will be excluded from the international community and be severed from its time and history. Articles 98 and 161 must be annulled from Egyptian law. Legal license for militants and religious officials to intimidate intellectuals in the Muslim world must be curtailed. The way should be cleared for reformists to express their ideas through the media and press without intimidation, threat or prosecution. Without this, I fear for the future of Islam and humanity.

ISLAMIC LAW AND HUMAN RIGHTS

Human rights, the expression and the concept, were never known during the medieval period when Islamic law was first established. Human rights, as a claim by any person, such as the right to worship as one chooses, the right to free speech, etc., were initially declared during the French Revolution (1789 C.E.). In time, the concept became widely accepted, especially when the human race suffered from the denial of human rights by totalitarian governments, fascistic parties, misleading media and tyranny in general. Today, human rights constitute an international call and a humanitarian creed to liberate people from any fear or tyranny, to free our capacities from any obstacles so that we may live in peace, spread peace and interrelate with the community, humanity and the cosmos.

It is necessary to realize that Muslims have neither one unified attitude toward Islamic law nor one clear understanding about human rights. Actually, in the Islamic world today, there are two movements, each one with its own understanding of Islamic law and human rights. As previously discussed, the first is fanatical, extremist and militant; the second is liberal, intellectual and enlightened.

The first movement, namely the fanatical, extremist, militant, believes that Islamic rights are primary to human rights. What are Islamic rights? It is a question answered only by the fanatics, the extremists and the militants, and specifically defined and detailed by their leaders, who believe they monopolize the truth and are entitled by God to impose the truth forcefully, even by the sword in jihād or holy war. They believe that Islamic law is revealed from God, without making any distinction between Islamic law and Islamic jurisprudence. God, they say, knows humankind and society better than man, and God revealed Islamic law to be enforced upon man for his own benefit and that of society. This movement argues that applying Islamic law strictly would refine society, instill justice and spread prosperity. They believe that neither humanity nor society has the right to legislate themselves. Laws were already legislated by God in the Qur'ān for all human beings, anytime and in every place.

Democracy is thought to be a Western system, not Islamic, according to this movement, and is considered heresy. The Islamic political system is based on *shūra* (consultation), which means that the ruler (the Caliph or the Imam) has the right to appoint counselors to offer advice when he wants it. However, he is not obliged to take their advice, even if there is consensus among them. His decision is seen as infallible, whether de jure (in the Shī'ite doctrine) or de facto (in the Sunnite doctrine). To the fanatical, extremist militant movement, humanity has no right to choose their own faith, unless they are non-Muslims and convert to Islam. And Muslims have no right to convert from Islam or else they will be subject to the death penalty.

This movement believes that no one has the right to free opinion or free speech. They believe that Muslims should mold themselves according to the traditions of their sect or community or group. They are to suppress their opinions and bond themselves to the community. Any different opinion expressed is considered an act against God and against the community. Such a person is considered to be at war with God and the community; thus, subject to the death penalty or to being murdered by any Muslim.

This movement believes that non-Muslims living in an Islamic country are obliged to behave the same as a Muslim and not to act, speak or declare a viewpoint that might be considered against Islam or Islamic traditions or the Islamic community. As part of the minority, non-Muslims have to obey the majority. And in non-Islamic countries, the majority—non-Muslims— are to behave toward minority Muslims as if Muslims were in an Islamic country, otherwise the fanatic, extremist militants claim discrimination.

This movement believes women are under the custody of a man, whether he be her father, brother, husband or son. A woman has no right to leave the house without permission from her custodian. If she is married, she has no right to work unless she has her husband's permission and then only in certain jobs, such as teaching girls, caring for women, and the like. A woman has no right to wear what she wants. She must don the veil or the *chadoor* (in Iran), and if she does not, she could be considered a heretic, which is punishable by death (as was declared in Iran). A woman has no right to drive a car, and if she does, she will be considered a rebel against the community, endangering herself and her husband, which happened in Saudi Arabia.

The liberal, intellectual, enlightened movement has another approach and totally different concepts and ideas about Islamic law and human rights. To this movement, human rights never contradict Islamic law. This movement stresses that there is a distinction between Islamic law and Islamic jurisprudence.

This movement believes that not all the legal rules mentioned in the Qur'ān are permanent, that some of them are temporary. A very specific example is slavery and slavery harems. Slavery and slave harems were mentioned in the Qur'ān; as previously cited, they were not abrogated, yet they are not applied today and are forbidden by law. Even though the principle was not clear to him and to the Muslims of his time, the second Caliph, 'Umar, stopped applying certain rules from the Qur'ān.

This movement believes that everyone has a share in political life. Public discussions and laws should be implemented only after extensive discussion and an open and free process of voting. Democracy is a must at every level and in every unit of society.

This movement believes that political actions are mere civil actions, not religious actions. The head of the state, ministers (state secretaries), governors and all other civil servants are not infallible. Their acts can be criticized and even canceled, if necessary.

This movement believes that all people have the right to choose their own faith without being threatened by the death penalty. Verses stating freedom of choosing one's faith have not been and never were abrogated from the Qur'ān. According to the Qur'ān, forcing someone to be or to become a Muslim against his will is distorting the meaning and the spirit of Islam and is a denial of human rights. Islam has no need for hypocrites or oppressed nonfree people.

This movement believes that everyone has the right to free speech and to express ideas and opinions the way he or she chooses. If these opinions prove to be correct, they will benefit all the community; if not, they should be debated decently and not suppressed by any means.

Finally, this movement believes that men and women have equal rights —the right to free speech, the right to work, and to drive a car. Women should never be under the custody of anyone. If humanity has obligations to God, it also has rights. Humanity's first and major right is to be free, with free mind and free conscience, rather than enslaved by anyone, any political power, any religious group or any false media.

To the liberal, intellectual, enlightened movement, jihād is self-control. If jihād is applied to war, it should only be applied for self-defense. To the liberal, intellectual, enlightened movement, each human being is a word of God and is entitled to every human right. To this movement, justice precedes punishment, the spirit is more important than the text and humanity is one community.

HEBA RAOUF EZZAT
1965–

Born and educated at Cairo University, Heba Raouf Ezzat is
Lecturer in the Faculty of Economics and Political Sciences, Cairo
University. Her writings focus on Islam, gender, democracy, and
human rights. She is Coordinator of the Civil Society Program at
the Center for Political Research and Studies at Cairo University,
Editor of the Global Civil Society Yearbook, and a member of
the World Economic Forum's Council of 100 Leaders.

On the Future of Women
and Politics in the Arab World

THE POLITICAL RE-DEFINED

Many writings have addressed the issue of women and politics in the
Arab world in particular, from the angle of an obvious deficit in women's
political participation in the MENA countries.

My argument here is that thinking about this topic should better start
by revising how the Social and the Political are analyzed, and whether
the dominant paradigm (that is fundamentally modernist) would really
"empower" women, and according to what definition—not of gender—but
essentially to what definition of power.

There is a need to develop tools and indicators to measure women's
present contribution and participation on the grass root level and in
everyday life, namely what can be named "informal politics" where socio-
political survival strategies take place. Informal politics are usually overlooked by dominant quota approaches that are focusing on official bodies,
ignoring the well established fact that they are not representative and
that even if few women have more seats and occupy more offices within
them, this would have little impact on the lives and the participation of the
majority of women unless a wider democratic transformation takes place.

If democracy is the end goal and women's liberation from injustice and
discrimination is the means, then women's "empowerment" should start
by developing a notion of power and politics that befits women in its logic
and its structure, accommodating their needs as well as their conditions
instead of requiring (or forcing) them to adapt to standard philosophical
assumptions and organizational structures that change their course of

life or demand a price for social and political participation that they are unwilling to pay.

One clear problem with the dominant paradigm is the stress on the public as a space of freedom and the private—namely the family—as a domain of oppression and discrimination, violence and exploitation. Such a vision does not reflect the vision of the majority of women in the Arab world, nor does it have the potential of taking root within their Islamic culture without drastic, or even devastating, externally imposed cultural change. A major problem with the approach to MENA is that it adopts many myths built on Orientalist stereotypes and ignores the changes that have occurred to the socio-economic situation of women in the last century. One recent report published by the World Bank criticized the main features of the "traditional gender paradigm" in its definition: that women are expected to marry early, be home makers and obey men who are bread-winners and mediators between women and the public sphere.[1] While the assumption that women marry early ironically overlooks the fact that the majority of young people can not afford marriage expenses, a situation that resulted in a sweeping phenomena of late marriage across the societies of the region, even in the Gulf states. On the other hand the negative evalu-ation of the expectation that women should be home makers is obviously rooted in a modernist and feminist approach that sees this role as under-mining women's public participation, fostering a patriarchal culture. It implies that women aspire to greater presence in the public space, not more efficiency in managing the problems, the texture and roles of the private family sphere.

The concern is that traditional dominant gender paradigm gives cen-trality of the family over the individual, an old modernist critic of organic societies, while we ironically find the dilemma of the post modern individu-alist condition grasping the attention of sociologists. One feels here that the field of comparative women studies, especially the literature on the Arab region, is lagging behind critical social theory. The report states that the work of women is still considered optional, not essential. This overlooks the fact that a segment of women may be free to choose work inside or outside their home, but that in practice this freedom is undermined not by men but by the economic necessity that forces women to work to share the responsibility of the household, sometimes against their own wish as women and as busy mothers.

Last but not least the report criticizes the imposition on women of the code of modesty, and norms controlling male-female interaction. The assumption is a new paradigm in which women marry late, feel no urge to become home makers, consider freedom as economic independence, paid work and liberation from the code of modesty!

---

1. *Gender and Development in the Middle East and North Africa: Women in the Public Sphere.* MENA Development Report 2004. Washington, DC: World Bank, 2004, pp. 94–96.

Many writings on gender and politics show concern that women are under-represented in the parliament and executive body, and even when they are ministers, they are likely to be assigned to ministries that reinforce their social roles and responsibilities. Although there is worldwide improvement in women's active participation in this field, the participation of Arab women is evaluated as being slow and ad hoc.[2] The obsession is with driving women out of home and getting them either in the labor market or in the seats of power, regardless of the stagnation on the side of democratic change. Many feminists decided to join the official and formal bodies of women in the region and make use of the authoritarian power delegated to those bodies to achieve change and see the feminist agenda applied, giving democratic demands less priority and human rights concerns less attention. Different figures have been co-opted and one can even talk about a *"feminization of authoritarianism"* that is taking place in the region in most of the countries.

It is a strategy abused by regimes to improve their image and at the same time delay the wider democratic transition. Tunisia and the Gulf political entities are but an example. In Egypt, Morocco, Bahrain, Qatar and other countries the official support of women's rights and appointment of women as ministers or executives or even judges serves only to obscure the rising authoritarianism of the regimes that is veiled by soft democratic rhetoric limited to the vocal level or reduced to trivial changes that are curbed by logistic and legal details. No power-sharing is taking place and political elites are well determined to monopolize authority.

The establishment of the Arab Women's Organization by Mrs. Mubarak, the First Lady of Egypt, to serve as a coordinating mechanism for the various women's issues and movements in the region is an example of such a quasi-feminist effort. The first summit of the Arab Women's Organization held in Cairo in 2001 claimed to help Arab women to attain their legitimate status as full-fledged partners in shaping both the present and future of their societies. At the first meeting, a plan of action addressed the common interests of all the participating countries, namely Egypt, Lebanon, Jordan, Syria, Sudan, Djibouti, Bahrain and Kuwait. The Organization had certain political legitimacy lent to it by its founders and its status within the Arab League. Since its inception, the Organization has held various forums to address a wide range of issues including women's legal and political rights, the image and the role of women in media and the growing role of women in national economic empowerment, all hosted by the first ladies in their respective countries. How democracy can be achieved by non-democratic regimes via the leading role of "first ladies" is a question that should be discussed.

---

2. *Paving the Road Towards Empowerment.* Amman, Jordan: UNIFEM Arab States Regional Office, 2002, p. 46.

EMPOWERING WOMEN BY DIS-EMPOWERING THE STATE?

Focusing on quantitative indicators that assess the percentage of women in decision-making positions in the executive, in the legislative, in the political parties, etc. provides either a gloomy picture of women's under representation in politics, or a bright picture about their rising political role and their emerging power. (The case of Morocco is seen as a striking example.)

A new definition of political participation should try to bridge the conceptual gap between the public and the private, and engage in re-defining the "Political" in terms of power relations rather than power structures, understanding that the engagement of citizens and the management of power relations on a day-to-day basis [are] mainly located outside official political bodies and structures especially when political participation is obstructed by despotism. Politics of everyday life should be the focus of attention and research, exploring how women—very much like their fellow male citizens—face oppression, violence, marginalization and discrimination.[3]

Attempting to "measure" and capture the "empowerment" of women by figures, percentages and numbers does not reflect the increasing "weakening" or dis-empowerment of the rights of women as citizens suffering from the lack of transparency and rising corruption within the bureaucracy as well as the new business sectors across the Arab world. They also fail due to rising enthusiasm and fascination with quantitative studies to direct enough brainstorming and research effort to qualitative strategic and critical studies that can understand the shortcomings, acknowledge the unintended negative consequences, and introduce new visions for changing the course of action.

The social indicators that were based mainly on an economic and formal approach to politics as well as to the concept of progress and the notion of rational choice originating from the behavioral era in social sciences continue to shape the methodology of the study of Arab women's "empowerment" in the political domain. These notions remain largely unchallenged despite the fact that politics and power have been dramatically changing as phenomena, moving away from the structural definition to being manifested in flows of power with rising globalization, trans-local relations and trans-national networks.

This prevailing paradigm when faced with the pressing question "Why are women not active politically?" usually provides a variety of answers including lack of political skills, cultural factors that tend to emphasize the traditional role of women as wives and mothers, poverty and/or lack of democracy. Based on these simplistic answers, national and global strategies

---

3. Jill Bystydzienski admits that politics and power are transforming in shape and content, yet in her study she still adopts the institutional indicators. See Jill Bystydzienski (ed.), *Women Transforming Politics: Worldwide Strategies for Empowerment*. Indianapolis: Indiana University Press, 1992, pp. 1–5.

are formulated to empower women and upgrade their political skills through a series of training programs, to create funds for supporting their campaigns, or to raise awareness about their role in the voting process. However, these strategies had little success compared to the cost and effort entailed. *I claim that women are not actively engaged in politics because the political domain is not a safe and secure space for them.*

In Arab countries where women can constitutionally and legally participate in politics, they are faced with a lot of challenges and uncertainties.

Where there is violence during elections and voters are prevented by force from reaching the ballots by supporters of other candidates and where clashes between the supporters of different candidates or with security forces result in heavy casualties or even the death of innocent civilians, it is expected that women feel discouraged from participating.

When women are candidates they are subject to harassment, and face physical and psychological threats. They also shy away from involvement to avoid accusations of political corruption due to the negative image of politicians in their respective societies.[4]

Hence the process of empowering women politically has to go hand in hand with democratization and the dis-empowerment of the authoritarian regimes of the region.

This should start by re-negotiating the power allocated to the state. It necessitates a re-formation of the conceptual tools starting from the definition of power to a more profound investigation of the transformation of the political at large. In many Arab countries and due to the political stagnation women prefer to address societal needs and to contribute to public life via parallel avenues of political participation embedded in their social environment.

Women's "human condition" needs to be addressed in a complex way, stressing the need for a new sustainable human development paradigm that is urgently needed to meet the challenge of socio-economic insecurity.[5]

A purely "women centered" agenda that is confined to women's participation in voting and running for elections fails to address wider political challenges.

As the personal and private can not be separated from the public, the civil, the economic and the political, we would then have to draw a map of complex relations where one dimension or factor can not be separated from the others. In this map it is not sufficient to make the personal political, but also investigate how women make the political personal. We need to develop tools to help build a new vision encompassing different and linked spheres of life of women and their complex relation, and the historic changes of their life conditions, as well as the plurality of their experiences.

4. Arab countries still suffer from political corruption of different degrees.
5. UNDP, *Human Development Report 1994*. Oxford: Oxford University Press, pp. 1–4.

The concept of "empowerment" that has been central in the gender streaming writings and programs focuses basically on "bringing some women to power" to represent women rather than "bringing additional power to women" or empower the majority of women. Here both the notion of power as well as the notion of representation should be revised in the light of the changing role of the state and the re-definition of politics in our era of the "network society" to encompass the social and civil dimension of day to day politics, and the influence exercised by communities, advocacy groups and social movements on policy making and decision taking.[6]

The state is no more the sole locus of power, and the theories of the state that used to explore the relation between the state and the society are shifting dramatically to an approach of analysis that explores the fusion of power and the dialectic relation between state and society that is transforming the state to match the expectations of people not to impose change from above.

The state is becoming an agent among others with the rising role of the civil society and the private sector. Policy networks and communication networks become the dominant pattern.[7]

Power as synonymous to state power and political participation in the representative sense no longer are the only means for the majority of women becoming more powerful and more politically active and more important: socially visible.[8]

Place itself is not fixed but rather becoming—in an information age —more irrelevant for the acquirement of knowledge and skills, and of the potential to become more "empowered." So how can we envision the future of comprehensive security in the light of these changes, and how can we seize the potentials and opportunities that this new historical context offers to marginalized women—especially the new generations in urban spaces and rural areas—to have more access to new avenues of empowerment and influence?

How can the voice of poor women, who form the majority of women in the Arab world, be heard, and how can we discover the power they already have and develop it? Does this necessitate reforming our notion of what political participation is about and shifting from a definition of democracy as the "politics of representation" to the more relevant and truly aspired "politics of presence"?

If power is also a complex entity that is based primarily on elementary forms of social relations and social capital, how can empowering the majority of women then build on the available social capital of networks and social solidarity and rescue some of the diminishing ones in a rapidly

6. Agnes Heller, "The Concept of the Political Revisited," in David Held, *Political Theory Today*. Oxford: Polity Press, 1995, pp. 332–335.

7. Salwa S. Gomaa (ed.), *Governance*. Cairo: Public Administration Research and Consultation Center (PARC), 2001, p. 14.

8. Gerald Gaus, *Political Concepts and Political Theories*. Boulder, Colorado: Westview Press, 2000, pp. 241–242.

modernizing urban society, and how can we introduce new notions of women empowerment that are grass-root based and public policy oriented?

In this context the role of civil society becomes political, not only social and civil, and the focus on local governance is the key to engaging more people in the public domain to influence policies that affect their day to day life. This does not mean that official political bodies should be neglected, nor undermined. On the contrary, this approach should strengthen the electoral process but also allow women to have constant influence and power over policy making and decision taking.[9]

Women's movements engaged in formal politics may risk being co-opted by the state, or making concessions regarding the wider democratic transformation, in order to guarantee the state support, secure legal changes and access to power (in the form of issuing new laws or securing quota for women),[10] whereas empowering women in the local communities to have a voice and to step into the public sphere to defend their interests can foster democracy in all its above mentioned complex dimensions in the long run sometimes even at the expense of dominating women's political elites against their will.

Efficient use of this strategy can help discover the individual and collective assets that have been overlooked. It can also alleviate poverty, and turn the traditional knowledge and cultural heritage into a source of economic power for legal and political participation, advocacy and even social mobility and national esteem.

Many writings on Gender and Development in the region celebrated the access to employment as a condition for political empowerment. Now with the failure of states to provide social welfare and the negative effects of the open market on the socio-economic conditions of many women, employment in a globalized private sector can form a new challenge for social citizenship rights. This reminds us that women's empowerment should always be contextualized in respective sectors and national conditions to allow critical assessment.

IMPLICATIONS FOR CURRENT DEBATES

The suggested reform in the paradigm can lead to substantial change in the nature of the debate on different aspects of women's political participation. We can state some of these potential changes:

1. Revising assessment indicators. There was great enthusiasm about the signing of the CEDAW by some Gulf states in the Arab region in the last few years, and about appointing women in high posts. Yet, again, how

9. Caroline Robb, *Can the Poor Influence Policy? Participatory Poverty Assessment in the Developing World.* Washington, D.C.: World Bank, 2002, pp. 90–91.
10. Mervat Hatem, "The Paradox of State Feminism," in Barbarar J. Naleson and Najma Chowdhury, *Women and Politics Worldwide.* New Haven: Yale University Press, 1994, pp. 226–242.

far does this reflect a democratic change in making? Figures sometimes obscure ruling elites' politics and corruptions. There is a theoretical (and moral) dilemma here: should this be celebrated as "empowerment" of women as citizens while Amnesty International and Transparency International annual reports show how basic human and political rights are violated in these countries?

In the second Arab Human Development Report 2003 titled *Building a Knowledge Society* a reference was made to the empowerment of women as an important factor in achieving the titled goal. Yet, again, small achievements here and there were celebrated on the basis of the same formal indicators, not pointing at all to the fact that in many cases the change was initiated by authoritarian regimes, and that the appointment of some women in high governmental and judicial executive posts was the price the state paid to abort an emerging independent women's movement that was replaced by formal bodies and councils of women funded by the state and receiving foreign aid to put the global agenda in action, accompanied by structural changes in the economy and in politics that dis-empower and impoverish the majority of women.[11]

2. Revising the quota debate: from political representation to political presence. There is an urgent need to shift towards women's "presence" in daily life politics in an age where information technology, media and mobility render the notions of power as well as politics more hybrid and linked with public policies and daily concerns of millions of women.

The preoccupation with quota and the debate about positive discrimination marginalize the majority of women and focus on elites and active politicians. Empowering women at large by engaging them in constant interest in the political process and the decision making and legislative agenda, pushing for improvement in their life opportunities and those of future generations, is indeed what democracy is about. Women in high positions in the political bodies also need to be supported, backed, as well as continuously affiliated with the majority of women they represent. There is little evidence that women in power are the strong advocates of women's rights. Social scientists and women's rights groups in the Arab world should develop tools and indicators to research the status of present political participation at the grass root level that might be overlooked by dominant quota approaches that are focusing mainly on representative bodies.

Women's economic participation in the informal sectors of economy forms up to 30% in some developing economies; thus the "informal" political sector and power-sharing "survival strategies to combat the feminization of political poverty" at the grass root level should be also given attention. It is there that many women are empowered in local communities and are active in innovating cultural and socio-political survival strategies. This is where real balances of power are determined in an age where

---

11. *Arab Human Development Report 2003*. New York: United Nations Publications, 2003.

primordial relations and networks are re-gaining importance and influence. The flow of power in a post-industrial era and the hybridity of many urban and rural spaces enable women to bridge easily the gap between the personal and the political. If we add to this the growing withdrawal of the welfare state from the domain of social services and formal sector employment, the presence of women's civil and social networks in the public domain becomes crucial more than ever and obviously would have political implications on the medium and long term.

3. *Bridging the gap between civil and political participation.* Nowadays new opportunities allow increasing numbers of young women in the Arab world, a world with a portion of young people over 60% of its population, to lobby, network and mobilize while choosing to integrate their public concerns into the space of their private daily life using technology, either by self-employment home business or by being actively engaged in promoting women's rights through the avenues of the cyberspace, while choosing to be a full time mother and housewife.

This "access" and "empowerment" through post-industrial science and technology can spare the new generations of Arab women many debates and controversies and allow them to have different asymmetric and plural paths of modernization in a post-modern era than what conventionally was thought of by adopting a uni-linear notion of progress, development and suffrage that sees the empowerment of women in the light of the Western historical model.

One of the paradoxes facing any observer of the political participation of women in the Arab world is the growing participation of women in the labor force, their growing access to executive positions, their engagement in civil society associations, but the simultaneous disengagement from politics either in respect of joining political parties or trade unions (for example, only 7.6% in a sample of executive women in official bodies and private sector businesses in Egypt are members of political parties).[12]

This requires finding avenues and programs to allow women to get engaged in political activism and civil forums.[13]

4. *Facing the cultural challenges and seizing the open opportunities of globalization.* Traditional culture is not the sole challenge they are facing on the social level as many studies imply, but rather the dichotomy that is increasingly conceived between that culture with its potential for reform on one hand, and the global cultural agenda of hegemony in a semi uni-polar system on the other hand. This requires embedding cultural and social reform in the Arab countries within a wider vision for a project of renaissance for the Arab world based on democracy and pluralism. A project that

12. Mohamed Shuman, *Working Women Leaders: Current Situation and Future Horizons.* Cairo: The Group for Democratic Development, 1999. (Arabic)

13. Zoheir Hatab, "Achieving the Incomplete Civility of the Lebanese Society," in Antoine Massara *et al.*, *Developing the Civil Society in Lebanon.* Beirut: Permanent Civil Peace Association, 1999, pp. 235–240.

would not distort the unifying role of the Arab culture across the region, and at the same time would allow cultural diversity to be a source of enrichment, not an obstacle to coherence, be it a diversity within, based on the multi-ethnic or multi-religious nature of some Arab states, or the diversity that results from the interaction with global cultures through IT, travel, tourism, or travel and diaspora networks.

5. Mainstreaming women's presence beyond elitism and statism. The situation of Arab women and their political participation has been overwhelmingly affected by small pressure groups of active women, networks between study centers and civil society activists, or official and semi-official state bodies, plans and initiatives.

These should give way to the formation of a much needed social movement of women's rights that would push for change.

Here one has to realize that the role of a progressive Islamic vision about the participation is crucial and has been developing for quite a while.

Here we stress that dominant religious opinions play a crucial role in dis-encouraging women from participating in politics, seeing it in a nutshell as a business for men only.

The focus has been—at best—on neutralizing religion in the discourse on women's political participation.

Sometimes formal religious opinions have been issued to support a more serious participation of women in the public sphere and in politics, only to face counter religious opinions from groups that oppose that participation. The cases of Kuwait and Egypt are exemplary.

It should be highlighted that there has been an effort to reform the religious discourse on women's political participation by prominent Islamic jurists, and there is an emerging voice of women scholars advocating an Islamic vision that stresses the importance of women's participation in public life and in politics.

In Egypt, Syria, Morocco, Tunisia and Sudan these voices are changing the nature of the debate, trying to avoid the intellectual context of polarization between the Islamists and the secularists on one hand, and the official religious opinions and the opinions of religious social movements on the other. There is an increasing awareness of the public and political role of women, and during the last decade prominent scholars have shown notable consideration of that role and wrote in support of it.

How religion becomes a force of progressive change is a question that should be addressed in an overdue debate on the philosophy, direction and core of an Arab vision of women's political participation placed within a wider debate on human development in the region.

The recent 2003 report on Arab Human Development stressed the importance of the political participation of women and celebrated their rising presence in official positions. It also stressed the role of religion in establishing a society of knowledge and liberty. These statements should fit into a new paradigm that would re-establish the connection between culture, religion and human rights/women's rights discourse and activism in the region.

Finally we have to stress the link between the empowerment of women and larger ambitions of change such as security, peace, stability, accountability and equal citizenship.

Not only are women affected by crisis and instability, to say nothing of war in Somalia, Iraq, Palestine, they suffer also from the uncivil situation in Algeria, and have direct interest in finding a solution by becoming a force for peace, reconciliation, and national unity.

As Mary Kaldor rightly points out, women in many countries in the South have been the vehicle for addressing security issues and pressing for peace.[14]

This dimension of international efforts that was clear since the 1976 Brussels International Tribunal on Crimes Against Women and [that] was integrated in global strategies and plans of action since the UN Mexico City Conference that launched the decade for women in 1975 has been forgotten in favor of political agendas. No politics is really possible without a state, an initial minimal process of presence and representation, not always available in some areas in the Arab world.[15]

THE ROAD AHEAD

The mere fact that we are aware of the shortcomings of the dominant paradigm and the need to develop and reform it should drive us to opening discussion on how to solve the paradoxes and bridge the methodological gap. We have three challenges to face:

1. Allowing space for democratic deliberation on the future of women. Women from all backgrounds, socio-economic contexts and academic disciplines should debate the future of Arab women's presence and their notion of a fair and equal democratic process that secures political spaces for their activity. If the standard paradigm failed to bridge the gap and resulted in plans of action that consumed money and effort and ended with poor results, this indicates the approaches were partial and particular. Only a comprehensive and collective effort can result in a more inclusive and powerful paradigm where women can discuss how they can be empowered in order to power-share democracy, on all levels.

Public debate is a necessary condition to form a strong civic culture, and an essential prerequisite for strong and sustainable presence of women in the public as well as the political sphere. The democratic imagination is re-constructed through debates and democratic deliberation, allowing different notions of democratic participation to take place on different levels.

---

14. Mary Kaldor, *Global Civil Society: An Answer to War?* Cambridge: Polity Press, 2003, pp. 87, 96.
15. Purna Sen, "Success and Challenges: Understanding the Global Movement to End Violence Against Women." *Global Civil Society Yearbook*. Oxford: Oxford University Press, 2003, pp. 119–146.

A major challenge in this context is that the social movements in the region have no common political agenda on women empowerment and its meaning nor even a shared "thin" conception of the nature of democracy they want to build and how to integrate women's participation within it.

2. *Celebrating the diversity in models of political participation and development.* The shifting nature of politics towards empowerment of civil bodies and networks and engaging women in politics requires a shift of focus from seeing women as victims of discrimination that need to be "empowered" to stressing their situation as political agents that have power and possess a potential but need to find in their individual context a way for new possibilities. This would require a re-imagination of the notion of politics as we stressed, and a more pluralistic conception of political presence, that would accommodate the different visions and discourses on women to become cross-fertilized and fruitful instead of contradictory and exclusivist.

So far theorizing political participation was done within the boundaries of social sciences. At best, it was linked to the central role of the state. It is worth mentioning here that the changing nature of the state power as the overarching actor in politics resulted in a confusion of researchers facing new phenomena. See how the emigration of many men in the seventies to the Gulf States resulted in the emergence of millions of mother-headed families. Is this to be seen as empowerment or disempowerment of women? Is this a reformation of the power relations in the family that would result in women's empowerment or the opposite? It remained unclear, simply because women were not consulted and the culture that allowed them to play new roles completely silenced.

If politics is to be re-structured, so is our imagery of average women. Here the shift should not be to an exclusive model of action but to one that moves flexibly within the overlapping spheres of the life of women to fulfill their need for speaking out their concerns, finding their way to solve their respective problems and implement their available assets and sources of power to achieve these goals. Celebrating diversity of strategies should allow women, groups and individuals, to "create" their own spaces of presence and "integrate" them in the structures of power on all levels. Innovation, rather than standardization, in thinking and acting, is a condition for integrating more women in the public sphere and helping them to feel safe and secure, supported by their social capital and networks.

The tragic irony of formal structural notions of politics that dominate the current paradigm is that it takes away women's freedom of choice in order to secure the implementation of ready-made solutions, another result of the mind set of the centrality of the state as a conceptual variable in the theoretical underpinnings of the current paradigm.[16]

---

16. J. P. Nettl, "The State as a Conceptual Variable," *World Politics*, Vol. XX, No. 4, July 1968, p. 559.

3. Re-assessing of the relation between the local and the global in Analysis. The complex notion of politics and participation should lead to a more complex evaluation of the positive and negative implications of globalization on the empowerment of Arab women at this historic moment.

The global actors in IR supported authoritarian political regimes that managed to provide the necessary "security" for the global market even if at the expense of freedom and individual dignity, and "safety" on the domestic and regional level. This remains one of the major challenges to the democratic transformation in the MENA countries.

Formed in 1988 in Malaysia and registered as a Non-Governmental Organisation (NGO) in 1993, Sisters in Islam (SIS) is a group of Muslim professional women committed to promoting the rights of women within the framework of Islam. The SIS mission statement notes: "The participation of Muslim women as full and equal partners in the ummah's socio-economic development and progress is the need of the day. . . . It is imperative that the female experience, thought and voice are included in the interpretation of the Quran and in the administration of religion in the Muslim world."

Chronology of a Struggle for Equal Rights

1. ISLAM AND POLYGAMY, 20 AUGUST 1990

Sisters in Islam welcome the decision of the Selangor Syariah Appeal Court Judgement in the case of **Aishah Abd Rauf vs Wan Mohd Yusof Wan Othman.** The judgement reflects the true spirit of the teachings of the Qur'an and true practice of polygamy.[1]

We would like to point out the popular misconceptions surrounding the Qur'anic verses on polygamy.

Many men believe that polygamy is a God-given right enshrined in the Qur'an; Many believe that Islam, by allowing polygamy has found the ideal solution to men's alleged insatiable sexual drive; and, many also believe that if a woman allows her husband to take on a second wife, she is assured of a place in heaven. The Selangor Syariah Appeal Court judgment of Aishah Abdul Rauf v Wan Mohd Yusof Wan Othman brought to public debate these misconceptions which have been mistakenly elevated to be the word of Allah.

---

1. Note: In the 1990 case of Aishah Abdul Rauf vs Wan Mohd Yusuf Wan Othman, the Syariah Appeal Court of Selangor unanimously overturned the lower court's decision to permit Wan Yusuf to take a second wife—stating that all conditions for polygamy are of "equal importance and should be proven independently."

A failure to fulfill one condition alone would have been sufficient for the lower court judge to reject the husband's application, it stated. Women's groups support the grounds of this judgment as they reflect the true message and spirit of the Quran and the provisions of the Islamic Family Law Act 1984.

From a series of press releases, Kuala Lumpur, Malaysia, 1990–2003.

Let us point out what the Qur'anic verses on polygamy actually say: "If you fear that you shall not be able to deal justly with the orphans, marry women of your choice, two or three, or four; but if you fear that you shall not be able to deal justly (with them) then only one" (Al Nisa', 4:3).

A subsequent verse states: "You are never able to be fair and just between women even if that were your ardent desire" (Al Nisa', 4:129).

It is clear from this verse that:

First, the Qur'an does not give men the blanket right to have more than one wife. Polygamy is not a right, but a responsibility to ensure that socio-justice be done to orphans. What Allah has granted is in fact a restriction on the existing practice of that time when men could marry as many wives as they wanted.

Second, because polygamy is not a right, Allah placed conditions on its practice. There is an overriding concern for justice in this short verse. Conditions are set to ensure that justice is done.

Condition A: Polygamy is permitted within the context of war and orphans. It is permitted only if the men fear they would not be able to deal justly with the orphans.

Condition B: The man who wants to be polygamous must have the capacity to be fair and just to all his wives. The verse is a call for just conduct towards women, not a right for men to fulfil their alleged lustful desires or their ego. And just treatment here means more than a man's financial capacity to support more than one wife. He must be fair in all ways, including the time, support and companionship he provides to the wives and children.

Condition C: If the man fears he cannot deal justly with all his wives, then Allah advocates that he should marry only one as this will prevent injustice. This is explicitly stated in the verse.

Third, it is often forgotten that there was a socio-historical context within which the verse was revealed. That context was a period of tragedy in Islam after the battle of Uhud when dozens of men from the still formative Muslim community in Medina were killed in one day. Numerous women and children were left without support. To deal with this problem, Allah revealed the verse permitting men to be polygamous.

Finally, we would like to emphasise that it is reprehensible for Muslims to say that polygamy is Islam's solution for men's alleged unbridled lust. Islam teaches self-control, self-discipline and self-purification. The solution to an immoral society, whether in the West or in the Muslim world, is not polygamy. The solution, as found in the Qur'an and the hadith, is a change of attitude from indulging in promiscuity to one of self-discipline and respect for the opposite sex.

We wish to emphasize that the clear intention in the Qur'an is to restrict polygamy.

Unfortunately, in practice, the restrictions imposed in the Qur'an have often not been applied and the context within which the verse was revealed has been completely overlooked.

2. IDEAL STATE OF MARRIAGE IN ISLAM, 20 OCTOBER 1996

The recent regulations introduced by the Jabatan Agama Islam Selangor (JAIS) to assist Muslim men to expedite their application for polygamy without the need to obtain consent from their existing wife or wives are a cause for concern. In the wake of recent calls for the better protection of rights of our Muslim women, the JAIS decision appears ill advised, if not an indication of misplaced priorities.

What is especially alarming is the rationale for it. It was reported that the regulations stem from the notion that polygamy is the right of the Muslim male; and what the regulations sought to do was merely to ensure that this alleged right is made more accessible.

It is clear that there is confusion over the intent of polygamy in Islam and on how the laws on polygamy should operate and be administered in this country.

First, a reading of verses 4:3 and 4:129 in the Quran clearly shows that polygamy is not a right in Islam but a responsibility to ensure that socio-economic justice be done to orphans. . . .

Second, because polygamy is not a right, Allah placed conditions on its practice, with an overriding concern that justice be done. . . .

It is clear that the intention of the Quran is to restrict polygamy; many theologians over the centuries have stated that, in fact, the Quran advocates monogamy as the original and ideal state of marriage in Islam.

Malaysia in the late 1970s and early 1980s embarked upon a remarkable programme of reformation of Islamic family laws under the doctrine of siasah syariah (in codification of the law, the state may choose opinions of differing schools to serve the best interest of the community), which introduced among others the restriction of polygamy to help ensure that justice is done as envisaged by the Quran.

The reform law laid down a set of conditions upon which it sought to assess that justice will be done. Consent of the existing wife or wives is one of the factors to be taken into consideration by the court.

Four conditions also need to be fulfilled: The proposed marriage is "just and necessary"; the applicant has the financial means to support his existing and future dependants; he would be able to accord equal treatment to all his wives; and the proposed marriage would not cause any harm to the existing wife or wives.

The law requires that the court summon the applicant and his existing wife or wives to be present at the hearing of the application. If under the new JAIS regulations consent of the existing wife is no longer needed, will this mean that she will not be consulted by the court as required by law?

Clearly the reformed law saw the necessity of consultation with the existing wife. Her experiences living in the same household would assist the court in ascertaining the measure of the man and on whether he would be able to fulfil the conditions required under the law before permission for polygamy is granted.

The spirit of the law reform on polygamy had taken a fresh step in affirming that justice in Islam would not be gender biased. However, in the implementation of the law, much of the spirit and intent of these reforms remain largely ignored because of prejudicial attitudes of a patriarchal society.

3. CONTROVERSY ON POLYGAMY, 8 JANUARY 2002

Not surprisingly, in the recent debate on the suggestion to re-legalize polygamy for non-Muslims, most women's groups and progressive minded men have reacted with outrage and condemned the proposal.

It is acknowledged that polygamy was legal for non-Muslim men in Malaysia until the enforcement of the Law Reform (Marriage and Divorce Act 1976) in 1982. Prior to its enforcement, unlimited and unconditional polygamy was recognized under the men's respective customary laws. The Law Reform Act was the outcome of the struggle of various women's groups in this country to put an end to the oppression and injustice suffered by women under unfair and outdated customary practices. Women's groups comprised of women from different races and religions, including some Muslim women, joined in the struggle against the abuse of polygamy and the discrimination against women. The pressure from the various women's groups led to the abolition of polygamy for non-Muslims, and certain attempts (not very effective) intended to control it among the Muslims. However, any effective measures against the abuse of polygamy among the Muslims were unfortunately condemned as "un-Islamic" due to a general mistaken notion that polygamy was a sacred male right guaranteed by Islam.

An argument that is being put forward in support of the suggestion for the re-legalization of polygamy for non-Muslims is that it would help to reduce social ills such as illicit affairs, prostitution and the birth of illegitimate children. However, the legality of polygamy has not put an end to these social ills among the Malay community. In some cases, it might even have contributed to the problem of social ills among young people who have been brought up in unhappy and neglected polygamous households. Therefore, the question that should be addressed in our society today is not whether polygamy should be re-legalized under the civil law for the non-Muslims, but whether it should still be continued under the Islamic family law for the Muslims, bearing in mind the true purpose of the Qur'anic injunctions on polygamy: "if you fear you cannot deal justly (with your wives), marry only one (wife)." The Qur'an is also the only holy scripture that contains the phrase "marry only one." The Muslims should have led the other communities in the struggle against polygamy and its abuses.

4. SELANGOR SYARIAH LAW ENACTMENT, 5 MAY 2003

Sisters in Islam welcomes the decision of the Selangor State government to tighten the procedure for polygamous marriages to ensure that justice is done.

The decision to require the man, his existing wife, his future wife and her guardian to appear before court allows the judge to determine the ability of the man to be just.

It is the first step in a series of procedures that should be in place to assess justice and to recognise that this can only be done in consultation with all concerned parties. It is not for the husband alone to decide.

Sisters in Islam urges that other procedural steps be adopted to evaluate whether the Islamic requirement that justice be served in a polygamous marriage can indeed be fulfilled by:

- Requiring all Syariah court judges to conform to the judgement of the Selangor Appeals Committee in Aishah Abdul Rauf vs Wan Mohd Yusof Wan Othman case which concluded that all four conditions, not just one, for polygamy under the Islamic Family Law are equally important and must be fulfilled. The four conditions—just and necessary, financial means, equal treatment and no harm caused to the existing wife—must be proven independently.

- Establishing that the existing wife's consent was given freely. The judge must establish during consultation with the existing wife whether her consent has been given freely or under duress. It has been common practice for the first wife to be threatened with divorce unless she gives her consent.

- Drafting a new application form to reflect the new requirements and ensuring that court officials are able to advise the husband accordingly. Husband must also provide proof of his statements—supporting documents on his income, liabilities, property. Currently, the Application Form is misleading as it presumes that permission for polygamy will be granted as a matter of course and husband need not submit any supporting documents.

- Providing a wife who cannot live in a polygamous marriage the choice to leave. A wife should not be forced to remain in a marriage different from the one she is contracted to.

- According the right of the first wife to her share of the matrimonial property (harta sepencarian) prior to the approval of the polygamous marriage. This is to ensure that her interests are protected and secured. We strongly feel that it is unjust that a wife who has struggled together with her husband is subsequently deprived of her rights when her husband marries another woman.

- Ensuring that the husband will provide monthly maintenance to wife and children. The husband's employer can be ordered to deduct a portion of the husband's salary for them. We propose that the State Government insert a paragraph which provides that the polygamous marriage should not directly or indirectly lower the standard of living enjoyed by the existing wife and dependents (similar to paragraph (e) of section 23(4) of the Islamic Family Law (Federal Territory) that was deleted). This is to ensure that at the very least, the financial security of the first wife and children is ensured.

The last two procedures must be a standard. The court need not wait for an application by the wife before giving the order but instead dispense with it as a matter of justice.

REFORM OF ISLAMIC LAW: THE CHANGING
STATUS OF WOMEN AND THE FAMILY

Muslim family law (laws governing marriage, divorce, and inheritance) is the heart of the *Sharia* and thus reflects the importance of the family in Islam. As noted in the previous sections, although modern legal reform began in the nineteenth century, Muslim family law remained largely unchanged until the twentieth century. Unlike other areas of Islamic law, the process of legal adaptation for Muslim family law has been characterized by the incorporation of selective changes based upon reform through a process of reinterpretation drawing on the Islamic legal tradition for its rationale and new provisions, rather than the replacement of Islamic law with Western-based codes. In this way Muslim family law from North Africa to Southeast Asia has undergone change.

The two major purposes of Muslim family law reforms have been 1) to improve the status of women and 2) to strengthen the rights of nuclear family members vis-à-vis those of the more distant male members of the extended family. Reforms have occurred in three areas: marriage, divorce, and inheritance.

Among the more significant changes in marriage laws are the discouragement of child marriages and the restriction of polygamy. The latter has been effected by such measures as requiring that a husband obtain judicial permission to take an additional wife and permitting a woman to include a stipulation in her marriage contract that gives her the right to divorce should her husband subsequently take another wife.

Divorce was perhaps the most crucial area of legal reform. Among the principal changes legislated were an expansion of the grounds upon which a woman may obtain a divorce and the restriction of the male's unilateral right of divorce.

However, family law reform has not occurred without a great deal of debate between conservatives and modernists on both methodological and substantive legal questions. At the heart of these debates are conflicting opinions about who should engage reform, how it should be accomplished, and what elements of the law may or may not be changed.

In 1955, the Commission on Marriage and Family Laws, consisting of six lay members and one representative of the *ulama*, was established. A majority report calling for reforms in marriage, divorce and inheritance was issued in 1956. However, Mawlana Ihstishām-ul-Haq wrote a vigorous dissenting opinion. The majority and minority reports provided the basis for a debate between modernists and traditionists. Finally, in 1961, Pakistan enacted *The Muslim Family Laws Ordinance*.

The Modernist Majority Report

We shall state briefly the reasons for the formation of this Commission. It is an indisputable article of Muslim creed professed by every Muslim that so far as the basic principles and fundamental attitudes are concerned, Islamic teaching is comprehensive and all-embracing, and Islamic law either actually derives its principles and sanctions from divine authority as revealed in the Holy Qur'ān or clear injunctions based on the Sunna. It is this belief which has been affirmed in the Objectives Resolution and the Constitution of Pakistan. It might be objected that if a well-defined code about Marriage and Family Laws already existed, where was the necessity of appointing a Commission for the purposes of any revision or modification? This question can be easily answered both by reference to the history of Muslim jurisprudence and the present-day circumstances. So far as the Holy Book is concerned, the laws and injunctions promulgated therein deal mostly with basic principles and vital problems and consist of answers to the questions that arose while the Book was being revealed. The entire set of injunctions in the Holy Qur'ān covers only a few pages. It was the privilege of the Holy Prophet to explain, clarify, amplify and adapt the basic principles to the changing circumstances and the occasions that arose during his lifetime. His precepts, his example and his interpretation or amplification constitute what is called Sunna. As nobody can comprehend the infinite variety of human relations for all occasions and for all epochs, the Prophet of Islam left a very large sphere free for legislative enactments and judicial decisions even for his contemporaries who had the Holy Qur'ān and the Sunna before their eyes. This is the principle of *ijtihād* or interpretative intelligence working within the broad framework of the Qur'ān and the Sunna.

From *The Gazette of Pakistan* (June 20, 1956), pp. 1198–99, 1202–03, 1230.

IJTIHĀD

Although there was primitive simplicity in the life of Arabia during the time of the Holy Prophet, his prophetic wisdom was conscious of the fact that there may be situations and problems not clearly envisaged in the Qur'ān, and that in such cases the Qur'ān could only lay down basic principles which could offer light and guidance even in unpredictable circumstances. He knew that his own explanations and amplifications too could not be expected to cover all details or encompass the novelty of situations and circumstances. He enjoined on his companions, to whom important duties were entrusted, to exercise their own rational judgment with a pure conscience if the Holy Qur'ān and the Sunna did not provide any precise guidance in any particular situation.

The great *Khalīfas* [Caliphs] and others endowed with wisdom and imbued with the spirit of Islam exercised *ijtihād* when the Muslim State and Society were developing. This is what Iqbāl, the great Philosopher and revivalist of Islam, calls the dynamic principle which according to him is a distinguishing characteristic of Islam. . . . No Muslim can believe that Islam is an outworn creed incapable of meeting the challenge of evolutionary forces. Its basic principles of justice and equity, its urge for universal knowledge, its acceptance of life in all its aspects, its world-view, its view of human relations and human destiny, and its demand for an all-round and harmonious development, stand firmly like a rock in the tempestuous sea of life.

NOT A CLERGY STATE

Many a nation of the West, after centuries of bitter conflict between the Church and the State, resorted to Secularism having despaired of divine guidance in the matter of law. Islam was never theocratic in the sense in which this term is used in the history of Western politics. For Islam life is an indivisible unity in which the spiritual and the mundane are not sundered. Religion, according to Islam, means life in the world lived with a spiritual attitude which sublimates all that it touches. For this very reason Islam never developed a church with ordained priests as a class separate from the laity. According to the Holy Qur'ān, the demands of God and the demands of Caesar are not to be satisfied separately because of mutual contradictions and conflicts as Islam recognizes no Caesars. As it countenances no kings who can do no wrong and who stand above the law, so it recognizes no priests. Some may be more learned in the Muslim law than others, but that does not constitute them as a separate class; they are not vested with any special authority and enjoy no special privileges.

PAKISTAN AND LEGAL REFORM

Pakistan was carved out of the Indian subcontinent by leaders of Muslim thought beginning with Sayyid Ahmad Khān and culminating in the person of Qaid-i-Azam Muhammed 'Alī Jinnāh. Islamic ideology was expounded by Iqbāl, with the firm conviction that Islam, properly understood and rationally interpreted, is not only capable of moving along with the progressive and evolutionary forces of life but also of directing them into new and healthy channels in every epoch. The creation of Pakistan was a revolutionary step, and all revolutions demand primary remolding of the educational system and the recasting of laws and the judicial system to fulfill the aspirations of a free and expanding life. But Pakistan, at its very inception, was faced with problems of sheer existence and self-preservation. Ugly situations created by the hostility of neighbors and economic chaos, for which Pakistan was not responsible, made the country concentrate its energies on problems of sheer subsistence, leaving little mental or material resources for educational reconstruction and legal and judicial reform. The work of legal and judicial reform requires intensive and extensive efforts over a period of time, and can be undertaken fruitfully only by a team of scholars and legal experts who possess a vast experience in the legal field, are conversant with Muslim law and jurisprudence and are progressive enough to believe that reconstruction and fresh adaptation of the basic injunctions of Islam are urgently needed to remedy the evils and remove the hurdles created by unsalutary traditions and customs masquerading in the garb of religion. The task entrusted to this Commission is of vital importance as legislation relating to human relationships cannot brook any further delay. The entire revision of our Procedural Law is likely to take a considerable time, and it is only right that a beginning should be made in this respect by tackling Family Laws first of all.

With respect to polygamy, which has become a hotly debated issue in every Muslim society, the commission has adhered to the Qur'ānic view. Polygamy is neither enjoined nor permitted unconditionally nor encouraged by the Holy Book, which has considered this permission to be full of risks for social justice and the happiness of the family unit, which is the nucleus of all culture and civilization. It is a sad experience for those who have practiced it and for those who have watched its tragic consequences that in most cases no rational justification exists and the practice of it is prompted by the lower self of men who are devoid of refined sentiments and are unregardful of the demands of even elementary justice. The Qur'ānic permission about polygamy was a conditional permission to meet grave social emergencies, and heavy responsibilities were attached to it, with the warning that the common man will find it extremely difficult, if not impossible, to fulfill the conditions of equal justice attached to it. The members of the Commission, therefore, are convinced that the practice cannot be left to the sweet will of the individual. It is thoroughly irrational to allow individuals to enter into second marriages whenever they please and then demand *post facto* that if they are unjust to the first wife and children, the wife and children should seek a remedy in a court of law. This is like allowing a preventible epidemic to devastate human health and existence and offering advice to human beings to resort to the medical profession for attempting a cure. Great evils must be nipped in the bud, and prevention is always more rational and more advisable than cure. The Commission is conscious of the fact that in rare cases taking of a second wife may be a justifiable act. Therefore it recommends that it should be enacted that anyone desirous of taking a second wife should not be allowed to do it without first applying to a Matrimonial Court for permission. If the court sees any rational justification in the demand of such a husband he may be allowed only if he is judged to be capable of doing justice in every respect to more than one wife and the children. To ask the first wife and her children to resort to a court for the demands of justice is unjust and impracticable in the present state of our society where women, due to poverty, helplessness, social pressure and suppression are not in a position to seek legal assistance. The function of the court is not merely to remove injustice when it is done. In our opinion a more vital function of the legal and the judicial system is to adopt measures that minimize the practice of injustice. Therefore permission of the Matrimonial Court for a contemplated second marriage, so that the demands of justice are fulfilled and guaranteed, is the fundamental reform proposed by the Commission. . . .

The Minority Report

But the selection of members of the Commission, made for the purpose of achieving this objective, is most disappointing and surprising. What greater injustice could be done to Islamic *Sharī'a* than entrusting the work of bringing the marriage laws into conformity with Islamic *Sharī'a* to a Commission the majority of whose members have neither the detailed knowledge of the Islamic teachings and injunctions nor are they versed in the interpretation and application of those laws. In this connection I was told that in constituting the Commission some of the members were included purely for the reason of their possessing legal and judicial experience, the women members were taken in on the ground that they were conversant with family problems and conditions more than men, and only one member was added to advise on *Sharī'a*. There was no apparent harm in utilizing diverse talents but in the meetings of the Commission every member, save myself, assumed the position of an expert authority on *Sharī'a* and an absolute *mujtahid*. Hence they all remained one and united in contravening the Holy Qur'ān and the Sunna and in ridiculing Muslim jurisprudence, and by calling their action an *ijma'* [Consensus] in the Report, they have debased this technical term of *Sharī'a*. . . .

The members of our Commission, who hasten to declare, so sweetly, the Holy Qur'ān and the Sunna as their source and fount, are neither prepared to perform the feat of codifying a new set of laws of jurisprudence in supersession of the existing one by generalizing from specific provisions, nor are they willing to be guided by the established laws of jurisprudence as their guiding star and beacon light. It is obvious, therefore, that to take personal and individual whims as the basis for the derivation of laws and principles is neither *fiqh* nor *ijtihād* but amounts to distorting the religion of God and the worst type of heresy. In spite of their blatant departure from the view of the Muslim commentators and jurists, no member of the Commission could take the place of Fakhruddīn Rāzī or Abū Hanīfa. This is the reason that certain recommendations, which reflect subservience to the West of some of the members and their displeasure with Islam, constitute an odious attempt to distort the Holy Qur'ān and the Sunna with a view to giving them a western slant and bias. . . .

In order to seek a justification for the arbitrary *ijtihād* of the Commission, the Introduction of the Report says this about the Holy Qur'ān and the Sunna:

> The Holy Qur'ān and the Sunna depict events and contain answers to the questions as they took place and arose while the Book was being revealed.

From *The Gazette of Pakistan* (August 30, 1956), pp. 1561–62, 1564–65, 1572–73, 1591–92.

As nobody can comprehend the infinite variety of human relations and situations for all occasions and for all epochs, the Prophet of Islam left a very large sphere free for legislative enactments and judicial decisions even for his contemporaries who had the Holy Qur'ān and the Sunna before their eyes. This is that principle of *ijtihād* or interpretative intelligence working within the broad framework of the Qur'ān and the Sunna.

It is a matter of surprise that persons utterly ignorant of elementary propositions concerning God, His Glory, the Prophethood, and the comprehensiveness and universality of religion, should have the temerity to write on such subjects. Perhaps our Introduction-writer does not know that the Qur'ān is the sacred Word of God and embodies His Divine Guidance, who has the fullest knowledge and embodies prescience of every minor event of every period and every epoch from the beginning of Time to its end. He knows all the infinite varieties of human relationship which can happen in any period for epoch in all futurity. Hence His revealed Book and His appointed Prophet with prophetic wisdom, all are based on the truth that until doomsday all teachings and injunctions of the Holy Qur'ān and the Sunna shall be the authoritative guidance and final work for all the infinity of events that may take place in this Universe. This is the basic and fundamental article of faith in Islam owing to which Islam is a religion for all times. If the scope of the Qur'ān and the Sunna were limited to the circumstances and events that arose during the Prophet's lifetime or while the Qur'ān was being revealed, then it would be meaningless to call the Holy Qur'ān and the Sunna as the revealed Word of God, and Islam as His Revealed Religion. It would then be more correct to dub the Qur'ān and the Sunna as the work and compilation of an individual who could not see beyond the limited horizon of his own time.

Their sole motive to malign the *'ulamā'* was that Muslims should ignore the *'ulamā'* and these so-called progressives should install themselves in the place of Ghazālī and Rāzī themselves. But in spite of the destructive propaganda Muslims had enough religious consciousness and feeling for faith to turn for religious guidance to the pious *'ulamā'* who possess the knowledge of *Sharī'a* and act upon it. It is an obvious fact that in all technical matters only experts and specialists are consulted. This prerogative of the specialist is not based on any racial or tribal ground but is rooted in reason. When people did not take any notice of the nontechnical *ijtihād* and opinions of these anglicized, West-ridden Sahibs, they started propaganda against the *'ulamā'* that they have created priesthood in Islam, so that their own opinion may have the right to encroach upon their domain. They should know that the *'ulamā'* have not got a special privilege of interpreting and quoting the Holy Qur'ān and the Sunna on the basis of any racial distinction. *'Ulamā'* is not the name of any race or tribe but everyone who has devoted the greater part of his life to the acquisition of knowledge on religious subjects is an *'ālim*. This right of theirs is based on their erudition and experience in exactly the same way in which the right of explaining and interpreting the provisions of the Pakistan Penal Code vests in lawyers and barristers only. It is obvious that the lawyers are not a tribe but they have studied law. The right of prescription and treatment belongs only to a doctor. As anyone who studies law is a lawyer or barrister, in the same way anyone who studies *Sharī'a* and religion is an *'ālim* no matter to what race or tribe he belongs.

The main cause of raising this question [of polygamy] is inferiority complex against the West and the desire to copy it blindly. Our young men and women, who happen to visit Europe, often find themselves in situations in which their country is ridiculed for permitting polygamy. Unable to think out for themselves, these young things readily take to the course of condemning polygamy as the greatest evil in society. It is in fact this class of persons who have, on their return from abroad, taken up arms against polygamy permitted by Islam in an attempt to copy the West and to uphold the condemnation to which they have pledged themselves while in foreign lands. In fact polygamy is not a matter for any human society to be ashamed of, nor does its abolition constitute any achievement of Europe that may be worth emulation by others. Moreover, if we cannot put Europe to shame for permitting free indulgence in adultery, we have no cause to blush at the permission granted by *Sharī'a* for lawfully marrying a second wife. The real comparison in this regard is that of contentment with one woman and this contentment is equally absent in Europe as well as in our own society. The difference is that we proceed to take a second wife by entering into a solemn agreement with her and accepting certain bona fide responsibilities in the form of *nikāh* [marriage], while they choose the unworthy and irresponsible course of playing with the chastity of women in return for a few coins. Thus it is clear that marrying a second wife in the lifetime of the first is nothing discreditable; the sin and the shame of it lies in indulging in adultery while living with a lawfully wedded wife—a practice which has not been declared a penal offense in any European country if it is committed with the consent of the woman involved. It is nothing but a sad demonstration of our own shortsightedness and inferiority complex that we feel shy of a just and reasonable injunction of our religion and do not venture to put others to shame for their glaring fault.

In short, we do not have the slightest excuse for imitating the ways of a people with a social setup and a legal system which tolerates sexual satisfaction by means other than marriage. It is indeed hard to imagine a worse type of blind imitation than the one we find in the present case wherein the women who have kicked up so much dust on the question of polygamy and the Commission which has supported their views have not chosen to utter a word against adultery or recommended it to be declared a penal offense, although this form of vice not only means a flagrant violation of the rights of the lawfully wedded wife but also constitutes a deprecation committed on the chastity of others. The question of adultery in this way becomes purely a question of matrimonial and family life in its bearing. The institutions so vociferously advocating the rights of women and the leaders who dub polygamy as the greatest bane on womanhood, would do well to take the trouble of going round the bazaars in Pakistan and cast a glance on the legions of prostitutes who are daily corrupting unmarried as well as married men in the thousands and breaking up many a happy home by sowing the seeds of hatred in the minds of young men against their innocent wives. In this background the conclusion is inescapable that polygamy is to be penalized while adultery is to be left to flourish free of all legal restrictions and that holy alliance between man and woman, as permitted by *Shari'a*, is to be declared a crime while moral depravity is to be left unscathed. . . .

A fatwa is a formal legal opinion or interpretation given by a jurisconsult (*muftī*) in response to a request from a judge (*qādī*) or an individual. Some modern Muslim governments have obtained *fatwas* to legitimate their reforms.

The Islamic Veil (Hijab)

Is wearing the veil obligatory for Muslim women regardless of the circumstances?

I. Yes, it is a strict obligation

ISLAM ONLINE FATWA BANK
Group of Muftis:

The hijab is not merely a religious symbol; the hijab has an indispensable function in the life of a Muslim woman. That function is protection of the Muslim woman and preservation of her honor and chastity. This means that a woman who wears hijab does not do this to declare her religion or distinguish herself. Rather, she wears it out of obedience to her Lord.

On the other hand, preventing hijab on the basis of preserving the secularity of the state is an illogical claim because secularism in a liberal community means that the state authority should be neutral in matters of religion. The government should neither accept nor reject, neither be for or against any religion. The state is to provide freedom of religion for all people.

One might further ask: If a non-Muslim woman chooses to dress modestly by covering her body and even her hair, would she be prevented from doing so by this ban? And if she is given the freedom to cover herself because she is not Muslim, why then is a Muslim woman not given the same freedom?

Excerpted from a report by Samir Khalil Samir, SJ in Asia Times, January 2, 2004. Copyright © 2003 Asia News. All rights reserved. Also Siyasa, December 31, 2003, p. 1.

(a) In this concern, the eminent Muslim scholar, Dr. 'Ali Jum'ah, Mufti of Egypt, states:

> A Muslim woman is obliged to wear hijab as soon as she reaches puberty, as indicated in the Qur'an, the Sunnah of the Prophet (peace and blessings be upon him) and the consensus of Muslim scholars from early ages of Islam up till now. Hijab is known to be essential and necessary in religion; it is not merely a symbol that distinguishes Muslims from non-Muslims. It is an obligation that forms part and parcel of the Islamic religion.
>
> Allah Almighty says: "O Prophet! Tell thy wives and thy daughters and the women of the believers to draw their cloaks close round them (when they go abroad). That will be better, so that they may be recognized and not annoyed. Allah is ever Forgiving, Merciful." (Al-Ahzab: 59)
>
> He also says: "And tell the believing women to lower their gaze and be modest, and to display of their adornment only that which is apparent, and to draw their veils over their bosoms." (An-Nur: 31)
>
> Also, the Prophet (peace and blessings be upon him) said to Asma', daughter of Abu Bakr (may Allah be pleased with them): "O Asma'! Once a girl reaches puberty, nothing of her body may be seen (by non-*mahrams*) except this and these (he pointed to his face and hands while saying so)."

(b) Sheikh Muhammad Husain Fadl Allah, a well-known Shiite jurist of Lebanon, also comments:

> Wearing hijab derives from religious commitment; it is in the same status of religious obligations in the way that incompliance with it constitutes a sin. Has secularism become so weak that the secular authorities fear a scarf, a turban, or a cross hanging from the neck to threaten its stability?

(c) Moreover, the eminent Muslim scholar, Sheikh Yusuf Al-Qaradawi, states:

> I completely reject and condemn the French resolution that prevents the Muslim female students from wearing hijab at school. By doing so, they force Muslim women to ignore the teachings of their religion and disobey Allah's commands.
>
> Claiming that hijab is a sign of religion is by no means acceptable, because a religious sign or symbol has no function but to declare the religious beliefs of the one who wears it, such as the cross for a Christian and the kippa for a Jew. They both have no function but to declare the religious beliefs of those who wear them. Hijab, on the other hand, has a religious function, namely, to protect Muslim women and preserve their chastity. It could not strike the mind of hijab-clad women to wear it for declaring their religious beliefs. Rather, they wear it in obedience to Allah's commands.
>
> Therefore, the hijab ban contradicts the principles of freedom and equality that have been asserted by the French Revolution and stipulated in all heavenly revealed religions and international charters of human rights. In fact, the hijab ban is a form of persecution against the committed

Muslim women; it infringes upon their freedom; it prevents them from their right to learn and work to the favor of non-Muslim and uncommitted Muslim women.

Real civilization is characterized by tolerance, so it has room for various races, religions, and ideologies. It does not tend to make people copies of a prototype. People should be brought up to the point of tolerance with one another in spite of their difference in religion, as the Glorious Qur'an teaches us in the following verse: "Unto you your religion, and unto me my religion." (Al-Kafirun: 6)

It hurts to hear the claims that one who wears hijab bears hostility towards others. What hostility can a woman who tries to protect her honor and who is committed to the teachings of her religion bear towards others? Hostility and enmity are never expected from a pious person, man or woman, who is conscious of Allah and fears Him.

It is true that the majority pass whatever laws they agree upon, according to the principles of democracy. Yet, just democracy cares for the rights of the minorities, whether religious or ethnic; it does not oppress the minorities. Were it so, the majority in a democratic society could get rid of the minorities under the name of democracy.

II. No, not necessarily in a non-Muslim State

Shaikh al-Azhar, Muhammad Sayyid Tantawi, declared before the French minister of internal affairs, Nicolas Sarkozy, who visited al-Azhar, the most famous religious university in the Islamic Sunnite world. On Dec. 30, 2003:

> The veil is a divine obligation for Muslim women. If it is not respected, God will pass judgement for it not being worn. No Muslim, ruling or ruled, has the right to oppose this obligation.
>
> However, this obligation is valid if Muslim women live in a Muslim state. Yet if they find themselves in a non-Muslim state (like France, for example) and their rulers want to adopt laws in opposition to the veil, it is their right; it is their right; it is their right. I repeat: it is their right, and I cannot oppose them.
>
> When Muslim women conform to the laws of a non-Muslim state, in terms of Islamic Shari'ah, they are under the conditions of he who obligates them (fî hukm al-mudtarr) and they do not, therefore, bear the responsibility (wizr) for the situation.

Sheikh Tantawi justified his opinion with the Qur'anic verse 173, chapter 2, from the Sura of the Cow (al-Baqarah): "In truth regarding beasts it is forbidden to kill them, to have contact with their blood, eat pork, and that which is called by another name other than that of Allah. And he who is forced, without desire or intention, will not sin. Allah is forgiving and merciful."

Muslim women forced by human law cannot, therefore, fear divine punishment. He added: "I wouldn't allow a non-Muslim to intervene in Muslim affairs; likewise I would not permit myself to intervene in non-Muslim affairs."

Bio-ethics

ORGAN DONATION

Date: 4/Aug/2002

Question: What does Islam say about organ donation during life or after death? Is this allowed in Islam?

Mufti: Dr. Muzammil Siddiqi

In his response to the question, Dr. Muzammil Siddiqi, former president of the Islamic Society of North America, states the following:

This question is very much debated by the jurists in past two decades. The Supreme Council of 'Ulama in Riyadh (in their resolution no. 99 dated 6 Dhul Qi'dah 1402) has allowed both organ donation and organ transplantation in the case of necessity.

The organ can be taken from the body of a living person with his/her consent and approval and also from the body of a dead person. In the case of a living person, the jurists have stipulated that this donation should not deprive him/her of vital organs. It should also not cause risk to his/her normal life.

The Fiqh Academy of the Muslim World League, Makkah also allowed organ donation and transplantation in its 8th session held between 28 Rabi'ul Thani and 7 Jumadal Ula, 1405.

The Fiqh Academy of the Organization of the Islamic Conference in Jeddah, during the year 1408, and the Mufti of Egypt Dr. Sayyed At-Tantawi also allowed the use of the body organs of a person who has died in an accident, if the necessity requires the use of any organ to cure a patient, provided that a competent and trustworthy Muslim physician makes this decision.

It is important to note that most of the jurists have only allowed the donation of the organs. They do not allow the sale of human organs. Their position is that the sale of human organs violates the rules of the dignity and honor of the human being, and so it would be haram in that case.

Some jurists suggest that because people have become too materialistic and it may not be possible to find a free organ, under necessity one can purchase the organs, but a Muslim should never sell his/her organs.

From islamonline.net.

BLOOD DONATION

Is blood donation permissible?

Answered by Mufti Muhammad ibn Adam, Darul Iftaa (Leicester, UK)

Question: We are a local newspaper based in Blackburn targeting the Asian communities in Lancashire and Greater Manchester. We have worked with the National Blood Service in promoting the donating of blood and as you will be aware there are misgivings within the Muslim community on this particular action. We would like you to provide us the Islamic view on this issue so we can try to tackle this topic through editorial and informative articles.

Answer: In the name of Allah, Most Compassionate, Most Merciful,

It is a well known principle of Shariah that all the organs and parts of a human body whether one is a Muslim or a non-Muslim are sacred and must not be tampered with. To take benefit from any part of a human without a need is unlawful (haram).

This also includes blood, for it is an integral part of a human. There are two reasons for the impermissibility of taking benefit from another person's blood. Firstly, it is sacred like all other parts of a human. Allah Most High says: "And verily we have honoured the children of Adam" (Surah al-Isra, V.70).

However, Islam is a religion of mercy and caters to all the problems faced by humanity. It acknowledges the needs of people, thus gives concessions and dispensations wherever needed. Allah Most High says: "On no soul does Allah place a burden greater than it can bear" (al-Baqarah, 286). The famous principle of Fiqh states: "Necessity makes prohibition lawful" (See: Ibn Nujaym, al-Ashbah wa al-Naza'ir, p. 85).

Hence, it can be said that blood transfusion is lawful as a necessity just as Islamic law has permitted women's milk for infants out of necessity, despite it being part of a human body.

The second reason was the impurity of blood. This has been discussed earlier in that impure and unlawful things become permissible in cases of need and necessity.

In light of the foregoing, it would be permitted to donate and transfuse blood under the following conditions:

a) The donor is mature and sane.

b) The donor willingly donates his blood. If he is compelled to do so, it will not be permissible.

From themodernreligion.com.

c) There is no apparent risk to the life or health of the donor.

d) There is absolute necessity in donating blood in that there is a definite risk to the life of a patient, and in the opinion of the medical expert, there is no other way in saving his/her life.

e) There is a need for it, that is, there is no risk to the life, but in the opinion of the experts, restoration of health may not be possible without it.

f) There is no reasonable alternative.

g) It is not for the sake of beautification or any other additional benefit.

h) Transfusion of blood must not be carried out by way of buying and selling, for trading in human parts is never permissible. However, if one is in need of blood desperately and the only means to obtain the blood is to purchase it, then only will it be permissible to pay for the blood. This is discussed further in the following section.

GENETIC ENGINEERING

FINAL STATEMENT & RECOMMENDATIONS
OF THE ISLAMIC ORGANISATION
FOR MEDICAL SCIENCES

In pursuance of the Islamic Organisation for Medical Sciences' efforts in dealing with medical and health issues through an Islamic perspective, as shown in the numerous seminars it has regularly organised.

And in view of the tremendous importance of the science of genetics and the scientific avenues it has opened up and their potential applications, with respect to the shaping of the present and future of mankind, the Islamic Organisation for Medical Sciences undertook to hold a special seminar to deal with this issue in depth, and to discuss all the facts and ramifications and possibilities associated with it, from the perspective of Islamic law.

With the grace of God, and under the kind care of His Highness, Sheikh Jaber al-Ahmed al-Jaber al-Sabah, the Emir of the State of Kuwait, the Eleventh Seminar was held in the State of Kuwait, to deal with the subject of "Genetics, Genetic Engineering, the Human Genes, and Genetic Treatment—An Islamic Perspective."

The Seminar was organised in association with the Islamic Fiqh Academy, Jeddah, the World Health Organisation Regional Office, Alexandria, and the Islamic Education, Science and Culture Organisation (ISESCO), during the period from 23 to 25 Jumada al-Akhirah 1419 AH, corresponding to 13 to 15 October 1998.

From islamset.com.

RECOMMENDATIONS

General Principles

1. God has created man in the best form and elevated him above all other creatures. Any tampering with man's basic constituents or subjecting his body to aimless genetic engineering experimentation would be in violation of man's God-given dignity, as asserted by the Quran (al-Isra 17:70).

2. Islam is a religion of knowledge and science, as confirmed in the Quran (al-Zumour 39:9), which imposes no restrictions on constructive scientific research. The outcome and the conclusion from such research should not, however, find their way into implementation before having considered in the light of Islamic legal principles and so long as they do not violate these principles they should be permitted. Genetic science and all its ramifications are, like any other field of knowledge, encouraged and supported by Islam, and Muslim scientists should be at the forefront of research and inquiry in this field.

3. Islam recommends the safe-guarding of human health, as stated in the Quran (al- Baqarah 2:195), and the avoidance of harm. Furthermore, treatment is specifically urged by Islam for hereditary as well as acquired diseases and ailments. This in no way conflicts with the Islamic teachings of perseverance and acceptance of God's will.

4. Every man, regardless of his genetic features, has the right to have his dignity and rights respected.

5. Nobody's genes should be the subject of research, treatment or diagnosis without having first carried out thorough and rigorous evaluation of the possible risks and benefits associated with such activity, while respecting the precepts of Islamic law in this regard and obtaining prior, conscious and free agreement of the person concerned. If the person concerned is not qualified to give such approval, it must be obtained from his guardian, putting the person's own interest first and foremost. If the person concerned is not in a position to grant his consent, no research on his genes must be carried out, unless this has an immediate and clear benefit for the person's own health.

6. The right of everyone to decide whether to be informed of the results of any genetic diagnosis or its effects must be fully respected.

7. All diagnosis of preserved genes or genes obtained for research purposes, or any other purpose, must be treated with full confidentiality. No such information must be divulged except in those cases indicated at the Third Seminar of the Islamic Organisation for Medical Sciences on professional confidentiality, held on 18 April 1987.

8. No one must be subjected to discrimination of any kind on the basis of his genetic identity, which might be intended to infringe on any of his rights or basic freedoms, or undermine his integrity.

9. No research on human genes or the applications of any such research, especially in the fields of biology, genetics or medicine, should take precedence over the rulings of Islamic law and the respect of human rights, basic liberties and human dignity of any individual or group of individuals.

10. Muslim countries are urged to venture into the area of genetic engineering by establishing research centres, working within the directives of Islamic law, to complement one another as much as possible, and grant qualifications to people to work in this field.

11. The Islamic Organisation of Medical Sciences is urged to form committees to study and monitor ethics of medical practice in every Muslim country as a step towards the formation of an Islamic federation for medical ethics in bio-technology.

12. Muslim ulema must prepare and publish research, in a simplified and accessible form, on scientific facts relating to genetics and genetic engineering and educate and enlighten the public.

13. Muslim countries are urged to include genetic engineering as part of the educational curricula at all levels of education, and give it more prominence at university and higher levels.

14. Muslim countries are urged to give more attention to genetics and genetic engineering in the national public media and give full and adequate coverage of the Islamic view of these sciences.

15. To ask the Islamic Organisation for Medical Sciences to monitor scientific progress in this field and to organise similar seminars to prepare and issue the required recommendations, if necessary.

Genetic Engineering

The Seminar agreed that genetic engineering may be used in the prevention, treatment or alleviation of diseases, whether in the form of genetic surgery in which genes are replaced by other genes or genes are implanted in the patient's cells, or when genes are planted in another body to obtain larger amounts of the same gene to be used in the treatment of certain diseases. Genetic engineering should not be used on germ cells, due to certain reservations from the Islamic legal point of view.

The Seminar finds no Islamic legal objection to the use of genetic engineering in the fields of agriculture and livestock, without ignoring, however, those voices that have recently warned of possible harmful long-term effects on man, animals, crop or the environment. The Seminar agreed that companies and factories producing animal or plant foods should make it clear to the public what is being offered for sale of those items that are genetically manufactured. The Seminar also recommends that countries should be fully vigilant in monitoring such products and complying with the relevant recommendations and decisions of the American Food and Medicine Association, the World Health Organisation, and the International Food Agency.

The Seminar recommends that institutions be established to protect and educate the consumer in Muslim countries.

CLONING

With the grace and blessings of God, the 9th Fiqh-Medical Seminar was successfully convened at Casablanca, Morocco, during 8–11 Safar 1418, corresponding to 14–17 June 1997, under the eminent auspices of the Commander of the Faithful, His Majesty King Hassan II. The theme of the seminar was "An Islamic View of Certain Contemporary Medical Issues," and it was held jointly with the Hassan II Institute for Scientific and Medical Research on Ramadhan, the ISESCO, the Islamic Fiqh Academy, and the World Health Organisation Regional Office. The Seminar discussed at length the medical aspects of this matter, and arrived at the following main conclusions relating to cloning:

1. In 1993, human twins were produced by the splitting method, which stimulates the fertilised egg to follow its natural course towards producing identical twins. Each of the initial two daughter cells would then behave as a new fertilised egg in its own right and would grow by dividing itself to form a separate foetus. If the two foetuses were planted in the womb, the result would be identical twins. The debate was not completed since the two scientists in charge of the experiment refrained from planting the eggs in the womb. In fact, they chose to experiment with a defective cell that would divide only until an early stage, due to the sensitivity and seriousness of experimenting with human foetuses. More time is, therefore, required to establish a proper ethical and legal framework for this type of work. The Seminar had no objections, in principle, to this method of fertilisation, but deemed it too early to evaluate its advantages and disadvantages. Of its immediate benefits is the application of diagnostic methods on either twin or some of its cells to establish their normalcy before introduction into the womb. It could also be useful in treating certain infertility cases, subject to all the controls governing test-tube baby procedures. The Seminar discussed thoroughly the new techniques of cloning, in the light of the case of Dolly the sheep, and looked at some of the consequences of producing a foetus (later to be born), which is an exact genetic copy of the

From islamset.com.

original, except for the presence of a very few cytoplasmic genes in the cytoplasm of the recipient egg.

2. It emerged that cloning would be fraught with risk, if ever its application is approved. The risks include the infringement on the individuality and identity of the person, undermining the stability of the social order, and the destruction of the bases of blood relationships and established age-old family ties, recognised by the Islamic Shari'ah and all other religions as the foundation of the family and of social order. This would have serious repercussions on the principles governing blood ties, marriage and inheritance, as well as on civil, criminal and other laws. Numerous hypotheses and possibilities were cited in this connection. . . .

4. The Seminar emphasised that Islam imposes no restrictions on scientific research, but considers it a religious duty and encourages it as a means of understanding God's traditions in His creation. However, Islam advocates that the doors of scientific study should not be left wide open for the application of the results of research in the public domain without proper examination by Shari'ah experts. Not everything that is practicable is necessarily applicable, but should be free of any harmful effects and in line with the rules of Shari'ah.

   Since some of the untoward effects do not become apparent until some time later, it is important to give full consideration and adequate time to the issues involved and take all possible precautions.

5. Based on these unanimously agreed on considerations, some participants were of the view that human cloning was not permissible in any way, shape or form. Others, however, thought that certain, present and future, exceptions may be made, if their benefits are proved and they could be accommodated by the Shari'ah, provided each case is considered on its own merits. . . .

8. The Seminar sees no objection to the application of cloning and genetic engineering techniques on plants and animals within the considered restrictions.

RECOMMENDATIONS

The Seminar passed the following recommendations:

I.   All cases introducing third parties into a marriage, whether a womb, an egg, a sperm or a cloning cell, are not permissible.

II. Ordinary human cloning, in which the nucleus of a living somatic cell from an individual is placed into the cytoplasm of an egg devoid of its nucleus, is not to be permitted. If exceptional cases emerge in the future, they should be considered to verify compliance with the Shari'ah.

III. All Muslim countries are called upon to formulate the necessary legislation to prevent foreign research institutes, organisations and experts
from directly or indirectly using Muslim countries for experimentation
on human cloning or promoting it.

IV. The Islamic Organisation for Medical Sciences and other similar bodies
are called upon to monitor all scientific developments in the field of
cloning and define its terminology and organise seminars and meetings,
as required, to determine and articulate the Islamic rulings and principles pertaining thereto.

V. Specialised committees should be set up to look into the ethics of biological research and adopt protocols for study and research in Muslim
countries, and prepare a document on foetal rights as a prelude to formulate legislation on the rights of the foetus.

Human Procreation

BIRTH CONTROL

Date: 6/July/2003

Question of Fatwa: What does Islam say about birth control? Is it true that sex cannot be used for pleasure and only for reproduction? I was under the impression that this view exists only in Christianity. Please give references from the Qur'an and Hadith. (Jazakum Allah khayran)

Mufti: Sheikh Ahmad Kutty

First of all, it should be clear that the preservation of the human species is unquestionably the primary objective of marriage, and such preservation of the species requires continued reproduction. Accordingly, Islam encourages having many children and has blessed both male and female progeny. However, it allows the Muslim to plan his family due to valid reasons and recognized necessities.

In his response to your question, Sheikh Ahmad Kutty, a senior lecturer and Islamic scholar at the Islamic Institute of Toronto, Ontario, Canada, states:

> Marriage in Islam is based not on one single objective or purpose such as procreation or sexual fulfillment. Rather, it is intended to cater to multiple purposes which include, above all, spiritual tranquility and peace, and cooperation and partnership in fulfilling the divine mandate. Let me explain this briefly.
>
> Islam, being a natural way of life, takes into account all of genuine human instincts such as physical, spiritual, intellectual, emotional, et cetera. It is for this reason that, unlike some other religious ideologies, Islam looks at sexuality positively. In other words, instead of attaching any taboo to sexual fulfillment, Islam teaches us to celebrate sexuality within the framework of a lawful union.
>
> The Prophet (peace and blessings be upon him) said, "You merit rewards of charity in your sexual union with your spouses!" His companions asked in surprise, "How shall we be getting rewards for fulfilling our natural instincts?" He asked, "What if someone were to fulfill his desire unlawfully; would he/she be punished for doing so?" They replied, "Certainly." Then he said, "Likewise, when one does it within the framework of marriage, he/she will be rewarded for it!"

From http://www.islam-online.net.

Although sexuality is one of the main purposes of marriage, it is not the sole one. According to the clear statement of the Qur'an, tranquility and peace through a successful union is considered the primary objective of marriage: "Among His signs is that He created for you spouses of your own kind in order that you may repose to them in tranquility and He instilled in your hearts love and affection for one another; verily, in these are signs for those who reflect (on the nature of the reality)" (Ar-Rum: 21).

In another place, Allah refers to the relationship between males and females in terms of partnership for achieving goodness and fulfilling the divine mandate for their lives. "The believers, males and females, are partners of one another; they shall jointly enjoin all that is good and counsel against all that is evil" (At-Tawbah: 71). And procreation of the human species is also another important purpose, although marriage is still valid if, for one reason or another, the stated purpose of procreation cannot be achieved.

Now coming to the issue of birth control, there is nothing in Islam that prohibits it so long as it is done consensually for valid reasons such as the following: putting off pregnancy until such time when the spouses are in a better position to shoulder the responsibilities of parenting, to allow for space between pregnancies in order to provide proper nurturing and care to existing children, et cetera.

Birth control is, however, forbidden or undesirable when it is resorted to as a permanent measure to prevent conception altogether; likewise, it is forbidden if resorted to for fear of poverty. Allah says, "Don't kill your children for fear of poverty; it is We who provide sustenance for them and you; verily killing them is a most heinous crime!" (Al-Isra': 31). After reflecting on this verse, scholars have concluded that practicing birth control for fear of poverty is unlawful since it implies weakness of faith and trust in Allah as the Provider and Sustainer of all beings.

ARTIFICIAL INSEMINATION

AN ISLAMIC APPROACH TO THE ISSUE OF ARTIFICIAL INSEMINATION

Dr. Muzammil Siddiqi, former president of the Islamic Society of North America, states:

Indeed, artificial insemination is one of the new issues on which Muslim scholars have recently done some Ijtihad in the light of some basic principles and values of the Qur'an and Sunnah.

Artificial insemination for conceptual purpose is generally needed in the situation when the husband is not able to deposit his semen inside his wife's genital tract. This procedure is allowed in Islam as long as it is between legally married couples during the life of the husband. The jurists

Excerpted, with slight modifications, from www.islam.ca.

have emphasized that under the Shari'ah, a wife is not allowed to receive the semen of her ex-husband after divorce or after his death.

The Islamic Reservations Against Third Party's Involvement

Stressing the irreparable harms that occur as a result of another donor's involvement in the process, it must be borne in mind that "Islam safeguards lineage by prohibiting Zina and legal adoption, thus keeping the family line unambiguously defined without any foreign element entering into it. It likewise prohibits what is known as artificial insemination if the donor of the semen is other than the husband. . . ."

Safe Lab Conditions Have to Be Ensured

In his commentary on this point, Dr. 'Abdul-Fattah Idrees, Professor of Islamic Jurisprudence at Al-Azhar University, states:

> Artificial insemination should be conducted under meticulous as well as safe laboratory conditions. The owners of those labs should be trustworthy people. The board of the Islamic Fiqh Council have agreed on the issue of artificial insemination as long as no other third party is involved. The council also stressed the necessity of carrying out the operation when both the husband and wife are alive. In supporting their view, the council cited the Hadith in which the Prophet, peace and blessings be upon him, is reported to have said: "No one of you should lag behind in seeking progeny because if he dies while having no children, his traces will be wiped out."
>
> In the light of this comprehensive fatwa, it's clear that what the 'Ulama focus on for the artificial insermination to keep its permissibility is [for it] to be conducted in a safe atmosphere where no slight cheating or deception takes place, and third party should not get involved in this process.
>
> If you have any further comments, please don't hesitate to write back!
>
> May Allah guide you to the straight path, and guide you to that which pleases Him, Amen.

SURROGATE MOTHERHOOD

Does Islam Allow "Surrogate Motherhood"?

Date: 19/May/2003

Question of Fatwa: What is the Islamic view of surrogate motherhood? Is a married couple allowed to use this procedure to have a child? (Jazakum Allah khayran)

Mufti: Sheikh Ahmad Kutty

Excerpted, with slight modifications, from www.islam.ca.

Answering your question, Sheikh Ahmad Kutty, a senior lecturer and Islamic scholar at the Islamic Institute of Toronto, Ontario, Canada, states:

> Surrogate motherhood is often euphemistically referred to as "hiring a womb." The procedure involves using the service of another woman to serve as a carrier for the fertilized ovum of a couple. The woman makes herself available to inject the fertilized ovum into her own womb and then carries the child to its full term on behalf of the other couple. It is often done in lieu of a specified remuneration or free of charge. People resort to this procedure either because a married woman who desires to have a child has problems in carrying her child to its full term or because of her desire to simply forgo the "trouble" of conception and labor.
>
> According to the rules of Shari'ah, surrogate motherhood as described above is not allowed, since it involves introducing the sperm of a male into the uterus of a woman to whom he is not married and, thus, it clearly falls under the specific category of transgressing the bounds of Allah as stated in the Qur'an: "Those who guard their private parts except from their spouses" (Al-Mu'minun: 5). "Whosoever goes beyond that are indeed transgressors" (Al-Mu'minun: 7).
>
> By introducing a third party into the family equation, this procedure throws into confusion the issue of the identity of the child. In Islam, every child has a right to a definite parentage, namely, that of a father and mother. In the case of surrogate motherhood, the question arises as to the identity of the real mother of the child thus conceived. Is she the genetic mother who provides the egg from which the child is born, or is she the woman whose womb serves as a carrier for the child? Such confusion is bound to affect the child emotionally as he will be torn between two mothers. Further, it may also lead to legal fights over the parentage of the child, as happened in the United States in the case of a child thus conceived in 1987.
>
> Finally, the entire procedure amounts to dehumanizing the process of human procreation by reducing womb down to the level of a commodity that can be bought or rented for service. Ultimately, such a process, yet again, violates the dignity and honor that Allah Almighty has bestowed on man and woman.

ABORTION

Date: 4/June/2002

Question of Fatwa: What is Islam's stance on abortion, as the issue is still controversial, especially among Muslims living abroad?

Mufti: Sheikh Yusuf Al-Qaradawi

From islamset.com.

As regards your question, the following is what the eminent Muslim scholar, Sheikh Yusuf Al-Qaradawi states in his well-known book, "The Lawful and the Prohibited in Islam":

> While Islam permits preventing pregnancy for valid reasons, it does not allow doing violence to it once it occurs.
>
> Muslim jurists have agreed unanimously that after the fetus is completely formed and has been given a soul, abortion is Haram. It is also a crime, the commission of which is prohibited to the Muslim because it constitutes an offense against a complete, living human being. Jurists insist that the payment of blood money (diya) becomes incumbent if the baby is aborted alive and then died, while a fine of lesser amount is to be paid if it is aborted dead.
>
> However, there is one exceptional situation. If, say the jurists, after the baby is completely formed, it is reliably shown that the continuation of the pregnancy would necessarily result in the death of the mother, then, in accordance with the general principle of the Shari'ah, that of choosing the lesser of two evils, abortion must be performed. The reason for this is that the mother is the origin of the fetus; moreover, her life is well-established, with duties and responsibilities, and she is also a pillar of the family. It would not be possible to sacrifice her life for the life of a fetus which has not yet acquired a personality and which has no responsibilities or obligations to fulfill.
>
> Imam al-Ghazzali makes a clear distinction between contraception and abortion, saying that contraception is not like abortion. Abortion is a crime against an existing being. It follows from this that there are stages of existence. The first stages of existence are the settling of the semen in the womb and its mixing with the secretions of the woman. Then comes the next gestational stage. Disturbing the pregnancy at this stage is a crime. When it develops further and becomes a lump, aborting it is a greater crime. When it acquires a soul and its creation is completed, the crime becomes more grievous. The crime reaches a maximum seriousness when it is committed after it (the fetus) is separated (from the mother) alive.

ISLAM AND ECONOMICS

In economics as in politics and law, most modern Muslim states have followed the West. However, the Quran and the *Sharia* do address themselves to economic questions of ownership, taxation, banking, distribution of wealth, and so on. The creation of Pakistan as an Islamic state set off research into the possibilities of an Islamic economy based on an Islamic banking system. Now Islamic banking has become extremely popular even with Western commercial banks, many of which have Islamic sections.

In our first selection, Āyatullāh Mahmūd Tāliqānī, a leader in Iran's (Islamic) revolution, discusses the major characteristics of Islamic economics. Khurshid Ahmad addresses a fundamental consideration facing developing Muslim nations: Is the direction of economic development to be based simply on the adoption of Western models, or should Muslim nations seek to reconstruct their societies on more indigenously rooted models of economic development? Is there an Islamic concept of development?

If Jamal 'Abd al-Nasir and the Ba'th Party advocated and used Islam to legitimate some form of state socialism as essential to bring about serious socioeconomic reform, Muslim economists such as M. 'Umar Chapra espouse alternative viewpoints. Chapra discusses the Islamic state and its resources for ensuring the social welfare of its citizens. Sayyid Muhammad Baqir al-Sadr, who along with Taliqani represents original Islamic research into the problem, explains the beneficial psychological aspect of a school of Islamic economics.

ĀYATULLĀH MAHMŪD TĀLIQĀNĪ
d. 1979

At his death he was the leader of Teheran's clergy. Long a voice for reform, Āyatullāh Tāliqānī was closely allied with the more intellectual and activist elements of Iranian society throughout the 1960's and 70's.

He was a founding member in 1961 of the Freedom Movement (*Nihdat-i Āzādī*) along with lay Islamic leaders such as Mehdī Bāzargān (a former engineering professor at Teheran University and the first Prime Minister appointed by Āyatullāh Khumaynī). Counted among the politically active clergy, he suffered repeated imprisonment. With the Āyatullāhs Khumaynī and Sharī'atmadārī, he was among the principal religious leaders in the revolution.

The Characteristics of Islamic Economics

When one considers the body of Islamic economic principles and laws and compares them with modern economic schools, the indisputable result is that Islamic economics cannot be compared with any of these scientific or practical schools in any way. Islamic economics have special features which can be summarized in the following principles.

First, Islamic economics recognizes individuals as the rightful owner of whatever is the result of their labor in the widest sense, and as the authorized possessor in exchange, within the limits of the special laws of Islam. . . . In this respect Islamic economics are not based on the foundation of the unlimited freedom of individual ownership, the result of which is uncontrolled capitalism. They are also not based upon common ownership the result of which might be the complete deprivation of ownership and of individual freedom, or like mixed or con-joined economies in which limits are confused and unknown. Rather the limits and conditions that characterize Islamic economics are compatible with human nature and with an equitable system and with the rights of all participants. Individual ownership is based on the innate and natural freedom of individuals, and cooperation is based on common needs and interests.

From Sayyid Mahmūd Tāliqānī, *Islām wa Mālikiyat* [Islam and ownership], trans. William Darrow (Houston, Texas: Islamic Distribution Center, n.d.), pp. 225–75.

Now the theory of capitalism and the theory of collectivism, when actually practiced, dispenses with all their theoretical principles. Capitalist countries, which are based on the principle of free and unlimited ownership, inevitably go down the road of unbridled capitalism, and as a result the nationalization of the means of production and of the large industries follows. On the other hand, the principles of collectivism, in spite of their rigidity, make individual ownership possible in practice to a limited extent in the areas of necessities such as housing and farm production, either by law or by tradition. These obvious violations show that these two views are not views actually applicable to real life, but are rather the products of the fluctuations of industrial economics in the past century in Western countries. They must, after the period of fluctuation, be judged according to the absolute scale of truth and natural rights.

Second, from the Islamic point of view, material attachments and economic relations are intertwined with modes of thought, innate characteristics, emotions and human instincts. . . .

Islam posits the connection between an organized system of limits on rights and attachments and the critical assessment of views, the strengthening of faith, the cultivation of consciences and human values. It has explained economic laws and rules according to this principle. . . .

Third, Islam has organized and systematized the limits of ownership and economic relations in terms of three characters: 1. individuals; 2. laws; and 3. government. As in other affairs, individuals are free to enjoy material things to the limit of their maturity and according to the dictates of their faith and the responsibility of their consciences. They can benefit and enjoy property as long as it does not belong to someone else. This freedom in the area of economic exchanges is limited to the right of ownership of things which are the product of one's labor. This sets the limits of the laws and the conditions of legitimacy in a transaction.

Islamic government is to be defined as the rule of the Imām, or his deputy, or the viceroy of God or someone He has sent. Islamic government has the right to limit the enjoyment and ownership of an individual even more than the rules permit, in the event that there is an opposition between the right of an individual and the right of society because the rightful rulers give precedence to and seek to ensure that social benefits prevail over individual benefits. . . .

Fourth, distribution like production, in the view of Islam, is the natural and innate right of the one who performs the labor, with the qualification that the individual is free in choosing such labor. Labor is the basis of the right of ownership. As a result of this the owner is free in the enjoyment and distribution of his possessions. The limitations and laws circumscribing the enjoyment and right of ownership, and the general supervision of the sage governor, is the guarantor of the systematization and limitation of distribution and preventor of unreasonable profit. Given this limitation and supervision, why is this right not given to the one who is the original laborer? As has been said before, it is against nature that the results of labor and the product of the effort of individuals who are created free should be at the will of capitalists or the government. Both the capitalists and government take away the independence and freedom and personality of individuals which are more valuable than anything, by giving food and limited means of livelihood in the same way they give machinery oil so that machines are prepared to produce more. If the laborer (i.e. the one who is the one authorized to enjoy and to distribute what he has) is not free and distribution (within necessary boundaries) is limited, then both the rightful owner is deprived of his right and human values go unrealized. These two are the principle motivations for good action and the appearance of talents. . . .

Fifth, based on the principles of Islamic economics, the right of possession and distribution of natural products, is based on the right of possession and distribution of natural resources, with the stipulation that the land and all natural products belong to everyone. Government which is the guardian and representative of the common good possesses the right of oversight and distribution. At a later stage the cultivation of the land and extraction from it in underground mines and making natural items productive such as rocks on the earth and running water and water and desert animals, all give the right to each individual who does these things, as long as these claims and relations obtain, to enjoy and distribute these products.

These rights, to the extent that there is no injury to the common good, are preserved, because resources and common things in nature belong to the public and their enjoyment is limited by the rights of the public. Therefore, if someone owns more than the average, and has more possibilities, the law of common ownership and the power of the government limits him and prevents him from misusing what is commonly held either in cultivation, extraction or making something productive. . . .

Given this form of limited freedom in transactions and the supervision of the government over commodities, the simple law of supply and demand in the usual capitalist understanding cannot direct transactions. This is because demand in the usual capitalist usage and in actuality depends upon the ability to buy things and on having money. But demand, on the basis of Islamic jurisprudence, arises out of what is actually required by necessity. Therefore supply and the actual making available of goods will be limited to what is actually required by necessity. The marketplace thus cannot become the toy of the greed of capitalists by which they open the way to false demand and oppressive profits.

Therefore these rights that arise out of natural resources and things, as a result of cultivation, discovery, or making something productive, are the prime source for the distribution of these resources and products. But these rights that are entailed are not sufficient basis for the right of absolute ownership of natural resources. The absolute right of ownership applies only to things that are agricultural products which are the actual result of labor and represent human effort . . . The result of labor whether in the form of commodities or exchanged for money is the basis of and motive for new activities. It leads to new activities, and the later labor is the result of the earlier and the earlier has a share in it. The share of those who work later on a product is limited to the labor they actually do or that is attached to the product. The laws of Islam have direct oversight in each affair and transaction and can intervene to negate what is inappropriate so that the protection of freedom prevents unlawful profit and stops unlawful methods.

These rights which are entailed in connection with the enjoyment and distribution that arise from natural resources are the special feature of Islamic economic principles. In practice, capitalism does not have a just and right means to have and distribute natural products. Because no matter how natural resources come into the possession of a capitalist, provided they do not belong to someone else, the capitalist has an absolute right of ownership (not a right which limits profits). . . .

Marxism adds the qualification that it entrusts the possession of natural resources by human beings to evolution, means of production and the course of history so that according to those conditions, the relations of men to those resources are conditioned or limited. Therefore the differences between capitalism and communism mainly concern industrial production, and natural resources are of minor concern in both these systems.

Islam has based the foundation and center of human life on natural resources and has not entrusted them either to the hands of powerful capitalists or to power of the evolution of the means of production. From the Islamic point of view the one who must have the natural resources which are the basis of human life is the worker, to the limit of his labor and always preserving the right of the society. . . .

Sixth, since natural resources, earth, water, forests, woods, lakes and mines are the foundation of life for human beings and all other animals, if the limitations on the rights and benefits derived from them are organized in a clear and just manner, then all other issues connected with the means of livelihood must also be systematized. Then the problems connected with economic relations would be greatly alleviated. Economists of the age of industrialization have devoted most of their attention to the problems of industrializaton and thus have not provided a just and clearcut manner of organizing and systematizing natural resources. . . .

Seventh, the right of ownership is based upon labor and arises from the right of using and holding natural resources. It is determined by Islamic laws in the context of transactions and exchanges. In the course of time death ends the right. Therefore after death no one still continues to have the right to enjoy one's possessions. . . .

At death the dying person has the right of determining the disposition of one-third of his wealth. It can be used for the rights of his relatives or by the way of charity. It is designed to take care of the right of society so that if his heirs do not have sufficient means or are not in the direct lines of inheritance, although they are entitled or if public needs make it desirable, the person who is on the verge of death can dispose of one third of his wealth as he sees fit according to these needs. The Qur'ānic law is that he has only right to make a will concerning one-third of his possessions. . . .

Eighth, Islamic law has also limited the ways in which possessions can be used after it has provided limits on ownership and benefits and on the rights of transaction and limited even the given rights by such means as required alms, setting aside a fifth of your income for religious purposes and charity. These limitations by necessity increase the production of useful commodities and also put wealth to work for the sake of economic progress and increasing employment. In the end it would prevent the use of factories and productive capacities in ways which are harmful and dangerous to individuals and society. . . .

Ninth, in the realm of Islam and under the supervision of its laws, workers and wage earners are not dominated by the capitalist layer of society and by the power of the government. This group has both personal freedom and freedom in their work. Their means of livelihood are supplied according to their own free work and given according to their needs.

Tenth, among the distinguishing features of the Islamic economic system is the protection of independence in financial exchanges and the cultivation of the personality of the individual within society. If we agree that the actual form of a society is nothing but the collection of the legal relationships of individuals and that social classes do not have any external reality and that individuals possess independence and personality while respecting the rights of others and finally that the establishment of communal rights and good relations is for the preservation of the individuals' independence (and not individuals for society), then we must agree that since individuals possess two personalities, an individual one and a social one, with regard to the individual personality, he has freedom of action and of enjoying the results of his labor. With regard to his social personality, such enjoyments and profits must be limited by the social good. But the idea of the social good does not mean that society possesses an independent legal personality and is somehow separate from the collectivity of individual rights. Government, in this view, must be like the representative and deputy of individuals and not the representative of a special class nor the possessor of a separate personality. Its purpose is nothing but the preservation of individual rights and of the collectivity of individuals. In this regard government does not have the right to deprive or limit the freedom and independence of individuals or the rights of some classes for the profit of another class in the name of the higher good of the government. . . .

Eleventh, Islam in the economic sphere, just as in the area of spiritual relations and social interactions, has fixed principles and dynamic rules and laws. The fixed principles are the foundation and basis of the dynamic rules and underpin communal interaction. The rules concerning specific issues and affairs which might come up must be applied according to the fixed and beneficial principles. On this basis, the rules of Islam are at once fixed and dynamic. The society which is administered by these principles and rules does not become static, outmoded or dependent. Old and new do not split asunder or separate in it. . . . This subjugation, and feeling of inferiority and of being at a loss that Muslims feel towards foreigners and the governments connected with them, which now appears among Muslims in all areas of action, is what has made them static and blocked the functioning of the Islamic economic system as it has everything else. . . .

Twelfth, thus according to what has been said, Islamic economics are founded on the principles of right and justice, and are not based on any special group or class. In fact, from the point of view of Islam the appearance of the features of classes is not a necessary inevitable thing or a irremediable social necessity. The appearance of classes is the result of the defect of individuals and society [due to their] not following right and just principles. It is the byproduct of transgression, oppression and colonialism. The form of society is only the reflection of individual relationships and individual relationships externalize the thoughts, minds and morals of persons. Let the thoughts and spirits of individuals change into any other form and the communal relations and social form must also change. *Indeed God does not change the condition of a people, until they have changed it for themselves* (Qur'ān 13: 11). Thus in history and in different areas in both large and small manifestations we can observe the appearance of societies bound together without class. This is a decisive proof that the appearance of classes is not an historical necessity. . . .

Thirteenth, the Qur'ān, before explaining the rules and laws about the organization and limitations on relations and financial attachments, turns the mind and ideology of the monotheist toward the foundation and original source of all rights and possessions which manifest themselves out of natural powers. This view, which is the conviction that all existence is created and belongs to the origin and creator and director of the world, is the principle of faith in *tawhīd*. Therefore He who possess the whole world has created man with the power of reason and the capacity for enjoyment, so that he can use his understanding and thought and limbs to investigate mysteries and to put to use whatever exists. In this regard the Qur'ān has introduced this thinking and powerful phenomenon that is man as the "viceroy" of God before giving man any other name or title. . . .

Therefore, every Muslim and monotheist, before his responsibilities of faith and those related to serving and preserving the rights of others, communal security and obeying rules, must do the will and commands of Him who is the rightful possessor. Man is both his possession and also his viceroy and deputy.

Fourteenth, since the monotheist recognizes himself as the representative of Him who possesses the world and the agent of His will and executor of His command and realizes that he is not entirely free and independent in his possessions, he cannot view what material and attachments he has independently of this. In this view what wealth and possessions he has are nothing but a means to reach humane aims and goals and a place in the other world.

The aim of acquiring wealth in economic relations or using it as a means for satisfying lust and animal desires is the result of the mental defects and dull-mindedness and the corruption of human beings. This defective mind-set is the most significant cause which gives to classes and groups which follow individuals of the same view in accumulating wealth in whatever way possible. This causes individuals to become merely the means for the production and profit and the accumulation of wealth. Any kind of tyranny and transgression in reaching this goal is approved of. Consequently the way toward progress and just production and distribution is blocked. These two views, that of acquiring wealth for its own sake and of using wealth for base purposes, have had an effect in all areas of spiritual and material life of man, and have been the special topic of discussion by prophets and the great benefactors of mankind and especially in the cultivation of the laws of Islam. One should not only see the struggle of religious leaders for such an evolution of thought and expansion of views as a topic for spiritual and ethical sermons, but should also realize the importance of developing towards such an attitude and of its effects in all aspects of human life. . . .

KHURSHID AHMAD
1934–

He was formerly associate professor of economics at the University of Karachi, a founder and Director-General of the Islamic Foundation (Leicester U.K.), and Federal Minister of Planning and Development, Government of Pakistan. He is currently Director of the Institute for Policy Studies, Islamabad, Pakistan.

Islam and the Challenge of Economic Development

A major challenge confronts the world of Islam: the challenge of reconstructing its economy in a way that is commensurate with its world role: ideological, political and economical. What does this demand: economic development with a view to "catch up" with the industrialized countries of the West, Capitalist or Socialist according to one's inclination and sympathy, or politico-economic dependence? Or does it demand total socio-economic reconstruction in the light of a basically different model, with its own set of assumptions, ideals and growth-path, something that would be unique and value-specific?

The Muslim countries suffer from widespread economic underdevelopment, i.e. non-utilisation and or under-utilisation of human and physical resources with consequent poverty, stagnation and backwardness.

The paradox of the Muslim world is that it is resource-rich, but economically poor and weak. Development planning has been introduced in a number of Muslim countries. In some, the art is now at a fairly advanced level. Nigeria, Egypt, Syria, Algeria, Iran, Pakistan, Malaysia, Indonesia are some of the instances in view. But in almost all these countries developmental effort is modelled after the prototypes of growth developed by the Western theorists and practitioners of planning and "sold" to the planners in the Muslim countries via international diplomacy, economic pressurization, intellectual mobilization and a number of other overt and covert means. Whatever be the source of inspiration—the Capitalist economies of the West or the Socialist models of Russia and China—no effort worth the name seems to have been made to re-think the basic issues of development economics in the light of the ideals and values of Islam and its world strategy.

From *The Challenge of Islam*, ed. Altaf Gauhar (London: Islamic Council of Europe, 1978), pp. 339–49.

How does this policy and the actual developments stand in relation to Islam? It would be correct to say that developmental policies have been, more or less, Islam-neutral. As against this unfortunate "fact," it is our submission that as far as Islam is concerned, it cannot be neutral *vis-à-vis* economic development. But there is no evidence to support that generally speaking, the policy makers derived any inspiration worth the name from Islam and tried to translate its economic ideals into development policies, some lip-service here and there notwithstanding. Actual policies have had no or little relation to Islam with the result that the economics of the Muslim world have failed to be transformed towards Islam and the deformities and inequities inherited from the colonial period and beyond have been generally aggravated. Muslim thinkers have criticised this state of affairs and have emphasised that Islam should be the main inspiration in their development thinking.

The primary task of any theory of development is to examine and explain the nature of the processes of development and factors responsible for it, to identify and analyse principal obstacles to development in a given situation, and to try to prescribe the most desirable and the most efficient ways and means to remove those obstacles and achieve various dimensions of economic development.

A major contribution of Islam lies in making human life and effort purposive and value-oriented. The transformation it seeks to bring about in human attitudes and *pari passu* in that of the social sciences is to move them from a stance of pseudo-value-neutrality towards open and manifest value-commitment and value-fulfilment. As such the first premises which we want to emphasise is that economic development in an Islamic framework as also Islamic development economics are rooted in the value pattern embodied in the Qur'ān and Sunna. This is our basic frame of reference.

Our second premise is that this approach clearly rules out a strategy of imitation. The Capitalist and the Socialist models cannot be adopted as our ideal-types, although we would like to avail ourselves of all those experiences of mankind which can be gainfully assimilated and integrated within the Islamic framework and can serve our own purposes without in any way impairing our values and norms.

But we must reject the archetypes of capitalism and socialism. Both these models of development are incompatible with our value system. Both are exploitative and unjust and fail to treat man as man, as God's vicegerent (*khalīfa*) on earth. Both have been unable to meet in their own realms the basic economic, social, political and moral challenges of our time and the real needs of a humane society and a just economy. Both are irrelevant to our situation, not merely because of the differences in ideological and moral attitudes and in socio-political frameworks, but also for a host of more mundane and economic reasons, like differences in relative resource bases, changed international economic situations, bench-mark differences in the levels of the respective economies, socio-economic costs of development, and above all, for the fundamental fact that the crucial developmental strategy of both the systems—industrialisation primarily through maximisation of investible surplus—is not suited to the conditions of the Muslim world and the demands of the Islamic social ideals.

Development economics is presently passing through a period of crisis and re-evaluation. It is coming under attack from a number of directions. An increasing number of economists and planners are becoming sceptical about the whole approach of contemporary development economics.

A much more critical approach deserves to be adopted towards the panaceas that have been "sold" to the Muslim countries.

On the positive side we submit that our approach should be ideological and value-oriented. In development economics, as in economics—or in any branch of human activity, there is an area which deals with technological relationships. But such technological relationships *per se* are not the be-all and end-all of a social discipline.

Technological relationships are important, and they should be decided according to their own rules. But technological decisions are made in the context of value-relations. Our effort is to weld these two areas and to make our values explicit and to assign to them the role of effective guide and controller for the entire system. This means that as against an imitative stance, our approach must be original and creative. It is only through a thorough understanding of the social ideals and values of the Qur'ān and Sunna and a realistic assessment of our socio-economic situation—resources, problems and constraints—that we can adopt a creative and innovative strategy for change. As such, our approach would be ideological as well as empirical and somewhat pragmatic—pragmatic not in the sense that ideals and values can be trimmed to suit the exigencies of the situation, but pragmatic in the sense that ideals and values are to be translated into reality in a practical and realistic way.

Islam stands for effort, struggle, movement and reconstruction—elements of social change. It is not merely a set of beliefs. it also provides a definite outlook on life and a programme for action, in a word, a comprehensive milieu for social reconstruction. We would, therefore, conclude this section by submitting some basic propositions about the dynamics of social change as they reveal themselves by reflection on the Qur'ān and Sunna. They also provide some indicators for goals of socio-economic policy.

a. Social change is not a result of totally pre-determined historical forces. The existence of a number of obstacles and constraints is a fact of life and history, but man is not subject to any historical determinism. Change has to be planned and engineered. And this change should be purposive—that is, sustained movement towards the norm or the ideal.

b. Man is the most active agent for change. All other forces have been subordinated to him in his capacity as God's vicegerent (*khalīfa*). Within the framework of the divine arrangement for this universe and its laws, it is man himself who is responsible for making or marring his destiny.

c. Change consists in environmental change and change within the heart and soul of man—his attitudes, his motivation, his commitment, his resolve to mobilize all that is within him and around him for the fulfilment of his objectives.

d. Life consists of a network of inter-relationships. Change means some disruption in some relationships somewhere. As such there is a danger of change becoming an instrument of disequilibrium within man and in society. Islamically oriented social change would aim at the least friction and disequilibria, and planned and co-ordinated movement from one state of equilibrium to a higher one, or from a state of disequilibrium towards equilibrium. As such, change has to be balanced and gradual and evolutionary. Innovation is to be coupled with integration. It is this unique Islamic approach which leads to revolutionary changes through an evolutionary trajectory.

These are some of the major elements of healthy social change through which Islam wants man and society to move from one height to another. The task before the Islamic leadership, intellectual as well as politico-economic, is clearly to formulate the objectives and strategy of change along with the ways of achieving it and also to establish institutions and inaugurate processes through which these policies could be actually implemented.

ISLAMIC CONCEPT OF DEVELOPMENT

Now we would like to elaborate on some of the essential elements of the Islamic concept of development.

Islam is deeply concerned with the problem of economic development, but treats this as an important part of a wider problem, that of total human development. The primary function of Islam is to guide human development on correct lines and in the right direction. It deals with all aspects of economic development but always in the framework of total human development and never in a form divorced from this perspective. That is why the focus, even in the economic sector, is on human development, with the result that economic development remains an integrated and indivisible element of moral and socio-economic development of human society.

The philosophic foundations of the Islamic approach to development . . . are as follows:

1. *Tawhīd* (God's unity and sovereignty). This lays down the rules of God-man and man-man relationship.

2. *Rububiyya* (Divine arrangements for nourishment, sustenance and directing things towards their perfection). This is the fundamental law of the universe which throws light on the divine model for the useful development of resources and their mutual support and sharing. It is in the context of this divine arrangement that human efforts take place.

3. *Khilāfa* (man's role as God's vicegerent on earth). This defines man's status and role, specifying the responsibilities of man as such, of a Muslim, and of the Muslim *umma* as the repository of this *khilāfa*. From this follows the unique Islamic concept of man's trusteeship, moral, political and economic, and the principles of social organisation.

4. *Tazkiyah* (purification *plus* growth). The mission of all the prophets of God was to perform the *tazkiyah* of man in all his relationships with God, with man, with natural environment, and with the society and state.

We would submit that the Islamic concept of development is to be derived from its concept of *tazkiyah*, as it addresses itself to the problem of human development in all its dimensions and is concerned with growth and expansion towards perfection through purification of attitudes and relationships. The result of *tazkiyah* is *falah*—prosperity in this world and the hereafter.

In the light of these foundational principles, different elements of the concept of development can be derived. We would submit the following as its essential features:

A. Islamic concept of development is comprehensive in character and includes moral, spiritual and material aspects. Development becomes a goal- and value-oriented activity, devoted to the optimisation of human well-being in all these dimensions. The moral and the material, the economic and the social, the spiritual and the physical are inseparable. It is not merely welfare in this world that is the objective; it is also the welfare that Islam seeks to extend to the life hereafter—and there is no conflict between the two. This dimension is missing in the contemporary concept of development.

B. The focus for developmental effort and the heart of the development process is man. Development, therefore, means development of man and his physical and socio-cultural environment. According to the contemporary concept, it is the physical environment—natural and institutional—that provides the real area for developmental activities. Islam insists that the area of operation relates to man, within *and* without.

C. Economic development is a multi-dimensional activity, more so in an Islamic framework. As efforts would have to be made simultaneously in a number of directions, the methodology of isolating one key factor and almost exclusive concentration on that would be theoretically untenable. Islam seeks to establish balance between the different factors and forces.

D. Economic development involves a number of changes, quantitative as well as qualitative. Involvement with the quantitative, justified and necessary in its own right, has unfortunately led to the neglect of the qualitative aspects of development in particular and of life in general. Islam would try to rectify this imbalance.

E. Among the dynamic principles of social life, Islam has particularly emphasized two: First, the optimal utilisation of resources that God has endowed to man and his physical environment and, secondly, their equitable use and distribution and promotion of all human relationships on the basis of Right and Justice. Islam commends the value of *shukr* (thankfulness to God by availing oneself of His blessings) and *'adl* (justice) and condemns the disvalues of *kufr* (denial of God and His blessings) and *zulm* (injustice).

In the light of this analysis, development process is mobilized and activated through *shukr* and *'adl* and is disrupted and distorted by *kufr* and *zulm*.

This is basically different from the approach of those who look upon production and distribution in an either/or relationship with the development process and is a much wider and more dynamic concept than that of the role of production and distribution in development. The developmental effort, in an Islamic framework, is directed towards the development of a God-conscious human being, a balanced personality committed to and capable of acting as the witness of Truth to mankind.

We may, therefore, submit that in an Islamic framework economic development is a goal-oriented and value-realising activity, involving a confident and all-pervading participation of man and directed towards the maximisation of human well-being in all its aspects and building the strength of the *umma* so as to discharge in the world its role as God's vicegerent on earth and as "the mid-most people." Development would mean moral, spiritual and material development of the individual and the society leading to maximum socio-economic welfare and the ultimate good of mankind.

M. 'UMAR CHAPRA
1933–

Born and raised in Pakistan, Dr. Chapra earned a doctorate in economics from the University of Minnesota. He has held academic posts in America and Pakistan, served as Senior Economist for the Pakistan Institute of Development Economics, and is currently Economic Advisor to the Saudi Monetary Agency.

The Islamic Welfare State

SOCIAL SECURITY AND EQUITABLE DISTRIBUTION OF INCOME AND WEALTH

It is the duty of the Islamic state to ensure a respectable standard of living for every individual who is unable to take care of his own needs and hence requires assistance. The Prophet clearly declared that: "He whom God has made an administrator over the affairs of Muslims but remains indifferent to their needs and their poverty, God will also be indifferent to his needs and poverty."[1] He also said that: "He who leaves behind him dependants, they are our responsibility"[2] and that "the ruler [state] is the supporter of him who has no supporter."[3] These and other similar *hadīths* lay down the gist of Islamic teachings in the realm of social security.

'Umar, the second Caliph, explaining distributive justice in Islam, emphasized in one of his public addresses that everyone had an equal right in the wealth of the community, that none, not even he himself, enjoyed a greater right in it than anyone else, and that if he were to live longer, he would see to it that even a shepherd on Mount Sinai received his share from this wealth. . . .

The Islamic concept of justice in the distribution of income and wealth does not require equal reward for everyone irrespective of his contribution to society. Islam tolerates some inequalities of income because all men are not equal in their character, ability, and service to society (Qur'ān 6: 165, 61: 71, and 43: 32). Therefore, distributive justice in the Islamic society, after (i) guaranteeing a humane standard of living to all members through

1. Abū-Dāwūd al-Sijistani, *Sunan Abū-Dāwūd* (Cairo: 'Isā al-Bābī al-Halabī, 1952), vol. 2, p. 122.
2. Ibid., p. 124.
3. Ibid., vol. 1, p. 481.

From "The Islamic Welfare State and Its Role in the Economy," in *Islamic Perspectives*, ed. Khurshid Ahmad and Zafar Ishāq Ansārī (Leicester: The Islamic Foundation, 1979), pp. 208–17.

proper training, suitable job, "just" wages, social security and financial assistance to the needy through the institution of *zakāt*, and (ii) intensifying the distribution of wealth through its system of dispersal of the estate of a deceased person, allows such differentials in earning as are in keeping with the differences in the value of the contribution made or services rendered to society.

The Islamic stress on distributive justice is so emphatic that there have been some Muslims who have been led to believe in absolute equality of wealth. Abū-Dharr, a companion of the Prophet, was of the opinion that it is unlawful for a Muslim to possess wealth beyond the essential needs of his family. However, most of the Prophet's companions did not agree with him in this extreme view and tried to prevail upon him to change his position. . . .

THE WHEREWITHAL

To live up to all the above obligations, the Islamic state would naturally stand in need of adequate financial resources. . . .

One principle which is clearly recognised by all jurists is that the state has no right to acquire resources by *confiscating* property duly possessed by individuals or groups. . . .

If the acquisition of resources through either confiscation or nationalisation without just compensation is to be ruled out then the primary sources left would be the following *in addition to the sale of relevant services*.

   i. *Zakāt*;

  ii. Income from natural resources;

 iii. Taxation; and

 iv. Borrowing.

i. *Zakāt*

To enable Muslims to bring to fulfilment a society which is like a single nuclear family, where wealth is equitably distributed and where the essential needs of all deserving individuals are met primarily by mutual help with the planning and organisational assistance of the state, Islam has instituted a powerful social security system giving it a religious sanctity which it enjoys nowhere else in the world. It is a part of the religious obligations of a Muslim to pay *zakāt* at a prescribed rate on his net worth or specified income flows to the *zakāt* fund. Of such great significance is the institution of *zakāt* in Islam that whenever the Qur'ān speaks of the obligation to establish prayers it also simultaneously stresses the obligation of Muslims to pay *zakāt*. The Prophet went so far as to declare that "whoever offers prayers but does not pay *zakāt*, his prayers are in vain."[4]

4. Abū-'Ubayd Qāsim ibn Sallām, *Kitāb al-Amwāl* (Cairo: at-Maktabah al-Tijāriyah al-Kubra, A.H. 1353), p. 354:919.

There is a general consensus among jurists that collection and disbursement of *zakāt* is essentially the responsibility of the Islamic state. This was the practice during the days of the Prophet and of the first two Caliphs, Abū-Bakr and 'Umar. Abū Bakr even used coercion against those who refused to pay *zakāt* to the state. . . .

However, even if the state collects *zakāt*, the proceeds are likely to be limited. Moreover, the expenditure heads for *zakāt* are clearly enumerated in the Qur'ān. Even though some jurists have widened somewhat the coverage of the expression *fī sabīl Allāh* (in the way of Allah), it can hardly be made to include all expenditure heads of the Islamic state. Thus, if the Islamic state is to live up to its obligations it must have access to the resources beyond the *zakāt* collection. . . .

ii. Income from Natural Resources

It has already been established that natural resources have been provided by God for the welfare of all people. The monetary benefit derived from these resources should, therefore, permeate to all people and should not under any circumstances be allowed to be diverted solely to certain individuals or groups. The acceptance of this principle does not necessarily restrict the management of these resources to the state alone. Whether the state or private enterprise should manage the exploitation of these resources should be determined by the criterion of efficiency. However, even if private enterprise is to manage and operate these resources the profit derived by it should not be more than what is justified by the services rendered and the efficiency attained.

In countries with abundant natural resources to contribute an adequate income to the state treasury to finance public expenditure (as is the case in some major oil-producing Muslim countries) there may be little need for additional sources of revenues. However, countries where income from this source is either not available, or if available, is not sufficient, the state would have to supplement its income by resorting to taxation and/or borrowing if necessary.

iii. Taxation

The right of the Islamic state to raise resources through taxes cannot be challenged provided that taxes are raised in a just manner and are within a certain "bearable" limit. This right is defended on the basis of the Prophetic saying that "in your wealth there are also obligations beyond the *zakāt*," and one of the fundamental principles of Islamic jurisprudence that "a small benefit may be sacrificed to attain a larger benefit and a smaller sacrifice may be imposed in order to avoid a larger sacrifice."

Most jurists have upheld the right of the state to tax. According to Marghīnānī, if the resources of the state are not sufficient, the state should collect funds from the people to serve the public interest because if the benefit accrues to the people it is their obligation to bear the cost. Abū Yūsuf also supports the right of the ruler to increase or decrease taxes depending on the ability of the people to bear the burden. However, only a just tax system has been held to be in harmony with the spirit of Islam. A tax system which is oppressive and too onerous as compared with the ability of the people to bear has been unanimously condemned. All rightly-guided caliphs, particularly 'Umar, 'Ali, and 'Umar ibn 'Abd al-'Azīz, are reported to have stressed that taxes should be collected with justice and kindness, that they should not be beyond the ability of the people to bear, and should not deprive the people of the basic necessities of life. . . .

In view of the goals of social justice and equitable distribution of income a progressive tax system seems to be perfectly in harmony with the goals of Islam. It must, however, be emphasized that from the discussion of the jurists what is relevant from the point of view of modern times is the right of the Islamic state to tax with justice. It would not be proper to conclude that taxation should be strictly confined to the items mentioned by the jurists. Circumstances have changed, and there seems to be the need for devising a tax system which is in harmony with the goals of Islam and yields sufficient revenue to allow a modern Islamic state to discharge its functions as a welfare state.

iv. Borrowing

If total revenue from all the above sources (including sale of services) is not sufficient, the Islamic state would stand in need of borrowing. In this case because of the Islamic injunction against interest, the borrowing would need to be free of interest.

For certain sound income-yielding projects amenable to sale of services and distribution of dividends it may be possible to raise funds on the basis of profit-sharing. However, the scope for this is limited in the case of most public projects. In case profit-sharing is not possible or feasible, the Islamic state may have to borrow funds, and this would be possible only if the private sector of the Muslim society is so highly inspired by the ideals of Islam that it is willing to forego the return. In modern acquisitive Muslim societies imbued perhaps more with hedonistic ideals of the economic man as conceived by Adam Smith rather than by the altruistic teachings of Islam, and with continuous erosion of the real value of savings because of the high rate of inflation, it may be expected that borrowing without any return may tend to be unproductive unless it is made compulsory.

"RICHEST" OR "IDEAL"

It may be contended here that all Islamic states may not have access to "adequate" resources to finance the functions discussed above and could not hence become "ideal." Here it is important to clarify that the "ideal" Islamic state should not be confused with the "richest" one. The ideal is to be construed in the light of general spiritual and material welfare attained for God's vicegerents within the framework of resources. Hence an Islamic state may be considered to have attained the position of "ideal" if it has at least (i) elevated the spiritual level of the Muslim society and minimised moral laxity and corruption; (ii) fulfilled its obligations for general economic welfare within the limits of its resources; and (iii) ensured distributive justice and has weeded out exploitation. Adequacy of resources is a relative term and is to be judged against attainable standards in the light of the stage of economic development.

NATURE AND IDENTITY

The above discussion indicates that the Islamic state is essentially a welfare state and is duty-bound to play an important role in the economy for the fulfilment of the goals of the *Sharī'a* in the economic field as briefly specified above. This welfare role is, however, to be played within the framework of individual freedom which Islam values greatly. The most important pillar of the Islamic faith is the belief that man has been created by God and is subservient to none but Him (Qur'ān 13:36) and that one of the primary objectives of the prophetic mission of Muhammad (peace be on him) is to release mankind from all burdens and chains enslaving it (7:157). This provides not only the essence of the Islamic charter for individual freedom from all bondage but also subjects man to the sovereignty of God in all aspects of life which essentially implies subordination of man to the moral law as specified in the Qur'ān and the Sunna.

Because man is born free, no one, not even the state, has the right to abrogate this freedom and to subject him to regimentation. . . .

It is to realise this norm of individual freedom that Islam has incorporated in its economic system the essential elements of free enterprise after conditioning it to its own norms and values. The institution of private property along with the market mechanism has been integrated into the Islamic system in such a manner that an "appropriate" part of the production and distribution of goods and services is left to individuals and voluntarily constituted groups enjoying freedom in their dealings and transactions. The profit motive has also been upheld as, besides being consistent with human nature, it provides the necessary incentive for efficiency in the use of resources which God has provided to mankind.

However, since social welfare has a place of absolute importance in Islam, individual freedom—though of considerable significance—does not enjoy a place independent of its social consequences. It is sacred only as long as it does not conflict with the larger social interest or the overall spiritual and material goals of Muslim society, or as long as the individual does not transgress the rights of others. Property can be owned privately but is to be considered a *trust* from God and is to be acquired and spent in accordance with the terms of the trust. The profit motive has also been subjected to certain moral constraints so that it serves individual interest within a social context and does not lead to economic and social ills or violate the Islamic goals of social justice and equitable distribution of income and wealth.

MIXED CAPITALISM? SOCIALISM?

All these various considerations make the Islamic state completely distinct from both the socialist and the capitalist systems. First of all, socialism, as conceived by Marx, is basically amoral and based on the concept of dialectical materialism; while capitalism, being a secular ideology is, at best, morally neutral. In contrast Islam lays emphasis on both the moral and the material aspects of life and erects the edifice of economic well-being on the foundation of moral values. The foundation being different, the super-structure is bound to be different too.

Moreover, Islam is also fully committed to human brotherhood with social and economic justice, to equitable distribution of income, and to individual freedom within the context of social welfare. Although both socialism and mixed capitalism also claim to pay allegiance to social justice, the concept of justice in socialism or mixed capitalism is not based on human brotherhood reinforced by inviolable spiritual criteria for social and economic justice. In fact, Marxist socialism under the influence of dialectics condones injustice done by one group to the other and even the annihilation of one group by the other. In *laissez faire* capitalism with its slogan of "Don't interfere, the world will take care of itself" there was no innate ideal of social justice to be attained through conscious state effort, while in mixed capitalism the roots of social justice lie in group pressures rather than in an intrinsic belief in human brotherhood.

Although capitalism also recognises freedom of the individual there are no spiritual constraints on this freedom. The constraints that do exist are determined primarily by the pressures of competition or the coercive power of the state, and secondarily by changing social norms without any spiritual sanctity. In the Islamic system, however, the individual is subject to inviolable spiritual values in all aspects of life, including the acquisition, spending and distribution of wealth. Islam normally recognises, like capitalism, the freedom of enterprise with the institution of private property, the market system and the profit motive, but it differs from capitalism because, as already indicated, property in Islam is a trust from God and man as trustee and vicegerent of God is responsible to Him and subject to His guiding principles.

Although both socialism and capitalism recognise equitable distribution of income, in capitalism this recognition is again an outcome of group press-ure while in socialism it is accompanied by negation of individual freedom. Islam achieves this equitable distribution within the framework of individual freedom but with spiritual and legal imperatives to safeguard public interest, moral constraints against unearned income, and social obligations to ensure a just distribution of income and wealth.

The Islamic welfare state is hence neither capitalist nor socialist. It is based on its own values and guided by its own goals. It has its own identity and bears no resemblance to any other form of state.

MUHAMMAD BAQIR AL-SADR
1933–1980

Born in Baghdad, Baqir al-Sadr, an intellectual, religious, and political leader, excelled in religious studies in Najaf and wrote his first book, *Our Philosophy*, in 1959. This was followed by *Our Economy* (1960), among the most influential twentieth-century books on Islamic economics, as well as other works on Quranic interpretation, jurisprudence, theology, and philosophy. A member of the *Jama'at al-Ulama* in Najaf, founded by his uncle Murtada Al Yasin in 1960, he published the review *al-Adwa'*. Baqir al-Sadr is also credited with having begun a reform of the courses of study in Najaf and had a project to reform the institution of religious leadership. His published fatwas are considered innovative. Two fatwas led to his elimination by Saddam Hussein's government. One prohibited membership in the Ba'th party and praying behind Imams who collaborated with the regime. The other called for open armed struggle against the regime. On April 8, 1980, he was liquidated along with his sister, Bint al-Huda.

The Psychological Role of Islam in Economic Development

My faith and conviction have grown that the umma has actively begun to open up to its true mission represented in Islam, and to realize, despite the various types of colonialist delusion, that Islam is the way of salvation and that the Islamic system is the natural framework within which it must achieve its life and release its potential. It is on the foundation of Islam that the umma must create its existence. . . .

The umma is living out a holy war (jihad) against backwardness and collapse, attempting politically and socially to move towards a better existence in a more firmly rooted entity with a richer and more prosperous economy. After all the attempts made, some wide of the mark, others less so, it is clear that the umma will never find the way except in following the Islamic line. It will never find the framework within which to work out the solution to problems of economic backwardness except in the economic framework of Islam.

Preface to second printing of M. B. Al-Sadr, Iqtisāduna, Dar al-Fikr, Beirut, 1974. Translated by John J. Donohue.

Mankind, beset by tormenting anxiety as it oscillates between the two world currents which are mining its path with bombs and rockets and all means of destruction, will never find salvation except at the one door to heaven which remains open, Islam.

When the Islamic world opened itself up to the life of European man and conceded the precedence of the latter and its leadership of the march of civilization, it turned from its authentic mission of conducting the life of mankind. The Islamic world accepted the European classification of the world according to economic criteria of rich and poor and found itself in the category of the poor countries which, in the logic of the Europeans, had no choice but to admit the leadership of the developed countries and allow them to breathe in their spirit and plan the way for the poor countries to rise up.

The Islamic world's subordination to the pioneering experience of European man in modern civilization found expression in three contemporaneous forms—forms which are still found in various parts of the Islamic world: 1. political subordination in the direct rule of economically advanced European peoples over backward peoples; 2. economic subordination which accompanied the setting up of politically independent entities for government in various countries. This found expression in giving room for European economy to perform its role on the stage of that country in various forms—exploiting raw materials, filling the void with foreign capital, monopoly of several economic services on the pretext of preparing the people of backward countries to bear the burden of the economic development of their country; 3. subordination in the program followed in many an attempt within the Islamic world to get free of the dominant European economy and to begin to think of relying on one's own power to develop the economy and overcome backwardness. It was impossible to conceive one's own understanding of the nature of the problem embodied in one's economic backwardness outside the framework of the European understanding of it. One found one's self called to choose the same program which European man followed in building his towering modern economy. . . .

The modern experiments at economic building in the Islamic world ordinarily faced two forms of experience in economic building in modern Western civilization, namely, free economy based on capitalism and planned economy based on socialism. Both of these forms had sizeable experience in constructing the modern European economy. For application in the Islamic world there was study to see which of the two forms merited to be followed as more capable of assuring success in the struggle of the umma against economic backwardness and in building an economy.

The Islamic world leaned towards capitalism because the capitalist axis of European influence was quicker to make inroads.

Then during the umma's political struggle with colonialism and its attempt to liberate itself from the capitalist axis, some of the experimental governments found that the European opposition to the capitalist axis was the socialist. Thus there developed another tendency leaning towards the choice of the second form for development (i.e., planning on a socialist base). It was a way of combining faith in European man as the pioneer for backward countries with the actual struggle against the politics of capitalism. The economic subordination of backward countries to the developed imposed faith in the European experience as pioneer, but the emotions provoked by the battle against the lived reality of colonialism clashed with the capitalist wing of this experience, so socialist planning was chosen as another form of the pioneer experience.

Each of the two tendencies has proofs to justify its point of view. The first usually argues that the great progress which the European capitalist countries have made, their levels of production and industry, is because of their free economies. They add that it is possible for backward countries, if they follow the same style and live the same experience, to shorten the road and make the leap to the desired level of economic development in a shorter time because they will profit from the expertise of the capitalist experiment of European man and use all the scientific capacities which it took him hundreds of years to gain.

The second tendency explains its choice for planned economy on a socialist base rather than a free economy because, although free economy was able to realize great gains and continued progress in technology and production and growth of domestic resources for pioneering European countries, it is not possible that it play the same role in backward countries today. Backward countries today face a formidable challenge in the great progress made by the Western states and at the same time are confronted with unlimited competition. . . .

Both tendencies, to explain their failure in the area of application, point to the artificial conditions created by the colonialists in the region in order to hinder the operation of development. Though they sense failure, they do not allow themselves to think of any program which might offer an alternative to the two traditional forms which modern European experience took in the East and in the West. And yet there is an alternative, ready made, alive in the theory and belief of the umma even though it has been segregated from practical application—the Islamic program (manhaj) and the economic system (nizam) of Islam.

Here . . . I merely wish to compare the two wings of European economy, capitalism and socialism, with Islamic economy from the point of view of their capacity to share in the battle of the Islamic world against backwardness and to offer a framework for its economic development. To judge this it is not sufficient to focus on the theoretical data of each of the two, but it is even more necessary to note in detail the objective conditions of the Islamic umma, and its psychological and historical composition.

NEED FOR A PROGRAM WHICH FORMS PART
OF AN INTEGRATED WHOLE

Since the umma is the field in which the economic program is applied, it is necessary to study the specificities and conditions of this field to see how effective the application of one or other of the systems may be.

The effectiveness of the free capitalist system or that of socialist planning in the European experience does not necessarily mean that the program in itself is effective and that wherever it is followed it will be equally effective. Rather, the effectiveness of the program may come from the fact that in Europe it formed part of an integrated whole and was a link in the chain of Europe's history. It is possible that if the program is isolated from its general frame and history that it will not be effective.

A comparative study of numerous economic schools and the possibility of their succeeding practically in the Islamic world bring to the fore a basic truth which must be the ground of any judgement. It is this: the need of an economic program for economic development is not merely the need for a framework for social organization which the state adopts and adheres to. No, economic development and the battle against backwardness require a framework which is capable of incorporating the umma and which stands on a base with which the umma can interact. The movement of the whole umma is a basic condition for the success of any development and of any comprehensive battle against backwardness. The movement of the umma expresses its growth, the growth of its will and the release of its inner talents. If the umma does not grow, there can be no process of development. The development of external resources and internal growth must go hand in hand.

The experience of European man is a clear historic expression of this truth. There was success on the material level because European peoples interacted with these programs in all aspects of life. The tendency of these programs was in accord with their aspirations and their psychology, formed during long years of assimilation and interaction.

When we want to choose a program or a general framework for economic development in the Islamic world, we must take this truth as a basis in choosing the ship capable of moving the umma and mobilizing all its potential for the battle against backwardness. We must take account of the feelings of the umma, its psychology, its history and its various intricacies. . . .

THE PSYCHOLOGICAL ELEMENT
AND THE RESORT TO NATIONALISM

There are, for example, particular psychological feelings concerning colonialism which the umma in the Islamic world experiences. There is doubt, suspicion and fear resulting from a long, bitter history of exploitation and struggle. These feelings cause the umma to recoil from the organization of European man. . . .

It was the clarity of this truth that made many of the political blocs in the Islamic world think of taking nationalism as a philosophy and foundation for civilization and as a basis for social organization. They were careful to bring forward slogans which were completely separated from the ideological entity of colonialism. Nationalism, however, is nothing but an historical and linguistic tie; it is not a philosophy with principles, nor a creed with foundations. By its very nature it is neutral concerning the various philosophies and social, ideological and religious schools. For this reason it has to adopt a specific point of view concerning the universe and life, and a particular philosophy on the basis of which it can formulate the main lines of its social organization, its renaissance and its civilization.

Apparently many of the nationalist movements felt this and realized that nationalism as raw material had need of adopting a certain social philosophy and system. They tried to reconcile nationalism with authenticity through the slogans they raised and thus cut it off from European man, so they called for Arab socialism. They called for socialism because they realized that nationalism alone was not sufficient; it needed a system. And they called for socialism in an Arab framework because they discerned the sensitivity of the umma to any slogan or philosophy tied to the world of colonialists. By describing socialism as Arab they tried to cover the foreign reality it represented from the historical and ideological point of view. But it was an unsuccessful cover; it did not fool the sensitivity of the umma because this uneasy framework was nothing but a purely external and formalistic framing of the foreign content represented in socialism. . . . The propagandists of Arab socialism were not able to distinguish between Arab socialism and Persian or Turkish socialism, nor could they explain how socialism differed merely by giving it this or that nationalist framework because the fact is that the content and substance were no different. This framework only expresses exceptions which differ from one people to another according to the type of traditions reigning among the people.

Despite the fact that the propagandists of Arab socialism failed to present a truly new content for this socialism by placing it in an Arab frame, still this action of theirs confirms what we stated earlier, namely that the umma, because of the sensitivity resulting from the era of colonialism, cannot construct a new renaissance save on an authentic base which is not connected in the mind of the umma with the colonialist countries themselves.

THE UMMA FEELS THAT ISLAM IS ITS PROPER EXPRESSION

It is here that the great difference emerges between the programs of European economy and the Islamic program. The European programs, in the mind of the umma, are tied to the man of the colonialist continent, no matter what framework is drawn up for them, but the Islamic program, in the mind of the umma, is bound up with its history and proper glory and expresses its authenticity with no imprint of the colonialist countries. The feeling of the umma that Islam is its proper expression, the title of its historic personality and the key to its former glory is considered an extremely weighty factor for success in its battle against backwardness for development when the program is derived from Islam and chooses the Islamic system as the framework for its point of departure.

Besides the complex feelings of the umma in the Islamic world towards colonialism and all programs connected with colonialist countries, there is also another complication which presents a sizeable difficulty blocking the success of new European economic programs applied in the Islamic world. It is the contradiction between these programs and the religious creed which Muslims live. Here . . . I merely want to underline this contradiction between the programs of European man and the religious creed of Muslim man, characterizing this creed as a living force in the Islamic world without giving any value judgement. Whatever our estimation of this force may be as a result of the disintegration and decline which followed from the action of colonialism against it in the Islamic world, it still has momentous influence in directing behaviour, shaping feelings and defining a point of view towards things. We acknowledged above that the operation of economic development is not merely one which the state adopts, puts into practice and legislates for; it is an operation in which the whole umma must participate and share in one way or another. If the umma senses a contradiction between the framework imposed for development and the creed which it still reverences and whose outlook on life it guards, at least on some points, then to the degree that it acts in accord with that creed it will recoil from contributing to the operation of development and from being drawn into the imposed framework.

The Islamic system, on the contrary, does not face this complication; it suffers no contradiction in this respect. Rather, if it is applied, it will find in the religious creed a huge support and a helping factor for the success of the development placed in its framework because the basis of the Islamic system is the rules of the Islamic Sharia and these are rules in the sanctity and inviolability of which the Muslim usually believes. He has an obligation to carry them out by force of his creed and his belief that Islam is a religion revealed by heaven to the seal of the prophets.

Without a doubt, the most important factor in the success of the programs adopted to organize social life is the respect which people have for them and their belief that these programs should be executed and applied.

ISLAMIC MORALS AND VALUES ARE DIFFERENT

There is in fact an Islamic morality alive to one or other degree in the Islamic world, and there is a morality of European economy which accompanied modern Western civilization and wove for it its general spirit and prepared the way for its success on the economic level. The two moralities differ substantially in their orientation, their point of view and their value systems. To the extent that the morality of modern Western man is sound for European economic programs, the morality of man in the Islamic world is incompatible with it. This morality has deep roots which cannot be extirpated by merely diluting the religious creed.

Planning—any planning for the battle against backwardness—must necessarily take into account the resistance of nature in the country for which the plan is intended, the degree to which it will resist operations of production. So too, account must be taken of the resistance of the human element and the extent to which it is in harmony with this or that plan.

European man looks always to earth, not to heaven. Even Christianity, the religion in which European man believed for hundreds of years, was not able to overcome his earthly tendency. Rather than the Christian raising his view to heaven, he was able to bring the God of Christianity down to earth and incarnate him in an earthly being.

The attempts to tie man's lineage to groups of animals and to explain humanity as an objective adaptation to the land and environment in which it lives, or the scientific attempts to explain the whole human edifice on the basis of productive forces which represent the earth and the potential within it, these attempts are nothing other than endeavors to bring God down to earth. This is their psychological signification. They are all morally tied to that deep-seated view in the soul of European man towards the earth, even though their style and scientific or mythical character may differ.

This view towards the earth allowed European man to give values to matter, resources and property which harmonize with his basic orientation.

The values rooted in European man over the ages expressed themselves in schools (*madhahib*) of sensual delight and pragmatism which inundated moral philosophic thinking in Europe. These schools, in as much as they were the product of European thought, registered great success in Europe. They had psychological significance and meaning for the general temper of the European soul.

FREEDOM IS A MATERIALISTIC ABERRATION

In the same way, European man's cutting of the true tie with his God and his looking to earth instead of to heaven snatched from his mind any true notion of a lofty presence on high or of limits imposed from outside the circle of his own self. This prepared him psychologically and noetically to believe in his right to liberty and to submerge himself in a flood of feelings of independence and individualism. . . .

Freedom played a principal role in European economy and the operation of development was able to use to advantage the deep-rooted feelings of European man concerning freedom, independence and individualism for the success of free economy; it was a means in accord with the deep-rooted tendencies in the souls and minds of European peoples . . .

We all know that the deep sentiment of freedom provided a basic con-dition without which many of the activities in the process of development would never have taken place—that condition was the absence of any feeling of moral responsibility.

Freedom itself was an instrument to open up European man to the concept of struggle because it set every man loose from all limits save that of the presence of the other person opposite him. Every individual, by his existence, formed a limit to the liberty of the other person. Thus the notion of struggle grew in the mind of European man, and this notion expressed itself on the philosophical level, as we saw, in the other basic thoughts which went to make up the mixture of modern Western civilization. This notion of struggle expressed itself in scientific and philosophical ideas on the struggle for existence as a natural law among all living beings or on the inevitability of class struggle within society or on dialectical movement and the explanation of the universe on the basis of thesis, antithesis and the synthesis arising out of the struggle between two contradictories. All these tendencies which bear a scientific or philosophical stamp are before all else an expression of the general psychological state and the vehement feelings of the man of modern civilization concerning struggle.

Struggle had a great effect in orienting modern European economy and the operations of development which accompanied it. This was so whether it took the individualist form and expressed itself in fierce unlimited competition between personal capitalist institutions and projects under a free economy, developing all resources through competition and struggle for existence, or whether it took the class form and expressed itself in rev-olutionary groups which took over the key positions of production in the country and moved all potential to the benefit of economic development.

This is the morality of European economy and on these grounds this economy was able to set itself in motion, achieve growth and register huge gains.

EASTERN MAN IS ORIENTED TO THE INVISIBLE

This morality differs from that which the umma in the Islamic world lives as a result of its religious history. Eastern man, brought up on the heavenly missions which lived in his lands, extensively educated in religion by Islam, naturally looks to heaven before he looks to earth. He accepts the invisible world before the world of matter and sense. His deep infatuation with the invisible world expresses itself on the level of thought in the life of Muslims by the orientation of thought in the Islamic world towards the intellectual spheres of human knowledge rather than those tied to sense reality.

This profound other-worldliness in the character of Muslim man limits the seductive force of matter for him and its capacity to impress him. This fact explains why man in the Islamic world, when he is deprived of moral motives for interacting with matter and finds no enticement to exploit it, tends to take a negative attitude towards it—an attitude which takes the form of asceticism at times, temperance at others or even laziness at others.

This other-worldliness has trained him to feelings of an unseen supervision which may express themselves in the pious Muslim's consciousness of his clear responsibility before God Almighty, or in the mind of another Muslim as a well defined and directed conscience. In any case, it keeps man in the Islamic world far from sensing personal freedom and moral freedom in the way European man does.

... AND TO THE COMMUNITY

This internal limitation felt by Muslim man has its moral base in the interests of the community in which he lives; consequently he feels a profound tie with the group to which he is related. There is harmony between him and the community, not struggle, the notion which dominates modern European thought. This notion of community reinforces the world framework of the mission of Islam for the Muslim and charges this mission with the responsibility of assuring its presence in the world and its extension in time and place. . . .

If we look on this morality which man in the Islamic world lives as a truth represented in the being of the umma, we can put it to use in the economic program within the Islamic world by placing that program in a framework which marches with that morality so that it may become a force of impulsion and movement just like the morality of modern European economic programs was a great factor in the success of those programs because of the harmony between the two.

The regard of man in the Islamic world towards heaven before earth could lead to a negative attitude to earth, its resources and goods— asceticism, moderation and laziness—if earth is separated from heaven. If, however, earth is clothed in the framework of heaven and action with nature is given the quality of duty and worship, then this otherworldly view is transformed for the Muslim man into active energy and impulsive force to participate to the greatest degree possible in raising the economic level. Instead of the coldness towards earth which the negative Muslim feels today, or the psychological anxiety which the active Muslim who follows the styles of free economy or socialism feels for the most part, even though he is a watered down Muslim, there will be generated a full harmony between the psychology of the man of the Islamic world and his anticipated positive role in the process of development.

The concept of internal limits and other-worldly supervision which prevents man in the Islamic world from living according to the European notion of freedom can help to avoid, to a great degree, the difficulties which spring from free economy and hinder economic development by providing moral justification for general planning.

Group ties and sensibilities can share in mobilizing the energies of the
Islamic umma for the battle against backwardness if the battle is waged
under a slogan which coincides with those sensibilities, such as jihad for
preserving the essence and existence of the umma. This is what the Quran
does when it says: Make ready for them all that you can (Sura viii, 60). The
order is to prepare all forces including the economic which are represented
by the level of production as part of the battle of the umma and its jihad
to preserve its existence and sovereignty.

This brings out the importance of the Islamic economy as an economic
program capable of using to advantage the morality of man in the Islamic
world and transforming it into a great impulsive and constructive energy
for operations of development and for success in sound planning for economic life.

When we adopt the Islamic system we will profit from this morality
and be able to mobilize it in the battle against backwardness, contrary to
what would happen if we adopted the programs in economy which are
psychologically and historically rooted in the ground of another morality.

STEWARDSHIP

Some European thinkers have begun to realize this truth and to take note
of it, acknowledging that their programs do not accord with the nature of
the Islamic world. . . . I would like to expand on this on another occasion,
for now suffice it to say that the orientation of man in the Islamic world
towards heaven does not in its authentic sense mean that man submits to
fate and relies on the conditions, opportunities and feelings of complete
incompetence concerning creativity and invention . . . rather this orientation of Muslim man is a true expression of the principle of the stewardship
of man on earth. By his very nature he inclines to see his position on earth
as an expression of his stewardship to God. I know of no concept richer
than this for affirming the capacity of man and his energies; it makes him
the absolute master of the universe. And I know of no concept further
removed from surrender and fate than the concept of stewardship to God
because stewardship gets to the bottom of the sense of responsibility concerning what one is made steward of. There is no responsibility without
liberty and a sense of choice and an ability to master circumstances.
Otherwise, what stewardship would this be if man was bound or remotely
controlled? For this reason, we say that clothing the earth in the framework
of heaven releases the energies of Muslim man and stirs up his potential,
whereas cutting earth off from heaven annuls the sense of stewardship and
fixes the view of Muslim man on earth in a negative way. . . .

ONE FOUNDATION FOR ALL—ISLAM

In addition to all that precedes, we would like to remark that taking Islam
as the basis for general organization allows us to set up all of our life, both

spiritual and social aspects, on one foundation because Islam extends to both, whereas many of the social programs other than Islam are limited to the social and economic relations in the life of man and his ideals. If we take our general program for life from human sources instead of the Islamic system, we leave the organization of the spiritual side unsatisfied. There is no sound source for the organization of our spiritual life except Islam. There is no way but to establish both sides, spiritual and social, on the foundation peculiar to Islam. Moreover, the two sides are not isolated from one another but interact to a great degree. This interaction makes it more sound and harmonious to set up the two on one base given the unmistakeable inter-connection of spiritual social activities in the life of man.

IV

ISLAM AND
CONTEMPORARY ISSUES

ISLAM AND DEMOCRACY

This section on the critical topic of Islam and democracy gives a fairly extensive sampling of thought, ranging from the conviction that popular participation is a crucial necessity for development to the fear that the unbridled liberty of Western democracy entails a neglect of the social values that distinguish Islam. Abū-l-'Alā' Mawdūdī, writing in the wake of European colonialism and its political and cultural impact, argued that Islam was incompatible with Western democracy, maintaining that Islam had its own foundation for democracy. Decades later, both he and his Islamic movement, the Jamaat-i-Islami, would accept and participate in the democracy movement and elections in Pakistan.

The debate continues today. Rachid Ghannouchi considers the challenge to Islamists in a non-Muslim society, while Muhammad Salim al-Awa puts the problem in broader terms, explaining how political parties can be beneficial to Muslim society. The theme of *shura* is central for many Muslims, as seen in Fathi Osman, who translates or reinterprets it in modern terms for modern times. Murad Hofmann wants Islam to realize its democratic potential, and Abdulaziz Sachedina emphasizes the need to get on with democratization and push aside reactionary religious spokesmen. Abdolkarim Soroush emphasizes the importance of justice, human rights, limited power, and tolerance for democratic religious governance. Despite the enthusiasm for democracy that exists among many Muslims, Abid Ullah Jan is a reminder that today there are those who remain critical of Western intentions and oppose attempts to Islamize Western democracy. Instead, they advocate the development of models of social and political organization based on Islamic values and principles. In any case, this cross section of Muslim thought puts to rest the stereotype that Islam is contrary to democracy.

ABŪ-L-'ALĀ' MAWDŪDĪ
1903–1979

Mawlānā Mawdūdī received an early traditional religious education, which was supplemented by his self-taught knowledge of Western thought. He pursued a career in journalism and in 1933 assumed editorship of *Tarjuman al-Qur'ān* [Exegesis of the Quran], which throughout the years served as a vehicle of his thought. He has been perhaps the most systematic modern Muslim writer, and his many writings have been translated into English and Arabic and circulated throughout the Muslim world. In 1941 Mawdūdī established the Jamā'at-i-Islāmī [the Islamic Association], an extremely well organized association committed to the reestablishment of an Islamic world order or society (politically, legally, and socially). Although originally against any form of nationalism and thus opposed to the establishment of Pakistan, Mawdūdī nevertheless migrated to Pakistan, after the partitioning, where the Jamā'at-i-Islāmī has been very active in politics.

Political Theory of Islam

With certain people it has become a sort of fashion to somehow identify Islam with one or the other system of life in vogue at the time. So at this time also there are people who say that Islam is a democracy, and by this they mean to imply that there is no difference between Islam and the democracy as in vogue in the West. Some others suggest that Communism is but the latest and revised version of Islam and it is in the fitness of things that Muslims imitate the Communist experiment of Soviet Russia. Still some others whisper that Islam has the elements of dictatorship in it and we should revive the cult of "obedience to the *Amīr*" (the leader). All these people, in their misinformed and misguided zeal to serve what they hold to be the cause of Islam, are always at great pains to prove that Islam contains within itself the elements of all types of contemporary social and political thought and action. Most of the people who indulge in this prattle have no clear idea of the Islamic way of life. They have never made nor try to make a systematic study of the Islamic political order—the place and nature of democracy, social justice, and equality in it. . . . some people have begun to present apologies on Islam's behalf. As a matter of fact, this attitude emerges from an inferiority complex, from the belief that we as

From *Islam: Its Meaning and Message*, ed. Khurshid Ahmad (London: Islamic Council of Europe, 1976), pp. 147–48, 158–61, 163–70.

262

Muslims can earn no honour or respect unless we are able to show that our religion resembles the modern creeds and it is in agreement with most of the contemporary ideologies. These people have done a great disservice to Islam; they have reduced the political theory of Islam to a puzzle, a hotchpotch. They have turned Islam into a juggler's bag out of which can be produced anything that holds a demand! Such is the intellectual plight in which we are engulfed. . . .

FIRST PRINCIPLE OF ISLAMIC POLITICAL THEORY

The belief in the Unity [*tawhīd*] and the sovereignty of Allah is the foundation of the social and moral system propounded by the Prophets. It is the very starting-point of the Islamic political philosophy. The basic principle of Islam is that human beings must, individually and collectively, surrender all rights of overlordship, legislation and exercising of authority over others. No one should be allowed to pass orders or make commands *in his own right* and no one ought to accept the obligation to carry out such commands and obey such orders. None is entitled to make laws on his own authority and none is obliged to abide by them. This right rests in Allah alone:

> The Authority rests with none but Allah. He commands you not to surrender to any one save Him. This is the right way (of life). (Qur'ān 12:40)

> They ask: "have we also got some authority?" Say: "all authority belongs to God alone." (Qur'ān 3:154) . . .

According to this theory, sovereignty belongs to Allah. He alone is the law-giver. No man, even if he be a Prophet, has the right to order others *in his own right* to do or not to do certain things. The Prophet himself is subject to God's commands:

> I do not follow anything except what is revealed to me. (Qur'ān 6:50)

Other people are required to obey the Prophet because he enunciates not his own but God's commands:

> We sent no messenger save that he should be obeyed by Allah's command. (Qur'ān 4:64) . . .

Thus the main characteristics of an Islamic state that can be deduced from these express statements of the Holy Qur'ān are as follows:

1. No person, class or group, not even the entire population of the state as a whole, can lay claim to sovereignty. God alone is the real sovereign; all others are merely His subjects;

2. God is the real law-giver and the authority of absolute legislation vests in Him. The believers cannot resort to totally independent legislation

nor can they modify any law which God has laid down, even if the desire to effect such legislation or change in Divine laws is unanimous;[1] and

3. An Islamic state must, in all respects, be founded upon the law laid down by God through His Prophet. The government which runs such a state will be entitled to obedience in its capacity as a political agency set up to enforce the laws of God and only in so far as it acts in that capacity. If it disregards the law revealed by God, its commands will not be binding on the believers.

THE ISLAMIC STATE: ITS NATURE AND CHARACTERISTICS

The preceding discussion makes it quite clear that Islam, speaking from the view-point of political philosophy, is the very antithesis of secular Western democracy. The philosophical foundation of Western democracy is the sovereignty of the people. In it, this type of absolute powers of legislation— of the determination of values and of the norms of behaviour—rest in the hands of the people. Law-making is their prerogative and legislation must correspond to the mood and temper of their opinion. If a particular piece of legislation is desired by the masses, howsoever ill-conceived it may be from a religious and moral viewpoint, steps have to be taken to place it on the statute book; if the people dislike any law and demand its abrogation, howsoever just and rightful it might be, it has to be expunged forthwith. This is not the case in Islam. On this count, Islam has no trace of Western democracy. Islam, as already explained, altogether repudiates the philos-ophy of popular sovereignty and rears its polity on the foundations of the sovereignty of God and the vicegerency (*khilāfa*) of man.

A more apt name for the Islamic polity would be the "kingdom of God" which is described in English as a "theocracy." But Islamic theocracy is something altogether different from the theocracy of which Europe has had a bitter experience wherein a priestly class, sharply marked off from the rest of the population, exercises unchecked domination and enforces laws of its own making in the name of God, thus virtually imposing its own divinity and godhood upon the common people. Such a system of government is satanic rather than divine. Contrary to this, the theocracy built up by Islam is not ruled by any particular religious class but by the whole community of Muslims including the rank and file. The entire Muslim population runs the state in accordance with the Book of God and the practice of His Prophet. If I were permitted to coin a new term, I would describe this system of government as a "theo-democracy," that is to say a divine demo-cratic government, because under it the Muslims have been given a limited popular sovereignty under the suzerainty of God. The executive under this

1. Here the *absolute right of legislation* is being discussed. In the Islamic political theory this right vests in Allah alone. As to the scope and extent of human legislation provided by the *Sharī'a* itself please see Mawdūdī, A.A., *Islamic Law and Constitution*, Chapter II: "Legislation and Ijtihād in Islam" and chapter VI: "First Principles of Islamic State."

system of government is constituted by the general will of the Muslims who have also the right to depose it. All administrative matters and all questions about which no explicit injunction is to be found in the *Sharī'a* are settled by the consensus of opinion among the Muslims. Every Muslim who is capable and qualified to give a sound opinion on matters of Islamic law, is entitled to interpret the law of God when such interpretation becomes necessary. In this sense the Islamic polity is a democracy. But, as has been explained above, it is a theocracy in the sense that where an explicit command of God or His Prophet aleady exists, no Muslim leader or legislature, or any religious scholar can form an independent judgement, not even all the Muslims of the world put together have any right to make the least alteration in it. . . .

God has laid down those limits which, in Islamic phraseology, are termed "divine limits" (*Hudūd-Allāh*). These limits consist of certain principles, checks and balances and specific injunctions in different spheres of life and activity, and they have been prescribed in order that man may be trained to lead a balanced and moderate life. They are intended to lay down the broad framework within which man is free to legislate, decide his own affairs and frame subsidiary laws and regulations for his conduct. These limits he is not permitted to overstep and if he does so, the whole scheme of his life will go awry.

Take for example man's economic life. In this sphere God has placed certain restrictions on human freedom. The right to private property has been recognized, but it is qualified by the obligation to pay *zakāt* (poor dues) and the prohibition of interest, gambling and speculation. A specific law of inheritance for the distribution of property among the largest number of surviving relations on the death of its owner has been laid down and certain forms of acquiring, accumulating and spending wealth have been declared unlawful. If people observe these just limits and regulate their affairs within these boundary walls, on the one hand their personal liberty is adequately safeguarded and, on the other, the possibility of class war and domination of one class over another, which begins with capitalist oppression and ends in working-class dictatorship, is safely and conveniently eliminated.

Similarly in the sphere of family life, God has prohibited the unrestricted intermingling of the sexes and has prescribed *purdah*, recognized man's guardianship of woman, and clearly defined the rights and duties of husband, wife and children. The laws of divorce and separation have been clearly set forth, conditional polygamy has been permitted and penalties for fornication and false accusations of adultery have been prescribed. He has thus laid down limits which, if observed by man, would stabilize his family life and make it a haven of peace and happiness. There would remain neither that tyranny of male over female which makes family life an inferno of cruelty and oppression, nor that satanic flood of female liberty and licence which threatens to destroy human civilization in the West. . . .

THE PURPOSE OF THE ISLAMIC STATE

The purpose of the state that may be formed on the basis of the Qur'ān and the Sunna has also been laid down by God. The Qur'ān says:

> We verily sent Our messengers with clear proofs, and revealed with them the Scripture and the Balance, that mankind may observe right measure; and We revealed iron, wherein is mighty power and (many) uses for mankind. (Qur'ān 57:25)

In this verse steel symbolizes political power and the verse also makes it clear that the mission of the Prophets is to create conditions in which the mass of people will be assured of social justice in accordance with the standards enunciated by God in His Book which gives explicit instructions for a well-disciplined mode of life. In another place God has said:

> (Muslims are) those who, if We give them power in the land, establish the system of *salāt* (worship) and *zakāt* (poor dues) and enjoin virtue and forbid evil and inequity. (Qur'ān, 22:41)

> You are the best community sent forth to mankind; you enjoin the Right conduct and forbid the wrong; and you believe in Allah. (Qur'ān 3:110)

It will readily become manifest to anyone who reflects upon these verses that the purpose of the state visualized by the Holy Qur'ān is not negative but positive. The object of the state is not merely to prevent people from exploiting each other, to safeguard their liberty and to protect its subjects from foreign invasion. It also aims at evolving and developing that well-balanced system of social justice which has been set forth by God in His Holy Book. Its object is to eradicate all forms of evil and to encourage all types of virtue and excellence expressly mentioned by God in the Holy Qur'ān. For this purpose political power will be made use of as and when the occasion demands; all means of propaganda and peaceful persuasion will be employed; the moral education of the people will also be undertaken; and social influence as well as the force of public opinion will be harnessed to the task.

ISLAMIC STATE IS UNIVERSAL AND ALL-EMBRACING

A state of this sort cannot evidently restrict the scope of its activities. Its approach is universal and all-embracing. Its sphere of activity is coextensive with the whole of human life. It seeks to mould every aspect of life and activity in consonance with its moral norms and programme of social reform. In such a state no one can regard any field of his affairs as personal and private. Considered from this aspect the Islamic state bears a kind of resemblance to the Fascist and Communist states. But you will find later on that, despite its all-inclusiveness, it is something vastly and basically different from the modern totalitarian and authoritarian states. Individual liberty is not suppressed under it nor is there any trace of dictatorship in it. It presents the middle course and embodies the best that the human society has ever evolved. . . .

ISLAMIC STATE IS AN IDEOLOGICAL STATE

Another characteristic of the Islamic State is that it is an ideological state. It is clear from a careful consideration of the Qur'ān and the Sunna that the state in Islam is based on an ideology and its objective is to establish that ideology. The state is an instrument of reform and must act likewise. It is a dictate of this very nature of the Islamic State that such a state should be run only by those who believe in the ideology on which it is based and in the Divine Law which it is assigned to administer. The administrators of the Islamic state must be those whose whole life is devoted to the observance and enforcement of this Law, who not only agree with its reformatory programme and fully believe in it but thoroughly comprehend its spirit and are acquainted with its details. Islam does not recognize any geographical, linguistic or colour bars in this respect. It puts forward its code of guidance and the scheme of its reform before all men. Whoever accepts this programme, no matter to what race, nation or country he may belong, can join the community that runs the Islamic state. But those who do not accept it are not entitled to have any hand in shaping the fundamental policy of the states. They can live within the confines of the State as non-Muslim citizens (*dhimmīs*). Specific rights and privileges have been accorded to them in the Islamic law. A *dhimmī's* life, property and honour will be fully protected, and if he is capable of any service, his services will also be made use of. He will not, however, be allowed to influence the basic policy of this ideological state. The Islamic state is based on a particular ideology and it is the community which believes in the Islamic ideology which pilots it. Here again, we notice some sort of resemblance between the Islamic and the Communist states. But the treatment meted out by the Communist states to persons holding creeds and ideologies other than its own bears no comparison with the attitude of the Islamic state. Unlike the Communist state, Islam does not impose its social principles on others by force, nor does it confiscate their properties or unleash a reign of terror by mass executions of the people and their transportation to the slave camps of Siberia. Islam does not want to eliminate its minorities, it wants to protect them and gives them the freedom to live according to their own culture. The generous and just treatment which Islam has accorded to non-Muslims in an Islamic State and the fine distinction drawn by it between justice and good and evil will convince all those who are not prejudiced against it, that the prophets sent by God accomplish their task in an altogether different manner—something radically different and diametrically opposed to the way of the false reformers who strut about here and there on the stage of history.[2]

THE THEORY OF THE CALIPHATE AND
THE NATURE OF DEMOCRACY IN ISLAM

I will now try to give a brief exposition of the composition and structure of the Islamic state. I have already stated that in Islam, God alone is the real sovereign. Keeping this cardinal principle in mind, if we consider the position of those persons who set out to enforce God's law on earth, it is but natural to say that they should be regarded as representatives of the Supreme Ruler. Islam has assigned precisely this very position to them. Accordingly the Holy Qur'ān says:

> Allah has promised to those among you who believe and do righteous deeds that He will assuredly make them to succeed (the present rulers) and grant them vicegerency in the land just as He made those before them to succeed (others).

The verse illustrates very clearly the Islamic theory of state. Two fundamental points emerge from it.

1. The first point is that Islam uses the term "vicegerency" (*khilāfa*) instead of sovereignty. Since, according to Islam, sovereignty belongs to God alone, anyone who holds power and rules in accordance with the laws of God would undoubtedly be the vicegerent of the Supreme Ruler and would not be authorised to exercise any powers other than those delegated to him.

---

2. This paper was written in 1939 and in it the author had dealt with the theoretical aspect of the problem only. In his later articles he has discussed the practical aspect as well. In his article on the "Rights of Non-Muslims in Islamic State" (see *Islamic Law and Constitution*, Chapter VIII, pp. 316–317). He writes:

> However, in regard to a parliament or a legislature of the modern conception, which is considerably different from *shūrā* in its traditional sense, this rule could be relaxed to allow non-Muslims to become its members provided that it has been fully ensured in the Constitution that:
>
> i. It would be *ultra vires* of the parliament or the legislature to enact any law which is repugnant to the Qur'ān and the *Sunna*.
> ii. The Qur'ān and the *Sunna* would be the chief source of the public law of the land.
> iii. The head of the state or the assenting authority would necessarily be a Muslim. With these provisions ensured, the sphere of influence of non-Muslims would be limited to matters relating to the general problems of the country or to the interests of minorities concerned and their participation would not damage the fundamental requirements of Islam.

The non-Muslims cannot occupy key-posts—posts from where the ideological policy of the state can be influences—but they can occupy general administrative posts and can act in the services of the state.

2. The second point stated in the verse is that the power to rule over the earth has been promised to *the whole community of believers*; it has not been stated that any particular person or class among them will be raised to that position. From this it follows that all believers are repositories of the Caliphate. The Caliphate granted by God to the faithful is the popular vicegerency and not a limited one. There is no reservation in favour of any family, class or race. Every believer is a Caliph of God in his individual capacity. By virtue of this position he is individually responsible to God. The Holy Prophet has said: "Everyone of you is a ruler and everyone is answerable for his subjects." Thus one Caliph is in no way inferior to another.

This is the real foundation of democracy in Islam. The following points emerge from an analysis of this conception of popular vicegerency:

A. A society in which everyone is a caliph of God and an equal participant in this caliphate, cannot tolerate any class divisions based on distinctions of birth and social position. All men enjoy equal status and position in such a society. The only criterion of superiority in this social order is personal ability and character. This is what has been repeatedly and explicitly asserted by the Holy Prophet:

> No one is superior to another except in point of faith and piety. All men are descended from Adam and Adam was made of clay.
>   An Arab has no superiority over a non-Arab nor a non-Arab over an Arab; neither does a white man possess any superiority over a black man nor a black man over a white one, except in point of piety. . . .

B. In such a society no individual or group of individuals will suffer any disability on account of birth, social status, or profession that may in any way impede the growth of his faculties or hamper the development of his personality. . . .

> Listen and obey even if a negro is appointed as a ruler over you.

C. There is no room in such a society for the dictatorship of any person or group of persons since everyone is a caliph of God herein. No person or group of persons in entitled to become an absolute ruler by depriving the rank and file of their inherent right of caliphate. The position of a man who is selected to conduct the affairs of the state is no more than this; that all Muslims (or, technically speaking, all caliphs of God) delegate their caliphate to him for administrative purposes. *He is answerable to God on the one hand and on the other to his fellow "caliphs" who have delegated their authority to him.* Now, if he raises himself to the position of an irresponsible absolute ruler, that is to say a dictator, he assumes the character of a usurper rather than a Caliph, because dictatorship is the negation of popular vicegerency. No doubt the Islamic state is an all-embracing state and comprises within its sphere all departments of life, but this all-inclusiveness and universality are based upon the universality of Divine Law which an Islamic ruler has to observe and enforce. The guidance given by God about every aspect of life will certainly be enforced in its entirety. But an Islamic ruler cannot depart from these instructions and adopt a policy of regimentation on his own. He cannot force people to follow or not to follow a particular profession; to learn or not to learn a special art; to use or not to use a certain script; to wear or not to wear a certain dress and to educate or not to educate their children in a certain manner. The powers which the dictators of Russia, Germany and Italy have appropriated or which Ataturk has exercized in Turkey have not been granted by Islam to its *Amīr* (leader). Besides this, another important point is that in Islam *every individual is held personally answerable to God.* This personal responsibility cannot be shared by anyone else. Hence, an individual enjoys full liberty to choose whichever path he likes and to develop his faculties in any direction that suits his natural gifts. If the leader obstructs him or obstructs the growth of his personality, he will himself be punished by God for this tyranny. That is precisely the reason why there is not the slightest trace of regimentation in the rule of the Holy Prophet and of his Rightly-Guided Caliphs; and

D. In such a society every sane and adult Muslim, male or female, is entitled to express his or her opinion, for each one of them is the repository of the caliphate. God has made this caliphate conditional, not upon any particular standard of wealth or competence but only upon faith and good conduct. Therefore all Muslims have equal freedom to express their opinions.

RACHID GHANNOUCHI
1941–

A Tunisian-born Islamic thinker and politic activist who was educated at Cairo University and the University of Damascus, Ghannouchi founded Tunisia's Islamic Tendency Movement in 1981 (Tunisia's largest Islamist party), later renamed Hizb al-Nahda (Renaissance Party) in 1988. Imprisoned twice during the 1980s, he has lived in exile in London since the early 1990s. Ghannouchi has been a major voice in the Islamic movement on political and social issues from Islam and democracy to women's rights in Islam.

The Participation of Islamists in a Non-Islamic Government

INTRODUCTION

This paper attempts to answer the question related to the position of Islam regarding the participation of its followers in establishing or administering a non-Islamic regime.

Prior to attempting to provide an answer to this question certain facts need to be underlined:

First: the fact that a concept for an Islamic government does exist, and that it is the religious duty of Muslims, both individuals and groups, to work for the establishment of such a government.

Second: the fact that such an Islamic government, in the circumstances under discussion, is non-existent, and that had it been in existence, a Muslim would have no option but to support it and work for the reformation of such elements of corruption as might exist within it.

Third: the fact that the present circumstances do not seem to favour the establishment of an Islamic government. So much effort has been exerted in order to establish such a government, and despite their failure so far, it is the duty of all Muslims to continue the effort and cooperate in order to fulfil Allah's commandment and establish justice on earth.

The Holy Qur'an says:

> O you who believe! stand out firmly for Allah, as witnesses to fair dealing, and let not the hatred of others towards you make you swerve to wrong

From Azzam Tamimi, ed., *Power-Sharing Islam* (London: Liberty for Muslim World Publications, 1993), pp. 51–63. Translated from the Arabic by Azzam Tamimi.

and depart from justice. Be just, that is next to piety, and fear Allah. For
Allah is well-acquainted with all that you do. (5:8)

In the same chapter, verse 49 reads: "Judge between them by what Allah
has revealed, and follow not their vain desires," while verse 44 reads: "Those
who do not judge by what Allah has revealed, they are unbelievers."

EXCEPTIONAL CIRCUMSTANCES

The scope of this discussion does not apply to the normal situation when
the Muslim community can establish the system of its intellectual, political,
economic, international and other relations on the basis of Islam and in
conformity with its faith and cultural heritage—the heritage which continues to be deep-rooted in the hearts and souls of Muslims despite the
attempts of Western colonial occupation to undermine its fundamental
principles.

The discussion here focuses on the exceptional situation when the
community of believers is unable to accomplish its goal of establishing the
Islamic government directly. In this case the community is faced with tough
options.

Realism and flexibility are among the most important features of
Islamic methodology. These features explain the fact that this religion is an
eternal way of life that is suitable for all times and all places. Furthermore,
the lives of human communities, including the community of Muslims,
are in continuous dynamism just like the life of an individual human being.
Fluctuations between health and sickness, victory and defeat, success and
failure, progress and slipping back, strength and weakness are only natural. Therefore, it is imperative that a religion which came for the purpose
of improving the life of all humans wherever and whenever they exist
should have the capacity to respond to all emerging situations and forms
of development through which the Muslim communities may pass. And
in doing so, such a religion would have to draw the main straight lines as
well as the bending ones; that is it would not just be content with drawing
the lines for the absolute fundamentals during normal circumstances, but
would also define the rules and mechanisms which ought to be followed
and observed during exceptional extra-ordinary circumstances. In this way
the believers remain in close contact with the fundamentals of the Shari'ah
(the revealed or canonical law of Islam) in the situations of both strength
and weakness.

POWER-SHARING IN A NON-ISLAMIC GOVERNMENT

The general rule in judging the acts of humans is that all actions are
permissible unless a prohibition is specified. The prohibition in this case is
derived from the commandment to implement the law of Allah and not to
resort to adopting laws other than His. It is therefore a must for all Muslims

to do what they can in order to obey Allah's commandment and establish His governance. But what if the Muslims are unable to do so? The rule is that we are obliged to do only that which we can:

No soul shall have a burden laid on it greater than it can bear. (2:233)

The Islamic government is one in which:

1. Supreme legislative authority is for the Shari'ah, that is the revealed law of Islam, which transcends all laws. Within this context, it is the responsibility of scholars to deduce detailed laws and regulations to be used as guidelines by judges. The head of the Islamic state is the leader of the executive body entrusted with the responsibility of implementing such laws and regulations.
2. Political power belongs to the community (*ummah*), which should adopt a form of *shura*, which is a system of mandatory consultation.

If this kind of government is possible, it is then the duty of the believers to spare no effort in establishing it. However, if this is not possible, what must the community do?

On the basis of the general fundamentals of Islam and its purposes of accomplishing the needs and serving the interest of the public (and these include the protection of faith, souls, wealth and the prevention of evils), it is incumbent upon the community of the faithful to avoid passivism and isolationism. Every Muslim has a responsibility toward the task of establishing the Islamic government. If such a task is not possible, then Muslims must endeavour to accomplish whatever can be accomplished.

Power-sharing in a Muslim or a non-Muslim environment becomes a necessity in order to lay the foundations of the social order. This power-sharing may not necessarily be based on Islamic Shari'ah law. However, it must be based on an important foundation of the Islamic government, namely shura, or the authority of the *ummah* (community), so as to prevent the evils of dictatorship, foreign domination, or local anarchy. Such a process of power-sharing may also aim to achieve a national or a humanistic interest such as independence, development, social solidarity, civil liberties, human rights, political pluralism, independence of the judiciary, freedom of the press, or liberty for mosques and Islamic activities.

Can any Muslim community afford to hesitate in participating in the establishment of a secular democratic system if it is unable to establish an Islamic democratic one? The answer is no. It is the religious duty of the Muslims, as individuals and as communities, to contribute to the efforts to establish such a system. In this way, the Muslims would seek the establishment of the government of rationale due to their inability to establish the government of Shara'—as Ibn Khaldoun put it.

DOCUMENTED CASES

Several events can be quoted from the Qur'an, the Sunnah and Islamic history to prove that Muslims, as individuals or as communities, are permitted to participate in establishing or administering non-Islamic governments in order to achieve good and avoid evil.

In one chapter of the Qur'an we are told the story of Yusuf (Joseph) who was thrown into the well by his brothers and was then rescued, to end up in the Pharaoh's palace in Egypt where he was subjected to trial and seduction. It is worth noting that this young man, who was imprisoned and mistreated, seized the moment when it was right and expressed readiness to take charge of the most important office in the Pharaoh's government, believing it was his duty to rescue many nations that were threatened by famine and drought. He did not wait for the Egyptian people to renounce paganism and embrace his unitarian religion so as to form the foundation for an Islamic government.

What that young man had in mind was the fact that religion has come to serve the people and fulfil their essential needs. Yusuf had the conviction that rescuing the people from starvation and consequently from annihilation could not wait. He saw that he was able to help, and he did help. Through his effective participation in administering the affairs of the people he performed his other responsibility of calling for Islam and admonishing the people to reform their lives and renounce evils.

The detailed narration of the story of Yusuf in the Qur'an is a clear testimony that his approach is commendable. What happened with Yusuf can happen to Muslims anywhere and at any time. In similar circumstances, Muslims have no option but to participate politically in establishing and administering non-Islamic governments in order to serve the interests of the *ummah* (community) and prevent evils. Failing to do so will lead to undermining these interests and to allowing evils to spread and dominate society.

The second example is that of the Negus (the Emperor of Ethiopia) who lived during the early years of Islam. The Prophet advised some of his companions who were being severely persecuted to migrate to Abyssinia describing the Negus as "the King in whose country none is wronged." The presence of the small Muslim community in Abyssinia resulted in the Negus embracing Islam, although he did not effect any amendments to his government in the direction of implementing the Shari'ah, as such an attempt could have threatened his kingship and endangered the lives of his guests. The story of that noble king has been documented in Islamic history and continues to be narrated to this day. The Prophet instructed his followers to perform a prayer for the King's soul when the news of his death reached them.

Commenting on this, Ibn Taymiyah said, "We know definitely that he could not implement the law of the Qur'an in his community because his people would not have permitted him to. Despite that, the Negus and all those who are similar to him found their way to the pleasure of Allah in eternity although they could not abide by the laws of Islam, and could only rule using that which could be implemented in the given circumstances.

The third example is that of *hilf al-fudul*, that is the pact or alliance of *al-fudul*. It was an agreement among several pre-Islamic Arab tribes to support the wronged, maintain close relations with relatives and take good care of them. The Prophet did witness the signing of the alliance prior to his prophethood, and said afterwards that if he were to be invited to a similar alliance in Islam he would have accepted without reservation. He further stressed that any good and noble contract made in *jahiliyah* (the pre-Islamic era) is automatically endorsed by Islam. It is thus concluded that the community of believers may participate in an alliance aimed at preventing injustice and oppression, at serving the interests of mankind, at protecting human rights, at recognising the authority of the people and at rotating power-holding through a system of elections. The faithful can pursue all these noble objectives even with those who do not share the same faith or ideology.

The fourth example is that of Umar ibn Abdul-Aziz. This ummayyad Caliph, whose rulership did not exceed two years, is considered by historians and scholars to be the fifth guided Caliph because of his piety and justice, although more than half a century separated him from the last of the four guided Caliphs. Although he was a king who inherited kingship, he was unhappy with the monarchy, and in principle did not approve of it. However, he could not alter the system and was unable to restore the right of the *ummah* in a consultative style government due to the accumulation of corruption over the years. Nonetheless, he managed to significantly reform many bad practices, and restored justice and fairness. By accepting the monarchy, which he did not approve of, he was able to do many good things, and no one said he was wrong or misguided in his actions.

CONTEMPORARY CONSIDERATIONS

An Islamic government is based on a number of values which if accomplished in their totality would result in a perfect or near-perfect system. But it may not be possible for all such values to be implemented, and therefore some must suffice in certain circumstances in order for a just government to exist. A just government, even if not Islamic, is considered very close to the Islamic one, because justice is the most important feature of an Islamic government, and it has been said that justice is the law of Allah.

Ibn 'Aqil defined *As-Siyasah Ash-Shar'iyah* (Islamic administrative policy) as the actions which bring the people closer to good and distance them from evil, even if such actions were not advocated by the Prophet or revealed from the Heavens.

He further explained that describing these actions using the phrase "those that conform with the Islamic law (*shar'*)" in order to imply that such actions should not contradict the Shar' is justified. However, if one means by such a phrase that such actions must specifically be mentioned in the Qur'an or the Sunnah (traditions of the Prophet), then this is wrong and can be taken to imply that the companions of the Prophet themselves went wrong. After all they initiated many new policies and took numerous measures in order to fulfil the needs of the society in response to new developments or changing circumstances.

In contemporary times, numerous examples can be cited to show that Islamic individuals and groups have entered into alliances in order to prevent evil or in order to serve the community within a non-Islamic framework. This is happening despite the fact that many scholars still insist that such measures should not be pursued. With due respect, these scholars make life difficult for the Muslims unnecessarily. Their opinions impose restrictions on a policy which is definitely permissible and lawful, and which is intended to equip the Muslims with the ability to react positively in situations that can be very difficult indeed.

To cite only a few examples of such situations:

First: About one third of the Muslims in the world are minorities in the countries they live in, that is to say they have no hope in the foreseeable future of governing their countries in an Islamic way. Many of these Muslim minorities face threats of exile or annihilation due to ethnic cleansing and other pressures. What options does Islamic jurisprudence have for them? Some people have been suggesting that such minorities should emigrate to countries that have Muslim majorities. If this was possible, and it is normally impossible, what good will it do them? Or is such a suggestion another plot against the Muslims in order to drive them out of their homes? There are those who advise Muslim minorities to isolate themselves and wait, but this too contradicts the very essence of the Islamic message which encourages the faithful to be positive, active and involved.

The best option for such minorities is to enter into alliances with secular democratic groups. They can then work towards the establishment of a secular democratic government which will respect human rights, ensuring security and freedom of expression and belief—essential requirements of mankind that Islam has come to fulfil.

The accomplishment of such important values in any society will immediately transform it, in the Islamic conception, from *darul-harb*, a land of hostility and war against Islam, to a land of peace and tranquillity. Al-Imam An-Nawawi defines the land of hostility (*darul-harb*) as the country in which the faithful cannot practice their religious duties freely, and consequently emigrating from it becomes an imperative duty. True democracies are not like this; they guarantee the freedom of worship and belief.

Second: There are many Islamic communities or movements that exist in countries that have Muslim majorities but which happen to be ruled by dictatorships claiming to be Islamic or by dictatorships hostile to Islam. Such Islamic movements may not be able to reform the regime or change it alone. Does the *shari'ah* (Islamic Law) object to cooperation and alliance between these movements and secular parties that also work and struggle to topple the dictatorships and establish secular democracies that would respect humans and guarantee their liberties? No, not at all.

Third: Similarly, the Islamic groups which exist in Muslim majority countries governed by dictatorships may be able to attract majority support from the public and establish an Islamic government. However, such a transition may incite hostility towards them from within their own country or from other countries, rendering the newly-formed Islamic government susceptible to oppression or other forms of pressures that may end with its collapse.

Is there any reason why such groups cannot agree or coordinate with secular groups in order to isolate the existing oppressive power and establish a secular democracy postponing the long-term objective of establishing an Islamic government until circumstances permit? Certainly, there is nothing against that.

It should be emphasised that the choice in this case is not between an Islamic government and a non-Islamic one, but between dictatorship and democracy.

Fourth: The Islamic groups which exist in countries colonised by foreign powers. Is there any reason why they should not form a united front with the secular groups in order to confront the common enemy in favour of a national alternative, in which the Muslims would have a better life than under the colonial authority? Certainly, there is nothing to prevent them from doing so.

CONCLUSION

If the establishment of the Islamic government is the short or long-term goal of every Islamic group in order to implement Allah's commandments, the *shari'ah* (Islamic Law) does take into consideration the possibility that such a goal may not be easily accomplished, and therefore an alternative is provided. Under exceptional circumstances, Islamic groups may forge alliances with non-Islamic groups in order to establish a pluralistic government system in which power is held by the majority party.

Such an alliance may also exist for the purpose of deterring aggression or getting rid, of a dictatorship. In all cases, the alliance must not include provisions that would in any way undermine Islam, or impose restrictions on those who work for Islam and who seek to establish its system in the land.

These arguments are based on:

- the principle of supporting that which brings good and suppressing that which produces evil,
- the rule that what an imperative duty is essentially dependent on is imperative in itself,

- the rule of consequences or outcomes,
- the principle of necessity.

What is most important is that a Muslim must remain positive and actively engaged in the effort to implement the revealed laws of Allah, whether partially or in their totality, depending on circumstances and resources. The essence of Allah's laws, for which all divine messages were sent, is the establishment of justice for mankind.

> "We sent aforetime our Messengers with clear signs and sent down with them the Book and the Balance (of right and wrong), that men may stand forth in justice. (57:25)

It should however be emphasised that the problem facing the concept of power-sharing does not lie in the difficulty of convincing the Islamists to accept democracy, pluralism and power-sharing. The current general trend in Islamic circles is to adopt power-sharing—even in a secular style government—as a means for achieving mutual goals such as national solidarity, respect for human rights, civil liberties, cultural, social and economic development, and the deterrence of external threats.

The real problem lies in convincing the "other," that is the ruling regimes, of the principle of "the people's sovereignty" and of the right of Islamists—just like other political groups—to form political parties, engage in political activities and compete for power or share in power through democratic means.

The punishment of the Islamic victors in the Tunisian and Algerian elections—which have regrettably been taking place with the consent of Western democracies and the support of local "secular theological elites" that are allied with the oppressive regimes in both countries—provides a decisive evidence that the root of the problem in the Muslim world lies in the hegemony of despotism. Our main task now is to combat despotism in favour of a genuine and true transition to democracy.

MUHAMMAD SALIM AL-AWA
1942–

Born in Cairo, he studied law at Alexandria University and earned his Ph.D. from the School of Oriental and African Studies (SOAS) at London University in 1972. He is a prominent lawyer, specializing in comparative law and Islamic law, and an activist in Egypt and the Arab world; his publications include *On the Political System of the Islamic State, The Crisis of the Religious Establishment,* and the award-winning *Islamic Jurisprudence on the Path of Renewal,* for which he was named Arab thinker of the year. Chair of the Egyptian Association for Culture and Dialogue, he has been a leading public intellectual and a founder and leader of the *Wasatiya* movement in Egypt since the 1980s.

Political Pluralism from an Islamic Perspective

In essence, pluralism means the recognition of diversity. Not only is it a reality which no sensible person can deny, but is a legitimate right for those with whom we may disagree or differ; a right that no person or authority can deny or take away. Pluralism usually takes an adjective derived from the topic of concern, and thus can be political, economic, religious, racial, or linguistic.

Pluralism already exists in nature among creatures and among their various species. In this sense, it is an expression of the marvellous divine achievement.

Allah says in the Holy Qur'an:

> It is He Who has produced you from a single soul: then there is a resting place and a repository. We detail Our signs for people who understand. It is He Who sends down rain from the skies, with it We produce vegetation of all kinds. From some We produce green crops, out of which We produce close-compounded grain. Out of the date-palm and its sheaths come clusters of dates hanging low and near. Then there are gardens of grapes, of olives and of pomegranates, each similar (in kind) yet different in variety. When they begin to bear fruit, feast your eyes upon the fruit and the ripeness thereof. Behold in these things there are signs for people who believe. (6:98–99)

From *Power Sharing Islam*, ed. Azzam Tamimi (London: Liberty for Muslim World Publications, 1993), pp. 67–76. Translated from the Arabic by Azzam Tamimi.

Allah also says:

Have you not seen that Allah sends down rain from the sky? With it We then bring out produce of various colours. And in the mountains are tracts white and red, of various shades of colour, and black intense in hue. And amongst humans and beasts and cattle they are also of various colours. Among His servants those who have knowledge truly fear Allah: for Allah is Exalted in Might, Oft-Forgiving. (35:27–28)

There is obvious and significant pluralism among humans—in their races, affiliations, responsibilities, performances, talents, faculties and powers.

Among His signs is the creation of the heavens and the earth, and the variations in your languages and your colours: verily in that are signs for those who know. (30:22)

O mankind! We created you from a single (pair) of a male and a female, and made you into nations and tribes, that you may know each other. Verily the most honoured of you in the sight of Allah is he who is the most righteous of you. And Allah has full knowledge and is well acquainted with all things. (49:13)

In this verse the Qur'anic expressions of "honoured" and "righteous" are used to indicate the existence of these who are honoured and those who are righteous, pointing to the fact that diversity is a reality, and that pluralism in the Divine scheme of evaluation does not necessarily mean accepting the members of a certain category while rejecting the members of other categories. By categories I mean the grades of "righteousness" and "honour," which are based on sincerity of belief and clarity of conviction.

If one recognises the pluralistic nature of humans, and recognises their rights to disagree and differ, one must inevitably, and without much effort, recognise pluralism in the political sphere. Why should this matter require clarification? And why does it seem to many observers of Islamic political thought that it rejects political pluralism and adopts monism, or the unitary vision, which in most cases leads to an unjust despotic rule or a permanent tyrannical government.

Islamic political thought appears to be distorted and misunderstood over this as well as over many other issues. There are usually three reasons for this distortion. The first is that writings on Islam and Islamic thought continue to be constrained by the unquestioning adoption of ancient writings (taqlid), copying them, building on them and considering them fundamentals and references for analogy (qiyas). These ancient writings describe the situation that existed during the times of those who wrote them, based on the writers' understanding and assessment. The judgement given therein is that of ancient writers based on their or their predecessors' interpretation or comprehension of the fundamentals of Islam.

The second reason is that writings on Islam and Islamic thought still revolve around the ancient occurrences in the history of Muslims. Researchers who tackle these occurrences in Muslim history usually pursue one of two ways. They either take an interest only in the best and most enlightened times, deriving lessons from them as if they were the entire history of the Muslims; or alternatively take an interest only in the worst events and gloomiest stages and then ascribe such gloominess to the entire history.

The third reason is that the advocates of an Islam-based reform for the deteriorating political, social and economic situations in the Muslim world do not bother to explain to the people the Islamic position with regard to the organisation of society. They avoid tackling essential problems and are usually content with the fact that they invite to the faith of the majority; the faith which they themselves believe in. They usually uphold true slogans but fall short of making the required effort to translate these slogans into reality. Many seek to justify this attitude by saying they suffer security restrictions and are denied the right to form political parties. Some of the groups which pursue moderate policies function without governmental approval and therefore cannot be protected from arbitrary measures. These occur without prior notice and without obvious reasons. On the other hand, members of extremist (radical) groups are on the run and can be shot dead wherever they are ambushed. If caught alive, they are usually indicted and sentenced without proper trial or defence.

The three aforementioned reasons require some consideration. If *taqlid* (the unquestioning adoption of ancient writings) is generally bad, it is worst when applied to political thinking. Ancient writings that are copied and imitated by contemporary writers are "relative." They should not be referred to in order to restrict or hinder the progress of the Islamic political movements. These movements to revive Islam have been in motion throughout history and should continue to be so.

Islamic history, or the history of the Muslims, with all its ups and downs, is certainly a good source of lessons and admonitions. However, it should not be used to create restrictive precedents, which should be followed to the finest detail if deemed to be good, or which would cause Islam itself to be rejected and its followers denounced if they were precedents of tyranny and oppression.

The excuses made by those who call for an Islam-based reform are in essence valid excuses but do not justify their abstention from explaining to the people what they call them to. Nor do such excuses legitimise the adoption of obscure and inexplicable concepts which oftenly reflect negatively on Islam itself. Hence, the stand of Islamic thought toward pluralism requires renewed clarification. It is necessary to prevent any of the aforementioned reasons from causing the people to think that those who call for an Islam-based reform stand against political pluralism or support tyranny or that they are preparing for a new era of despotism cloaked in religion and protected by it!

It is important that those who call for Islam-based political reform do not miss the fact that the most extreme forms of oppression and the worst types of tyranny in history were those resulting from the interpretation of religion so as to satisfy the ambitions or desires of oppressors. Many tyrannical practices resulted from the distortion of religions, introducing into them things that did not belong to them. The history of humanity, irrespective of religion, stands witness. Hence, it is important to underline the truth about Islam's position toward political pluralism. Islam considers "differing" to be a genuine human right and an essential requirement of diversification.

The appropriate approach to Islamic political thought in contemporary times is—now as it has always been—to thoroughly examine Islamic fundamentals. The purpose would be to determine what the fundamentals obligate, and to suggest the means and methods believed to accomplish the fulfilment of such obligations. The means and methods that prove to be sound and reliable are endorsed, and those that prove to the contrary should be replaced. By doing so, we would be pursuing a sound jurisprudential rule, namely: "any course of action which fails to accomplish its targeted goal is invalid."

The examination of Islamic fundamentals in this manner is termed *ijtihad*, which is governed in *fiqh* (jurisprudence) by scholastic aptitude, and in politics by the ability to serve the interests of the people. After all, securing the rights and liberties of the public is the essential foundation of obtaining good and averting evil.

Exercising political *ijtihad* for the purpose of organising and administering the state has never stopped throughout the history of Islam. However, whenever Islamic *shari'ah* was excluded from government, creative efforts to develop Islamic jurisprudence were frozen and jurists ceased to practise juristical explanation. Consequently, governors—as Ibn Qayim Al-Jawziyah put it—invented and introduced bad practices, thinking that *shari'ah* was inadequate or incapable of serving the interests of the people. Hence, Ibn Qayim Al-Jawziyah suggested that "wherever there is justice, that is the law and religion of Allah."

Others such as Ibn 'Aqil Al-Hanbali suggested that the Islamic policy is that which does not contradict the verdict of the Revelation. He stressed that those who claim that Islamic policy approves only that which is stated in the Revelation commit two mistakes: the first is that their claim is not supported in any way by evidence from the Qur'an or the Sunnah (traditions of the Prophet), and the second is that by claiming this they put the Prophet's companions and their successors in the wrong. The companions and their successors did exercise whatever they deemed to serve the interests of the people so long as it did not contradict the Revelation. But they did not restrict themselves to the revealed texts alone.

The question which we need to ask ourselves is: what do revealed texts or Islamic fundamentals obligate the people to do in the running of their daily affairs, and what do they forbid them from doing? Has a specific method been outlined in order for the people to fulfil such obligations and avoid such prohibitions? Before answering this question, one must testify that what *shari'ah* obligates must be observed. All such obligations must strictly be obeyed and failing to do so constitutes a major sin that persists so long as the obligations continue to be neglected or ignored.

To answer the above question, it is necessary to begin with emphasising that Islamic references do not outline a specific path for mankind to pursue in order to attain the political objectives stated in the Qur'an and the Sunnah.

The fundamental principles of the Islamic state can be summarised in the following points:

1. In neither the Qur'an nor the Sunnah does Islam prescribe a specific system of government. Nevertheless, it clearly defines the values and guidelines the *ummah* (community) should adhere to and rulers should abide by. In addition to other nomenclature, these values may be referred to as "general rules" or "comprehensive issues". In the political field, this is compatible with the nature of Islamic legislations which are characterised by complete flexibility. This in itself is an important prerequisite of applicability through extrapolation and deduction.

2. Choosing the ruler was the cornerstone in the organisation of the Islamic state when it was first established. Nevertheless, Islam at that time had only prescribed *shura* (consultation) as a method for making the choice. What matters is that the *ummah* (community) should be able to exercise its free will in choosing and appointing the ruler. This is exactly how the four guided Caliphs were chosen. The actual procedure is left for the community to determine, and may therefore differ from time to time and from one place to another.

   Perhaps the best procedure in our time is the election of the head of state and of the people's representatives through direct free elections. All citizens should have the right to participate, and appointment to the office should be for a limited period. No group or individual should be excluded from the process or deprived of the right to nominate themselves or elect others.

3. Freedom is an indispensable Islamic value, guaranteed and considered to be instinctive. Political freedom, in Islam, is a branch of a general fundamental right: the freedom to choose. The Prophet said: "Let not any of you be a characterless person, saying: I do what the people do— if they do good I do good, and if they do bad I do bad." Voicing one's opinion is not just permissible but is an Islamic duty. Scholars of *usul* (fundamentals) define a *wajib* (duty) as being "the action that is imperatively demanded" and consider a person who fails to execute such an action to be a sinner.

4. Equality before the law and equity in the treatment of citizens and in the assessment of their rights and liberties are essential Islamic values. Such values should under no circumstances be abandoned.

5. Enjoining what is right and forbidding what is wrong are Islamic duties applicable to all fields of life. They are obligatory upon individuals and groups. Allah says in the Qur'an: "Let there arise out of you a band of people inviting to all that is good, enjoining what is right and forbidding what is wrong." (3:104) He also says in the same chapter: "You are the best of peoples evolved for mankind. Enjoining what is right, forbidding what is wrong, and believing in Allah." (3:110)

6. Rulers are accountable to the community and are responsible for looking after its affairs. This responsibility was endorsed, in action, by the Prophet himself. No ruler succeeding the Prophet has the right to claim an immunity that the Prophet himself did not enjoy.

In order for these political values to be accomplished in today's society, they require a guarantee of protection, and that is nothing else but political pluralism. This conclusion stems from the fact that Islamic fundamentals (sources) provide universal or general values which leave the *ummah* (community) unrestricted and capable of creative thinking and unlimited search for the best means of organisation and re-organisation. These include the means necessary for preserving the *ummah*'s right to live under the banner of Islamic values and for preventing rulers from becoming tyrants and oppressors.

It is only common sense that these means should vary from time to time and from one location to the other. For instance, a community that is under colonial control may have to resort to methods inapplicable to other places, or to means that were never employed by previous generations or other communities. Under certain circumstances, it may be feasible to borrow from the experiences and methods of other cultures if these are thought to guarantee and protect rights and freedoms.

In one of the best remarks ever made by a prominent scholar of Islam, Ibn Qayim Al-Jawziyah said: "Some scholars categorise government into *shari'ah* (law) and *siyasah* (politics) in the same manner as they categorise *deen* (religion) into *shari'ah* and *haqiqah* (reality), or as some may categorise *deen* (religion) into *'aql* (reasoning) and *naql* (tradition); but all these categorisations are wrong. Politics, reality, methodology and reasoning are all categorised into two classes: right and wrong. *Shari'ah* accepts and supports all that which is right and opposes and rejects that which is bad or corrupt. This is one of the most important and useful fundamentals."

Islamic political thinkers are confronted with two arguments used by some Islamists when they talk about political pluralism or multi-party politics. Both arguments are easily refutable and do not in any way undermine the credibility of the above discussion.

The first argument is the claim by some researchers that Islam does not know party politics. This, indeed, is a meaningless argument. If Islam does not "mention" something, this indicates one of two things: either that it is not stated anywhere in the traditional sources or that Muslims have never practised it throughout their history.

In the first case, the non-mentioning of something implies that it is permitted. The only exception to this rule is the subject of worship which is not realisable or comprehensible by man, and in whose case non-mentioning implies prohibition. It is self-evident that political pluralism does not fall into the category of subjects that are beyond the comprehensibility of man; it is neither an act of worship nor a ritual of any kind. Actually, it falls into the category of changing circumstances in which interests are determined by logic and reasoning.

In the second case, the fact that earlier Muslims did not practise it is not a valid argument against pluralism. Even the very early generation of Muslims, the Prophet's companions, introduced new measures, means and methods that were not known during the time of the Prophet himself. It is only natural that Muslims should respond to changes and developments at all times and in all circumstances.

Furthermore, the history of Islam witnessed the birth of several political groups such as the *Khawarij*, the *Shi'ah*, and the *Mu'tazilah*, each of which then gave rise to various other sub-divisions. Such partisanship or factionalism became a common political feature of the Muslim society. Scores of different jurisprudential and ideological schools have emerged since the early days of the Islamic civilisation. They tolerated each other and coexisted. Therefore, there is no reason why political diversification or pluralism cannot be recognised and tolerated.

The second argument stems from the claim that the Qur'an has condemned factionalism, division and disagreement. Qur'anic verses are usually quoted to substantiate this claim. They include the following:

> They have cut off their affair (of unity) between them into sects: each party rejoices in that which it has. (23:53)

> As for those who divide their religion and break up into sects, you have no part in them in the least. (6:159)

Actually, this argument is nothing but a manipulation and a distortion of the Qur'anic text. As the Qur'an condemns "parties" in these instances, it commends them in others. One can quote several examples including the following:

> As for those who turn to Allah, His Messenger, and the believers, it is the Party of Allah that must certainly triumph. (5:56)

[T]hey are the Party of Allah. Truly it is the Party of Allah that will achieve
success. (58:22)

Then We roused them, in order to test which of the two parties was best
at calculating the term of years they had tarried! (18:12)

It is clearly unacceptable to quote only the verses in which "parties" are
condemned, as this is bound to make one arrive at the wrong conclusion.

The other side of this argument is the claim some contemporary
Islamists make, quoting Qur'anic verses which describe the *ummah* as a
single community, to show that Islam does not permit the formation of
political parties. They quote verses such as "Verily, this ummah of yours is
a single ummah." (21:92)

In fact what this verse, and all other verses that are similar to it, implies
is the oneness in religion, which is sincere worship of and submission to the
Creator alone without assigning partners with Him or below Him. Hence,
applying this concept so as to imply political oneness, as opposed to political pluralism, clearly involves a distortion of the meaning.

Contemporary *ijtihad* must inevitably arrive at supporting the concept
of political pluralism, even if for the sake of argument, such a concept was
not known before. Parties which call for that which is right and good, and
which serve the interests of the public are included in the Qur'anic description of the believers. "[T]hey are the Party of Allah. Truly it is the Party of
Allah that will achieve success." (58:22) Parties which oppose the commands of Allah and His Messenger and which harm the interests of the
public come under the Qur'anic description. "[T]hey are the party of Satan.
Truly, it is the party of Satan that will lose." (58:19)

An Islamic state incurs no reproach today by licensing political parties
and permitting political pluralism. However, it may—and probably it
should—stipulate that these parties must abide by the values of Islam and
respect its provisions. Apart from that, political parties are free to call for
the political, social or economic programmes they deem feasible. Islam does
not object to this state of affairs.

Rather, I believe that the existence of political parties in the present
circumstances will promote the progress and development of Muslim
societies, and will bolster the freedom of expression in them. This will also
serve as a safety valve to prevent despotism or check despotic tendencies.
After all, most—if not all—of these societies have been suffering from some
form of despotic rule.

The jurisprudence of Islamic fundamental principles is based on a grand
rule, namely that "what a duty is essentially dependent upon is itself a
duty." Is it possible for any political system to be set up at the present time
while denying the people the right to differ or disagree, or denying them
the right to the freedom of expression or the right to congregate and organise public meetings?

The only correct answer to this question is "no." The principles of Islamic jurisprudence, the logic of political interests and history stand witness to the fact that as far as Islam is concerned political pluralism is a necessity.

This conclusion should receive special attention by thinkers within the contemporary Islamic Movement and by those involved in political activities. On the one hand, it is our responsibility to explain the true position of Islam on these matters, but at the same time we should seek to gain the confidence of the public in order to promote the Islamic civilizational political project.

FATHI OSMAN
1928–

Egyptian-born scholar and a graduate of Cairo and of Al-Azhar University, he received a doctorate from Princeton University and taught in the Muslim world as well as in the United States. For many years, Fathi Osman was editor of *Arabia* magazine as well as Vice President of the American Association of Muslim Social Scientists. His publications include *Islamic Legal Thinking Between the Permanent Divine Sources and the Changing Juristic Contributions, Islamic Thought and Human Change, The Muslim World: Issues and Challenges, Jihad: A Legitimate Struggle for Human Rights*, and *The Children of Adam*.

Shura and Democracy

Shura means a serious and effective participation in making a decision, and the practices of the Prophet proved that it cannot be merely a formal or ceremonial exercise. The Muslim people and those "who are entrusted with authority from among them by them" (Quran 4:59) are bound by the goals and general principles of the Islamic law that secure human dignity and that sustain and develop all human beings: their life, families and children, minds, freedom of faith, and their private or public possessions. Those who are entrusted with authority by the people are always referred to in the Quran in the plural, which suggests that they form organizational bodies and are not considered as individuals (Quran 4:59, 83).

Differences may naturally emerge within these bodies which are entrusted with authority, or between them and the people or groups among them. The parties at variance are referred to the guidance of God and the Conveyor of His message which may be presented and decided in the most appropriate way, whenever this becomes necessary, by a supreme court.

Democratic mechanisms can provide the practical ways for implementing shura. Islam urges Muslims to adopt all human wisdom, as the Prophet's tradition reported by Tirmidhi indicates. Among the fundamentals of jurisprudence is a valuable rule that states: "Whenever there is a certain means that can lead only to the fulfillment of an obligation, the practice of such a means becomes an obligation in itself." The outstanding jurist Ibn al-Qayyim has stated that the ways of reaching a given goal are not necessarily limited to what the Quran and Sunna may indicate, and

From *The Children of Adam: An Islamic Perspective on Pluralism* (Washington, D.C.: Center for Muslim-Christian Understanding, Occasional Paper Series, 1996), pp. 547–59.

"whenever justice comes forth by any way, there is God's law and command and good acceptance."[1]

ELECTION

The head of a contemporary Muslim state can be elected directly by the people or by the parliamentary representatives of the people, or can be nominated by those representatives as a candidate for or against whom the public then votes. Any procedure can be followed, depending on its merits and the given circumstances, and Islam can accept any that is in the interests of the people. The first four caliphs were chosen in different ways, but in the end they went to the public in the mosque to obtain their approval in the form of bay'a. Bay'a is a mutual pledge from the ruler to follow Shari'a and earn the public's approval and support through his services, and from the people to support the ruler and advise him.[2] In a contemporary democratic procedure, the voting of the electorate and the oath made by the elected head of state take the place of the original bay'a.

When several candidates contest a position, the public choice is determined by the majority of votes, another democratic mechanism. Even when one candidate for the position is nominated by the parliament or decides to be a candidate, a majority of voters may be required to elect the candidate.

The Quran frequently states most people lack knowledge or moral commitment and may fail to make the right decision (e.g., Quran 5:49, 6:116, 7:187, 10:60, 92, 11:17, 12:40, 68, 103, 13:1, 16:38, 17:89, 25:50, 30:6, 8, 30, 34:28, 36, 37:71, 40:57, 59, 61, 45:26). But, the Quran never teaches that a reliance on a few persons necessarily yields perfect decisions. A majority can make mistakes, but their mistakes are most likely fewer than the mistakes of one or a few. Making mistakes is human; all that is required from human beings is that they make a serious effort to find out what is right and use accumulated knowledge and experience to avoid error where possible. Cooperation in reaching these objectives saves time and energy, and it provides a reasonable chance for mutual correction and for a sensible revision of any decision that proves wrong when in practice. Many precedents can be found in the life of the Prophet and the early caliphs about decisions made according to the majority, even when they differed from the leader's view. When Caliph 'Umar selected six candidates for the caliphate to succeed him after he was stabbed, he instructed them to follow the candidate from among themselves who would receive the majority of votes. A Prophet's tradition urges the individual to yield to greatest number (al-sawad al-a'zam) when there is a serious split (reported by Ibn Hanbal and Ibn Majah).

---

1. Ibn Qayyim al Jawziyya, Abu Abd-Allah Muhammad ibn Abi Bakr, I'lam al-Muwaqqi'in (Cairo: al-Muniiriyya Press, n.d.), 4: 267–69.
2. Abu Ya'la Muhammad ibn al-Husayn al-Mutamad, text published in Ibish, 1966, p. 224.

One may ask: "Isn't following the Quran and Sunna sufficient and the safest way?" To which one can easily answer, the Quran and Sunna provide the general laws, but the human mind is entrusted with the details and specifics for coping with the unceasing changes in human society. Human beings know what may be beneficial and fair for a given time and place, and the more people involved in such collective thinking and discretion, the fewer the mistakes made. Terms of reference and guidelines, in addition to procedural and ethical safeguards, reduce human error.

The election of the representatives of a people to a parliamentary body is also based on winning a majority of voters. If the principles of "one person one vote" fails to achieve a fair representation for an ethnic or religious minority or of women, each group can be allotted a certain number of seats in the parliament proportional to their numbers, which may be contested in broader constituencies or in the country as a whole. The parliament is responsible for legislation, as well as for guarding the interests of the executive body. Decisions of the parliament and its committees are made by the majority of the voting members. A public referendum on matters of special importance may be decided by the legislature or by a given number of voters through an established procedure. Decisions of the executive body or any of its departments or branches are also determined by a majority of voting members.

Voting can be the means for choosing the governing boards for workers' unions, professional and student associations, philanthropic and other organizations, as well as for making decisions on their boards. There is no better way of learning the public's views and interests than through a vote, in spite of its limitations or abuses. The same is true even of technical decisions among professionals, in schools, factories, companies, or other bodies, and even of reaching decisions in a court of several judges or judge and jury.

The argument that voting means giving the same value to the judgment of the most knowledgeable person and that of the most ignorant one can be answered by saying that the common interest of the people can be determined by any individual of ordinary civic abilities and experience. Campaigns for candidates and laws and the mass media provide valuable information for a serious voter. The judgment of an older experienced person who is uneducated may be more reasonable than of a young university graduate.

As women are equal to men in their social rights and responsibilities according to the Quran (9:71), and a woman can, according to prominent jurists, be a judge, she is naturally eligible to vote. The Quranic verse that makes a male witness equal to two female witnesses for documenting a credit contract is restricted to the special case where a woman might not be familiar with such a transaction and its legal requirements "so that if one of them should make a mistake, the other could remind her" (2:282). It is obvious from the Quranic text, from the historical context, and from the jurisprudential principle that "legal rule follows its reason: if the reason continues to exist, the legal rule continues to exist; and if the reason ceases to exist, the legal rule follows," that the verse is not meant to apply to an educated business woman, nor to areas of common interest which do not require specific expertise of knowledge.

Non-Muslims enjoy equal human rights and dignity and are eligible for voting the same as Muslims as soon as they reach the required age and if they have no mental disability. A Muslim majority should have no misgivings about a non-Muslim voting, since votes are taken regarding matters related to common sense, not to a particular faith. In addition, voting would be proportional to the minority population and cannot hurt majority interests or beliefs. The right to vote should be equally shared by all ethnicities, whether Muslims or not.

Elections require several candidates to choose from, whether such a choice is for the parliament or for a board of a union, association or other organization. Some Muslims argue against such a procedure citing a Prophet's tradition that disqualifies anyone who asks for a public position (as reported by Ibn Hanbal, al-Bukhari, Muslim, Abu Dawud, and al-Nasa'i). According to commentators and jurists, this can be interpreted as a warning against asking for a public position for personal benefit, without considering the responsibilities of the office or the ability of the seeker. Only someone fully aware of what the position entails and having the abilities to fulfill those tasks can seek office by indicating his or her credentials for it, as was done by the Prophets Yusuf (Joseph) and Sulayman (Solomon (12:55, 38:35). Caliph Umar nominated six candidates, from which one had to be chosen by the majority as a candidate for the caliphate. It goes without saying, that presenting the candidate's merits and qualifications for the position and criticizing others should follow legal and ethical principles. The requirements for a candidate and what may bar have to be decided in the light of social ideals and circumstances.

Women can be members of parliament, ministers in the government, judges, and military and police officers, according to their merits and credentials, since they share with men the right and responsibility to do what is right and avoid doing what is wrong (9:71). The Quran mentions the Queen of Sheba (27:28–44), with no indication of Quranic disapproval of a female head of state. On the contrary, the Quran describes her strong personality and capable leadership. She did not ignore the leading persons in her country when making important decisions, and they respected her wisdom and leadership. The tradition that says the Prophet expected a Persian failure because they had a queen (reported by Ibn Hanbal, al-Bukhari, al-Tirmidhi, al-Nasa'i) was informative not legislative, and should not be taken out of context. However, nothing in the tradition indicates that it represented a law of God that must be observed by Muslims; it could simply have been a personal view. The Prophet expressed an opinion that was not meant to be binding as a part of God's teachings.

Non-Muslims have the right and the duty to occupy positions in the legislature, the government, and administration, the judiciary, and the military forces. A modern state is ruled by institutions not by individuals, and non-Muslims naturally work within these bodies. The non-Muslim is equal to a Muslim as a witness (5:106), and can be a minister with executive power (wazir tanfidh), according to al-Mawardi, but not a plenipotentiary minister (wazir tafwid) with absolute power. There were non-Muslim ministers and top officials in medieval Muslim states such as Egypt and Andalusia. No single person, even the head of the state, should have absolute power in a modern state; the non-Muslim judge has to apply the same state code of laws, whatever his or her beliefs may be. A non-Muslim can also be included with Muslim judges in a multi-judge court. Areas that are related or close to the faith such as family matters, inheritance, and charity endowments (awqaf) can be assigned to a judge of the litigant's own faith.

THE MULTI-PARTY SYSTEM: THE OPPOSITION

Political parties are essential for democracy, as they help people establish their views about persons and policies. The individual can find himself or herself helpless to oppose those who enjoy governmental authority, especially in a modern state where advanced technology provides a formidable tool for suppressing opponents and influencing public opinion. The multi-party system has proved to be the most if not the only democratic formula, since the one-party system has never produced any real or effective opposition, and such opposition has rarely been able to grow outside the party system through individuals contacting masses directly.

The Quran urges that groups be found to enjoin the doing of what is right and to forbid the doing of what is wrong (3:104). The word umma in the Quran does not always mean the whole universal body of believers, as is often assumed, but it can merely mean a group of people (e.g., 3:113, 5:66, 6:108, 7:38, 159, 164, 28:23), especially when the word is connected with the preposition "from," as in the above-mentioned verse 3:104: "And let there be from among you a group (umma) that calls to good and enjoins the doing of what is right." The Arabic word "umma" can be used for groups of different sizes, and it is sometimes used in the Quran for the whole Muslim community (e.g., 3:110, 2:113, 21:92, 23:52), but it is also used for limited groups (e.g., 5:66, 7:159, 164, 28:23), or even for one leading person who has his followers (16:120).

This does not deny the fundamental unity of the people, since political differences are human and inevitable and should not affect public unity if they are properly handled in an objective and ethical way. As politics often represents an area of human discretion (ijtihad), the Quran assumes that Muslims may face differences and even disputes (4:59), and they are guided to settle them conceptually and morally according to their terms of the

Quran and Sunna. Various legitimate human approaches to interpret the divine texts may naturally emerge.

The early Muslims had their conceptual differences from time to time, beginning with the argument about who should become leader after the Prophet's death. Their political differences were represented in certain groups which openly expressed their views in a public meeting at "al-Saqifa," a spacious area that had a sort of roof (saqf in Arabic) among the homes of the clan Banu Sa'ida in Medina which was apparently allocated for tribal gatherings. Later, Muslims have had their several theological groups (e.g., the Ahl al-Sunna, al-Shi'a, al-Khawarij) with different political ideas and juristic schools. These differences should not in any way damage public unity.

Accordingly, Muslims can form several Islamic political parties, all of them committed to Islam, but with different concepts or different ways in carrying out their legitimate political activities, or they may have different programs of reform when they rule. Although establishing parties on ethnic grounds or out of personal or family considerations ought not be encouraged from the Islamic point of view, it may be acceptable in given circumstances, however, as a fact of life.

Non-Muslims and secularists, whether they are Muslims or not, can also have their own political parties to present their views, defend their interests, and guard the human rights and dignity of all the children of Adam, as the Quran teaches. The Quran indicates that all the People of the Book are responsible for enjoining the doing of what is right and forbidding the doing of what is wrong (3:114, 5:78–79).

Women can join any party or form their own. Political fronts and alliances may involve Islamic parties and others in certain circumstances or for certain issues, and various parties can join in coalitions to form a government. Diversity in political thinking and practice, against a background of unity, is a fundamental organizational requirement to achieve pluralism. An unreasonable number of parties can reduce the efficiency and effectiveness of governance, however, and create difficulties in gaining a majority in the parliament, in forming a coalition to secure such a majority, when no single party can secure it, and in presenting a strong opposition. This is a challenge for the multi-party system which some democracies face. It should be handled through political prudence and moral responsibility rather than by any legal restrictions arbitrarily decided or executed.

An opposition is indispensable to a democratic system, and should not raise any suspicion in the Muslim mind. It is needed to scrutinize the practices of the government and to provide an alternative if the party in power loses the confidence of the people. The opposition does not oppose for the sake of mere opposition; it should join in a united front during times of national crisis, and it should praise the government when it does something commendable. Under the early caliphs, opposing views were known and recorded. They have to be put forth even if they cannot prevail, for their validity and value may later be realized.

THE LEGISLATIVE FUNCTION

Some Muslims argue that since God is the Lawgiver, there should be no legislative body in an Islamic state. In fact, the legislature specifies and establishes the details of the required laws; the Quran and the Sunna provide only general principles and rules. In the case of the Quran and Sunna, different interpretations and jurisprudential views might appear regarding a certain text because of its language or its relation to other relevant texts. It is essential that a certain interpretation or jurisprudential view should be adopted by the state as a law, and what this is to be has to be decided by the legislature, so that the courts are not left to enforce inconsistent rules, according to the discretion of each different judge, something about which the well-known writer Ibn al-Muqaffa' complained in his time.

What is allowed by the Islamic law al-mubah is extensive, and such a limitless number of allowed acts ought to be organized in a certain way: making them mandatory, or forbidden, or optional according to changing circumstances in different times and places. The public interest has also to introduce new laws not specified in the Quran and Sunna, which may be needed under new and different times or places. They must not contradict any other rule in the divine sources, nor the general goals and principles of Shari'a. Many laws are required in a modern state to regulate traffic, irrigation, construction, transportation, roads, industry, currency, importing and exporting, public health, education, etc; they have only to be provided according to considerations of public interest or in the light of the general goals and principles of Shari'a. No text in the Quran or the Sunna deals specifically with all the emerging human needs until the end of this life. Even the Prophet expected that some cases that may come before a judge would not find a specific solution in the Quran or Sunna, and the judge would then have to use his own discretion and judgment (ijtihad), which is naturally enlightened by the spirit of Shari'a and its general goals and principles. Such a juristic or judicial discretion (ijtihad) may have to be generalized and codified as state law and not left to the individual discretion of the judiciary.

Changing circumstances also influence understanding of a legal text and develop new needs that require new legislation. Applying the goals and general principles of Islamic law to changing social needs has been called in the Islamic law "the conduct of state policies according to Shari'a (al-siyasa al-shari'iyya). The prominent jurist Ibn al-Qayyim stated that wherever a sign of justice appears there is God's law and command and good acceptance, since God only sent the conveyors of His messages and brought down His books to secure justice in people's dealings with one another, and thus any procedure that secures justice should be followed. This outstanding jurist states, "We do not see that a just policy can be different from the comprehensive Shari'a, but it is merely a part of it . . . since if it is just, it is inseparable from Shari'a."[3]

A legislature, then, is a necessary and legitimate institution for a modern Islamic state, and it allows all components of the sociocultural and political pluralism to participate in making state laws. Democracy works within the dominant sociocultural circumstance, and the people will not accept a decision against their beliefs, as long as they are committed to them. As democracies assume that natural law or social contract or human rights supersede any human legislation, a modern Islamic state may always assume in general and with no need for explicit repetition in every case that God's guidance has supremacy over any legislation. This can be secured by the legal experts in the legislature and the administration, and through educational institutions and the information services of the media, in addition to judicial control of the supreme court.

INSTITUTIONAL AND PUBLIC SUPERVISION

The legislature also watches over the practices of the executive body, looks into any complaint or failure, and introduces any necessary legislation for reform. The principle of "checks and balances" organizes state powers and guards the public interest through an organizational and ethical climate of cooperation.

The Quran requires that even God's guidance has to be clarified to people before one becomes responsible for any deliberate deviation from it (e.g., 4:115, 47:25, 33). Those from among the people who are entrusted with authority by the people have to respond to people's questions about their practices, while the people have the responsibility to ask the authorities about any of their common concerns and worries (4:86). Mass communication has to be secured, together with its freedom in fulfilling its responsibilities to inform. Legal and ethical safeguards ought not to hinder creativity. If the mass media are within the public sector and controlled in any way by the government, political parties and candidates for public office should be given equal time to address the voters.

The supreme court has judicial control over the legislature and executive in order to secure Shari'a goals and principles and the constitutional provisions and framework (4:59). It and the whole judiciary as well should be independent and protected against any interference or pressure. Courts provide the strongest protection for the rights of the individuals and the different components of sociocultural and political pluralism against any violation of their rights, whether from any one against the other, or from the state authorities.

3. See note 1.

MURAD HOFMANN
1931–

Born Catholic in Germany, he completed his doctorate in German law at Munich University in 1957 and earned an LL.M. degree in American law from Harvard Law School in 1960. He served in the German Foreign Service and as an officer in NATO. Hofmann embraced Islam in 1980 and subsequently served as German ambassador to Algeria and then Morocco, retiring in 1994. An accomplished speaker and a prolific writer, Hofmann wrote many books, including *The Diary of a German Muslim*, *Islam 2000*, *Voyage to Mecca*, and *Islam in the Third Millennium*.

Democracy or *Shuracracy*

He who says that democracy is disbelief, neither understands Islam, nor democracy.
Sheikh Yusuf al-Quaradawi in the
London newspaper *Ash-Sharq
al-Awsat*, February 5, 1990

We do not view democracy as an alternative to Islam, or as better than Islam. We view democracy as an Islamic principle that was taught and practiced by Prophet Muhammad and his companions.
Radwan Masoudi in the first issue
of the Washingtonian periodical
Muslim Democrat, May 1999

We have now reached the question to which every discussion of "political Islam" invariably leads: what is democracy to Islam? That this subject is still the source of discordant tunes will surprise nobody. But critical Muslim voices are becoming weaker—the voices of those who used to treat democracy as a rival religion, and therefore associated it with infidelity (*nizam al-kufr*) or polytheism (*shirk*), because democracy meant worshipping, as supposedly, the sovereign, both the individual citizen and his State.[1] Nevertheless, Sayyid Qutb's radical rejection of democracy, "*Milestones*," is being continuously reprinted: a book whose powerful punch and radical bite can only be compared to the Communist Manifesto (1848), and which caused Gamal Abd al-Nasser to execute him in 1966. Qutb had been afraid

---

1. Qutb, p. 61.

From *Religion on the Rise*, ch. 6 (Beltsville, MD: Amana Publications, 2001), pp. 90–103. Used by permission of the publisher.

that a parliamentary democracy, even in an Islamic State, might eventually legalize what the *Shari'ah* prohibits (like charging interest).

One may wonder why Qutb was more suspicious of parliamentary democracy than of other forms of government when suspecting abuse of authority. The answer to this question is easy: just as in the case of human rights, when it comes to the issue of "democracy," highly emotional associations tend to play tricks on Muslims. The main reason probably is that they were introduced to democracy in a questionable form and by the powers that were "civilizing" them through colonization. Democracy was seen as a skillful method for alienating them from their own religious traditions. This has left a bad taste in their mouth for generations to come when thinking of "democracy."

For Muslims, the semantics alone are offensive. They translate the term "democracy" etymologically correctly as "people's rule"—sovereignty of the people—and by doing so make the word immediately anathema, because the sole and only sovereign is of course God, the Creator, alone. Explaining the practical meaning of sovereignty (*hakim iyya*) is therefore absolutely of prime importance. As can be expected, for Sayyid Qutb any form of legislation had divine character, and therefore, any legislative act of parliament constituted a manifest act of blasphemous presumption and rebellion against God.[2] In short: for him a parliamentary institution did not have any conceivable Islamic use.

His opponents, chiefly among them Muhammad Asad, M.S. Ashmawi, Fathi Osman, Rashid Ghannouchi, Hassan al-Turabi and Jeffrey Lang, explain that rule of God (*hukm Allah*) obviously cannot mean that God is doing the job of everyday governing for His people on earth. Sovereignty here rather refers to the sovereignty of God's Word (Qur'an) and Law (*Shari'ah*). This being granted, the question remains how man, how the Muslims can best implement the divine Revelation received.[3]

According to Hassan al-Turabi, "gray eminence of the Sudan," the Islamic ideal is a democratic Islam, since "Islam rejects absolute authority, hereditary authority, and the authority of one single individual."[4] Also to Fathi Osman, those who readily dismiss democracy as un-Islamic only reveal their ignorance of Islam or of democracy—or of both. He goes on to maintain that playing Islam and democracy off against each other is unfair—to both.[5]

Not only unfair, but also totally false is the allegation that democracy needs to be accompanied by secularism. (If this were so, democracy would indeed be unacceptable for Islam.) Democracy and secularism are anything but synonymous, on the contrary. Great Britain, Germany, Italy, Austria, Ireland, Sweden, Norway, Denmark, the Netherlands, Belgium and other

2. Qutb, p. 61.
3. Osman (1994), p. 70; Lang (1995), p. 191; Tamimi (1998), p. 35.
4. al-Turabi (1992), p. 19.
5. Osman (1996), S. 58.

non-secular States, aren't they all solidly democratic? Hence in Islam, a "theodemocracy" (Mawdudi) is a definite possibility.[6]

For Muslims, "people's rule" would be unacceptable if it really meant that the people can enact whatever they like, simply by virtue of having a majority in parliament. But this hypothesis does not even reflect the Western theory of democracy, which also distinguishes rule of the people from rule of the mob. For this reason, Western constitutions not only protect their citizens from the State, but also the State from its own citizens' license, and minorities from the majority.

Western democracies all know some constitutional norms that transcend the law by being considered immutable. For German constitutional scholars, it is therefore plausible that there could even be such a thing as unconstitutional constitutional law, resulting from forbidden attempts to change what must not be changed. The situation would not be much different in an Islamic democracy, since an Islamic parliament when engaging in legislation will always feel the breath of the Shari'ah on its neck and refrain from violating it.[7]

Instead of mindlessly stumbling over offensive vocabulary like "people's rule," Muslims should realize that the primary goal of democracy —preventing the abuse of power through a systematic control of government and a balance of power—is a key Islamic concern. How to improve and ensure better welfare of the people, equality, and justice? In an Islamic democracy, this goal would be addressed primarily by acknowledging the Qur'an as the supreme constitutional norm. (This would be the first cornerstone of an Islamic democracy.)

This Islamic constitution would provide the yardstick against which Muslim judges, members of a supreme court, would have to measure all bills passed by legislative bodies. (Second cornerstone.)

The Qur'anic foundation for an Islamic parliament (third cornerstone) is the twice repeated reference to the necessity of "consultation" (*ash-shura*) in *Surah Al 'Imran (3:159)*, and *Surah ash-Shura (42:38)*. The latter *surah* being eponymous prompted the Algerian party leader Shaykh Mahfoudh Nahnah to suggest that the Islamic form of democracy be called *Shurakratiyya*.

According to verse (3:159), the Prophet himself was under obligation to "consult the believers in [current] affairs." With Verse (42:38), the obligation to seek counsel covers the entire community of believers and is elevated to the importance of prayer and charity. Accordingly, those are rewarded ". . . who (conduct) their affair by mutual consultation." This innocuous phrase potentially is of paramount legal significance, even though historically, ever since the Umayyad dynasty in Damascus (until 750), the consultative principle has been neglected over long centuries of despotism. (Little consolation that the Occident for long did no better.)

---

6. al-Turabi (1992), p. 24.
7. al-Turabi (1992), p. 19.

Contemporary Muslims do not deny their duty to consult, nor do they overlook the fact that in modern mass societies consultation is only feasible via representative bodies (*majalis ash-shura*), as even Moses realized[8] (Cornerstone number four.)

But which is the Islamic way of choosing people's representatives? If, as is the norm in most Muslim core states, the ruler appoints them into an advisory council, the authority to be controlled is controlling itself. For that reason, more and more Muslims are calling for free and general elections of their representatives.[9] (Cornerstone number five.)

One obstacle practicing democracy this way is the Islamic principle not to nominate oneself for political office. To do so was regarded with such disapproval that Muhammad would never appoint as governor anyone who campaigned for the job.[10] As far as I can see, applying this *sunnah* to an election campaign does not mean that a candidate, once nominated by the *Ummah*, could not speak up for his cause (and thus invariably for himself); however, he must not put his name up for election himself.

Another question yet to be settled is whether consultations between government and representative assembly should be considered binding or not.[11] Making them binding is first and foremost supported by the fact that the Qur'an views each and every individual human being, man and woman, as God's deputies (*khulafa*) on earth. (That is why the chief executive should not be called *khalifa* but *amir*.)[12] Everybody is a Caliph! (In that sense, something like "sovereignty of the people" indeed exists even in Islam.)

The binding nature of consultation can of course be based directly on the *Sunnah* of the Prophet because Muhammad honored the results of consultation even if he personally had disagreed: before the battle of Badr (624), he followed the advice of al-Khabab ibn al-Mundhir to post the Muslims before and not (as intended by him) behind the water wells. Before the "Battle of the Trench" (627), Muhammad heeded the then most outrageous counsel of Salman al-Farsi to dig defensive trenches all around *al-Madinah*. Once, on the eve of the battle at mount Uhud (625) at the outskirts of *al-Madinah*, the Prophet abided by the result of consultations against his better judgment. The ambitious Muslims lost, because their majority had overruled Muhammad's advice and engaged the overwhelming besiegers from Makkah in open battle without having the necessary discipline for it.[13] (The binding nature of consultation forms cornerstone number six.)

While the Qur'an itself assumes that Muslims can be of different opinions (4:59), they seem to be obsessed with a desire for internal harmony,

---

8. 7:155.
9. Osman (1996), p. 43.
10. *al-Bukhari*, vol. 8, no. 715, vol. 9, no. 58 and 261.
11. Osman (1996), p. 83, supports the binding nature.
12. Every man is seen as God's deputy according to 2:30; 6:165; 24:55; 27:62; 35:39.
13. Cf. Haikal, pp. 219, 221, 232, 242, 252, 254.

as if disputes were to be averted no matter what. This quest for unanimity in unity can be so strong that it becomes almost authoritarian.[14] It also comes through in the fear that political pluralism might provoke ugly confrontations between Muslim parties (as in Malaysia). This misgiving is partly due to the fact that most Muslims expect Qur'an and *Sunnah* to give clear and definite (and therefore indisputable) answers to every conceivable question, also in politics. Does it not say: *"Nothing have We omitted from the Book"* (6:38) and *"This day have I perfected your religion for you"* (5:3)? In view of that, differences of opinion are easily seen as a sign of ill.

This interpretation overlooks the fact that Islam has found its perfection only in religious matters, that is faith (*aqida*), worship (*'ibada*) and morality (*akhlaq*). This means that differences in opinion are permissible, legitimate, and even unavoidable, when no specific rules of the *Shari'ah* but broad Islamic principles (*maqasid*) are applied to fields like agriculture, military strategy, or economic policy. Only, debate should never degenerate into splitting hairs.[15] Did Muhammad not state: "The differences among the learned members of my community are a grace of God"?[16] There had actually been many heated arguments among the Prophet's followers on political and military issues and, in settling the question of succession, even fighting. 'Umar, 'Uthman and 'Ali, the 2nd, 3rd and 4th Caliphs, were assassinated.

Even if Muslim anxieties about keeping internal peace are warranted, they do not constructively address the question of what to do in the event the desired political consensus among brothers simply won't materialize. Many Muslims hesitate to let majority decisions carry the day in situations of stalemate because they misjudge the legislative discretion of a Muslim parliament in two opposite ways: they overestimate it by recalling *Surah al-An'am (6:116)* which states, *"If you follow the common run of those on earth, they will mislead you away from Allah's path."* In reality, however, in a true Islamic democracy no representative body would ever be permitted to diverge from, or modernize, issues long since settled by the Qur'an or the *Sunnah*—no matter how large the majority.

On the other hand, the room for parliamentary discretion in a Muslim setting is frequently underestimated, because the role of an Islamic parliament is not limited to finding divine Muslim law in the Qur'an and the *Sunnah* (and perhaps codifying it). Rather, it has long been recognized that there is room, and even a need, for additional man-made laws dealing with new issues on which the *Shari'ah* remained silent—as long as such legislation is compatible with the principles (*maqasid*) of the Qur'an and

14. Osman (1996), S. 55.
15. So Osman (*Human Rights*, 1996), p. 11. The harmfulness of differing opinions is derived from the following *ahadith: al-Bukhari* no. 4.468, 5.434, 5.717, 6.510, 9.67, 9.39; and *Sahih Muslim* no. 6447. This may be partly due to fear of religious innovation (cf. *Muslim, Sahih*, no. 6450).
16. The Prophet warns of destructive hairsplitting in *hadith* no. 6450. in *Sahih Muslim*.

the *Sunnah* and therefore does not contradict the spirit of the *Shari'ah*.[17] (Cornerstone number seven.) After all, there is a practical need for technical regulations governing, for instance, road building, customs duties, hygiene, occupational safety standards, and so forth. No Muslim State has been able to function without legislation supplementing the penal code of the *Shari'ah* with additional misdemeanors and crimes (*ta'zir*). This, as an accepted practice, goes back to the Abbasid Caliphate where early on a kind of Islamic secularism emerged in the form of two parallel legal systems: on one level there was the divine *Shari'ah*, the domain of legal scholars. On another level, administrative law and supplementary criminal law, emancipated (to put it mildly) from the former, evolved at the "discretion" of the respective rulers. This way, for instance, non-Qur'anic methods of punishment such as incarceration and fines were eventually introduced.

This juxtaposition of executive and legislative, together with the judiciary, equally anchored in Islam, constitutes a veritable separation of powers also for an Islamic democracy. (Cornerstone number eight.) This would find its most striking expression in a direct or indirect election of the Head of State. Islamic tradition, in accordance with the Prophet's role in the Qur'an, mandates that one single (male) individual be at the helm of the State—no revolutionary council, no supreme soviet, no politburo. This head of government should be the most righteous among the citizens qualified for the position, since only a Muslim who believes in the divine nature of Qur'anic norms can be expected to observe and defend them. (Cornerstone number nine.)

The chief executive, on the other hand, called Grand *Vizier* in the Ottoman Empire, does not necessarily have to be either a Muslim, or male. (Cornerstone number ten.)

In spite of the positive example set by the Queen of Sheba in *Surah al-Naml (27)*, many Muslims still believe, though, that a State run by a woman chief executive could never prosper. This is because Prophet Muhammad, commenting on a concrete historical situation in imperial Persia, had expressed skepticism about whether the daughter who had just succeeded Emperor Chosroes II would be a successful ruler. (Her tenure did indeed turn out to be rather brief.) But this rather popular tradition may be read as more informative than normative, as sort of a judicial *obiter dictum*. At the same time it is a rather weak, if not altogether apocryphal tradition. . . .

Be that as it may, with Benazir Bhutto (1988) and Begum Khaleda Zia (1991), the Muslim world has by now produced more female heads of government than Germany, France, Great Britain and the United States combined.

The history of the Prophet's early successors demonstrates that the Head of State of an Islamic State is to be elected without a procedure fixed

---

17. Muhammad, after all, did not want Muslims to emulate him in each and every respect. Cf. Muslim, Sahih, no. 5830 and 5831.

once and for all. (Cornerstone number 11.) Abu Bakr, his first successor, was elected after a heated argument between the Muslims from Makkah and those of al-Madinah, 'Umar, the second successor, was appointed by acclamation. The third successor, 'Uthman, emerged from an electoral council of six. It follows that Islam understands monarchy, too, only as an elected monarchy. Any new king must be confirmed, at least by acclamation, and preferably through the described *baya'*—the process by which the successor to the throne and the people's representatives enter into not merely a symbolic, but a substantial contract spelling out their mutual rights and obligations.

The foregoing discussion offers compelling proof that Islam cannot be considered, in itself, hostile to democracy. Rather it contains ten cornerstones, or basic building blocks, by which the foundation of an Islamic democracy can be put into place. The counter argument, which assumes a singular, genetic flaw in Muslims with regard to democracy, qualifies as postmodern racism. One might just as well dismiss the French as essentially unfit for democracy, considering their motley collection of five republics, two empires, two monarchies and a Communist commune over as little as 200 years. A sounder argument to make is not based on myth: alas, as a religion, Islam has not had any significant impact on the political history of the Muslim world since 661, nor does it have any on the contemporary political landscape from *Maghrib* to *Mashriq*.

An Islamic democracy would not be a copy of the Westminster one, since the Arab-Islamic world knows its own unique forms of pluralism, confederation, civil society, and distribution of power which are indigenous to it alone. After all, even in the West, Westminster only exists in Westminster. At any rate, it is utterly unacceptable that democracy be defined in such a way that it excludes religious societies, i.e., societies intent on drawing political consequences from their faith. If this were the case, most North Americans would be poor democrats because de-Christianization is not an American, but only a European, phenomenon. One wonders, by the way, about the democratic spirit of those who welcome Christian parties in Germany and Italy, while questioning the democratic credentials of Islamic parties in the Muslim world, such as in Tunisia (*Mouvement de Tendence Islamique*), or Algeria (*Front Islamique du Salut*).

Concluding—not from Islam itself but from political history—that Muslims are afflicted by some congenital democratic disability would be a fallacy as well. After all, there is no region in this world, whether Christian, Confucian, Buddhist, Hindu, Jewish, or Islamic, that has not had its share of problems with democracy, most of them to this very day. Sub-Saharan Africa, China, most other parts of Asia and some Latin American countries have yet fully to arrive in the democratic camp. The Europeans, too, experienced many setbacks in their centuries–long journey towards democracy. . . .

Currently, it is primarily Muslim opposition groups headquartered abroad who stake their hopes for Islam back home on democratic control mechanisms. And yet, expecting the ruling powers in the Muslim world to show a genuine interest in democracy means misjudging human nature. True, nowadays hardly any governments can safely do without projecting a democratic façade (*ad-dimuqratiyya shikliyya*), but that is as far as it usually goes. Surprisingly, in a recent book with the pessimistic title *Democracy Without Democrats?* edited by Ghassan Salamé, most of the mostly Western authors nevertheless arrive at the optimistic conclusion that democracy is very gradually gaining ground inside the Muslim world as well.

If so, Islam owes this development to a number of distinguished personalities who have contributed bit by bit, each in his own way, to creating the foundations for a democratic blueprint. First and foremost among them are the Persian Jamal ad-Din al-Afghani (1838–1897), the Egyptian Muhammad Abdu (1849–1905), the Syrians Abdurrahman al-Kawakibi (1849–1903) and Rashid Rida (1865–1935), the Algerian Malik Bennabi (1905–1973), the Austrian Muhammad Asad (1900–1992),[18] the Egyptian Fathi Osman, who now lives in California, the Sudanese politician Hassan al-Turabi, the Tunisian Rashid Ghannoushi,[19] currently living in exile in London, as well as Jeffrey Lang, an American Muslim mathematician (and Arabist) in Kansas.

The forces that had been most strenuously resisting the Muslims' warming to democratic mechanisms are gradually losing their influence over the contemporary intra-Islamic debate on democracy. I am referring to the Journalist Abul 'Ala Mawdudi (1903–1979), founder of the Indo-Pakistani cadre-party Jama'at-e-Islami; Hassan al-Banna (1904–1949), founder of the Muslim Brotherhood (ikhwan al-muslimun), as well as Sayyid Qutb (1906–1966), their "chief ideologue." Curiously enough, since his execution, certain governments have feared him more for his ideological impact than during his lifetime. All three can be considered the legitimate heirs of Shah Waliyullah (1703–1762) and Muhammad 'Abd al-Wahhab (1703–1787), the two great inspirational figures and renewers of Islam in the early modern age.

In his breathless work *Milestones*, Sayyid Qutb wrote, "We ought not . . . start looking for similarities with Islam and the current systems or in current religions or current ideas. We reject these systems in the East as well as in the West. We reject them all."[20] This was thoroughly consistent with his premise that all existing States, the so-called Muslim States included, were still—or again—tarrying in the pre-Islamic world of unbelief

---

18. Nobody has spurred on Muslim organization more vigorously than Muhammad Asad (a.k.a Leopold Weiss) in his *The Principles of State and Government in Islam*, first published 1961 in California and only 107 pages long. In it, he arrived at the well documented conclusion that an Islamic state could be conceived along the lines of the American form of presidential government.

19. The most important book by Ghannouchi relevant to our topic is *Al-hurriya al-'amma fi-l-daula al-islamiyya (Public Liberties in the Islamic State)*.

20. Qutb, pp. 117 f.

(*jahiliyya*).[21] That this train of thought has not yet lost its impact became evident in a heated debate, as late as 1994, in the German magazine *Al-Islam* on the pros and cons of voting in parliamentary elections.[22]

Believe it or not, only 30 years after *Milestones*, the contemporary Muslim Brotherhood leadership committed itself in writing to the following elements of an Islamic state: written State constitution; general elections to determine the head of state, for a limited term; multi-party system, i.e. political pluralism; parliamentarianism; independent judiciary; and also the Muslim women's right to vote and to be elected.[23] With that in mind, Fathi Osman's wish that the Muslims will soon abandon their fruitless "*Shura*-Democracy polemics"[24] may well be fulfilled. Those doing an incredulous double take over this would be better off accepting the fact that the Islamic world is—and historically always has been—far from static.[25]

These observations should be reason enough for Western critics to reevaluate their often negative attitude towards Muslim opposition groups in Europe which are trying to change the political status quo in their home countries by adopting a democratic discourse. These "Islamist" movements have much in common with Western grass roots movements supporting civil rights, women's liberation, environmental protection, and ethnic concerns.[26]

These Islamic movements in the West are united with many a thoughtful Occidental observer in their assessment that today's societies have but three options: (i) To pursue the "Project Modernity" in the spirit of rationalist enlightenment as if nothing had happened—a prescription for disaster. (ii) To surrender to a postmodern cultural relativism and lead a life without meaning. Or (iii) to revive the transcendental links of their religions. Many young Islamic academics consider the "Project Modernity" a bankrupt paradigm and view postmodernism as an intellectual dead end. For this reason, they opt for the religion of their fathers. What is dangerous about that?

That they politicize Islam into an ideology of liberation and progress is their reasoned reaction to previous colonial domination. To them, Islam is an instrument of motivation, legitimization, and justification, which is true

---

21. Qutb, p. 67.
22. Burhan Kesici, "Wählen oder nicht? [To Vote or Not to Vote?]," in: *Al-Islam*, 1994, no. 2, p. 12, argued in favor of participating. In the next edition (p. 23), two letters to the editors voiced strong disagreements: voting constituted an endorsement of the rule of the people, hence a rejection of Qur'an and *Shari'ah*.
23. "The Muslim Brotherhood's Statement on *Shura* in Islam and the Multi-Party System in an Islamic Society"; "Statement of the Muslim Brotherhood on the role of Muslim Women in Islamic Society and Its Stand on the Women's Right to Vote, Be Elected and Occupy Public and Governmental Posts and Work in General." in: *Documentation, Encounters*, vol. 1, no. 2, Markfield, LE (UK) 1995, p. 100 and p. 85.
24. Osman (*Human Rights*, 1996), p. 24.
25. Schulze has shown this even for the 18th century.
26. According to Pinn, p. 70.

for religion everywhere. With their involvement in social work, they counter "me-societies" with the solidarity of a "we-society" that has always been characteristic of Islam, a community defined by common conduct (group prayer, public fasting, communal pilgrimage, tax for the poor). Where dire circumstances cause such movements to slide into formal illegality, one should not rush into denying them their right to resistance against State oppression which is, after all, guaranteed by Christian and Islamic teaching (42:40) alike.[27]

And yet it is understandable when the West suspects that groups committing acts of violence, although defensively, and those prone to it, would not deliver on democracy if they were to seize power themselves. Would the escalation of violence and counter-violence leading up to a successful democratic revolution not spiral into a renewed suppression of opposition, now by the former underdogs?

Indeed, groups prepared to use violence will typically follow the 8th century example of the Abbasid rebellion against Umayyad tyranny and "excommunicate" their adversaries, so to speak, by disputing their Muslim credentials. Such groups are also likely to idealize a Golden Islamic Period of their choice, claim a Messianic mission, monopolize the correct interpretation of the Qur'an and the *Sunnah*, and operate with deceivingly simple slogans of little practical use, like *"lâ hukma illa'llah"* (all sovereignty is with God).

Until the contrary is proven, it will therefore be difficult to dispel the suspicion that among politically active Muslims there are Islamists, rightly called that way, who are using Islam for their own varied purposes. Why should the Muslim world be capable today of making vanish the very phenomenon of religious hypocrisy (*nifaq*) which figured so prominently even in *al-Madinah* during the Prophet's lifetime and plays such a great role in the Qur'an?

Not to be overlooked: there are specific Muslim political opposition movements, active world-wide, like al-Hizb at-Tahrir (Party of Liberation), which renounce violence out of principle, even where it would be justified in legal theory or advantageous in practical terms. These groups follow the example of the Prophet in pre-Islamic Makkah. Even though the persecution of the small initial Muslim community was severe there, Muhammad did not call to arms. He preferred his companions to emigrate, some first to Ethiopia and then all to *al-Madinah*, rather than mounting armed resistance. It is perhaps to be expected that these groups face especially hard prosecution, because certain governments perceive their attractive tactical pacifism as even more dangerous than terrorist attacks.

"Islamic movements" based and operating in the Occident itself, for the most part, are dominated by Western-educated academics—mostly scientists

---

27. The *sunnah* recommends much, but not unlimited patience with tyrants: *al-Bukhari*, vol. 9, no. 257 and following; *Rassoul, Hadith* no. 7053 and following; *Muslim* no. 4551 and following.

and medical doctors—who appreciate the rule of law as practiced in the United States and Europe and follow Western methods in dealing with academia, the political scene, and the media. There is no justification whatsoever to paint even such well-integrated Muslim groups with the suspicion of lacking sincere conviction as far as democracy and the rule of law is concerned. At present, among Muslims worldwide, there is no greater democratic potential to be found than in these youthful, Western-based Islamic groups. As even Edward Luttwak concedes: "Islamists are the only viable opposition against anti-democratic governments."[28] Their "fundamentalism" is not a "fad," but the choice of an entire generation.

In 1992, during a discussion in Washington, D.C., Hassan al-Turabi put it squarely: "If you want to keep Islam at a distance, you have to stay away from the ballot boxes!"[29] There can indeed be no doubt that in every Muslim country throughout the world, democratic Islamic parties would now win free and fair elections, if there were such a thing.

28. Quoted by Osman (*Human Rights*, 1996), p. 25.
29. al-Turabi (1992), p. 21.

ABDULAZIZ SACHEDINA
1942–

Born in Tanzania, Sachedina studied at Aligarh Muslim University in India and Ferdowsi University in Iran, and he obtained his Ph.D. from the University of Toronto. He has written extensively on Islamic law, ethics, and theology, concentrating for more than a decade on social and political ethics, including interfaith and intrafaith relations and Islamic biomedical ethics. Professor of Religious Studies at the University of Virginia and a prolific author, Sachedina has publications that include *Islamic Messianism, Human Rights and the Conflicts of Culture, The Just Ruler in Shiite Islam*, and *The Islamic Roots of Democratic Pluralism*.

Why Democracy, and Why Now?

After the atrocities of September 11, many of us who are Muslim intellectuals living and working in North America made a discovery that deepened the horrors of that terrible day. We learned, to our intense dismay, that some of the Muslim organizations around us were getting their notions about Islam from imported Middle Eastern or South Asian preachers who pushed a deeply illiberal "us against them" worldview and reviled the proposition that Muslims should learn the basic civic virtues and responsibilities of life in a free, democratic, and pluralist society. Claiming to care only about safeguarding the "purity" of Islam, these preachers of intolerance continue to promote seclusion and mistrust and to slander those of us Muslims who disagree with them as "enemies of Islam."

Seclusion and mistrust lead nowhere, and least of all to the promotion of Islam. The truth is that Muslims today—wherever they live—can only benefit from hearing *more*, not less, about the opportunities connected with democratic civil society, the inspiring demands that flow from civic responsibility, and the ideas that undergird government by consent and ordered liberty. Muslim intellectuals who can help their brothers and sisters critically rethink their political heritage and find their way to a free and faithful future have never been more urgently needed—or more threatened with irrelevance—than they are today.

Worse yet, this irrelevance is at least partly self-inflicted. If the voices of those who could stir discussion of freedom and democracy are silent or unintelligible, the preachers of intolerance will win by default. That must not be allowed to happen.

Too many of us—occupying comfortable, even privileged positions in the academy or the professions, enjoying the freedoms of life in democratic societies—have been "absent without leave" from what should be the fight of our lives: the struggle for liberty of Muslim peoples. This must not continue: Our absence must end, and our silence must stop.

Democracy means, among other things, that people can demand an accounting from their leaders, whether political, religious, or cultural. Have our safe jobs in the ivory tower made us forget our moral responsibility to the community? Can we not see that our indifference to the political and intellectual empowerment of average people—whether on the streets of Cairo and Karachi or around the corner at our local mosque—has allowed the most backward elements among the traditional religious leadership, the ulama, to come far too close to setting themselves up as the sole custodians of political and social education? Their ideas might be foolish, benighted, and far from authentically Islamic, but they know how to speak the language of the people, and they are gaining an alarming amount of traction in the Muslim street.

Given that staggering fact, can we afford to wrap our own message in an arcane academic argot that the average Muslim, intelligent but not a specialist, finds impenetrable? The reactionaries among the ulama all too often use populist-sounding rhetoric to prop up retrograde and conformist attitudes toward existing unfree governments. Muslim autocrats need their court preachers to lend a veneer of Islamic legitimacy to dictatorship, and the ulama (at least in the Sunni world) need the rulers to keep the money flowing to the religious establishment.

The preachers may not have the people's best interests at heart, but they know how to talk the people's talk. It is this sociological fact that needs our undivided attention today. The answer to the question "Why democracy, and why now?" must be sought in the moral numbness and political indifference to injustice that prevail today across far too large a swath of the Muslim world.

Let me be clear: Fostering a positive understanding of democratic ideals within an Islamic framework will take the best efforts that a host of intellectual specialists can muster. For this is not a matter of superficial "Islamizing" verbiage, but rather of a deep and comprehensive effort to show both the learned and the lay in Muslim societies that democratic ideas can and must be thought from within the authentic ethical culture of Islam and its teachings about the awesome accountability of human beings in this world and the next.

We need to learn how to guide ourselves and our community back to the sources, to the living heart of Islamic belief, and take seriously the emphasis that we find there on building nurturing, constructive relationships of justice and charity at all levels of human existence. By taking Islam seriously in this way, I believe, we will come to see perhaps more clearly than ever that the kinds of relationships our faith enjoins us to build cannot exist without respect for the equal dignity of all human persons and a broad appreciation for the God-given liberty of the human conscience.

I also believe that we will find ulama—and here I am thinking especially of the rising generation among them—who are willing to make this journey with us, who are not pathologically distrustful of intellectuals or hopelessly compromised by too close a proximity to power, and who will agree about much of that which constitutes the common good. Their help will be crucial in dismantling political and religious authoritarianism and building democratic institutions.

One need not be a secularist in order to seek a practical consensus on the basis of which peoples of diverse backgrounds and religious opinions can relate fairly with one another. To engage the more tractable elements among the ulama in fruitful ways, and to outargue the extremists, we need to do a better job of learning about and discussing classical Islamic traditions so that we can meet religious interlocutors and opponents on their own ground, and not allow anyone to dismiss us as "outsiders" to our own religion. It's fine for us to produce critical scholarship in sociology and anthropology that wins plaudits from our colleagues in the Western universities where we teach. Yet we must also learn to challenge and persuade a Muslim community at large—and this includes many Muslims living in the West—that still mistakes the rantings of Sayyid Qutb and Maulana Maududi (neither of whom was much of an Islamic scholar and both of whom came from secular educational backgrounds, by the way) for the last word in "authentically Islamic" thought about the modern world.

We also need to care about what is being taught in Muslim seminaries and theological faculties, and we need to study—carefully and in detail —how these teachings affect the political thinking of Muslim peoples. On subjects such as the rights of women or non-Muslim minorities, too many ulama and too many seminaries are disseminating illiberal, antidemocratic attitudes and attacking anything that smacks of rationality and tolerance.

In 2002, I spent eight months in Iran. During my stay, I had intense conversations with scholars at Islamic seminaries and Iranian universities alike. I came away convinced that we Muslim intellectuals living in the West absolutely must end our irrelevance and take up the crucial role that only we—or more precisely, our ideas—can play in renewing the way Muslims think about politics and society. Unless and until our critical scholarship is translated and disseminated to the seminaries and theological faculties of the Muslim world—and to Islamic institutions right here in our own backyards—it is impossible for me to see how the reformist renewal that we all hope and pray for can take off and change the future.

It is in light of all this that we should appreciate the work that is being done by some dissident scholars in Iran and Egypt. They are writing in Persian and Arabic, and speaking directly to people who long to understand how their religion is relevant to modern times, and desperate to hear of word of hope as they labor under oppression. Autocrats can and do make the lives of these brave scholars very hard. But even one article by one of them—a critique, perhaps, of the spuriously "Islamic" arguments that the local religious establishment uses to justify its absolutism and obscurantism —does the work of thousands of books that we produce here: That's how much evidence there is to show that Muslim dissident scholarship in Western languages has not reached the people who can rethink Islamic theology and Islamic juridical traditions by applying modern findings about the study of religion.

As Muslim scholars who wish to assist the culture of tolerance in the Muslim world and help our fellows in their search for truth, we require not only cultural legitimacy in order to reach intelligent Muslim audiences, but also the means to transmit our research in languages that can carry our ideas to a wide public outside the West.

Speaking of matters closer to home, I believe that there are a number of scholars here in the United States whose work could foster better inter-faith and intercommunal relations and lead to badly needed change in our own local Muslim communities. We've seen narrow–mindedness propagated here and abroad for a quarter-century, and we know that buckets of petrodollars still grease the way for extremist individuals and organizations that traduce Islam while claiming to promote it. Overcoming their false appeals and winning acceptance for "dissident" thought will be a long-term project, but that is all the more reason to get started now. We should all leave here tonight thinking of ways to reach out to our community, to combat the confusion of obscurantism with faithfulness to Islam, and to counteract the intolerance and bigotry that are taught in too many Muslim institutions in America, Europe, Asia, Africa, and the Middle East.

I have no illusions that any of this will be easy. Backwardness and extremism have powerful backers with deep pockets—just look at who gets invited to speak at so many Muslim gatherings in the West. But that is our challenge, and more, our sacred duty.

ABDOLKARIM SOROUSH
1945–

Born in Tehran and initially trained as a pharmacologist and philosopher, Abdolkarim Soroush studied history and philosophy of science, particularly the philosophy of Karl Popper and Thomas Kuhn, in the United Kingdom. During the months preceding the Islamic revolution of Iran, Soroush had a major role in the gatherings of young Muslims, opponents of the Shah's regime, that took place in the London *imam-barah*. His book *Dialectical Antagonism*, a compilation of his lectures delivered in the *imam-barah*, was published in Iran. When the revolution began in 1979, Soroush returned to Iran. In the spring of 1980, Soroush was appointed a member of the Council for the Cultural Revolution, established by Āyatullāh Khumayni, but resigned in 1982. Soroush became a member of Iran's Academy of Sciences in 1990 and was Dean of the Research Institute for Human Sciences in Teheran. His writings and audiotapes on social, political, religious, and literary subjects delivered all over the world are widely circulated in Iran and elsewhere. He has been a Visiting Professor at Harvard University, Yale University, and Princeton University.

Tolerance and Governance: A Discourse on Religion and Democracy

1. THE PRINCIPLES OF A RELIGIOUS DEMOCRATIC GOVERNMENT: A SYNOPSIS

"The Idea of Religious Democratic Government" . . . alluded to a number of pivotal principles that are of cardinal significance to the architecture of religious democracy:

A. The combination of religion and democracy is an example of the concordance of religion and reason. Thus, the efforts and experiments of religiously sympathetic thinkers in the latter domain will be of use in the former. It is evident that such attempts are at once religious, useful, and well-precedented. They are by no means tainted by antireligious intentions or treacherous tendencies to supplant religiosity with worldliness.

From Ahmad Sadri and Mahmoud Sadri, eds., *Reason, Freedom, and Democray in Islam* (Oxford University Press, 2000), pp. 131–155.

B. The combination of religion and democracy is a metareligious artifice that has at least some extrareligious epistemological dimensions. Therefore, the exclusive reliance on the religious laws and myopic focus on intrareligious adjudications [*ijtihad-e fiqhi*] in order to confirm or reject democratic religiosity are ill-considered and unsound.

C. Whether we consider democracy as a successful method to delimit power, attain justice, and achieve human rights or as a value that tacitly embraces all those objectives, it is the religious understanding that will have to adjust itself to democracy not the other way around; justice, as a value, can not be religious. It is religion that has to be just. Similarly, methods of limiting power are not derived from religion, although religion benefits from them. In any case the question of whether or not democracy has the above advantages can only be decided outside religion, prior to its acceptance, and as a prelude to its understanding. The same reasoning holds for the relationship of religion and human rights, which is—not unlike the debate on free will—a theological and metareligious argument that influences the understanding and acceptance of religion.

D. In autocratic governments, the right of arbitration is left to the power and will of the few; in democratic governments, it is left to the dynamic common wisdom; in religious society, it is left to religion.

E. In a religious society, it is not religion per se that arbitrates, but some understanding of religion which is, in turn, changing, rational, and in harmony with the consensual and accepted extrareligious criteria.

F. Religious society is the supporter, sponsor, source, and succor of the religious politics. Without a religious society, the religious democratic government would be inconceivable.

The above synopsis provides a valid starting point and a correct formulation of—if not an actual solution to—the problem of the combination of religion and democracy. The present argument, unlike the writings of some Islamic thinkers, makes no attempt to place the entire weight of the conceptual edifice of democracy upon the frail shoulders of such (intrareligious) precepts as consultation [*shura*], consensus of the faithful [*ijma'*], and oath of loyalty to a ruler [*bei'at*]. Rather, the discourse on religious government should commence with a discussion of human rights, justice, and restriction of power (all extrareligious issues). Only then should one try to harmonize one's religious understanding with them.

2. SHARED NOTIONS OF JUSTICE, HUMAN RIGHTS, AND LIMITED POWER IN DEMOCRACY AND IN RELIGION

In the opinion of believers, justice is at once a prerequisite for and a requirement of religious rules. A rule that is not just is not religious. Justice, in turn, aims to fulfill needs, attain rights, and eliminate discrimination and inequity. Thus, justice and human rights are intimately connected. The rights concerning government, power, and the just relationship between the ruler and the ruled are among the most significant elements of these rights. Therefore, the effort to restrain and restrict power is closely related to the establishment of justice and human rights. Indeed, the two efforts are in such constant exchange and harmony that any trouble or tension in one reverberates in the other. Justice, then, is a metareligious category, and the right and acceptable religion should, inevitably, be just. The same is true of other categories such as discovery and derivation of methods of just government, distribution and restriction of power, and the specific instances of human rights.

All of the above issues have, primarily and logically, a rational—not a religious—origin. Religion (in itself) and religious understanding (religion for us) rely on these rational precepts. Once the status of reason, particularly the dynamic collective reason, is established; once the theoretical, practical, and historical advances of humanity are applied to the understanding and acceptance of religion; once extrareligious factors find an echo within the religious domain; and finally, once religion is rationalized, then the way to epistemological pluralism—the centerpiece of democratic action—will be paved.

Sober and willing—not fearful and compulsory—practice of religion is the hallmark of a religious society. It is only from such a society that the religious government is born. Such religiosity guarantees both the religious and the democratic character of the government. Democracy needs not only sobriety and rationality but liberty and willing participation. The above rationality (which is not to be adopted halfheartedly) is realized when the innerreligious and outerreligious domains are harmonized. This rational sensibility permits the transformation and variation of religious understanding. The acknowledgment of such varieties of understanding and interpretation will, in turn, introduce flexibility and tolerance to the relationship of the ruling and the ruled, confirm rights for the subjects, and introduce restraints on the behavior of the rulers. As a result, the society will become more democratic, humane, reasonable, and fair. Expansion and contraction of knowledge, its constant renewal, the perception of truth as an elusive labyrinthine path, the recognition of man as a tarnished, slothful, and fallible creature who, nevertheless, possesses an array of natural rights have all been among the necessary prerequisites for and epistemological and anthropological foundations of democracy. If these same principles are included in religious knowledge and respected by religious people, the result will be religious democracy. Practical and governmental regulations and social relationships are born out of theoretical presuppositions, just as branches feed on roots. The root of democracy is a novel insight that humanity has gained about itself and the limitations of its knowledge. Wherever this seed is allowed to germinate, the external manifestations of democracy will, inevitably, bloom.

3. THE PARADOX OF "DEMOCRATIC RELIGIOUS GOVERNMENT": A CRITICAL EXCHANGE

Some critics, however, have deemed the idea of democratic religious government preposterous. They point to such phenomena and rules as gender and belief inequality in the Moslem societies, theocracy, the absolute authority of the jurisconsults, designation of death penalty on apostates, the regarding of infidels as impure, dogmatism of beliefs, and the general inflexibility of the rules of religious decrees as evidence of the inherent animosity of religion and religious government toward democracy. They further accuse the adherents of the compatibility of democracy and religion, of ignorance about the true nature of religion. (See Mr. Hamid Paydar's "The Paradox of Islam and Democracy," *Kiyan*, no. 19.)

Three dark and dangerous errors dim the horizon of judgment of the above thesis. First, Democracy is equated with extreme liberalism. Second, religious jurisprudence [*shari'ah*] is severed from its foundations, quoted out of context, and then presented as evidence. Third, and most important, religious democratic government is equated with religious jurisprudential [*fiqhi*] government and attacked as a monolithic whole. It should be unequivocally stated that all three assumptions are erroneous.

If the debate is over the compatibility of the religious jurisprudential government, with democracy, then the sponsors of the above-mentioned regime themselves avoid the title of democracy; they even take great pride and delight in opposing it, because they consider democracy as a fruit of the secular Western culture. The excerpts the critics quote from the declarations of some religious scholars and orators in order to portray religious democracy as a "paradox" reveal the critics' misperception of religious democracy, which they identify with the religious jurisprudential government.

The truth, however, is that religious law [*shari'ah*] is not synonymous with the entirety of religion; nor is the debate over the democratic religious government a purely jurisprudential argument. Moreover, jurisprudential statements are different from epistemological ones, and no methodic mind should conflate the two realms. Evidently, a jurisprudential conception of Islam has so occupied certain minds that epistemological arguments are allowed to pose as jurisprudential propositions. Democracy itself, in some circles, is treated as a religious practice, subject to ritual prescription or proscription.

Democracy is comprised of a method of restricting the power of the rulers and rationalizing their deliberations and policies, so that they will be less vulnerable to error and corruption, more open to exhortation, moderation, consultation; and so that violence and revolution will not become necessary. Separation of powers, universal compulsory education, freedom and autonomy of the press, freedom of expression, consultative assemblies on various levels of decision making, political parties, elections, and parliaments are all methods of attaining and securing democracy. Conversely, a nation that is illiterate, unfamiliar with its rights, and unable to attain them, in other words, a nation deprived of the right to criticize and choose, will be unable to achieve democracy.

Agnosticism and indecision, however, are by no means necessary foundations of or prerequisites for democracy. On the contrary, constant review, critique, and renewal of ideas and beliefs, followed by emendation, calibration, and transformation of the policies and decisions of rulers and their powers are among the routine responsibilities of democratic societies. There is no doubt that a democracy is engaged in an interminable process of choosing and examining, while a religious society believes that it has made a crucial choice and that it has the answer within its reach: it has chosen the path of religiosity and has determined to live in the shade of a religious belief. However, this preliminary decision of religious societies paves the way to innumerable subsequent decisions and arduous trials. From there on, it is religious understanding that needs to undergo constant examination. It will have to pass through difficult cycles of contraction, expansion, modification, and equilibrium:

> On the path of love, a hundred hazards lie, beyond oblivion, yet;
> So you won't say: once I reach my life's end, I'll have escaped.

The venerable author of the essay on "Paradox of Islam and Democracy" observes: "Islam and democracy can not be combined, unless Islam is thoroughly secularized." This belief stems from the assumption that relativistic liberalism and democracy are identical. Democracy, however, does not require believers to abandon their convictions, secularize their creed, and lose faith in divine protection. Why should a religion that is freely and enthusiastically adopted be cast away? Why shouldn't the believers be allowed to strengthen and spread their belief? The practice that truly violates democracy is not embracing a faith but the imposition of a particular belief or punishment of disbelief. Needless to say, these practices are impermissible and undesirable in a democratic religious government. (Although some may condone them under a jurisprudential religious government.)

Mr. Paydar regards the principle of free choice as prior to human fallibility and considers the realm of ideas as "the most important manifestation of human free choice." He proposes that human beings are free to choose religion or irreligion at any time and under any conditions, thus equating freedom with indecision. The logical flaws of such an argument notwithstanding, one may point out that it still does not mean that a self-determining religious society is unfree or that religion and democracy are incompatible. It seems Mr. Paydar has not noticed that freedom does not necessitate permanent ambivalence and inability to reach, or act upon, a decision. Embracing a faith, relying upon it, committing to it, and believing in it—independent and autonomous decisions—are not contrary to the freedom of choice. This is the meaning of the theological dictum "Self-imposed restraint is no restraint!"

It is not the assumption of free will or the belief in the fallibility of human beings in liberal societies that causes religion to abdicate the office of final judgment. Nor are these assumptions responsible for the neutrality of the liberal government and prevalence of the scientific and practical evaluation of religion. There is another epistemological fact that is partly responsible for this separation: Liberal philosophers consider metaphysical arguments unverifiable and unfalsifiable. Consequently, they deem controversy over the truth or falsehood of religious beliefs futile and interminable. They point to the permanence, doctrinal rigidity, and plurality of divergent religious practices as historical evidence. Therefore, they advocate peaceful coexistence of a multiplicity of belief systems. Their neutral stance enables them to dismiss the interreligious strife as a futile pursuit of truth in the quagmire of delusions. Or else, they view the variety and plurality of beliefs as consistent with a divine plan to distribute heavenly guidance in many disguises.

However, let's remind ourselves that these same liberal societies, their unshakable belief in the freedom of the will and fallibility of man notwithstanding, will never relinquish the reins of decision making concerning lucid and well-examined affairs to the popular whim. Nor do they warrant indiscriminate reexamination of all things. No liberal government would base its modern technology upon the Aristotelian physics or reexamine such obsolete theories as the Flogeston theory of combustion, which prevailed before the oxygen theory of combustion. Nor would it experimentally expose people to such deadly diseases as plague and small pox. No one is allowed, under the penalty of law, to free those accursed demons from their enchanted dungeons. In the meantime, a colorful assortment of religious creeds is allowed to multiply and spread. In other words, although the state in liberal governments stays neutral toward religious claims, it does not remain impartial concerning scientific achievements. It is true, then, that the liberal society is no longer a religious society but a scientific one. The same status accorded to religion and religious certitude in religious societies is ascribed to science in liberal societies. The experimental, verifiable, and falsifiable scientific rules have deservedly reached such a grandeur and glory that no freedom-loving thinker would contemplate their arbitrary castigation, just as no wise and vigilant person would relegate the judgment of those scientific rules to laymen and dilettantes. Science, however fallible as a human achievement, has been so well elaborated, thanks to courageous and free human critique and refinement, that it has attained an unassailable status. This exalted position of science has not diminished human free will and dignity, nor has it curtailed, in the least, the liberal identity of the society. If in these societies religion is not an equal partner with science, it is not because liberalism considers human beings as autonomous decision makers and allows them to constantly change their religion but because it does not recognize science and religion as analogous bodies of knowledge. And this is established epistemologically, not through popular vote. Therefore, the religious attitude (relegating the judgment to the shared religious knowledge) maintains the same epistemological relationship to democracy as does the scientific attitude (relegating judgement to the shared wisdom of practitioners). Another error of Mr. Paydar is equating freedom of choice with indecision, ambivalence, irresolution, and an absence of a basis for judgment, thus declaring religion and democracy incompatible. However, religious knowledge is, potentially, as open to criticism as scientific knowledge; the authority of religion in religious knowledge is as invalid as the authority of science in the scientific knowledge. Contraction and expansion of scientific knowledge and religious knowledge share the same vicissitudes and trajectories.

Mr. Paydar has (incorrectly) surmised that liberalism is neutral on the subjects of science or religion. He has equated liberalism's skeptical credo of fallibility of human knowledge with utter neutrality. It is true that the liberal society has taken the above principles as the groundwork of its life and belief; however, in practice, as a result of those very criticisms, the society has adopted specific positions with respect to science and religion and no longer countenances their infringement.

The prophets of the liberal philosophy are not only Mill, Locke, Rousseau, Smith, Bayle, Voltaire, and (among contemporaries) Rawls and Friedman; but Kant, Hume, and—among contemporaries—Russell, Quine, and Carnap as well. The latter group should be included among the founders and supporters of the liberal society because they share the belief that unraveling the intricate knots of metaphysical questions is improbable. They go even farther by declaring any involvement with metaphysical subjects as exceeding the boundaries of rationality altogether. However, had religion enjoyed as popular an epistemological niche as science and had it not been weakened by the philosophical and scientific forays of the Western scholars, the society could have, conceivably, remained both "religious" and democratic, just as it has remained "scientific" and democratic.

Parting with metaphysics meant, for the West, parting with all of its requisites: the church and the clergy, divine laws, ethics, religious strictures, clerical government, and pious submission. In short, every religious institution that oversaw the temporal affairs in any way was abandoned. It was such a rupture that, in Kant's words, liberated humanity from its "infancy" and placed the destiny and determination of all affairs in its hands. Thereafter, man reached an unprecedented centrality (even Godliness) in world history. Liberal freedom was freedom from the fetters of religion and metaphysics. It was freedom from divine guardianship. This freedom had an epistemological and rational basis. Liberal philosophers did not discover man's fallibility and free will. They discovered the irrelevance of metaphysics. This, their most important achievement, combined with the advent of scientific knowledge and free economy, shaped the liberal society. But, atheism, by itself, does not entail emancipation from tyranny and totalitarianism. Communism, too, professed atheism but it fostered an utterly ruthless form of dictatorship. Thus, democracy is neither a result of atheism nor an ally of it. Equating liberalism and democracy signifies, at once, great ignorance of the former and grave injustice toward the latter. The liberal democratic society has plural foundations. Its many bases, while not mutually conflicting, are far from being mutually indispensable. It is, therefore, logically possible to separate them. The idea of democratic religious society is a result of logical decoupling of democracy and liberalism. As such, it is analogous to the attempts of the social democrats to separate democracy from capitalism.

The opponents of religious democracy usually conclude that since liberalism is identical with or a requirement of democracy and since religiosity has no affinity with liberalism; therefore, religiosity can not coexist with democracy. However, as we have argued above, the premise is not correct.

ABID ULLAH JAN
1965–

A political analyst from Pakistan who graduated from the University of London, Abid Ullah Jan writes extensively on democracy, Islam, and terrorism, including *A War on Islam?* and *The End of Democracy.*

Compatibility: Neither Required nor an Issue

> Can Islam produce a comparable religious argument in support of modernity and democracy? The answer is that we do not know. We must hope and pray that it can and will. But this we do know: If it is true, as some still say, that liberal democracy is inseparable from secularism, liberal democracy has a very dim future in a world of resurgent religion.[1]
>
> Richard John Neuhaus

Much of the recent literature on Islam focuses on the question of whether Islam is or can be made compatible with democracy, an inquiry closely related to (but not as vigorously researched as) finding out if incompatibility is really as much a threat as is being presented. Interestingly, no one asks what will happen if Muslims are allowed to form their own institutions and models on the basic principles of Islam which can, at the very least, serve as an antidote to anti-Westernism and global insecurity.

Instead the focus has been on the misconception that only a "soft," "civil" and "moderate" Islam can live with free elections, tolerate a free press, grant equal rights to women, tolerate secular authorities, and the rest. Although there is little agreement on this subject, one of the earmarks of "soft" Islam is the assumption that only it can coexist with democratic political institutions.

Events and discussions surrounding developing constitutions for Iraq and Afghanistan suggest that Western leaders and political thinkers raise the prospect of submissive dictatorships into unpredictable nations. Thus

---

1. Richard John Neuhaus, "Democracy vs. Religion," published at www.zenit.org. ZENIT is an International News Agency based in Rome whose mission is to provide objective and professional coverage of events, documents, and issues emanating from or concerning the Catholic Church for a worldwide audience, especially the media.

Reprinted by permission of the author.

democracy and reform are now strongly linked to some newly invented versions of Islam for preserving the new order.

Lack of interest in granting the right to self-determination to Muslim countries has been rationalized by the assertion that Islam is not compatible with democracy unless it is reformed. Those who argue that a governance mechanism based on the basic principles of Islam vis-à-vis sovereignty, legislation and due place for *Shari'ah* will turn Muslim countries to police states do not feel equally disturbed that few rulers in the Muslim world have been democratically elected and that many who speak of democracy and "moderation" actually believe only in self-perpetuation at all costs.

The baseless threat of an Islamic State has contributed to support for these repressive regimes. In fact, there can never be truly representative governments in the Muslim world as long as the influential players from outside continue to look at Islam in compatible and incompatible terms with democracy. The subsequent repression, desperation and violence in these societies are blamed on "Islamists," thus confirming all scare mongering theories.

SETTING THE CONTEXT

To avoid a long-term conflict, instead of working hard to make relevant to Islam a concept that is so problematic even within western political culture,[2] we need to do a realistic threat assessment of the Islamic State based on the fundamental principles of Islam to take the steam out of the argument that an Islamic State might suppress opposition, lack tolerance, deny pluralism, and violate human rights.

For example, one needs to find out the elements of threat in the following broad outline: In today's world, a Modern Islamic Republic is

a. Modern—that it must include all the organs of a "state craft" vis-à-vis legislative, executive, judiciary and press;

b. Islamic—that there should be no law, regulation or decision (nothing) against the Qur'an and the *Sunnah*, and

c. A Republic and a Welfare State—the state must be responsible for the welfare of every citizen.

If these aspects are practically implemented in Muslim states, the so-labelled "rejectionists" would be left with no ground to seek to topple governments through violent revolutions. There would be no threat to the stability of their societies and to global politics.

The need is to prove that the issue of compatibility is irrelevant. What is important to prove is that if democracy ensures legitimacy of the government, accountability, transparency, and the rule of law, so does Islam.

2. Joseph Farah, "Taking America Back," Thomas Nelson Inc. 2003.

There is a need to compare the fear of perceived repression in a so far non-existent Islamic State with the established democracies vis-à-vis their ways of legitimising war on Iraq, their passing Islamophobic anti-terrorist legislations, and their abusive incarceration of political prisoners in modern-day concentration camps.

Muslims need not be forced to one way or the other Islamize western democracy. They need freedom to develop models of social and political organization, based on Islamic values and principles that are suitable for the complexities of modern societies. Muslims would long have found their ways to reasserting the values of Islam in public life against the stagnant tyrannies, provided the natural evolution of Muslim societies had not been derailed by the destructive impact of continued colonialism.

Compatibility of democracy with Islam must not mean endorsement of all that comes from non-Muslim societies and rejecting the core of Islam. The Islamic model might well have certain elements in common with western democratic institutions, such as elections to determine public opinion; but, if it genuinely reflects Islamic goals and priorities, it will be quite different in key respects.

Most importantly, Muslims' primary goal is to develop, establish and nurture a society driven by Faith. The structure of government becomes secondary to this goal. Unfortunately, each of the major Muslim governments has drifted from this foundation and the Muslim world faces a two-pronged crisis of Faith: a general lack of Faith among the masses, and an abandonment of Faith among the educated elite for materialist aims. Simply, Muslims are proving themselves no less capitalist than the capitalists.

An Islamic democracy would first need to be able to exist without inheriting any of the shackles of its predecessors. Besides, unless it is born from the faith of the masses and the elite, any attempts to implement any sort of Islamic rule will be an unwelcome imposition on a population not ready for it. No legitimate government can be implemented with a top-down approach, and an Islamic democracy is no exception.

An Islamic model, however, does not mean a threat to global security and others' interest at all. The need is to understand that a true Islamic model would neither be a threat to non-Muslims nor will it be exactly according to the formulaic definitions of *Khilafah* of some contemporary Islamic groups.

Before agreeing on deep and extensive changes within the Muslim world for compatibility with democracy, we need to go a bit deeper to see what principles of democracy we are comparing with Islam and also if we are not comparing two incomparable concepts or systems in the first place.

The debate over compatibility of democracy with Islam intensified just after the end of the Cold War. In 1992, when the campaign was reshaping, Amos Perlmutter, a leading light in US foreign policy, had no hesitation in writing in the *Washington Post*: "Is Islam, fundamentalist or otherwise, compatible with liberal, human rights-oriented, Western-style, representative democracy? The answer is clearly no."[3]

It was the time when the "democratic" world chose to shut its eyes on abrupt suspension of elections in Algeria and used a massive military operation to restore the Emir of Kuwait to his throne.

The cultural assessment of Islam—asking if culture, values and attitudes of ordinary Muslims obstruct the democratization process in Muslim countries—smacks of barely-disguised racism. The encompassing message of Islam and its application over all aspects of human life—as a *Deen* (a politico-socio-economic whole), not merely a religion—makes the core principles of democracy (except the strings of human sovereignty and secularism) just one of its many components. It is unjustified in the first place to attempt to find out if Islam fits into the democratic design. It is something akin to fitting the whole into its component parts.

This line of argument serves three objectives:

a. to justify indefinite occupations on the grounds that developing democratic institutions in an inhospitable environment of Islam is a lifelong task;

b. to support authoritarian regimes on the ground that they are not pressured towards democracy because they are supposed to respect their "cultural specificity"; and

c. to justify the campaigns for diluting Islam with the objective to eliminate its challenge to maintaining the status quo.

"REBUILDING" ISLAM FOR DEMOCRACY

Muslims have many reasons to believe that democracy's compatibility with Islam is yet another stunt to highlight that Islam does not care about human freedoms, whereas secular democracy has made the people sovereign and supreme. That is why despite admitting, "there is nothing about it [Islam] that immutably contradicts democracy," Daniel Pipes criticizes Muqtedar Khan for ducking the question, "whether Islam and democracy are essentially incompatible," because Pipes believes the *Shari'ah* makes it incompatible.[4] Actually, such an argument is based on the anticipation of Muslims to claim that Islam and democracy are incompatible.

It seems that democracy is more compatible with Islam than the policies of the US and its allies. Those who criticize Islam do not explain why the US should assist the Muslim world in bringing real democratic revolution when it can retain control through unrepresentative rulers, whom it can

3. Amos Perlmutter, "Islam and Democracy Simply Aren't Compatible," *International Herald Tribune*, Paris, January 21, 1992.

4. Daniel Pipes, "The Rock Star and the Mullah, Debate: Democracy and Islam," a PBS debate between Daniel Pipes and Muqtedar Khan. http://www.pbs.org/wnet/wideangle/shows/junoon/debate.html.

force to chase "terrorists" on its behalf, and whom it can use as secular bulwarks against the so-perceived Islamic challenge to the status quo.

Muslims' obligation to live by Islam has been turned into a cause to designate Islam as constituting multi-headed monsters. However, the Islamic State, particularly a single Islamic State that implements the fundamentals of Islam, is the non-Muslim world's only safe guarantee against terrorism and anti-Westernism. If it met the *Shari'ah* requirements, it would be able to control *Jihad*, which has always been seen as a state activity. Those who perforce have to carry on an unprecedented "private" *Jihad* because of oppression will be bound to follow the decisions of the Islamic State on whether or not their struggle constitutes a *Jihad*.

Although it is some specially drafted brand of Islam that is touted to be compatible with democracy, moderation and a conciliatory approach are indeed part of the Islamic path. At the same time, Islam is as much a "religion of militancy," as the US justified all aggression after 9/11. Islam does teach to turn the other cheek to oppression and injustice. Nevertheless, Islam has nothing against modernisation, and it can accept certain elements of modern-day democracy. To be precise: a) Islam does not accept the concept of sovereignty belonging to the people as legislation can be derived only from the Qur'an and *Sunnah* and b) Islam cannot be reconciled with secularism.

Secularism assumes that all religions have value, or that none do. Islam includes as integral to its belief its own correctness and the falseness of other belief systems, though their practitioners are under protection. Although Islam literally means "acceptance," and Kufr "rejection," there is no concept of compulsion or per force conversion to Islam (Al-Qur'an 2:256).

For those who accept Islam, they have to do it completely without any ifs and buts (Al-Qur'an 2:208). They also have to live every moment of their life according to the revealed standards (5:44–47) and they cannot accept or reject parts of the Qur'an (2:85). Thus, "soft" or "civil" Islam is a compromise somehow between Islam and non-Islam. This is unfair both to Muslims, who are denigrated, and to non-Muslims, who are being misled about what Islam actually demands. An honourable co-existence is possible between Muslims and the rest, but only on parity and co-acceptance. Muslims may aspire for it, but the US and former colonialists would prefer to maintain the present master-client relationship.

ISLAMIC VALUES VS. SECULARISM

Some Muslims, undoubtedly, marvel when they find a tenet of Islam matching the concept of democracy and proudly declare that Islam is compatible with democracy. Similarly, others quickly reject Islam when it challenges the godless and spiritually bankrupt aspects of democracy. In fact, if we take out the goodness of democracy, we will see that the Qur'an identified all these social and political values 1400 years ago.

Khaled Abou El Fadl has rightly identified these values as "pursuing justice through social cooperation and mutual assistance (the Qur'an 49:13; 11:119); establishing a non-autocratic, consultative method of governance; and institutionalizing mercy and compassion in social interactions (6:12, 54; 21:107; 27:77; 29:51; 45:20)."[5] Yet these fine values can never be fostered in an environment that throws religion out of the public square and which has now been turned into a cornerstone for democracy.

Actually, when religion is thrown out, permanent norms are replaced with a broad, generic perspective called secularism, an over-arching principle under which falls a variety of systems: Positivism, Hedonism, Pragmatism, Pluralism (and its corollary, Relativism), Existentialism and Humanism. One has to study the far-reaching impact of this denial of the eternal and the transcendent on every aspect of society. The fundamental conviction of secularism that *this time* and *this place* are all there is and there is no eternal dimension leads to a kind of personality and ultimately a society in which fostering the values of justice and mercy becomes almost impossible. When there is no eternity, no eternal perspective, there are left no absolutes or abiding principles by which to evaluate human actions and values.

In the end we may have secular democracy but with a despair hardly any different under the secular Baathist regime in Iraq or communists in former Soviet Union. Islam bears no grudge with democracy, but when *the ontological* position of secularism is taken to its logical conclusion, we come to the remainder of its cardinal points that have no place in Islam: There is no ultimate significance to human life, there are no ultimate consequences and there are no ultimate answers to the human predicament. Humankind lives out its existence in a sphere that is bound inexorably by this space and time.

Any thinking person who adopts a worldview dependent upon secularism must ultimately embrace a philosophy of despair, for according to such a belief system *there is no tomorrow*—ultimately. Some of the practical results are before us. More than 531,000 Americans attempt suicide each year. Suicide accounts for more deaths than homicide, and is the eighth leading cause of death in the US. Doctors say depression is as disabling as end stage heart disease.[6] They believe it is particularly important to treat children and adolescents for depression—because their brains "learn to be depressed like they learn to ride a bicycle." At the top level, the unjust and hypocritical foreign policy of the US government is just another reflection of the rot at the core.

5. Khaled Abou El Fadl, "Islam and the Challenge of Democracy," *Boston Review* 2003. See http://bostonreview.mit.edu/BR28.2/abou.html.

6. In 2000, suicide was the 11th leading cause of death in the United States. Suicide was the 3rd leading cause of death among young people 15 to 24 years of age, following unintentional injuries and homicide. National Institute of Mental Health Care, Bethesda, Maryland 20892, US. Figures updated April 11, 2003.

The increasing stress on making secularism part and parcel of democracy makes it incompatible with Islam, which demands living and judgment according to the revealed standards. Of course, theoretically democracy is supposed to offer the greatest potential for promoting justice and protecting dignity. Countries such as Canada would go on to establish even *Shari'ah* courts. However, a closer examination of prevailing democracies clearly suggests that in the absence of an environment developed in accordance with the basic principles of Islam, it is impossible for human beings to discharge many of their responsibilities that lead to a just social order.

Establishing a just order through democracy alone is impossible because it is not the end in itself as the war lords in the US would like us to believe. Democracy is a fraction of the means to human governance, human development, stable patterns of human interactions and, above all, the purpose of human existence. It can never reach the abiding influence of Islamic faith on the common relations of mankind in the affairs of everyday life; its deep power over the masses, its regulation of their conception of rights and duty, its suitability and adaptability to the ignorant savage and the wise philosopher are characteristic features which democracy can learn from Islam. Fraction always benefits from the whole. Democracy is a fraction of the total, encompassing message of Islam.

On the other hand, Islam is an organic unity, whereby the stress on good actions is not at the expense of correctness of faith. While some religions may praise faith at the expense of deeds and others exhaust various acts to the detriment of correct belief, Islam is based on correct faith and righteous actions. Means are important as the end and ends are as important as the means. Together they live and thrive.

Let us clearly understand the relation of governance with the teaching of Islam. Democracy has finally come to be ineffective and meaningless unless divorced from religion or married with secularism. That is the reason that not only democracy is meaningless but also Islam becomes meaningless where end is severed from means. In Islam, faith cannot be divorced from the action. There cannot be a full government in operation without any reference to faith. In Islam, right knowledge must be transferred into right action to produce the right results.

Theoretically, both Islam and democracy establish a basis for pursuing justice and making the authorities accountable to all. The objective is to resist the tendency of the powerful to render themselves immune from judgment. Unfortunately, this is exactly what secular democracy has failed to deliver. According to Khaled Abou El Fadl, "if a political system has no institutional mechanisms to call the unjust to account, then the system is itself unjust, regardless of whether injustice is actually committed or not."[7] We witness the same happening in the US despite the much vaunted accountability mechanism in the Constitution. Many inquiries from Waco

---

7. Ibid., Khaled Abou El Fadl, "Islam and the Challenge of Democracy."

to Ruby Ridge, Flight 108, Oklahoma City bombing, September 11 and Anthrax mailing have been completely misdirected to avoid accountability and justice at the highest echelons.

DEBATING COMPATIBILITY IS MISLEADING

The Islamic concept of submission and subsequent accountability both to Allah and the people is more powerful in that it unconditionally subordinates human will to His will and law. It is an ontological requirement and not a condition of any secular contract.

Discussing the compatibility of Islam with democracy is misleading because it takes the focus away from the fact that we did not witness the miracle of secular democracy as a political system with its godless institutional mechanisms to call the unjust to account. If the criminal law does not assign punishment for a man in position of power, it is simply unjust—quite apart from whether that crime is ever committed or not. The world has lived long under the illusion that it is a moral good in and of itself that a democracy at least offers the possibility of redress. "At least offering" is not the answer to what human societies actually need for good governance.

As far as the idea of the popular vote, equal rights, special status of human beings etc. is concerned, no one has any quarrel with the idea of democracy in the Muslim world. It is the idea of sovereign people flouting Qur'anic injunctions and the *Sunnah* that is a matter of concern for Muslims.[8]

The misleading claims that Islam is against democracy and secularism is indispensable imply two things: First, that Islam is threatening democracy, while in reality real democracy and Muslims' right to self-determination have never been promoted in Muslim countries. Secondly, that Islam is inherently anti-Western and the West cannot live with it, which is clearly not the case.

According to the common Western view, Islam and democracy are antithetical because there is no place for secularism in Islam. To the question, "can democracy only succeed in a nation where there is a separation of religion and state?" scholars, like Muqtedar Khan on the one end of a conceptual spectrum and Daniel Pipes on the other, state that secularism may be a desirable, but not a necessary precondition in order to foster state neutrality in a multi-religious society.[9]

---

8. It might be argued that it depends on who is interpreting the Qur'an. The rule of thumb in this regard in the present times is: do not focus too much on who is interpreting the Qur'an; try to find out why. No sincere attempt at interpretation misleads. Confusion arises when interpretation is done to justify a pre-conceived idea, such as justifying homosexuality. Imagine if Muslim homosexuals, such as the Al-Fatiha group in the US, can go to this extreme, justifying other issues through the Qur'an becomes much easier for those with some agenda.

9. Daniel Pipes, "The Rock Star and the Mullah Debate: Democracy and Islam," a PBS debate between Daniel Pipes and Muqtedar Khan. http://www.pbs.org/wnet/wideangle/shows/junoon/debate.html.

However, experience shows that this is not the case. Reality is very different from opinions. A look at the developments over the last 13 years suggests that two consistent themes in much of the contemporary analysis of world affairs have been the impending clash of civilizations and the need for the secularization of the Muslim world.

Indeed, the call to secularize Islam as a means of averting a clash of civilizations is really the first salvo in such a clash. It is a fashionable mantra to suggest that invading Muslim states could transform the Muslim world by bringing the long-denied liberal democracy to them. US Deputy Defense Secretary Paul Wolfowitz is one of the many proponents of secularism. He publicly declared in March 2002 that democracy is incomplete without being secular. In this regard, he believes, "Turkey can be an example for the Muslim World."[10]

Analysts and reporters are helpless before influence of the sources that shape their mindset. For example, reporters from the *Chicago Tribune* wrote, "Washington, we are told, wants to foster secular democracy in Iraq, but alas, the Islamists are resisting."[11] Headlines in the *Hindu* read, "Democracy impossible without secularism."[12] Ramesh Sharma writes, "Democracy should uphold secular ethos."[13] Furthermore, secularism is considered the soul of democracy. Writing in *Dawn*, Dr. Syed Jaffar Ahmed says, "Secularism played a pivotal role in shaping the modern democratic states. . . . It has been accepted as a universal principle for engineering democratic nations."[14] Karen Litfin of the University of Washington goes a step further and argues that even "Sovereignty is inseparable from the secular worldview that has been emblematic of modernity."[15]

With this mindset, any reference to Islam becomes far more painful for many than Mr. Bush's declaration of war on Afghanistan and Iraq, which eventually took more than 100,000 lives and continues to subjugate

10. Jim Garamone, "Wolfowitz Says Turkey's Example Important to Muslim World," American Forces Press Service, July 2002. http://www.defenselink.mil/news/Jul2002/n07152002_200207154.html.
11. Copyright 2003 Chicago Tribune Company, *Chicago Tribune* April 23, 2003, Wednesday, Chicago Final Edition Section: News; Pg. 1; Zone: C Length: 1504 Words Headline: Imams Exercise Newfound Clout; Mosques Gaining Postwar Power. Byline: By Paul Salopek, *Tribune* Foreign Correspondent. *Tribune* Foreign Correspondent Tom Hundley in Qatar contributed to this report.
12. Staff reporter, "Democracy Impossible without Secularism," *The Hindu*, Wednesday, March 27, 2002.
13. Sharma Ramesh. "Democracy Should Uphold Secular Ethos," *The People's Review*, July 11–17, 2002. http://www.yomari.com/p-review/2002/07/11072002/demo.html.
14. Dr. Syed Jaffar Ahmed, "Secularism in the Dock," *Dawn*, July 13, 2003.
15. Karen Litfin. "Secularism, Sovereignty and the Challenge of Global Ecology: Towards a New Story," page 2. Paper prepared for presentation at the workshop on "The Global Ecological Crisis and the Nation State: Sovereignty, Economy and Ecology," Joint Sessions of Workshops of the European Consortium on Political Research, Grenoble, France, 6–11 April 2001.

millions against their will.[16] The reason is the lies that shaped a policy and the baseless threat associated with the establishment of an Islamic state. This fear of Islam is so overwhelming that it blinds most to the injustices and discrimination carried out for denying Muslims an opportunity to self-rule.

Unfortunately, the blind commitment to democracy in the Muslim world is limited to a simple formula: if the secularists take control of the State through elections, it is democracy. However, if people associated with religion succeed to do the same, it is totalitarianism. The secularists then have to become legitimate dictators and usurpers of power to avoid aspiring Muslims from coming to power "democratically."

Samuel P. Huntington's argument for the destabilizing effects of modernization and for the stabilizing effects of institutionalization undermines his own pessimistic view of the incompatibility of Islam with democratic norms. He ignores Western double standards of democracy for the Muslim world and instead points to the revival of "Islamic fundamentalism" as the fundamental reasons for his pessimism.[17] Yet throughout the movements for Islamic revival, we have yet to see the promotion of any values which are against the positive aspects of democracy.

No one is aiming to undermine democratic values. Given the wide range of Islamic responses, the appeal in Muslim countries to unconventional forms of political conduct, including mass uprisings and rioting, is not due to any inherent intolerance of Islam toward democracy and the peaceful settlements of disputes. Islam has always been a source of protest against oppression.

Some Islamic groups do not aim their rejectionist approach towards the West per se for its democratic values but for its domination and continued interference in their domestic affairs. From Indonesia to Algeria, there are numerous examples of religious parties trying to contest elections and come to power through the routine political process. However, the Western-supported repressive measures of Mubarak, the butchery of the Algerian junta and military control in Turkey are some examples that annoy the religious opposition for not finding a level playing field for a real contest.

For Muslims, democracy is not an alternative to Islam because the few golden principles of democracy are already part of Islam. These principles cannot replace Islam's comprehensive package for all spheres of human life. Islam, nevertheless, remains a challenge to the present most exploited form of democracy as we witness today because it has the potential to let human beings develop the most perfect governance mechanism.

16. Editorial, *New York Times*, November 14, 2003. What hurt *NY Times* the most is: "it [Afghanistan's proposed constitution] says that no law can be contrary to the sacred religion of Islam. And it says the members of the Supreme Court should be educated in either civil law or Islamic law, a provision that raises the possibility of more judges who base their rulings on the Koran rather than civil law."

17. Samuel P. Huntington, "Will More Countries Become Democratic?" *Political Science Quarterly* 99 (Summer 1994): 193–218.

It is not that Muslims should embrace secular values for democracy and break up their life into temporal public and religious private spheres. "The Ultimate Reality, according to the Qur'an, is spiritual, and its life consists in its temporal activity. The spirit finds its opportunities in the natural, the material, and the secular. All that is secular is therefore sacred in the roots of its being."[18] It can be understood in the light of the fact that man-made laws could be implemented in an Islamic State with the intention to benefit the community when they emerge from the *Shari'ah* or, to put it another way, the *Shari'ah* would not or could not be opposed to these laws if there is no violation of its limits.

MUSLIMS NEED A BREAK

There is no need to prove that Islam is compatible with democracy or democracy with Islam. All positive aspects of modern democracy are already part of the teachings of Islam just as Prophet Jesus is a fundamental part of Islamic belief and so Muslims do NOT have to be Christians to believe in Prophet Jesus—son of Mary. It is only the institutional structure and other aspects evolved with social evolution that Muslims have to accommodate fully for consolidating an Islamic State.

The US and its allies should not be a hurdle to the establishment of Islamic States. While some so-labelled Islamists are rejectionists, most will be critical and selective in their relations with the West, generally operating on the basis of national interests and showing a flexibility that reflects understanding of the globally interdependent world. The West should demonstrate by word and action its belief that the right to self-determination and representative government extends to all Muslim countries if these reflect the popular will and do not directly threaten Western interests.

Co-acceptance is the key. Policies of the Western governments should do away with the unnecessary fear of Islamic States and must accept the ideological differences between Islam and the rest to the greatest extent possible.

Just as the transformation of Western feudal monarchies to democratic nations was a long, drawn-out process among contending factions with competing interests and visions, so would Islamic democratization proceed by experimentation, and necessarily involves both success and failure. Keeping the bloody and so far failed US adventure in Afghanistan in mind, one can safely say that a little recognition of the Taliban, intellectual input and support for developing an administrative set up on the principles of Islam would have been a good experiment for Islamic democracy as well as successful anti-terrorism efforts.

---

18. Allama Muhammad Iqbal, *The Reconstruction of Religious Thought in Islam*, IAP, 1989, p. 123.

Those who fear the unknown, exaggerating how inhumanly an Islamic State will act once in power, have enough misconceptions to do so. However, if one worries that a democratic Islamic State might suppress opposition, lack tolerance, deny pluralism, and violate human rights, the same concern must apply equally to the plight of those who are living under the most repressive Western-sponsored regimes in the Muslim world. It must be clear that it is definitely not Islam that hinders transformation to democracy nor Islamic principles that justify their never-ending oppression.

If supporting Muslims is not possible, they need to be left alone to shatter the myths of Islam's incompatibility with democratic values through developing Islamic models. These will be general and tentative of necessity, and will need to be tested and refined through historical experience when implemented, which is how social institutions develop; but they will at least be built on sounder foundations than any form of democracy transplanted from western discourse.

If the curse of imposed dictatorships is lifted, promotion of the "war within Islam" for pitting Muslims against each other is called off, and the demonization of Islam is withheld for a while, Muslims have the ability to engage with each other and make a far more constructive contribution to Muslim political discourse than they can by seeking to "Islamise" western-style democracy.

The discussion over compatibility yields nothing. Proving or disproving the threat aspect of an Islamic State would, however, be very helpful. If implementing Islam is not a threat to global peace and security, Muslims must be left alone to exercise their right to self-determination and living by Islam without undue interference from outside. The irrelevant debate about its compatibility with democracy only complicates the fact that liberal democracy is not the end of history and irrespective of any incompatibility, Muslims have the right to live by revealed Islam—not the one refurbished by some institute in Washington.

ISLAM AND THE WEST: CLASH AND DIALOGUE

Samuel Huntington's reflections on the clash of civilizations have given new impetus to an old theme, and the rise of a belligerent anti-Western Islam would seem at first to second his opinion. Such is not the case; there are serious efforts at what is labeled the dialogue of civilizations. Here we have included selections that reflect both the classic positions and some important contemporary refinements of the theme Islam and the West. By any standards, the Iranian revolution was a watershed, affecting politics and society within Muslim countries and relations between the Muslim world and the West. The establishment of the Islamic Republic of Iran, with Āyatullāh Khumaynī's definition of Islamic government as governance by the jurisprudent, proved both revolutionary and contentious. Anwar Ibrahim adds a new dimension, emphasizing the present Asian consciousness characterized by a more positive attitude toward one's own tradition and a self-confidence that is essential for any real dialogue; also, he looks East as well as West. Abdallah Laroui faults the Arab intellectuals for not fulfilling their critical role in change, while Muhammad Shahrur reacts to present extremism by calling for a complete reform of the seventh-century Bedouin culture, which became a religion. 'Alī Sharī 'atī presents Husayn's martyrdom as an authentic model of social and political protest and a key element for mobilization in the present context. Ayatollah Khatami gives a quiet updated rendition of the themes of "reason" in the West and "soul" in the East, which are integrated by listening and talking. Seyyed Hossein Nasr represents the polar opposite of Shariati with his critique of secularism and the need for the West to learn from Islam. T. J. Winter, warning that the Islamic world is going through a devastating period of transition, provides a trenchant critique of Muslim extremism and the need for the mainstream majority to engage in a process of inner activism and reform.

ĀYATULLĀH RŪHULLĀH KHUMAYNĪ
(1900–1979)

After completing his studies at Qum, a major center of religious learning in Iran, under Shaykh 'Abd al-Karīm Hā'iri Yazdī, the Āyatullāh Khumaynī taught philosophy, ethics, and law. In 1963, he emerged as a critic of the Shah in his sermons at the Faydīya Madrasa (religious school) in Qum. The Āyatullāh Khumaynī was arrested and from 1964 lived in exile, fifteen years in Iraq and later France. He became a symbol for and leader of the opposition movement. In February 1979, the Āyatullāh Khumaynī returned to Teheran to establish the Islamic Republic of Iran.

Islamic Government

In the name of God, the merciful and the compassionate, whose help we seek. God, lord of the universe, be thanked and God's prayers be upon Muhammad, the best of mankind, and upon all his kinsmen.

FOREWORD

The Governance of the Jurisprudent is a clear scientific idea that may require no proof in the sense that whoever knows the laws and beliefs can see its axiomatic nature. But the condition of the Muslim society, and the condition of our religious academies in particular, has driven this issue away from the minds and it now needs to be proven again.

Since its inception, the Islamic movement was afflicted with the Jews when they started their counter-activity by distorting the reputation of Islam, by assaulting it and by slandering it. This hag continued to our present day. Then came the role of groups that can be considered more evil than the devil and his troops. This role emerged in the colonialist activity which dates back to more than three centuries ago. The colonists found in the Muslim world their long-sought object. To achieve their colonialist ambitions, the colonists sought to create the right conditions leading to the annihilation of Islam. They did not seek to turn the Muslims into Christians after driving them away from Islam because they do not believe in either. They wanted control and domination because they were constantly aware during the Crusades wars that the biggest obstacle preventing them from attaining their goals and putting their political plans on the brink of an abyss was Islam with its law and beliefs and with the influence it exerted

From *Islamic Government*, trans. Joint Publications Research Service (Arlington, Va.: National Technical Information Service, 1979), pp. 1a–3, 10, 13–14, 17–18, 20–22.

on people through their faith. This is why they treated Islam unjustly and harbored ill intentions toward it. The hands of the missionaries, the orientalists and of the information media—all of whom are in the service of the colonialist countries—have cooperated to distort the facts of Islam in a manner that has caused many people, especially the educated among them, to steer away from Islam and to be unable to find a way to reach Islam.

Islam is the religion of the strugglers who want right and justice, the religion of those demanding freedom and independence and those who do not want to allow the infidels to dominate the believers.

But the enemies have portrayed Islam in a different light. They have drawn from the minds of the ordinary people a distorted picture of Islam and implanted this picture even in the religious academies. The enemies' aim behind this was to extinguish the flame of Islam and to cause its vital revolutionary character to be lost, so that the Muslims would not think of seeking to liberate themselves and to implement all the rules of their religion through the creation of a government that guarantees their happiness under the canopy of an honorable human life.

They have said that Islam has no relationship whatsoever with organizing life and society or with creating a government of any kind and that it only concerns itself with the rules of menstruation and childbirth. It may contain some ethics. But beyond this, it has no bearing on issues of life and of organizing society. It is regrettable that all this has had its bad effect not only on the ordinary people but also among college people and the students of theology. They misunderstand Islam and are ignorant of it. Islam has become as strange to them as alien people. It has become difficult for the missionary to familiarize people with Islam. On the other hand, there stands a line of the agents of colonialism to drown Islam with clamor and noise.

So that we may distinguish the reality of Islam from what people have come to know about it, I would like to draw your attention to the disparity between the Qur'ān and the *hadīth* books on the one hand and the (theological) theses on the other hand. The Qur'ān and the *hadīth* books, which are the most important sources of legislation, are clearly superior to the theses written by religious interpreters and legists because the Qur'ān and the *hadīth* books are comprehensive and cover all aspects of life. The Qur'ān phrases concerned with society's affairs are many times the phrases concerned with private worship. In any of the detailed *hadīth* books, you can hardly find more than three or four chapters concerned with regulating man's private worship and man's relationship with God and few chapters dealing with ethics. The rest is strongly connected with social and economic affairs, with human rights, with administration and with the policy of societies. . . .

What we are suffering from currently is the consequence of that misleading propaganda whose perpetrators got what they wanted and which has required us to exert a large effort to prove that Islam contains principles and rules for the formation of government.

This is our situation. The enemies have implanted these falsehoods in the minds of people in cooperation with their agents, have ousted Islam's judiciary and political laws from the sphere of application and have replaced them by European laws in contempt of Islam for the purpose of driving it away from society. They have exploited every available opportunity for this end. . . . In the prophet's time, was the church separated from the state? Were there at the time theologians and politicians? At the time of the caliphs and the time of 'Alī, the Amīr of the faithful, was the state separated from the church? Was there an agency for the church and another for the state?

The colonialists and their lackeys have made these statements to isolate religion from the affairs of life and society and to tacitly keep the *'ulamā'* of Islam away from the people, and drive people away from the *'ulamā'* because the *'ulamā'* struggle for the liberation and independence of the Muslims. When their wish of separation and isolation is realized, the colonialists and their lackeys can take away our resources and rule us. I tell you that if our sole concern is to pray, to implore and mention God and never go beyond, colonialism and all the agencies of aggression will never oppose us. Pray as you wish and call for prayer as you wish and let them take what God has given you. The final account is to God and God is the only source of strength and might. When we die our reward will come from God—if this is our thinking, then we have nothing to be concerned with or to fear. . . .

Need for Continued Implementation of Laws

. . . Because Islam is immortal, it must be implemented and observed forever. If what was permissible by Muhammad is permissible until the day of resurrection and what was forbidden by Muhammad is forbidden to the day of resurrection, then Muhummad's restrictions must not be suspended, his teachings must not be neglected, punishment must not be abandoned, tax collection must not be stopped and defense of the nation of the Muslims and of their lands must not be abandoned. The belief that Islam came for a limited period and for a certain place violates the essentials of the Islamic beliefs. Considering that the implementation forever of laws after the venerable prophet, may God's prayers be upon him, is one of the essentials of life, then it is necessary for government to exist and for this government to have the qualities of an executive and administrative authority. Without this, social chaos, corruption and ideological and moral deviation would prevail. This can be prevented only through the creation of a just government that runs all aspects of life.

ISLAMIC SYSTEM OF GOVERNMENT

Distinction from Other Political Systems

The Islamic government is not similar to the well-known systems of government. It is not a despotic government in which the head of state dictates his opinion and tampers with the lives and property of the people. The prophet, may God's prayers be upon him, and 'Alī, the Amīr of the faithful, and the other Imāms[1] had no power to tamper with people's property or with their lives. The Islamic government is not despotic but constitutional. However, it is not constitutional in the well-known sense of the word, which is represented in the parliamentary system or in the people's councils. It is constitutional in the sense that those in charge of affairs observe a number of conditions and rules underlined in the Qur'ān and in the Sunna and represented in the necessity of observing the system and of applying the dictates and laws of Islam. This is why the Islamic government is the government of the divine law. The difference between the Islamic government and the constitutional governments, both monarchic and republican, lies in the fact that the people's representatives or the king's representatives are the ones who codify and legislate, whereas the power of legislation is confined to God, may He be praised, and nobody else has the right to legislate and nobody may rule by that which has not been given power by God. This is why Islam replaces the legislative council [branch] by a planning council that works to run the affairs and work of the ministries so that they may offer their services in all spheres.

All that is mentioned in the book (Qur'ān) and in the Sunna is acceptable and obeyed in the view of the Muslims. This obedience facilitates the state's responsibilities, however when the majorities in the constitutional monarchic or republican governments legislate something, the government has to later exert efforts to compel people to obey, even if such obedience requires the use of force.

The Islamic government is the government of the law and God alone is the ruler and the legislator. God's rule is effective among all the people and in the state itself. All individuals—the prophet, his successors and other people—follow that Islam, which descended through revelation and which God had explained through the Qur'ān and through the words of His prophet, and has legislated for them.

The venerable prophet, may God's peace and prayers be upon him, was appointed ruler on earth by God so that he may rule justly and not follow whims. God addressed the prophet through revelation and told him to convey what was revealed to him to those who would succeed him. The prophet obeyed the dictates of this order and appointed 'Alī, the Amīr of the faithful, as his successor. He was not motivated in this appointment by the fact that 'Alī was his son-in-law and the fact that 'Alī had performed weighty and unforgettable services but because God ordered the prophet to do so.

Yes, government in Islam means obeying the law and making it the judge. The powers given to the prophet, may God's peace and prayers be

---

1. Imām: For Shī'ītes, the Imām is the successor of the prophet Muhammad and thus the religio-political leader of the Islamic community. Ithnā' 'Asharīte (Twelver) Shī'ī Islam recognizes twelve Imāms who are descendants of Muhammad through 'Alī, his son-in-law and first Imām.

upon him, and to the legitimate rulers after him are powers derived from God. God ordered that the prophet and the rulers after him be obeyed: "Obey the prophet and those in charge among you." There is no place for opinions and whims in the government of Islam. The prophet, the Imāms and the people obey God's will and *Sharī'a*.

The *Sharī'a* and reason require us not to let governments have a free hand. The proof of this is evident. The persistence of these governments in their transgressions means obstructing the system and laws of Islam whereas there are numerous provisions that describe every non-Islamic system as a form of idolatry and a ruler or an authority in such a system as a false god. We are responsible for eliminating the traces of idolatry from our Muslim society and for keeping it away from our life. At the same time, we are responsible for preparing the right atmosphere for bringing up a faithful generation that destroys the thrones of false gods and destroys their illegal powers because corruption and deviation grow on their hands. This corruption must be wiped out and erased and the severest punishment must be inflicted upon those who cause it. In his venerable book, God describes Pharaoh as "a corrupter." Under the canopy of a pharonic rule that dominates and corrupts society rather than reform it, no faithful and pious person can live abiding by and preserving his faith and piety. Such a person has before him two paths, and no third to them: either be forced to commit sinful acts or rebel against and fight the rule of false gods, try to wipe out or at least reduce the impact of such a rule. We only have the second path open to us. We have no alternative but to work for destroying the corrupt and corrupting systems and to destroy the symbol of treason and the unjust among the rulers of peoples.

This is a duty that all Muslims wherever they may be are entrusted—a duty to create a victorious and triumphant Islamic political revolution.

Need for Islamic Unity

On the other hand, colonialism has partitioned our homeland and has turned the Muslims into peoples. When the Ottoman State appeared as a united state, the colonialist sought to fragment it. The Russians, the British and their allies united and fought the Ottomans and then shared the loot, as you all know. We do not deny that most rulers of the Ottoman State lacked ability, competence and qualifications and many of them ruled the people in a despotic monarchic manner. However, the colonialists were afraid that some pious and qualified persons would, with the help of the people, assume leadership of the Ottoman State and (would safeguard) its unity, ability, strength and resources, thus dispersing the hopes and aspirations of the colonialists. This is why as soon as World War I ended, the colonialists partitioned the country into mini-states and made each of these mini-states their agent. Despite this, a number of these mini-states later escaped the grip of colonialism and its agents.

The only means that we possess to unite the Muslim nation, to liberate its lands from the grip of the colonialist and to topple the agent governments of colonialism, is to seek to establish our Islamic government. The efforts of this government will be crowned with success when we become able to destroy the heads of treason, the idols, the human images and the false gods who disseminate injustice and corruption on earth.

The formation of a government is then for the purpose of preserving the unity of the Muslims after it is achieved. . . .

Need for Rescuing Wronged and Deprived

To achieve their unjust economic goals, the colonialists employed the help of their agents in our countries. As a result of this, there are hundreds of millions of starving people who lack the simplest health and educational means. On the other side, there are individuals with excessive wealth and broad corruption. The starving people are in a constant struggle to improve their conditions and to free themselves from the tyranny of the aggressive rulers. But the ruling minorities and their government agencies are also seeking to extinguish this struggle. On our part, we are entrusted to rescue the deprived and the wronged. We are instructed to help the wronged and to fight the oppressors, as the Amīr of the faithful ('Alī) instructed his two sons in his will: "Fight the tyrant and aid the wronged."

The Muslim *'ulamā'* are entrusted to fight the greedy exploiters so that society may not have a deprived beggar and, on the other side, someone living in comfort and luxury and suffering from gluttony. . . .

The opinion of the Shī'ī concerning the one who is entitled to lead the people is known since the death of the prophet and until the time of the disappearance (of the Shī'īte leader). To the Shī'ī the Imām is a virtuous man who knows the laws and implements them justly and who fears nobody's censure in serving God.

Ruler in Time of Absence

If we believe that the laws concerning the establishment of the Islamic government are still present and that the *Sharī'a* denounces chaos, then we must form the government. Reason dictates that this is necessary, especially if an enemy surprises us or if an aggressor who must be fought and repelled attacks us. The *Sharī'a* has ordered us to prepare for them all the force that we can muster to scare God's enemy and our enemy, and it encourages us to retaliate against those who attack us with whatever they attack us. Islam also calls for doing the wronged justice, for wrenching his rights and for deterring the unjust. All this requires strong agencies. As for the expenses of the government that is to be formed for the service of the people—the entire people—these expenses come from the treasury house, whose revenues consist of the land tax, the one-fifth tax and the tax levied on Jews and Christians and other resources.

Now, in the time of absence, there is no provision for a certain person to manage the state affairs. So what is the opinion? Should we allow the laws of Islam to continue to be idle? Do we persuade ourselves to turn away from Islam or do we say that Islam came to rule people for a couple of centuries and then to neglect them? Or do we say that Islam has neglected to organize the state? We know that the absence of the government means the loss and violation of the bastions of the Moslems and means our failure to gain our right and our land. Is this permitted in our religion? Isn't the government one of the necessities of life? Despite the absence of a provision designating an individual to act on behalf of the Imām in the case of his absence, the presence of the qualities of the religious ruler in any individual still qualify him to rule the people. These qualities, which are knowledge of the law and justice, are available in most of our jurisprudents in this age. If they decide, it will be easy for them to create and establish a just government unequalled in the world.

Rule of Jurisprudent

If a knowledgeable and just jurisprudent undertakes the task of forming the government, then he will run the social affairs that the prophet used to run and it is the duty of the people to listen to him and obey him.

This ruler will have as much control over running the people's administration, welfare and policy as the prophet and Amīr of the faithful had despite the special virtues and the traits that distinguished the prophet and the Imām. Their virtues did not entitle them to contradict the instructions of the *Sharī'a* or to dominate people with disregard to God's order. God has given the actual Islamic government that is supposed to be formed in the time of absence (of Caliph 'Alī ibn Abi Tālib) the same powers that he gave the prophet and the Amīr of the faithful in regard to ruling, justice and the settlement of disputes, the appointment of provincial rulers and officers, the collection of taxes and the development of the country. All that there is to the matter is that the appointment of the ruler at present depends on (finding) someone who has both knowledge and justice.

The Rule of the Jurisprudent (*wilāyat i-faqīh*)[2]

The above-mentioned must not be misunderstood and nobody should imagine that the fitness of the jurisprudent for rule raises him to the status of prophecy or of Imāms because our discussion here is not concerned with status and rank but with the actual task. The rule here means governing the

2. *Wilāyat i-faqīh* (Guidance of the jurisprudent): During the absence (*ghaybat*) of the Imām and a formal Islamic government, Shī'ī political theory developed the belief that the jurisprudent(s) should provide guidance (*wilāyat*) for the Islamic community. Shī'ī religious leaders differ significantly in their interpretations. For Āyatullāh Sharī'atmadārī *et al.*, the jurisprudents provide moral guidance. For Āyatullāh Khumaynī *wilāyat* means governance itself by an individual *faqīh* who assures Sharī'ah rule.

people, running the state and applying the laws of the *Shari'a*. This is a hard task under which those qualified for it buckle without being raised above the level of men. In other words, rule means the government, the administration and the country's policy and not, as some people imagine, a privilege or a favor. It is a practical task of extreme significance.

The rule of the jurisprudent is a subjective matter dictated by the *Shari'a*, as the *Shari'a* considers one of us a trustee over minors. The task of a trustee over an entire people is not different from that of the trustee over minors, except quantitatively. If we assume that the prophet and the Imām had been trustees over minors, their task in this respect would not have been very different quantitatively and qualitatively from the task of any ordinary person designated as a trustee over those same minors. Their trusteeship over the entire nation is not different practically from the trusteeship of any knowledgeable and just jurisprudent in the time of absence.

If a just jurisprudent capable of establishing the restrictions is appointed, would he establish the restrictions in a manner different from that in which they were established in the days of the prophet or of the Amīr of the faithful? Did the prophet punish the unmarried fornicator more than one hundred lashes? Does the jurisprudent have to reduce the number to prove that there is a difference between them and the prophet? No, because the ruler, be he a prophet, an Imām or a just jurisprudent, is nothing but an executor of God's order and will.

The prophet collected taxes: The one-fifth tax, the alms tax, the tax on the Christians and the Jews and the land tax. Is there a difference between what the prophet and the Imām collected and what the present-day jurisprudent should collect?

God made the prophet the ruler of all the faithful and his rule included even the individual who was to succeed him. After the prophet, the Imām became the ruler. The significance of their rule is that their legal orders applied to all and that the appointment of, control over and, when necessary, dismissal of judges and provincial rulers was in their hands.

The jurisprudent has this same rule and governance with one difference —namely that the rule of the jurisprudent over other jurisprudents is not so that he can dismiss them because the jurisprudents in the state are equal in terms of competence.

Therefore, the jurisprudents must work separately or collectively to set up a legitimate government that establishes the strictures, protects the borders and establishes order. If competence for this task is confined to one person, then this would be his duty to do so corporeally, otherwise the duty is shared equally. In case it is impossible to form that government, the rule does not disappear.

The jurisprudents have been appointed by God to rule and the jurisprudent must act as much as possible and in accordance with his assignment. He must collect the alms tax, the one-fifth tax, the land tax and the tax from Christians and Jews, if he can, so that he may spend all this in the interest of the Muslims. If he can, he must implement the divine strictures. The temporary inability to form a strong and complete government does not at all mean that we should retreat. Dealing with the needs of the Muslims and implementing among them whatever laws are possible to implement is a duty as much as possible.

ANWAR IBRAHIM
1947–

A Malaysian religious and political activist and intellectual, he established the Malaysian Islamic Youth Movement (ABIM) in 1972, a social movement and organization that pressed for Islamization of Malaysian life, educational reform, and social justice. He became the most influential youth leader and political activist in Malaysia and a prominent Muslim leader internationally. He joined the ruling UMNO party (United Malays National Organization) in 1983 and quickly went on to hold a series of cabinet-level positions, culminating in his becoming Deputy Prime Minister. In 1998 he was removed from power by the Prime Minister and tried for sedition and corruption. His trial and conviction drew international attention as well as criticism from human rights organizations and many international leaders. In 2004, his conviction was overturned and he was released.

The Need for Civilizational Dialogue

In all the literary traditions of mankind, the love story is the most enduring, for love brings forth the best, and also the worst in man. In *Romeo and Juliet*, Shakespeare rends our hearts with the story of love's entanglement with loyalty. Anguished by the acrimony and bitterness of the family feud, Juliet is prepared to forsake her family for love:

> Deny thy father, and refuse thy name;
> Or, if thou wilt not, be but sworn my love,
> And I'll no longer be a Capulet.

In the encounter between the civilizations of the East and the West, generations of the intelligentsia from the East—the Muslims, the Hindus, the Confucianists—have been caught in an equally tormenting predicament, a predicament of a different kind yet more profound and far-reaching: whether to remain loyal to one's traditions or to depart for a way of life perceived as superior. They generally fall into two distinct categories. There were those who forswore everything from the West because of their passionate and tenacious hold on everything from their own traditions. And then there were those who, overwhelmed by the dazzling light of Western civilization, became renegades to condemn their own.

From *The Need for Civilizational Dialogue* (Washington, D.C.: Center for Muslim-Christian Understanding, Occasional Paper Series, 1995), pp. 1–5.

341

The theme is still very much alive, although it has evolved into more complex alignments reflecting the political changes and intellectual milestones of the [nineteenth] century. Now, a new debate is brewing. But this time the exotic and moribund East has been transfigured into an energetic and menacing Asia, threatening the lifestyles and the very foundations of the industrial West.

During the late nineteenth and early twentieth century, the European writers on Southeast Asia conjured an image of "the lazy native" to form an ideology to justify colonialism. Today, a new image is being distilled in the mass media and popular travel writings: Asia is an economic juggernaut and the continent is a vast sweat shop. Asian values are said to be responsible not only for the frugality, discipline, diligence and vigour of the people, but also for the excesses and autocratic tendencies of the ruling elites. The fear of competition has been transposed into an impending clash on a civilizational scale.

On the other hand, Asian spokesmen, in their eagerness to fend off criticism, often indulge in stereotyping the West. The West is nothing more than a moral wasteland. Crime, depravity and licentiousness are the order of the day. It is a lost society of aimless wandering souls.

It is against this background that we must engage ourselves in civilizational dialogue, for we fear that protracted mutual miscomprehension will lead to a supplanting of the Cold War with more insidious forms of confrontation. Indeed, this dialogue has become an imperative at a time when the world has shrunk into a global village. For it is a pre-condition for the establishment of a convivencia, a harmonious and enriching experience of living together among people of diverse religions and cultures.

Some four decades ago the historian Arnold Toynbee published a small volume, containing extracts of historical works, including a section from Josephus' *History of the Romano-Jewish War*. That section was titled by Toynbee as *The Conflict of Civilizations* (A.D. 66). Thus the idea of a clash of civilization is not altogether new. The question, however, is not whether civilizations will necessarily clash, rather whether civilizations ought to clash. For us, the divine imperative as expressed in the Qur'an is unambiguous. Humanity has been created to form tribes, races and nations, whose differences in physical characteristics, languages and modes of thought are but the means for the purpose of *lita'arafu*—"getting to know one another." On the other hand, in the narrative of modernity, the story of the encounter is less straightforward. It is the progressive globalization of a particular language of discourse issuing from the Renaissance and the Enlightenment, that being the only true and possible discourse for mankind. It is the light of reason against the darkness of magic and superstition, of dynamism against sterility, of civilization against barbarism.

True, the age of the civilizing mission is over and no one talks about it any longer without a touch of remorse or embarrassment. But at any rate the undertone is as resounding, and in our day it has metamorphosed into a *mission democratrice*. That enterprise, implied or expressed, has acquired the status of a dogma in foreign relations. It is being espoused with great sophistication, ready to be enforced with the mightiest fire power known in human history.

By the same token, the East is no less worthy of blame. The recent successes of the economies of Asia, and the growing self-confidence of the people, have on occasions given rise to overtones of arrogance and trumpets of triumphalism. In the process, they betray their most enduring value, that of humility before the vastness of human endeavor and the totality of creation.

We are already in fundamental agreement, in that we subscribe to the universal quest for truth and the pursuit of justice and virtue. We rejoice in beauty, both within ourselves and in what surrounds us. We long for knowledge, peace and security amid the mysteries and uncertainties of the universe. In our disjointed world, therefore, with so much ugliness, violence and injustice, there cannot be a nobler aim and vocation than the realization of values which unify humanity, despite the great diversity of climes and cultures.

The poignancy in the question posed by T. S. Eliot: "Where is the knowledge we have lost in information?" is even more profoundly felt today than when it was first raised. And no community has suffered more wrong from the information explosion than the Muslims. The gullible consumer of the mass media of today would form the impression that the Muslim world is only populated by stern and menacing fundamentalists. The fact of the matter is, the Muslim is not without a sense of humor, and his civilization has produced plenty of love stories. For example, from the Moroccan coast of the Atlantic to the tiny Merauke island of Indonesia in the Pacific, Muslim children are raised with the enchanting tale of love between Laila and Majnun. As the story goes, the young man was scorned and ridiculed for his obsession with the maiden, because to the eyes of the world Laila was hideous in physical appearance. In response to this, the youth always replied: "To see the beauty of Laila, one requires the eyes of Majnun."

Looking at our co-religionists, we tend to be Majnun most of the time. But we are also deeply aware that the Muslim world is not without its excesses and internal contradictions. The negative image of Muslims to the rest of the world is to a great extent the result of the failure of many Muslims themselves to realize and manifest their own ideals. Ignorance, injustice, corruption, hypocrisy and the erosion in moral rectitude are quite prevalent in contemporary Muslim societies.

The decision of this University to initiate studies and research programmes concerning Islam in Southeast Asia comes at a critical time when Islam itself needs the platform to project its positive aspects. The experience of contemporary Islam in Southeast Asia has much to contribute not only to Muslims in other regions but possibly also to the world at large. This is due to the fact that the devout Southeast Asian Muslim practices his religion in the context of a truly multicultural world. Especially in Malaysia, a Muslim is never unaware of the presence of people of other faiths; as friends, colleagues, collaborators, partners or even competitors.

The challenges before Muslims, like people of other traditions in Asia today, are indeed great. They must endeavor to alleviate ignorance, disease, and destitution. They have to battle corruption and arrest moral decay. They have to strengthen the institutions of civil society to ensure order and stability, as well as protect the individual from the unwarranted denial of his rights. Indeed, these are the imperatives of all the great religious traditions, and one could do no greater disservice than to invoke the name of tradition to justify excesses, injustices and authoritarianism in society. In this regard, the renewal of traditions must mean reliving their ideals—truth, justice and compassion—and not resurrecting past aberrations, of the depraved and the decadent.

As Asia renews itself, it must have the confidence to appreciate and learn from what is truly great in Western civilization. Indeed, in the traditions of the West, there are other languages of discourse apart from the one presented since the Renaissance. If the dialogue between Asian and Western civilizations is to become productive, Asians must transcend the pain and bitterness following their earlier encounters. The Islamic world must surely look beyond the Crusades and the era of colonialism. For its part, the West has probably to look at the East and the rest of the world in a new light, a perspective illuminated by a profound empathy for the predicament of the rest. The prospect for productive engagement and cultural enrichment must take the place of the fear of competition. In this enterprise no region should be totally forgotten for reasons of economic backwardness, for that would be tantamount to moral abdication.

The global convivancia that is to be the primary motif of civilizational dialogue is not alltogether new. Centuries before us Dante envisaged the establishment of the "universal community of human race": a community dedicated to justice and the realization of man's intellectual potential. Several times in the past it was experienced as a living reality, and as the origin of the term denotes, Spain under Moorish rule represents one of its crowning fulfillments.

It is an irony of our time that as the world becomes smaller, the consciousness of the division and divide among human community magnifies: the East and the West, the North and South, the powerful and the marginalized. Much of this division has come about and is perpetuated by the practice of polity that has become totally identified with the exercise of power, and leadership that is increasingly divorced from ethical concerns and morality. Enduring peace and security of the world must be built not upon religious, cultural, economic or political hegemonies but on mutual awareness and concern. For understanding brings respect, and respect prepares the way for love. Love, like truth, liberates and takes us onto a higher kind of loyalty, onto what is true, just and virtuous.

ABDALLAH LAROUI
1933–

Historian and philosopher as well as Professor Emeritus at
Université Mohammed V in Rabat, Morocco, he has published
extensively in French and Arabic on Islam, modernity, and intellectuals of the Arab world. His publications include *Islam et
histoire: essai d'épistémologie*; *Islam et modernité*; and *The Crisis
of the Arab Intellectual: Traditionalism or Historicism?*

The Crisis of the Arab Intellectual: Traditionalism or Historicism?

[We do] not treat culture per se; rather [we treat] the problems of Arab
society with culture as the means of approach . . . to lay bare one of the
foremost obstacles impeding the evolution of that society. . . . However
important one thinks the crisis of the Arab intelligentsia, it still would not
merit the attention it has been given if it did not symbolize and reveal a
crisis of society as a whole.

How are all the contradictions of society combined in the crisis of the
intelligentsia? How does the intellectual's disarray bear witness to the
inefficiency and stagnation of society?

Arab intellectuals think according to two rationales. Most of them
profess the traditionalist rationale (salafi); the rest profess an eclecticism.
Together these tendencies succeed in abolishing the historical dimension.
But if the intellectual erases history from his thought, can he erase it from
reality? Of course not; history as past and present structure informs the
present condition of the Arabs quite as much as it does that of their adversaries. Ahistorical thinking has but one consequence: failure to see the real.
If we translate this into political terms, we may say that it has the effect of
confirming dependence on all levels. This goes without saying for eclecticism which opens itself to every outside influence. But traditionalist thought
is no less dependent in spite of its pretensions. Indeed how can it oppose
modern technology, modern economic and social systems, and modern
intellectual schools when it is incapable of understanding them and has not
the slightest possibility of inventing competitive systems? Dependency, visible or concealed, means not only exploitation, loss of liberty, and damage

From Abdallah Laroui, *The Crisis of the Arab Intellectual: Traditionalism or Historicism?*
Translated from the French by Diarmid Cammell (Los Angeles: University of California Press,
1977, 153–176).

to the pride and material interests of a nation, but also and above all the continuance and exacerbation of historical retardation.

Many historians of colonization have subscribed to the foregoing conclusion; it has been corroborated by economic studies on countries attempting to emerge from underdevelopment in a neo-colonial framework. Production figures have actually increased, investments have been made, but the human, social, and intellectual phenomenon of underdevelopment has not diminished in the least.

This bitter truth notwithstanding, the great majority of Arab intellectuals continue to lean toward salafiyya and eclecticism and, what is even stranger, believe they enjoy complete freedom to appropriate the best among the cultural products of others: the freedom of a Stoic slave! The only way to do away with these two modes of thought consists in strict submission to the discipline of historical thought and acceptance of its assumptions. We have already defined some of these. Some of them determine historicism: truth as process, the positivity of the event, the mutual determination of facts, the responsibility of the agents. Others delimit historicism: the existence of laws of historical development, the unicity of the meaning of history, the transmissibility of acquired knowledge, the effectivity of the intellectual's and the politician's role. These different points have been analyzed more or less briefly in the preceding pages, and we drew the conclusion that today the Arabs may find the best school of historical thought in Marxism, read in a certain manner. Nevertheless, this conclusion is not easily accepted. Submission to the discipline of history is resented by most Arab intellectuals as a loss of responsibility and freedom, inasmuch as the goal of their activity, over and above their specific aims, would already be known. Perpetually to play the role of pupil is in their eyes another slight, since they are asked to play the uncreative role of making good a retardation. . . .

It is hardly necessary to recall that only historical understanding confers logic and density to action; it alone liberates politics from aimless tactical relativism, permitting the individual to conceive long-term plans and to rid himself of the most tenacious illusion. . . .

If things are as clear as we have indicated, to what (over and above his psychology) may we attribute the Arab intellectual's indecision, which he has already protracted over decades?

The intellectual is molded by a culture; the latter is born of a consciousness and politics. Now there are two types of alienation: the one is visible and openly criticized, the other all the more insidious as it is denied on principle. Westernization indeed signifies an alienation, a way of becoming other, an avenue of self-division (though one's estimation of this transformation may be positive or negative, according to one's ideology). But there exists another form of alienation in modern Arab society, one that is prevalent but veiled: this is the exaggerated medievalization obtained through quasi-magical identification with the great period of classical

Arabic culture. The cultural policy of all Arab states combats the alienation of Westernization by two means: the sanctification of Arabic in its archaic form and the vulgarization of classic texts (the resurrection of the cultural legacy). . . .

For all objective observers, the true alienation is this loss of self in the absolutes of language, culture and the saga of the past. The Arab intellectual blithely plunges into them, hoping thus to prove his perfect freedom and to express his deepest personality. Here then are found the inward chains binding him to a present he yet claims to repudiate. Historical consciousness alone will allow him to free himself of them. Then he will see reality, perhaps for the first time. He will see that the absolutes he worships are alien to him, for they may be interiorized only through intellectual analysis and synthesis, that is through voluntary effort—never through inward understanding and intuition. . . .

If we continue to associate, as we nearly always do, the future of the Arab peoples with fidelity to these absolutes, then we shall have to conclude that Arabizing (or medievalizing) alienation is the worst of all and that the campaign waged for so many years against the alienation of Westernization (a successful campaign, it must be acknowledged) serves only to camouflage an ever-growing cultural retardation. . . .

Medievalization is the result of a cultural policy, but whose policy? With this question we have reached the social basis of a cultural situation that, despite its destructive aspects, in self-perpetuating.

We offer here a few brief remarks that make no claim to get to the root of the matter. The vast domain of the Arabs comprises a baffling diversity of circumstances . . . I shall limit myself to observations drawn from experience of the Maghrib; from these the reader may generalize where he sees fit.

I have described elsewhere the principal characteristics of the national State dominated by the petite bourgeoisie, whose ideology is "technologism" and whose mainstay is a closed bureaucracy closely controlled by its primary means of centralization and defense: the army. Nasser's Egypt and Ben Bella's Algeria have served as prototypes. Since then, many other Arab states have reached this stage—notably Syria and Iraq. Other states, such as Libya, the Sudan, and South Yemen, which might seem to qualify, do not altogether merit inclusion on account of the weakness of their bureaucracies and hence of their States, or on account of their economic and demographic weakness; for foreign policy and explicit ideology are not defining criteria of the national State. . . . Therefore we may say that the type of national State we have described, some bold but marginal experiments in the Arabian Peninsula notwithstanding, continues to be the most advanced form of political organization in the Arab countries.

Let us be quite clear on this point: the petite bourgeoisie, which politically dominates the national State, takes first place in all Arab political entities, even when it possesses neither power nor economic preponderance nor military backing in countries such as Morocco, Saudi Arabia, Jordan and the Gulf Emirates. We find public administration, the technical services of public and private organizations, teaching and culture in the hands of the petite bourgeoisie, so that, in power or out of power, it is this class that delimits the intellectuals' horizon and defines cultural policy. . . .

Can the intellectual elite which fashions the petite bourgeois State transcend the narrow confines of its immediate interests and bring itself to desire a society better prepared for rapid evolution . . . ?

The revolutionary intellectual, necessarily of petite bourgeoisie origin, belongs to a small minority of that uncommitted intellectual elite that is satisfied with expressing its lived situation and does not attempt to transcend it even in thought. Now a role falls to this revolutionary intellectual; historically determined by the practice of others, this role is a possibility— not a transcendent duty or a destiny. It may or may not be filled, just as Arab society may one day be modernized or may drag out the moribund existence of an alleviated Middle Ages. The role consists in presenting the general program of modernization of Arab thought and society. . . . Comparison with what exists elsewhere in the world can lead the Arab intellectual beyond romanticism toward positive thought. . . .

How can he play his part? By once and for all repudiating the romanticism, the utopianism and the exclusivism of the petite bourgeoisie, by taking a clear and distinct position vis-à-vis language, history and tradition; by becoming aware of history. . . . Even within the petite bourgeoisie there are racial or cultural minorities that have no interest in seeing the present situation perpetuated—especially as it accumulates failures within and without. These groups can objectively transcend the limits of the national State, but they have always lacked the organization, the will and the intellectual training that would enable them to imagine an order different from the one in which they live. Some of them are probably ready to accept any program that can show them a convincing image of a different order, one more open to the future. Although education is kept under surveillance, although information is censured and culture manipulated, the system is not perfectly closed and cannot be. It falls therefore to the revolutionary intellectuals, however small their number, to hold ready that program that is capable of guiding the Arabs toward the path of the future.

Let us say plainly that this program does not exist today. Clearly it has nothing to do with the economic program offered by the local progressives in each of the Arab countries, nor is it the rhetorical program of those who believe that Arab unity is an accomplished fact rather than an eventuality or a possibility. The former lacks historical depth; the latter lacks rationality. We are referring to a total program that adopts a clear and consistent position toward the absolutes of traditionalist thought, the problems of minorities, democracy at the state level and at the level of local communities, unity in its real historical framework, the national State and its primarily cultural policy, etc.—in short, a program giving a rational analysis of the past, the present, and the foreseeable future of the Arabs. Thus at last will traditionalism and eclecticism be truly defeated and transcended. . . .

Progressive intellectuals form a minority of the Arab intelligentsia, even if, through a favorable combination of circumstances, they succeed in transcending the petite bourgeois point of view, they make their way with difficulty on account of the counterpressure exerted by the Palestinian problem. Why?

Here we have no alternative but to acknowledge a real external influence . . . the world does not grant the Arab position an equitable hearing even when this position is presented in a purely historicist framework and is no longer predicated on an immutable and transcendent right. . . .

The progressive Arab intellectual must accept the Palestinian drama as a fact and the attitudes of others (rational or irrational) as facts, and he must define his position with regard to the cardinal problem of the Arabs: their historical retardation. He must not invert the terms by defining his position vis-à-vis historical retardation with an eye to the attitudes of others vis-à-vis the Palestinian question. This is a difficult position, certainly —in the present circumstances even heroic. Without taking it, however, there is little hope that the Arabs will find their place in the modern world.

The Arab world has known but one revolution—the national revolution—that comprised several others: intellectual (the discovery of the worth of human individuality), social (the discovery of democracy), economic (the discovery of social calculation and the concern for production). But because of this very confusion between goals and aspirations, none of them has been truly realized. The Arab society of today is heterogeneous: different epochs, temporalities, and humanities are placed side by side therein. Believers in continuous revolution use this indistinction to justify their desire to compress time. However, this compression necessarily implies that all the attainments of the successive revolutions of modern history should be ideologically interiorized. The idea of continuous revolution means two things: it means that on the level of ideology the various phases of development are inescapable; in practice, it implies the possibility of bypassing certain phases. It consequently supposes the effectivity of the role of the intellectual minorities—otherwise it is meaningless.

The more a society is retarded, the more its revolutionary elite should be cultured, progressive, conscious of all the qualitative leaps that have occurred in the life of humanity. In the modern period humanity has experienced a religious reform, a democratic revolution, an industrial revolution. Each of these has expressed, in a particular domain, the evolution of society as a whole; from them derive breaks in thought (also called revolutions)—scientific, rationalist, historicist—that have given rise to ideologies whose most complete expressions were liberalism and Marxist socialism.

The more a society lags behind other societies, the more are the goals of revolution diversified and deepened; the more the intellectual is conscious of this retardation, the greater are his reponsibilities and the more frequent are temptations to escape into illusion and myth; the more a revolution must be all embracing, the more distant and improbable it seems. Such indeed is the situation of the Arab revolutionary. The various struggles for freedom—individual, communal, national—which the bourgeoisie of the national State nowhere forced to a conclusion, now devolve upon him. If things remain as they are today, the Arabs' retardation, despite an ever increasing gross national product, will be exacerbated—linguistically, culturally, ideologically. Foreign Marxists will increasingly tend to believe that the Arab revolution is unattainable; and when it finally happens, it will be reckoned fortuitous.

Confronted with this less than encouraging situation, the Arab intellectual must objectively appraise what he has hitherto called his political commitment, which has often induced him to play hide-and-seek with his convictions for the sake of practical results. His only truly positive role is to be radical in the exact sense of the term—whatever the short-term cost. The ideological and cultural front has always been calm in the Arab countries, because this is a domain in which all social strata have coexisted in a common adoration of absolutes. If this calm endures, it is likely that the Arabs will be the last to wake up to history—perhaps sharing this destiny with the Indians, who, since Gandhi, have likewise taken the religion on tradition as a national ideology.

To put an end to the traditionalist mentality requires much modesty; above all, it requires acceptance of a common fund of ideas and a willingness to identify oneself only through one's tone. Our modern culture will be derived; let us accept the fact if it is the path to realization. We must in any case pay the price of a long decadence. We have already paid heavy tribute to an empty cultural nationalism that is all the more distressing when one thinks of the extraordinary modesty—perhaps feigned—of the Chinese, as they at last realize the dreams of several generations of intellectuals fated never to see the coming of the day. Strange indeed are certain proclamations announcing a special competency in the art of manufacturing "civilization!"

All too long has the Arab intellectual hesitated to make radical criticisms of culture, language, and tradition. Too long has he drawn back from criticizing the aims of local national policy, the result of which is a stifling of democracy and a generalized dualism. He must condemn superficial economism, which would modernize the country and rationalize society by constructing factories with another's money, another's technology, another's administration. When it comes to the problems of minorities and local democracy, he must cease from censoring himself for fear of imperiling an apparent national unity. The Arab revolutionary intellectual has too long applauded the call to Arab unity, all the while accepting and sometimes justifying the fragmentation that is reality.

Everyone subscribes to a unity founded on feelings; a unity founded on economy is condemned as being too slow to transpire. There are those who prefer to panegyrize Arab unity rather than bring it about. Only an historical critique can put an end to such seductions.

This critique must be carried out on two levels: first, the Arab states, within those territorial organizations to which each revolutionary intellectual belongs. Second, the Arab unitary movement: this must be structured, liberated from every consideration of or dependence on local interests, freed from the limitations of current political practice, and given the major role of criticizing and evaluating the actions, organizations, and policies of the Arab states insofar as they influence the future of the Arabs. Thus will it safeguard the rights of the future as revealed by positive analysis, recalling always the shared interests of the community whenever the tendency to consider local, sectional, and transitory interests threatens to gain the upper hand.

Necessarily assuming many forms, this labor will in any case accomplish the modernization of Arab society, whatever the ultimate result of the unitary movement in which victory or failure is assured to nobody.

Today, outside his personal successes the Arab revolutionary intellectual must lead an unhappy life, because his society is living in an infrahistorical rhythm. He will not put an end to his anguish until he clearly expresses what he knows to be the prerequisites for radical renovation and then defends them with all his strength, thus bringing finally to a close the long winter of the Arabs.

MUHAMMAD SHAHRUR
1938–

Born in Damascus, Shahrur studied in Damascus and Moscow, and he earned a doctorate at University College in Dublin, Ireland. A civil engineer, he joined the faculty at the University of Damascus in 1972. In 1990, Shahrur published *The Book and the Qur'an*, an 800-page treatise, which became a best-seller in the Arab world, calling upon Muslims to reinterpret Islam through a fresh reading of the Quran that is not shackled by medieval interpretations and jurisprudence. Thus, his basic approach is to reread Islam in the context of historical developments. Labeled by some an Islamic Martin Luther, he has also provoked much criticism.

Islamic Culture in Danger

Q: After the events of September 11 the world discovered a discourse, alleging affiliation with Islam, calling for killing and hatred among religions and peoples. What are the ideological and cultural impulses (*muntalaqat*) driving this current which Ben Laden, al-Qa'ida and the Taliban have come to represent today, and what is its relation to Islam?

A: Terrorism is the misplaced use of violence. Certainly there are political reasons for violence including the policy of the USA in our region. But there are also causes connected with the problematics present in Islamic culture. We are bearers of a sick culture which produces violence. . . . When I say that our Islamic culture is sick, I do not mean Islam as a religion; I mean the culture which is circulating today and which is represented in people's minds with Islamic religion. One of the causes of our backwardness is this sick culture, hence the necessity of treating it.

When I hear Ben Laden I get fed up not from him personally, but because he is the spokesman for this sick culture. What happened on September 11 is an indication that Islam today is in crisis. Taliban thought is present in every country, and the books which the Taliban studied and derived their principles from are studied in all the Shari'a colleges in the Islamic world. The difference is that the Taliban applied them; the others

Interview conducted by Muhammad Ali al-Attasi. Translated from the Arabic by John J. Donohue. In his books and studies Dr. Muhammad Shahrur tries to present contemporary readings of the Qur'an and pose searching questions concerning the crisis of Islamic culture and the ways to revivify and reform it.

have not yet done so, but the foundations of the thought are one and the same, and I as a Muslim feel ashamed that Islam should end up as Taliban. Until now no official Islamic institute has dared to delve seriously into the impulses behind all those who practice violence. Because in such a case it would have to reconsider the bases of Islamic jurisprudence and the way of interacting with the Book of God and this is something for which they are absolutely not prepared.

The Muslim ulama in the official religious institution have never exposed to criticism or rebuttal the theoretical impulses and the cognitive structure of the Islamic *jihadi* movements. Indeed this official Islamic institution is incapable of entering into ideological confrontation with the theorists of the Qa'ida organization because the latter would defeat them since they both come out of the same ideological school. He who exercises violence and he who does not both come out of the same principles and impulses (*muntalaqat*) which comprise the principle of abrogation (*nasikh* and *mansukh*) and the reasons for revelation (*asbab al-nuzul*) and the principle of analogy (*mabda'a al-qiyas*). The present Arab intellect is an analogical intellect and an analogical intellect does not create or produce any knowledge. It is based on the authentic model of the seventh century. This model is treated analogically in a repetitious fashion. Arab thought is repetitious; it repeats itself through analogy which is the only domain for exercising the intellect.

The Islam we have today with its concept of what is necessarily fixed in religion and the concept of free-will (*qadariyya*) and fatalism (*jabariyya*) and the definition of fate and divine decree and the foundations of Islamic jurisprudence and the Sunna, this Islam drew up its general concepts in the Umayyad era and was framed and written down and took its final form in the Abbasid era.

We need a cultural reformation from within. We have to reconsider the concept of sunna and the concept of consensus and the concept of analogy and abrogation (*nasikh* and *mansukh*) and liberty and authority and the people who bind and loose and other concepts of a human stamp. There is no other solution. Islamic culture is in crisis; it is in peril.

Q: Can I understand from your words that Ben Laden is more consistent with himself, more representative and sincere concerning these principles of jurisprudence (*fiqh*) than the representatives of official Islam?

A: Certainly. As an example let's take the principle of abrogation. Well, [look at] all the verses from the Book of God which speak of wisdom and exhortation to good like:

Let there be no compulsion in religion. Truth stands out clear from error. (2.256)

And say: "The truth is from your Lord." Let him who will believe, and let him who will reject it. (18.29)

All these verses are abrogated (*mansukh*). They are read only and not observed. The abrogation of these verses did not come from Ben Laden or from the Organization of al-Qa'ida, or from the Muslim Brothers. The abrogation is prior to them. These verses were abrogated by a verse called the verse of the Sword from the Surat al-Tawba

> Then when the Sacred Months have passed, then kill the *Mushrikûn* wherever you find them, and capture them and besiege them, and prepare for them each and every ambush. But if they repent and perform *Prayer* and pay *Zakât*, then leave their way free. Verily, God is Oft-Forgiving, Most Merciful. (9.5)

If we wish to fight terror and fight violence we must reconsider the principle of abrogation in the Book of God; otherwise things will continue as they are and the production of blind violence will continue in the same form. . . .

Q: If we leave aside the concept of abrogation for now and treat the subject of murder for apostasy, what possibility of revising this subject do you see at present?

A: Here we must distinguish between political apostasy and creedal apostasy, since creedal apostasy in the sense of changing religion has no connection with society, and its divine punishment is in the Book of God. The basis for life is permissibility and the basis for death (blood) is prohibition except what God permits. God does not permit killing the apostate. God it is who gives life and takes it away.

Concerning political apostasy we must return to the central state in the prophetic era and discuss the appeal (*da'wa*) from the purely political angle. Before the coming of the Messenger the Arabs had no central state. The Apostle came and called to Unicity (*tawhid*) and to a new religion. He ended his appeal by founding a central state with its capital at Madina. There all those who supported the Apostle and entered into his appeal and became his followers were called believers (*mu'minun*).

> O Prophet! God is Sufficient for you and for the believers who follow you. (8.64)

> And when the believers saw the Confederate forces, they said: "This is what God and His Messenger had promised us. (33.22)

Islam as a concept is much broader than faith. From the political point of view there was a party called the believers which formed and founded the state. Accordingly, in the political consciousness of the people at that time, anyone who wanted to form a state had to become a prophet. al-Aswad al-'Anzi before the death of the Messenger is the most famous who claimed prophecy in Yemen because he wished to separate from the central state, thus the Prophet's order to kill him. In the separatist political apostasy there is fighting and killing. Likewise after the death of the Messenger several attempts at separation took place and those responsible had to claim prophecy; given the political mentality it meant that they wished to found a new party. . . .

In this case it is natural for the central state to defend its existence. In the wars of apostasy, the apostasy was political so Abu Bakr fought them according to the logic of political apostasy in which there is fighting and killing. When the sole income into the state was the wealth of the alms-tax (*zakat*), any resistance to paying it meant separation. . . .

Q: For centuries on end, the People of the Book were forced to pay the head tax (*jizya*) which is mentioned in the Qur'an. Where are we today in regard to this?

A: There is one verse in the Qur'an which speaks of the head tax, in Surat al-Tawba:

> Fight against those who believe not in God, nor in the Last Day, nor forbid that which has been forbidden by God and His Messenger and those who acknowledge not the religion of truth among the People of the Book, until they pay the *jizyah* with willing submission, and feel themselves subdued. (9.29)

The concept of head tax is a purely political concept and the Commander of the Faithful was so-called in the past because the believers, followers of the Messenger, were those who founded the state and political power was in their hands. The treasury was called the treasury of the Muslims because the State whose Commander of the Faithful was Umar ibn al-Khattab contained Christians and Jews and as an equivalent for the money which was taken from Muslims in the name of *sadaqat* and *zakat*, there was money taken for the treasury of the state from Jews and Christians in the name of head tax. This money was spent on all.

Now believers and non-believers have become citizens and the state does not have need of the *sadaqat* or the *jizya* because it has its special budget and numerous taxes, so the concept of *jizya* and *dhimmis* (protected people) has been completely abrogated for the good of the concept of citizen. All pay taxes to the state; taxes are the common denominator for all individuals of the society. Every man pays his *sadaqat* according to his religious convictions without interference from the state. The concept of head tax is completely historical; no one is calling for its return today.

Q: This leads us to what some Islamic currents are doing today, namely calling People of the Book infidels. What is your opinion on this?

A: In the Qur'an we have People of the Book and those of the People of the Book who have become infidels. These are two completely different things. Those of the People of the Book who became infidels are those who attacked and fought against the Prophet. In the Qur'an the phrase always comes as "Those among the People of the Book who became infidels," not all the People of the Book. . . .

The concept of *kufr* is not clear in Islamic literature (*adabiyat*). There is confusion between faith and infidelity (*kufr*). A country in which there are no believers should not be called an infidel country but a country of non-believers; otherwise all the world becomes your enemy. If you say that non-Muslim believers are infidels, this is exactly like the saying of Bush today that he who is not with us is against us. It is not correct for any man who is a believer to fight people because they are not believers. It is possible to fight people because of land or for interests or because of political differences, but it is not right for you to fight them because they are not believers and are not followers of the Muhammadan message. . . .

The question today is how can we interact with the People of the Book in the best way, regarding them with a human regard. If for instance we continue in the exegesis of Surat "al-Fatiha," which we recite with every *rak'a* in our prayers in accord with the old principles of *fiqh*, which explains that "those who earn Thy anger" (*maghdub 'alayhim*) are the Jews and "those who go astray" (*dallin*) are the Christians whereas the *maghdub* and the *dallin* are those who deviated from the straight path. The one who kills a person is among the *maghdub* and the polytheists are the *dallin*. The *maghdub* and the *dallin* could be among the followers of Muhammad or among those who do not follow Muhammad. This exegesis was laid down when there was a strong state which regarded its subjects of the People of the Book with a regard of domination and haughtiness and pity, not the regard of equality.

Today the state of citizens and the state in which there is no constraint in religion is the just form, more lofty than the state of believers and the *dhimmis*, which was the first form of the state. In the state of citizens there is no difference between a believing Muslim and a Christian as long as they both pay their taxes. But there is a difference in faith. The pillars of faith for a believer are fasting and prayer; these are separate from the state but not from the society. . . .

Q: We come now to the question of *jihad* in Islam and its relation to the use of violence and fighting in the way of God. What is your reading of this thorny problem in Islam?

A: Before I answer this question I would like to explain the difference between the two words '*ibad* and '*abid*. The word of God Most High previously to the people of the earth is that all people are '*ibad* of God and not '*abid*:

> Mankind were but one community then they differed (later), and had not it been for a Word that went forth before from your Lord, their difference would have been settled between them. (10.19)

So people obey God by fulfilling his will and they disobey him by free choice. For this he created them. The believers are *'ibad allah*, the rebellious are *'ibad allah* and the atheists are *'ibad allah*, all people are *'ibad allah*, he created them and left them in several verses the freedom to choose obedience or disobedience, faith or infidelity; then he promised them an encounter to reward the good choices and punish the bad.

The word *'abada* in the Arabic language is of the verbs with opposite meanings; it bears the meaning of obedience or disobedience, and here there is a big difference between *'ibad* and *'abid*.

> And I created the jinns and humans that they may serve Me. (51.56)

That is, he created them to be free *'ibad*, not *'abid* and not as some say for prayer and fasting.

Now for *jihad*, there are two types; this is in the saying of the Almighty:

> God does not forbid you to deal justly and kindly with those who fought not against you on account of religion and did not drive you out of your homes. God loves those who deal with equity. (60.8)

There is *jihad* in the way of God. It is *jihad* to lift off constraint from people, that is, that the word of God Most High is in the way of freedom of choice for all people, not just for believers. So fighting in the way of God is fighting in the way of non-constraint generally and non-constraint in religion in particular. A country where people are constrained to pray or where women are forced to wear the veil, the word of God is at a low level, and the country where people are prevented from praying or where women are prohibited from wearing the veil, the word of God is at a low level. *Jihad* in the way of God is against tyranny and for the freedom of people one and all and to lift constraint from them. This came as an obligation for the followers of Muhammad only; it is not right to oblige others to it unless they so wish. This *jihad* has several forms and the use of force may be a stage of *jihad* or one of its forms, but there is also *jihad* with wealth and word and speaking the truth. However, for the use of force and violence there are objective conditions stipulated as to international relations, the balance of political and military forces, etc.

As for the second type of *jihad* and fighting, it is in the way of not being evinced from their abode (*diyar*). Here the people of the abode fight, Muslim believers and Christians and others, not just the followers of Muhammad. This is not fighting in the way of God but in the way of land and abode.

Q: Are you convinced that there are conditions regulating the use of violence in *jihad*? Is every type of violence allowed when the situation is like the state of occupied Palestinian lands today?

A: There are three conditions for that which come in the following verses of Surat al-Baqara:

> The sacred month is for the sacred month, and for the prohibited things, there is the Law of Equality. Then whoever transgresses the prohibition against you, you transgress likewise against him. And fear God, and know that God is with the pious. (2. 194)

Here we remark that we should not be the ones who begin the enmity and that we fear God in our enemies if we are the stronger; if we are the weaker, then we should practice all forms of *jihad* and know how to use violence so that we don't put ourselves in jeopardy. For example, if we fight America today with force we will lose. But we can spend our wealth as do the Zionist lobbies in the United States.

In what pertains to the Palestinian people, their struggle against Israel is just. But their being in the right does not mean that they are always correct in the way they conduct the struggle against Israel. Any military action or operation of martyrdom unaccompanied by a mature political idea is vain and a loss of blood and wealth.

When the operation of martyrdom becomes an institution, this is an error. This institution can be turned over to secondary goals which may be criminal as in the case of Ben Laden. The desire for martyrdom is not transformed into an institution; the decision of martyrdom is an individual decison. God is the giver of life and no one other than God has the right to take it. According to their logic, it has not been confirmed that the Messenger sent anyone to his death; rather he would say to them: he who fights with dedication and is killed, paradise is his. For instance the Syrian pilot who flew his Mig into an Israeli plane, his command did not order him to do it; he took the decision himself. I esteem that decision highly and his command honored him afterwards.

Q: But are we always forced to go back to religion? Why today in all our political struggles is Islam dragged into the battle by the Muslims themselves?

A: No. Islam is not susceptible to politicization and if it is politicized, the State that does it will die. The Book of God sufficed for setting up a human society; it does not suffice for setting up a state with historical and geographical limits. It inspires with universals and general laws and it needs additions and not explanations, as they say. And these additions the Messenger set up to build his state and his society in the Arab peninsula in the seventh century. At present these additions are civil law and parliaments.

Q: But most of the Islamic political currents call for setting up a state today on the same bases on which it stood in the era of the Messenger and the Rightly Guided Caliphs.

A: The problem here is in the analogy of the seen for the unseen (*qiyas al-shahid 'ala al-gha'ib*). For example, all the political measures which the

Messenger undertook and the Rightly Guided Caliphs took are not Islamic law and cannot be used for analogy. All the measures in building the state and organizing the society and the wars and the military decisions were worldly political measures and cannot be used for analogy. . . .

Here today we don't direct our blame to this purely political decision nor do we use it for analogy. The Prophet Muhammad in his time took the military and political decisions connected with conditions in his era. We have no connection with those decisions. The problem here is that the Prophetic sunna requires redefinition.

The great problem for Muslims is that the Arab bedouin culture which prevailed in the seventh century in the Arab peninsula was transformed entirely into religion, from clothes and manners to social customs, food, even music. For instance, the tambourine which was the only musical instrument prevalent is transformed in our day to Islamic music. Even eating dates has become Islamic and the one who played a methodological role in transforming this culture into religion is al-Shafi'i.

When Islamic ideological thought speaks of Islamic music and Islamic architecture and Islamic art of the story and Islamic poetry, this denomination and this thought resemble Communist ideological thought. The only difference between them is that the first is believing, the second atheist. Ben Laden in 1998 formed an international ideology; the Islamic International spread to many countries.

When one-dimensional culture is imposed as the axis and effort is expended to ideologize all aspects of society, the result will be a totalitarian terrorist rule.

Q: Dr. Shahrur, you have a special theory with regard to the sovereignty (*hakimiyya*) of God and those who speak of it. Can you give us a summary?

A: The *hakimiyya* of God in its absolute pure form exists only with God. All the attempts to apply it are purely human activities with no relation to God or his *hakimiyya* because they are authoritarian operations with historical and geographical limits. Everyone who claims that he represents the *hakimiyya* of God is misled and corrupt; they claim this to cover over oppression and expropriate liberties.

In what concerns the *hakimiyya* of God, there are five points I would like to expose:

1. God does not share his rule with anyone, and everyone who does not share with anyone in his rule is inimical to God in his *hakimiyya*.

2. God, as the verse says, . . . "cannot be questioned as to what He does, while they will be questioned" (21.23).
   Everyone who puts himself beyond all questioning is inimical to God in his *hakimiyya*.

3. God, according to the verse, . . . "is doer of what He will" (11.107 also 85.16).

Every man who places himself in a position to do as he wishes is inimical to God in his *hakimiyya*.

4. God is Lord of the heavens and the earth, and every man who supposes that the country and the *'ibad* are his personal property is inimical to God in his Lordship.

5. God almighty is God of the worlds, and every man who demands absolute obedience from others is inimical to God in his divinity.

Every ruling system should be devoid of these five matters, that is, a pluralist system, the system of parties and opposition, opinion and contrary opinions, a system of interrogation. Consequently the State is a contract between the power and citizens by way of a constitution which should guarantee not falling into these five matters.

Today there are three solutions: let the *umma* fall into oblivion, or abandon Islam, or work to reform it. Otherwise I can only wish the regimes and rulers of the Arabs from the Ocean to the Gulf a pleasant sojourn and long security, as long as the problem of liberty remains incurable in the heads of the people as in the structure of the regimes. In our history the concept of tyranny is deep rooted and the concept of liberty is merely the contrary of slavery. This concept today has need of creativity, but the creativity has not yet come.

The son of a prominent religious preacher, he was active in the struggle against the Shah. In 1959 he went to Paris where he earned a doctorate in sociology at the Sorbonne and also became heavily involved in Iranian and Third World opposition movements. He later joined the Freedom Movement (*Nihdat-i Āzādī*) along with Āyatullāh Tāliqānī and Mehdī Bāzargān. He lectured at the University of Mashhad and subsequently at the Husayniya-i Irshad, a religious center in Teheran, where he drew large crowds and became very popular among the politically and religiously committed youth. The center was closed down, and Sharī'atī was arrested. Finally, after an international campaign, he was released and allowed to go to England, where shortly after his arrival, he died of a heart attack.

On Martyrdom (*Shahadat*)

In order to understand the meaning of *shahadat*, the ideological school from which it takes its expression and its value should be clarified. The concept of *shahadat* should be studied within the context of the school of thought and action which it is based upon, and in the school of thought of which Husayn is the manifestation par excellence. In the flow and struggle of human history, Husayn is the standard bearer of this struggle and his Karbala, a battlefield among battlefields, is the only link uniting the various fronts, the various generations and the various ages, throughout history from the beginning until the present moment and flowing into the future.

Husayn's meaning becomes clear when we understand his relationship to that movement beginning with Abraham. . . . This meaning should be made clear if Husayn's revolution is to be interpreted. To view Husayn and the battle of Karbala as isolated from historical and social circumstances would lead us to view the man and the event purely as an unfortunate, if not tragic, occurrence of the past, and something to cry about (and we certainly do continue to cry) rather than as an eternal and transcendent phenomenon. To separate Karbala and Husayn from their historical and ideological context is to dissect a living body, to remove only part of it and to examine it in exclusion from the living system of the body.

Excerpted from a lecture delivered by Alī Sharī'atī on *Shahadat* at the Husayniyah Irshad in 1970. The English translation was published in the volume *Jihad and Shahadat: Struggle and Martyrdom in Islam*, edited by Mehdi Abedi and Gary Legenhausen, the Institute for Research and Islamic Studies, Houston, Texas, 1986.

. . . Throughout the whole history of humanity, religious movements may be divided into two classes. Whether these movements are related to the contents of the religion and the conduct of the prophets and founders of the religion, or to the social class connections of the leaders of the religion and to what they were calling the people to do, all the historical prophets, whether true or false, as well as anyone who has begun a religious movement, are divided into two different classes. The first group consists of the links of the religious chain which began with Abraham. [These links in the] chain of prophets, from the historical point of view, are nearer to us and therefore we know them better. They consist of prophets whose view of society arose from the most deprived social and economic class of society. As Muhammad has said, and history shows us, all of these prophets were either shepherds, or simple hungry artisans and workers. These prophets stand in sharp contrast with the messengers of the other group of founders of intellectual and moral schools of thought, such as those which arose in China, India and Iran, and the scientific and ethical schools of Athens. This latter group without exception was composed of aristocrats. They arose from the noble, powerful and comfortable classes of their society. . . .

The mission of the non-Abrahamic messenger is always founded on the existing power structure so that power supports these messengers' ideas. The Abrahamic prophets, on the other hand, were always supported by the ordinary people against the powerful rulers of their time. . . .

The Prophet of Islam was appointed to complete the movement which has existed throughout history in opposition to deception, falsehood, polytheism, discord, hypocrisy, aristocracy and class differences. This was made a goal of the struggle by the announcement that all humanity is of one race, one source, one nature and of one God. Equality was declared for all; and with philosophical disputation as well as fighting against the economically powerful regime, social equality was upheld. Madinah was the ideal city, a model for every Islamic community. . . .

After the death of the Prophet, the deviation which was so very slight at first developed generation after generation. The distance between honesty, rectitude, truth and justice progressed so far in fourteen or fifteen years that by that time Uthman, like a magnetic pole, attracted all the counter-revolutionary agents who were scattered about, he gathered them at the center of Islamic power and Islamic movement. . . .

As we move forward in time the true base of the Islamic revolution becomes increasingly weakened, while in contrast, the base of neo-*jahiliya* and the internal enemies grow ever stronger until we reach the age of Imam Hasan, the eldest son of Ali and Fatima. . . . Hasan has no authority. . . . [He] sits in resistance to a reawakened neo-*jahiliya* . . . as the model of loneliness and isolation in Islamic society, even in the Madinah of the Prophet, he clearly shows that the Truth-seeking party in Islam is utterly shattered. . . .

Husayn inherits the Islamic movement. . . . There is nothing left for Husayn to inherit, no army, no weapons, no wealth, no power, no force, not even an organized following. Nothing at all. . . .

So now, sixty years after the *hijrah*, all of the powers are in possession of the oppressive ruler. Values are determined solely by the regime. Ideas and thoughts are developed by agents of the regime. Brains are washed, filled and poisoned with material presented in the name of religion. Faiths are altered, bought, paralyzed. If none of these efforts prove successful, faith is cut off with a sword. It is this power which Husayn must now face, a power which controls thought and religion, and which has at its disposal the Qur'an, wealth, weaponry, armies, the tools of propaganda, and the inheritance of the Prophet. Husayn appears with empty hands. He has nothing. What can he do? . . .

Husayn has two ways open before him—he could say "No, I cannot start a political fight against the Umayyad tribe because a combat like that needs an army and I have no power so I have to just sit down and perform an intellectual, a mental *jihad*." But Imam Husayn cannot choose this solution. . . .

Imam Husayn, as a responsible leader, sees that if he remains silent, Islam will change into a mere civil religion. Islam will be changed into a military-economic power and nothing more. Islam will become as other regimes and powers. . . . It is for this reason that Imam Husayn now stands between two inabilities. He can neither remain silent nor can he fight. . . . Husayn must fight, but he cannot.

It is so wonderful that it is so clear to intellectuals . . . that the response to the question "What is to be done?" is "Nothing," because the result of any action is defeat. Nothing can be done. . . .

There is only one man, a lonely man, who says "Yes." And what is that "yes"? It is a response behind which lies total inability, total weakness in a time of darkness and silence, against oppression and tyranny, an aware and faithful man who still has the responsibility of the *jihad*. . . .

Suddenly a spark appears in the darkness and bursts into flame! The radiant visage of a "martyr who walks upon the earth." . . .

A man emerges from Fatimah's house. Alone, friendless, with empty hands he confronts the terror of darkness and the sword. He has only one weapon—death. But he is the son of the family which has learned the art of dying well in the school of life. . . .

The great teacher of *shahadat* has now arisen in order to teach those who consider the *jihad* to pertain only to those who have ability and who think that victory lies only in conquest, that *shahadat* is not a loss; it is a choice, a choice whereby the warrior sacrifices himself on the threshold of the temple of freedom and the altar of love and is victorious. . . .

Shahadat in our culture and in our religion is not a bloody and tragic occurrence. In other religions and tribal histories, *shahadat* refers to the sacrifice of the heroes who are killed in the battles with the enemy. It is considered to be a sorrowful accident full of misery. Those who are killed in this way are called martyrs and their death is called martyrdom. But in our culture, *shahadat* is not a death which is imposed by an enemy upon our warriors. It is a death which is desired by our warriors, selected with all of the awareness, logic, reasoning, intelligence, understanding, consciousness and alertness that a human being can have. . . .

Look at Husayn! He releases his life, leaves his town and rises up in order to die because he has no other means by which to struggle to condemn and disgrace the enemy. He selects this way in order to pull aside the curtains which deceive by covering the ugly faces of the ruling power. If he cannot defeat the enemy in this way, at least he can disgrace them. If he cannot conquer the ruling power, he can at least condemn it by injecting the new blood and the belief of *jihad* into the dead bodies of this second generation after the revolution revealed by the Prophet.

He is an unarmed, powerless and lonely man. But he is still responsible for the *jihad*. He has no other means except to die, having himself chosen a "red death". Being Husayn makes it his responsibility to perform the *jihad* against all that is corrupt and cruel. He has no other means at his disposal for his *jihad* but his own death. He leaves his home only to enter the place of execution. We see how well he carried this out with his accurate plans, reasoning, a glorious and well-planned departure, movement and migration. Stage by stage, he clears the way, explaining the aim which he is moving toward with his unique selection of companions—men who had come to die with him—as well as members of his family. These are all of the things that he possesses in this world and he leads them to be sacrificed at the altar of *shahadat*. . . .

He who has no arms and no means has come with all of his existence, his family, his dearest companions, so that his *shahadat* and that of his whole family will bear witness to the fact that he carried out his responsibility at a time when truth was defenseless and unarmed. He bears witness that nothing more than this could be done. . . .

It is in this way that the dying of a human being guarantees the life of a nation. His *shahadat* is a means whereby faith can remain. It bears witness to the fact that great crimes, deception, oppression and tyranny rule. It proves that truth is being denied. It reveals the existence of values which are destroyed and forgotten. It is a red protest against a black sovereignty. It is a shout of anger in the silence which has cut off tongues.

Shahadat bears witness to that which some would rather let remain hidden in history. It is a symbol of that which must exist. It is bearing witness to what is taking place in this silent and secret time, and finally *shahadat* is the only reason for existence, the only sign of being present, the only means of attack and defense and the only manner of resistance so that truth, right and justice can remain alive at a time and under a regime in which uselessness, falsity and oppression rule. All of the bases have been defeated. All of the defenders and faithful followers have been massacred.

To be human is to stand at the threshold of decline in the face of the danger of dying forever. All of these miracles are performed by *shahadat*: arising and bearing witness.

Sixty years after the *hijrah*, a savior would appear and arise upon this black and silent graveyard. And Husayn, aware of his mandate which human destiny has placed upon his shoulders, leaves Mecca without hesitation and moves toward his place of *shahadat*. . . .

Shahadat, in summary, in our culture, contrary to other schools where it is considered to be an accident, an involvement, a death imposed upon a hero, a tragedy, is a grade, a level, a rank. It is not a means but is a goal itself. It is originality. It is completion. It is lift. It itself is mid-way to the highest peak of humanity and it is a culture.

In all ages and centuries, when the followers of a faith and an idea have power, they guarantee their honor and lives with *jihad*. But when they are weakened and have no means whereby to struggle, they guarantee their lives, movement, faith, respect, honor, future and history with *shahadat*. *Shahadat* is an invitation to all generations, in all ages, if you cannot kill your oppressor, then die.

AYATOLLAH MOHAMMAD KHATAMI
1942–

He was born into a clerical family in Ardakan in central Iran; his father was the Grand Ayatollah Ruhollah Khatami. After religious studies in Qom, Khatami entered the University of Isfahan in 1965 to study philosophy, followed in 1969 by graduate studies in education at the University of Teheran. Two years later, he returned to Qom to pursue further religious studies in Islamic law, jurisprudence, and philosophy. In Qom he became more immersed in political activity. In 1978, on the eve of the Iranian revolution, he was chosen to lead the Hamburg Islamic Institute in Germany, which played a pivotal role in organizing revolutionary activity among the Iranian diaspora. From 1982 to 1992, he served as Minister of Culture and Islamic Guidance, and then in 1992 he was appointed assistant to Iran's President and head of the National Library of Iran. He was elected President of the Islamic Republic of Iran on May 23, 1997, with over two-thirds of the popular vote and reelected for a second term in 2001. He has published several books and articles, including *Islam, Liberty and Development* and *From the City-World to the World-City.*

Dialogue Between East and West

The phrase 'dialogue among civilizations and cultures', which should be interpreted as conversing with other civilizations and cultures, is based upon a definition of truth which is not necessarily at odds with the well-known definitions of truth that one finds in philosophical texts. Dialogue among civilizations requires listening to and hearing from other civilizations and cultures, and the importance of listening to others is by no means less than talking to others. It may be in fact more important.

Talking and listening create a conversation; one side addresses the other side, and speech is exchanged. . . . The world of science is not the world of speeches and addresses. . . . But the world of art and the world of religion are the world of addressing. We are addressed by a work of art, and in religion, words of God address man. That is why the languages of mysticism and religion are linked together by genuine and profound ties, and why the earliest specimens of art that have been created by man are also specimens of Sacred Art. Man is addressed again and again in the Bible and in the Holy Quran, and it is with this call that the individual human being is elevated and becomes a person. . . .

Text of an address to the European University Institute, Florence, on March 10, 1999.

[T]he important point here is that in the concept of religious address, when man is being addressed by God on a general and universal level, and not in specific terms of religious teaching and codes of conduct, none of his psychological, social or historical aspects are really being addressed. What is addressed is man's true, non-historic and individual nature, and that is why all the divine religions are not quintessentially different. The differences arise from religious laws and codes of conduct that govern the social and judicial life of human beings.

Now we must ask ourselves who is this person that is being addressed.

Recounting the fascinating story of philosophical anthropology, and the episodes dealing with self-knowledge and self-discovery, would take several long nights in the Thousand and One Nights of the history of philosophy. Some of these tales were first told in the East and some originated in the West. It is significant to note that the Eastern tales explain the Oriental side of man's being while the Western tales reveal the properties of his Occidental side. Man is in fact the meeting point of the soul's East and the reason's West. Denying the existence of any part of his essence would impair our understanding of the significance of his being. In our effort to grasp the meaning of the person, we should watch out not to fall into the trap of individualism, or into that of collectivism. Even though the views expressed by Christian thinkers have helped the modern concept of the individual to crystallize, this should not be taken to mean that there exists a natural link between the two views. Just as the profound attention focused on the meaning of the person as the recipient of the Divine Word should not be credited, in my view, to the influence of personalism. Of course, it has been said by everyone that in modern society, it is individual human beings who are the criterion and the yardstick for all institutions, laws and social relations, and that civil rights and human rights are in fact nothing other than the rights of this same individual. On the other hand, collectivism, which was launched vis-à-vis individualism, was formulated by multiplying the same concept of the individual, and therefore the two ideologies have the same philosophical foundation. For this reason we consider, from our position of spiritual wisdom, the antagonism between individualistic liberalism and collectivist socialism to be superficial and incidental. The concept of the person can be easily explained in terms of Islamic mysticism. The Islamic mystics consider man to be a world unto himself, a microcosm. Man's originality does not emanate from his individuality or his collectivity. His originality is solely due to the fact that it is him, and him alone, who is addressed by the Divine Call. With this address, man's soul transcends its boundaries, and with the transcendence of his soul, his world also becomes a world of justice and humanity.

Anyone who examines even briefly the meandering course of philosophy from its beginnings to the present will clearly notice the continuous swing of the philosophers, from one extreme to the other. The last swing, the last link in the chain, is modernity. This word, which seemingly is the latest term to be derived from the Latin *modernus*, was apparently first used in the nineteenth century. But the Latin word itself has been in use for more than fifteen centuries, and it was only in the nineteenth and twentieth centuries that modernity was applied to a wide range of concepts in such diverse fields as philosophy, art, science, history and ethics. The common denominator in all these concepts is the cataclysm that shook the very foundations of man's existence and thinking towards the end of the Middle Ages. It was a cataclysm that pushed man and the world into a new orbit. Man and the contemporary world (so far as it is affected by man's ideas) result from this modern orbit into which they were sent in the aftermath of the Middle Ages. This new orbit was labelled 'modern' in those times, but today we call it the Renaissance. Italy played a decisive role in the birth of the Renaissance. Although many books and essays have been written to describe and explain this great milestone, there is still a definite need for philosophers, historians and scientists to think and talk about it.

The sole aim of the Renaissance was not to revive classical Greek culture. Its principal aim was—as already pointed out by a number of thinkers—to revitalize religion by giving it a new language and fresh ideas. The Renaissance defined the man of religion not as someone who would contemptuously turn his back on the world in order to repress it, but as somebody who would face the world. The Renaissance man of religion turns to the world just as the world awaits him with open arms, and this reciprocal openness and opening up of the world and man constitute the most fundamental point about the Renaissance, and inherently it is a religious event aimed at conserving, reforming and propagating religion, and not opposed to it or against it.

But this great event ended up, in due course, somewhere diametrically opposed to the original intention. The opening of the world was transformed into violent conquest and subjugation. This violent conquest did not remain limited to mastering nature. Its fires soon spread to human communities. What came to be known in the socio-political history of Europe as colonialism is the result of extending the domineering attitude of man towards nature and the natural sciences, to men—modernity without adopting a humanitarian and ethical approach.

The critique of modernity that I propose is undertaken from a vantage point and angle which are profoundly different from the position of its well-known critics, especially in the domain of philosophy. Someone who sets out to prune a tree should not cut the very branch he is standing on. That is exactly how some of the philosophers of our time are behaving in their critique of modernity. By denying Reason any dialectical authority, they turn it either into a weapon that destroys everyone and everything, itself included, or transform it into a blunt and rusted sword that can only become a museum piece. One cannot use Reason as a critical weapon without accepting its authority and without recognizing its limits.

The critique of pure reason, which opened a new chapter in Western philosophy and may be taken to mean the critique of everything and all concepts including pure reason itself, only becomes possible if reason is endowed with authority. Without the authority of reason—which should be discussed at length and with precision in some other venue and at a more appropriate time, without forgetting to discuss its relationship to domination and power—it will not be possible to have a clear picture and concept of such vital political issues as human rights, peace, justice and freedom. And without this clear concept, our efforts for the establishment of these ideals will not succeed. But this should not be interpreted as a call to rationality and European style logocentrism that preceded post-modernism. Because of the fact that Europe has given birth to modern rationality, it should feel a stronger responsibility for criticizing it and finding a solution to prevent its destructive consequences.

Europe has itself fallen prey to its over-reliance on rationality, and is today engaged, through its thinkers and philosophers, in totally discrediting its own rationality. The Orient, which etymologically speaking has given rise to a number of words pertaining to order and a sense of direction, can undertake, in the course of a historical dialogue with the West aimed at reaching a mutual understanding, to call on Europe and America to exercise more equilibrium, serenity, and contemplation in their conduct, thus contributing to the establishment of peace, security and justice in the world.

The exuberance and vitality of European culture stem from its critical approach towards everything, itself included. But the time has come for Europe to take another step forward and view itself differently, as others see it. This should not be taken to mean that Europe should forget its great cultural heritage or that it should turn to a new type of obscurantism. It is rather an encouragement to European culture and civilization to embark on new experiences to gain a more precise knowledge of global cultural geography. In Orientalism, we find that the East is treated as an object of study, rather than as 'the other side' of a dialogue. For a real dialogue among civilizations to take place, it is imperative that the East should become a real participant in the discussions and not just remain an object of study.

This is a very important step that Europe and America need to take towards the realization of the 'dialogue-among-civilizations' project. Of course this is not a one-way invitation. We too, as Iranians, as Muslims and as Asians, need to take major steps towards gaining a true knowledge of the West, as it really is. This knowledge will help us to improve our economic and social way of life. Taking such bold steps by us and by Europeans would require a character trait that was first recognized and promoted in Europe by the Italians.

Renaissance historians have written that as a result of the continuous contacts of the Italians with Byzantium and the Islamic world, the people of Italy developed a sense of tolerance. The Italians had been familiar with Islamic civilization since the time of the Crusades, and they admired it.

Speaking of the historical past without any reference to the future would be an idle academic exercise, whereas it is imperative upon us, for the sake of helping human communities and improving the state of the world, to find out how the relations of Asian countries, and especially those of the Muslim countries, with Europe stand today. Why? Because Muslims and Europeans are next-door neighbours, and nations, unlike individuals, cannot choose their neighbours. Therefore, apart from moral, cultural and humanitarian reasons, Islam and Europe must, by force of historic and geographical circumstance, get to know one another better, and then move on to improve their political, economic and cultural relations. Our futures are inseparable because our pasts have been inseparable. Even today, in our schools of philosophy, the views of Plato, Aristotle, and Plotinus, and those of Descartes, Kant, Hegel and Wittgenstein from among the modernists are taught alongside the views of al-Kindi, Farabi, Ibn Sina (*Avicenna*), Suhrawardi and Mulla Sadra. If the great civilizations of Asia view themselves today in a Western mirror and get to know one another through the West, it was Islam that served in the not-too-distant past as a mirror to the West; it was a mirror in which the West could see its own past and its own philosophical and cultural heritage. If dialogue is not a simple choice but a necessity for our two cultures, then this dialogue should be conducted with the true representatives of Islamic culture and thought. Otherwise, what good will it do for the West to talk with a few 'Westoxicated' types who are themselves no more than inferior and deformed images of the West? This would not be a dialogue; it would not even amount to a monologue. A profound, thoughtful and precise dialogue with Islamic civilization would be helpful in finding fair and practical solutions to some of the grave problems that beset the world today. The crisis of the family, the crisis in the relationship of man and nature, the ethical crisis that has developed in scientific research, and many more problems of this nature should be among the items on the agenda of an Islamic–European dialogue.

Dialogue is such a desirable thing, because it is based on freedom and free will. In a dialogue, no idea can be imposed on the other side. In a dialogue, one should respect the independent identity of the other side and his or her independent ideological and cultural integrity. Only in such a case can dialogue be a preliminary step leading to peace, security and justice.

In the meanwhile, conducting a dialogue with Iran has its own advantages. Iran is a door-to-door neighbour with Europe on one side, and with Asia on the other. Thus Iran is the meeting point of Eastern and Western cultures, just as man is the meeting point of the soul's East and the reason's West. The Persian heart and the Persian mind are brimful with a sense of balance, affection and tolerance, and for this reason, Iranians are the advocates of dialogue and adherents to justice and peace.

SEYYED HOSSEIN NASR
1933–

Educated in Iran and the United States, Nasr graduated from
the Massachusetts Institute of Technology and Harvard
University. Nasr taught at Teheran University until 1979 and
founded the Iranian Academy of Philosophy. He is University
Professor of Islamic Studies at George Washington University.
A prolific author, he has made major contributions to the field
of Islamic and Iranian studies and been a leader in a school
of thought known as the perennial philosophy. Among his
many publications are *Man and Nature: The Spiritual Crisis of
Modern Man, Islam: Religion, History and Civilization,
Philosophy of Seyyed Hossein Nasr,* and *Islam and the Plight
of Modern Man.*

Reflections on Islam and
the West: Yesterday,
Today and Tomorrow

. . . We wish to reflect and meditate on the question of the relation between
Islam and the West in the future on the basis of the past. In discussing this
most important and timely issue, and in light of what has already been paid,
we must pause and ask again what we mean by the two terms Islam and
the West. Which Islam and which West are we considering? Is it traditional
Islam as practiced by the majority of Muslims, the Islam of pious men
and women who seek to live in the light of God's teachings as revealed in
the Quran and in surrender to His will? Or is it modernist interpretations
that seek to interpret the Islamic tradition in view of currently prevalent
Western ideas and fashions of thought? Or yet, is it the extreme forms
of politically active Islam that, in exasperation, before dominance by non-
Islamic forces both outside and inside the borders of most Islamic countries,
takes recourse to ideas and methods of certain strands of recent Western
political history, including, in some cases, terrorism, which is against
Islamic law and which was not invented by them?

Nor is the reality of the West in any way homogeneous. In fact,
practically the only political unity observed in the West these days appears
in the hatred of Islam, as shown in the case of Bosnia and Chechnya, where

From Seyyed Hossein Nasr, *Islam and the Plight of Modern Man* (London: Longman, 2000),
pp. 267–84.

one observed for a long time, with very few exceptions, the uniformity of silence, indifference, and inaction by various voices in the West in the face of the worst kind of human atrocities. Otherwise, the opposition of forces and diversity of what is usually called the West are so blatant as to hardly need mention. But since it is ignored in many quarters that speak of global order based on what they call Western values, it must be asked if the West is characterized by Trappist and Carthusian monks or European and American agnostic or atheistic "intellectuals" on university campuses or in the media. One wonders if the Westerners are those who still make pilgrimage to Lourdes in the thousands, or those who journey, also in the thousands, to Las Vegas or the home of Elvis Presley. This diversity and even confrontation within the West are of the greatest importance not only for those in Europe and the United States who speak of confrontation with the Islamic world on the basis of the idea that there is an at least relatively unified West, but also for the Muslims, at least some of whom are in general fully aware of deep divisions not likely to be integrated into unity soon but which are in fact on the verge of creating disorder and chaos within the very fabric of Western societies.

Also, religiously speaking, the diversity in the two worlds is not of the same degree. The vast majority of the Islamic world still lives within the Islamic worldview. Everyone considers the Quran as the Word of God, the Prophet as His messenger, and the reality of God, His Names and Attributes as unquestioned realities. In contrast, in the West, beyond common commercial interests of various nations and groups that unify them, there is a much greater division concerning the most fundamental issues, such as the reality or denial of the reality of God, the origin of humanity, the nature and origin of ethics, and even the sacredness and the origin of life itself, over which some people are willing to kill those whom they consider to be participating in murder by terminating the life of a fetus. Muslims might be fighting over the question of political authority and the types of laws that should govern Islamic society, but very few differ concerning the belief that God is still sitting on His Throne (al-'arsh) and is the ruler of the universe.

On the contrary, in the West there is less political fighting today after several centuries of bloody revolutions and upheavals, but there is also the deepest struggle and almost revolution on the question of values and ethics, not to speak of theology itself. On both sides of the debate concerning Islam and the West, it is important to remember these and many other dimensions and forms of diversity, although . . . it is not possible to deal in depth with them. Lest one forget, it must be recalled that even on the question of the nature of the Bible and its meaning, there is more difference between people of the Bible belt and many skeptical and deconstructionist professors in the universities in that very region than there is between the view of the former and what Muslims consider the Bible to be throughout the whole of the Islamic world. . . .

THE ELEMENTS OF CONFLICT TODAY

The basic reality underlying the relation of Islam and the West is the already mentioned fact that, in contrast to earlier Western expectations, the Islamic religion is still fully vibrant and Islamic civilization is still alive, even if greatly weakened. In contrast to all those late nineteenth- and early twentieth-century Western students of Islam, especially missionaries, who predicted the imminent demise of Islam, the religion shows much more vitality today than many others. The very existence of the Islamic world, which negates so many assumptions of the postmedieval and modern Western worldview, such as individualism, secular humanism, and the superiority of human rights over divine rights and humanly devised laws over Divine Law, appears as a formidable challenge to a West that considers its own historical develop-ment as the only acceptable path follow for all other peoples on the globe. Otherwise, they are branded as medieval and backward and are identified with all kinds of other pejorative connotations prevalent in the modern world. Were Islam to have simply surrendered to Western patterns of think-ing and acting, as do so many Muslim modernists, there would have been no confrontation between the two worlds.

The reason for the conflict is the very reality of another civilization that wishes to follow its own principles and develop according to its own inner life and dynamic rather than on the basis of externally imposed norms that, according to many voices, now threaten the West itself. Today, the situation is not like the period of the cold war, when the West and the com-munist worlds were threatening each other's very existence, for the Islamic world cannot and does not threaten the West militarily, politically, or even economically in any conceivable way. On the contrary, the West controls the most vital economic resources of Muslim nations, benefits from all conflicts in that world through the sale of vast quantities of arms, and prac-tically dictates its wishes in many parts of the Islamic world.

In debates about the threat of the Islamic world, rarely do the Western media present the real issues of basic importance in Muslim eyes, such as the loss of Muslim lands, especially in Palestine, on the basis of exclus-ive historic claims that deny the claims of the other side. These historical claims are, in fact, of such a nature that were they to be pursued elsewhere they would, through the same logic, require non-native Americans to return to its original inhabitants much of the land captured only a century or two ago through one of the most successful conquests in human history of the type that some now call "ethnic cleansing." How tragic it is that Jews and Muslims could have lived in harmony with each other in days of old but cannot do so in the future if one accepts this exclusivist logic without considering the views of the other side of the confrontation. Other issues include the fact that many nations in the West not only control the most important economic asset of much of the Islamic world—oil —but also want in a thousand and one ways to recover the money they have paid for it, whether through the sale of arms or the creation of safe markets.

Nor is the West, in the sense of Western governments and of course non well-meaning individuals and organizations, seriously interested in the welfare of the Islamic world, unless it coincides, as is to be expected, with its own geopolitical and economic interests, as seen so clearly in the attitude of the West toward democracy in the Islamic world or the unbelievably hypocritical manner in which concerns for human rights are applied whenever it is to the interest of this or that power but never when it goes against the political and commercial interests of those same powers. How many people who keep talking about Islamic terrorist threats ever bother to ask why a twenty-year-old person should, at the prime of his youth, give up his/her life so easily and so voluntarily? What is lacking that causes such extreme actions? Terrorism of any kind, whether committed by Muslims, Christians or Jews, is heinous and against the teachings of all three religions. When it does occur, it is necessary not only to condemn it, which one must, but also to go behind the immediate events and ask why such acts are being or have been carried out. Today, as far as the Islamic world is concerned, the causes behind such terrible acts are the loss of hope, unbearable pressures (often supported directly or indirectly by the West), and desperation before forces that are destroying one's religion and civilization. Hatred is a fire that consumes and annihilates, but the fire cannot be put out unless one inquires about its causes. Otherwise, as soon as one fire is put out, another is ignited.

There is no possibility of creating understanding between the West and the Islamic world until, on the Western side, people realize that the very absolutization of the West's particular worldview at a particular moment in time, when combined with powerful economic "interests" that are usually against the interest of others, brings about impatience with and even hatred of other worldviews. This has happened to such an extent that today many people in the West who are opposed to friendship with the Islamic world, because of their own political or economic agendas, also oppose any mention of the harmony and peace that dominated most of the life of Jews and Christians within the Islamic world before modern times. They even seek to arouse Christian and Jewish enmity against Islam, although many of them are not themselves, for the most part, serious followers of either religion.

As for Muslims, they must stop identifying the aggressively secularist force and crass commercial interests of the West with the whole of the West and remember that, although the West is predominantly secular, there has survived in the West to this day important Christian and also Jewish elements whose worldviews, despite transient worldly interests in some quarters, are close to that of Islam. Between the Islamic world and the secularist West there can be no deep harmony and accord, for there are no common transcendent principles between them, just as there are none between Hindus and Confucians or Buddhists and the secularist worldview. There can only be peace based upon mutual respect on the human level. Needless to say, this respect is not given by many Westerners to any Muslims who, rather than emulating a West lost to an even greater degree in the maze of its own errors, seek to live Islamically in a serious manner. Nor is it given by most Muslims to Westerners with spiritual principles—with the major difference, however, that Islam is not a threat to the Western way of life but only to Western interests within the Islamic world itself. Tapes of the Quran are not about to invade the airwaves of Europe and the United States as the crudest products of Western pop culture are invading the East, while Western secularism is seeking in a virulently aggressive manner to impose not only its technology, but also its half-dying world-view, through that technology, upon the non-Western world, especially the Islamic.

TO OVERCOME OBSTACLES TO UNDERSTANDING

It is here that, for people of good faith on both sides of this divide and also for Christians living in the Islamic world and Muslims living in the West, a more profound question, as far as its long-term impact is concerned, arises. It is the question of understanding and accord between Islam and Christianity, and to the extent possible Judaism, both across the frontiers of the West and the Islamic world and also within their borders. The Muslims, whom the Serbs and Russians were massacring until recently in the name of Christianity, have a lot more in common with the Serbs as far as religion is concerned, as exemplified by such Orthodox masters as St. Maximus the Confessor and St. Gregory of Palamas, than do the Serbs with many not only secularized Westerners but also completely modernized Christians, some of whom admit freely that they do not even believe in the virgin birth of Christ or his historical authenticity, to which Muslims cling as truths revealed in the Quran. To talk of the West and Islam and to identify characteristically the modern West with Christianity, which it has enfeebled to the degree observable today, is to gloss over a cleavage that would make all serious mutual understanding well-nigh impossible.

It is true that modernism has marginalized Christianity to an ever-greater degree since the Renaissance. Yet Christianity, as well as Judaism in the West, continues to survive as a living reality and in its evangelical form at least there has been even a revival of Christianity in recent time in the Occident. If one looks at the situation in depth, one sees that they have a great deal more in common with Muslims who believe in God, accept the moral injunctions of the Ten Commandments and seek to live a life centered upon prayer and the reality of the other world to which Christ referred in that most forgotten of his utterances, "Seek ye first the Kingdom of God," than with people whose mother tongue is English, French, German, or some other European language but who share nothing of the Christian worldview, whether it be of this world or the next. If a new awareness of this truth is to be created in the context of the present anti-Islamic current in the West, which speaks sometimes as if we were living at the time of St. Bernard of Clairvaux rather than of deconstructionism, relativism, and a general hatred of serious religion, which is tolerated only if completely divorced from public life, there would be a greater possibility for a serious accord between most of the Islamic world and, at least, a West if not what is called the West as defined by economic and geopolitical interests that are pursued at all costs, whether these "interests" also accord with the interests of others or not. The achievement of this awareness is so laudable that it must be pursued fully by all people of good faith on both sides, despite many obstacles on the way.

On the Christian side, the first important consideration is, of course, a theological one. Despite so many ecumenical meetings since the Second World War between Christians and Muslims, sometimes along with Jews, few Christians accept Islam as an authentic religion or revelation and the Prophet as the receiver of a major message from Heaven coming after Christ. There is much diplomatic courtesy, but little theological acceptance, especially by more traditional and conservative elements of Christianity, who are, in fact, closest to Muslims and best understand the meaning of a sacred scripture that is immutable and of divine origin and of ethical laws that, coming from God, are not meant to evolve with "the times" but to determine "the times" whenever and wherever they might be. This tragic paradox is similar to the case of the environment, in which conservative Christians, who emphasize more than others the sanctity of human life from its conception in the mother's womb, are much more indifferent to forces that are destroying the whole natural environment and the web of life that supports also human life, than many of those who would have difficulty with the very notion of the Sacred.

Granted, accepting the authenticity of Islam is more difficult for Christianity than the acceptance of the authenticity of Christianity is for Islam, which, while denying the Trinity and Incarnation, accepts the divine origin of the Christic message and considers Christ as the supreme prophet of inwardness preceding the Prophet of Islam. Nevertheless, the question of mutual acceptance must be faced squarely. The greatest support in the world today for traditional Christian and Jewish beliefs comes from Islam and, in fact, throughout the ages Islam has permitted its Jewish and Christian minorities in its midst to practice their religion freely, the result of which is witnessed by the depth of piety and authenticity of eastern Christianity and Oriental Judaism today.

The task that lies ahead is for religious leaders of the three religions to realize and have the courage to assert these truths, despite the tragic problems of Palestine that have cast such a shadow upon Muslim-Jewish relations and a triumphalism in certain quarters that would still seek to prove the glory of Christianity through the fact that it was the religion of a civilization that became the most powerful—but at the same time the most secularized—civilization in the world. From the Islamic point of view, how tragic it is that while Muslims protected the Jewish people throughout most of their history and provided a haven for them after their expulsion from Spain after the Reconquest, they have had to pay so dearly for the barbaric atrocities of Hitler. Likewise, how sad it is to observe that, even at the height of their power and before the modern colonial period, Muslims never practiced "ethnic cleansing" against the many Christian minorities in their midst; they recently had to suffer a new wave of ethnic cleansing similar to that of Spain after 1492, while the official modern West—and of course not the many concerned Westerners, the West that declares loudly to be the champion of human rights—looked on for a long time without taking a single serious step because those being cleansed in Bosnia or massacred in Chechnya were Muslims and not Christians or Jews.

Despite these tragedies that have darkened the scene, the attempt must nevertheless be made by Christian and Jewish leaders on one side, and Islamic leaders on the other, to reach a profound accord not on the basis of a secular humanism that has already demonstrated its poverty, nor of simple political niceties carried out for the sake of expediency, but on the foundation of the certitude that the followers of these religions are all the children of Abraham and pray to the same God. Muslim leaders, as well as Jewish and Christian ones, bear the deep responsibility of undertaking every effort possible in this direction. More specifically, Muslims, often wary of ecumenical discussions because of their subsequent results and effects, must realize how difficult the task of the acceptance of Islam as an authentic revelation is for a serious Christian theologian and not simply castigate the Christian because he cannot accept the authenticity of the Islamic revelation as easily as can Islam the revelations of Judaism and Christianity.

A second major obstacle that affects the whole of the modern West, much of modernized Christianity and, to some extent, Western Judaism is the assumption that all civilization must follow the secularizing trajectory of Western history since the Renaissance. In fact, most of the dialogue carried out between Christians and Muslims today is colored by the presence of that silent third partner: anti-religious secularism. The debate is not like the one in which Nicholas of Cusa participated at the end of the fifteenth century. How easier would it have been, in fact, if a Ghazzālī, a Maimonides, and a St. Thomas were to carry out religious dialogue! From the Islamic point of view, what is difficult to understand is how various tenets of Christianity are changing so rapidly to the extent that some want to change the name and gender of Christ, whom they now call Christa. When modernism began, Christianity, especially in its Catholic form, stood as the critic and opponent of modernism, whereas now many voices in the churches have become accomplices to the spread of the very ideas that have opposed the most fundamental tenets of the authentic Christian faith. The result is the constant change of even basic elements of the faith, so that it is difficult to understand with whom one is dialoguing. On the one hand, Christianity presents itself to Islam as a powerful spiritual force that, in reality, still dominates the West and its value system, and, on the other hand, under the pressure of modern secularist ideas, much of Christian theology is changing with incredible rapidity, and what has survived of Christian ethics in Western society is disappearing with an unprecedented speed.

The present situation is one in which Islam still sees God as sitting upon "His Throne" (al-'arsh) ruling over the universe and Islamic society, as one in which the practice of religion is so intense as to incorporate the whole of life, and where the vast majority of Muslims still perform their daily prayers, fast, and perform other rites promulgated by the Divine Law (Shari'ah). In the West, in contrast, many question the very nature and function of God, and in many European countries only about 10 percent of the people attend church at least once a week. Rarely is this great difference of actual practice of religion taken into account in current inter-religious dialogue, and the agenda is carried out in which many Christians simply identify themselves with the West, as if the case of religion in the two worlds were the same. It is as if a country in Africa or Asia were to carry out trade talks with the United States without paying any attention to the present disparity in economic activities in the two countries.

As in the case of trade, so in the case of religion. The actual religious situation must be considered and such baseless slogans as Islam being medieval and Christianity being modern must be put aside, at least by serious Christian thinkers. When France was medieval, it was called the elder daughter of the Church and produced great theologians, Christian art, and deep piety, whereas today only 10 percent of French people go to church regularly. St. Thomas Aquinas has been succeeded at the Sorbonne by such men as Derrida and Foucault, and Notre Dame has been "superseded" by the Centre Pompidou! Christian thinkers, at least Catholic and Orthodox ones, should be the last to try to look upon Islam in a pejorative and degrading manner by calling it "medieval" or expecting Islam to undergo a so-called reform that would simply follow the path of the West, ending up with an officially Lutheran Sweden, in which church attendance a few years ago was less than 5 percent. A new appreciation of the eternal values of religion and the sapience that lies at its heart must be cultivated to allow serious dialogue to take place with Islam, one which would also strengthen what remains of traditional religions in the Occident.

Finally, a third major obstacle to be confronted is missionary activity, not as it was practiced in the days of old, but as it has been practiced by Western Christian missionaries since the colonial period and to this day. Both Christianity and Islam are traveling religions that claim to bear a global message, and neither religion can demand from the other that it discontinue "preaching unto the nations." In the days of old, the material power behind the religious message of the two religions was more or less the same, in total contrast to what one observes today, where Western

Christian missionary activity in the Islamic world is accompanied often, but not always, by enticement of the most worldly kind, usually relying upon the products of the very civilization that has marginalized Christianity. There is usually a Bible in one hand and syringes or sacks of rice in the other, along with a schooling system that is more successful in secularizing than Christianizing its students. There are, of course, remarkable exceptions, but not all the missionaries are a Père de Foucault who, living in poverty, went into the North African desert to be a witness of Christ among Muslims. Rather, in many areas missionary activity continues to be the instrument of Western secular interests, as it was during the colonial period. Almost everywhere in Africa and Asia converted populations are as much protagonists of the secularized modern West as they are of the message of Christ, which they often understand in an already secularized form.

It is interesting to note in this context that Eastern Christians have not usually displayed the same missionary zeal as Western Christians, whose aggressive missionary spirit is due not only to Christianity but also to the Graeco-Roman civilization, for which everyone other than themselves was a barbarian. This fact was also demonstrated in that Christian and Jewish heresy, Marxism and communism, and continues to be seen in the zeal with which secular humanists, no longer defending Christianity, go about with the same missionary zeal within the Islamic world to convert the Muslims to the secularist perspective. These several types of missionary activity, in fact, meet in some places, such as in American and European institutions of learning in the Islamic world, many of which started as Christian missionary schools and are now supposedly bastions of secularist education.

To understand how great an obstacle is the missionary issue in the context of its being wed to the modern West and its being supported by great wealth created by means of modern finance and technology that, to put it mildly, have little to do with Christian poverty, one should look for a moment at the situation if roles were reversed. How would devout Christians feel if Islam carried out missionary activity not from the position of worldly weakness, as it does now as Christians did in the Roman empire, but from the position of incomparable economic strength? How would they react if Muslims invited Christians to dialogue while promising anyone who embraced Islam free oil for their cars, free hospital care, and access to an educational system that would guarantee them high position in their countries, whose governments were so much under the influence of the Islamic world that they could not stop such types of aggressive missionary activity?

There is no doubt that these obstacles exist, but from both the Western Christian and Muslim side there must be an attempt to overcome them if there is to be any real accord and peace between the two sides. Muslims, especially, while acting from the background of much greater weakness politically, economically, and militarily, must nevertheless open all the doors possible to genuine dialogue and understanding with those Christians who put the kingdom of God above that of Caesar. How sad it is that many of the most devout Muslims are distrustful of even well-intentioned Christians, whom they identify simply with the modern West, concerning which they have the right to be suspicious. How tragic that in the West the more conservative and traditional a Christian, the more he is likely to be ignorant of Islam, while some leaders of such groups describe Islam in terms of the anti-Christ. Ecumenism then often remains in the hands of those who are willing to change the very foundations of their faith to bring about worldly understanding with followers of other religions, or one might say those who would readily sacrifice that peace "which passeth all understanding," that is, peace with God and in God, for a worldly peace that God does not allow anyway under these conditions, for there can never be peace on earth without harmony and peace with Heaven.

CONCLUDING REMARKS

Finally, it is necessary to assert once again that, for those seriously concerned with the future of humanity and not simply with passing exigencies in addition to egotistical calculations and short-term "interests," the question of Islam and the West must be cast in a new mold. Both sides must understand that there cannot be an integration of two diametrically opposed worldviews, that is, Islam and modern secularism, but, as mentioned, at best mutual and not simply one-sided respect on the human level and the creation of a modus vivendi based upon lack of aggression of one side against the other, which includes refraining from plundering the wealth and the land and seeking to demolish the culture of the other side. But both Islam and the West must also understand that there can be, and in fact needs to be, a true meeting of minds and hearts between Christians, Jews, and Muslims who, after all, share many fundamental principles of their respective worldviews and who all face a much greater danger of a mortal threat from Western secularist culture, including its outposts in the Islamic world, than they do from each other.

To accomplish this end, the atmosphere must be cleared through earnest effort on all sides, and such terms as fundamentalism, extremism, and radicalism must be restudied and defined not in the light of immediate political interests but of the truth. The practice of first anathematizing and demonizing a word and then simply using it against whomever one does not like at the moment is hardly the way of achieving any understanding or accord. What is needed is, indeed, the truth of that peace of which Christ spoke as being immanent to man's nature and that Muslims identify as one of the Names of God. It is only the shining of the light of truth upon the dark clouds of today's horizon that can make possible an accord between the people of faith in both worlds. Furthermore, one hopes, on the basis of such an accord, that a way of living and acting between Islam and the West would come about based upon mutual respect rather than greed parading as human concern or hatred passing itself as religious righteousness.

In any case, as Christians well know, what God has united should not and cannot be rent asunder by human beings. The destiny of the West, and especially the Christian West, as well as Judaism, and Islam are intertwined and connected by profound bonds that cannot be severed in the long run and can only be loosened temporarily at great cost to all. Let us hope that the current situation will provide the opportunity for people of good intentions on both sides to pursue the vital issue of relations between Islam and the West in light of permanent truths and not transient whims and fancies based upon the desire for power, greed and self-assertion.

wa'Llāhu a'lam

T. J. WINTER (ABDAL HAKIM MURAD)
1960–

Born Timothy J. Winter in 1960, he studied at the prestigious
Westminster School in London and later at the University of
Cambridge, where he graduated with first class honors in Arabic
in 1983. Lecturer at the University of Cambridge, he focuses his
work on Muslim-Christian relations, Islamic ethics, and the study
of the orthodox Muslim response to extremism. He is particularly known for his translations, especially his al-Ghazali series,
including al-Ghazali's *On Death and What Comes After* and *On
Disciplining the Soul.*

The Poverty of Fanaticism

"Blood is no argument," as Shakespeare observed. Sadly, Muslim ranks are
today swollen with those who disagree. The World Trade Center, yesterday's symbol of global finance, has today become a monument to the
failure of global Islam to control those who believe that the West can be
bullied into changing its wayward ways towards the East. There is no real
excuse at hand. It is simply not enough to clamor, as many have done, about
"chickens coming home to roost," and to protest that Washington's acquiescence in Israeli policies towards Palestine is the inevitable generator of
such hate. It is of course true—as Shabbir Akhtar has noted—that powerlessness can corrupt as insistently as does power. But to comprehend is
not to sanction or even to empathize. To take innocent life to achieve a goal
is the hallmark of the most extreme secular utilitarian ethic, and stands at
the opposite pole of the absolute moral constraints required by religion.

There was a time, not long ago, when the "ultras" were few, forming
only a tiny wart on the face of the worldwide attempt to revivify Islam.
Sadly, we can no longer enjoy the luxury of ignoring them. The extreme
has broadened, and the middle ground, giving way, is everywhere dislocated
and confused. And this enfeeblement of the middle ground, of the moderation enjoined by the Prophetic example, is in turn accelerated by the
opprobrium which the extremists bring not simply upon themselves, but
upon committed Muslims everywhere. For here, as elsewhere, the preferences of the media work firmly against us. David Koresh could broadcast
his fringe Biblical message from Ranch Apocalypse without the image of
Christianity, or even its Adventist wing, being in any way besmirched. But

From Joseph E. B. Lombard, *Islam, Fundamentalism, and the Betrayal of Tradition* (Indiana:
World Wisdom, Inc., 2004), pp. 283–95.

when a fringe Islamic group bombs Swedish tourists in Cairo, the stain is instantly spread over "militant Muslims" everywhere.

If these things go on, the Islamic movement will cease to form an authentic summons to cultural and spiritual renewal, and will exist as little more than a splintered array of maniacal factions. The prospect of such an appalling and humiliating end to the story of a religion which once surpassed all others in its capacity for tolerating debate and dissent now seems a real possibility. The entire experience of Islamic work over the past fifteen years has been one of increasing radicalization, driven by the perceived failure of the traditional Islamic institutions and the older Muslim movements to lead the Muslim peoples into the worthy but so far chimerical promised land of the "Islamic State."

If this final catastrophe is to be averted, the mainstream will have to regain the initiative. But for this to happen, it must begin by confessing that the radical critique of moderation has its force. The Islamic movement has so far been remarkably unsuccessful. We must ask ourselves how it is that a man like Nasser, a butcher, a failed soldier, and a cynical demagogue, could have taken over a country as pivotal as Egypt, despite the vacuity of his beliefs, while the Muslim Brotherhood, with its pullulating millions of members, should have failed, and failed continuously, for six decades. The radical accusation of a failure in methodology cannot fail to strike home in such a context of dismal and prolonged inadequacy.

It is in this context—startlingly, perhaps, but inescapably—that we must present our case for the revival of the spiritual life within Islam. If it is ever to prosper, the "Islamic revival" must be made to see that it is in crisis, and that its mental resources are proving insufficient to meet contemporary needs. The response to this must be grounded in an act of collective *muḥāsaba*, of self-examination, in terms that transcend the ideologized neo-Islam of the revivalists, and return to a more classical and indigenously Muslim dialectic.

Symptomatic of the disease is the fact that among all the explanations offered for the crisis of the Islamic movement, the only authentically Muslim interpretation, namely, that God should not be lending it His support, is conspicuously absent. It is true that we frequently hear the Qur'ānic verse which states that "God does not change the condition of a people until they change the condition of their own selves" (13:11). But never, it seems, is this principle intelligently grasped. It is assumed that the sacred text is here doing no more than to enjoin individual moral reform as a precondition for collective societal success. Nothing could be more hazardous, however, than to measure such moral reform against the yardstick of the *fiqh* (jurisprudence) without giving concern to whether the virtues gained have been acquired through conformity (a relatively simple task), or proceed spontaneously from a genuine realignment of the soul. The verse is speaking of a spiritual change, specifically, a transformation of the *nafs* (soul or self) of the believers—not a moral one. And as the Blessed Prophet never tired of reminding us, there is little value in outward conformity to the rules unless this conformity is mirrored and engendered by an authentically righteous disposition of the heart. "No one shall enter the Garden by his works," as he expressed it. Meanwhile, the profoundly judgmental and works-oriented tenor of modern revivalist Islam (we must shun the problematic buzzword "fundamentalism"), fixated on visible manifestations of morality, has failed to address the underlying question of what revelation is *for*. For it is theological nonsense to suggest that God's final concern is with our ability to conform to a complex set of rules. His concern is rather that we should be restored, through our labors and His grace, to that state of purity and equilibrium with which we were born. The rules are a vital means to that end, and are facilitated by it. But they do not take its place.

To make this point, the Holy Qur'ān deploys a striking metaphor. In Sūra *Ibrāhīm*, verses 24 to 26, we read:

> Have you not seen how God coineth a likeness: a goodly word is like a goodly tree, the root whereof is set firm, its branch in the heaven? It bringeth forth its fruit at every time, by the leave of its Lord. Thus doth God coin likenesses for men, that perhaps they may reflect. And the likeness of an evil word is that of an evil tree that hath been torn up by the root from upon the earth, possessed of no stability.

According to the scholars of *tafsīr* (exegesis), the reference here is to the "words" (*kalima*) of faith and unfaith. The former is illustrated as a natural growth, whose florescence of moral and intellectual achievement is nourished by firm roots, which in turn denote the basis of faith: the quality of the proofs one has received, and the certainty and sound awareness of God which alone signify that one is firmly grounded in the reality of existence. The fruits thus yielded—the palpable benefits of the religious life—are permanent ("at every time"), and are not man's own accomplishment, for they only come "by the leave of its Lord." Thus is the sound life of faith. The contrast is then drawn with the only alternative: *kufr*, which is not grounded in reality but in illusion, and is hence "possessed of no stability."

This passage, reminiscent of some of the binary categorizations of human types presented early on in Sūra *al-Baqara*, precisely encapsulates the relationship between faith and works, the hierarchy which exists between them, and the sustainable balance between nourishment and fructition, between taking and giving, which true faith must maintain.

It is against this criterion that we must judge the quality of contemporary "activist" styles of faith. Is the young "ultra," with his intense rage which can sometimes render him liable to nervous disorders, and his fixation on a relatively narrow range of issues and concerns, really firmly rooted, and fruitful, in the sense described by this Qur'ānic image? Let me point to the answer with an example drawn from my own experience. I used to know, quite well, a leader of the radical "Islamic" group, the

Jamāʿāt Islāmiyya, at the Egyptian university of Assiut. His name was Hamdī. He grew a luxuriant beard, was constantly scrubbing his teeth with his traditional toothstick, and spent his time preaching hatred of the Coptic Christians, a number of whom were actually attacked and beaten up as a result of his sermons. He had hundreds of followers; in fact, Assiut today remains a citadel of hard-line, Wahhābī-style activism.

The moral of the story is that some five years after this acquaintance, providence again brought me face to face with Shaykh Hamdī. This time, chancing to see him on a Cairo street, I almost failed to recognize him. The beard was gone. He was in trousers and a sweater. More astonishing still was that he was walking with a young Western girl who turned out to be an Australian, whom, as he sheepishly explained to me, he was intending to marry. I talked to him, and it became clear that he was no longer even a minimally observant Muslim, no longer prayed, and that his ambition in life was to leave Egypt, live in Australia, and make money. What was extraordinary was that his experiences in Islamic activism had made no impression on him—he was once again the same distracted, ordinary Egyptian youth he had been before his conversion to "radical Islam."

This phenomenon, which we might label "*salafī* burnout," is a recognized feature of many modern Muslim cultures. An initial enthusiasm, gained usually in one's early twenties, loses steam some seven to ten years later. Prison and torture—the frequent lot of the Islamic radical—may serve to prolong commitment, but ultimately, a majority of these neo-Muslims relapse, seemingly no better or worse for their experience in the cult-like universe of the *salafī* mindset.

This ephemerality of extremist activism should be as suspicious as its content. Authentic Muslim faith is simply not supposed to be this fragile; as the Qur'ān says, its root is meant to be "set firm." One has to conclude that of the two trees depicted in the Qur'ānic image, *salafī* extremism resembles the second rather than the first. After all, the Companions of the religion's founder were not known for a transient commitment: their devotion and piety remained incomparably pure until they died.

What attracts young Muslims to this type of ephemeral but ferocious activism? One does not have to subscribe to determinist social theories to realize the importance of the almost universal condition of insecurity which Muslim societies are now experiencing. The Islamic world is passing through a most devastating period of transition. A history of economic and scientific change which in Europe took five hundred years is, in the Muslim world, being squeezed into a couple of generations. For instance, only thirty-five years ago the capital of Saudi Arabia was a cluster of mud huts, as it had been for thousands of years. Today's Riyadh is a hi-tech megacity of glass towers, Coke machines, and gliding Cadillacs. This is an extreme case, but to some extent the dislocations of modernity are common to every Muslim society, excepting, perhaps, a handful of the most remote tribal peoples.

Such a transition period, with its centrifugal forces which allow nothing to remain constant, makes human beings very insecure. They look around for something to hold onto, something that will give them an identity. In our case, that something is usually Islam. And because they are being propelled into it by this psychic sense of insecurity, rather than by the more normal processes of conversion and faith, they lack some of the natural religious virtues, which are acquired by contact with a continuous tradition, and can never be learned from a book.

One easily visualizes how this works. A young Arab, part of an oversized family, competing for scarce jobs, unable to marry because he is poor, perhaps a migrant to a rapidly expanding city, feels like a man lost in a desert without signposts. One morning he picks up a copy of the fundamentalist writer Sayyid Qutb from a newsstand, and is "born-again" on the spot. This is what he needed: instant certainty, a framework in which to interpret the landscape before him, to resolve the problems and tensions of his life, and, even more deliciously, a way of feeling superior and in control. He joins a group, and, anxious to retain his newfound certainty, accepts the usual proposition that all the other groups are mistaken.

This, of course, is not how Muslim religious conversion is supposed to work. It is meant to be a process of intellectual maturation, triggered by the presence of a very holy person or place. Repentance (*tawba*), in its traditional form, yields an outlook of joy, contentment, and a deep affection for others. The modern type of *tawba*, however, born of insecurity, often makes Muslims narrow, intolerant, and exclusivist. Even more noticeably, it produces people whose faith is, despite its apparent intensity, liable to vanish as suddenly as it came. Deprived of real nourishment, the activist's soul can only grow hungry and emaciated, until at last it dies.

THE ACTIVISM WITHIN

How should we respond to this disorder? We must begin by remembering what Islam is for. As we noted earlier, our religion is not, ultimately, a manual of rules which, when meticulously followed, becomes a passport to paradise. Instead, it is a package of social, intellectual, and spiritual technologies whose purpose is to cleanse the human heart. In the Qur'ān, the Lord says that on the Day of Judgment, nothing will be of any use to us, except a sound heart (*qalb^{un} salīm*). And in a famous *hadīth*, the Prophet, upon whom be blessings and peace, says: "Verily in the body there is a piece of flesh. If it is sound, the body is all sound. If it is corrupt, the body is all corrupt. Verily, it is the heart." Mindful of this commandment, under which all the other commandments of Islam are subsumed, and which alone gives them meaning, the Islamic scholars have worked out a science, and *'ilm*, of analyzing the "states" of the heart, and the methods of bringing it into this condition of soundness. In the fullness of time, this science acquired the name *taṣawwuf*, in English "Sufism"—a traditional label for what we might nowadays roughly but more intelligibly call "Islamic psychology."

At this point, many hackles are raised and well-rehearsed objections voiced. It is vital to understand that mainstream Sufism is not, and never has been, a doctrinal system, or a school of thought—a *madhhab*. It is, instead, a set of insights and practices which operate within the various Islamic *madhhabs*; in other words, it is not a *madhhab*, it is an *'ilm*, a science. And like most of the other Islamic sciences, it was not known by name, or in its later developed form, in the age of the Prophet (upon him be blessings and peace) or his Companions. This does not make it less legitimate. There are many Islamic sciences which only took shape many years after the Prophetic age: jurisprudence (*uṣūl al-fiqh*), for instance, or logic (*manṭiq*), or the innumerable technical disciplines of *ḥadīth*.

Now this, of course, leads us into the often misunderstood area of *sunna* (Prophetic custom) and *bid'a* (innovation), two notions which are wielded as blunt instruments by many contemporary activists, but which are often grossly misunderstood. The classical Orientalist thesis was of course that Islam, as an "arid Semitic legalism," failed to incorporate mechanisms for its own development, and that it petrified upon the death of its founder. This, however, is an antisemitic nonsense rooted in the ethnic determinism of the nineteenth-century historians who had shaped the views of the early Orientalist synthesizers (Muir, Le Bon, Renan, Caetani). Islam, as the religion designed for the end of time, has in fact proved itself eminently adaptable to the rapidly changing conditions which characterize this latest and most "entropic" stage of history.

What is a *bid'a*, according to the classical definitions of Islamic law? Many are familiar with the famous *ḥadīth*: "Beware of matters newly begun, for every matter newly begun is innovation, every innovation is misguidance, and every misguidance is in Hell." Does this mean that everything introduced into Islam that was not known to the first generation of Muslims is to be rejected? The classical *'ulamā'* do not accept such a literalistic interpretation. Let us take a definition from Imām al-Shāfiʿī, an authority universally accepted in Sunnī Islam. Imām al-Shāfiʿī writes:

> There are two kinds of introduced matters (*muḥdathāt*). One is that which contradicts a text of the Qur'ān, or the *sunna*, or a report from the early Muslims (*athar*), or the consensus (*ijmā'*) of the Muslims: this is an "innovation of misguidance" (*bid'at ḍalāla*). The second kind is that which is in itself good and entails no contradiction of any of these authorities: this is a "non-reprehensible innovation" (*bid'a ghayr madhmūma*).

This basic distinction between acceptable and unacceptable forms of *bid'a* is recognized by the overwhelming majority of classical *'ulamā'*. Among some, for instance al-'Izz ibn 'Abd al-Salām (one of the half-dozen or so great *mujtahids* of Islamic history), innovations fall under the five axiological headings of the *sharī'a*: the obligatory (*wājib*), the recommended (*mandūb*), the permissible (*mubāh*), the offensive (*makrūh*), and the forbidden (*ḥarām*).

Under the category of "obligatory innovation," Ibn 'Abd al-Salām gives the following examples: recording the Qur'ān and the laws of Islam in writing at a time when it was feared that they would be lost, studying Arabic grammar in order to resolve controversies over the Qur'ān, and developing philosophical theology (*kalām*) to refute the claims of the Mu'tazilites. Category two is "recommended innovation." Under this heading the *'ulamā'* list such activities as building *madrasas*, writing books on beneficial Islamic subjects, and in-depth studies of Arabic linguistics. Category three is "permissible," or "neutral innovation," including worldly activities such as sifting flour, and constructing houses in various styles not known in Medina. Category four is the "reprehensible innovation." This includes such misdemeanors as overdecorating mosques or the Qur'ān. Category five is the "forbidden innovation." This includes unlawful taxes, giving judgeships to those unqualified to hold them, and sectarian beliefs and practices that explicitly contravene the known principles of the Qur'ān and the *sunna*.

The above classification of *bid'a* types is normal in classical *sharī'a* literature, being accepted by the four schools of orthodox *fiqh*. There have been only two significant exceptions to this understanding in the history of Islamic thought: the Ẓāhirī school as articulated by Ibn Ḥazm, and one wing of the Ḥanbalī *madhhab*, represented by Ibn Taymiyya, who goes against the classical *ijmā'* on this issue, and claims that all forms of innovation, good or bad, are un-Islamic.

Why is it, then, that so many Muslims now believe that innovation in any form is unacceptable in Islam? One factor has already been touched on: the mental complexes thrown up by insecurity, which incline people to find comfort in absolutist and literalist interpretations. Another lies in the influence of the well-financed neo-Ḥanbalī *madhhab* called Wahhābism, whose leaders are famous for their rejection of all possibility of development. In any case, armed with this more sophisticated and classical awareness of Islam's ability to acknowledge and assimilate novelty, we can understand how Muslim civilization was able so quickly to produce novel academic disciplines to deal with new problems as these arose.

Islamic psychology is characteristic of the new *'ulūm* which, although present in latent and implicit form in the Qur'ān, were first systematized in Islamic culture during the early Abbasid period (750–945). Given the importance that the Qur'ān attaches to obtaining a "sound heart," we are not surprised to find that the influence of Islamic psychology has been massive and all-pervasive. In the formative first four centuries of Islam, the time when the great works of *tafsīr*, *ḥadīth*, grammar, and so forth were laid down, the *'ulamā'* also applied their minds to this problem of *al-qalb al-salīm*. This was first visible when, following the example of the second generation of Muslims, many of the early ascetics, such as Sufyān ibn 'Uyayna, Sufyān al-Thawrī, and 'Abdallāh ibn al-Mubārak, had focused their concerns explicitly on the art of purifying the heart. The methods they recommended were frequent fasting and night prayer, periodic retreats, and a preoccupation with *murābaṭa*: service as volunteer fighters to defend the border castles of north Syria. This type of pietist orientation was not in the least systematic during this period. It was a loose category embracing all Muslims who sought salvation through the Prophetic virtues of renunciation, sincerity, and deep devotion to the revelation. These men and women were variously referred to as *al-bakka'ūn*, "the weepers," because of their fear of the Day of Judgement, or as *zuhhād*, ascetics, or *'ubbād*, "unceasing worshipers."

By the third century, however, we start to find writings which can be understood as belonging to a distinct devotional path. The increasing luxury and materialism of Abbasid urban society spurred many Muslims to campaign for a restoration of the simplicity of the Prophetic age. Purity of heart, compassion for others, and a constant recollection of God were the defining features of this trend. We find references to the method of *muḥāsaba*: self-examination to detect impurities of intention. Also stressed was *riyāḍa*: self-discipline.

By this time, too, the main outlines of Qur'ānic psychology had been worked out. The human creature, it was realized, was made up of four constituent parts: the body (*jism*), the mind (*'aql*), the spirit (*rūḥ*), and the self (*nafs*). The first two need little comment. Less familiar (at least to people of a modern education) are the third and fourth categories.

The spirit is the *rūḥ*, that underlying essence of the human individual which survives death. It is hard to comprehend rationally, being in part of Divine inspiration, as the Qur'ān says: "And they ask you about the spirit; say, the spirit is of the command of my Lord. And you have been given of knowledge only a little" (17:85). According to the early Islamic psychologists, the *rūḥ* is a non-material reality which pervades the entire human body, but is centered on the heart, the *qalb*. It represents that part of man which is not of this world, and which connects him with his Creator, and which, if he is fortunate, enables him to see God in the next world. When we are born, this *rūḥ* is intact and pure. As we are initiated into the distractions of the world, however, it is covered over with the "rust" (*rān*) of which the Qur'ān speaks. This rust is made up of two things: sin and distraction. When these are banished through the process of self-discipline, so that the worshiper is preserved from sin and is focusing entirely on the immediate presence and reality of God, the rust is dissolved, and the *rūḥ* once again is free. The heart is sound; and salvation, and closeness to God are achieved.

This sounds simple enough. However, the early Muslims taught that such precious things come only at an appropriate price. Cleaning up the Augean stables of the heart is a most excruciating challenge. Outward conformity to the rules of religion is simple enough; but it is only the first step. Much more demanding is the policy known as *mujāhada*: the daily combat against the lower self, the *nafs*. As the Qur'ān says: "As for him that fears the standing before his Lord, and forbids his *nafs* its desires, for him, Heaven shall be his place of resort" (79:40). Hence the Sufi commandment: "Slaughter your ego with the knives of *mujāhada*." Once the *nafs* is controlled, then the heart is clear, and the virtues proceed from it easily and naturally.

Because its objective is nothing less than salvation, this vital Islamic science has been consistently expounded by the great scholars of classical Islam. While today there are many Muslims, influenced by either Wahhābī or Orientalist agendas, who believe that Sufism has always led a somewhat marginal existence in Islam, the reality is that the overwhelming majority of the classical scholars were actively involved in Sufism. The early Shāfi'ī scholars of Khurāsān; al-Ḥākim al-Nīsābūrī, Ibn Fūrak, al-Qushayrī, and al-Bayhaqī, were all Sufis, who formed links in the richest academic tradition of Abbasid Islam which culminated in the achievement of Imām Ḥujjat al-Islām al-Ghazālī. Ghazālī himself, author of some three hundred books, including the definitive rebuttals of Arab philosophy and the Ismā'īlīs, three large textbooks of Shāfi'ī *fiqh*, the best-known tract of *uṣūl al-fiqh*, two works on logic, and several theological treatises, also left us with the classic statement of orthodox Sufism: the *Iḥyā' 'ulūm al-dīn* (*The Revivification of the Religious Sciences*), a book of which Imām Nawawī remarked: "Were the books of Islam all to be lost, excepting only the *Iḥyā'*, it would suffice to replace them all."

Imām Nawawī himself wrote two books which record his debt to Sufism, one called the *Bustān al-'ārifīn* (*Garden of the Gnostics*), and another called *al-Maqāṣid*. Among the Mālikīs, too, Sufism was the almost universally followed style of spirituality. Al-Ṣāwī, al-Dardīr, al-Laqqānī and 'Abd al-Wahhāb al-Baghdādī were all exponents of Sufism. The great Mālikī jurist of Cairo, 'Abd al-Wahhāb al-Sha'rānī, defines Sufism as follows:

> The path of the Sufis is built on the Qur'ān and the *sunna*, and is based on living according to the morals of the prophets and the purified ones. It may not be blamed, unless it violates an explicit statement from the Qur'ān, *sunna*, or *ijmā'*. If it does not contravene any of these sources, then no pretext remains for condemning it, except one's own low opinion of others, or interpreting what they do as ostentation, which is unlawful. No-one denies the states of the Sufis except someone ignorant of the way they are.

For Ḥanbalī Sufism one has to look no further than the revered figures of 'Abdallāh Anṣārī, 'Abd al-Qādir al-Jīlānī, Ibn al-Jawzī, and Ibn Rajab.

In fact, virtually all the great luminaries of medieval Islam—al-Suyūṭī, Ibn Ḥajar al-'Asqalānī, al-'Aynī, Ibn Khaldūn, al-Subkī, Ibn Ḥajar al-Haytamī;

tafsīr writers like Bayḍāwī, al-Ṣāwī, Abu'l-Su'ūd, al-Baghawī, and Ibn Kathīr; doctrine specialists such as al-Taftazānī, al-Nasafī, al-Rāzī—all wrote in support of Sufism. Many, indeed, composed independent works of Sufi inspiration. The *'ulamā'* of the great dynasties of Islamic history, including the Ottomans and the Moghuls, were deeply infused with the Sufi outlook, regarding it as one of the most central and indispensable of Islamic sciences.

Further confirmation of the Islamic legitimacy of Sufism is supplied by the enthusiasm of its exponents for carrying Islam beyond the boundaries of the Islamic world. The Islamization process in India, black Africa, and Southeast Asia was carried out largely at the hands of wandering Sufi teachers. Likewise, the Islamic obligation of *jihād* has been borne with especial zeal by the Sufi orders. All the great nineteenth century jihādists, 'Uthman dan Fodio (Hausaland), al-Sanūsī (Libya), 'Abd al-Qādir al-Jazā'irī (Algeria), Imām Shāmil (Daghestan) and the leaders of the Padre Rebellion (Sumatra), were active practitioners of Sufism, writing extensively on it while on their campaigns. Nothing is further from reality, in fact, than the claim that Sufism represents a quietist and non-militant form of Islam. However, it has always been utterly different from modern, wild extremism, in that it is rooted in mercy and justice, forbidding the targeting of civilians, and conforming to the ethical ideal of the just war. Sufism forms no part of modern terroristic radicalism.

With all this, we confront a paradox. Why is it, if Sufism has been so respected a part of Muslim intellectual and political life throughout our history, that there are, nowadays, angry voices raised against it? There are two fundamental reasons here. Firstly, there is again the pervasive influence of Orientalist scholarship, which, at least before 1922 when Louis Massignon wrote his *Essai sur les origines de la lexique technique*, was of the opinion that something so fertile and profound as Sufism could never have grown from the essentially "barren and legalistic" soil of Islam. Orientalist works translated into Muslim languages were influential upon key Muslim modernists—such as Muhammad 'Abduh in his later writings—who began to question the centrality, or even the legitimacy, of Sufi discourse in Islam. Secondly, there is the emergence of the Wahhābī *da'wa*. When Muhammad ibn 'Abd al-Wahhāb, some two hundred years ago, teamed up with the Saudi tribe and attacked the neighboring clans, he was doing so under the sign of an essentially neo-Khārijite version of Islam. Although he invoked Ibn Taymiyya, he had reservations even about him. For Ibn Taymiyya himself, although critical of the excesses of certain Sufi groups, had been committed to a branch of mainstream Sufism. This is clear, for instance, in Ibn Taymiyya's work *Sharḥ futūḥ al-ghayb*, a commentary on some technical points in the *Revelations of the Unseen*, a key work by the sixth-century saint of Baghdad, 'Abd al-Qādir al-Jīlānī. Throughout the work Ibn Taymiyya shows himself to be a loyal disciple of al-Jīlānī, whom he always refers to as *shaykhunā* ("our teacher"). This Qādirī affiliation is confirmed in the later literature of the Qādirī *ṭarīqa* (order), which records Ibn Taymiyya as a key link in the *silsila*, the chain of transmission of Qādirī teachings.

Ibn 'Abd al-Wahhāb, however, went far beyond this. Raised in the wastelands of Najd in Central Arabia, he had inadequate access to mainstream Muslim scholarship. In fact, when his *da'wa* appeared and became notorious, the scholars and *muftīs* (judges) of the day applied to it the famous *ḥadīth* of Najd:

> Ibn 'Umar reported the Prophet (upon whom be blessings and peace) as saying: "Oh God, bless us in our Syria: O God, bless us in our Yemen." Those present said: "And in our Najd, messenger of God," but he said, "O God, bless us in our Syria; O God, bless us in our Yemen." Those present said, "And in our Najd, messenger of God." Ibn 'Umar told that he thought he said on the third occasion: "Earthquakes and dissensions (*fitna*) are there, and the horn of the devil shall arise in it."

And it is significant that almost uniquely among the lands of Islam, Najd has never produced scholars of any repute.

The Najd-based *da'wa* of the Wahhābīs, however, began to be heard more loudly following the explosion of Saudi oil wealth. Many, even most, Islamic publishing houses in Cairo and Beirut are now subsidized by Wahhābī organisations, which prevent them from publishing traditional works on Sufism, and remove passages in other works considered unacceptable to Wahhābist doctrine.

The neo-Khārijite nature of Wahhābism makes it intolerant of all other forms of Islamic expression. However, because it has no coherent *fiqh* of its own—it rejects the orthodox *madhhabs*—and has only the most basic and primitively anthropomorphic theology, it has a fluid, amoeba-like tendency to produce divisions and subdivisions among those who profess it. No longer are the Islamic groups essentially united by a consistent *madhhab* and the Ash'arī or Māturīdī doctrine. Instead, they are all trying to derive the *sharī'a* and doctrine from the Qur'ān and the *sunna* by themselves. The result is the appalling state of division and conflict which disfigures the modern Wahhābī condition.

At this critical moment in our history, the *umma* has only one realistic hope for survival, and that is to restore the "middle way," defined by that sophisticated classical consensus which was worked out over painful centuries of debate and scholarship. That consensus alone has the demonstrable ability to provide a basis for unity. But it can only be retrieved when we improve the state of our hearts, and fill them with the Islamic virtues of affection, respect, tolerance, and reconciliation. This inner reform, which is the traditional competence of Sufism, is a precondition for the restoration of unity and decency in the Islamic movement. The alternative is likely to be continued, and agonizing, failure.

JIHAD DEFINED AND REDEFINED

Post 9/11, many have questioned whether Islam is a religion of violence or of peace. Jihad has often been central to this issue and debate. Jihad (to strive or struggle) is a concept with multiple meanings and usages throughout history, from the spiritual struggle to lead a moral life to armed warfare. In recent times, jihad has been used to legitimate or attempt to justify acts of resistance and liberation as well as extremism and global terrorism. Sherman Jackson reviews and analyzes the meanings of jihad in the modern world, placing jihad in its historical context, from the Quran and early conquests to the interpretation of Sayyid Qutb (executed in 1966), whose writings have inspired many modern militants. Jackson is followed by a selection from Sayyid Qutb, the godfather of militant jihad, in which he sets out his ideological vision of the obligatory role of militant jihad in Islam. Muhammad Abdel Salam al-Farag, influenced by Qutb's writings, wrote the *Neglected Duty*, a tract that provided the worldview and rationale for the assassins of Egypt's president Anwar Sadat (d. 1981). The chain of militant jihad continued and was transformed into an ideology for pan-Islamic, global jihad by Abdullah al-Azzam, a mentor of Osama Bin Laden. Though not qualified as a mufti (or legal expert), Osama Bin Laden issued a fatwa for a jihad against America and its allies, maintaining that it is the individual duty of every Muslim. The covenant of HAMAS (acronym for the Islamic Resistance Movement), its ideological credo, sets forth the role of jihad in the pursuit of its mission and realization of its goal in Palestine/Israel.

In contrast, Muhammad Shams al-Din, a prominent Shiite religious leader in Lebanon writing in the context of the Lebanese civil war and civil resistance to the Israeli military presence in southern Lebanon as well as the use of armed violence by some Islamic movements, argues that armed violence is ineffective. Ayatollah Muhammad Fadlallah comments on jihad and armed combat in the context of the September 11 attacks, the Palestine conflict, and the issue of violence versus dialogue. Khaled Abou El Fadl speaks of a legacy that is forgotten by many today or denied by extremists such as Bin Laden, the Quranic distinction between the meaning of jihad as struggle and use of the word *qital* for fighting and warfare. Finally, a selection of fatwas on jihad, terrorism, suicide bombing, and martyrdom illustrates a diversity of opinions by religious scholars.

SHERMAN JACKSON
1956–

Born in Philadelphia, Sherman Jackson studied at the University
of Pennsylvania where he received his doctorate in 1990.
Professor of Arabic and Islamic Studies at the University of
Michigan, Jackson specializes in Islamic law and jurisprudence
and is President of Shariah Scholars Association of North
America. His publications include *Islamic Law and the State: The
Constitutional Jurisprudence, The Boundaries of Theological
Tolerance in Islam*, and *Islam and the Black American*.

Jihad and the Modern World

I. INTRODUCTION

"Islam is a religion of peace." This is certainly the mantra that has
inundated us from almost every quarter since the horrifying events of
September 11, 2001. From president George W. Bush to local, national and
even international Muslim spokespersons, the peaceful nature of Islam has
been reiterated time and again. Of course, this has not gone unchallenged.
Skeptics, polemicists, even opportunists of various stripes, have repeatedly
warned against accepting too uncritically what they hint at being a "newfound, politically correct" depiction of a religion that includes, *inter alia*,
a scripturally mandated institution of armed violence and a holy book that
exhorts its adherents, at least on the face of it, to "slay 'them' wherever you
find them."[1] Today, years after the tragedy, emotions and rhetoric on both
sides have subsided a bit. But there is still a perduring suspicion among
many Americans—including many Muslim Americans—when it comes to
the question of Islam, violence and the relationship between Muslims and
non-Muslims.

I shall limit myself to only one of the products of the modern encounter
between the Muslim world and the West, namely the claim that Islam is
a religion of peace. I propose to explore the credibility of this claim via
a treatment of jihad, as the religiously sanctioned institution of armed
violence in Islam. I shall focus on jihad not from the perspective of *jus in
bello*, i.e., the rules and regulations governing the conduct of combatants
in war, but rather from the perspective of *jus ad bellum*, the causes and

1. Qur'ân, 2: 191. All translations of Qur'ânic material in this essay will be my own.

Versions of this paper were delivered at the University of Wisconsin–Madison in December
2001, the University of Michigan–Flint in March 2002, and the University of Nevada–Las
Vegas in April 2002.

justifications for going *to* war. My aim shall be to determine the normative role, function and status of jihad not in the abstract but, first, as an institution at Islamic law, and, second, in the very particular context of the modern world. This latter concern implies, of course, that context and circumstances are relevant to the enterprises of interpreting and applying the rules of Islam. . . .

IV. JIHAD

a. Jihad Among the Arabs at the Time of Revelation

In 1991, professor Fred Donner of the University of Chicago published an insightful article under the title "The Sources of Islamic Conceptions of War." This was part of an edited volume entitled *Just War and Jihad: Historical and Theoretical Perspectives on War and Peace in Western and Islamic Traditions.*[2] In this article, professor Donner began by questioning the propriety of relying solely on the Qur'ân, the Sunna or the books of Islamic law for an understanding of the substance and the logic underlying the medieval Muslim concept of jihad. Rather, according to professor Donner, the Muslim valuation and articulation of jihad were just as much, if not more, a product of *history* as of religion. This insight yielded two extremely important implications. First, just as Islamic theology, philosophy and jurisprudence had been informed by perspectives brought by Hellenized and other converts from the world of Late Antiquity, so had jihad, in its classical formulation, been informed by such Roman-Byzantine concepts as "charismatic victoriousness," according to which God would aid the expansionist endeavors of the empire against all enemies of the religion or the state.[3] Second, and more important, the whole Qur'ânic rationale undergirding the verses on jihad could be seen as resting on a particularly intractable reality in 7th century Arabia. Speaking of this reality, professor Donner writes,

> In this society, war (*harb*, used in the senses of both an *activity* and a *condition*) was in one sense a normal way of life; that is, a "state of war" was assumed to exist between one's tribe and all others, unless a particular treaty or agreement had been reached with another tribe establishing amicable relations.[4]

As an historian of Late Antiquity and early Islam, professor Donner could substantiate this view on the basis of several historical sources. The Qur'ân itself, however, confirms this reality and confers the additional advantage of providing a glimpse into the early Muslim perception of the

2. ed. J. Kelsay and J. T. Johnson (New York: Greenwood Press, 1991), 31–70.

3. *Just War and Jihad: Historical and Theoretical Perspectives on War and Peace in Western and Islamic Traditions*, 34.

4. Ibid., 34. Emphasis added.

world around them. It should be noted in this context that it matters little whether we accept the Qur'ân as divine revelation or not. For whether it came from God or Muhammad or anywhere else, it certainly reflected the social, historical and political realities of 7th century Arabia.

Several verses of the Qur'ân depict Arabia's general "state of war." For example, "Do they not see that We established a safe haven (in the Sacred Mosque) while people all around them were being snatched away?"[5] Similarly, "And remember when you were a small, marginalized group in the land living in fear that the people would snatch you away."[6] The 106th chapter appears to be devoted entirely to the twin themes of societal fear and security:

> For the comforting of Quraysh [the tribe of the Prophet],
> the comfort of (being able to complete) the winter and summer caravans.
> Let them, then, worship the Lord of this House,
> Who banished their hunger with food and their fear with security.

It was, indeed, Arabia's endemic "state of war" that drove the pre-Islamic Arabs in desperation to institute the so-called Forbidden Months (al-Ashhur al-hurum), a pan-Arabian treaty of non-aggression, subsequently ratified by the Qur'ân, that outlawed all acts of war initiated during the 11th, 12th, 1st and 7th months of the lunar year. This particular sequence was pegged to the time of the annual pilgrimage to Mecca, which took place in the 12th lunar month. The Forbidden Months gave potential pilgrims ample time to travel from their homes to Mecca, spend the needed time carrying out the rites of the pilgrimage, and then make it back to their homes unmolested by any and all raiders or brigands. The 7th Forbidden Month provided the same for those who wished to travel to Mecca during the off-season for a "lesser pilgrimage."

Other verses in the Qur'ân suggest that part of the reason many of the Prophet's contemporaries hesitated to follow him was their fear that they would lose the support of their tribes and allies and thus be rendered fair game for all attackers. For example, Qur'ân 28:57 reads: "They say, 'If we follow the guidance with you we shall be snatched from our land.'" Similarly, 3:173 describes the nascent Muslim community as "Those whom the people warned, 'Verily all the people have lined up against you, so fear them!'" These and numerous other verses clearly indicate that war, as an *activity* or a *condition*, was the assumed status among groups in the Prophet's 7th century Arabia. In a sense, one might say that Arabia only survived as an entity by virtue of a primitive version of the Cold War "balance of terror."

5. 29: 67.
6. 8: 26.

The fact that certain groups and individuals in Arabia feared losing the support of their tribes is actually much more germane to our discussion than appears at first blush. For the dynamic underlying this fear actually explains an often overlooked aspect of the Qur'ânic discourse and rhetoric on jihad. Far from depicting the early Muslims as a brave and warlike people, one of the most consistent Qur'ânic criticisms of them is directed at their unwillingness to fight. It is in fact this need to overcome this unwillingness that explains in large part the pungency and urgency of the Qur'ânic injunctions to fight. "Fighting is prescribed for you, but you despise it."[7]

> Say [O Muhammad], If your fathers, your sons, your brothers, your wives, your close associates or moneys that you have earned or businesses whose stagnation you fear or homes with which you are pleased are more beloved to you than God and His Messenger and waging jihad in His path, then wait until God sends forth His command. And God does not guide a people who are corrupt.[8]
> You shall not find a people who (truly) believe in God and the Last Day maintaining loving relations with those who strive to undermine God and His Messenger, be the latter their fathers, sons, brothers or close associates.[9]

In a similar vein, this time showing a sense of indulgence:

> God does not forbid you to have friendly, mutually respectful relations with those who have not attacked you because of your religion and have not turned you out of your homes. God simply forbids you to take as your patrons those who attack you because of your religion or turn you out of your homes or conspire with others to turn you out of your homes.[10]

What these (and numerous other verses) depict is the early Muslims' deep sense of divided loyalties between Islam, on the one hand, and "the old order," at the center of which stood the tribe, tribal alliances and the presumed state of war, on the other. What the early Muslims had trouble accepting was not fighting in general (to which they were as used as anyone else in Arabia) but fighting that pit them against kith and kin. Ultimately, their wish was that they would be able to reconcile the old and the new order in such a way that enabled them to enjoy the benefits of both. From the Qur'ân's perspective, however, this could not be done without lending support, directly or indirectly, to the very forces whose existence and way of life included an active ideological and military opposition to Muhammad. Thus, the Qur'ân sets out to break the early Muslims' emotional, psychological and even material dependency on the "old order"

7. 2: 216.
8. 9: 24.
9. 58: 22.
10. 60: 8.

by forcing them to affirm their commitment to Islam by way of a willingness to fight—in accordance with the existing norm—for the life and integrity of the new religion.

In sum, by revealing those verses in which the believers are commanded to wage jihad, the Qur'ân was not introducing the obligation to fight *ab initio*. On the contrary, the Qur'ân was simply responding to a pre-existing state of affairs by effectively redirecting energies that were already being expended. Moreover, peace, i.e., the repelling of aggression, rather than conversion to Islam was the ultimate aim of this fighting. This is clearly indicated by several verses, scattered throughout the Qur'ân, that clearly envision a *terminus ad quem* other than conversion or annihilation: "If they incline towards peace, then you incline thereto, and place your trust in God;"[11] and, "Fight them until there is no oppression and religion is solely for God. And if they desist, then let there be no aggression except against the transgressors."[12] Even more elaborately, this time speaking of a group of "interlopers" who had made a career of playing both ends against the middle, now supporting Muhammad, now colluding against him,

> They wish that you would reject faith as they have, so that you would all be equal. Do not accept them as patrons until they migrate to join you in the path of God. If they refuse to migrate, then seize them and slay them wherever you find them, and do not accept them as patrons nor as helpers. Except for those who arrive at the home of a tribe with whom you have a treaty, or who come to you in a state of contrition that will not permit them to fight you or to fight against their own . . . If they avoid you and do not fight you and declare themselves to be in a state of peace with you, then these people We do not give you permission to fight.[13]

Based on this admittedly narrow sample, it seems clear that the *raison d'être* behind the Qur'ânic injunction to fight was clearly connected with the very specific necessity of preserving the *physical* integrity of the Muslim community at a time and place when fighting, sometimes preemptively, sometimes defensively, was understood to be the only way to do so. To be sure, Qur'ânic injunctions to fight often take on the *appearance* of a call to Holy War, i.e., war based solely on a difference of religion. But this is simply because the only people Muhammad and the early Muslims had to fear were non-Muslims. As de Tocqueville writes of 19th century France, "The *unbelievers* of Europe attack the *Christians* as their *political* opponents rather than as their *religious* adversaries."[14] To the casual observer, however, such a conflict, though politically motivated, would

11. 8: 61.
12. 2: 193.
13. 4: 89–90.
14. *Democracy in America*, 2 vols. (New York: Vintage Books, 1990), 1: 314. Emphasis mine.

simply show Christians on one side and unbelievers on the other, a Holy War to most eyes, if there ever was one. Yet, when the Prophet Muhammad died in Medina, at the height of his power, he died in debt to a Jew. Famous Companions of his, men like Hudhayfah b. al-Yamâm, married Jewish women. The second Caliph, 'Umar, under whose reign the Muslim empire expanded more than it did under any other reign, was killed by a Christian in Medina. Clearly, on these facts, if the unbelief of the unbelievers rather than their real or perceived hostility towards the Muslims had been the object of those verses in which the Muslims were commanded to "slay them wherever you find them," certainly Muhammad and his Companions would have understood this, and at the time, there would have been nothing to prevent them from carrying this order out.

In sum, even before the Prophet Muhammad, Arabia was characterized by an overall "state of war." The advent of the Prophet's mission only altered this by altering the categories with which the various groups and individuals identified. From this point on, in the absence of a peace treaty (which the Qur'ân both sanctioned and sanctified) there would exist only the blurriest of distinctions between "non-Muslims" and "hostile forces." This is the backdrop and *raison d'être* against which all the Qur'ânic material on jihad must be read.

b. Jihad in the Classical Juristic Tradition

Turning to the post-Prophetic era, classical jurists unanimously divided jihad into two main modalities. The first we may refer to as "aggressive jihad," which is pro-active and, according to the majority, constituted a communal requirement to be carried out at least once every year. The second modality was the "defensive jihad," which was waged whenever Muslim lands were attacked. This jihad was actually a much more serious affair than its counterpart, inasmuch as many of the stipulations and restrictions governing aggressive jihad were dropped in the case of defensive jihad. For example, the Muslim ruler did not have to announce the obligation to join the defensive jihad nor conscript soldiers for its prosecution. Similarly, all those groups who were normally exempt from participating in the aggressive jihad, e.g., women, minors, the elderly, young men who had not been granted permission by their parents, were *required* to participate in defensive jihad.

For our purposes of trying to determine the credibility of the claim that Islam is a religion of peace, we may ignore the defensive jihad. For no one would accuse Islam, or any other religion for that matter, of not being a peaceful religion simply because it insisted on defending itself. We shall thus restrict the remainder of our discussion to the aggressive jihad.

As I intimated above, the aforementioned "state of war" was not restricted to Arabia. It characterized the pre-modern world in general. In his book, *Violence and Civilization*, Jonathan Fletcher writes of Europe in the Middle Ages: "individual lords *had* to engage in warfare to save themselves and their families. If they did not, then sooner or later they would be overtaken by another lord and have to submit to his rule or be killed."[15] As late as the 19th century, Alexis de Tocqueville would reveal vestiges of this perspective in the United States. Relating the fears about how the country would be affected if Indians monopolized the Western frontier, he cites a contemporary view to the effect that "It is . . . in our interest that the new states should be religious, in order that they may permit us to remain free."[16] In other words, according to this understanding, only Christians would permit other Christians to remain free. In the case of the Muslim empire, an identical assumption would collude with the presumed "state of war" and produce a sense of mission that was reinforced by the overall medieval thirst for conquest. Jihad, for its part, like the Roman-Byzantine "charismatic victoriousness," would lend itself well to these ambitions and these concerns.

Still, the Muslim conquests were neither for the sole purpose of conversion nor annihilating the infidel. In addition to the fact that non-Muslims paid higher taxes—and thus non-conversion operated to the financial advantage of the state—the rules of jihad stipulated that non-Muslims remained free to practice their religion upon payment of the so-called *jizya*, or "income tax," in exchange for which the Muslim state incurred the responsibility to protect them from outside attack. While the imperial quest for empire invariably informed the policies of every Muslim state, Muslim juristic writings continued to reflect the logic of the "state of war" and the assumption that only Muslims would permit Muslims to remain Muslims. They continued to see jihad not only as a means of guaranteeing the security and freedom of the Muslims but as virtually the *only* means of doing so. For even peace treaties were usually the result of one's surrender to demands that had been imposed by a real or anticipated defeat by the sword.

To take one example, the juridical writings of the Spanish jurist Ibn Rushd the Elder (d. 520/1122), a major legal authority and grandfather of the celebrated Averroës of Western fame, clearly reflect the influence of the perceived "state of war." Because Ibn Rushd perceived it to be impossible for Muslims to live as Muslims outside of Muslim lands, he insisted that it was forbidden for Muslims to take up residence abroad. In fact, he even banned travel to non-Muslim countries for purposes of commerce, going so far as to urge the ruler to build check-points and light-houses to stop Muslims from leaving the lands of Islam. As for individuals in non-Muslim countries who converted to Islam, Ibn Rushd insisted that they were religiously obligated to migrate to a Muslim polity. On this understanding,

---

15. J. Fletcher, *Violence and Civilization: An Introduction to the Work of Norbert Elias* (Cambridge: Polity Press, 1997), 33. Emphasis not added.
16. *Democracy*, 1: 307.

it comes as no surprise that Ibn Rushd endorsed the traditional doctrine on aggressive jihad as a communal obligation. During the course of his discussion, however, it becomes clear that his ultimate consideration was the security of the Muslims rather than either conquest or conversion. After exhausting the point that jihad is a communal obligation, Ibn Rushd comes to the following conclusion:

> So, whenever we are placed beyond the reach of the enemy and the outlying districts of the Muslim lands are secured and the gaps in their fortifications are filled, the obligation to wage jihad falls from all the rest of the Muslims.[17]

The purpose of jihad, in other words, is to provide for the security and freedom of the Muslims in a world that kept them under constant threat. This may be difficult for many, especially Americans, to appreciate today. But we should remind ourselves that throughout the Middle Ages, while one could live as a Jew in Morocco, a Christian in Cairo, or even a Zoroastrian in Shirâz, one could not live as a Muslim in Paris, London or the Chesapeake Bay. Indeed, the "Abode of Islam/Abode of War" dichotomy, cited *ad nauseam* by certain Western scholars as proof of Islam's inherent hostility towards the West, was far more a *description* of the Muslim peoples of the world in which they lived than it was a *prescription* of the Islamic religion per se.[18]

c. Jihad in the Modern World

As we proceed to our discussion of the legal status of jihad in modern times, I should like to clarify the meaning of the claim that Islam is a religion of peace. "Religion of peace" does not imply that Islam is a pacifist religion, that it rejects the use of violence altogether, as either a moral or a metaphysical evil. "Religion of peace" connotes, rather, that Islam can countenance a state of permanent, peaceful coexistence with other nations and peoples who are not Muslims. In other words, contrary to the belief that Islam can only accept a world that is entirely populated by Muslims and, as such, Muslims must, as a religious duty, wage perpetual jihad against non-Muslims, Islam can peacefully coexist with non-Muslims. This position is no more than the result of an objective application of principles of Islamic jurisprudence which no jurist or activist, medieval or modern, has claimed to reject.

17. *Al-Muqaddimât*, 4 vols. (Beirut: Dâr al-Fikr, n.d.), 1: 374 (on the margins of *al-Mudawannah al-kubrâ*).
18. Indeed, the concept and function of the "Abode of Islam/Abode of War" dichotomy has been grossly exaggerated and often misrepresented. For example, the towering Shâfi'î jurist Abû al-Hasan al-Mâwardî (d. 450/1058) includes among the definitions of the "Abode of Islam" (*Dâr al-Islam*) any land in which a Muslim enjoys security and is able to isolate and protect himself, even if he is unable to promote the religion.

We have seen that a perennial "state of war" informed both the Qur'ânic and the classical articulations of jihad. In effect, this "state of war" constituted what Muslim jurists refer to as the custom or prevailing circumstances underlying the law. The assumed relationship, in other words, among nations and peoples in both the Qur'ân and pre-modern Islamdom was one of hostility. In such a context, jihad emerged as the only means of preserving the physical integrity of the Muslim community. The 20th century has introduced, however, major changes to this situation. Beginning with the Covenant of the League of Nations after WW I and culminating in the signing of the United Nations Charter after WW II, the territorial integrity of every nation on earth has been rendered inviolable. In effect, this development dismantled the general "state of war" and established peace as the assumed and normal relationship between all nations. This was an unprecedented development in the history of the world, certainly as Muslims had known it. For, again, the assumed relationship between Muslims and the peoples surrounding them had always been one of hostility. This fundamental difference between the prevailing reality of pre-modern and modern times both justifies and requires a different interpretation and application of all scriptural and juridical injunctions that command Muslims to wage jihad against non-believers. Contrary to the situation dictated by a prevailing "state of war," under a "state of peace," there is no obligation to wage aggressive jihad. Classical law manuals *do not* reflect this view (Ibn Rushd being the exception that proves the rule); nor should one expect them to. For not only was peace not the prevailing medieval order, it was part of the medieval "unimaginable." By contrast, numerous modern jurists, from Rashîd Ridâ to 'Abd al-Wahhâb Khallâf to Wahbah al-Zuhaylî, have confirmed Islam's commitment to peaceful coexistence with non-Muslims.[19]

To be sure, this manner of argument will appeal to many liberal-minded observers, Muslim and non-Muslim alike. It is in fact a common practice among those who argue for change and reform in Islam to insist that this or that change wrought by modern developments requires a different interpretation and/or application of Islamic law. It should be noted, however, that the shift from a "state of war" to a "state of peace" is much more easily achieved on paper than it is on the ground. And, according to the relevant principle of Islamic jurisprudence, the only changes in prevailing circumstances that can serve as a cause for changes in the law are those that are actually *realized* in the lives of the people. The fact that a community of lawyers or Muslim intellectuals, based on the state of *discussion* in their respective fields, conclude that the world has shifted from a "state of war" to a "state of peace" is not sufficient to establish this as a probative

19. See, e.g., Muhammad Rashîd Ridâ, *Tafsîr al-manâr*, 12 vols. (Beirut: Dâr al-Kutub al-'Ilmîyah, 1420/1999), 10: 257–91; 'Abd al-Wahhâb Khallâf, *al-Siyâsah al-shar'îyah* (Cairo: Matba'at al-Taqaddum, 1397/1977), 64–84; Wahbah al-Zuhaylî, *al-Fiqh al-islâmî wa adillatuh*, 9 vols. (Damascus: Dâr al-Fikr, 1417/1996), 9: 925–41.

change in custom. This is clearly established by al-Qarâfî in a passage dealing with the effect of custom on the status of expressions used as formulae for divorce:

> It is not enough that the jurist believes that a particular expression has become customary (as a formula for divorce). For his belief of what has become customary may stem from his training in the *madhhab* and his persistent study and disputation in the law. Rather, for an expression to become customary is for the common folk of a particular locale to understand one thing only whenever they hear it, not from the mouth of a jurist but from one of their own and according to their use of this expression for this particular purpose. This is the "becoming customary" that is sufficient to transform the literal meaning of an expression to a legally binding meaning based on custom.[20]

Two important implications emerge from this. First, the shift from the "state of war" to the "state of peace" cannot be simply asserted but must be confirmed on [the] ground. As such, there may arise disagreements among Muslims regarding the obligation to wage jihad, not over whether or not jihad remains an obligation even under a "state of peace," but over whether or not an actual "state of peace" exists. Second, the major powers, especially the United States as the lone superpower, bear an enormous responsibility towards the world community, inasmuch as their policies and actions, more than those of others, have the capacity to confirm or undermine the newly established and admittedly fragile "state of peace." To the extent that powerful nations flout Article I of the UN Charter, they actually contribute to the re-emergence of the medieval "state of war," with all that that implies in terms of relations among nations.

1. The Counter View. The terrorist attacks of September 11 have put Muslim leaders and intellectuals, especially those in the West, on the defensive, a corollary to which has been a rush to extirpate all traces of violence from Islam. This is understandable, given the enormous pressure being applied by the media and government agencies in search of assurances from Muslims. But there is also a dangerous side to this approach. For it carries the potential to radicalize the Muslim masses by undermining the credibility of Muslim leaders and intellectuals, who come to be seen as being more interested in appeasing the government-media complex than in defending the integrity of Islam and Muslims. In the end, the very people who are being pressured by the government-media complex to explain away and provide alternatives to extremist and wrong-minded views end up losing the

---

20. *Tamyîz*, 243. Divorce in traditional Islamic law was not a judicial proceeding but was initiated by the husband's uttering a "pronouncement of divorce." Since the expressions used in these pronouncements were not dictated by scripture, much ink was spilled over the question of which expressions constituted "pronouncements of divorce." This is the point of al-Qarâfî's argument.

masses and thus consigning them to the very views that they are supposed to be displacing.

The views of the so-called Muslim Radicals cannot be simply ignored out of fear of bringing Islam under indictment. Nor can they be dismissed as the mindless rantings of a tiny, vociferous fringe or the politically motivated dribble of simpletons who just don't understand the grand and glorious tradition of classical Islam. For, rightly or wrongly, these views constitute the going opinion in many quarters. And the authors of these views are often men of immense standing who wield enormous authority in the Muslim world and beyond. If the American government-media complex or American Muslim apologists can condemn or dismiss these views as extreme or unfounded, it should surely be no more difficult for the latter to dismiss their detractors as un- or insufficiently Islamic. Clearly, a more productive approach would be to search for ways of drawing Muslim Radicals into a logic that is both shared and esteemed by them and capable of serving as a basis for moving them beyond the blind and reckless radicalism that often characterizes their views.[21]

Given the limitations of space, I shall be able to engage the view of only one such Radical, by many accounts, the most important of them. This is the redoubtable Sayyid Qutb, chief ideologue of the Muslim Brotherhood, who was executed by the Egyptian government in 1966 and whose commentary, *In the Shade of the Qur'ân*, is perhaps *the* most widely-read Qur'ânic exegesis in the Muslim world. Indeed, for those who think that I might be conveniently avoiding Usâmah b. Lâdin, a child born in the Arab world twenty years from now will probably know little more of Usâmah than his name. At some point in his life, however, if religious, that child will probably be exposed to, if not imbibe, the writings of Sayyid Qutb. Whereas Usâmah b. Lâdin's effectiveness is linked almost exclusively to his ability to tap into the shared, negative experience of modern Muslims, Qutb grounds his views in a meticulously crafted methodology of Qur'ânic interpretation, which he holds up as the best, if not the only, way to read the Qur'ân. Perhaps more than any other Muslim thinker in modern times, his interpretive efforts have succeeded in sustaining the argument that the heirs of the classical tradition have bowed to the modern secular state's attempt to "domesticate" Islam, to borrow the term of Stephen L. Carter. According to Carter, in response to religion's higher calling, on the basis of which it may oppose the material interests of the state, "the state tries to move religion from a position in which it threatens the state to a position in which it supports the state."[22] This is largely the basis upon

21. One should note that even if it should be concluded that jihad against America *is* a communal obligation, this would not justify the *terrorist* attacks of September 11. For the law of jihad does not condone terrorism, which Islamic law basically defines as publicly directed violence against which the reasonable citizen, Muslim or non-Muslim, is unable to take safe-keeping measures.

22. Stephen Carter, *God's Name in Vain: The Wrongs and Rights of Religion in Politics* (New York: Basic Books, 2000), 30.

which Qutb has been able to appeal to the masses as an alternative to the classical tradition.

As a modern Revivalist, Qutb all but ignores the classical tradition of the *madhhabs* and relies almost exclusively on the Qur'ân. Based on his reading of Qur'ân 9: 29, he insists that waging jihad against the People of the Book (Jews and Christians) is a permanent, communal obligation upon the Muslims.

> Fight those who do not believe in God and the Last Day and do not forbid that which God and His Messenger have forbidden and do not practice proper religion, among those who were given the Book until they pay the poll-tax and they are subdued.

According the Qutb, the ninth chapter, in which this verse appears, was among the last to be revealed. As such, this verse constitutes the last and final stage of development in the Qur'ânic doctrine on Muslim–non-Muslim relations. While Qutb was not a jurist trained in the classical tradition, contrary to the popular stereotype about Muslim Radicals, he was also not a literalist. Rather, he insists on a "dynamic" reading of the Qur'ân, reminiscent of the position of the classical jurists exemplified in the above-cited al-Qarâfî and Qûtah. According to this "dynamic" reading, the concrete circumstances on the ground are to inform both the interpretation and application of the text. In Qutb's own words,

> The legal rules of Islam are, and always will be, subject to a certain dynamism in accordance with the Islamic approach. And it is not possible to understand the texts of scripture in isolation from this reality. Indeed, there is a fundamental difference between reading the verses of scripture as if they existed in a vacuum and reading them in their dynamic context in accordance with the Islamic approach.[23]

In this particular case, however, Qutb insists that as *an historical fact* Jews and Christians have always proved themselves to be hostile to Muslims. As proof, he adduces several verses from the Qur'ân, which he takes to constitute scriptural evidence of the inherent beliefs and attitudes of Jews and Christians (rather than as a scriptural description of the attitude of particular Jews or particular Christians at particular places and times). In addition, he relates a series of historical events, from the Crusades to modern colonialism. From this it becomes clear that it is Qutb's belief that Jews and Christians (which one senses he uses as a catch-all for the West) are inherently hostile towards Muslims that informs his reading of 9: 29. This belief, moreover, is so strong and overpowering that it preempts all other possibilities, including those established by the Qur'ân itself. For example, at 5: 82, the Qur'ân states, "You will find those who are most closely drawn to the Believers in love to be those who say, 'We are

23. *Fî zilâl al-qur'ân*, 6 vols. (Cairo: Dâr al-Shurûq, 1417/1996), 3: 1631.

Christians.'" Similarly, speaking this time of both Jews and Christians, Qur'ân 3: 113–14 states, "They are not all the same. Among the People of the Book are those who stand at night reciting the words of God and prostrating. They believe in God and the Last Day, they command what is good and forbid what is evil and they strive in the path of righteousness. Indeed, they are among the righteous."

What all of this suggests is that Qutb's understanding of the Qur'ânic doctrine on Muslim–non-Muslim relations is as informed by his own reading *into* the text as it is by his attempt to extract meaning *from* the text. For the Qur'ân clearly establishes *a range* of possible attitudes and behaviors on the part of Jews and Christians towards Muslims. Moreover, at least as many if not more exegetes, classical and modern, hold chapter five (which speaks of Christian love for Muslims) to be the last-revealed chapter as hold chapter nine to be so. As such, on purely formal grounds, one could just as rightly argue that chapter five reflects the final teaching on Muslim–non-Muslim relations. What brings Qutb to privilege 9: 29 and to construe it in the manner he does seems to be his *historical assessment*, based in part on his own experience, of the attitude of Jews and Christians towards Muslims. On this assessment, one would have to admit that whether we employ his "dynamic" method or the classical jurisprudence exemplified by al-Qarâfî, Qutb is certainly correct in the conclusion he draws. But it is equally true, on both approaches, that this conclusion could be overturned, assuming a different *historical assessment*. In other words, assuming that Jews and Christians are no longer active enemies of Muslims, or that there are political mechanisms in place that prevent them from acting on this hostility, even Qutb (or his followers), *on his own methodology*, could be convinced to modify his interpretation of 9: 29. In sum, assuming an overall "state of peace," even Qutb might be forced to concede that there is no obligation to wage jihad against Jews and Christians.

Having said this much, there does appear to exist one potential stumbling block. This is Qutb's insistence that the only realities to which Muslims are obligated to respond in adjusting their interpretations and applications of scripture are those that are the result of Muslim efforts.[24] In other words, developments such as the League of Nations or the United Nations, which were not the products of strictly Muslim efforts, are of no probative value in interpreting the Qur'ân or deducing the rules of Islamic law. To be sure, there is a glaring (and redeeming) weakness in this position. For even the most casual acquaintance with the sources of Islam reveals that this principle cannot claim to derive from the Qur'ân or the practice of the Prophet. Indeed, the Prophet can easily be shown to have endorsed all kinds of realities that were not the products of Muslim efforts, from the system of tribal alliances to the Forbidden Months to honoring pagan marriages contracted before Islam. In short, what matters in legal

---

24. For Qutb's entire discussion on 9: 29, see *Zilâl*, 3: 1619–50.

deliberations is, *ceteris paribus*, the concrete situation on the ground, not the agency via which that situation is brought into being. As such, the transformations effected by the U.N. Charter should be deemed no less probative than those effected by the pre-Islamic pagan Arabs.

V. CONCLUSION

I have argued that Islam is a religion of peace. I have based this argument on the assertion that a prevailing "state of war," rather than difference of religion, was the *raison d'être* of jihad and that this "state of war" has given way in modern times to a global "state of peace" that rejects the unwarranted violation of the territorial sovereignty of all nations. Assuming the factual verity of this "state of peace," even Radicals like Sayyid Qutb could be convinced of the veracity of my argument affirming Islam's fundamental commitment to peace. Ironically, however, it is precisely here that a superpower like the United States is put in a position to contribute directly to the Muslim valuation of jihad in the modern world. Lamentably, U.S. actions such as the 1999 bombing of Sudan and Afghanistan, its acquiescence in the face of Israeli incursions into south Lebanon and the Occupied Territories, its talk of an impending invasion of Iraq and its saber-rattling with Iran all undermine the credibility of any presumption of a new world "state of peace." Still, I would argue, these unfortunate challenges notwithstanding, the *principle* of territorial inviolability continues to enjoy general recognition throughout the world community. And it is this general recognition that sustains my commitment to the doctrine that Islam is a religion of peace.

In the end, however, whether Islam actually functions on the ground as a religion of peace will depend as much on the *actions* of non-Muslims as it does on the *religious understanding* of Muslims. Muslims will have to make a more courageous and assiduous commitment to the principle that recognizes changes in circumstances as a basis for changes in the law, what Sayyid Qutb himself referred to as the "dynamic" method of interpretation. Muslims will also have to avoid the fallacy of assuming that the realities of yesterday pass automatically into today or that the factual or historical assessments of the Muslims of the past constitute authoritative doctrines that are binding on the Muslims of the present. As for non-Muslims, they will have to make a more conscious and sustained effort to conduct their military, economic and political affairs in a fashion that actually confirms the new world order of the United Nations Charter, by respecting the dignity and territorial integrity of Muslim and other nations, including variations on what the U.N. Charter refers to as "Trust Territories."[25] They will have

---

25. Article 77 reads: "(1) The trusteeship system shall apply to such territories in the following categories as may be placed thereunder by means of trusteeship agreements: (a) territories now held under mandate; (2) territories which may be detached from enemy states as a result of the Second World War; and (3) territories voluntarily placed under the system by states responsible for their administration."

to refrain from acting in a manner that expresses or implies aggression and pushes the world back toward the dark ages of the "state of war." For under the latter condition, the aggressive jihad of the premodern world will find both practical justification and religious sanction. In these our times of weapons of mass destruction, spiraling conflicts and renewed aggression, let us hope that all of us, Muslims and non-Muslims alike, will recognize just how quickly we may be moving toward the abyss and, in light of this, seize the opportunity to make our respective contributions to a better, safer world.

SAYYID QUTB
1906–1966

Egyptian literary critic, novelist, poet, Islamic activist, and the godfather of modern revolutionary Islamic ideology, he was both a respected intellectual and religious writer. His works included an influential multivolume commentary on the Quran, *In the Shade of the Quran*, and *Milestones*, which sets forth Qutb's revolutionary vision. It would be difficult to overestimate the role played by Qutb in the reassertion of militant jihad, from the assassins of Egypt's President Anwar Sadat to Osama Bin Laden and al-Qaeda.

Jihad in the Cause of God

When writers with defeatist and apologetic mentalities write about "Jihad in Islam," trying to remove this "blot" from Islam, then they are mixing up two things: first, that this religion forbids the imposition of its belief by force, as is clear from the verse, "There is no compulsion in religion" (2:256), while on the other hand it tries to annihilate all those political and material powers which stand between people and Islam, which force one people to bow before another people and prevent them from accepting the sovereignty of God. These two principles have no relation to one another nor is there room to mix them. In spite of this, these defeatist-type people try to mix the two aspects and want to confine Jihad to what today is called "defensive war." The Islamic Jihad has no relationship to modern warfare, either in its causes or in the way in which it is conducted. The causes of Islamic Jihad should be sought in the very nature of Islam and its role in the world, in its high principles, which have been given to it by God and for the implementation of which God appointed the Prophet—peace be on him—as His Messenger and declared him to be the last of all prophets and messengers.

The way to establish God's rule on earth is not that some consecrated people—the priests—be given the authority to rule, as was the case with the rule of the Church, nor that some spokesmen of God become rulers, as is the case in a "theocracy." To establish God's rule means that His laws be enforced and that the final decision in all affairs be according to these laws.

The establishing of the dominion of God on earth, the abolishing of the dominion of man, the taking away of sovereignty from the usurper to revert it to God, and the bringing about of the enforcement of the Divine Law

From http://www.islamistwatch.org/texts/qutb/Milestones/jihad.html.

(Shari'ah) and the abolition of man-made laws cannot be achieved only through preaching. Those who have usurped the authority of God and are oppressing God's creatures are not going to give up their power merely through preaching; if it had been so, the task of establishing God's religion in the world would have been very easy for the Prophets of God! This is contrary to the evidence from the history of the Prophets and the story of the struggle of the true religion, spread over generations.

This universal declaration of the freedom of man on the earth from every authority except that of God, and the declaration that sovereignty is God's alone and that He is the Lord of the universe, is not merely a theoretical, philosophical and passive proclamation. It is a positive, practical and dynamic message with a view to bringing about the implementation of the Shari'ah of God and actually freeing people from their servitude to other men to bring them into the service of God, the One without associates. This cannot be attained unless both "preaching" and "the movement" are used. This is so because appropriate means are needed to meet any and every practical situation.

Because this religion proclaims the freedom of man on the earth from all authority except that of God, it is confronted in every period of human history—yesterday, today, or tomorrow—with obstacles of beliefs and concepts, physical power, and the obstacles of political, social, economic, racial and class structures. In addition, corrupted beliefs and superstitions become mixed with this religion, working side by side with it and taking root in peoples' hearts.

If through "preaching" beliefs and ideas are confronted, through "the movement" material obstacles are tackled. Foremost among these is that political power which rests on a complex yet interrelated ideological, racial, class, social and economic support. Thus these two—preaching and the movement—united, confront "the human situation" with all the necessary methods. For the achievement of the freedom of man on earth—of all mankind throughout the earth—it is necessary that these two methods should work side by side. This is a very important point and cannot be over-emphasized.

If the actual life of human beings is found to be different from this declaration of freedom, then it becomes incumbent upon Islam to enter the field with preaching as well as the movement, and to strike hard at all those political powers which force people to bow before them and which rule over them, unmindful of the commandments of God, and which prevent people from listening to the preaching and accepting the belief if they wish to do so. After annihilating the tyrannical force, whether it be in a political or a racial form, or in the form of class distinctions within the same race, Islam establishes a new social, economic and political system, in which the concept of the freedom of man is applied in practice.

It is not the intention of Islam to force its beliefs on people, but Islam is not merely "belief." As we have pointed out, Islam is a declaration of the freedom of man from servitude to other men. Thus it strives from the beginning to abolish all those systems and governments which are based on the rule of man over men and the servitude of one human being to another. When Islam releases people from this political pressure and presents to them its spiritual message, appealing to their reason, it gives them complete freedom to accept or not to accept its beliefs. However, this freedom does not mean that they can make their desires their gods, or that they can choose to remain in the servitude of other human beings, making some men lords over others. Whatever system is to be established in the world ought to be on the authority of God, deriving its laws from Him alone. Then every individual is free, under the protection of this universal system, to adopt any belief he wishes to adopt. This is the only way in which "the religion" can be purified for God alone. The word "religion" includes more than belief; "religion" actually means a way of life, and in Islam this is based on belief. But in an Islamic system there is room for all kinds of people to follow their own beliefs, while obeying the laws of the country which are themselves based on the Divine authority.

Anyone who understands this particular character of this religion will also understand the place of Jihad *bis saif* (striving through fighting), which is to clear the way for striving through preaching in the application of the Islamic movement. He will understand that Islam is not a "defensive movement" in the narrow sense which today is technically called a "defensive war." This narrow meaning is ascribed to it by those who are under the pressure of circumstances and are defeated by the wily attacks of the orientalists, who distort the concept of Islamic Jihad. It was a movement to wipe out tyranny and to introduce true freedom to mankind, using resources according to the actual human situation, and it had definite stages, for each of which it utilized new methods.

If we insist on calling Islamic Jihad a defensive movement, then we must change the meaning of the word "defense" and mean by it "the defense of man" against all those elements which limit his freedom. These elements take the form of beliefs and concepts, as well as of political systems, based on economic, racial or class distinctions. When Islam first came into existence, the world was full of such systems, and the present-day Jahiliyyah also has various kinds of such systems.

When we take this broad meaning of the word "defense," we understand the true character of Islam, and that it is a universal proclamation of the freedom of man from servitude to other men, the establishment of the sovereignty of God and His Lordship throughout the world, the end of man's arrogance and selfishness, and the implementation of the rule of the Divine Shari'ah in human affairs.

As to persons who attempt to defend the concept of Islamic Jihad by interpreting it in the narrow sense of the current concept of defensive war, and who do research to prove that the battles fought in Islamic Jihad were all for the defense of the homeland of Islam—some of them considering the homeland of Islam to be just the Arabian peninsula—against the aggression of neighboring powers, they lack understanding of the nature of Islam and its primary aim. Such an attempt is nothing but a product of a mind defeated by the present difficult conditions and by the attacks of the treacherous orientalists on the Islamic Jihad.

Can anyone say that if Abu Bakr, 'Umar or 'Othman had been satisfied that the Roman and Persian powers were not going to attack the Arabian peninsula, they would not have striven to spread the message of Islam throughout the world? How could the message of Islam have spread when it faced such material obstacles as the political system of the state, the socio-economic system based on races and classes, and behind all these, the military power of the government?

It would be naive to assume that a call is raised to free the whole of humankind throughout the earth, and it is confined to preaching and exposition. Indeed, it strives through preaching and exposition when there is freedom of communication and when people are free from all these influences, as "There is no compulsion in religion"; but when the above-mentioned obstacles and practical difficulties are put in its way, it has no recourse but to remove them by force so that when it is addressed to people's hearts and minds they are free to accept or reject it with an open mind.

Since the objective of the message of Islam is a decisive declaration of man's freedom, not merely on the philosophical plane but also in the actual conditions of life, it must employ Jihad. It is immaterial whether the homeland of Islam—in the true Islamic sense, Dar ul-Islam—is in a condition of peace or whether it is threatened by its neighbors. When Islam strives for peace, its objective is not that superficial peace which requires that only that part of the earth where the followers of Islam are residing remain secure. The peace which Islam desires is that the religion (i.e. the Law of the society) be purified for God, that the obedience of all people be for God alone, and that some people should not be lords over others. After the period of the Prophet—peace be on him—only the final stages of the movement of Jihad are to be followed; the initial or middle stages are not applicable. They have ended, and as Ibn Qayyim states, "Thus, after the revelation of the chapter 'Bratt,' the unbelievers were of three kinds: adversaries in war, people with treaties, and Dhimmies. The people with treaties eventually became Muslims, so there were only two kinds left: people at war and Dhimmies. The people at war were always afraid of him. Now the people of the whole world were of three kinds: one, the Muslims who believed in him: two, those with whom he had peace (and from the previous sentence we understand that they were Dhimmies); and three, the opponents who kept fighting him."

These are the logical positions consonant with the character and purposes of this religion, and not what is understood by the people who are defeated by present conditions and by the attacks of the treacherous orientalists.

God held back Muslims from fighting in Mecca and in the early period of their migration to Medina, and told them, "Restrain your hands, and establish regular prayers, and pay Zakat." Next, they were permitted to fight: "Permission to fight is given to those against whom war is made, because they are oppressed, and God is able to help them. These are the people who were expelled from their homes without cause." The next stage came when the Muslims were commanded to fight those who fight them: "Fight in the cause of God against those who fight you." And finally, war was declared against all the polytheists: "And fight against all the polytheists, as they all fight against you"; "Fight against those among the People of the Book who do not believe in God and the Last Day, who do not forbid what God and His Messenger have forbidden, and who do not consider the true religion as their religion, until they are subdued and pay Jizyah." Thus, according to the explanation by Imam Ibn Qayyim, the Muslims were first restrained from fighting; then they were permitted to fight; then they were commanded to fight against the aggressors; and finally they were commanded to fight against all the polytheists.

With these verses from the Qur'an and with many Traditions of the Prophet—peace be on him—in praise of Jihad, and with the entire history of Islam, which is full of Jihad, the heart of every Muslim rejects that explanation of Jihad invented by those people whose minds have accepted defeat under unfavorable conditions and under the attacks on Islamic Jihad by the shrewd orientalists.

What kind of a man is it who, after listening to the commandment of God and the Traditions of the Prophet—peace be on him—and after reading about the events which occurred during the Islamic Jihad, still thinks that it is a temporary injunction related to transient conditions and that it is concerned only with the defense of the borders?

In the verse giving permission to fight, God has informed the Believers that the life of this world is such that checking one group of people by another is the law of God, so that the earth may be cleansed of corruption. "Permission to fight is given to those against whom war is made, because they are oppressed, and God is able to help them. These are the people who were expelled from their homes without cause, except that they said that our Lord is God. Had God not checked one people by another, then surely synagogues and churches and mosques would have been pulled down, where the name of God is remembered often." Thus, this struggle is not a temporary phase but an eternal state—an eternal state, as truth and falsehood cannot co-exist on this earth. Whenever Islam stood up with the universal declaration that God's Lordship should be established over the entire earth and that men should become free from servitude to other men, the usurpers of God's authority on earth have struck out against it fiercely and have never tolerated it. It became incumbent upon Islam to strike back and release man throughout the earth from the grip of these usurpers. The eternal struggle for the freedom of man will continue until the religion is purified for God.

The command to refrain from fighting during the Meccan period was a temporary stage in a long journey. The same reason was operative during the early days of Hijra, but after these early stages, the reason for Jihad was not merely to defend Medina. Indeed, its defense was necessary, but this was not the ultimate aim. The aim was to protect the resources and the center of the movement—the movement for freeing mankind and demolishing the obstacles which prevented mankind from attaining this freedom.

The reasons for refraining from fighting during the Meccan period are easily understood. In Mecca preaching was permitted. The Messenger—peace be on him—was under the protection of the Banu Hashim and hence he had the opportunity to declare his message openly; he had the freedom to speak to individuals and to groups and to appeal to their hearts and minds. There was no organized political power which could prevent him from preaching and prevent people from listening. At this stage there was no need for the use of force.

In the early Medinite period fighting was also prohibited. The reason for this was that the Prophet—peace be on him—had signed a pact with the Jews of Medina and with the unbelieving Arabs in and around Medina, an action which was necessary at this stage.

First, there was an open opportunity for preaching and persuasion. There was no political power to circumscribe this freedom; the whole population accepted the new Muslim state and agreed upon the leadership of the Prophet—peace be on him—in all political manners. In the pact it was agreed by all parties that no one would make a treaty of peace or declare war or establish relations with any outsider without the express permission of the Prophet—peace be on him. Thus, the real power in Medina was in the hands of Muslim leadership. The doors were also open for preaching Islam and there was freedom of belief.

Secondly, at this stage the Prophet—peace be on him—wanted to conserve all his efforts to combat the Quraish, whose relentless opposition was a great obstacle in spreading Islam to other tribes which were waiting to see the final outcome of the struggle between the two groups of the Quraish. That is why the Prophet—peace be on him—hastened to send scouting parties in various directions. The first such party was commanded by Hamza bin Abdul Muttalib, and it went out during the month of Ramadan, only six months after the Immigration.

After this, there were other scouting parties, one during the ninth month after Hijra, the next in the thirteenth month the third sixteen months after Hijra, and in the seventeenth month he sent a party under the leadership of Abdullah bin Jahash. This party encountered some resistance and some blood was shed. This occurred during the month of Rajab, which was considered a sacred month. The following verse of Chapter Baqara refers to it:

They ask you about fighting in the sacred months. Say: Fighting in them is a great sin, but to prevent people from the way of God, and to reject God, and to stop people from visiting the Sacred Mosque, and to expel people from their homes are a much greater sin, and oppression is worse than killing. (2:217)

During Ramadan of the same year, the Battle of Badr took place, and in Chapter Anfal this battle was reviewed.

If this stage of the Islamic movement is viewed in proper perspective, then there is no room to say that the basic aim of the Islamic movement was "defensive" in the narrow sense which some people ascribe to it today, defeated by the attacks of the treacherous orientalists!

Those who look for causes of a defensive nature in the history of the expansion of Islam are caught by the aggressive attacks of the orientalists at a time when Muslims possess neither glory nor do they possess Islam. However, by God's grace, there are those who are standing firm on the issue that Islam is a universal declaration of the freedom of man on the earth from every authority except God's authority, and that the religion ought to be purified for God; and they keep writing concerning the Islamic Jihad.

But the Islamic movement does not need any arguments taken from the literature, as it stands on the clear verses of the Qur'an:

They ought to fight in the way of God who have sold the life of this world for the life of the Hereafter; and whoever fights in the way of God and is killed or becomes victorious, to him shall We give a great reward. Why should not you fight in the way of God for those men, women and children who have been oppressed because they are weak and who call "Our Lord! Take us out of this place whose people are oppressors, and raise for us an ally, and send for us a helper." Those who believe fight in the cause of God, while those who do not believe fight in the cause of tyranny. Then fight against the friends of Satan. Indeed, the strategy of Satan is weak. (3: 74–76)

Say to the unbelievers that if they refrain, then whatever they have done before will be forgiven them; but if they turn back, then they know what happened to earlier nations. And fight against them until there is no oppression and the religion is wholly for God. But if they refrain, then God is watching over their actions. But if they do not, then know that God is your Ally and He is your Helper. (8: 38–40)

Fight against those among the People of the Book who do not believe in God and the Last Day, who do not forbid what God and His messenger have forbidden, and who do not consider the true religion as their way of life, until they are subdued and pay Jizyah. The Jews say: "Ezra is the Son of God," and the Christians say: "The Messiah is the Son of God." These are mere sayings from their mouths, following those who preceded them and disbelieved. God will assail them; how they are perverted! They have taken their rabbis and priests as lords other than God, and the Messiah, son of Mary; and they were commanded to worship none but One God. There is no deity but He, glory be to Him above what they associate with Him! They desire to extinguish God's light with their mouths, and God intends to perfect His light, although the unbelievers may be in opposition. (9: 29–32)

The reasons for Jihad which have been described in the above verses are these: to establish God's authority in the earth; to arrange human affairs according to the true guidance provided by God; to abolish all the Satanic forces and Satanic systems of life; to end the lordship of one man over others since all men are creatures of God and no one has the authority to make them his servants or to make arbitrary laws for them. These reasons are sufficient for proclaiming Jihad. However, one should always keep in mind that there is no compulsion in religion; that is, once the people are free from the lordship of men, the law governing civil affairs will be purely that of God, while no one will be forced to change his beliefs and accept Islam. . . .

MUHAMMAD ABDEL SALAM AL-FARAG
1954–1982

He was an ideologue of Egypt's Islamic Jihad (the group that assassinated Egypt's President Anwar Sadat) and a former member of the Muslim Brotherhood disaffected by its moderate posture. Al-Farag's tract, *The Neglected Duty*, was heavily indebted to Sayyid Qutb's militant writings and provided the worldview and ideology of Islamic Jihad. At the heart of al-Farag's message and mission was a call to "true believers" to wage jihad against Egypt's "un-Islamic state" and its leader in order to establish an Islamic state. Al-Farag was executed April 15, 1982, along with the four assassins of Sadat.

The Forgotten Duty

(§68) THE ENEMY WHO IS NEAR AND THE ENEMY WHO IS FAR

It is said that the battlefield of *jihād* today is the liberation of Jerusalem since it is (part of) the Holy Land. It is true that the liberation of the Holy Land is a religious command, obligatory for all Muslims, but the Apostle of God—May God's Peace be upon Him—described the believer as "sagacious and prudent" (*kayyis faṭin*), and this means that a Muslim knows what is useful and what is harmful, and gives priority to radical definitive solutions. This is a point that makes the explanation of the following necessary:

(§69) First: To fight an enemy who is near is more important than to fight an enemy who is far.

Second: Muslim blood will be shed in order to realize this victory. Now it must be asked whether this victory will benefit the interests of an Islamic State? Or will this victory benefit the interests of Infidel Rule? It will mean the strengthening of a State which rebels against the Laws of God. . . . These Rulers will take advantage of the nationalist ideas of these Muslims in order to realize their un-Islamic aims, even though at the surface (these aims) look Islamic. Fighting has to be done (only) under the Banner of Islam and under Islamic Leadership. About this there is no difference of opinion.

(§70) Third: The basis of the existence of Imperialism in the Lands of Islam are (precisely) these Rulers. To begin by putting an end to imperialism is not a laudatory and not a useful act. It is only a waste of time. We must concentrate on our own Islamic situation: we have to establish the

From Johannes J. G. Jansen, *The Neglected Duty* (New York: Macmillan, 1986).

Rule of God's Religion in our own country first, and to make the Word of God supreme. . . . There is no doubt that the first battlefield for *jihād* is the extermination of these infidel leaders and to replace them by a complete Islamic Order. From here we should start.

(§71) THE ANSWER TO THOSE WHO SAY THAT IN ISLAM *JIHĀD* IS DEFENSIVE ONLY

Concerning this question it is proper that we should refute those who say that *jihād* in Islam is defensive, and that Islam was not spread by the sword. This is a false view, which is (nevertheless) repeated by a great number of those who are prominent in the field of Islamic missionary activities. The right answer comes from the Apostle of God—God's Peace be upon Him—when he was asked: "What is *jihād* for God's cause?" He then said: "Whosoever fights in order to make the Word of God supreme is someone who (really) fights for God's cause." To fight is, in Islam, to make supreme the Word of God in this world, whether it be by attacking or by defending. . . .

Islam spread by the sword, and under the very eyes of these Leaders of Unbelief who conceal it from mankind. After the (removal of these Leaders) nobody has an aversion (to Islam). . . .

It is obligatory for the Muslims to raise their swords under the very eyes of the Leaders who hide the Truth and spread falsehoods. If (the Muslims) do not do this, the Truth will not reach the hearts of Men. . . .

(§76) THE VERSE OF THE SWORD (QUR'ĀN 9.5)

Most Koran commentators have said something about a certain verse from the Koran which they have named the Verse of the Sword (Qur'ān 9.5). This verse runs: "Then when the sacred months have slipped away, slay the polytheists wherever ye find them, seize them, beset them, lie in ambush for them everywhere."

The Qur'ān scholar Ibn Kathīr noted in his commentary on this verse: "Al-Daḥḥāk ibn Muzāḥim said: 'It cancelled every treaty between the Prophet—God's Peace be upon Him—and any infidel, and every contract and every term.' Al-'Ūfī said about this verse, on the authority of Ibn 'Abbās: 'No contract nor covenant of protection was left to a single infidel since (this) dissolution (of treaty obligations) was revealed.'"

(§77) The Qur'ān scholar Muḥammad ibn Aḥmad ibn Muḥammad ibn Juzayy al-Kalbī, the author of (a Qur'ān commentary entitled) *Tafsīr al-Tashīl li-'Ulūm al-Tanzīl*, says: "The abrogation of the command to be at peace with the infidels, to forgive them, to be (passively) exposed to them and to endure their insults preceded here the command to fight them. This makes it superfluous to repeat the abrogation of the command to live in peace with the infidels at each Qur'anic passage (where this is relevant). (Such a command to live in peace with them) is found in 114 verses in 54 surahs. This is all abrogated by His word: "Slay the polytheists wherever ye find them" (Qur'ān 9.5) and "Fighting is prescribed for you" (Qur'ān 2.216).

Al-Ḥusayn ibn Faḍl says: "This is the verse of the sword. It abrogates every verse in the Qur'ān in which suffering the insults of the enemy is mentioned." It is strange indeed that there are those who want to conclude from Qur'ān verses that have been abrogated that fighting and *jihād* are to be forsworn.

(§78) The Imām Abū 'Abdallāh Muhammad Ibn Ḥazm who died in AH 456 says in (his book entitled) *Al-Nāsikh wa-'l-Mansūkh* (The Abrogating and the Abrogated Passages from the Qur'ān), in the Chapter "On Not Attacking the Infidels": "In 114 verses in 48 surahs everything is abrogated by the Word of God—Exalted and Majestic He is—: 'Slay the polytheists wherever ye find them' (Qur'ān 9.5). We shall discuss this whenever we come across it, if God—Exalted He is—permits." End of quotation.

(§79) The scholar and Imām Abū al-Qāsim Hibbat Allāh ibn Salāmah says on "Slay the polytheists wherever ye find them": "The third verse is indeed the third verse, and it is this verse which is the verse which abrogates. But it abrogates 114 verses from the Qur'ān and then the end of it abrogates the beginning of it, because the verse ends with: 'If they repent and establish the Prayer and pay the Zakāt, then set them free' (Qur'ān 9.5, end of the verse)." (This quotation is taken from) a book (entitled) *Kitāb al-Nāsikh wa-'l-Mansūkh.*

(§80) "SO WHEN YOU MEET THOSE WHO HAVE DISBELIEVED, LET THERE BE SLAUGHTER" (QUR'ĀN 47.4)

Al-Suddī and Al-Ḍaḥḥāk say: "The Verse of the Sword was abrogated by: 'So when you meet those who have disbelieved, (let there be) slaughter until ye have made havoc of them, bind them fast, then (liberate them) either freely or by ransom' (Qur'ān 47.4). This verse is harsher on the infidels than the Verse of the Sword." Al-Qatāda, however, has the opposite opinion, and I do not know anyone who disagrees with the opinion that it is abrogated except Al-Suyūṭī who says in his book (entitled) *Al-Ittifāq*: "At the time when the Muslims were weak and few in number the command was to endure and to suffer. Then this command was abrogated by making fighting obligatory. In reality this is, however, not really abrogation, but it is to be regarded as 'causing to forget.' Did not God—Exalted He is—say (in Qur'ān 2.106): '. . . or We cause (the Messenger) to forget?'"

The thing that is forgotten is the command to fight, until the time when the Muslims are strong. When, however, the Muslims are weak, the legal ruling is that it is obligatory to endure insults. This weakens a view about which so many are so enthusiastic, namely, that the verse (Qur'ān 47.4) on this point is abrogated by the Verse of the Sword (9.5). It is not like that. On the contrary, it is caused to be forgotten.

(Al-Suyūṭī) also said: "Some mention that verses like (Qur'ān 2.109 which runs): 'So overlook and pay no attention until God interveneth with His Command' do not address a specific group of people at a specific time and with a specific aim. Hence (the command embodied in this verse) is not abrogated but it is postponed until a certain time." Here ends the quotation from Al-Suyūṭī.

(§81) In spite of Al-Suyūṭī's disagreement with all the preceding opinions, there is no room for doubt that to adopt the first opinion is correct. Moreover, whoever thinks that the view that nonabrogation of the verses of pardon and forgiveness (like 2.109) means that we are free to neglect the two duties of (1) jihād and (2) urging to what is reputable and prohibiting what is not, is mistaken.

It certainly also does not mean that the duty of jihād has come to an end, because the Apostle of God—God's Peace be upon Him—says: "Jihād continues (mādin) until the day of Resurrection." Professor Dr. 'Abd al-Wahhāb Khallāf says in his book (entitled) 'Ilm Uṣūl al-Fiqh (The Science of the "Roots" of the Islamic Legal System) on p. 227: "Since it continues until the Day of Resurrection this indicates that it will remain (a duty) as long as the World remains."

To do away with jihād with the argument that it was caused to be forgotten does not only put an end to fighting for this religion but it also puts an end to the intention (nīyah) of fighting for this religion. The danger of that is apparent from the saying of the Apostle of God—God's Peace be upon Him—: "Someone who does not fight for his religion, or someone whose soul does not talk to him encouraging him to fight for his religion, dies as a pagan."

It is, moreover, generally agreed upon that in order to wage jihād the Muslims must have strength. But how can this strength be realized when you abolish the duty of jihād? Does not God—Praised and Exalted He is—say: "If they intended to go forth, they would make some preparation for it; but God is adverse to their being stirred up and hath made them laggards" (Qur'ān 9.46). The fact that you are not willing to go forth has as a consequence your neglecting to prepare (for it). From where now will a Muslim who has abolished the duty of jihād get the means for obtaining strength? Does not the Apostle of God say: "When people yearn for money and wealth, and conclude their bargains upon credit, and neglect the waging of jihād for God's cause, and hold on to the tails of their cows, then God will send a plague upon them from heaven, and He will not remove it from them until they return to their religion?" . . .

(§83) THE MECCAN AND THE MEDINAN SOCIETY

There are those who allege that we live in a Meccan society, thereby endeavoring to obtain for themselves the permission to abandon the waging of jihād for God's cause. Whoever puts himself in a Meccan society in order to abandon the religious duty of *jihād* must also refrain from fasting and prayer (since the Revelations about these duties were only given after the Apostle had emigrated from Mecca to Medina in 622 AD), and he must enrich himself by asking usury since usury was not forbidden until the Medinan period.

The truth of the matter is that (the period in) Mecca is the period of the genesis of the Call (to Islam). The Word of God—Praised and Exalted He is—(Qur'ān 5.3): "Today I have perfected your religion for you, and have completed my goodness towards you, and have approved Islam as your religion" abrogates these defeatist ideas that have to be substantiated by the argument that we are Meccans. We are not at the beginning of something, as the Prophet—God's Peace be upon Him—was at the beginning (of the establishment of Islam), but we (have to) accept the Revelation in its final form.

We do not live in a Meccan society, and neither do we live in a Medinan society. When you wish to know in what kind of society we live, consult the paragraph on "The House in Which We Live" (§18).

(§84) FIGHTING IS NOW A DUTY UPON ALL MUSLIMS

When God—Praised and Exalted He is—made fasting obligatory, he said (Qur'ān 2.183): "Fasting is prescribed for you." In regard to fighting he said (Qur'ān 2.216): "Fighting is prescribed for you." This refutes the view of whoever says that *jihād* is indeed a duty and then goes on by saying: "When I have fulfilled the duty of engaging in missionary activities for Islam (*da'wah*), then I have fulfilled the duty (of *jihād*), because (engagement in missionary activities for Islam) is *jihād* too." However, the (real character of this) duty is clearly spelled out in the text of the Qur'ān: It is fighting, which means confrontation and blood.

The question now is: When is *jihād* an individual duty? *Jihād* becomes an individual duty in three situations:

(§85) First, when two armies meet and their ranks are facing each other, it is forbidden to those who are present to leave, and it becomes an individual duty to remain standing, because God—Exalted He is—says: "O ye who have believed, when ye meet a hostile party, stand firm, and call God frequently to mind" (Qur'ān 8.45) and also: "O ye who have believed, when ye meet those who have disbelieved moving into battle, turn them not your backs" (Qur'ān 8.15).

Second, when the infidels descend upon a country, it becomes an individual duty for its people to fight them and drive them away.

Third, when the Imām calls upon a people to fight, they must depart into battle, for God—Exalted He is—says (Qur'ān 9.38-39): "O ye who have believed, what is the matter with you? When one says to you: 'March out in the way of God,' ye are weighed down to the ground; are you so satisfied with this nearer life as to neglect the Hereafter? The enjoyment of this nearer life is in comparison with the Hereafter only a little thing. If ye do not march out He will inflict upon you a painful punishment, and will substitute (for you) another people; ye will not injure Him at all; God over everything has power." The Apostle—God's Peace be upon Him—says: "When you are called upon to fight, then hasten."

With regard to the lands of Islam, the enemy lives right in the middle of them. The enemy even has got hold of the reins of power, for this enemy is (none other than) these rulers who have (illegally) seized the Leadership of the Muslims. Therefore, waging *jihād* against them is an individual duty, in addition to the fact that Islamic *jihād* today requires a drop of sweat from every Muslim.

(§87) Know that when *jihād* is an individual duty, there is no (need to) ask permission of (your) parents to leave to wage *jihād*, as the jurists have said; it is thus similar to prayer and fasting.

(§88) THE ASPECTS OF *JIHĀD* ARE NOT SUCCESSIVE PHASES OF *JIHĀD*

It is clear that today *jihād* is an individual duty of every Muslim. Nevertheless we find that there are those who argue that they need to educate their own souls, and that *jihād* knows successive phases; and that they are still in the phase of *jihād* against their own soul. They offer as proof the doctrine of Imām Ibn al-Qayyim, who distinguished three aspects in *jihād*:

1. *Jihād* against one's own soul
2. *Jihād* against the Devil
3. *Jihād* against the infidels and the hypocrites

(§89) This argument shows either complete ignorance or excessive cowardice, because Ibn Al-Qayyim (only) distinguished *aspects* in *jihād*; he did not divide it into successive phases. Otherwise we would have to suspend the waging of *jihād* against the Devil until we finished the phase of *jihād* against our own soul. The reality is that the three (aspects) are aspects (only) that follow a straight parallel course. We, in our turn, do not deny that the strongest of us in regard to faith, and the most zealous of us in regard to waging *jihād* against his own soul is the one (of us) who is the most steadfast.

Whoever studies the Biography (of Muḥammad) will find that whenever (a state of) *jihād* was proclaimed, everybody used to rush off for God's cause, even perpetrators of great sins and those who had (only) recently adopted Islam.

It is reported that (once) a man embraced Islam during the fighting and fell in the battle, thus dying a martyr, and the Apostle—God's Peace be upon Him—said: "A small work, a great reward."

(§90) (There is also) the story about Abū Miḥjan al-Thaqafī (who was guilty of a great sin since he was) addicted to wine, while his bravery in the war against Persia was famous.

Ibn al-Qayyim also made mention that the Tradition "'We returned from the Small *Jihād* to Great *Jihād*'—and then someone said: 'What is the Great *Jihād*, O Apostle of God?'—and then (Muhammad) said: 'The *jihād* against the soul,'" is a fabricated Tradition, see (the book by Ibn Al-Qayyim entitled *Kitāb*) *Al-Manār*.

The only reason for inventing this Tradition is to reduce the value of fighting with the Sword, so as to distract the Muslims from fighting the infidels and the hypocrites.

(§91) FEAR OF FAILURE

It is said that we fear to established the State (because) after one or two days a reaction will occur that will put to an end everything we have accomplished.

The refutation of this (view) is that the establishment of an Islamic State is the execution of a divine Command. We are not responsible for its results. Someone who is so stupid as to hold this view—which has no use except to hinder Muslims from the execution of their religious duty by establishing the Rule of God—forgets that when the Rule of the Infidel has fallen everything will be in the hands of the Muslims, whereupon (*bi-mā*) the downfall of the Islamic State will become inconceivable. Furthermore, the Laws of Islam are not too weak to be able to subject everyone who spreads corruption in the land and rebels against the Command of God. Moreover, the Laws of God are all justice and will be welcomed by everyone, even by people who do not know Islam.

In order to clarify the position of the hypocrites in their enmity towards the Muslims and to put at peace the hearts of those who fear (this) failure (we quote) the Word of the Lord in Surah 59, (verses 11 and 12): "Hast thou not seen those who have played the hypocrite saying to their brethren the People of the Book who have disbelieved: 'Surely, if ye are expelled, we shall go out with you, we shall never obey anyone in regard to you, and if ye are attacked in war, we shall help you?' God testifieth that they are lying. If they are expelled, they will assuredly not go out with them, and if they are attacked in war, they will help them, and if they do not help them, they will certainly turn their backs in flight and then they will not be helped (and gain a victory)."

This is God's promise. When the hypocrites see that the power is in the ranks of Islam they will come back in submission, so we will not be deceived by these voices that will quickly fade away and be extinguished. . . . The position of the hypocrites will be equal to that of the enemies of Islam. God—Exalted He is—says: "(O ye who have believed), if ye help God He will help you (and give you victories) and He will set firm your feet" (Qur'ān 47.7).

(§92) THE COMMAND

There are some who excuse themselves (from participating in *jihād*) because of the lack of a commander who will lead the course of *jihād*. There are also people who make (the execution of) the divine command to *jihād* dependent upon the presence of a commander or a Caliph. . . .

The people who hold these opinions are the same people who have made (proper) leadership impossible and who have stopped the course of *jihād*. Yet the Apostle—God's Peace be upon Him—urges the Muslims, according to the texts of His Traditions, to entrust the (military) leadership to one of them.

Abū Dāwud transmits in the chapter on *jihād* (in his Collection of Traditions) that the Apostle—God's Peace be upon Him—says: "When three (of you) go out on a journey, then make one of them the commander (*amīr*)." From (the text of) this (Tradition) one can conclude that the leadership over the Muslims is (always) in their own hands if only they make this manifest. (The Apostle)—God's Peace be upon Him—says: "Whosoever is put at the head of a group in which there is someone who is more agreeable to God than him himself, is disloyal to God and His Apostle and the Muslim Community." This Tradition is transmitted by Al-Ḥākim. Its reliability is pointed out by Al-Suyūṭī.

(§93) (This means that the command) must go to the best Muslim. (The Apostle)—God's Peace be upon Him—says to Abū Dharr: "You are weak. This is (to our) security!" (The command) must be in the hands of the strongest, which is a relative matter. Our conclusion is that the leader of the Muslims. . . .

Whoever alleges that the (proper) leadership has been lost has no case, because the Muslims can (always) produce leaders from amongst themselves. If there is something lacking in the leadership, well, there is nothing that cannot be acquired. It is (simply) impossible that the leadership disappears (from amongst us).

(§94) Sometimes we may find a *fiqh* scholar who does not know anything about modern circumstances and (military) command and organization; and sometimes we find the opposite, but all this does not discharge us of the duty from organizing proper leadership, by getting the most suitable from amongst us into the position of leadership, through mutual consultation (*shūrā*). The qualities which such a leader may lack can be supplemented.

So now there can be no valid excuse for any Muslim for neglecting the duty of *jihād* which has been thrown upon his shoulder. We must seriously begin to organize *jihād* activities to return Islam to this nation and to establish an Islamic State, and to exterminate the idols who are only human and who have not (yet) found in front of them anyone who has subdued them with the Command of God—Praised and Exalted He is.

ABDULLAH AL-AZZAM
1941–1989

Born in Palestine, he was both a scholar and a *mujahid* (the Emir of Jihad), important to the development of contemporary Islamic radicalism with its notion of a pan-Islamic, global jihad. Al-Azzam studied theology at Damascus University and received his doctorate in jurisprudence from al-Azhar University. After teaching Islamic law briefly at the University of Jordan, he taught at King Abdul Aziz University in Jeddah, Saudi Arabia, where he met Osama Bin Laden. He subsequently went to Peshawar, Pakistan, to join the jihad against the Soviet occupation of Afghanistan. He was killed in an unsolved assassination in 1989. His writings and sermons have lived on as an inspiration to Muslim extremist movements.

Join the Caravan

PART THREE: CLARIFICATIONS
ABOUT THE ISSUE OF JIHAD TODAY

Praise be to Allah, Lord of the Worlds. Blessings and peace be upon the noblest of Messengers, Muhammad, and upon all his family and companions.

1. We have spoken at length about the status of jihad today in Afghanistan, Palestine, and other usurped Muslim lands of the like. We have confirmed what has been agreed upon by the earlier (salaf) and latter (khalaf) generations of hadith scholars, exegetes, jurists, and scholars of religious principles (usul), namely that: "When a span of Muslim land is occupied, jihad becomes individually obligatory (fard 'ayn) on the inhabitants of that piece of land. The woman may go out without her husband's permission with a mahram, the one in debt without the permission of the one to whom he owes, the child without his father's permission. If the inhabitants of that area are not sufficient in number, fall short, or are lazy, the individually obligatory nature of jihad extends to those around them, and so on and so on until it covers the entire Earth, being individually obligatory (fard 'ayn) just like salah, fasting, and the like so that nobody may abandon it."

2. The obligation of jihad today remains fard 'ayn until the liberation of the last piece of land which was in the hands of Muslims but has been occupied by the Disbelievers.

From http://www.religioscope.com/info/doc/jihad/azzam_caravan_5_part3.htm.

3. Some scholars consider jihad today in Afghanistan and Palestine to be fard kifayah. We agree with them in that jihad in Afghanistan for the Arabs was initially fard kifayah. But the jihad is in need of men, and the inhabitants of Afghanistan have not met the requirement which is to expel the Disbelievers from Afghanistan. In this case, the communal obligation (fard kifayah) is overturned. It becomes individually obligatory (fard 'ayn) in Afghanistan, and remains so until enough Mujahideen have gathered to expel the communists in which case it again becomes fard kifayah.

4. There is no permission needed from anybody in the case of an individual obligation (fard 'ayn), according to the principle, "there is no permission necessary for an individual obligation (fard 'ayn)."

5. A person who discourages people from jihad is like the one who discourages people from fasting. Whoever advises an able Muslim not to go for jihad is just like the one who advises him to eat in Ramadan while he is healthy and in residence.

6. It is best to shun the company of those who hold back from jihad and not to enter into arguments with them, for this would lead to idle disputation and hardening of the heart. Shaykh al-Islam Ibn Taymiyyah says, "And avoidance comprises: avoiding evil and evil people, and similarly shunning those who call for innovation in religion, and sinful people and those who associate with such people or assist them in those endeavours. Similar is the case of the person who abandons jihad and from whom there is no benefit in associating with, for in this case we are liable to punishment for not having helped him by co-operating in matters of righteousness and piety.

"The adulterers, homosexuals, those who abandon jihad, the innovators and the alcoholics, as well as those who associate with them are a source of harm to the religion of Islam. They will not cooperate in matters of righteousness and piety. So whoever does not shun their company is, in fact, abandoning what he has been commanded to do and is committing a despicable deed."

IMPORTANT NOTES REGARDING
APPLICATION OF THE ORDINANCE

1. When we call people for jihad and explain to them its ordinance, it does not mean that we are in a position to take care of them, advise them, and look after their families. The concern of the scholars is to clarify the Islamic legal ruling. It is neither to bring people to jihad nor to borrow money from people to take care of the families of Mujahideen. When Ibn Taymiyyah or Al-'Izz Ibn 'Abd As- Salam explained the ruling concerning fighting against the Tartars, they did not become obliged to equip the army.

2. Carrying out religious obligations is necessary according to one's capability. Pilgrimage, for example, is compulsory on those who are able to perform it. "And it is an obligation on mankind towards Allah to perform the Pilgrimage of the House for whoever is able to do so."

Similarly, jihad must be performed according to one's ability, as mentioned in the Qur'an,

> There is no blame on the weak, nor on the ill, nor on those who cannot find anything to spend, when they have shown goodwill toward Allah and His Messenger. There is no censure upon the righteous. Allah is Oft-Forgiving, Most Merciful. Nor (is there any blame) on those who, when they came to you to be mounted, you said to them, "I cannot find anything on which to mount you." They turned away, their eyes flowing with tears, out of grief that they did not have anything to spend (in the path of Allah).

Ibn al-'Arabi said,

> This second verse is the strongest of evidence for the acceptability of the excuse of one who is in poverty or has a valid need which holds him back from jihad, provided goodwill has been identified in his conduct while claiming the inability.

Qurtubi said in his tafsir,

> The verse is a basis for the dismissal of obligation from the incapable, so that whoever is incapable of performing a deed is exempted from it, sometimes by doing something else in its place, and sometimes by merely having the resolution and will to do it. There is no difference in this respect between a person who is incapable physically, and one who is financially unable. This verse is explained by the words of Allah, (translated) "Allah does not impose upon any soul a burden beyond its capability."

In Sahih Muslim, it is reported that the Prophet (may Allah bless him and grant him peace) said, "In Madinah are people who are with you whenever you travel any distance or traverse a valley. They were held back by (valid) excuses." According to another narration, "they were held back by illness."

Qurtubi said, "The majority of scholars are of the view that anybody who cannot find anything to spend in jihad is not obliged to spend."

Tabari inferred, "There is no blame (i.e. sin) on those with chronic diseases, who are incapable of travelling and fighting, nor on the ill, nor on those who do not find anything to spend to take them to jihad."

Ibn Taymiyyah said, "The commands, retributions, expiations and so on of the Islamic law are intended to be implemented according to capability."

ADDING TO THE TEXTS OF SCHOLARS
ALREADY MENTIONED

1. Those with valid excuses are absolved of the sin of sitting back from jihad. Those validly excused include:

a) somebody with a wife and children who do not have income from any other source nor have anybody besides him who could support and maintain them. But if he is able to allocate provision for them for the duration of his absence, then he is sinful if he sits back. Every Muslim should reduce his spending and be frugal with his earnings until he is able to go out for jihad.

b) somebody who was unable, after much effort, to obtain a visa to come to Pakistan.

c) somebody whose government denied him a passport or prevented him from leaving from the airport.

d) somebody who has parents who do not have anybody besides him to support and maintain them.

THE QUESTION OF INTERROGATION BY POLICE AUTHORITIES UPON RETURN OF THE MUJAHID TO HIS HOMELAND FROM JIHAD

This point is never an excuse because it is a matter of suspicion and uncertainty. Jihad is a certainty and the fear of interrogation by the Intelligence is a matter of doubt. In fact, even if he is certain that the Intelligence will interrogate him, this is not an excuse, which absolves him from the sin of sitting back from jihad. The excuse of coercion which is admissible in the shari'ah and which would absolve him of the sin of abandoning an obligation is "direct coercion which threatens loss of life or limb," that is, torture involving death or severance of a limb.

Similarly, fear of police authorities in the country whose passport he holds, even if he is sure that when he returns they will detain him and kill him or sever his limb, is not an acceptable excuse before Allah because in this case he is obliged to forsake his country and live in the land of jihad.

> Those whose souls the angels take while they are wronging themselves—(the angels) say to them, "What was the matter with you?" They reply, "We were weak and oppressed in the land." (The angels) say, "Was not Allah's earth spacious enough that you could emigrate therein?" Then, the abode of those people shall be Hell—how evil a destination it is! Except for such weak and oppressed men, women and children who were neither able to come up with a stratagem (to emigrate) nor shown any way (to do so)—those Allah will surely pardon, and Allah is Most Pardoning, Oft-Forgiving.

THE ISSUE OF ARAB WOMEN PERFORMING JIHAD IN AFGHANISTAN

Arab women may not come without a non-marriageable male guardian (mahram). Their duties are confined to education, nursing, and assisting refugees. As for fighting, Arab women may not fight because until now, Afghan women are not participating in the fighting.

THE ISSUE OF SOMEBODY WHO HAS A HANDICAP (SUCH AS THE CRIPPLE) WHICH PREVENTS HIM FROM FIGHTING BUT DOES NOT PREVENT HIM FROM WORKING IN OTHER SPHERES

The individual obligation is not dismissed from a cripple or from an invalid whose illness is not serious because they are capable of working in the spheres of health and education which is a broad field. The Mujahideen are now more in need of propagators than they are in need of food, weapons, and medicine.

Ibn al-Humam said, "As for the one who is not able to go out for fighting, he must go out to swell the ranks for this will help terrorise the enemy." So if going out to swell the ranks is obligatory, then how about going out to teach the Mujahideen the regulations of their religion? This is more obligatory and more strongly compulsory.

A WORD TO THOSE WITH FAMILIES

In conclusion: We tell those with families that they may not leave their families and go out for jihad without ensuring provision for them and without ensuring that somebody will take care of them. Thus, whoever wishes to go out now with his family should realise that we are not able to take care of him. He should therefore check with the Islamic centres close to him or with well-wishers until he is able to guarantee provision for his family. The poor people with families must therefore determinedly look for somebody who could financially support their families for the duration of their absence. They should urgently hasten to take care of their financial affairs, then go out for jihad.

Born in Riyadh, Saudi Arabia, Bin Laden received a degree in public administration in 1981 from King Abdul-Aziz University. His religious worldview was influenced by Saudi Arabia's Wahhabi-brand of Islam as well as the militant ideas of Sayyid Qutb and Abdullah al-Azzam. From 1979 to 1982, he vigorously supported the Afghan jihad against Soviet occupation of Afghanistan, later creating al-Qaeda, "the base," to organize and track the channeling of fighters and funds for the Afghan resistance. Bin Laden's opposition to the American-led coalition in the Gulf War of 1991 placed him on a collision course with the Saudi government and the West. Assuming a leadership role in international terrorism, he issued a Declaration of Jihad in 1996 to drive the United States out of Arabia and in 2000 formed the World Islamic Front for the Jihad Against Jews and Crusaders. Bin Laden and al-Qaeda have been behind the September 11 attacks and many other acts of global terrorism.

Text of Fatwa Urging Jihad Against Americans (1998)

Praise be to God, who revealed the Book, controls the clouds, defeats factionalism, and says in His Book "But when the forbidden months are past, then fight and slay the pagans wherever ye find them, seize them, beleaguer them, and lie in wait for them in every stratagem (of war)"; and peace be upon our Prophet, Muhammad Bin-'Abdallah, who said "I have been sent with the sword between my hands to ensure that no one but God is worshipped, God who put my livelihood under the shadow of my spear and who inflicts humiliation and scorn on those who disobey my orders." The Arabian Peninsula has never—since God made it flat, created its desert, and encircled it with seas—been stormed by any forces like the crusader armies now spreading in it like locusts, consuming its riches and destroying its plantations. All this is happening at a time when nations are attacking Muslims like people fighting over a plate of food. In the light of the grave

Statement signed by Sheikh Usamah Bin-Muhammad Bin-Ladin; Ayman al-Zawahiri, leader of the Jihad Group in Egypt; Abu-Yasir Rifa'i Ahmad Taha, a leader of the Islamic Group; Sheikh Mir Hamzah, secretary of the Jamiat-ul-Ulema-e-Pakistan; and Fazlul Rahman, leader of the Jihad Movement in Bangladesh. Published in Al-Quds al-'Arabi on February 23, 1998. Reprinted with thanks to S. Suwellam, Arab Electronic Journal.

situation and the lack of support, we and you are obliged to discuss current events, and we should all agree on how to settle the matter.

No one argues today about three facts that are known to everyone; we will list them, in order to remind everyone:

First, for over seven years the United States has been occupying the lands of Islam in the holiest of places, the Arabian Peninsula, plundering its riches, dictating to its rulers, humiliating its people, terrorizing its neighbors, and turning its bases in the Peninsula into a spearhead through which to fight the neighboring Muslim peoples.

If some people have formerly debated the fact of the occupation, all the people of the Peninsula have now acknowledged it.

The best proof of this is the Americans' continuing aggression against the Iraqi people using the Peninsula as a staging post even though all its rulers are against their territories being used to that end, still they are helpless. Second, despite the great devastation inflicted on the Iraqi people by the crusader-Zionist alliance, and despite the huge number of those killed, in excess of 1 million . . . .despite all this, the Americans are once again trying to repeat the horrific massacres, as though they are not content with the protracted blockade imposed after the ferocious war or the fragmentation and devastation.

So now they come to annihilate what is left of this people and to humiliate their Muslim neighbors.

Third, if the Americans' aims behind these wars are religious and economic, the aim is also to serve the Jews' petty state and divert attention from its occupation of Jerusalem and murder of Muslims there.

The best proof of this is their eagerness to destroy Iraq, the strongest neighboring Arab state, and their endeavor to fragment all the states of the region such as Iraq, Saudi Arabia, Egypt, and Sudan into paper statelets and through their disunion and weakness to guarantee Israel's survival and the continuation of the brutal crusade occupation of the Peninsula.

All these crimes and sins committed by the Americans are a clear declaration of war on God, his Messenger, and Muslims. And ulema have throughout Islamic history unanimously agreed that the jihad is an individual duty if the enemy destroys the Muslim countries. This was revealed by Imam Bin-Qadamah in "Al-Mughni," Imam al-Kisa'i in "Al-Bada'i," al-Qurtubi in his interpretation, and the shaykh of al-Islam in his books, where he said, "As for the militant struggle, it is aimed at defending sanctity and religion, and it is a duty as agreed. Nothing is more sacred than belief except repulsing an enemy who is attacking religion and life."

On that basis, and in compliance with God's order, we issue the following fatwa to all Muslims.

The ruling to kill the Americans and their allies—civilians and military —is an individual duty for every Muslim who can do it in any country in which it is possible to do it, in order to liberate the al-Aqsa Mosque and the holy mosque from their grip, and in order for their armies to move out of all the lands of Islam, defeated and unable to threaten any Muslim. This is in accordance with the words of Almighty God, "and fight the pagans all together as they fight you all together," and "fight them until there is no more tumult or oppression, and there prevail justice and faith in God."

This is in addition to the words of Almighty God, "And why should ye not fight in the cause of God and of those who, being weak, are ill-treated and oppressed—women and children, whose cry is 'Our Lord, rescue us from this town, whose people are oppressors; and raise for us from thee one who will help!'"

We—with God's help—can on every Muslim who believes in God and wishes to be rewarded to comply with God's order to kill the Americans and plunder their money wherever and whenever they find it. We also call on Muslim ulema, leaders, youths, and soldiers to launch the raid on Satan's U.S. troops and the devil's supporters allying with them, and to displace those who are behind them so that they may learn a lesson.

Almighty God said, "O ye who believe, give your response to God and His Apostle, when He calleth you to that which will give you life. And know that God cometh between a man and his heart, and that it is He to whom ye shall all be gathered."

Almighty God also says, "O ye who believe, what is the matter with you, that when ye are asked to go forth in the cause of God, ye cling so heavily to the earth! Do ye prefer the life of this world to the hereafter? But little is the comfort of this life, as compared with the hereafter. Unless ye go forth, He will punish you with a grievous penalty, and put others in your place; but Him ye would not harm in the least. For God hath power over all things."

Almighty God also says, "So lose no heart, nor fall into despair. For ye must gain mastery if ye are true in faith."

HAMAS is the Arabic acronym for "the Islamic Resistance Movement" (*Harakat al-Muqawamah al-Islamiyya*), an offshoot of the Muslim Brotherhood (MB) movement that originated in Egypt in 1928. The MB was not politically active in Palestine and Jordan until rather late; it focused on building an impressive social, religious, educational, and cultural infrastructure in both the Gaza Strip and the West Bank.

HAMAS was legally registered in Israel in 1978 by Shaikh Ahmed Yassin, the movement's spiritual leader, as an Islamic Association by the name *Al-Majma' al-Islami*, whose religious preaching and social work widened its base of supporters and sympathizers. When the MB opted for large-scale militancy by creating HAMAS, with the aid and encouragement of Israeli authorities, it appeared as a counterweight to the Palestinian Liberation Organization (PLO). HAMAS began as an underground movement, but with the first uprising (*intifada*) in 1987, it became public and emphasized its Palestinian character and patriotism. It professed to be not just a parallel force but an alternative to the almost absolute control of the PLO and its factions over the Palestinians in the Territories. In August 1988, HAMAS published the *Islamic Covenant* (its ideological credo), which presented its policy against both Israel and the national movement of the PLO.

The Covenant of the Islamic Resistance Movement HAMAS

"In the Name of the Most Merciful Allah Israel will exist and will continue to exist until Islam will obliterate it, just as it obliterated others before it."
the Martyr, Imam Hassan al-Banna,
of blessed memory

"The Islamic world is on fire. Each of us should pour some water, no matter how little, to extinguish whatever one can without waiting for the others."
Sheikh Amjad al-Zahawi,
of blessed memory

Note: The text has been shortened somewhat by omission of repetitive ideas and some citations. The full text may be found at http://www.yale.edu/lawweb/avalon/mideast/hamas.htm.

INTRODUCTION

Praise be unto Allah, to whom we resort for help, and whose forgiveness, guidance and support we seek; Allah bless the Prophet and grant him salvation, his companions and supporters, and to those who carried out his message and adopted his laws—everlasting prayers and salvation as long as the earth and heaven will last. Hereafter:

O People:

Out of the midst of troubles and the sea of suffering, out of the palpitations of faithful hearts and cleansed arms; out of the sense of duty, and in response to Allah's command, the call has gone out rallying people together and making them follow the ways of Allah, leading them to have determined will in order to fulfill their role in life, to overcome all obstacles, and surmount the difficulties on the way. Constant preparation has continued and so has the readiness to sacrifice life and all that is precious for the sake of Allah.

Thus it was that the nucleus (of the movement) was formed and started to pave its way through the tempestuous sea of hopes and expectations, of wishes and yearnings, of troubles and obstacles, of pain and challenges, both inside and outside. When the idea was ripe, the seed grew and the plant struck root in the soil of reality, away from passing emotions, and hateful haste. The Islamic Resistance Movement emerged to carry out its role through striving for the sake of its Creator, its arms intertwined with those of all the fighters for the liberation of Palestine. The spirits of its fighters meet with the spirits of all the fighters who have sacrificed their lives on the soil of Palestine, ever since it was conquered by the companions of the Prophet, Allah bless him and grant him salvation, and until this day.

This Covenant of the Islamic Resistance Movement (HAMAS) clarifies its picture, reveals its identity, outlines its stand, explains its aims, speaks about its hopes, and calls for its support, adoption and joining its ranks. Our struggle against the Jews is very great and very serious. It needs all sincere efforts. It is a step that inevitably should be followed by other steps. The Movement is but one squadron that should be supported by more and more squadrons from this vast Arab and Islamic world, until the enemy is vanquished and Allah's victory is realized. . . .

Hamas (means) *strength and bravery* (according to) Al-Mu'ajam al-Wasit: c1.

DEFINITION OF THE MOVEMENT

Article One

The Islamic Resistance Movement: The Movement's programme is Islam. From it, it draws its ideas, ways of thinking and understanding of the universe, life and man. It resorts to it for judgement in all its conduct, and it is inspired by it for guidance of its steps.

Article Two

The Islamic Resistance Movement is one of the wings of Moslem Brotherhood in Palestine. Moslem Brotherhood Movement is a universal organization which constitutes the largest Islamic movement in modern times. It is characterised by its deep understanding, accurate comprehension and its complete embrace of all Islamic concepts of all aspects of life, culture, creed, politics, economics, education, society, justice and judgement, the spreading of Islam, education, art, information, science of the occult and conversion to Islam.

Article Three

The basic structure of the Islamic Resistance Movement consists of Moslems who have given their allegiance to Allah whom they truly worship—"I have created the jinn and humans only for the purpose of worshipping"—who know their duty towards themselves, their families and country. In all that, they fear Allah and raise the banner of Jihad in the face of the oppressors, so that they would rid the land and the people of their uncleanliness, vileness and evils. . . .

Article Four

The Islamic Resistance Movement welcomes every Moslem who embraces its faith, ideology, follows its programme, keeps its secrets, and wants to belong to its ranks and carry out the duty. Allah will certainly reward such one.

Article Five

By adopting Islam as its way of life, the Movement goes back to the time of the birth of the Islamic message, of the righteous ancestor, for Allah is its target, the Prophet is its example and the Koran is its constitution (Abraham, verses 24–25).

Article Six

The Islamic Resistance Movement is a distinguished Palestinian movement, whose allegiance is to Allah, and whose way of life is Islam. It strives to raise the banner of Allah over every inch of Palestine, for under the wing of Islam followers of all religions can coexist in security and safety where their lives, possessions and rights are concerned. In the absence of Islam, strife will be rife, oppression spreads, evil prevails and schisms and wars will break out. . . .

Article Seven

As a result of the fact that those Moslems who adhere to the ways of the Islamic Resistance Movement spread all over the world, rally support for it and its stands, strive towards enhancing its struggle, the Movement is a universal one. It is well-equipped for that because of the clarity of its ideology, the nobility of its aim and the loftiness of its objectives (The Table, verse 48).

The Islamic Resistance Movement is one of the links in the chain of the struggle against the Zionist invaders. It goes back to 1939, to the emergence of the martyr Izz al-Din al Kissam and his brethren the fighters, members of Moslem Brotherhood. It goes on to reach out and become one with another chain that includes the struggle of the Palestinians and Moslem Brotherhood in the 1948 war and the Jihad operations of the Moslem Brotherhood in 1968 and after. . . .

Article Eight

Allah is its target, the Prophet is its model, the Koran its constitution: Jihad is its path and death for the sake of Allah is the loftiest of its wishes.

Article Nine

The Islamic Resistance Movement found itself at a time when Islam has disappeared from life. Thus rules shook, concepts were upset, values changed and evil people took control, oppression and darkness prevailed, cowards became like tigers: homelands were usurped, people were scattered and were caused to wander all over the world, the state of justice disappeared and the state of falsehood replaced it. Nothing remained in its right place. Thus, when Islam is absent from the arena, everything changes. From this state of affairs the incentives are drawn.

As for the objectives: They are the fighting against the false, defeating it and vanquishing it so that justice could prevail, homelands be retrieved and from its mosques would the voice of the mu'azen emerge declaring the establishment of the state of Islam, so that people and things would return each to their right places and Allah is our helper. . . .

Article Ten

As the Islamic Resistance Movement paves its way, it will back the oppressed and support the wronged with all its might. It will spare no effort to bring about justice and defeat injustice, in word and deed, in this place and everywhere it can reach and have influence therein.

Article Eleven

The Islamic Resistance Movement believes that the land of Palestine is an Islamic Waqf consecrated for future Moslem generations until Judgement Day. It, or any part of it, should not be squandered: it, or any part of it, should not be given up. Neither a single Arab country nor all Arab countries, neither any king or president, nor all the kings and presidents, neither any organization nor all of them, be they Palestinian or Arab, possess the right to do that. Palestine is an Islamic Waqf land consecrated for Moslem generations until Judgement Day. This being so, who could claim to have the right to represent Moslem generations till Judgement Day? . . .

It happened like this: When the leaders of the Islamic armies conquered Syria and Iraq, they sent to the Caliph of the Moslems, Umar bin-el-Khatab, asking for his advice concerning the conquered land—whether they should divide it among the soldiers, or leave it for its owners, or what? After consultations and discussions between the Caliph of the Moslems, Omar bin-el-Khatab and companions of the Prophet, Allah bless him and grant him salvation, it was decided that the land should be left with its owners who could benefit by its fruit. As for the real ownership of the land and the land itself, it should be consecrated for Moslem generations till Judgement Day. Those who are on the land are there only to benefit from its fruit. This Waqf remains as long as earth and heaven remain. Any procedure in contradiction to Islamic Sharia, where Palestine is concerned, is null and void.

Verily, this is a certain truth. Wherefore praise the name of thy Lord, the great Allah (The Inevitable, verse 95).

Article Twelve

Nationalism, from the point of view of the Islamic Resistance Movement, is part of the religious creed. Nothing in nationalism is more significant or deeper than in the case when an enemy should tread Moslem land. Resisting and quelling the enemy become the individual duty of every Moslem, male or female. A woman can go out to fight the enemy without her husband's permission, and so does the slave without his master's permission. . . .

Article Thirteen

Initiatives, and so-called peaceful solutions and international conferences, are in contradiction to the principles of the Islamic Resistance Movement. Abusing any part of Palestine is abuse directed against part of religion. Nationalism of the Islamic Resistance Movement is part of its religion. . . .

There is no solution for the Palestinian question except through Jihad. Initiatives, proposals and international conferences are all a waste of time and vain endeavors. The Palestinian people know better than to consent to having their future, rights and fate toyed with. . . .

Article Fourteen

The question of the liberation of Palestine is bound to three circles: the Palestinian circle, the Arab circle and the Islamic circle. Each of these circles has its role in the struggle against Zionism. Each has its duties, and it is a horrible mistake and a sign of deep ignorance to overlook any of these circles. . . .

Since this is the case, liberation of Palestine is then an individual duty for every Moslem wherever he may be. On this basis, the problem should be viewed. This should be realised by every Moslem. . . .

Article Fifteen

The day that enemies usurp part of Moslem land, Jihad becomes the individual duty of every Moslem. In face of the Jews' usurpation of Palestine, it is compulsory that the banner of Jihad be raised. To do this requires the diffusion of Islamic consciousness among the masses, both on the regional, Arab and Islamic levels. It is necessary to instill the spirit of Jihad in the heart of the nation so that they would confront the enemies and join the ranks of the fighters. . . .

It is important that basic changes be made in the school curriculum, to cleanse it of the traces of ideological invasion that affected it as a result of the orientalists and missionaries who infiltrated the region following the defeat of the Crusaders at the hands of Salah el-Din (Saladin). The Crusaders realised that it was impossible to defeat the Moslems without first having ideological invasion pave the way by upsetting their thoughts, disfiguring their heritage and violating their ideals. Only then could they invade with soldiers. This, in its turn, paved the way for the imperialistic invasion that made Allenby declare on entering Jerusalem: "Only now have the Crusades ended." General Gorout stood at Salah el-Din's grave and said: "We have returned, O Salah el-Din." Imperialism has helped towards the strengthening of ideological invasion, deepening, and still does, its roots. All this has paved the way towards the loss of Palestine. . . .

Article Sixteen

It is necessary to follow Islamic orientation in educating the Islamic generations in our region by teaching the religious duties, comprehensive study of the Koran, the study of the Prophet's Sunna (his sayings and doings), and learning about Islamic history and heritage from their authentic sources. . . .

Article Seventeen

The Moslem woman has a role no less important than that of the Moslem man in the battle of liberation. She is the maker of men. Her role in guiding and educating the new generations is great. The enemies have realised the importance of her role. They consider that if they are able to direct and bring her up the way they wish, far from Islam, they would have won the battle. That is why you find them giving these attempts constant attention through information campaigns, films, and the school curriculum, using for that purpose their lackeys who are infiltrated through Zionist organizations under various names and shapes, such as Freemasons, Rotary Clubs, espionage groups and others, which are all nothing more than cells of subversion and saboteurs. . . .

Article Eighteen

Woman in the home of the fighting family, whether she is a mother or a sister, plays the most important role in looking after the family, rearing the children and embuing them with moral values and thoughts derived from Islam. She has to teach them to perform the religious duties in preparation for the role of fighting awaiting them. That is why it is necessary to pay great attention to schools and the curriculum followed in educating Moslem girls, so that they would grow up to be good mothers, aware of their role in the battle of liberation. . . .

Article Nineteen

Art has regulations and measures by which it can be determined whether it is Islamic or pre-Islamic (Jahili) art. The issues of Islamic liberation are in need of Islamic art that would take the spirit high, without raising one side of human nature above the other, but rather raise all of them harmoniously and in equilibrium. . . .

Article Twenty

Moslem society is a mutually responsible society. The Prophet, prayers and greetings be unto him, said: "Blessed are the generous, whether they were in town or on a journey, who have collected all that they had and shared it equally among themselves."

The Islamic spirit is what should prevail in every Moslem society. The society that confronts a vicious enemy which acts in a way similar to Nazism, making no differentiation between man and woman, between children and old people—such a society is entitled to this Islamic spirit. Our enemy relies on the methods of collective punishment. He has deprived people of their homeland and properties, pursued them in their places of exile and gathering, breaking bones, shooting at women, children and old people, with or without a reason. The enemy has opened detention camps where thousands and thousands of people are thrown and kept under sub-human conditions. Added to this are the demolition of houses, rendering children orphans, meting cruel sentences against thousands of young people, and causing them to spend the best years of their lives in the dungeons of prisons. . . .

To counter these deeds, it is necessary that social mutual responsibility should prevail among the people. The enemy should be faced by the people as a single body which if one member of it should complain, the rest of the body would respond by feeling the same pains.

Article Twenty-One

Mutual social responsibility means extending assistance, financial or moral, to all those who are in need and joining in the execution of some of the work. Members of the Islamic Resistance Movement should consider the interests of the masses as their own personal interests. They must spare no effort in achieving and preserving them. . . .

Article Twenty-Two

For a long time, the enemies have been planning, skillfully and with precision, for the achievement of what they have attained. They took into consideration the causes affecting the current of events. . . .

Article Twenty-Three

The Islamic Resistance Movement views other Islamic movements with respect and appreciation. . . .

Article Twenty-Four

The Islamic Resistance Movement does not allow slandering or speaking ill of individuals or groups, for the believer does not indulge in such malpractices. . . .

NATIONALIST MOVEMENTS IN THE PALESTINIAN ARENA

Article Twenty-Five

The Islamic Resistance Movement respects the Nationalist Movements in the Palestinian arena and appreciates their circumstances and the conditions surrounding and affecting them. . . .

Article Twenty-Six

In viewing the Palestinian nationalist movements that give allegiance neither to the East nor the West, in this positive way, the Islamic Resistance Movement does not refrain from discussing new situations on the regional or international levels where the Palestinian question is concerned. It does that in such an objective manner revealing the extent of how much it is in harmony or contradiction with the national interests in the light of the Islamic point of view.

Article Twenty-Seven

The Palestinian Liberation Organization is the closest to the heart of the Islamic Resistance Movement. It contains the father and the brother, the next of kin and the friend. The Moslem does not estrange himself from his father, brother, next of kin or friend. Our homeland is one, our situation is one, our fate is one and the enemy is a joint enemy to all of us.

Because of the situations surrounding the formation of the Organization, of the ideological confusion prevailing in the Arab world as a result of the ideological invasion under whose influence the Arab world has fallen since the defeat of the Crusaders and which was, and still is, intensified through orientalists, missionaries and imperialists, the Organization adopted the idea of the secular state. And that its how we view it.

Secularism completely contradicts religious ideology. Attitudes, conduct and decisions stem from ideologies.

That is why, with all our appreciation for **the Palestinian Liberation Organization**—and what it can develop into—and without belittling its role in the Arab-Israeli conflict, we are unable to exchange the present or future Islamic Palestine with the secular idea. The Islamic nature of Palestine is part of our religion and whoever takes his religion lightly is a loser. . . .

Article Twenty-Eight

The Zionist invasion is a vicious invasion. It does not refrain from resorting to all methods, using all evil and contemptible ways to achieve its end. It relies greatly in its infiltration and espionage operations on the secret organizations it gave rise to, such as the Freemasons, the Rotary and Lions Clubs, and other sabotage groups. All these organizations, whether secret or open, work in the interest of Zionism and according to its instructions. They aim at undermining societies, destroying values, corrupting consciences, deteriorating character and annihilating Islam. It is behind the drug trade and alcoholism in all its kinds so as to facilitate its control and expansion.

Arab countries surrounding Israel are asked to open their borders before the fighters from among the Arab and Islamic nations so that they could consolidate their efforts with those of their Moslem brethren in Palestine.

As for the other Arab and Islamic countries, they are asked to facilitate the movement of the fighters from and to it, and this is the least thing they could do. . . .

Article Thirty

Writers, intellectuals, media people, orators, educators and teachers, and all the various sectors in the Arab and Islamic world—all of them are called upon to perform their role, and to fulfill their duty, because of the ferocity of the Zionist offensive and the Zionist influence in many countries exercised through financial and media control, as well as the consequences that all this leads to in the greater part of the world.

Article Thirty-One

The Islamic Resistance Movement is a humanistic movement. It takes care of human rights and is guided by Islamic tolerance when dealing with the followers of other religions. It does not antagonize anyone of them except if it is antagonized by it or stands in its way to hamper its moves and waste its efforts.

Under the wing of Islam, it is possible for the followers of the three religions—Islam, Christianity and Judaism—to coexist in peace and quiet with each other. Peace and quiet would not be possible except under the wing of Islam. Past and present history are the best witness to that.

Article Thirty-Two

World Zionism, together with imperialistic powers, tries through a studied plan and an intelligent strategy to remove one Arab state after another from the circle of struggle against Zionism, in order to have it finally face the Palestinian people only. Egypt was, to a great extent, removed from the circle of the struggle, through the treacherous Camp David Agreement. They are trying to draw other Arab countries into similar agreements and to bring them outside the circle of struggle.

The Islamic Resistance Movement calls on Arab and Islamic nations to take up the line of serious and persevering action to prevent the success of this horrendous plan, to warn the people of the danger emanating from leaving the circle of struggle against Zionism. Today it is Palestine; tomorrow it will be one country or another. . . .

Article Thirty-Three

The Islamic Resistance Movement, being based on the common coordinated and interdependent conceptions of the laws of the universe, and flowing in the stream of destiny in confronting and fighting the enemies in defence of the Moslems and Islamic civilization and sacred sites, the first among which is the Aqsa Mosque, urges the Arab and Islamic peoples, their governments, popular and official groupings, to fear Allah where their view of the Islamic Resistance Movement and their dealings with it are concerned. . . .

Article Thirty-Four

Palestine is the navel of the globe and the crossroad of the continents. Since the dawn of history, it has been the target of expansionists. . . .

Expansionists have more than once put their eye on Palestine which they attacked with their armies to fulfill their designs on it. Thus it was that the Crusaders came with their armies, bringing with them their creed and carrying their Cross. They were able to defeat the Moslems for a while, but the Moslems were able to retrieve the land only when they stood under the wing of their religious banner, united their word, hallowed the name of Allah and surged out fighting under the leadership of Salah el-Din al-Ayyubi. They fought for almost twenty years and at the end the Crusaders were defeated and Palestine was liberated. . . .

This is the only way to liberate Palestine. There is no doubt about the testimony of history. It is one of the laws of the universe and one of the rules of existence. Nothing can overcome iron except iron. Their false futile creed can only be defeated by the righteous Islamic creed. A creed could not be fought except by a creed, and in the last analysis, victory is for the just, for justice is certainly victorious. . . .

Article Thirty-Five

The Islamic Resistance Movement views seriously the defeat of the Crusaders at the hands of Salah el-Din al-Ayyubi and the rescuing of Palestine from their hands, as well as the defeat of the Tatars at Ein Galot, breaking their power at the hands of Qataz and Al-Dhaher Bivers and saving the Arab world from the Tatar onslaught which aimed at the destruction of every meaning of human civilization. The Movement draws lessons and examples from all this. The present Zionist onslaught has also been preceded by Crusading raids from the West and other Tatar raids from the East. Just as the Moslems faced those raids and planned fighting and defeating them, they should be able to confront the Zionist invasion and defeat it. This is indeed no problem for the Almighty Allah, provided that the intentions are pure, the determination is true and that Moslems have benefited from past experiences, rid themselves of the effects of ideological invasion and followed the customs of their ancestors.

THE ISLAMIC RESISTANCE MOVEMENT
IS COMPOSED OF SOLDIERS
Article Thirty-Six

While paving its way, the Islamic Resistance Movement emphasizes time and again to all the sons of our people, to the Arab and Islamic nations, that it does not seek personal fame, material gain, or social prominence. It does not aim to compete against any one from among our people, or take his place. Nothing of the sort at all. It will not act against any of the sons of Moslems or those who are peaceful towards it from among non-Moslems, be they here or anywhere else. It will only serve as a support for all groupings and organizations operating against the Zionist enemy and its lackeys.

The Islamic Resistance Movement adopts Islam as its way of life. Islam is its creed and religion. Whoever takes Islam as his way of life, be it an organization, a grouping, a country or any other body, the Islamic Resistance Movement considers itself as their soldiers and nothing more.

We ask Allah to show us the right course, to make us an example to others and to judge between us and our people with truth. "O Lord, do thou judge between us and our nation with truth; for thou art the best judge" (Al Araf, Verse 89).

The last of our prayers will be praise to Allah, the Master of the Universe.

SHAIKH MUHAMMAD MAHDI SHAMS AL-DIN
1936–2000

Born in Najaf where his Lebanese father was pursuing religious studies, Muhammad Mahdi followed a course of studies at Najaf and from 1961 to 1969 worked as a representative of Ayatullah Muhsin al-Hakim in the central Euphrates region. He returned to Lebanon in 1969 to aid Imam Musa al-Sadr, leader of the Shiite community, in founding the Supreme Islamic Shiite Committee. As the first deputy to Imam al-Sadr, he became the de facto head of the institution when the Imam disappeared while on a visit to Libya in 1978. In 1983 Shams al-Din began the comprehensive civil resistance against the Israelis in southern Lebanon. A proponent of dialogue and renovation, he established schools, institutes, orphanages, and an Islamic university.

On the Political Utility
of Using Armed Violence

A study of the use of armed violence reveals its inefficacy as a political tool.

Political organizations of various tendencies, secular and Islamic, all over the world are immersed in the use of armed violence against ruling regimes, contending parties and even against civil society. A close look at the results shows beyond all doubt that armed violence is not a succesful expedient for political action, neither as a means for expressing political opinion and obtaining legitimate presence in society nor for gaining political victory in a dispute.

There are several examples of this both in Islamic and non-Islamic movements. If we review the experience of armed violence which the Islamic Movement immersed itself in during the last decades against others and against one another, we see that armed violence does not lead to any true political victory. In all these attempts armed violence failed to achieve any victory for Islam or the Islamic Project, in whole or in part.

Even within the Islamic world in a country in which the Islamic Movement practiced armed violence, this style failed to achieve any notable gain in propaganda or mobilization.

The consequences of this style were not only failure and futility, but even worse, great harm to the Islamic project.

We mention some instances.

From *The Fiqh of Armed Violence In Islam* (Beirut: International Foundation for Study and Publication, 2001). Translated by John J. Donohue.

1. THE ACCUSATION OF TERRORISM

This style revivified and tacked onto Islam and the Islamic Movement the age-old accusation that Islam was spread by the sword and that Muslims are retarded when it comes to establishing relations and creating conviction through dialogue, just at the time when the idea of change through dialogue, mutual consent and democratic style has taken root on a world level.

Islam is free of these two accusations; it prohibits terror and deception even in times of war and it represents the largest and broadest appeal for dialogue known to human history.

It is this style which may enable Muslim opponents of the Islamic project to present world opinion with a preconceived idea of the Islamic system which would be imposed should the Islamic Movement succeed in getting power in this or that Islamic country. This creates a state of psychological enmity and refusal of the Islamic Movement and the Islamic political project. This enmity is openly expressed to Muslims under the present regimes.

2. OVERBURDENING CIVIL SOCIETY

This style overburdens civil society because it is loyal to the Islamic Movement and supports it or at least is not opposed to it, but it has need of the ruling regime which may not enjoy respect and sanctity but does provide security and the needs of daily life and that regime is exposed to upset, convulsion and collapse as a result of the use of armed violence.

So much for violence against regimes. But when violence is used against the institutions of civil society and against contending politicial parties, we believe that the political harm is greater and more burdensome.

It is self-evident that civil society is the umma and its fusion with the organization (*tanzim*) is considered the basis of its power, success and stability. The organization cannot achieve any victory without this fusion with the umma. Were the organization to achieve victory in isolation from the umma, it would be difficult to hold on to; it would be lost or collapse.

If it holds onto the victory by ruling over a state or dominating a region, a city or a quarter, its hold will be possible only by suppression and that traps the Islamic Movement into the style of oppressor (Taghut).

3. ISOLATION OF THE ISLAMIC MOVEMENT
FROM THE GENERAL COURSE OF POLITICS

This style was one of the causes blocking the Islamic Movement from entering political alliances and forming fronts with other political forces in order to confront regimes.

It also widened the gap between the Islamists with their mass base—both politically and from a human point of view—and other forces with their bases. It created an atmosphere of extreme caution among all other political forces. The conviction grew that Islamists do not believe in cooperation with others, do not believe in the legality of a multi-party system and politic, do not recognize the right to opposition and difference, and do not believe in sharing governance with others if they can do it alone, even though it be by force.

This is what isolates the Islamic Movement in many cases from the general flow of politics in its country.

4. ALLIANCE WITH REGIMES

This style pushed the Islamic Movement into relationships and alliances with regimes marked by their own particular policies arising from their regional and international situation and then the Movement takes on the very political characteristics of the regimes it intended to war against.

That is because armed action needs much money and weapons and other services to transport people and weapons. None of these organizations can furnish the necessary money from their own sources, so this or that organization is forced to contact this or that state to receive finance and arms and other services.

The goals of the financing states are different. These states may have their own political agenda against the regime targeted for violent action or against some of the political parties or groups there or they may want to fend off violence or political notoriety from themselves by financing and arming violent actions in other regions, or they may want to show that they are capable of making things move in the region, or may be trying to show that they have international notoriety. Or they may have goals which are less neat or more abominable than those mentioned, like pushing this or that Islamic organization to ally with a secular party against another Islamic organization to wage war and fight against it.

A relationship like this puts the Islamic Movement in contradiction with itself in that it wars against a non-Islamic position or one opposed to the Islamic project in cooperation with a position which is similar or worse than the position it is fighting.

It is not in a position which enables it to have its own way in this relationship; it is imprisoned because it does not possess the force to do anything other than becoming more reliant on the party offering finance and support. Because as soon as this party feels a lack of loyalty, it will cut off support and finance.

5. FACTIONALISM AND FRAGMENTATION

This style with the relationships it requires for finance and armament may open up broad possibilities within the command for independent marginal operations on the part of some leaders in conjunction with the state itself, another state or center of influence, another regional or international force with a view to individual material gain or to achieve some particular influence within the organization.

This is what leads, in many cases, to the so-called "struggle of the wings of revolutionary movements within the parties or centers of power" and this leads to breaking up the group into small groups and factions.

These are some of the effects of using armed violence. This presentation of the exegencies of armed violence and its effect on civil society and on the Islamic Movement itself reveals that the matter is not only useless but goes beyond this to harm the political project by squandering possibilities, creating obstacles and causing harm to the moral reputation of Islam and Muslims.

DEFENSE OF THE STYLE OF ARMED
VIOLENCE AND THE REPLY

It may be said in reply to what we have mentioned that the use of this style achieved "political presence" for the Islamic Movement in the [public] square; "extracted recognition" of it as an important political force. Without this style the Islamic Movement would not have achieved this "presence" for itself nor obtained "recognition."

This allegation is untrue. What proof is there that political "presence" and "recognition" by the society and other political forces of the Islamic Movement could not be had by peaceful, conscious, political activity based on wisdom and exhortation on the popular level, the mobilization of the masses and cooperation with forces sharing, even partially, a common goal. We are sure that the opposite is true relying on many experiences of other Islamic Movements in all parts of the world and on the experience of the Islamic Movement in its creation and growth.

Peaceful political action may be slow in achieving results and may demand greater expenditure of effort and more sacrifice, but it leads certainly to more permanent results and sounder consequences.

The use of armed violence may hasten political recognition and may hasten the political prominence and prestige of the leadership and their significance for the media, but all that comes at the cost of the reputation of Islam and opportunities for the success of the Islamic Movement and the safety of the workers and *mujahīdin* with a heavy cost of blood and possessions. Armed violence achieves one profit; it makes the Islamic Movement a problem for the ruling regime and the contending party. This is true beyond all shadow of doubt.

When we search for political utility, we must look at all aspects of the reality. If we do that, we will see another aspect or dimension to armed violence, namely at the same time it creates a problem for civil society and places a heavy burden on it which it may or may not be able to bear. But whether or not civil society does not wish to strike at the Islamic Movement to defend itself when the Movement's use of violence causes harm to its stability and system of life, still it rejects violence and condemns it and refuses to bear its material, political and moral cost. For that reason it keeps a cautious or negative silent attitude concerning the Islamic project in its entirety. It remains neutral before the crises and setbacks the Islamic Movement exposes it to.

This is in addition to the destruction of public and private property that armed violence causes to society and the dispersal and emigration of the population and the killing and wounding of many because of the lethal nature of modern weapons and the organization of the population and the institutions of modern society which make institutions of public service in society easy goals for destruction. The damage is not limited to the intended goal but goes beyond it to the society and its institutions. These negative results are against the Islamic Movement and against Muslim Civil Society because of the use of the style of armed violence which we saw leads to no real political victory. This confirms the political uselessness of this style; moreover it confirms that it is harmful to the creation of the Islamic Movement, its journey and its political project.

This requires that the Islamic Movement distance itself from political action and not take it as a style and method of action in any aspect whatever, based on the pragmatic measure apart from its legitimacy or illegitimacy from the point of view of *fiqh* [Islamic law]. Even if we were to suppose it realizes some political gains, certainly these are not proportionate to the harm and loss it causes to the Islamic Movement and to Muslim Civil Society and the Islamic Project.

SAYYID MUHAMMAD HUSAIN FADLALLAH
1935–

He was born in Najaf, Iraq; Fadlallah's father was a prominent Shiite scholar. In 1966, after twenty-one years of studying in Najaf, Muhammad Husain Fadlallah went to Lebanon in 1966 to work in East Beirut. When the Lebanese civil war forced him to leave the area, he moved to the southern suburbs. In 1983 he achieved notoriety as the "spiritual father" of Hizballah and was the target of an attempted assassination attributed to the CIA. Fadlallah founded the Mabarrat Association (orphanages, social and medical centers, schools, and mosques). He also opened a religious school in the Sayyida Zainab neighborhood in Damascus, where he teaches regularly. Fadlallah, a prolific author, is among the leading Āyatullāhs of the Shiite community, an advocate of interreligious dialogue and Shiite institutional reform.

We Must Think Before We Act; September 11 Was a Gift to the U.S. Administration

Question: The present state of affairs weighs heavy on us. It brings up questions about what has been happening since September 11 up to the present—about the problem of political Islam and Ben Laden and the Afghan school and what they have wrought—about the attitude of men of religion. What does Your Eminence make of all this?

Answer: First of all, anyone who is familiar with the political background in the region and in the world will most likely complain of injustice and uncover the hatred for America because of its policy. Things have arrived at such a point that people feel let down. There is no use of acting. Even the popular movements and the resistance, whether armed or political, move but remain in the same spot; they have no means of arriving at any decisive results.

In addition, the Arab region and all the Third World including the Islamic region are living in a state of oppression affecting all the people. It all fits under the title of intelligence services and martial law. A man can tremble in fright when he even thinks of freedom because he fears there is some apparatus to detect thought, like a lie detector. There are people who

Interview conducted by Abbas Baydun and Ziyad Majid. From the yearly supplement of *al-Safir*, Dec. 2001. Translated by John J. Donohue.

seize on some personage or a party by compulsion. Destruction is inflicted on the Palestinians daily. And there at the end of the tunnel stands America who pays all expenses with the injustice it lives.

What is going on is not extraordinary. It is a very human response to this arrogant pressure. In this context some Islamic currents moved. They read Islam in the verses on *jihad* and the *hadith* on unbelievers and the attitude to unbelief, and they may have read some history marked by violence. Thus they arrived at the conclusion that they should shorten the road to the goal by violent action. This may make some feel good psychologically, but it overlooks whether or not this action would lead to the goal. This is the problem with this tendency—its understanding of movement towards Islamic goals. The problem in some of this understanding of Islam is that they mix the vehemence of an idea in confronting another idea and the violence of means. It is natural that when an idea debates another idea or when an idea rejects another idea, there is vehemence in thought. Thought must be vehement in presenting all the details which will bring down the other thought when it is a question of thought struggling with thought. But while Islam affirms the vehemence of the idea, it acts on the basis of human means. This is what we notice in the Qur'an when we read:

> Surely, disbelievers are those who said: "God is the third of the three." (5.73)

> or: Surely, in disbelief are they who say that God is the Messiah, son of Maryam. (5.17)

But we read alongside that:

> Verily, . . . you will find the nearest in love to the believers those who say: "We are Christians." That is because amongst them are priests and monks, and they are not proud. (5.82)

> Say: "O people of the Scripture: Come to an agreement between us and you." (3.64)

> And argue not with the people of scripture unless it be in a way that is better, save with such of them as do wrong; and say: we believe in that which has been revealed unto you; our God and your God is one and unto Him we surrender. (29.46)

> Invite to the Way of your Lord with wisdom and fair preaching, and argue with them in a way that is better. (16.125)

So the vehemence of an idea should not mean violence of style, yet there is a certain mentality, uneducated, unconscious and not open which confuses the vehemence of the idea with violence in style.

That is one aspect; the other is that the East and the Third World, confronted with stifling crises and so many cases of collapse and break-down, are searching for a hero, a savior, an avenger. This is why it was so easy to stir up certain yearnings as an alternate for the hero—threats stated with vigor, or movements here and there which give the impression that a force is on the way which will solve the problem and alleviate some of the conditions. We have noticed this, beginning in the fifties until now. The umma has become addicted to personages whose qualifications were not called into doubt, but they had not the stature to prevent violence or to embody the umma in their person. And yet the umma accepted them as its personification and when an Islamic personage died we had the habit of saying that Islam died, or when an Arab personage died, that the Arabs died and collapsed, and the like.

This is why the phenomenon of Ben Laden with all his personal traits gave the impression of many marvels. There was no discussion of details because the details were not clear at least in as far as style, culture, the nature of the organization, and so forth were concerned. There was some-thing here which seemed to manifest that violence executed with vigor projected the image of overcoming the vigor of a great power.

Zeal transformed wishes into facts and this man was able to extend his reach to the Islamic world. He was able to get through to large groups of apprentices because the affair for them was exactly as in tribal society, namely vengeance without regard for content.

The inflated importance these were living made them sure that after their victory over the USSR in Afghanistan they could achieve victory over America although the situation differed greatly. They didn't study the objec-tive conditions which made their victory in Afghanistan possible; there was a world war against the USSR.

Their inflated importance created a state of euphoria remote from reality and from any organized plan detailed in particulars, and so the explosions occurred. Perhaps it was the first moment in the Islamic and non-Islamic world, in the world of the miserable that there was joy—a moment of joy because American vigor fell. A moment accompanied by an atmo-sphere usually seen only on the stage or in movies. The President of the USA could not land his plane in Washington, the vice-president with most of the American administration went into hiding. America for moments or for hours was reeling.

There was joy coming from the sense of revenge and malice and what not. Then things began taking their normal course. The difference between the Third World and the great powers, America in the lead, is that we in the Third World when faced with difficulty give in, but when the great, advanced States—without regard for the content of their progress—face problems they study them and see how they can reap the greatest gain from them. And that is what happened. America promptly suspected the Islamicists and Ben Laden was ready-made for the American media. Perhaps security and other data supported the claim, true or false—we are not held to account by law. There was only Afghanistan there with Ben Laden and the Qa'idah organization. And because the Taliban rebelled against their first masters who with the Pakistan administration created them and worked with them just as they worked with Saddam. Negotiations followed negotiations to hand over Ben Laden and his Qa'idah. They knew psychologically the Taliban would refuse. And so the scape goat was ready for the slaughter. They convinced the NATO countries to participate in the war on the claim that it was defensive. People imagined the Taliban would hold out and that America would be mired down in the morass of Afghanistan as the USSR had been.

But we knew America. Had it entered Afghanistan alone and had there been no Afghan group fighting the other with American airpower and other help, then there was possibility of being mired down. But the Afghan opposition to the Taliban was ready and Pakistan withdrew its support, leaving the Taliban alone to face a world war and so the Taliban fell. The world war continues against this fabled region which America with its media was able to inflate so the victory would appear cut to proper size.

In sum, by this action the Islamists—if they were the ones who did it—were able to offer America a service it could not have had for billions of dollars, while they thought they were going to bring down America.

Question: Your answer opens the way to many questions. Leaving aside the profound political analysis we just heard on the movement of Ben Laden and his fall, Ben Laden argues, in a way, from Islam and the Qur'an, and he argues from a certain jurisprudence (*fiqh*). It is the *fiqh* of seclusion which your Eminence calls the "*fiqh* of backwardness."

Answer: If we go back to the *fiqh* of violence in Islam, first we note that the main title placed at the head of this *fiqh* is *jihad* and combat. If we delve into this title, we find a verse that says:

> And fight in the Way of God those who fight you (2.190)

which means that the question is one of self-defense or defense of the society targeted.

> And what is wrong with you that you fight not in the Cause of God, and for those weak (4.75)

The battle is for deprived or persecuted groups.

> And fight them until there is no more *Fitnah* (8.39)

This means any sedition concerning religion, fighting in the way of freedom, since we do not use modern technical terms lest we move those to convert them from their religion by pressure, coercion and killing; "religion is God's" (1.18) means Islam should be chosen freely. Therefore, fighting in the Qur'anic text is not in the sense of attacking. . . .

From this we understand that the concept of *jihad* contains nothing of hostile combat. When we study the question of Islam's view of the other, the other at that time was Jew or Christian. We read "word of agreement" (*kalamat al-siwa*) is the one God, even though we differ on the nature of the unity, and the unity of humanity, namely that man cannot be lord of man and come to an agreement. History indicates that Islam embraces the other and does not interfere with its basic notion. Perhaps there were problems between Muslims and Christians and Jews, just like there were problems between Muslims themselves and Christians themselves and Jews. The proof is that Jews and Christians are found in Islamic countries all through history and they live as do Muslims. Perhaps there have been misgivings about their entering into the body of leaders because they do not believe in this notion of leadership. . . .

We note in the verse we read

> And argue not with the people of the Scripture (Jews and Christians), unless it be in (a way) that is better. (29.46)

When they wrong you, react as wronged to wronger. As for those who seek dialogue, dialogue with them on what is better.

> Say "We believe in that which has been revealed to us and revealed to you; our God and your God is One, and to Him we have submitted." (29.46)

This is the logic of conviviality and reconciliation which tells you that there is common ground between us; come let us proceed from there.

Therefore, the Islamic discourse is not one of enmity but of humane reconciliation open to the other. Still there remains something which makes those protest action like this; they say that the American people, just like the American administration, are responsible because they pay taxes to this administration. This is absurd because it is natural for all people to pay taxes to protect their interests or from fear of negative results. We know that many of the American people are not content with the administration; many did not elect this administration or its president. Here is a point, the verse which says

> No one bears another's load. (6.165)

The responsibility in Islam is individual; you are not permitted to hold a man responsible for the crime of another no matter how closely they be related. In the light of this we cannot place the responsibility of the administration on the American people, just as we cannot bear the responsibility

of the people who were present in the airplanes or in America itself, going
there for commerce or tourism or whatever. . . .

> For this reason we disavow this question and say that neither law, intel-
> ligence or religion accepts it. We oppose American policy but we do not
> oppose it in this way because the American people have no connection with
> the crimes of their administration. For that reason we say that the error is
> in the application. . . .

The Qur'an tells you, follow the style which will change your enemies
into friends. This is Islam in its humane magnanimity. Imam Ali says that
people are of two types, either a brother in religion or a peer in creation.
The Prophet says: kindness is not bestowed on a thing save it adorns it, nor
removed without defacing it.

God is tender, He loves kindness and bestows on kindness what he
bestows not on violence. So to understand that violence is the sole means
for change, without regard for the dynamic of the means, is not Islamic *fiqh*,
nor is it Islam in its humane magnanimity.

This is why I said when they were speaking about Islamic fundamentalism and saying Islam is fundamentalist and the like, I said to them: do
not transfer the Western concept to Islamic reality. Islam is not fundamentalist in the Western sense because fundamentalism stands on two elements:
the first is to do away with the other; the second is considering violence
as the one means of action. When we read the discourses of Islam to the
people of the Book, we see it did not do away with the people of the
Book and when we read "give what is better" and "dispute about what is
better" and "Say, my servants say what is better," we do not find violence.
Violence in Islam is like a surgical operation resorted to when the life
of the sick person is threatened. Violence to the one who imposes violence
on you.

Question: Many societies in the Third World are subject to American
injustice. I think of Latin American societies and there was an expression
of violence and much agitation, but it was of a different type. Don't you
think that the phenomenon of violence is tied to the Islamic world, not
to others?

Answer: Since the fifties I have been following most of the nationalist,
patriotic and Islamic movements. They have no method in style. All these
movements took their style from Marxism and found their common ground
in the Israeli occupation of Palestine. Violence entered the region with
this occupation and the political projects which through coup after coup
entangled the Arab world in the Cold War between East and West. Here
and there elements of nationalism and patriotism entered. For that reason
how can we explain all the violence? Islam had no part in it. Islam was
not a party in the Lebanese war, nor in the war in Yemen, nor in any other
war because political Islam did not enter until after the leftist currents

weakened, in the sense that people resorted to violence in the name of Islam because of the objective conditions.

Question: On the basis of your Eminence's words, Islam present and contemporary which was formed after the colonial period was also formed in conditions of Western violence, whether colonialist or revolutionary. Don't you think that contemporary Islamic movements, knowingly or not, are the heirs of Western violence, colonial or revolutionary?

Answer: There is a point we should recognize, namely that any movement, Islamic or national or secular, generally lives according to its means and its spirit, according to the mentality of those in charge. The Islamic world is a dynamic and variegated world. There are Islamists with an avant-garde education, close to the age, and there are those who lack this education and live in the past. There are Islamists born in a period of violence and this violence can burn their whole being and they bring an Islam with no conception of its culture and elements to be a subject to arouse the people. For this reason you cannot condemn activist Islam in all its models. There is no doubt that there are models of Islam which have a contemporary balanced view (I don't like to use the terms moderate and extremist as consumer labels). But the problem is that the regimes and the arrogant Western plans behind them have become preoccupied with moderate activist Islam more than with extremist Islam, just like the Israelis.

Question: Who, for instance, belongs to the moderate current?

Answer: The Muslim Brothers, for example, who have started to express themselves along rational, moderate lines. . . . They lived a period of violence in the days of Abd al-Nasir, if we may say that, and they begat several other groups, but the Brothers have taken their distance from them. The same as with the left. Aren't there parties coming from the left? They took some things from Marxism but then went beyond it, like the nationalists. Were we not saying in the forties "Arabs over all" like Hitler? On this basis, when we study the subject, we note that no room is left for moderate Islamists so that they might take their liberty. In Egypt and every Islamic country no Islamic religious party is allowed. When this party has a political vision (whether correct or erroneous), why don't they give it liberty within the system? Is it because the Islamists do not consider anyone not in their party or group as Muslim? This is not true. None of the Islamists say that if you do not belong to their party, you are not a Muslim. This notion has created a state of reaction which is storing up violence for the future. Would that some of these states gave freedom to the Islamists and then set limits to this freedom as they do for other parties; then there would be no problem. On the contrary. . . .

Question: Does Your Eminence think there is a possibility that there are some movements which under the banner of Islam get well-connected in the society and then act like all violent groups and sometimes like Mafia, allowing everything and violating everything? Don't they realize this harms

Islam? Every time one of these movements is really present or when a movement, Islamic or other, gets a hold somehow on the relations of this society and exposes itself to a test, there is a danger, theoretically and in principle. Maybe this test will hurt it. Can Islam with its idealism tolerate this type of action?

Answer: There is a broad title, namely that no idea can protect itself from its adherents; no law can protect itself. The man of thought protects the idea; the man of law protects the law. Islam grew up in a society variegated in the variety of culture and even in the variety of spiritual initiatives. Why talk only about Islam and not ask about tribal societies and the confessionalism present among non-Muslims, the ethnic groups present even in civilized societies like Yugoslavia which lived under Marxist rule. How did they become as they are now? . . . And so on. There are societies connected with a tangled history, a history with anarchical concepts and styles. For this reason we cannot undertake an engineering operation grouping all these people on the basis that they are Muslims, for example. No. True, they are Muslim, but this one understands Islam in his way, and that one in his.

It is not permitted for Muslims who think in a balanced way, the way of those who want to be realist to cooperate with others. The regimes will not let them; the violence present in the other parties does not let them; the sensibilities present in competition and even in elimination. Elimination is not limited to Islamists; every band with a foot in the arena tries to eliminate the others. Were there not operations of elimination in the fifties and the sixties, even within the secularist currents? The operation of elimination is human, not in any deep sense of man but from man's perception of power. For that reason I say: let's open the way for the clear voices, let's give an opportunity to the Islamists who are 60% open, encourage them, work with them, especially with this new Islamic tendency which tries to open out to others, even though there be some misgivings. This Iran, for instance, cooperates with Russia and India and tries to be with Armenia against Azerbaijan which is Islamic and Shiite. Internally there is also a struggle, but it indicates that there is political vitality. The style here or there may be inappropriate because this is the first attempt in the history of Iran at this type of political life in which people exercise their rights, play their role and express their opinion, etc. Naturally there are negative elements, but the line is positive.

Now in our Islamic reality the Islamists are seriously thinking of cooperating with Communists. Hizballah, for instance, despite all the question marks, meets with all groups, with Communists, with nationalists, with the Kata'ib and other Christians also. Perhaps a positive point is marked up here and a negative point there, but the sense of it all is that there is a new atmosphere which the grass roots accept. In the beginning the grass roots would not accept that an Islamist sits with a Communist; now that is acceptable. At the beginning of the last century, the nationalist, for example, was an infidel in a certain manner. Now the nationalists are in alliance with the Islamists. The Palestinian cause has grouped them all.

The responsibility of all tendencies including the secularist is that they not try to collect negative points to combat Islam, nor should the Islamists try to collect negative points against the others. Let them all converge on positive points. Let us all encourage the positive points of the other; perhaps these positive points will help us avoid the negative to arrive at understanding if not reunion. The problem is that we still have psychological hang-ups regarding one another. No one trusts the other, fearing a hidden agenda. We have a famous saying of the Prophet: had you discovered one another, you would not have hidden. People fear what may be hidden. If a Muslim speaks with a Christian in Lebanon, he will ask whom he is following and what he wants from me; he looks for something negative because he is not prepared to believe him and encounter him.

Question: In religious thought there are absolutes which are difficult to call into question. Islam considers itself religion and world (*din wa dunya*) and tries to cover all aspects and angles of society. In your opinion is it capable of developing and adapting to the age and to the questions posed; can it accept the principle of doubt and reject absolute certainty?

Answer: Among the things I proposed in my conferences at the American University is that nothing is sacred in dialogue. I said that God dialogues with the devil as well as with the angels. The Qur'an is a book of dialogue, dialogue with polytheists, with Jews, with Christians, with hypocrites . . . dialogue is the matter which forms the backbone of the humanist creed. I have a book *Dialogue in the Qur'an*. [On the one hand dialogue can raise doubts about one's religion]; on the other, doubt is not unbelief. We relate from one of the Imams of *Ahl al-Bayt*, Imam Sadiq, that a person came and said to him: a man doubts God and His messenger . . . then the Imam continued: he becomes an infidel only if he renounces. As long as he continues in moving his doubt forward toward certainty, he is not considered an infidel. . . .

Question: But there are those who search in faith, like Nasr Hamid Abu Zayd, and they are met with accusations of infidelity and threats.

Answer: I wrote once in the newspaper *al-Sha'b* that I do not agree with this style, even in the case of Salman Rushdie. I have a saying: "Give the other thought freedom and you will cause it to recoil; persecute it and you will cause it to spread." . . .

Question: It appears that the lesson we learn from what is going on in Iraq and what took place in Afghanistan is that there is a suicidal consciousness which continues to imagine that in the age of globalization it is possible for heroism or chivalry to conquer the world. The defeat of America is the defeat of the world. We can imagine that this suicidal comportment is that of despair, in a way, and a feeling that there is a problem without a solution. There is also suicidal comportment in combat, both individual and group. This style is becoming dominant and it brings the threat of another suicide, the suicide of the Palestinian entity. No matter what your Eminence may think of Yasir Arafat, absolutely nothing indicates that the end of the Palestinian entity would be useful to anyone.

Answer: This is a side of the picture. If we study the society as a whole, the group that thinks like this is not large. There is, for instance, a group of intellectuals open to globalization, with reservations concerning culture . . . there is also a group of non-intellectuals, like merchants and others. What we see in Iraq or in Afghanistan is that the Afghans are not like this, and the Iraqis are displaced in the world . . . the question is that there is a feeling that the West is taking hold of our world. This creates a state of frustration and a state of suicide and despair. This is present not only on the level of politics. Otherwise how can you explain the phenomenon of suicide in America? How can you explain the case of a student who carries a weapon to kill his comrades or his teachers? How can you explain what happened in Switzerland and what happens in Ireland?

This state is not limited to a given society nor is it the state of Islam or the East only. Rather whenever humans feel they are hemmed in on all sides—thought, sensibility, feeling—and even regarding economy and politics, they feel they can do nothing. A state of tension is produced which may need to remain because if the tension abates, especially concerning Palestine, it means death. Tension is an expression of a mental state which can transform you into vital, dynamic energy. Yes, the content of the tension may be erroneous. In our Arab and Islamic world we are passing through a period of transition, because we have much energy which possesses thought, culture and realism, but it has not found the atmosphere which will allow it to reach fruition. The Palestine problem, for instance, entered the world and cannot be neglected. Israel does not want to become another state in the region until it gains as much as possible inside Palestine and outside. This is what makes her try to gain whatever she can in the changing international situation while still concerned with a solution or a settlement, because the lack of a settlement will be of no use to her in the future.

The problem with the Palestine cause, despite its legendary spirit of patience, persistence, endurance and *jihad*, is the lack of coordination. The problem is that violence goes off in dubious directions. Any military operation, even in a state of revolution, must be politically accountable. The parties that have control may represent two different mentalities, revolutionary and traditional. They have to get together. But don't forget the international siege at this stage in the world war which I call the Third American War. America is now acting to kill all movements which have any force, especially if that force comes from a sacred state of mind— Islamic. This is what makes it raise its voice concerning Hamas and Jihad and Hizballah. There is an American-Israeli strategy working to eliminate any possibility of the strong in the Arab world lest they harm American interests. . . .

I am not pessimistic because I say that this world represents a case requiring a Caesarian operation. We spoke of the negative aspects of what happened, but over against that America lost its assurance of security. I am convinced that all this American war against so-called terrorism in the world can lead to some results restraining terror, but it will produce the most vicious possible reaction because it is increasing oppression. We know that the organizations they call terrorist and organizations espousing violence were born in exactly the same climate as this. . . .

Question: When we look at Shiite history, we note that for hundreds of years it was apprehensive regarding the state and politics and this apprehension led to a practical situation which though it had no theoretical base did separate the practice of religion from that of politics. Maybe for this reason the Shiites had the capacity for forbearance (*hilm*). Does not your Eminence consider that being drowned in politics leads to a loss of this forbearance on the one hand, and on the other prevents sympathy for Shiism (*tashayyu'*) from being the broad cloak or spacious tent for all the persecuted and oppressed?

Answer: Why separate the Shi'a from the State? Because Shiite thought considers the state illegal and regards rulers as tyrants. But at the same time the Shi'a were open, for instance, in the revolt of the twenties in Iraq against the English and officially in the interest of the Ottomans who persecuted the Shi'a. Also the Shi'a stood with the Palestinian cause. There is a Shiite openness, though it ebbs and flows. International forces come along and try to spread fanaticism against them and there are groups who try to be open towards them.

As for Shiite forbearance, there is in the Shiite creed the awaited Mahdi "who will fill the earth with justice and equity as it is filled with injustice and tyranny." International justice opposite international injustice. This idea is now making its way in dynamic thought so that we prepare conditions for the awaited Imam and make a State of justice here and a State of justice there. We adopt the mission of justice in the world and we stand with all just causes and against causes of injustice in the world. This Shiite movement confirms forbearance in some of its positions and moves in the way of forbearance.

Question: Aren't you apprehensive about every State and every party, your Eminence?

Answer: No, I look to the positive aspects. I learn from Christ who when he passed a decaying dog and the people talking with him said, "How awful the stench," Isa said, "How white its teeth." I think we must look to the bright side of the picture. I have a poem. I haven't memorized it, but I think of it: these stars were created by God to inspire man that there is no absolute evil, all evil bears spots of light and these spots of light gather to point to the dawn. In our Arab world the singers are still singing "O Night!" I don't hear anyone singing "O Dawn!"

KHALED ABOU EL FADL
1963–

Born in Kuwait of Egyptian parents, he holds degrees from Yale
University (B.A.), University of Pennsylvania Law School (J.D.),
and Princeton University (M.A./Ph.D.). Abou El Fadl also
received formal training in Islamic jurisprudence in Egypt and
Kuwait. He is Professor of Law at the UCLA School of Law; his
publications include *Islam and the Challenge of Democracy*; *The
Place of Tolerance in Islam*; *Speaking in God's Name: Islamic
Law, Authority and Women*; and *Rebellion and Violence in
Islamic Law*.

Islam and Violence:
Our Forgotten Legacy

When it comes to the issue of Islam and violence, I must confess that, as a
Muslim intellectual, I find myself in a bit of a bind. Islam, as expounded
in the classical books of theology and law, does not bear a message of
violence. In fact, *salam* (peace and tranquility) is a central tenet of Islamic
belief, and safety and security are considered profound divine blessings to
be cherished and vigilantly pursued. The absence of peace is identified in
the Qur'an as a largely negative condition; it is variously described as a trial
and tribulation, as a curse or punishment, or, sometimes, as a necessary
evil. But the absence of peace is never in and of itself a positive or desirable
condition. The Qur'an asserts that if it had not been for divine benevolence,
many mosques, churches, synagogues, and homes would have been
destroyed because of the ignorance and pettiness of human beings.[1] Often,
God mercifully intervenes to put out the fires of war, and save human beings
from their follies.[2]

The Islamic historical experience was primarily concerned not with
war-making, but with civilization-building. Islamic theology instructs that
an integral part of the divine covenant given to human beings is to occupy
themselves with building and creating, not destroying life. The Qur'an
teaches that the act of destroying or spreading ruin on this earth is one
of the gravest sins possible. *Fasad fi al-ard*, which means to corrupt the
earth by destroying the beauty of creation, is considered an ultimate act of

---

1. Qur'an 22:40.
2. Qur'an 5:64.

Reprinted by permission of the author.

blasphemy against God.[3] Those who corrupt the earth by destroying lives, property, and nature are designated as *mufsidun* who, in effect, wage war against God by dismantling the very fabric of existence.[4] In addition, the Qur'an states that God has made people different and diverse, and that they will remain so until the final day. Accordingly, human diversity is part of the divine plan, and the challenge is for human beings to co-exist and inter-act despite their differences.[5] The Qur'an proclaims in unequivocal fashion: "God has made you into many nations and tribes so that you will come to know one another. Those most honored in the eyes of God are those who are most pious."[6] From this, classical Muslim scholars reached the reason-able conclusion that war is not the means most conducive to getting "to know one another." Thus, they argued that the exchange of technology and merchandise is, in most cases, a superior course of action to warfare. In the opinion of most classical jurists, war, unless it is purely defensive, is not to be preferred, and must be treated as a last resort because war is not a super-ior moral virtue. Perhaps because of these moral imperatives, the Islamic civilization excelled in the sciences, arts, philosophy, law, architecture, and trade—and Islam entered into areas such as China, Indonesia, Malaysia, the Philippines, and sub-Saharan Africa primarily through traveling merchants and scholars, and not through warfare.

Despite this rich doctrinal and historical background, the dilemmas of a modern Muslim intellectual persist. For one, this tolerant and humani-tarian Islamic tradition exists in tension with other doctrines in the Islamic tradition that are less tolerant or humanitarian. Many classical Muslim scholars, for instance, insisted on a conception of the world that is bifur-cated and dichotomous. Those scholars argued that the world is divided into the abode of Islam (*dar al-Islam*) and abode of war (*dar al-harb*); the two can stop fighting for a while, but one must inevitably prevail over the other. According to these scholars, Muslims must give non-Muslims one of three options; either become Muslim, pay a poll tax, or fight. These classical scholars were willing to tolerate differences as long as the existence of these differences did not challenge Muslim political supremacy and dominance. This dichotomous and even imperialist view of the world, however, did not go unchallenged. So, for instance, many classical scholars argued that instead of a two-part division of the world, one ought to recognize a third category, and that is the abode of non-belligerence or neutrality (*dar al-sulh* or *al-'ahd*)—an abode that is not Muslim, but that has a peaceful relationship with the Muslim world. In addition, many classi-cal jurists argued that, regardless of the political affiliation of a particular territory, the real or true abode of Islam is wherever justice exists (*dar al-'adl*), or wherever Muslims may freely and openly practice their religion.

3. For instance, see Qur'an 2:27, 205; 5:32; 13:25.
4. Qur'an 2:27; 13:25.
5. Qur'an 11:118.
6. Qur'an 49:13.

Therefore, it is possible for a territory that is ruled by non-Muslims and where Muslims are minority to be considered part of the abode of true Islam.

But the fact that the Islamic scholastic tradition is not unitary, and that it is often diverse and multi-faceted is hardly surprising. What is surprising and often aggravating is the extent to which Islamic debates in the modern age have become politicized and polarized. It is difficult for a contemporary Muslim scholar to take a position on Islam and violence without becoming the subject of suspicion and even accusations as to his loyalties and commitments. For instance, if a contemporary Muslim scholar emphasizes the imperatives of tolerance and peaceful co-existence in Islam, or emphasizes the importance of moral commitments over political expedience, or perhaps condemns terrorism, this is often understood as a thoroughly political position. Such a scholar becomes susceptible to accusations of being a sell-out to the West, pro-Israeli, pro-government, or of being insufficiently sensitized to the suffering of the Palestinians, Kashmiris, Chechnyans, or any other oppressed Muslim population.

The real challenge that confronts Muslim intellectuals is that political interests have come to dominate the public discourse, and to a large extent, moral discourses have become marginalized in modern Islam. In many ways, since the onslaught of colonialism and its aftermath, Muslims have become largely pre-occupied with the attempt to remedy a collective feeling of powerlessness and a frustrating sense of political defeat, often by engaging in highly sensationalistic acts of power symbolism. The normative imperatives and intellectual subtleties of the Islamic moral tradition are not treated with the analytic and critical rigor that this tradition rightly deserves, but are rendered subservient to political expedience and symbolic displays of power.

Elsewhere, I have described this contemporary doctrinal dynamic as the predominance of the theology of power in modern Islam, and it is this theology that is a direct contributor to the emergence of highly radicalized Islamic groups, such as the Islamic Jihad or al-Qa'ida.[7] Far from being authentic expressions of inherited Islamic paradigms, or a natural outgrowth of the classical tradition, these are thoroughly a byproduct of colonialism and modernity. Such groups ignore the history of the Islamic civilization, with all its richness and diversity, and reduce Islam to a single dynamic—the dynamic of power. They tend to define Islam as an ideology of nationalistic defiance to the other—a vulgar form of obstructionism to the hegemony of the Western world. Therefore, instead of Islam being a moral vision given to humanity, it is constructed into the antithesis of the West. In the world constructed by these groups, there is no Islam; there is only opposition to the West.

---

7. Khaled Abou El Fadl, "Islam and the Theology of Power Islam," 221 *Middle East Report* (Winter 2001); 28–33.

I am not implying that resistance to Western cultural hegemony, or fighting oppression, is illegitimate. But the type of Islam that the radicalized groups offer is akin to a perpetual state of emergency where expedience trumps principle, and illegitimate means are consistently justified by invoking higher ends. In essence, what prevails is an aggravated siege mentality that suspends the moral principles of the religion in pursuit of political power. In this siege mentality, there is no room for analytical or critical thought, and there is no room for seriously engaging Islamic intellectual heritage. There is only room for bombastic dogma, and for a stark functionalism that ultimately impoverishes Islamic heritage.

This, perhaps, is nowhere as clearly apparent as in the treatment of the issue of jihad and violence in modern Islam. Jihad is a core principle in Islamic theology; it means to strive, to apply oneself, to struggle, and persevere. In many ways, jihad connotes a strong spiritual and material work ethic in Islam. Piety, knowledge, health, beauty, truth, and justice are not possible without jihad—without sustained and diligent hard work. Therefore, cleansing oneself from vanity and pettiness, pursuing knowledge, curing the ill, feeding the poor, and standing up for truth and justice even at great personal risk are all forms of jihad.

The Qur'an uses the term jihad to refer to the act of striving to serve the purposes of God on this earth, which includes all the acts mentioned above. Importantly, the Qur'an does not use the word jihad to refer to warfare or fighting; such acts are referred to as *qital*. While the Qur'an's call to jihad is unconditional and unrestricted, such is not the case for *qital*. Jihad is a good in and of itself, while *qital* is not. Therefore, every reference in the Qur'an to *qital* is restricted and limited by particular conditions, but exhortations to jihad, like the references to justice or truth, are absolute and unconditional. Consequently, the early Muslims were not allowed to engage in *qital* until God gave them specific permission to do so. The Qur'an is careful to note that Muslims were given permission to fight because they had become the victims of aggression.[8] Furthermore, the Qur'an instructs Muslims to fight only those who fight them and not to transgress for God does not approve of aggression.[9]

In addition, the Qur'an goes on to specify that if the enemy ceases hostilities and seeks peace, Muslims should seek peace as well. Failure to seek peace without just cause is considered arrogant, and sinful. In fact, the Qur'an reminds Muslims not to pick fights, and not to create enemies because the fact that a particular party does not wish to fight Muslims and seeks to make peace is a Divine blessing. God has the power to inspire in the hearts of non-Muslims a desire for peace, and Muslims must treat such a blessing with gratitude and appreciation, not defiance and arrogance.[10]

8. Qur'an 22:39; 60:8; 2:246.
9. Qur'an 2:190, 194; 5:87.
10. Qur'an 4:90.

In light of this Qur'anic discourse, classical Muslim jurists debated what would constitute a sufficient and just cause for fighting non-Muslims. Are non-Muslims fought because of their act of disbelief or only because they pose a physical threat to Muslims? Most classical jurists concluded that the justification for fighting non-Muslims is directly proportional to the physical threat they pose to Muslims. In other words, if they do not threaten or seek to harm Muslims, then there is no justification for acts of belligerence or warfare. Similarly, relying on a precedent set by the Prophet, classical Muslim jurists held that non-combatants, like children, women, people of advanced age, monks, hermits, priests, or anyone else who does not seek to or cannot fight Muslims, are inviolable and may not be targeted even during ongoing hostilities.[11] The existence of these doctrines is crucial for assessing the relationship between Islam and violence. But the reality is that the impact of such doctrines entirely depends on how modern Muslims choose to understand, develop, and assert them. Perhaps it is painfully obvious that regardless of how rich, humanistic, and moral the Islamic tradition is in fact, this tradition will be of very limited usefulness if it is not believed and acted upon by Muslims today. But herein is the true travesty of modern Islam, and the agony of every honest Muslim intellectual. It is fairly well-known that non-Muslims suffer from much ignorance and prejudice about the Islamic doctrine of jihad, its meaning, and effect. Unfortunately, however, much of this ignorance is shared by Muslims themselves about their own tradition. For example, many Muslims today do not know the difference between jihad and *qital*, or are woefully ignorant about the rules for the conduct of war in Islam. Even worse, when contemporary Muslim scholars rise to emphasize the numerous moral and humanistic aspects of the Islamic tradition, they are accused by their fellow Muslims of being Westernized or of seeking to appease the West. The real danger is that in this highly polarized and politicized climate, much of what is authentically Islamic and genuinely beautiful will be lost or forgotten for a long period to come.

11. It is reported that the Prophet used to instruct his armies not to hurt a non-combatant or needlessly destroy property or vegetation. It is also reported that after a battle, upon finding the corpse of a woman, the Prophet became very upset, and reproached his army for killing a non-combatant.

FATWA

Jihad

Question: What does the term "Jihad" mean to you as Muslims?

Answer: by Sheikh 'Atiyyah Saqr

First, we would like to start with stating that Islam does not call for violence; rather it abhors all forms of violence and terrorism, whether against Muslims or non-Muslims. Islam, moreover, calls for peace, cooperation, and maintaining justice, and provides for the happiness and welfare of humanity as a whole. This fact is declared in the Qur'an when Allah says: "Allah commands justice, the doing of good, and liberality to kith and kin, and He forbids all shameful deeds, and injustice and rebellion: He instructs you, that ye may receive admonition" (An-Nahl: 90).

Islam makes it obligatory upon Muslims to stand by the oppressed regardless of their race, color, religion or affiliation and say NO to the oppressor and ask him to respond to the voice of reason and justice.

As regards the question you posed, we would like to cite for you the fatwa issued by the eminent Muslim scholar Sheikh 'Atiyyah Saqr, former Head of Al-Azhar Fatwa Committee, that reads:

> "Jihad" is one of the words that have been misused due to misunderstanding its true meaning. The word "Jihad" is derived from the Arabic word "Jahd" which means fatigue or the word "Juhd" which means effort. A Mujahid is he who strives in the Cause of Allah and exerts efforts which makes him feel fatigued. The word "Jihad" means exerting effort to achieve a desired thing or prevent an undesired one. In other words, it is an effort that aims at bringing about benefit or preventing harm.
>
> Jihad can be observed through any means and in any field whether material or moral. Among the types of Jihad are struggling against one's desires, the accursed Satan, poverty, illiteracy, disease, and fighting all evil forces in the world.
>
> There are many religious texts that refer to these types of Jihad. Among the forms of Jihad is defending life, property or honor. Those who die while engaging in Jihad are considered to be martyrs, as confirmed by Hadith. Jihad is also done to avert aggression on home countries and on all that is held sacred, or in order to face those who try to hinder the march of the call of truth.
>
> In Islamic Shari'ah, Jihad in the Cause of Allah means fighting in order to make the Word of Allah most high, and the means for doing so is taking up arms in addition to preparation, financing and planning strategies. A large number of people are supposed to take part in Jihad including farmers, craftsmen, traders, doctors, engineers, workers, security

From: http://www.islam-online.net/fatwa/english/FatwaDisplay.asp?hFatwaID=18243.

men, preachers, writers and all those who directly or indirectly participate in the battle.

This type of Jihad was a major concern of Muslims in the beginning of the formation of the Islamic community, and a lot of verses of the Glorious Qur'an and the Hadith advocated and encouraged it. Almighty Allah says: "March forth, whether you are light (being healthy, young and wealthy) or heavy (being ill, old and poor) and strive with your wealth and your lives in the Cause of Allah" (At-Tawbah: 41). Jihad is considered an individual duty (Fard 'Ein), on all Muslims who are capable and fit to fight, in the event of being invaded by the enemy, and is considered a collective duty (Fard Kifayah) in the event of not being invaded. However, if the Imam (leader) calls to Jihad, people must respond to his call. This is evident from Allah's Saying, "O you who believe! What is the matter with you, that when you are asked to march forth in the Cause of Allah (i.e. Jihad) you cling heavily on the earth?" (At-Tawbah: 38), and the Hadith narrated by Al-Bukhari and Muslim, "When you are called to Jihad, then go forth."

A question arises: is taking up arms the only means to spread Islam? Fighting originally had two main objectives: the first one was to ward off an actual or an anticipated aggression, and the second one was to clear the hurdles in the path of Da'wah (call for Islam). The battles of Badr, Uhud, Al-Khandaq and others are examples of staving off actual aggression and some of them were fought in order to aid the oppressed. Almighty Allah says: "But if they seek your help in religion, it is your duty to help them" (Al-Anfal: 72). The conquest of Makkah was undertaken for the purpose of staving off an expected aggression after the Quraish had violated its covenant with the Prophet, peace and blessings of Allah be upon him, in Al-Hudaybyah; this was also the case of the expedition of Tabûk and other expeditions. It also cleared the obstacles placed in the path of Islam by enabling the Muslims to leave Madînah and spread the call to Islam all over the world because Islam is a universal message. Since Jihad was legalized in Islam and the Prophet, peace and blessings be upon him, said that he was sent by Allah to wage war against disbelief and that his sustenance was "tied" to his spear, as related by Ahmad on the authority of Ibn 'Umar, then we have to understand that Islam advocated acquiring the highest degree of power, and the reason for this is that Islam, at that time, was a newly rising power and was expected to be "attacked" by the already existing powers to prevent it from competing with them over power—a conflict that is common to all ages.

Therefore, the new entity had to be defended in order to prove its strength and deliver its message. If Islam were a local temporary call, taking up arms would be just for the purpose of defense, but Islam is a universal call that had to reach the whole world. However, the only means at that time was traveling, which was and still is fraught with dangers; so taking up arms was necessary to prevent the enemies from standing in the path of the Islamic call.

While arms were necessary to remove the hurdles in the past, their sole mission now is to defend Islam against those who want to harm it and harm those who embrace it. As for spreading Islam, there are several means that spare people the trouble of traveling, such as newspapers, books, the Internet and other means that have known no borders, although they may be controlled to some extent. However, radio stations have become of such power and prevalence that they can reach people while being at home or even in bed, and they can neither be prevented by any authority, nor held back by any door or border.

The superficial understanding of the legality of fighting contained in the verses of the Glorious Qur'an and the Prophet's Hadiths may give the impression that Islam has been spread by force and that if it had not been for force, Islam would not have existed or become predominant in many countries or embraced by such a large number of people. But how could this be said about Islam which is the religion of mercy? Allah Almighty says: "But if the enemy inclines towards peace, do thou also incline towards peace and trust in Allah" (Al-Anfâl: 61). The Prophet also says: "O people! Do not wish to face the enemy (in a battle) and ask Allah to save you (from calamities) but if you should face the enemy, then be patient and let it be known to you that Paradise is under the shades of swords."

The call to Islam is not meant to be imposed on anyone; people are completely free to make their choice. In fact, creeds can never be propagated by a dagger. Allah Almighty says to Noah: "Shall We compel you to accept it when you are averse to it?" (Hûd: 28). Allah says to Muhammad, peace and blessings be upon him: "Wilt thou compel mankind against their will to believe!" (Yûnus: 99); many other verses convey the same meaning.

While there are texts that explicitly indicate the absolute order to fight, there are others that restrict it to whether it is for the purpose of staving off an aggression, preventing an expected aggression or making it a punishment for violating a covenant. Allah Almighty says: "Fight in the cause of Allah those who fight you, but do not transgress limits" (Al-Baqarah: 190). And says: "But if they violate their oaths after their covenant and taunt you for your faith, fight thee the chiefs of unfaith" (At-Tawbah:12). In fact, the previous verse specifies the meaning of the verses: "And fight the pagans all together as they fight you all together" (At-Tawbah: 36). And: "And slay them wherever ye catch them."

As for those who call for taking up arms to change the current state of the Islamic communities, we have previously said that any means of reform based on violence will not achieve its goals. In addition to this, exercising power requires extensive preparation and planning including a careful study of all existing circumstances before taking such a step, i.e. calling arms. However, this should not be understood as undermining the importance of Jihad in its general sense. Jihad will continue till the end of days in all its forms and through all its means. This is evident from the Hadith narrated by Abu Dawûd: "Jihad will continue from the day I was sent by Allah till the last people of my nation fight against the Antichrist (Dajjâl), it will neither be stopped by oppression nor abstention." This Hadith denotes the continuance of Jihad in all fields including armed Jihad is an integral element; this fact is evident from referring to fighting against the Antichrist.

Terrorism

Question: Does Islam support terrorism? If yes, is the act justified by Islam?

Answer: by Sheikh Dr. Ahmad 'Abd al-Latîf

For your question regarding terrorism, the answer depends on the meaning applied to this word. If the meaning is to assassinate children and women and innocents who have not engaged in fighting, then Islam has a clear rule about it: that it is unlawful, even during times of war.

But if the meaning goes to those who defend their religion, their creed and their land, as it is now being applied in Palestine in their fight against the Jews, then Islam's rule in this case is also clear: that you can not call such actions as terrorism but as a struggle (Jihâd) in the defense of Islam.

From: islamtoday.net.

Suicide Bombings and Martyrdom

SUICIDE BOMBERS ARE MARTYRS

Opinion of Shaikh Yusuf al-Qaradhawi, president of the European Council for Fatwa and Research

The martyrdom operations carried out by the Palestinian factions to resist the Zionist occupation are not in any way included in the framework of prohibited terrorism, even if the victims include some civilians.

This is for several reasons:

First of all, due to the colonialist, occupational, racist, and [plundering] nature of Israeli society, it is, in fact, a military society. Anyone past childhood, man or woman, is drafted into the Israeli army. Every Israeli is a solider in the army, either in practical terms or because he is a reservist soldier who can be summoned at any time for war. This fact needs no proof. Those they call "civilians" are in effect "soldiers" in the army of the sons of Zion.

Second, Israeli society has a unique trait that makes it different from the other human societies, and that is that as far as the people of Palestine are concerned, it is a "society of invaders" who came from outside the region—from Russia or America, from Europe or from the lands of the Orient—to occupy Palestine and settle in it. . . .

Those who are invaded have the right to fight the invaders with all means at their disposal in order to remove [the invaders] from their homes and send them back to the homes from whence they came. . . . This is a *Jihad* of necessity, as the clerics call it, and not *Jihad* of choice. . . . Even if an innocent child is killed as a result of this *Jihad*—it was not intended, but rather due to the necessities of the war. . . . Even with the passage of time, these [Israeli] so-called "civilians" do not stop being invaders, evil, tyrants, and oppressors. . . .

Third . . . It has been determined by Islamic law that the blood and property of people of *Dar Al-Harb* [the Domain of Disbelief where the battle for the domination of Islam should be waged] is not protected. Because they fight against and are hostile towards the Muslims, they annulled the protection of his blood and his property.

Fourth, the Muslim clerics, or most of them, have agreed that it is permissible to kill Muslims if the army that attacks the Muslims hides behind them, that is, uses them as barricades or human shields, and sets them at the front so that the fire, arrows, or spears of the Muslims will

Taken from MEMRI.org, July 24, 2003.

harm them first. The clerics have permitted the defenders to kill these innocent Muslims, who were forced to stand at the head of the army of their enemies. . . . Otherwise the invading army will enter and annihilate their offspring and their harvests. There was no choice but to sacrifice some [of the Muslims] in order to defend the entire [Muslim] community. . . . Therefore, if it is permitted to kill innocent Muslims who are under coercion in order to protect the greater Muslim community, it is all the more so permissible to kill non-Muslims in order to liberate the land of the Muslims from its occupiers and oppressors.

Fifth, in modern war, all of society, with all its classes and ethnic groups, is mobilized to participate in the war, to aid its continuation, and to provide it with the material and human fuel required for it to assure the victory of the state fighting its enemies. Every citizen in society must take upon himself a role in the effort to provide for the battle. The entire domestic front, including professionals, laborers, and industrialists, stands behind the fighting army, even if it does not bear arms. Therefore the experts say that the Zionist entity, in truth, is one army.

Sixth, there are two types of *Fatwas*: *Fatwas* concerning a situation of calm and choice, and *Fatwas* concerning a situation of distress and necessity. It is permissible for a Muslim, when in a situation of extreme necessity, to do what is prohibited to him [in circumstances allowing] choice. . . . Thus, one of the clerics has espoused the rule: "Necessities permit prohibitions." Our brothers in Palestine are, without a doubt, in a situation of extreme necessity to carry out martyrdom operations in order to unsettle their enemies and the plunderers of their land and to sow horror in their hearts so that they will leave, and return to the places from whence they came. . . .

What weapon can harm their enemy, can prevent him from sleeping, and can strip him of a sense of security and stability, except for these human bombs—a young man or woman who blows himself or herself up amongst their enemy? This is a weapon the likes of which the enemy cannot obtain, even if the U.S. provides it with billions [of dollars] and the most powerful weapons, because it is a unique weapon that Allah has placed only in the hands of the men of belief. It is a type of divine justice on the face of the earth . . . it is the weapon of the wretched weak in the face of the powerful tyrant. . . .

Those who oppose martyrdom operations and claim that they are suicide are making a great mistake. The goals of the one who carries out a martyrdom operation and of the one who commits suicide are completely different. Anyone who analyzes the soul of [these two] will discover the huge difference between them. The [person who commits] suicide kills himself for himself, because he failed in business, love, an examination, or the like. He was too weak to cope with the situation and chose to flee life for death.

In contrast, the one who carries out a martyrdom operation does not think of himself. He sacrifices himself for the sake of a higher goal, for which all sacrifices become meaningless. He sells himself to Allah in order to buy Paradise in exchange. Allah said: "Allah has bought from the believers their souls and their properties for they shall inherit Paradise."

While the [person who commits] suicide dies in escape and retreat, the one who carries out a martyrdom operation dies in advance and attack. Unlike the [person who commits] suicide, who has no goal except escape from confrontation, the one who carries out a martyrdom operation has a clear goal, and that is to please Allah. . . .

A CONTRARY OPINION: SUICIDE BOMBERS ARE NOT MARTYRS

Following the bombing of Muhaya Residential Compound in Riyadh, Saudi Arabia, in November 2003, one of the three Shaikhs being held in custody for inflammatory preaching, Sheikh Nasser Al-Fahd, asked to go on TV to withdraw his previous fatwas.

He said the attack was a sin and the bombers were not martyrs because they violated Islam by killing both Muslims and non-Muslims under the state's protection, murdering women and children, harming security and wealth, distorting the image of jihad (holy war) and Islam, and "provoking enemies of Muslims."

"Blowing oneself up in such operations is not martyrdom; it is considered suicide. How can they kill Muslims, innocent people, and squander wealth in the country of Islam?"

Sheikh Nasser Al-Fahd told viewers that the merits of carrying arms in the name of jihad depended on the outcome. The Riyadh bombings, he said, had terrible consequences and were therefore wrong.

"We see the results, Muslims and innocent were killed, homes destroyed, Muslims terrorized. The judgment is clear."

Asked about Saudi youth trying to enter Iraq to fight U.S.-led forces, he said: "No, no, I don't agree. Fighting in Iraq is sedition. . . . They don't know who the killer is and who the victim is."

Sheikh Nasser Ibn Hamad Al-Fahd withdrew several fatwas (opinions) advocating militancy, describing them as "a grave mistake" in the interview broadcast on Saudi television.

Another of the three, Sheikh Ali Al-Khudair, had previously recanted on television. Sheikh Al-Khudair said the bombing of the Al-Muhaya Compound in Riyadh which killed at least 18 people including women and children had tarnished the image of Islam and harmed dawa work. He expressed his deep sorrow for issuing fatwas that incited terror attacks.

From Saudi Arabian Information Resources of November 23, 2003. Sheikh Nasser Al-Fahd recants and condemns suicide bombings in Riyadh.

He also withdrew fatwas he had issued declaring infidel Saudi thinkers Turki Al-Hamad, Mansour Al-Naqeedan and Abdullah Abusamh.

Sheikh Al-Khudair's statement signals a major turnabout in the attitude of scholars supporting Al-Qaeda, and observers expect other scholars to follow suit.

News of the interview with Al-Khudair, conducted by Sheikh Aaid Al-Qarni, spread quickly throughout the Kingdom. Al-Khudair had earlier issued edicts declaring attacks against Saudi security forces halal or permissible.

He had also praised the 19 terror suspects wanted by Saudi security authorities and acknowledged his relation with some of them. In the interview, Al-Khudair declared only rulers were in a position to declare jihad.

"It is not allowed to rise up against rulers unless they commit flagrant violations against Shariah," he said.

Appearing on Saudi state television, Sheikh Ali Al-Khudair said of his previous fatwas, or religious edicts, calling for attacks on the West: "If I had the choice I would not have said them. I hope that, God willing, I have time to correct them."

Al-Khudair also said the November 8 suicide bombing of a residential compound housing foreign workers—most of them Arabs—in Riyadh was "the work of criminals."

GLOBAL VOICES: ISSUES OF IDENTITY

Contemporary Muslim experiences globally reveal deep-seated tensions and issues of identity formation. The role of Islam and its relationship to culture, ethnicity, and pluralism continue to engage Muslim intellectuals and activists in predominantly Muslim countries and in the West. Tariq Ramadan emphasizes the need for Arabs and Muslims worldwide to move beyond attitudes of victimization and non-responsibility and to overcome the tendency to place all the blame for their political, economic, and social problems on the West.

Osman Bakar addresses the realities of globalization and the need for a civilizational pluralism in a multi-civilizational world. He examines the role of ethnicity in the Quran and the civilizational marriage of ethnicity and religiosity, using the Malay experience as a case study. Nurcholish Madjid, drawing on another Southeast Asian experience (that of Indonesia), examines the Quranic roots for religious pluralism, tolerance, and respect.

Integral to Islamic reform and Islamic civilization is the role of reason in Islam and the process of individual reasoning and reinterpretation (*ijtihad*). Muqtedar Khan revisits what he calls "the fear and skepticism in Islamic jurisprudence," which tend to limit reasoning to analogical reasoning, arguing for a new understanding of reason that goes beyond those that prevailed in the early centuries of Islam. Ali Mazrui places the discussion of the reinterpretation of Islam in light of expanding human knowledge in global perspective in terms of the struggle to reconcile faith and conscience as he dialogues with two friends in Canada and Kenya. He argues that just as God's prophets and revelations came incrementally in the past, so too "history is a continuing revelation of God."

TARIQ RAMADAN
1964–

Swiss-born professor of Islamic studies and philosophy, Muslim leader and activist, he taught at Fribourg University in Switzerland and at the University of Notre Dame. The revocation of his visa by the U.S. government, which then prevented him from taking up the distinguished Luce Professorship at Notre Dame, became an international issue. He is described by *Time* magazine as one of the one hundred most likely innovators of the twenty-first century and is the author of *The Muslims in a Secular Environment*, *To Be a European Muslim*, and *Western Muslims and the Future of Islam*.

The Arab World and the Muslims Faced with Their Contradictions

For almost a century the Arab world seems immobilised, rooted in its failures as much as in its divisions. No other region in the world has remained so rooted, nailed to its social, political and economic deficiencies to the point of suffocation. It is practically impossible, from Morocco to Iraq or in Saudi Arabia (and in the wider Muslim world), to find spaces where a truly free political opinion can be expressed, where economic well being exists for the majority of men and women, where literacy is the rule rather than the exception. And there is no upturn on the horizon; dictatorships are perpetuating themselves and taking on the appearance of dynasties (whether royal or republican) while the economic situation continues to deteriorate for the majority of people. A sad reality, a sad lot.

The temptation is high, in the heart of this reality, to blame the collapse on the Other, the exploiter, the rich, the West, and no bones are ever made about, throughout the Arab and Islamic world, eliciting all the arguments available to "explain" the situation this way. From old political colonisation to the modern forms of economic control, from the divisions maintained to the cultural imperialism imposed, from governments to multinationals who dictate their will to dominate from their Western base, the causes are clear and the situation understood: Muslims are suffering from a multi–faceted form of oppression.

While the policies imposed by the industrialised countries, the (de)regulation dictated by international institutions (IMF, World Bank, WTO) or indeed the murderous voracity of the Multinationals of the North should indeed be methodically criticised and denounced; to remain constantly routed in this argument of non responsibility and victimisation which has become the norm in the Muslim world is just not good enough. It is as if the constant incantatory and demonizing reference to the "Other," to "this West that oppresses and hates us," has become the only emotional and intellectual outlet that enables people to accept and justify their condition. Without much doubt, the key to the inaction and regression within the Muslim World might be found in the analysis of this attitude.

IN THE ARAB WORLD

The colonial era naturally saw the birth of numerous resistance movements who opposed the illegitimate foreign presence: some proclaimed exclusively nationalist ideals, others added or preferred a link with internationalism, socialism or communism while others were driven by Islam. The daily and tangible character of the domination meant the terms and objectives of any resistance became explicit: in one way or another, in Algeria, Tunisia, Egypt or in Syria, political freedom was sought. During the last 50 years, the situation has changed considerably and it must be admitted that the opposition movements as much as the general population have barely updated their analysis or renewed their strategy for the struggle against dictatorships and economic decline. The repression is certainly terrible and the run–down state of the economy very pronounced, but that cannot justify the passiveness, resignation and the lack of valid alternatives proposed: an alternative to the choice between violent opposition (the radical Islamist groups) or compromising resignation to the rules of the game imposed by the North, its financial institutions and its multinationals (a very watered-down take on "social democracy")[1] seems inconceivable.

Yet what is more serious are the divisions between the various opposition movements that the powerful are happy to exploit. The opposition movements, whether struggling in the name of socialism, communism or Islam, have to this day been incapable of seeing their struggle in terms of common fundamental values; demands for rights and citizenship, even in the terms of the cultural identity that they all share. The absence of dialogue between the leaders of the resistance movements and the repetition of old ideological arguments to the point of overdose are preventing the evolution and renewal of critical thought in the Arab and Muslim world. Political projects are sadly lacking, strategies for resistance are muddled, critical debates are pathetically old and superficial. To which one has to add, a patent lack of communication and explanations that really take into account the reality of the Western world, its own questions and fears. As

1. In order to be accepted on the international scene, even those known as the "democratic Muslims" or the "moderate Islamists" in Turkey have had to yield to the requirements of the structural adjustment programs imposed by the IMF.

a result, the Arab world appears divided and in particular isolated in relation to its difficulties as much as to its hopes, and the blame lies first and
foremost with its political classes as much as with its intellectuals.

If one listens in on the dominant views of Arab society, one thing
becomes immediately clear: the cause of all woes is "Israel." Nothing
works, it is thought, since the creation of the Zionist state: war, division,
people suffering and dying, like the Palestinians. The unconditional support
of the US to Israel as well as the absence of political courage from the
EU confirms in the eyes of the majority the relationship that the West
maintains with the Arabs and the Muslims. That is, a relationship founded
on domination, manipulation, rejection, even hatred. While it must be
stressed that if the Palestinian question *is a* central issue (for the Middle
East as well as in the consciousness of all Muslims), it cannot serve as
an alibi. The oppression of the Palestinian people, without land or state,
and the arrogance of successive Israeli governments, who have adopted a
rampant policy of occupation by its colonisers and well equipped forces,
are more and more revealing of the dysfunction of the Arab world than the
causes of that dysfunction.

The spectacle that we are offered by the leaders of the Arab world, for
the most part autocratic, divided to the point of sheer madness, loving of
their own power alone, valets for the financial manna of the industrialised
countries, pawns in their game, deaf to the cries of their own peoples and,
deep down, indifferent and opportunistic toward the Palestinian cause,
is pathetic. The people themselves have fallen into this trap that is the
overbearing influence of the Palestinian question: for every serious crisis,
the day after new massacres, a wave of emotion mobilises them for a time
and permits them to express their frustrations, but one sees absolutely no
structured thought about change. The powers that be are happy to simply
control the street and its passions: no overall vision of reform, no regional
political project, no popular national or trans-national movement to break
up their cosy political base. From Sabra to Chatila to Jenine, a lot of
emotion yet so little political vision: for how long?

The Palestinian question should be seen as a part of the problem.
It translates into a desire for national liberation, demanding a legitimate
political independence and seems to remain the model for engagement and
the demands of the majority of resistance movements in the Arab world.
Yet one hardly hears anything about the nature of the economic stakes, the
logic of neo-liberal globalisation, the ways of forming a multidimensional
and trans-national form of resistance.

While at the state level, all attempts at building economic alliances have
failed (such as the "grand Maghreb"[2] or the G8 of the Muslim countries),
one can only note the failure of Muslim resistance movements to take into
account the international dynamics of the global justice movement. Not

2. Great North Africa.

only are partnerships practically nonexistent on a national level (between the different movements and above and beyond religious, agnostic or atheist affiliations), but the void has become the norm in relations between the countries of the South and on a wider international level. Politically nourished from within national realities, cultural resistance ends up being only a demand to be different. In the face of a globalisation that wipes it out, the Arab-Muslim world seems only motivated by a hope for a political and cultural liberation which would supposedly protect its local particu- larities (Islam, cultures, languages etc): the expression of this hope in itself reveals the level of the lack of understanding of contemporary issues.

THE MUSLIMS OF THE WORLD

The absence of a world vision for change is at the same time the cause and the consequence of a very restricted understanding of what is resistance and of a view of Islam void of its universalism. The paradox is deep and the circle has become vicious: in fact, in Muslim conscience, Islam should be lived as a universal reference point that, because it is not presented as being exclusive, invites and forces the individual to recognise and build with and from diversity. However, the feeling of being dominated and isolated that prevails today leads the majority of Muslims to construct themselves by affirming their "otherness." They are incapable of relating to the universal dimension of their principles that would enable them to build bridges with the Other (with another civilisation, culture, religion or philosophy) and to bring to the fore, out of respect for what is different, common fundamental values. The latter are numerous and even if their source (revelation or reason) or expression is different (expressed out of the primacy of responsibility or on the contrary of right), that should not legitimate an absence of dialogue and partnership. Besides it is this absence that downstream reinforces the tendency to define oneself in opposition to the "other" and leads to the impasse that betrays this universal (Islamic) outlook by hiding behind domination and closing oneself off.

The immediate consequence of adopting this posture is the elaboration of a caricaturist view of the other. It is never repeated enough how often the view of the West is superficial, confused and largely mistaken. The difference between governments, peoples and institutions is rarely made; the legitimacy of the values of the West is denied by way of a denunciation of their deficient and hypocritical application and in the end its culture is rejected as a result of a partial, overly simplified criticism of its domination. What is troubling is that this theoretical rejection is itself contradicted in practice on a daily basis by attraction to the Western way of life. This contradiction is said to be illustrative of the nature of the crisis of con- science that faces the contemporary Muslim world; incapable of defining itself other than in the negative image of a caricaturised West, one ends up feeling that they have betrayed themselves every time they find themselves living the values of the other. These are explicit symptoms of a profound alienation.

We can better understand the difficulties that the Muslim world faces today when we try to explain ourselves and communicate better. To tell one's values, one's demands, one's hopes has become a challenge. Either we insist on the essence of our common values and we give the impression to most people of betraying ourselves or we insist on difference and we reinforce the sense of differentiation and of inevitable conflicts. To remain oneself, communicate with the other and to have the confidence to take on the idea of "us" is an experience Muslims often don't have the means to live today. The problem is profound and its origins can be found firstly in the disappearance of a cultural dialogue between Muslims themselves. The law schools, streams of thought, ulemas and intellectuals have practically ceased debating and we hardly progress beyond a discussion about the Islamic legitimacy of ideas. An often nervous, blighted intellectual discussion ends up forbidding itself the right to self-criticise because to do so would be seen as treachery. The logic stays the same: to recognise the validity of the other's criticism is to be or to become unfaithful to oneself. Muslims will not find the energy to renew and reform if they cannot seek to escape from this harmful logic. Self criticism, for example, by denouncing the behaviour of some so-called Islamic states, to distinguish oneself from the acts of certain radical or obtuse Muslim groups, to recognise the weaknesses of contemporary Muslim thought as well as its unacceptable discrimination (towards poverty, women, certain minorities, etc) is a vital first step.

At this point it has to be said that a certain number of Muslims whom one would have hoped to push forward reforms have, on the contrary, slowed down, even prevented their realisation. At the heart of the contemporary crisis, we find Muslim intellectuals who are torn from their Islamic ideals or who live with such a need for acceptance by the West that they end up, in the name of a self criticism gone astray, simplifying the debate and comforting the West in its dominant certainties, whether about its caricatures or its ancient and indeed contemporary suspicions. Far from creating a bridge between two worlds, they implicitly deny the legitimacy of one of the partners to speak about its universal principles. Acknowledged and envied in Western intellectual circles, they have often lost all legitimacy amongst Muslims, but what is more serious is that certain amongst them have become objective allies of the most obtuse Islamaphobes. Yet another paradox of this period of crisis which forces us to identify the nature of criticism: who is talking and from where? In the name of what? And, fundamentally, why?

ENCOURAGING SIGNS

The outlook is not all bad: studies and work on the ground carried out in recent years in the Arab world, Africa and Asia as well as within Muslim groups in Europe and North America, have shown signs of significant change. The younger generations from Dakar to Djakarta are beginning to "connect" to the world. The new means of communication are beneficial in that they enable more and more exchanges of information and experiences. In virtual contact with international resistance movements, and more and more in alignment with the dynamics of the West, Muslims of the world are seeing their horizons broaden and the possibility for partnerships. Alternatives have been experimented with in Indonesia, Malaysia, Bangladesh and in numerous Muslim countries in Africa, such as the creation of small to medium sized businesses or development co-operatives, practically unheard of in the West. Enough is not said about the importance of the participation of Western based Muslims in the alter globalisation movement; by remaining true to themselves, to the universal dimension of their message and its principles, while building ties with the fundamental dynamics of Muslim countries, establishing diversified partnerships, they open the way to a new perception of the self and will in time be able to go beyond the old divisions.

Those who are engaged in the struggle know full well that the road will be a long one, that labels and suspicions remain the norm. But it is up to them to face up to their responsibilities at this time when new partnerships are being forged. It is up to them, allied to the forces of the South, to develop a global vision of reform[3]; it is up to them to take up the universality of Muslim values and to set the terms for an *equitable dialogue* with the West; it is up to them to finally engage in a demanding and fruitful internal debate where constructive self-criticism is permitted. Their responsibilities are immense and we are only at the beginning of the journey: for the Muslim conscience it means that the political liberation of Jerusalem, occupied by another, cannot make us forget the need for an ideological, economic, and political liberation of Mecca by our own wanderings, alienated and betrayed.

3. The international symposium of Muslims in the francophone world (CIMEF), which brings together various intellectuals and associations from Canada, Africa and Europe, has been working on this for more than 3 years. The debates that ensued during its first meetings were about, amongst other things, a reformist understanding of Islamic principles, secularism and globalisation after 11 September 2001.

OSMAN BAKAR
1946–

Born and raised in Petaling Jaya, Malaysia, Osman bin Bakar was educated in Malaysia, at London University, where he obtained his B.Sc. and M.Sc. in mathematics and received his doctorate in Islamic philosophy from Temple University in America. He served as the Deputy Vice Chancellor/Vice President of Academics and the first (1992) holder of the Chair of the Professor of Philosophy of Science at the University of Malaya (Kuala Lumpur). From 2000 to 2005 he was the holder of the Malaysia Chair for the Study of Islam in Southeast Asia in the Center for Muslim-Christian Understanding at Georgetown University. Among his publications are *The History and Philosophy of Islamic Science, Islam & Civilizational Dialogue, Tawhid & Science*, and *Classification of Knowledge in Islam: A Study of Islamic Philosophies of Science.*

Islam and the Malay Civilizational Identity: Tension and Harmony Between Ethnicity and Religiosity

INTRODUCTION

Following the fateful encounter centuries ago between an Islam that was globalizing itself to the furthest corners of the earth and the Malay race long known for its openness to cultural influences both from its east and its west, a new Malay civilizational identity was born. The objective of this inquiry is made necessary by the contemporary concern for the future of the world's multi-civilizational character. This concern is expressed in the form of questions that raise doubts about the direction in which our global order is presently moving. Are we reaffirming the principle of civilizational pluralism or are we abandoning it? Are we advocating dialogues of civilizations in pursuit of global peace or are we promoting clashes of civilizations that will lead to global chaos? Apparently, in the past several years there has been a lot of talk going on all over the globe on the subject of dialogues, conflicts and clashes of civilizations. But to the dismay of many people, one major consequence of the September 11 tragedy, itself advanced in certain circles in the West as convincing proof that a clash

Reprinted by permission of the author.

of civilizations has already taken place, the nascent global movement for dialogues of civilizations is losing momentum while the more localized movement in America for clashes of civilizations appears to be gaining momentum and dangerous influence in the corridors of power.

We maintain the position that dialogue of cultures and civilizations is a moral virtue worth pursuing and defending at all times and in all kinds of situations no matter what happens to the world. We may even venture to claim that dialogue of cultures and religions has become an imperative in our day. In Islamic religious terminology, such dialogues have become *fardu kifayah*, meaning a societal obligation to be fulfilled by individuals and groups capable of delivering success to these dialogues. If the study of Malay civilizational identity could contribute to the contemporary global discourse on dialogue of civilizations, it is because it affirms at least three things. Firstly, Malay civilization is a major world civilization in its own right. Secondly, it is a major branch of the global Muslim civilization. Thirdly, the historical shaping of the Malay identity contributed by many cultures and civilizations provided an excellent instance of Islam the religion fulfilling the very purpose of its existence, namely a civilizational synthesis out of diverse cultural elements guided by the principle of *tawhid* (unity).

A SPIRITUAL ANTHROPOLOGY: THE PLACE AND ROLE OF ETHNIC IDENTITY

Certainly the Qur'an's spiritual anthropology is as much interested in the division of humans into spiritual types as in the division of the human species into racial and ethnic groups. In this discussion we are primarily interested in the later division but focusing on its civilizational significance. The Qur'an has emphasized this anthropological fact but with a spiritual bias in the following terms: "O humankind! We created you from a single (pair) of a male and a female, and made you into nations and tribes that you may know each other. Verily the most honored of you in the sight of God is the most righteous of you. And God has full knowledge and is acquainted (with all things)."[1] In maintaining that there is a definite purpose to the diversity and pluralism in the ethnic composition of humankind, the Qur'an has accorded a religious legitimacy to the place and role for ethnic consciousness and identity in the organization of human society and the global community. Having an ethnic consciousness and identity is something natural to human beings. Because of the natural human tendencies to be attached to one's ethnic group, ethnicity is one of the natural principles of human social organization. Islam which claims to be regulating human life in conformity with the nature of things would be the last to say that ethnic loyalty is necessarily opposed to the universal goals of religion. Far from seeking to abolish ethnic feelings and identity from the human consciousness, which would be practically impossible, Islam prefers giving

1. *The Qur'an*, Chapter 49, Verse 13.

recognition to their usefulness in serving religion's higher spiritual and moral purpose as embodied in the above quoted Qur'anic verse.

Islamic perspectives on the meaning and function of ethnic identity are perhaps best summed up by the Qur'anic verse earlier cited. The verse rationalizes the existence of ethnic identities and proposes the only sane way they can coexist peacefully in the world. The main purpose of ethnic pluralism is not the cultivation and affirmation of ethnic particularism for its own sake and glory but the fostering of inter-ethnic and inter-cultural acquaintance and understanding directed to serve a universal purpose that is ultimately divine. By and through "knowing one another" as envisaged by the Qur'an, ethnic groups and nations would be moved to go beyond ethnocentrism to embracing a spiritual universalism. What does the Qur'an mean by "knowing one another"? The Qur'an does not explain, but the philosophical meaning of the verse helps us to grasp the intended objects of this mutual knowledge and understanding. Philosophically what the verse is telling us is that God has created multiplicity and diversity out of unity, and He wants to lead multiplicity and diversity back to unity. This is precisely the divine purpose in the creation of both the natural and human worlds. Originating from the first human couple, God has created the human family, which has grown into a large tree with a multitude of ethnic branches. Each ethnic branch possesses an identity of its own with its specific characteristics that distinguish it from other branches. Consequently, the ethnic branches, each possessing a kind of soul and collective consciousness, are able to know one another.

The Qur'an looks upon both languages and ethnic identities as among the wonders of creation. Further, the Qur'an maintains that God has sent a messenger to every nation and the divine message brought was always in the language of his folk. These teachings of the Qur'an make it quite clear that an Islamic anthropology worthy of its name would be interested not only in the scientific significance of the variety of human languages and ethnic groups but also in their spiritual significance. By knowing one another in the deepest sense of the word, the ethnic branches will come to understand the true purpose of them having ethnic identities. Their goals are to acknowledge both their commonalities and differences and to recognize what these signify for inter-ethnic living. The commonalities are the universals that need to be strengthened and the differences are the particulars that need to be respected. What are these commonalities? The Qur'anic verse under discussion mentions the most important of them. First, we have a common human ancestor. Second, in consequence of the first, all ethnic groups form branches of the same human family tree. Third, we are all God's creatures answerable to Him. Fourth, our worth and dignity as humans before God are evaluated on the basis of our piety and righteousness and not our ethnic origins. The science of anthropology would reveal many more commonalities, but this issue is not our concern here. If the Qur'an has mentioned only those commonalities, it is primarily because humans tend to forget easily or belittle those facts and thus need to be reminded of their importance and true significance.

What are the particulars that differentiate the ethnic branches from one another? The same Qur'anic verse mentions only one of them, namely as a broad category consisting of the specific characteristics that define their ethnic identity. Of course, if we are to itemize these characteristics, we may end up with a good number of them. Physical characteristics, language, customs, culture, and manners are to be counted among the most important of them. Even the religion an ethnic group has embraced may be domesticated by its defining characteristics so as to produce a new religious culture unique to its geographical region.

ETHNICITY AND RELIGIOSITY
IN A CIVILIZATIONAL MARRIAGE

Islam claims to be the last of the divinely revealed religions and also the only religion to have explicitly stated from its very beginning it has been sent to the whole of humankind. According to Prophet Muhammad, all prophets of God before him had been sent to specific peoples, meaning that their respective messages from Heaven have likewise been targeted at specific audiences. He alone had been given a universal message meant for the whole world. What actually happened in history had turned out to be quite different. A few religions like Judaism and Hinduism and Taoism continue to be identified exclusively with specific ethnicities, Judaism with the Jewish people alone, and Hinduism overwhelmingly with the Indian race and Taoism with the Chinese. Some others have grown to become world religions identified with many ethnic groups. Interestingly, religions in this category like Buddhism and Christianity have become minority religions in their own respective birthplaces but found their largest concentration of followers in far away lands, the former in the Far East and the latter in Europe and the Americas. From the point of view of ethnic complexity that characterizes the global demographic makeup of each of the world religions, Christianity and Islam stand out prominently above the rest. These two sister religions in the Abrahamic family are the only real world competitors for adherents. . . .

Religions which have adherents scattered in numerous ethnic groups have manifested themselves in a variety of forms producing all kinds of local cultures with a religious coloring. Conversely, an ethnic group that over time has overwhelmingly opted to embrace a new religion finds itself deeply immersed in the complex process of cultural fusion. The process involves all the things that usually go into the working of what I call a civilizational marriage between ethnicity and religiosity. In conformity with the ideals and the code of practical conduct favored by the new religion, an ethnicity may have to discard some of its old beliefs and practices deemed no longer reconcilable with the new. It is obvious that conversion always necessarily involves the acceptance of new beliefs and practices. However, for the most part the process is not about discarding the old for the new, but about reconciling the old with the new, reinterpreting the old in the light of the new with the view of producing a new cultural synthesis.

As all marriages go, it is about partnerships in the pursuit of certain goals in life. In the case of civilizational marriages of the kind with which we are interested here, the partners are an ethnic branch and a religion. This marriage between an ethnicity and a religiosity will have its cultural offspring. Clearly, the success of the marriage calls for the inter-play of two geniuses, an ethnic genius and a religious genius. The quality of such marriages tends to vary with ethnicities and religiosities. Talking about the performances of Christianity and Islam in such marriages in history, no less an authority than Arnold Toynbee, a leading modern authority on civilization studies, has made the observation that Islam had achieved a far greater success than Christianity. This essay does not permit us to go into a detailed discussion of this very important issue, especially in the light of many Christians in America depicting Islam as an evil religion. However, since the issue of success in question has relevance to our discussion of Malay Islam as a civilizational marriage between Malay ethnicity and Islamic religiosity, we will say a few words about the Islamic genius which we think explains Islam's relative success in overcoming racism and maintaining inter-ethnic harmony within its own cultural boundaries as well as in the preservation of indigenous cultures. A major portion of that genius has already been discussed at length when we talk about Islam's legitimization of ethnic identities. Another aspect of the Islamic genius pertains to its ability to produce orderly and peaceful cultural fusions and cultural synthesis as history has witnessed it in so many instances. One such instance, and indeed a major one by world standards, was the Southeast Asian historical phenomenon of a cultural synthesis between Malay ethnicity and Islamic religiosity that was to produce what may be legitimately called Malay Islam.

MALAY ISLAM: THE MARRIAGE BETWEEN
MALAY ETHNICITY AND ISLAMIC RELIGIOSITY

A heavenly religion like Islam needs earthly instruments such as in the form of ethnicities in order to become a living reality in the lives of human beings and in the ordering of human societies. For that reason, Islam has come to sanctify the role of ethnicities in civilization building. It was the destiny of the Arabs to become the first ethnicity to enter into a civilizational marriage relationship with Islam. This is not to say that Islam has become completely Arabised to emerge into a purely Arab religion that somehow will later be followed by the non-Arabs. Two things have guaranteed that there will always be an objective and an ideal Islam that is not to be exhausted by one interpretation such as the Islam as understood and practiced by the Arabs. One is the Qur'an whose original content is preserved to every word and every letter until the end of the world. The other is the Prophet's own life or Sunnah which has an intrinsic value that transcends space and time in serving as a practical model to be emulated by every generation of Muslims anywhere on earth. The Prophet may be an Arab, but as a universal model for all believers coming from numerous ethnic branches, his Sunnah is one from which the elements of Arabness have been detached though the boundaries are not always clear to many people.

Apart from these two guarantees, the expansion of Islam beyond the Arabian Peninsula was swift like lightning as if in a hurry to dispel any illusion that it is purely an Arab religion. A new major ethnicity entering the fold of Islam was the Persians. The Malays were a later addition, more than six centuries after the Arab conversion to Islam. Like the Persians, the Malays had quite a rich pre-Islamic civilization as a result of extensive encounters and interactions with Hindu and Buddhist civilizations. Before Islam, the Malays had entered into a civilizational marriage with Hinduism and later Buddhism. Considering this fact, the Malays' conversion to Islam entailed for them the complex process of re-evaluating their pre-Islamic heritage and establishing an ethical-legal system and socio-political order in the light of the new religion, and creating a new cultural synthesis. Syed Muhammad Naguib al-Attas has termed this process *Islamization* which he has divided into an earlier phase dominated by jurists and theologians and a later phase dominated by the Sufis.[2] Al-Attas' identification of the two phases of Islamization is of relevance to our discussion of the emerging Malay-Islamic civilizational identity.

An important question to ask in this connection pertains to the beginnings and the formative period of Malay-Islamic civilization. When can we identify the beginning of this new civilization, and what was the dominant element of Islam that shaped its formative period? It seems safe to say that there is some sort of a universal pattern according to which regionalized Islamic civilizations have been founded and developed in different parts of the world. Everywhere whenever Islam was to develop and grow into a distinct civilization, it began with the organization of its followers into a religious community in accordance with its revealed laws collectively termed the Shari'ah. The beginning of Islam as a civilization may be identified with the founding of the first Muslim community in Medina following the Prophet's *hijrah* to the city from Mecca. In Medina laws for the new community had been revealed in stages. The Prophet had also established a socio-political order with clear guidelines for inter-faith living and cooperation for the city-state's different religious communities who as fellow citizens were to have common rights and responsibilities. It was here that seeds of the new civilization were sown. It is therefore justifiable to identify the beginning and formative period of Islamic civilization with the establishment of the Shari'ah.

---

2. Syed Muhammad Naguib al-Attas, *Preliminary Statement on a General Theory of the Islamization of the Malay-Indonesian Archipelago* (Kuala Lumpur, 1969).

In the case of Malay-Islamic civilization, its beginning and formative period may be identified with the founding and growth of the first Malay-Muslim kingdom in Pasai at the turn of the thirteenth century. If jurists and theologians had flourished in the royal courts during this formative period as witnessed by the famous medieval world traveler Ibn Battutah and as asserted by al-Attas, it was because they were the experts in the much needed Shari'ah. Many things old and new—beliefs, practices, and institutions—had to conform to the requirements of the Shari'ah including the feudal system of kingship. Objections may be raised that the Shari'ah is hardly compatible with such a political system. But the traditional Malay ulama generally took the position that it was acceptable in the context of the time as long [as] nothing stood above the Shari'ah, the rulers included. Tensions between the new legal thought and the local *adat* needed to be resolved as well, and to a large extent harmonization had been achieved. When Islam spread to the other islands in the Archipelago and new centers of Muslim power were established, this phase of Islamization repeated itself to varying degrees of fervor and success.

A civilization is not complete until the cosmos, the arts and the sciences, and literature have also been cultivated in the light of its world-view, epistemology and value-system heralding the birth of a new intellectual tradition. Thus we have the later phase of Islamization that was to be dominated by the Sufis. They were mainly the ones who had undertaken the task of resolving the conceptual overlappings and confusions between the old and new ideas such as pertaining to cosmological and eschatological beliefs. The pre-Islamic Malay cosmos seen mainly through the prism of an Olympian Greek-type mythology in its decadent stage was gradually Islamized. Thanks to the metaphysical doctrines and a profound spiritual knowledge in their possession, the Sufis were intellectually and spiritually well equipped to deal effectively with the problems posed by pre-Islamic Malay mysticism. As was generally true of Sufism in the rest of the Muslim world during the period of Muslim history under consideration, the Malay Sufis also excelled in literature and dominated the cultivation of the traditional arts and sciences. At the level of ideas, the center and the peak of the Malay-Islamic intellectual synthesis was the seventeenth century Aceh.

TENSION AND HARMONY BETWEEN
ETHNICITY AND RELIGIOSITY

Generally speaking, the traditional Malays under Islam had achieved considerable success in creating harmony between ethnicity and religiosity in practically every branch of civilization. Malay-Islamic civilization was very much a living reality with an identity that clearly distinguishes it from both the pre-Islamic Malay civilizational identity and other branches of the global Islamic civilization. It is an undeniable fact that tensions in one form or another have always existed between Malay ethnicity and Islamic religiosity during the past seven to eight centuries of their civilizational marriage. This is only to be expected since both ethnicity and religiosity have their demands and needs. However, it is to the credit of both the ethnic genius of the Malays and the spiritual genius of Islam that over the greater part of the civilizational domain, harmony has prevailed to this day.

Various factors may upset the delicate balance that a particular culture and civilization has attained between ethnicity and religiosity. Due to both external and internal factors, perceptions, understandings and appreciations of religiosity may change such as those brought about by new interpretations of the religion. In response to the various forces and phenomena that seem to challenge its civilizational identity, an ethnic-religious based culture may take various measures aimed at preserving and strengthening that identity. It is also possible that identity itself is thoroughly examined even to the point of unintentionally creating a civilizational crisis. In the modern period, we can see some of these factors at work such as the large-scale entry of Chinese and Indian immigrants to Malaysia under British colonial rule. It was under the perceived threat of this flooding of immigrants to the Malay-Islamic civilizational identity that the Malays sought a political protection through the Federal constitution upon the country's independence. The constitutional definition of Malay in Islamic terms needs to be understood in the light of the centuries old Malay-Islamic civilizational identity that is responding to the challenges of the modern world.

NURCHOLISH MADJID
1939–2005

Born in East Java, Indonesia, into a family of Islamic scholars, Nurcholish Madjid received his early education at his father's madrasah (school) and Darul Ulum *pesantren* (school). He completed his Quranic studies, along with English and secular subjects, at Pondok Modern "Darus Salam" Gontor in 1960 and received a B.A. in Arab literature in 1968 at Syarif Hidayatullah, Jakarta, Indonesia. A prominent student activist leader, Madjid served as the General Chairman of the Indonesian Muslim Students Association from 1966 until 1971, President of United Islamic Students of Southeast Asia, and assistant to the Secretary General of the International Islamic Federation of Students Organization. In 1978 Madjid went to the United States, where he earned a Ph.D in Islamic studies at the University of Chicago in 1984.

A gifted and prolific writer and charismatic speaker, Nurcholish Madjid became a prominent and respected voice for Islamic reform. His support for pluralism and democracy made him a prominent public intellectual in both Indonesia and the broader Muslim world. In addition to founding Paramedina Foundation, a major reform organization, and serving as the Rector of Paramadina Mulya University in Indonesia since 1998, he was also a member of the Indonesian National Commission for Human Rights and many international organizations.

Islamic Faith and the Problem of Pluralism: Relations Among the Believers

Almost all universal religions, particularly those with a great number of followers (Islam, Christianity, Hinduism and Buddhism), have adherents in Indonesia. This makes Indonesia, as Indonesians themselves usually acknowledge, a plural society. Also, Indonesians often proudly refer to the high degree of the religious tolerance they have. Given this situation, they even consider themselves unique among the nations in this world. And one—if not the most important—fundamental factor that is considered to contribute to this positive situation is *Pancasila* (Five Principles), the ideology of the nation. . . .

Nurcholish Madjid, *The True Face of Islam* (Voice Center Indonesia, 2003).

Actually, the plurality in Indonesian society is not unique. Particularly during the modern era, in practice there is no society that is not unique in terms of having different groups of believers (consisting of a great number of religious followers), except in certain cities like the Vatican, Mecca, and Medina. Even in Islamic countries in the Arab World, which were formerly the centers of Christianity and Judaism, the significant religious minorities of Christians and Jews have remained there up until now. In fact, those countries developed into the countries in which Muslims became the majority citizen, only after they had undergone a long natural process of Islamization, which took place for centuries. Though it appears that the Arab Muslims managed to liberate those countries when they brought Islam with them, what they actually carried out was socio-political reforms. One of the most important reforms was the affirmation of religious freedom, instead of the compulsory conversion of non-Muslim subjects into Islam (which would certainly oppose the basic principles of Islam).

The only exclusivist policy is that non-Muslims are not allowed to live in the compounds of Mecca and Medina (Hijâz). This policy, which was initiated by 'Umar ibn al-Khattâb, was expanded by the Wahhâbî Saudis, who established modern Saudi Arabia. Apart from these two compounds, however, Christian and Jewish minorities still can be found in almost all Islamic countries. This can be explained not only from the historical and sociological points of view, but also more fundamentally from the perspective of Islamic doctrine. It shows the consistency of Muslim societies in practicing the Islamic teachings on religious plurality.

CONCEPTS OF THE ONENESS AND THE TRUTH

Deeply rooted in the consciousness of the Muslim worldview is that Islam is a universal religion, a religion for everyone. It is true that this awareness also belongs to believers of other religions (the Jews deny the universal validity of Christianity and Islam, and Christians deny the universal validity of Judaism and Islam). However, it is only fair to say that for Muslims, this awareness bears with it a socio-religious attitude that is unique, which is very different from the attitudes of other religious believers, except since the beginning of the twentieth century.

Without depreciating the depth of Muslim faith regarding the truth of their belief (an attitude that will necessarily be held by a believer of any religious system), the unique attitude of Muslim believers in relation to other religions is characterized by tolerance, freedom, transparency, justice, fairness and honesty. To date, these principles have been quite clearly observable in the contemporary Muslim societies, but quite phenomenally so in the classical Muslims (salaf). The basic principles are derived from teaching points in the Holy Book which explain that the universal Truth is naturally one, though the physical manifestations of it may vary. Additionally, anthropology explains that in the beginning man was one, because man held onto the truth, which is only one. But later this view started to differ because many interpretations of the oneness of the truth developed. These differences became sharper because of certain vested interests, that is, the desire of certain groups to succeed at the expense of others. The unity of the origin of human beings is visualized in God's saying: "All mankind were once but one single community, and only later did they begin to hold divergent views," and His saying:

> All mankind were once one single community; then God raised up the prophets as bearers of glad tidings and of warnings, and with them revealed the Scripture with the truth, that it might judge between mankind concerning that wherein they differed. And only those unto whom (the Scripture) was given differed concerning it, after clear proofs had come unto them, through hatred one of another. And God by His leave guided those who believe unto the truth of that concerning which they differed: for God guides unto a straight path him that wills [to be guided].

The starting point of the oneness of the universal truth is the concept of God as One or *tawhîd* (which literarily means "to believe in One"). From the beginning of their existence, humans professed *tawhîd*, which is symbolized both in Adam and by his faith. Adam is considered the first human and the first prophet and messenger on earth by the Semitic religions (Judaism, Christianity, and Islam). Certainly the empirical truth of this proposition requires comprehensive and scientific anthropological research. For this reason, it is no wonder if there is one research confirming this proposition of the Holy Book, as enthusiastically expressed by Muhammad Farîd Wajdî, a Muslim thinker from Egypt, a follower of Muhammad 'Abduh's renewal movement at the beginning of the twentieth century, concerning a finding of a scholar:

> The activities of the Orientalists in India should be regarded as a part of their brilliant achievements. We should not forget that the most prominent among them is Dr. Max Muller, a German anthropologist, whose greatest contribution was deciphering Sanskrit. Dr. Muller proved that human communities in earlier times already adopted a pure monotheism, but the idolatry which prevailed among them was the result of the acts of the religious leaders who competed against one another. Therefore the result of Dr. Muller's research justifies the truth of the scientific miracle of the Qur'ân. It is so because there are definite texts in the Qur'ân (the texts which are quoted above—NM) regarding the matter which was finally discovered by Dr. Max Muller through his research and study.

The most important consequence of pure *tawhîd* is the complete submission or self-surrender to God the One, without doing the same for any other purpose, object, or person except Him. This is *al-islâm*, the essence of all true religions. The following is an explanation by Ibn Taymîyah, a famous figure of Islamic reform:

> The (Arabic) word "al-islâm" contains the meaning of the words "al-istislâm" (self-surrender) and "al-inqiyâd" (submission, obedience) and also contains the meaning of the word "al-ikhlâs" (sincerity). . . . Therefore it is necessary in Islam to submit oneself to God the One, leaving behind submission to others. This is the essence of our saying, "There is no god but God" (lâ ilâh illa 'l-Lâh). If one submits to God, while at he same time submitting himself to others, then he is a polytheist.

Therefore, it is emphasized in the Qur'ân that the tasks of God's messengers are to deliver the teachings of God the Almighty or *tawhîd* as well as the teachings regarding man's obligation to obey God alone:

> We never sent any apostle before you [O, Muhammad] without having revealed to him that there is no god save Me, therefore worship Me [alone].

Since the principles taught by the messengers and the prophets are the same, the followers of them are one single community. In other words, the concept of the unity of the basic teachings lays a foundation for the concept of the unity of prophecy, which then brings about the concept of one faithful community. This is affirmed by God's saying:

> Verily, this community of yours is one single community, since I am the Sustainer of you all. Therefore worship Me [alone].

It has been mentioned by Ibn Taymîyah that the word *al-islâm* carries the meaning of the words *al-istislâm* (self-surrender) and *al-inqiyâd* (submission, obedience). From the formal aspect of religious obligation, this is expressed in the act to worshiping nothing but the One, that is, God. Briefly and in conclusion, *al-islâm* teaching in the generic sense is the core and the essence of all religions of the prophets and the messengers. Ibn Taymîyah states:

> Because the origin of religion, that is *al-islâm*, is one, even though its *sharî'ah* varies, the Prophet Muhammad says in valid hadiths, "Our religion and the religion of the prophets is one," and "All the prophets are paternal brothers, [even though] their mothers are different," and "The nearest of all the people to Jesus, the son of Mary, is me."

From this perspective, we begin to understand better the description in the Qur'ân that to hold on to any religion except *al-islâm* or to devote oneself without total submission and surrender to God is not genuine and is therefore illegitimate. What I would like to argue here is that although someone may be socially dubbed "Islamic" or "Muslim," if their attitude is not *al-islâm*, they are categorized religiously as ingenuine and are denied legitimacy Affirmation of this in the Qur'ân is found in the famous saying of God: "*The only true faith in God's sight is* al-islâm." For a comparative study regarding the meaning of Islâm, the following is the complete translation of the verse by Muhammad Asad, one of the best-known modern commentators on the Qur'ân:

> Behold, the only [true] religion in the sight of God is [man's] self-surrender unto Him (al-islâm); and those who were vouchsafed revelation aforetime took, out of mutual jealousy, to divergent views [on this point] only after knowledge [thereof] had come unto them. But as for him who denies the truth of God's messages—behold, God is swift in reckoning!

If we look at the above verse carefully, the implication is that the former communities who received scriptures from God through His messengers and prophets, namely, those were technically called Ahl al-Kitâb (People of the Book), did know and understand that the core of the true religion is the act of total submission to God, which is the original meaning of the Arabic word islâm. On this matter, Muhammad Asad writes:

> Most of the classical commentators are of the opinion that the people referred to are followers of the Bible, or of parts of it—i.e., the Jews and the Christians. It is, however, highly probable that this passage bears a wider import and relates to all communities which base their views on a revealed scripture, extant in a partially corrupted form, with parts of it entirely lost.
>
> . . . All these communities at first subscribed to the doctrine of God's oneness and held that man's self-surrender to Him (islâm in its original connotation) is the essence of all true religion. Their subsequent divergences were an outcome of sectarian pride and mutual exclusiveness.

RELIGIOUS PLURALITY

Given the principles above, it can be argued that the Qur'ân essentially teaches the concept of religious plurality. To be sure, this does not necessarily mean an affirmation of the truth of all religions in their actual practices (in this respect, many of the actual religious practices of the Muslims are not correct because they basically contradict the teachings of the Qur'ân, such as their practice of deifying other human beings or creatures, whether they are dead or alive). However, the teaching of religious plurality emphasizes the basic understanding that all religions are free to be practiced, yet the believers, individually or collectively, have to be responsible for their practices. This attitude can be interpreted as an expectation of all religions: because—as mentioned above—all religions initially upheld the same principle, that is, the necessity of man to submit totally to God the One, those religions whether due to their internal dynamism or their encounter with one another, would eventually find their own original truth, leading them all to "one meeting point," "a common platform," or using the Qur'ânic term, "kalîmah sawâ," as indicated by one of the God's commands to the Prophet Muhammad:

Say: "People of the Book, let us come to an agreement (*kalîmah sawâ'*): that we will worship none but God, that we will associate none with Him, and that none of us shall set up mortals as deities besides God."

For a comparison, the following is Asad's translation of the verse:

Say: "O followers of earlier revelations! Come unto that tenet which we and you hold in common (*kalîmah sawâ'*): that we shall worship none but God, and that we shall not ascribe divinity to aught beside Him, and that we shall not take human beings for our lords beside God."

Because of the parallelism between the attitude to "worship none but God" and the concept of *al-islâm* in terms of its generic meaning explained by Ibn Taymîyah (that is, before *islâm* becomes the proper noun for the Prophet Muhammad's religion), thus the meeting point for all religions is *al-islâm* in that generic sense. In other words, the total and genuine submission to God the One, without association to anything else, is the only correct and true religious act. Thus others are denied and hence the affirmation in the Qur'ân:

He that chooses a religion other than *islâm* (self-surrender to God), it will not be accepted from him and in the world to come he will surely be among the losers.

Besides the generic meaning of *al-islâm* as mentioned above, A. Yusuf Ali makes a very pertinent comment:

The Muslim position is clear. The Muslim does not claim to have a religion peculiar to himself. Islam is not a sect or an ethnic religion. In its view all religion is one, for the Truth is one. It was the religion preached by earlier Prophets. It was the truth taught by all the inspired Books. In essence it amounts to a consciousness of the Will and Plan of God and a joyful submission to that Will and Plan. If anyone wants religion other than that, he is false to his own nature, as he is false to God's Will and Plan. Such a one cannot expect guidance, for he has deliberately renounced guidance.

From the original meaning of the term *al-islâm* described above, we begin to gain a better understanding regarding the following God's saying:

Verily, those who believe [in this divine writ], as well as those who follow the Jewish faith, and the Christians, and the Sabians—all who believe in God and the Last Day and do righteous deeds—shall have their reward with their Lord; and no fear need they have, and neither shall they grieve.

The immediate understanding regarding this quote is that believers, be they Muslims, Jews, Christians or Sabians, as long as they believe in God and in the Judgment Day (on which day man will be accountable in God's court, and on which day God will deal with everyone personally), and based on their belief and their good deeds, will be guaranteed to "go to Heaven" and be "free from the fire of Hell."

The above-quoted verse interested many *tafsîr* experts and produced much controversy. For some it is difficult to reconcile this verse with the common view that everyone who denies the Prophet Muhammad is "*kâfir*" (an infidel), that "the infidels shall not go to heaven," and that they "shall not be free from the fire of Hell." Therefore, one of the *tafsîr* books which is considered as a standard reading material in Indonesian *pesantrens*, that is, *Tafsîr Baydâwî*, explains that those "who shall have their reward with their Lord; and no fear need they have, and neither shall they grieve" are:

> Those among [the followers of earlier revelations] who had believed in God and the Day of Judgment and done righteous deeds in their respective religions before their religions were abrogated (*mansûkh*), and within their hearts they had confirmed the starting point (*al-mabda'*) and the final destination (*al-ma'ad*), and acted according to their religious laws. There is also another view [that holds that this verse refers to]: whoever they are from the infidels who have sincerely attuned to faith and truly converted to *al-islâm*.

Meanwhile, as a comparison, Yusuf Ali gives a different interpretation of the verse by saying: "As God's Message is one, Islam recognized true faith in other forms provided that it be sincere, supported by reason, and backed up by righteous conduct." This comment is very much in line with the explanation given by Muhammad Asad:

> The above passage—which recurs in the Qur'ân several times—lays down a fundamental doctrine of Islam. With a breadth of vision unparalleled in any other religious faith, the idea of "salvation" is here made conditional upon three elements only: belief in God, belief in the Day of Judgment, and righteous action in life. The statement of this doctrine at this juncture —that is, in the midst of an appeal to the children of Israel—is warranted by the false Jewish belief that their descent from Abraham entitles them to be regarded as "God's chosen people."

In other words, according to Muhammad Asad, the above God's saying affirms that anyone, whether they be a descendant of the Prophet Abraham, like the Jews (and Quraysh in Mecca), or not, can obtain salvation as long as they have faith in God and Judgment Day, and they do good deeds. This certainly correlates with God's explanation to the Prophet Abraham when he was taken to be the leader of humankind and when Abraham asked pleadingly: "And what of my descendants?" Then God replied, "My covenant does not apply to the evil-doers." It is clear that salvation is awarded not based on factors of descent, but based on faithfulness to God and the Day of Judgment, and the carrying out of good deeds. This is a principle that is much emphasized in the Qur'ân.

Furthermore, regardless of the different interpretations above, the above God's saying, in its relation to various principles explained in many other of His sayings, has created a unique attitude of Muslims in the face of other religious believers. This is the attitude based on the awareness of religious pluralism, tolerance, openness, and fairness, as apparently shown in the history of Muslims. This principle is reflected in the concept of the "People of the Book" (Ahl al-Kitâb).

The Jews and the Christians are often mentioned in the Qur'ân. As is obvious from God's sayings above, the Sabians and the Zoroastrians are mentioned as well. Further, the concept of the "People of the Book," both in Islamic political history—as in the Mogul Empire in India—and in the explanations made by some 'ulamâ', is extended to include other groups who have a holy book. In this regard, Yusuf Ali, for example, doubts whether those who call themselves Sabians and lived in Harran, North Mesopotamia, can be grouped as "People of the Book" because they were Syrian star-worshippers who belonged to Hellenistic society. However, Yusuf Ali believes that the concept of "People of the Book" can be extended "to cover earnest followers of Zoroaster, the Vedas, Buddha, Confucious and other teachers of moral law." The following is his complete explanation:

> The pseudo-Sabians of Harrân, who attracted the attention of Khalifa Ma'mûn al-Rashîd in 830 AD by their long hair and peculiar dress, probably adopted the name as it was mentioned in the Qur'ân, in order to claim the privileges of the People of the Book. They were Syrian star-worshippers with Hellenistic tendencies, like the Jews contemporary with Jesus. It is doubtful whether they had any right to be called People of the Book in the technical sense of the term. But I think that in this matter (though many authorities would dissent) the term can be extended by analogy to cover earnest followers of Zoroaster, the Vedas, Buddha, Confucious and other Teachers of moral law.

This point of view correlates with that of Muhammad Rashîd Ridâ', a famous Islamic reformer from Egypt, whose opinion was cited by 'Abd al-Hamîd Hakîm, a figure of Sumatran Thawalib from Padang Panjang, Sumatra. According to 'Abd al-Hamîd Hakîm, Rashîd Ridâ' was once asked about the marriage law between a Muslim male and a polytheist female, and he answered:

> The polytheist women whom God forbids (Muslims) to marry within a verse of the sûrah al-Baqarah are the Arabic polytheist women. This is the view that is chosen and much supported by the prominent tafsîr expert, Ibn Jarîr al-Tabarî; and that the Magians, the Sabians and the idolaters amongst the Indians, Chinese and Japanese are the followers of the holy books containing monotheism (tawhîd) up until now.

The view that the "holy books" belonging to the Indians, the Chinese and the Japanese contain the teaching of monotheism is still a bone of dispute among the experts. However, if those "holy books" are understood in terms of "their original version or teaching," then such a view is in line with the "finding" of Max Muller, supported by Muhammad Farîd Wajdî, cited above. Rashîd Ridâ' and 'Abd al-Hamîd Hakîm argue that based on the description in the Qur'ân, God sent a messenger to each community. Some of the messengers were described and some were not, and their duties were to deliver the same teaching of monotheism. For this reason, 'Abd al-Hamîd Hakîm affirms that:

> Essentially, the difference between us (Muslims) and the People of the Book is like the difference between the monotheists who are pure in their religious attitude toward God and act in accordance with the Qurân and the Sunnah on the one side and those who make unlawful innovation (bid'ah) on the other, straying from both (the Qurân and the Sunnah), which were left to us by the Prophet Muhammad.

Having described the principles above, it is clear to me that Islam teaches the attitude to behave inclusively within society, which acknowledges that a society's plurality is caused among others by the religious plurality of its members.

OPENNESS, RESPECT AND TOLERANCE

As pointed out previously, apart from the Mecca-Medina compounds, the Islamic world has witnessed the significant non-Muslim minority groups. The existence of these groups has been a proof of the openness, respect and tolerance of Muslims, from the classical time to the present. Muslims, as clearly seen from their (pure) religious teachings, are the mediators (Ar. wâsit) among many groups of people, and are expected to be the fair and just witnesses to all groups. This is the reason why the classical Muslims were so open, inclusive, and encouraging of other groups while they were in power. In this regard, it is interesting to consider the following long quote from Max I. Dimont, an expert of the Jews history, who wrote about the Jews experience in the classical Muslim society:

> When the Jews confront the open society of the Islamic world, they are 2,500 years old as people. . . .
>   Nothing could have been more alien to the Jews than this fantastic Islamic civilization that rose out of the desert dust in the seventh century. Yet nothing could have been more the same. Though it represented a new civilization, a new religion, and a new social milieu built on new economic foundations, it resembled the packaged "intellectual pleasure principle" presented to the doors of Hellenistic society to them. Now Islamic society opened the doors of its mosques, its schools, and its bedrooms for

conversion, education, and assimilation. The challenge for the Jews was
how to swim in this scented civilization without drowning, or in the
language of modern sociology, how to enjoy the somatic, intellectual, and
spiritual comforts offered by the dominant majority without disappearing
as a marginal minority.

The Jews did what came naturally. They fired the old scriptwriters and
hired a new set of specialists. Instead of rejecting the Muslim civilization,
they accepted it. Instead of keeping themselves apart, they integrated.
Instead of becoming parochialized fossils, they joined the new swinging
society as sustaining members. Arabic became their mother tongue; wine,
women, and secular songs their pastime avocations; philosophy, mathematics, astronomy, diplomacy, medicine, and literature, their full-time
avocations. The Jews never had it so good.

I include this long quote to illustrate how transparent the classical
Muslim society was, to the point that even the Jews, who are often
mentioned rather cynically in the Qur'ân, still could enjoy the Islamic
civilization. Besides Dimont, other experts on Jewish civilization also admit
that the Jews experienced their Golden Age under Islamic civilization.

For those who understand the concept of "Islamic spirit," Dimont's
description is nothing unusual. Part of the mission of the Prophet Muhammad
was to proclaim Islam as God's mercy for all. Therefore, regarding the
relationship with believers from other religions, God told the Muslims to
be kind and fair to those who are not oppressive:

> God does not forbid you to be kind and equitable to those who have
> neither made war on your religion nor driven you from your homes. God
> loves the equitable. But he forbids you to make friends with those who
> have fought against you on account of your religion and driven you from
> your homes or abetted others to drive you out. Those that make friends
> with them are wrongdoers.

In this regard, Yusuf Ali gives an explanation on the spirit of the verse:

> Even with Unbelievers, unless they are rampant and out to destroy us and
> our Faith, we should deal kindly and equitably, as is shown by our holy
> Prophet's own example.

In line with that, God decrees the faithful not to be involved in the
unhealthy disputation with the People of the Book, except to those who try
to inflict wrongdoing:

> And dispute ye not with the People of the Book, except with means
> better [than mere disputation], unless it be with those of them who inflict
> evildoing: but say, "We believe in the revelation which has come down to
> us and in that which came down to you; Our God and your God is one;
> and it is to Him we [all] surrender ourselves."

The principles discussed above serve as the basis of a great number of political policies of religious freedom in the Islamic world. The principles of religious freedom in the classical Muslim society are similar to modern ideals. It is even not exaggerating to suggest that religious freedom in the modern times is a consistent advanced development of that of the classical Islam. An example of the practices of religious freedom during the classical period of Islam was reflected in an agreement between 'Umar Ibn al-Khattâb and the people of Jerusalem or Bayt al-Maqdis, al-Quds (it was also called Aelia), after that holy city had been liberated by Muslim soldiers. The following is a complete translation of the agreement:

> In the name of God, the Most Compassionate, the Most Merciful.
> This is the guarantee of safety granted by the servant of God, 'Umar, the Commander of the believers, to the people of Aelia (al-Quds):
> He guarantees their personal safety, and the safety of their belongings, their churches and crosses—whether they are in a good or a bad condition —and for all their co-religionists. Their churches shall not be seized or damaged, and nothing shall be taken from their churches or from their property, nor shall their crosses or even the smallest possession be removed from their churches. They shall not be harassed because of their religion, and none of them shall be harmed. No Jew will be allowed to live with them in Aelia.
> The people of Aelia will have to pay a poll-tax (*jizyah*) as the inhabitants of other cities (in Syria) do. They have the authority to expel from Aelia the Romans and brigands (*al-Lasût*). Those (of the Romans) who leave shall be granted safety for themselves and their belongings until they reach a safe destination, and those among them who want to stay shall be safe on the condition that they pay the *jizyah* like the people of Aelia. If any of the people of Aelia want to leave with the Romans, take their belongings with them, and leave behind their churches and crosses, they and their churches and crosses shall be protected until they reach their own place of safety (Byzantium). Those among the local inhabitants (the Syrians) who have been in the city (Aelia) since before the war (i.e. the war in which Syria was liberated by the Muslim soldiers—NM) shall have the option of either staying on condition that they pay the *jizyah* like the people of Aelia or if they so wish, they shall be allowed to live with the Romans or go back to their original homes. No tax shall be collected front them until they have gathered their harvest (i.e. they are able to pay it—NM).
> This writing is placed under the guarantee of God and the covenant of the Prophet, of the caliphs, and of the believers, on condition that the people of Aelia pay their due tax.
> Witnessed by: Khâlid ibn al-Walîd, Amr ibn al-'Ass, 'Abd al-Rahmân ibn 'Awf, Mu'âwiyah ibn Abî Sufyân. Written in the year 15 (Hijrîyah).

The agreement between 'Umar and the people of Jerusalem was actually consistent with the spirit of the agreement that the Prophet Muhammad had made with the people of Medina, including the Jews, immediately after he returned from Mecca during the Hijrah (migration). This agreement was later known as the Medina Charter. Modern scholars are very impressed with it because it is the first official political document that put forward the principles of religious and economic freedoms. Moreover, the Prophet made a particular agreement that guarantees the freedom and safety of the Christians at all times and in all places. In order to get a brief overview of the agreement, the following is a quote from the first part of the agreement made by the Prophet:

> In the name of God, the Most Compassionate, the Most Merciful, and from Whom comes all help. This agreement was written by Muhammad ibn 'Abd Allâh, the messenger of God.
>
> To all Christians,
>
> This is the document for humankind written by Muhammad ibn 'Abd Allâh, as a bearer of glad tidings and of warnings, as a holder of God's trust for His creatures, so that man shall have no reason against God after (the coming of) God's apostles, as God is the Most Exalted and the Most Wise.
>
> This is written for the followers of Islam and those who adopt Christianity from the East and the West, near and far, Arabs and non-Arabs, the known and the unknown, a document made by him (the Prophet) as a covenant for them (the Christians).
>
> Whoever violates the agreement in this document, deviates from it, and disobeys what has been stipulated, then spoils God's agreement, breaks His covenant, insults His religion, which will result in a curse upon him, whether he is a ruler or not among the Muslims and the Believers.
>
> If a priest or a traveler takes shelter in a mountain or in a valley or in a cave or in a building or in a desert or in a church, I am behind them to protect them from any hostility towards them, by my soul, my supporters, the holders of my religion, my followers, as they (the Christians) are my citizens and under my protection.
>
> I will protect them against anything that displeases them according to the obligations placed upon the supporters of this covenant, that is, to pay the *jizyah* (the poll-tax), except those who are *musta'min* (i.e. those who are treated as non-residents, and therefore are exempt from paying tax—NM).
>
> They (the Christians) shall not be forced or coerced. There shall be no change to their buildings, or to their monasteries, or to their shrines, or to their surroundings. No building within their synagogues or churches shall be demolished, nor shall the property of their churches be taken to build mosques or houses for Muslims. Whoever commits such things breaks God's covenant and opposes His messenger.

Such is the way the Prophet Muhammad provided the example of how to live life according to one of the Islamic ideals, which is brotherhood among human beings with faith in God. As mentioned above, the Muslims have the obligation to bring as many people as possible to God's way in order to achieve their ideals. However, acts should be in accord with the soul and the spirit of the ideals of brotherhood; hence God Himself reminded the Prophet and all of the believers that to force others to accept the truth is not right. The faithful have been commanded to accept the plurality of human society as a reality as well as a challenge.

MUQTEDAR KHAN
1966–

Born and raised in India where he earned a degree in engineering and an MBA, he later received his doctorate in government and international relations from Georgetown University in 2000. On the faculty at the University of Delaware, he is the author of *American Muslims: Bridging Faith and Freedom, Jihad for Jerusalem: Identity and Strategy in International Relations*, and the forthcoming *Islamic Democratic Theory: Theory Philosophy and Debates*. His website is www.ijtihad.org.

Reason and Individual Reasoning

The term "ijtihad" itself means to strive hard. But it has been widely used to imply independent reasoning in the development of Islamic jurisprudence. The contemporary understanding, shared widely by formally trained Islamic jurists, defines ijtihad as an intellectual tool that seeks to articulate Islamic laws about issues on which the Quran and the Sunna are decidedly silent. This standard and orthodox conceptualization of ijtihad theoretically limits the role of reason to analogical thinking on mundane matters, even though most Islamic thinkers do use reason quite judiciously in the interpretation of revelation. The point that is often ignored in discussions of ijtihad, its meaning, role, scope and functions, is that the conceptualization of ijtihad itself is the product of ijtihad. The development of the *'usul al-fiqh*, the principles of jurisprudence, and the systematic articulation and rank ordering of the sources of Islamic Law—Quran, Sunna, ijma, ijtihad, *'urf* and *maslaha*—are all products of an ijtihad much wider in scope than its standard understanding. In a remarkably curious development, a conceptually wider process of ijtihad has spawned a rather meek theory of ijtihad.

Taking a second look at the discussion between Imam Shafii and his interlocutor on the Quranic sources of ijtihad,[1] one is amazed at how Imam Shafii is able to build a whole theory out of a single verse. We are turning to Imam Shafii because he has arguably left the most enduring and unshakeable impact on the structure of Islamic legal thinking and in particular on the theory of ijtihad. In his response to the question, "Is

---

1. See Imam Shafii, *Risala*, trans. Majid Khadduri (Johns Hopkins University Press, 1961), pp. 295–303. All references to Imam Shafii are from this book.

Reprinted by permission of the author.

ijtihad permitted in the Quran?" Imam Shafii derives the instrument from only one verse of the Quran and then supports it with just one other.

> Turn then thy face in the direction of the Sacred Mosque: wherever you are turn your faces in that direction. (2:144)

> It is He who maketh the stars for you, that you may guide yourself with their help. Through the darkness of land and sea. (6:97)

The first verse invites the individual to figure out the direction of the Holy Mosque and the second essentially confirms the role of reason in this process. Indeed, the second verse in an interesting way suggests that independent reasoning can also be seen as grasping nontextual indications from Allah, and the following quote from Imam Shafii himself confirms this:

> God, glorified and praised be He, has endowed men with reason by which they can distinguish between differing viewpoints, and He guides them to the truth either by texts or by indications. (p. 302)

The Quran is full of verses that repeatedly invite and exhort believers to use their reason, to reflect and to use their observation to read the signs of Allah in order to understand the divine law (7:176, 10:24, 30:8, 30:21, 34:46, 39:42, 59:21, 45:13, 3:191; for the text of these verses see footnote).[2] It is mystifying why these direct invitations to use reason were not used by the great scholar to explain ijtihad and instead he used verses which required a considerable degree of deductive reasoning to justify and validate his point. For example, the full text of the second verse that Imam Shafii uses has awesome potential:

> It is He who maketh the stars for you, that you may guide yourself with their help. Through the darkness of land and sea. *We detail Our signs for people who know.* (6:97)

The part that the great Imam left out, presented in italics, to my mind is a clear indication that there are great details that can be inferred from

2. Text of Quranic verses cited in the editorial:

> Tell the tale so that they may reflect (7:176).
> Thus do We explain the signs in detail for those who reflect (10:24).
> Do they not reflect in their own minds? (30:8).
> Verily in that are signs for those who reflect (30:21), (39:42).
> And reflect (within yourself) (34:46).
> Such are the similitudes which we propound to men so that they may reflect (59:21).
> In that are signs indeed for those who reflect (45:13).
> And contemplate the creation in the heavens and the earth (3:191).
> We have, without doubt, sent down the message; and We will assuredly guard it from corruption (15:9).

Allah's signs. What the traditional scholars can dispute is the methodology of eliciting those details. For the mystics these details have to be gleaned through gnostic experiences. For the theologian they may be confined only to the Sunna. But I insist that reason can provide us deep understanding of the details in God's signs (10:24). The enormous knowledge and details about Allah's creation accumulated by natural sciences can only be a realization of this Quranic prophesy. I believe that the great Imam did not include the implication of the rest of the *ayah* in his discussion of ijtihad because the formative scholars, in my understanding, did not see ijtihad as a function of human potential for rational thought, but rather as human interference in the legislation of divine law. This can be easily understood since the term "ijtihad" was used only when reason was exercised to articulate aspects of the law and not when conducting scientific research or even when advancing political theories—an exercise eminently fraught with danger and prone to error. Therefore, they sought to minimize human participation in the articulation of the Sharia to the minimum—to only those issues about which the sources are silent.

The use of reason within Islamic jurisprudence has a curious quality to it. The argument that only when one does not find injunctions in the Quran and the Sunna on a particular issue can we turn to reason to seek divine indications suggests that reason does not play any role in discerning these same principles and laws from the Quran and Sunna. Indeed, this suggestion is explicit since the process of understanding Islamic principles from the Quran and Sunna is said to depend more on linguistic sciences than on reasoning. The process of divining principles and laws from texts and relating it to the present context is deemed as an exercise that depends solely on the knowledge of language and historical context (*asbab al-nuzul*). The role of reason in this process is not recognized. It is supposed to be a constant in the equation, even though the fact that differences in interpretation are imminent is accepted and has led to the development of different *madhahib* attests to the inevitable role of individual reasoning in discerning the Sharia. What, if not reason, is the cause for differences in understanding if the grammar of the language as well as historical contexts are already agreed upon?

I think that the theory of ijtihad is also an implicit theory of reason. It does not completely acknowledge the critical function of reason in cognition and understanding. Indeed, it is one of the reasons why reason came to be seen as an alternative to revelation by later Muslim scholars. As if the sacred texts and reason are two different sources of truth, the former infallible and the latter imperfect. Reason is invoked only if texts are silent. And if the texts have spoken, then reason must be silenced. The general rumor that the door of ijtihad has been closed gained ground after the early scholars declared the process of Sharia development complete, which meant that the texts had now spoken on all issues possible and therefore ijtihad and reason were of no use to Muslims. Because the theory of ijtihad does not recognize the cognitive aspect of reason, it does not realize that texts are inaccessible without reason. *Texts can speak only through reason and to reason.* Without it they are silent. This major oversight has made scholars of Sharia and fiqh suspicious and even afraid of reason. It was seen as a source of impurity, as a means of human dabbling in things divine, therefore needing to be tamed and confined. Thus reason came to be understood not as an essential cognitive human process without which no intelligent task was possible, but as a peripheral source to be accessed rarely and with caution. It is from here on that reason became exogenous to revelation and then a competitor and even a threat to the integrity of revelation.

The significance, even the primacy that the Quran attaches to reason, is easy to understand. It is constantly appealing to human reason to recognize and understand the true meanings of life. The Quran does not appeal to humanity's linguistic skills or to its history (except as illustration), but appeals to its cognitive capacity to convey the divine message. Yet when it comes to codifying this message, and that is the role of jurists, reason and its potential are astonishingly minimized by scholars. In an ironic way, one can argue that the theory of reason implicit in the theory of ijtihad is a transgression. It places institutional barriers between the receptacle (reason) and the message (Quran). The various stipulations in the theory of ijtihad about when, how, and who can conduct it are clearly products of free thinking that merely reflect the fears of the scholars and their distrust of reason. None of these stipulations about the qualifications of the mujtahid and the reduction of the role of reason to analogical reasoning can be derived from the Quran or the Sunna.

The widely quoted Hadith about how the conversation between the Prophet Muhammad (pbuh) and the companion who was appointed Governor of Yemen, which acts as the traditional source for ijtihad, does not describe his qualifications.[3] We can only surmise that the individual was a companion, trusted by the Prophet and deemed worthy of public/political office. But the standards developed later stipulate that before an individual can do ijtihad, he must have the knowledge of Islam, Sunna, fiqh, and *'usul al-fiqh*. He must be able to differentiate between authentic and spurious *ahadith*, between *hadith al-hasan* and *hadith al-da'if*, he must know the principles of ijma, the injunctions of *qiyas*, must be aware of the verses of the Quran that are considered as abrogated by some scholars and so on and so forth, not to mention pious, pure, and above reproach.[4] One wonders if the companion deemed fit by the Prophet to do ijtihad as governor of Yemen will be considered fit by the jurists. In other words, can the jurists add to what the Prophet has stipulated? Are they allowed to institute innovative conditions prompted by their fears of

3. *Sahih Muslim*, hadith no. 976.
4. For a list of qualifications of a *mujtahid*, see Hasbullah Haji Abdul Rahman, "The Origin and Development of Ijtihad to Solve Modern Complex Legal Problems," in *Hamdard Islamicus*, xxi, 1 (January–March 1990), pp. 8–9.

reason? Indeed the hadith itself does not exclude any Muslim from using his/her personal judgment. I am confident that the jurists cannot produce even a single Quranic verse or an authentic hadith which can exclude any Muslim from exercising his/her own reason to understand Islamic texts and to extrapolate on issues about which the sources are silent.

There is another interesting element to the theory of ijtihad. It is discourse dependent. The theory and practice of ijtihad have meaning only within the discursive universe of the jurists. It is and has been an issue only for the self-styled articulators and arbitrators of Islamic law. Other Muslim intellectuals, scholars, scientists, and philosophers have not been too concerned with the theory, or with the closing or opening of the doors of ijtihad. One does not see Ibn Khaldun too concerned with whether ijtihad is allowed or not, whether he is qualified to practice it or not. Similarly other major Muslim thinkers like Ibn Rushd, Ibn Arabi, not to mention philosophers like Ibn Sina and Al-Farabi, felt free to use their reason on all matters including those that impinged on Sharia issues. A possible reason for this is that while the philosophers were keen that society in general become enlightened and capable of independent thought, the jurists sought to confine the power/right to think to a select few, supposedly in the interests of guarding the authenticity of the Islamic message—an unnecessary caution since Allah (swt) has Himself promised to guard and protect his message (15:9). In many ways, the theory of ijtihad is a disciplinary tool that seeks to establish the sovereignty of a particular type of scholarship and discourse over how Islam is understood. Those thinkers who choose to challenge or ignore it have often been labeled heretic or at least outside the "legitimate core."

We are not really concerned with a reformulation of the theory of ijtihad. The purpose of this discussion is to place the evolution of the theory in perspective and rescue reason from the prisons of this theory and restore it to its Quranic glory. Reason, as Imam Shafii himself suggests, is Allah's greatest gift to humanity. Without reason the human agent is nothing but a beast incapable of conceiving or realizing his/her divine purpose. Reason is the singular element that constitutes the human and enables everything else. Even the Quran needs reason to make itself available to us. Without humanity's cognitive faculty and without the underlying rationality in the Quran that makes it a consistent and understandable message, there would be no direct connection between God and his vice regent.

The limitation of reason in the theory of ijtihad has had an adverse effect on the very theory of knowledge in Islam. The epistemological dilemma of using reason for practical and other purposes such as medicine, while circumscribing it in Islamic studies in order to conserve legal thinking, has led Muslims to reach and maintain mutually contradictory positions. For example, nearly all Muslim thinkers, particularly those grounded in the Islamic traditions and genre, maintain the unity of knowledge as a fundamental epistemological truth. These same Muslims continue to maintain a stated or implicit boundary between secular and sacred knowledges. Reason reigns in the former while the latter is supposed to be ruled by revelation. Indeed, traditions and metaphorical thinking masquerade as revelation in the realm of sacred knowledge. The most significant consequence of this double-think has led to the decline of both forms of knowledges in the Muslim World. There is no doubt in my mind that the decline or rather stagnation of Islamic thought in all realms is due to the leash that the *fuqaha* have placed on reason.

The fear and skepticism of reason in Islamic jurisprudence are difficult to understand. Reason is as much from God as is revelation. Indeed, Imam Shafii's allusion to "indications from Allah" is a nice way of describing reason. Perhaps it is through reason that Allah is actively involved in the lives of his creation. It is important for the revitalization of Islamic civilization that the relationship between reason and revelation be properly understood. They are not ontologically similar to be compared. To place reason and revelation in opposition to each other is silly, to say the least. Revelation is a source; reason is a tool. The sources of the Sharia are like *data* that need to be processed into *information* that can be used in specific conditions. The activity of processing general data into particularized information is carried out by reason. Thus while reason on its own is empty, revelation without reason is inaccessible. Thus reason and revelation are inseparable. Rather than competing, they complement and strengthen each other.

In conclusion, we must remember that the theory of ijtihad is operating with a very narrow conception of reason and therefore the limits it poses on individual reasoning cannot stand up to critical scrutiny. Reason is much broader and more vital in scope than analogical reasoning or as a tool of jurisprudence—it is *essential* to understanding. Therefore, if Islamic civilization is to be based on an understanding of divine principles, it must first make itself comfortable with reason and the widespread use of individual reasoning. Our understanding of reason and its potential has grown far beyond the rudimentary conceptions of reason prevalent in the formative years of Islamic jurisprudence. Importantly, with the advent of the scientific age, reason has clearly demonstrated its power and its centrality to knowledge production; indeed, to the very process of perceiving, understanding, and negotiating reality. It is time we saw what the Islamic legal understanding of reason is: a limited conceptualization reflecting the politics and fears of a particular era. It is time we opened the doors of ijtihad not just to allow individual reasoning in legal issues, but to make reason one of the central arbiters in all issues. There is no dichotomy between reason and revelation. Revelation without reason is meaningless, and reason without revelation can be content-less. Both are essential to help us decipher Islamic rules for our times.

ALI A. MAZRUI
1933–

Born in Kenya, he studied at Manchester University in England (B.A.) and Columbia University in New York (M.A.), and he earned his doctorate at Oxford University. An expert on Africa and Islam in Africa, he has authored more than twenty books and hundreds of articles. Mazrui is Director of the Institute of Global Cultural Studies and Albert Schweitzer Professor in the Humanities, State University of New York at Binghamton; Andrew D. White Professor-at-Large Emeritus, Cornell University; and Chancellor, Jomo Kenyatta University of Agriculture and Technology, Kenya. His many publications include *The Africans: A Triple Heritage*, *Governance and Leadership: Debating the African Condition*, and *Cultural Forces in World Politics*.

Human History as Divine Revelation: A Dialogue

A MUSLIM IN SEARCH OF NEW ANSWERS

Let me elaborate a little on my e-mail to Rafii of July 23, 2003. I was explaining to Rafii what were the grounds for reinterpreting Islam in the light of changing circumstances and expanding human knowledge.

The reason why Islam recognizes so many prophets (*nabiyyun*) and so many messengers or apostles (*rusul*) is because Allah reveals himself in installments across time and across space. The Prophet Muhammad was the last prophet (*nabii*), but was he the last messenger (*rasul*)? Let us accept that he was also the last *rasul* in the form of a human person. But could *Time* be a continuing cosmic *rasul* or at least *risala*? Is history a continuing revelation of God?

If God reveals Himself incrementally, and if history is a continuing revelation of God, should we not re-examine the message of Muhammad in the light of new installments of Divine Revelation? The early Muslims of the first century of Hijra would not have understood much about distant galaxies. So Allah talked to them in simple terms about our own moon (as if it was the only moon) and about the sun in the Milky Way (as if it was the only sun). Fourteen centuries ago the Arabs were overwhelmed by the Almighty as the creator of our own universe. Today we know that what

From a dialogue between Ali A. Mazrui in the U.S.A., Muhammad Yusuf Tamim in Canada, and Rafii Abdalla Salim Shikely in Kenya, July–August 2003.

God created was a billion times greater than that. Should we not reinterpret the verses about the sun and the moon in the Qur'an in the light of our new understanding of astronomy?

If we need to reinterpret Qur'anic verses about astronomy, why can we not reinterpret Islamic verses about ancient punishments (*hudud*)? The expansion of human knowledge is not only about the stars. It is also about human beings themselves and their behaviour. If we now know more about the causes of crime, we also know more about the limits of culpability and guilt. We know that poverty, bad parenting, a sense of injustice, racial discrimination, chemical imbalance in the human body, a bad neighbourhood and bad social environment can all be contributing factors towards turning a human being towards crime. In recent times God has been telling us that Satan is not the only source of evil. Societies often create their own Satans.

From these conclusions I proceed to the belief that some verses of the Qur'an were about events during the Prophet's own time and other verses were eternal in purpose. I illustrated with the verses about Abu Lahab ("father of the flame"). I believe the Prophet's contemporaries knew that the verses were about the Prophet's uncle Abd al-Uzza bin Abdul Muttalib. In the Prophet's own time it was understood that the verses were about a *specific individual enemy of Islam*.

I like your efforts to reinterpret "Abu Lahab" in a more timeless fashion. You are doing precisely what I am recommending—reinterpreting Qur'anic verses in ways which would give them a timeless relevance.

The Sudanese theologian Mahmood Muhammad Taha had argued about the two messages of Islam—the time-specific message and the eternal. The Nimeiry Government executed the old man in 1985 in the name of Islamic *hudud*. Please read Taha's book, *The Second Message of Islam* (Northwestern University Press—originally written in Arabic).

If God has been teaching human beings in installments about crime and punishment, and if there were no police, prisons, forensic science, or knowledge about DNA fourteen centuries ago, the type of punishments needed had to be truly severe enough to be a deterrent. Hence the *hudud*. Since then God has taught us more about crime, its causes, the methods of its investigation, the limits of guilt, and the much wider range of possible punishments.

Did the Prophet Muhammad say, "My people will never agree on error"? If so you can take it for granted that Muslims of the future will *never* agree that the amputation of the hand is a suitable punishment for a thief under any circumstances. I have predicted that. Please tell your grandchildren that I predicted that. Tell them long after I am dead and gone. I have not the slightest doubt that the Islam of your grandchildren will never include penal amputation of the hands of thieves.

I know you think highly of the *Sahaba*. We revere them as the first converts to Islam and as supporters of our prophet (pbuh). But we must not forget that the *Sahaba* were not themselves *prophets*; most of them were not even *saints*. As ordinary human beings they were the usual mixture of vices and virtues. That is why three of the first of Islam's four Caliphs were assassinated. That is also why there was an Arab civil war within little more than a decade after the Prophet's death—with the Prophet's widow Aisha fighting the Prophet's cousin Ali! This was not saintly behavior! Have we been idealizing the *Sahaba* too much?

ON PUNISHMENT AND PIETY

If you have not yet read my annual letter 27 (early 2003), please turn to the section about the death penalty. It should be obvious from that section why I do not think that a verdict of "guilty" in a death penalty case is enough to justify execution. The experience of Illinois demonstrates how wide the margin of error can be. Hence the relevance of forensic evidence like finger-printing and now DNA. And even now we still make mistakes on whether the accused is guilty even if the accused confesses.

If a serial killer is really proven guilty, I do not think that we should kill him in order to save the tax payer's money. I do not believe in killing human beings as an economy measure. Executions as a budgetary device are not to be recommended.

Supposing you were an Islamic judge dealing with cases of adultery, have you considered how many of your closest relatives you would be forced to execute if they were found guilty of adultery? To my knowledge I shudder to think how many of my loved ones in Mombasa qualify for execution under the *hudud* if these are not reinterpreted. I would rather leave their punishment to God rather than to the state.

You keep on asking what our expanding knowledge of the galaxies has to do with the death penalty. You completely misunderstood my e-mail to Rafii of July 23. The summarized five points were not about the *hudud* alone. I was explaining to Rafii why it was necessary to reinterpret Islam *generally*—not just its ancient punishments. I was explaining to Rafii where I was coming from paradigmatically.

Rafii now wants me to write a book about theology; you, on the one hand, feel that I am not qualified. You are both right. The history of knowledge reveals two basic methods of argument. One is by reference to authority (Abu Hureira or At-Tabari); the other is from reason and logic. I may be strong on reason and logic, but I am still weak on traditional Islamic authority. You are right. The march of Islamic knowledge requires both shoulders of authority and the gift of independent reasoning. Your maternal grandfather combined both forms of analysis, may he rest in peace.

You say Islam is pro-science. Muslims have not been pro-science for hundreds of years. That is why we are left behind. How many Muslims have won the Nobel Prize for medicine, chemistry, physics or economics? Please check from any major encyclopedia—like the Britannica. Contrast that with how many Jews have won the different categories of the Nobel

Prize. There are more than a billion Muslims in the world, and less than twenty million Jews.

You may feel that the Nobel Prize is not a good measurement of scientific excellence. Well, which inventions of the modern world come from Muslim scientists? The conquest of the small pox? The battle against malaria? The control of hypertension? The invention of the steam engine? The first automobile? The ability to fly? The space craft and landing on the moon? The new field of bio-technology? The computer? If Islam has been irrelevant in all these steps, should not Muslims be concerned?

If Pakistan captured Hindus in one of their wars, do you really think that Pakistanis are justified in regarding their captives as *slaves* unless they convert to Islam?

If Turkey captured Greeks in Cyprus or in one of their other conflicts, do you really think that would constitute legitimate grounds for enslavement? What if India reciprocated in kind with Pakistani prisoners and Greece with Turkish prisoners? What about Iraqi prisoners in Iranian prison camps? Are they fair for bondage and enslavement?

If you say "Yes" to most of the above questions, let me ask you one additional question. Are you convinced that the rest of the modern world would accept such a system of values? I am using this as a test of how far you are in touch with contemporary realities and opinion even in the Muslim world alone.

With regard to whether I am entitled to have an opinion about Islam independently of medieval jurists or of your own preferred recent theologians, who says a well educated Muslim believer does not have the right to address his or her mind to the troubling contradictions of Islam? Any *fatwa* about who is qualified to interpret Islam is itself subject to challenge. It is a *fatwa* about what constitutes an authoritative *fatwa*.

I regard my humble mind as Allah's gift to me. I refuse to accept the proposition that anyone in Riyadh (Saudia) or Riyadha (*Lamu*) who is learned about medieval Islamic jurists is necessarily better qualified to interpret Islam than the modest but trained intellect which Allah has given me. I believe it would be a betrayal of God's gift to me if I followed theological authority blindly.

On the issue of amputation of the hands of thieves, are you sure it is my beliefs that have to take a back seat? Apart from Saudi Arabia, Nigeria and Sudan, that kind of punishment has *de facto* been rejected by one billion Muslims in the world. If, as the Prophet argued, the ummah would never agree on an error, you may take it for granted that the ummah will never (now and in the future) agree with punishing thieves with amputation of the hand. Take it from me and from your grandchildren. Large-scale amputation of hands for thieves will *never* be restored as a legitimate penalty in the modern world.

You mention the relatively low crime rate during the days of the prophet. There was also low crime rate in China, India, Persia and Africa.

There are also differences in levels of population. If there was one murder in Medina fourteen centuries ago, that was the equivalent proportionally to 800 murders in New York City in the year 2003.

When the Prophet Muhammad (pbuh) died, the population of the whole of Arabia was still to be counted in thousands rather than millions. There is a huge difference between the size of the population of the world today and what it was fourteen centuries ago. During my own lifetime of seventy years the population of Kenya has grown roughly six hundred percent (i.e., from less than five million to about thirty million). Population growth affects issues of stability and law and order in complex ways. The huge expansion of the size of the human race is additional evidence that God reveals Himself in installments.

ON SCIENCE AND RETARDATION

Allah has blessed the Muslim world with plenty of petroleum. But how many large Muslim oil companies do you know which are capable of independently drilling for oil, processing it, refining it and marketing it world wide? Where are the Muslim technological and organizational skills?

In the last three centuries how many scientific inventions or discoveries are we able to attribute to Muslims? Islamic science flourished when Muslims were prepared to learn from others—such as learning mathematics from Indians, philosophy from the Greeks, architecture from the pre-Islamic Persian empire. The Muslim world began to decline when it allowed itself to be imprisoned within the walls of medieval legalism, and took refuge in nostalgia for a bygone age.

It is humiliating that a Jewish state of about six million people can reduce to military impotence an Arab population which is fifty times Israel's size and a Muslim population nearly two hundred times the size of the Jewish state. The Jews have left us far behind in science, technology, organization, economic skill and power. Their religion is much older than ours, but they have not resisted creative change in spite of centuries of discrimination—or perhaps because of it.

Muslims are being victimized militarily in Iraq, Afghanistan, Palestine, Kashmir, Chechnya, Bosnia, Kosovo, and potentially in Iran, Syria, Somalia, Sudan, etc. Our slowness in learning and our resistance to reform have made us soft targets and vulnerable to the might of others. Is there a way out of this predicament?

CONCLUSION

I was intrigued by your suggestion that there were regular prisons and police in Arabia fourteen centuries ago. I am not being sarcastic when I say I would like to be corrected with evidence. I had assumed that most Islamic punishments fell into the following categories:

(a) Executions

(b) Amputations

(c) Freeing a slave or paying another fine

(d) Compensation to crime victims

(e) Flogging (whipping)

(f) Stoning

(g) Exile

Some of the above are Mosaic, some Qur'anic, while others found their way into the Shari'a Code from other sources. But you now tell me that there were *prisons*. Was I wrong in my assumption that the Qur'an did not prescribe prison terms (e.g., six years for first offender in robbery; seven years for zakat-evasion; ten years in prison for not fasting during Ramadhan). I am not being sarcastic. I am just illustrating possible sentences.

If the prison option was available in "seventh century Arabia," I am more puzzled than ever as to why such severe physical punishments on the body (*hudud*) were necessary. But of course God knows best.

Finally, I would appreciate your comments on the distinction between *nabii* (prophet) and *rasul* (messenger). Am I wrong in my assumption that the Islamic emphasis is that Muhammad was *Khatami nabiyyun* (the last of the prophets) and not *Khatami rusul* (the last of the messengers)? I sincerely seek your theological help (with authoritative sources) on this distinction.

My struggle to find new meanings in Islam has nothing to do with a desire to be "controversial." There are millions of Muslims like me who are disturbed by the *hudud*. I am repeatedly accosted by fellow Muslims who are embarrassed by Northern Nigeria's experimentation with the *hudud*. Much as I love Nigeria, what Northern Nigerians are attempting in the name of the Shariah is infinitely more "controversial" than my own humble views on the matter.

Your fellow Muslims who criticize the *hudud* in Nigeria or Sudan are struggling with their souls. They see in Sierra Leone people with hands chopped off because of drunken rebels. They see in Sudan people with chopped hands because of the Shariah. Muslims like me are struggling to reconcile our faith with our conscience. This is not a gimmick in "controversy." It is the anguish of the soul.